Security and Privacy Assurance in Advancing Technologies:
New Developments

Hamid R. Nemati
The University of North Carolina, USA

INFORMATION SCIENCE REFERENCE

Hershey · New York

Director of Editorial Content:	Kristin Klinger
Director of Book Publications:	Julia Mosemann
Acquisitions Editor:	Lindsay Johnston
Development Editor:	Myla Harty
Publishing Assistant:	Natalie Pronio
Typesetter:	Natalie Pronio
Production Editor:	Jamie Snavely
Cover Design:	Lisa Tosheff

Published in the United States of America by
Information Science Reference (an imprint of IGI Global)
701 E. Chocolate Avenue
Hershey PA 17033
Tel: 717-533-8845
Fax: 717-533-8661
E-mail: cust@igi-global.com
Web site: http://www.igi-global.com

Library of Congress Cataloging-in-Publication Data

Security and privacy assurance in advancing technologies : new developments /
Hamid R. Nemati, editor.
       p. cm.
  Includes bibliographical references and index.
  Summary: "This book provides a comprehensive collection of knowledge from
experts within the field of information security and privacy and explores the
changing roles of information technology and how this change will impact
information security and privacy"--Provided by publisher.
  ISBN 978-1-60960-200-0 (hardcover) -- ISBN 978-1-60960-202-4 (ebook) 1.
Information technology--Security measures. 2. Management--Technological
innovations. I. Nemati, Hamid R., 1958-
  HD30.2.S437 2011
  005.8--dc22
                        2010046637

British Cataloguing in Publication Data
A Cataloguing in Publication record for this book is available from the British Library.

This book is dedicated to my beloved parents. I love you guys.

Table of Contents

Chapter 23
Do You Know Where Your Data Is? A Study of the Effect of Enforcement Strategies on

    Ian Reay, University of Alberta, Canada
    Patricia Beatty, University of Alberta, Canada
    Scott Dick, University of Alberta, Canada
    James Miller, University of Alberta, Canada

Detailed Table of Contents

Chapter 1

Hui-min Ye, University of Vermont, USA
Sushil K. Sharma, Ball State University, USA
Huinan Xu, Ernst & Young, USA

Internet has become a major medium for information transmission, how to detect hot topic on web, track the event development and forecast emergency is important to many fields, particularly to some government departments. On the basis of the researches in the field of topic detection and tracking, we propose a model for hot topic discovery that will pick out hot topics by automatically detecting, clustering and weighting topics on the websites within a time period. Based on the idea of stock index, we also introduce a topic index approach in following the growth of topics, which is useful to analyze and forecast the development of topics on web.

Chapter 2

Lee Novakovic, Murdoch University, Australia
Tanya McGill, Murdoch University, Australia
Michael Dixon. Murdoch University, Australia

Computer security is a major issue facing the world we inhabit. Computer systems in a multitude of institutions and organizations hold our personal information. Furthermore, we rely on the safe working of computer systems to not only protect that data, but allow us to take advantage of the benefits technology has to offer. This research project investigated the roles of ease of use, facilitating conditions, intention to use passwords securely, experience and age on usage of passwords, using a model based on the Unified Theory of Acceptance and Use of Technology. Data was collected via an online survey of computer users, and analyzed using PLS. The results show that there is a significant relationship between ease of use of passwords, intention to use them securely and the secure usage of passwords. Despite expectations, facilitating conditions only had a weak impact on intention to use passwords securely and did not influence actual secure usage. Computing experience was found to have an effect on intention to use passwords securely, but age did not. The results of this research lend themselves to assisting in policy design and better understanding user behavior.

Chapter 3

Joanne H. Pratt, Joanne H. Pratt Associates, USA

Considerable research shows that personal information privacy has eroded over the last 30 years. Prior research, however, takes a consumer-centric view of personal information privacy, a view that leads to the conclusion that the individual is responsible for his/her own information. This research presents a comprehensive personal information privacy model of extra-organizational data sharing and use in ecommerce and social networking. It incorporates how data is actually passed and leaked to entities of which the individual has no knowledge and no control. This research presents support for the existence of legal, illegal, and legally-grey area extra-organizational parties and the need for more complete comprehension of personal information privacy. In addition, the research identifies the magnitude of privacy violations in spite of legal and self-protection policies. The model can serve as a guide for privacy research and for social discussion and legislation to manage and regulate use of data once collected.

Chapter 4

Hamid R. Nemati, The University of North Carolina, USA
Thomas Van Dyke, The University of North Carolina, USA

Companies today collect, store and process enormous amounts of information in order to identify, gain, and maintain customers. Electronic commerce and advances in database and communication technology allow business to collect and analyze more personal information with greater ease and efficiency than ever before. This has resulted in increased privacy concerns and a lack of trust among consumers. These concerns have prompted the FCC to call for the use of Fair Information Practices in electronic commerce. Many firms have added privacy statements, formal declarations of privacy and security policy, to their e-commerce web sites in an attempt to reduce privacy concerns by increasing consumer trust in the firm and reducing the perceived risk associated with e-commerce transactions. This article describes an experiment designed to determine the efficacy of that strategy.

Chapter 5

Kent D. Boklan, Queens College, USA

We expose a potential vulnerability in the common use of password-based cryptography. When employing a user-chosen password to generate cryptographic keys which themselves are larger than the digest size of the underlying hash function, a part of the resulting key is produced deterministically and this, in turn, may lead to an exploitable weakness.

Chapter 6

Based on an actual company, this case focuses on Business Continuity Planning issues for a small but growing software company, Municipal Software Solutions, Inc. (MSS). The firm experienced a catastrophic fire which completely eliminated all aspects of the information systems infrastructure, including the software product code repository, the client access infrastructure, the hardware operations center, and the software design facility. Fortunately, no one was harmed, and the firm survived despite the fact that it did not have a formal disaster recovery plan in place. MSS was very lucky. The case can be used in conjunction with coverage of risk assessment concepts in the context of the availability component of systems reliability and trust of services management. Accordingly, it is appropriate for use in courses covering information systems security, accounting information systems, or IT audit.

Chapter 7

Every email that originates from outside of an organization must go through a series of firewalls and gateways before reaching the intended recipient inside the organization. During this journey, each email may get scanned for possible viruses or other malicious programming codes. In some cases, the e-mail may also receive a score based on the possibility of spam content. On any stage of this processing email can be quarantined, or moved to a spam folder for the future possible analysis or simply deleted. Understandably, such complex structure helps secure the company's internal infrastructure, however, e-mails have become an important tool in marketing for many e-commerce organizations and if marketing e-mails do not get to their intended receiver, the sending company will be disadvantaged. Therefore, from the point of view of the sender of an e-mail, it is important to understand the faith of the e-mail that was sent and whether it was received as intended. In this case study, we describe an e-mail bounce back system that was developed by a major e-commerce company in order to understand whether its e-mail based marketing was successful in delivering the intended message to its customers. In addition to the describing the development of the system, security and privacy issues are also discussed.

Chapter 8

Compliance with regulatory guidelines and mandates surrounding information security and the protection of privacy has been under close scrutiny for some time throughout the world. Smaller organizations have remained "out of the spotlight" and generally do not hire staff with the expertise to fully address issues of compliance. This case study examines a project partnership between an information-technology (IT) consultant who specializes in small business and a diminutive medical practice that sought support with compliance issues surrounding a research study it was conducting. Other small medical practices were contributing to the research; consequently, information sharing while concurrently adhering to the regulations of the Health Insurance Portability and Accountability Act (HIPAA) of 1996 was a significant aspect of the project. It was also critical that numerous other security and privacy legislative requirements were met. The issue of data security is often neglected in IT instruction. This case study provides a foundation for examining aspects of information security from the perspective of the small-business IT consultant.

Chapter 9

This study reviews the progress made by the introduction of the Payment Card Industry (PCI) compliance rules in the USA. Available data indicate that compliance has grown but several issues remain unresolved. These are identified within, along with an analysis of the feasibility of several solutions to the challenges that have hampered compliance with the Payment Card Industry rules. These solutions are evaluated by the extent to which they can help the merchants meet their business objectives while still safeguarding the credit card data. The first solution involves upgrading the current PCI standards as suggested by the PCI council. The second solution would require moving the burden of credit card information storage to the credit card companies and member banks, as suggested by the National Retail Federation. A third option reflects a socially responsible approach that protects the interests of all stakeholders. The study concludes by suggesting the way forward.

Chapter 10

This study investigates the relationships between the contextual factor of national culture and information security concerns in the global financial services industry (GFSI). Essentially, this study attempts to expand the breath of information provided in the recent 2009 Deloitte Touche Tohmatsu (DTT) survey, which reported such issues in the financial services industry. The inference from the 2009 DTT survey was that information security concerns across GFSI are being informed solely by industry-related standards or imperatives. As such, perceptions and attitudes towards such issues were thought to remain unchanged in differing contexts. Results from this study's analysis showed that the perceptions of information security concerns in GFSI compared reasonably well, but also varied by some national cultural attributes to debunk such a claim. Corporate managers in the industry may benefit from this research's findings as they formulate country-wide information security policies and strategies. As well, insights from this current effort indicate that it would be erroneous for practitioners to accept that entities in the financial services hold exactly the same view on information security issues in their industry. Future research avenues are discussed.

Effective information security extends beyond using software controls that are so prominently discussed in the popular and academic literature. There must also be management influence and control. The best way to control information security is through formal policy and measuring the effectiveness of existing policies. The purpose of this research is to determine 1) what security elements are embedded in Web-based information security policy statements and 2) what security-related keywords appear more frequently. The authors use these findings to propose a density measure (the extent to which each policy uses security keywords) as an indicator of policy strength. For these purposes, they examine the security component of privacy policies of Fortune 100 Web sites. The density measure may serve as a benchmark that can be used as a basis for comparison across companies and the development of industry norms.

Chapter 12

Computer hackers, both individually and as a group, have been identified as a primary threat to computer systems, users, and organizations. Although hacker groups are complex socio-technical systems, much extant research on hackers is conducted from a technical perspective and at an individual level of analysis. This research proposes a research model composed of five dimensions and their relations in order to study hacker's social organization in the whole socio-technical context. Based on this model, the researcher applies network analysis methods to disclose the structure and patterns of a significant and complex hacker group, Shadowcrew. Network analysis tools are applied for data processing and data analysis. Three network measures: degree centrality, cognitive demand, and eigenvector centrality, are utilized to determine the critical leaders. Out-degree centrality is employed to analyze the relations among the five dimensions in the research model.

Chapter 13

Secure e-mail standards, such as Pretty Good Privacy (PGP) and Secure / Multipurpose Internet Mail Extension (S/MIME), apply cryptographic algorithms to provide secure and private e-mail services over the public Internet. In this article, we first review a number of cryptographic ciphers, trust and certificate systems, and key management systems and infrastructures widely used in secure e-mail standards and services. We then focus on the discussion of several essential security and privacy issues, such as cryptographic cipher selection and operation sequences, in both PGP and S/MIME. This work tries to provide readers a comprehensive impression of the security and privacy provided in the current secure e-mail services.

    Dulal C. Kar, Texas A&M University-Corpus Christi, USA
    Hung L. Ngo, Texas A&M University-Corpus Christi, USA
    Clifton J. Mulkey, Texas A&M University-Corpus Christi, USA
    Geetha Sanapala, Texas A&M University-Corpus Christi, USA

It is challenging to secure a wireless sensor network (WSN) because its inexpensive, tiny sensor nodes do not have the necessary processing capability, memory capacity, and battery life to take advantage of the existing security solutions for traditional networks. Existing security solutions for wireless sensor networks are mostly based on symmetric key cryptography with the assumption that sensor nodes are embedded with secret, temporary startup keys before deployment thus avoiding any use of computationally demanding public key algorithms altogether. However, symmetric key cryptography alone cannot satisfactorily provide all security needs for wireless sensor networks. It is still problematic to replenish an operational wireless sensor network with new sensor nodes securely. Current research on public key cryptography for WSNs shows some promising results, particularly in the use of elliptic curve cryptography and identity based encryption for WSNs. Although security is essential for WSNs, it can complicate some crucial operations of a WSN like data aggregation or in-network data processing that can be affected by a particular security protocol. Accordingly, in this paper, we summarize, discuss, and evaluate recent symmetric key based results reported in literature on sensor network security protocols such as for key establishment, random key pre-distribution, data confidentiality, data integrity, and broadcast authentication as well as expose limitations and issues related to those solutions for WSNs. We also present significant advancement in public key cryptography for WSNs with promising results from elliptic curve cryptography and identity based encryption as well as their limitations for WSNs. In addition, we also discuss recently identified threats and their corresponding countermeasures in WSNs.

    Ming Yang, Jacksonville State University, USA
    Monica Trifas, Jacksonville State University, USA
    Guillermo Francia, III, Jacksonville State University, USA
    Lei Chen, Sam Houston State University, USA
    Yongliang Hu, Taizhou University, China

Information security has traditionally been ensured with data encryption techniques. Different generic data encryption standards, such as DES, RSA, AES, have been developed. These encryption standards provide high level of security to the encrypted data. However, they are not very efficient in the encryption of multimedia contents due to the large volume of digital image/video data. In order to address this issue, different image/video encryption methodologies have been developed. These methodologies encrypt only the key parameters of image/video data instead of encrypting it as a bitstream. Joint compression-encryption is a very promising direction for image/video encryption. Nowadays, researchers start to utilize information hiding techniques to enhance the security level of data encryption methodologies. Information hiding conceals not only the content of the secret message, but also its very existence. In terms of the amount of data to be embedded, information hiding methodologies can be classified into low bitrate and high bitrate algorithms. In terms of the domain for embedding, they can be classified into spatial domain and transform domain algorithms. In this chapter, we have reviewed various data encryption standards, image/video encryption algorithms, and joint compression-encryption methodologies. Besides, we have also presented different categories of information hiding methodologies as well as data embedding strategies for digital image/video contents.

One of the most devastating forms of attack on a computer is when the victim doesn't even know an attack occurred. After some background material, various forms of man in the middle (MITM) attacks, including ARP spoofing, fake SSL certificates, and bypassing SSL are explored. Next, rootkits and botnets, two key pieces of crimeware, are introduced and analyzed. Finally, general strategies to protect against such attacks are suggested.

Chapter 17

Fair exchange between parties can be defined as an instance of exchange such that either all parties involved in the exchange obtain what they expected or neither one does. We examine a protocol by Micali that provides fair contract signing, where two parties exchange their commitments over a pre-negotiated contract in a fair manner. We show that Micali's protocol is not entirely fair and demonstrate the possibilities for one party cheating the other by obtaining the other party's commitment and not offering theirs. A revised version of this protocol by Bao which provides superior fairness by handling some of the weaknesses is also discussed. However, both these protocols fail to handle the possibilities of a replay attack. Our prior work improves upon these protocols by addressing the weakness that leads to a replay attack. This journal extends our prior work on fair electronic exchange by handling a type of attack which was not handled earlier and provides a brief survey of the recent work related to the field of fair electronic exchange. We also discuss the application of cryptography to our protocol which includes implementation of hybrid cryptography and digital signature algorithms based on elliptic curves to achieve features like confidentiality, data-integrity and non-repudiation.

    Feng Zhu, University of Alabama in Huntsville, USA
    Wei Zhu, Intergraph Co, USA

In pervasive computing environments, service discovery is an essential step for computing devices to properly discover, configure, and communicate with each other. We introduce a user-centric service discovery model, called PrudentExposure, which automates authentication processes. Traditional authentication approaches requires much users' involvement. PrudentExposure encodes hundreds of authentication messages in a novel code word form. Moreover, we discuss how a progressive and probabilistic model can protect both users' and service providers' privacy. Perhaps the most serious challenge for pervasive service discovery is the integration of computing devices with people. In a challenging case, both users and service providers want the other parties to expose sensitive information first. Our model protects both users and service providers.

    Madhu V. Ahluwalia, University of Maryland Baltimore County, USA
    Aryya Gangopadhyay, University of Maryland Baltimore County, USA
    Zhiyuan Chen, University of Maryland Baltimore County, USA

Association rule mining is an important data mining method that has been studied extensively by the academic community and has been applied in practice. In the context of association rule mining, the state-of-the-art in privacy preserving data mining provides solutions for categorical and Boolean association rules but not for quantitative association rules. This paper fills this gap by describing a method based on discrete wavelet transform (DWT) to protect input data privacy while preserving data mining patterns for association rules. A comparison with an existing kd-tree based transform shows that the DWT-based method fares better in terms of efficiency, preserving patterns, and privacy.

    Hamidreza Amouzegar, K. N. Toosi University of Technology, Iran
    Mohammad Jafar Tarokh, K. N. Toosi University of Technology, Iran
    Anahita Naghilouye Hidaji, Infotech Pars Company, Iran

This article presents an automata SOA based security model against competitive intelligence attacks in e-commerce. It focuses on how to prevent conceptual interception of an e-firm business model from CI agent attackers. Since competitive intelligence web environment is a new important approach for all e-commerce based firms, they try to come in new marketplaces and need to find a good customer-base in contest with other existing competitors. Many of the newest methods for CI attacks in web position are based on software agent facilities. Many researchers are currently working on how to facilitate CI creation in this environment. The aim of this paper is to help e-firm designers provide a non-predictable presentation layer against CI attacks.

Chapter 21
Xunhua Wang, James Madison University, USA
Hua Lin, University of Virginia, USA

Unlike existing password authentication mechanisms on the web that use passwords for client-side authentication only, password-authenticated key exchange (PAKE) protocols provide mutual authentication. In this article, we present an architecture to integrate existing PAKE protocols to the web. Our integration design consists of the client-side part and the server-side part. First, we implement the PAKE client-side functionality with a web browser plug-in, which provides a secure implementation base. The plug-in has a log-in window that can be customized by a user when the plug-in is installed. By checking the user-specific information in a log-in window, an ordinary user can easily detect a fake log-in window created by mobile code. The server-side integration comprises a web interface and a PAKE server. After a successful PAKE mutual authentication, the PAKE plug-in receives a one-time ticket and passes it to the web browser. The web browser authenticates itself by presenting this ticket over HTTPS to the web server. The plug-in then fades away and subsequent web browsing remains the same as usual, requiring no extra user education. Our integration design supports centralized log-ins for web applications from different web sites, making it appropriate for digital identity management. A prototype is developed to validate our design. Since PAKE protocols use passwords for mutual authentication, we believe that the deployment of this design will significantly mitigate the risk of phishing attacks.

Chapter 22
Wasim A. Al-Hamdani, Kentucky State University, USA

This work introduces three models to measure information security compliance. These are the cardinality model, the second's model, which is based on vector space, and the last model is based on the priority principle. Each of these models will be presented with definitions, basic operations, and examples. All three models are based on a new theory to understand information security called the Information Security Sets Theory (ISST). The ISST is based on four basic sets: external sets, local strategy sets, local standard sets, and local implementation sets. It should be noted that two sets are used to create local standard sets—local expansion and local creation.

Chapter 23
Ian Reay, University of Alberta, Canada
Patricia Beatty, University of Alberta, Canada
Scott Dick, University of Alberta, Canada
James Miller, University of Alberta, Canada

Numerous countries around the world have enacted privacy-protection legislation, in an effort to protect their citizens and instill confidence in the valuable business-to-consumer E-commerce industry. These laws will be most effective if and when they establish a standard of practice that consumers can use as a guideline for the future behavior of e-commerce vendors. However, while privacy-protection laws share many similarities, the enforcement mechanisms supporting them vary hugely. Furthermore, it is unclear which (if any) of these mechanisms are effective in promoting a standard of practice that fits with the social norms of those countries. We present a large-scale empirical study of the role of legal enforcement in standardizing privacy protection on the Internet. Our study is based on an automated analysis of documents posted on the 100,000 most popular websites (as ranked by Alexa.com). We find that legal frameworks have had little success in creating standard practices for privacy-sensitive actions.

Preface

It is unmistakably apparent that we in the midst of a "technological revolution" that has profound implications for all aspects of our lives. This revolution has transformed our lives in way unimaginable in less than a decade. We are able to communicate more freely and effortlessly with one another, make more informed decisions, and have a higher standard of living, all, resulting from advances in Information Technologies (IT). More people are employed generating, collecting, handling, processing and distributing information than any other profession and in any other time (Mason 1986). IT has made us more productive in our workplaces, has brought us closer, transformed our lives and has helped in redefining who we are as humans. Its impacts can be felt in the ways in which we relate, interact, and communicate not just with one another but also the way we interact with the technology itself. To some extent, information technologies have become "information appliances". Yet, we are only at the threshold of what is to come and many experts believe that we have only seen the tip of the iceberg. The dizzying pace of advances in information technology that characterize this revolution promises to transform our lives even more drastically than what we can conceive. Technology has redefined our relationships with businesses we interact with and governmental agencies representing us. Our world has been altered so irrevocably that we are no longer able to conduct our lives without it. But perhaps the most sweeping aspect of this revolution can be found in how we perceive and identify ourselves as individuals and eventually in how we will interact with one another. Consequently, we are on the verge of the biggest societal transformation in the history of mankind traced directly to advances in the information technology. This transformation will most likely create new opportunities and challenges we have yet to fathom. Information defines us. It defines the age we live in and the societies we inhibit. Information is the output of our human intellectual endeavors which inherently defines who we are as humans and how we conduct our lives. New technologies make possible what was not possible before. This alters our old value clusters whose hierarchies were determined by range of possibilities open to us at the time. By making available new options, new technologies can and will lead to a restructuring of the hierarchy of values (Mesthene, 1968). Mason (1986) claims that unique challenges facing our modern societies are the result of the evolving nature of information itself. This evolving nature of information requires us to rethink the way we interact with one another. Although this technological revolution has brought us closer and has made our lives easier and more productive, paradoxically, it has also made us more capable of harming one another and more vulnerable to be harmed by each other. Our vulnerabilities are the consequence of our capabilities. Mason argues that in this age of information, a new form of social contract is needed in order to deal with the potential threats to the information which defines us. Mason (1986) states "Our moral imperative is clear. We must insure that information technology, and the information it handles, are used to enhance the dignity of mankind. To achieve these goals we much formulate a new social contract, one that insures everyone the right to fulfill his or her own human potential." (Mason, 1986, p 26). This new social contract has profound implications for the way our society views information and the technologies that support them. For technology to enhance the "human dignity", it should assist humans in exercising their intellects ethically. But is it possible to achieve this without assuring the trustworthiness of information and the integrity of the technologies we are using? Without security that guarantees the trustworthiness of information and the integrity of our technologies, ethical uses of the information cannot be realized. This implies that securing information and ensuring its privacy are inherently intertwined and should be viewed synergistically. In order for us to take full advantage of the possibilities offered by this new interconnectedness, organizations, governmental agencies, and individuals must find ways to address the associated security and privacy implications. As we move forward, new security and privacy challenges will likely to emerge. It is essential that we are prepared for these challenges in order to take full advantage of the opportunities. With the emergence of the new paradigm in information technology, the role of information security and privacy will evolve. Therefore, whilst advances in information technology have made it possible for generation, collection, storage, processing and transmission of data at a staggering rate from various sources by government, organizations and other groups for a variety of purposes, concerns over security of what is collected and the potential harm from personal privacy violations resulting from their unethical uses have also skyrocketed. Therefore, understanding of pertinent issues in information security and privacy vis-à-vis technical, theoretical, managerial and regulatory aspects of generation, collection, storage, processing, transmission and ultimately use of information have never been more important to researchers and industry practitioners alike. Understanding and studying salient issues of Information security and privacy is a complex and multifaceted undertaking. As a result, it has received considerable attention from researchers, developers and practitioners from a verity of different perspectives and backgrounds. Information security and privacy have been viewed as one of the foremost areas of concern and interest by academic researchers and industry practitioners from diverse fields such as engineering, computer science, information systems, psychology, sociology, the law and management. In this preface, we will consider how advances in information technologies have ushered an unprecedented explosion in data that define us and discuss why understanding of the security and privacy issues relating to this data is essential in any meaningful examination the role of technology in our lives. To achieve this, we will define information security and privacy and will discuss important defining issues currently dominating each. We will conclude by looking ahead in an attempt to seek clues as how this technological revolution will impact this field.

An Ocean of Data

A byproduct of pervasiveness of Information Technology in our daily lives is the amazingly large amount of data currently being generated. According to IBM, worldwide data volumes are currently doubling every two years (IDC, 2010). Data experts estimate that in 2002 the world generated 5 exabytes of data. This amount of data is more than all the words ever spoken by human beings. The rate of growth is just as staggering – the amount of data produced in 2002 was up 68% from just two years earlier. The size of the typical business database has grown a hundred-fold during the past five years as a result of internet commerce, ever-expanding computer systems and mandated recordkeeping by government regulations. The rate of growth in data has not slowed. International Data Corporation (IDC) estimates that the amount of data generated in 2009 was 1.2 million Petabytes (IDC, 2010). (A Petabyte is a million gigabytes.) (IDC Report, 2010). Although this seems to be an astonishingly large amount of data, it is paled in compression to what IDC estimates that amount to be in 2020. IDC estimates that the amount of data generated in 2010 will 44 times as much as this year to an incomprehensible amount of 35 Zettabytes (A Zettabyte is 1 trillion gigabytes). IDC reports that by 2020, we will generate 35 trillion gigabytes of data. Moreover, that amount probably doubles every two years (Hardy, 2004). This astonishingly large growth in data, according a survey by US Department of Commerce, can be traced to the ever increasing number of Americans who are online on daily basis and are engaged in several activities, including engaging in online purchases and e-commerce, conducting banking online, learning, entertaining each other and being entertained by others and above all interacting socially. According the Neilson (Neilson 2010), Americans spend almost 25% of their time online on social networking sites and blogs, up 43 percent from one year earlier and they spend a third their online time (36 percent) communicating and networking across social networks, blogs, personal email and instant messaging (Lawson, 2010). A recent Neilson study (Nielson 2010) revealed that activities that generate larger and more private data are on the rise. Table 1 summarizes the findings.

Almost everything that we do in our daily lives can generate a digital footprint. Whether we are using credit cards, surfing the Internet or viewing a YouTube video, we are generating data. IDC senior vice president, John Gantz states: "About half of your digital footprint is related to your individual actions—taking pictures, sending e-mails, or making digital voice calls. The other half is what we call the 'digital shadow'—information about you—names in financial records, names on mailing lists, web surfing histories or images taken of you by security cameras in airports or urban centers. For the first time your digital shadow is larger than the digital information you actively create about yourself." Our digital shadow, the sum of all the digital information generated about us on a daily basis, now exceeds the amount of digital information we actively create ourselves (IDC, 2010). This digital footprint including

Table 1. Top 10 Sectors by share of U.S. Internet time

RANK	Category	Share of Time June 2010	Share of Time June 2009	% Change in Share of Time
\multicolumn{5}{}{**Top 10 Sectors by Share of U.S. Internet Time**}				
1	Social Networks	22.7%	15.8%	43%
2	Online Games	10.2%	9.3%	10%
3	E-mail	8.3%	11.5%	-28%
4	Portals	4.4%	5.5%	-19%
5	Instant Messaging	4.0%	4.7%	-15%
6	Videos/Movies	3.9%	3.5%	12%
7	Search	3.5%	3.4%	1%
8	Software Manufacturers	3.3%	3.3%	0%
9	Multi-category Entertainment	2.8%	3.0%	-7%
10	Classifieds/Auctions	2.7%	2.7%	-2%
11	Other	34.3%	37.3%	-8%

Source (http://blog.nielsen.com/nielsenwire/online_mobile/what-americans-do-online-social-media-and-games-dominate-activity/)

our digital shadow represents us, as humans, it represents who we are, and how we conduct our lives. It needs to be secured, protected, and managed appropriately.

The growth in Internet usage has offered businesses and governmental agencies the opportunity to collect and analyze information in ways never previously imagined. "Enormous amounts of consumer data have long been available through offline sources such as credit card transactions, phone orders, warranty cards, applications and a host of other traditional methods. What the digital revolution has done is increase the efficiency and effectiveness with which such information can be collected and put to use" (Adkinson, Eisenach, & Lenard, 2002).

The proclamation about data volume growth is no longer surprising, but continues to amaze even the experts. For businesses, more data isn't always better. Organizations must assess what data they need to collect and how to best leverage it. Collecting, storing and managing business data and associated databases can be costly, and expending scarce resources to acquire and manage extraneous data fuels inefficiency and hinders optimal performance. The generation and management of business data also loses much of its potential organizational value unless important conclusions can be extracted from it quickly enough to influence decision making while the business opportunity is still present. Managers must rapidly and thoroughly understand the factors driving their business in order to sustain a competitive advantage. Organizational speed and agility supported by fact-based decision making are critical to ensure that an organization remains at least one step ahead of its competitors. According to Kakalik and Wright (1997), a normal consumer is on more than 100 mailing lists and at least 50 databases. A survey of 10,000 Web users conducted by Georgia Institute of Technology concludes that "Privacy now overshadows censorship as the No. 1 most important issue facing the Internet" (Machlis 1997). A UCLA study released on February 2003, reported that 88.8% of the respondents said that they were somewhat or extremely concerned when purchasing online.

The gathering of data for data mining purposes was initially an attempt by companies to learn as much as possible about their customers so that they could provide customized or personable service and increase sales. The development and use of computer/data technology helped speed this process as it made the gathering and analyzing process easier. However, recent developments have caused the individual to lose control over that data about them. As technology advanced, the tools became more invasive, thorough and accuracy increased. It is possible that this data, available to anyone (individuals, businesses, governments) can be manipulated in such a way as to produce an in-depth profile of an individual or group.

Concerns have arisen regarding the use of data mining, as an individual has to interpret the results and data or knowledge gained can be taken out of context. For example, the US government utilizes some very powerful surveillance tools to gather data about its citizens. There are legitimate concerns regarding accuracy of data and privacy of the material these tools produce. The use of data mining technologies to make sense of this fata can provide limited and inaccurate results. What is the cost of a mistake? Is it a type one or type two error? What if you wrongly accuse an innocent person or allow a guilty person to go free? What percentage of accurate results is acceptable? Is an 85% accuracy rate good? If you are sending out a flyer or picking a stock then yes it is. If you are deciding if a person should be questioned and possibly detained by the police is that percentage still acceptable? What if you are one of the 15% wrongly accused? What are the implications? (Under the Patriot Act, if the accused is an immigrant they may be detained indefinitely). These are questions that must be seriously considered. The end-users of the technology must understand these concerns and the limitation of the technology they employ.

Information Security

Until recently, information security was exclusively discussed in terms of mitigating risks associated with data and the organizational and technical infrastructure that supported it. A common motivation for corporations to invest in information security is to safeguard their confidential data. This motivation is based on the erroneous view of information security as a risk mitigation activity rather than a strategic business enabler. No longer should information security be viewed solely as a measure to reduce risk to organizational information and electronic assets, it should be viewed as way the business needs to be conducted. To achieve success in information security goals, an organization's information security program should support the mission of the organization. Information security is concerned with the identification of an organization's electronic information assets and the development and implementation of tools, techniques, policies, standards, procedures and guidelines to ensure the confidentiality, integrity and availability of these assets. Although Information Security can be defined in a number of ways, the most salient definition is set forth by the U.S. government. The National Institute of Standards and Technology (NIST) defines Information Security based on the 44 United States Code Section 3542(b) (2), which states "Information Security is protecting information and information systems from unauthorized access, use, disclosure, disruption, modification, or destruction in order to provide integrity, confidentiality, and availability." (NIST, 2003, p3). The Federal Information Security Management Act (FISMA, P.L. 107-296, Title X, 44 U.S.C. 3532) defines Information Security as "protecting information and information systems from unauthorized access, use, disclosure, disruption, modification, or destruction" and goes on to further define Information Security activities as those "carried out in order to identify and address the vulnerabilities of computer system, or computer network" (17 U.S.C. 1201(e), 1202(d)). The United States' National Information Assurance Training and Education Center (NIATEC) defines information security as "a system of administrative policies and procedures for identifying, controlling and protecting information against unauthorized access to or modification, whether in storage, processing or transit" (NIATEC, 2006). The overall goal of information security should be to enable an organization to meet all of its mission critical business objectives by implementing systems, policies and procedures to mitigate IT-related risks to the organization, its partners and customers (NIST, 2003). The Federal Information Processing Standards Publication 199 issued by the National Institute of Standards and Technology (NIST, 2004) defines three broad information security objectives: "Confidentiality", "Integrity" and "Availability". This trio of objectives sometimes is referred to as the "CIA Triad".

The Information Systems Security Association (ISSA) has been developing a set of Generally Accepted Information Security Principles (GAISP). GAISP include a number of information security practices, including the need for involvement of top management, the need for customized information security solutions, the need for periodic reassessment, the need for an evolving security strategy and the need for a privacy strategy. This implies that information security should be viewed as an integral part of the organizational strategic mission and therefore, requires a comprehensive and integrated approach. It should be viewed as an element of sound management in which cost-effectiveness is not the only driver of the project. Management should realize that information security is a smart business practice. By investing in security measures, an organization can reduce the frequency and severity of security-related losses. Information security requires a comprehensive approach that extends throughout the entire information life cycle. The management needs to understand that without a physical security, information security would be impossible. As a result, it should take into considerations a variety of issues, both technical and managerial and from within and outside of the organization. The management needs to realize that this comprehensive approach requires that the managerial, legal, organizational policies, operational, and technical controls work together synergistically. This requires that senior managers be actively involved in establishing information security governance.

Effective information security controls often depend upon the proper functioning of other controls, but responsibilities must be assigned and carried out by appropriate functional disciplines. These interdependencies often require a new understanding of the tradeoffs that may exist, which means achieving one may actually undermine another. The management must insist that information security responsibilities and accountability be made explicit and the system owners have responsibilities that may exist outside their own functional domains. An individual or work group should be designated to take the lead role in the information security as a broad organization wide process. This requires that security policies be established and documented, and the awareness among all employees be increased through employee training and other incentives. This requires that information security priorities be communicated to all stakeholders, including customers, and employees at all levels within the organization to ensure a successful implementation. The management should insist that information security activities be integrated into all management activities, including strategic planning, capital planning. Management should also insist that an assessment of needs and weaknesses should be initiated and security measures and policies should be monitored and evaluated continuously. Information security professionals are charged with protecting organizations against their information security vulnerabilities. Given the importance of securing information to an organization, this is an important position with considerable responsibility. It is the responsibility of information security professionals and management to create an environment where the technology is used in an ethical manner. Therefore, one cannot discuss information security without discussing the ethical issues fundamental in the development and use of the technology. According to a report by the European Commission (EC, 1999, p. 7) "Information Technologies can be and are being used for perpetrating and facilitating various criminal activities. In the hands of persons acting with bad faith, malice, or grave negligence, these technologies may become tools for activities that endanger or injure the life, property or dignity of individuals or damage the public interest." Information technology operates in a dynamic environment. Considerations of dynamic factors, such as advances in new technologies, the dynamic nature of the user, the information latency and value, systems' ownerships, the emergence of a new threat and new vulnerabilities, dynamics of external networks, changes in the environment, the changing regulatory landscape, should be viewed as important. Therefore the management should insist on an agile, comprehensive, integrated approach to information security.

Information is a critical asset that supports the mission of an organization. Protecting this asset is critical to survivability and longevity of any organization. Maintaining and improving information security is critical to the operations, reputation, and ultimately the success and longevity of any organization. However, information and the systems that support it are vulnerable to many threats that can inflict serious damage to an organization resulting in significant losses. The concerns over information security risks can originate from a number of different security threats. They can come from hacking and unauthorized attempts to access private information, fraud, sabotage, theft and other malicious acts or they can originate from more innocuous sources, but no less harmful, such as natural disasters or even user errors.

David Mackey, IBM's Director of security intelligence estimates that IBM recorded more than 1 billion suspicious computer security events in 2005. The damage from these "security events" can range from loss of integrity of the information to total physical destruction or corruption of entire infrastructure that support it. Damages can stem from the actions of a variety of sources, such as disgruntled employees defrauding a system, careless errors committed by trusted employees, to hackers gaining access to the system from outside of the organization. Precision in estimating computer security-related losses is not possible because many losses are never discovered, and others are "swept under the carpet" to avoid negative publicity. The effects of various threats vary considerably: some affect the confidentiality or integrity of data while others affect the availability of a system. Broadly speaking, the main purpose of information security is to protect an organization's valuable resources, such as information, hardware, and software. Any information security initiative aims to minimize risk by reducing or eliminating threats to vulnerable organizational information assets. The National Institute of Standards and Technology (NIST, 2003, p. 7) defines risk as "…a combination of: (i) the likelihood that a particular vulnerability in an agency information system will be either intentionally or unintentionally exploited by a particular threat resulting in a loss of confidentiality, integrity, or availability, and (ii) the potential impact or magnitude of harm that a loss of confidentiality, integrity, or availability will have on agency operations (including mission, functions, and public confidence in the agency), an agency's assets, or individuals (including privacy) should there be a threat exploitation of information system vulnerabilities,". "Risks are often characterized qualitatively as high, medium, or low" (NIST, 2003, p 8). The same publication defines threat as "…any circumstance or event with the potential to intentionally or unintentionally exploit a specific vulnerability in an information system resulting in a loss of confidentiality, integrity, or availability," and vulnerability as "…a flaw or weakness in the design or implementation of an information system (including security procedures and security controls associated with the system) that could be intentionally or unintentionally exploited to adversely affect an agency's operations (including missions, functions, and public confidence in the agency), an agency's assets, or individuals (including privacy) through a loss of confidentiality, integrity, or availability" (NIST, 2003, 9). NetIQ (2004) discusses five different types of vulnerabilities that have direct impact on the governance of information security practices. They are: exposed user accounts or defaults, dangerous user behavior, configuration flaws, missing patches and dangerous or unnecessary service. An effective management of these vulnerabilities is critical for three basic reasons. First, an effective vulnerability management helps reducing the severity and growth of incidents. Second, it helps in regulatory compliance. And third and the most important reason can be summed by simply saying, it is a "good business practice" to be proactive in managing the vulnerabilities rather than be reactive by trying to control the damage from an incident.

The importance of securing our information infrastructure also applies to the government of the United States. The U.S. Department of Homeland Security (DHS) identifies a Critical Infrastructure (CI) as "systems and assets, whether physical or virtual, so vital to the United States that the incapacity or destruction of such systems and assets would have a debilitating impact on security, national economic security, national public health or safety, or any combination of those matters." According a recent report by the DHS titled The National Strategy for Homeland Security, which identified thirteen CI's, disruption in any component of a CI can have catastrophic economic, social and national security impacts. Information Security is identified as a major area of concern for the majority of the thirteen identified CI's. For example, many government and private-sector databases contain sensitive information which can include personally identifiable data such as medical records, financial information such as credit card numbers, and other sensitive proprietary business information or classified security-related data. Securing these databases, which form the back bone of a number of CI's, is of paramount importance.

Losses due to electronic theft of information and other forms of cybercrime against such databases can amount to tens of millions of dollars annually. In addition to specific costs can be incurred as the result of malicious activities such as identity theft as a result of data breaches (such as theft of hardware or system break ins, or virus attacks or denial of service attacks), one of the major consequences of dealing with a security attacks is the decrease in customer and investor confidence in the company. This is an area of major concern for the management. According to an event-study analysis using market valuations to assess the impact of security breaches on the market value of breached firms, announcing a security breach is negatively associated with the market value of the announcing firm. The breached firms in the sample lost, on an average, 2.1 percent of their market value within two days of the announcement – an average loss in market capitalization of $1.65 billion per breach. The study suggests that the cost of poor security is very high for investors and bad for business. Financial consequences may range from fines levied by regulatory authorities to brand erosion. As a result, organizations are spending a larger portion of their IT budget in information security. A study by the Forrester Research Group estimated that in 2007 businesses across North America and Europe will spend almost 13% of their IT budgets on security related activities. The same report shows the share of security expenditure was around 7% in 2006.

It is obvious that information security is a priority for the management, as it should be. Regardless of the source, the impact on organization can be severe ranging from interruption in delivery of services and goods, loss of physical and other assets, loss of customer good will and confidence in the organization to disclosure of sensitive data. Such sensitive data breaches can be very costly to the organization. However, recent research shows that investing and upgrading information security infrastructure is a smart business practice. By doing so, an organization can reduce the frequency and severity of losses resulting from security breaches in computer systems and information technology infrastructure. Information Security is not just a technology issue. It encompasses all aspects of business from people to processes to technology. Bruce Schneier founder and editor of Schneier.com states that "If you think technology can solve your security problems, then you don't understand the problems and you don't understand the technology." Information Security involves consideration of many interrelated fundamental issues to consider. Among them are technological, developmental and design, and managerial considerations. The technology component of information security is perhaps the easiest to develop and implement. The technological component of information security and privacy is concerned with the development, acquisition, and implementation of hardware and software needed to achieve information security. The developmental and design component of information security deals with issues related techniques and methodologies used to proactively design and develop systems that are secure. The managerial and personnel component focuses on the complex issues of dealing with the human elements in information security and privacy. It deals with policies, procedures and assessments required for the management of the operation of security activities. Undoubtedly, this is the hardest part of the information security to achieve since it requires a clear commitment to security by an organization's leadership, assignment of appropriate roles and responsibilities, implementation of physical and personnel security measures to control and monitor access, training that is appropriate for the level of access and responsibility, and accountability.

Information Privacy

Privacy is defined as "the state of being free from unsanctioned intrusion" (Dictionary.com, 2010). Westin (Westin, 1967) defined the right to privacy as "the right of the individuals… to determine for themselves when, how, and to what extent information about them is communicated to others." The Fourth Amendment to the U.S. Constitution's Bill of Rights states that "The right of the people to be secure in their persons, houses, papers, and effects, against unreasonable searches and seizures, shall not be violated." This belief carries back through history in such expressions from England, at least circa 1603, "Every man's house is his castle." The Supreme Court has since ruled that "We have recognized that the principal object of the Fourth Amendment is the protection of privacy rather than property, and have increasingly discarded fictional and procedural barriers rested on property concepts." Thus, because the Amendment "protects people, not places," the requirement of actual physical trespass is dispensed with and electronic surveillance was made subject to the Amendment's requirements (Findlaw. com, 2010). Generally the definitions of privacy in regards to business are quite clear. On the Internet, however, privacy raises greater concerns as consumers realize how much information can be collected without their knowledge. Companies are facing an increasingly competitive business environment which forces them to collect vast amounts of customer data in order to customize their offerings. Eventually, as consumers become aware of these technologies, new privacy concerns will arise, and these concerns will gain a higher level of importance. The security of personal data and subsequent misuse or wrongful use without prior permission of an individual raise privacy concerns and often end up in questioning the intent behind collecting private information in the first place (Dhillon & Moores, 2001). Privacy information holds the key to power over an individual. When privacy information is held by organizations, which have collected the information without the knowledge or permission of the individual, the rights of the individual are at risk. By 1997, consumer privacy had become a prominent issue in the United States (Dyson, 1998). In practice, information privacy deals with an individual's ability to control and release personal information. The individual is in control of the release process: to whom information is released, how much information is released and for what purpose the information is to be used. "If a person considers the type and amount of information known about them to be inappropriate, then their perceived privacy is at risk" (Roddick & Wahlstrom, 2001). Consumers are likely to lose confidence in the online marketplace because of these privacy concerns. Businesses must understand consumers' concern about these issues and aim to build consumer trust. It is important to note that knowledge about data collection can have a negative influence on a customer's trust and confidence level in online businesses.

Privacy concerns are real and have profound and undeniable implications on people's attitude and behavior (Sullivan, 2002). The importance of preserving customers' privacy becomes evident when we study the following information: In its 1998 report, the World Trade Organization projected that worldwide Electronic Commerce would reach a staggering $220 billion. A year later, Wharton Forum on E-commerce revised that WTO projection down to $133 billion. What accounted for this unkept promise of phenomenal growth? Census Bureau, in its February 2004 report states that "Consumer privacy apprehensions continue to plague the Web and hinder its growth." In a report by Forrester Research, it is stated that privacy fears will hold back roughly $15 billion in e-commerce revenue. In May 2005, Jupiter Research reported that privacy and security concerns could cost online sellers almost $25 billion by 2006. Whether justifiable or not, consumers have concerns about their privacy and these concerns have been reflected in their behavior. The Chief Privacy Officer of Royal Bank of Canada said "Our research shows that 80% of our customers would walk away if we mishandled their personal information." Privacy considerations will become more and more important to customers interacting electronically with businesses. As a result, privacy will become an import business driver. People (Customers) feel "violated" when their privacy is invaded. They respond to it differently, despite the intensity of their feelings. Given this divergent and varied reaction to privacy violations, a lot of companies still do not appreciate the depth of consumer feelings and the need to revamp their information practices, as well as their infrastructure for dealing with privacy. Privacy is no longer about just staying within the letter of the latest law or regulation. Sweeping changes in attitudes of people regarding their privacy will fuel an intense political debate and put once-routine business and corporate practices under the microscope. Two components of this revolution will concern businesses the most, rising consumer fears and a growing patchwork of regulations. Both are already underway. Regulatory complexity will grow as privacy concerns surface in scattered pieces of legislation. Companies need to respond quickly and comprehensively. They must recognize that privacy should be a core business issue. Privacy policies and procedures that cover all operations must be enacted. Privacy Preserving Identity Management should be viewed as a business issue, not a compliance issue.

Information Security and Privacy Issues

Information security and privacy will be everyone's business, not just IT's. This change in the way companies view and approach information security and privacy will be driven primarily due to consumer demand. Consumers will demand more security for information about them and will insist on better ethical uses of that information. This demand will drive business profitability measures and will ultimately manifest itself as pressure on the government and other regulatory agencies to pass tougher and more intrusive legislation and regulations, resulting in greater pressure on the business organizations to comply and to demonstrate a commitment to information security and privacy. Therefore to be successful, organizations need to focus on information security not just as an IT issue rather as a business imperative. They need to develop business processes that align business, IT and security operations. For example, information security considerations will play more of a prominent role while considering offshoring, collaborations and outsourcing agreements. In the same vein, business partners must prove that their processes, databases and networks are secure. This will also have an important implication for the outsourcing/offshoring agreements and collaborations. The need for more vigilant and improved policies and practices in monitoring insiders who may be leaking or stealing confidential information will become more apparent. The black hat will become the norm. Hacking will be increasingly become a criminal profession and will no longer be the domain of hobbyists. Attacks will be more targeted, organized and will have a criminal intent meant to steal information for profit.

Regulatory and compliance requirements will continue to plague organizations. Regulations and laws will have direct impact on IT implementations and practices. Management teams will be held accountable. Civil and criminal penalties may apply for non-compliance. Security audits will become more widespread as companies are forced to comply with new regulations and laws. The regulatory agencies and law enforcement will become more vigilant in enforcing existing laws such as HIPAA, Sarbanes-Oxley Act, etc.

Identity management will continue to be the sore spot of information security. The use of identity federations will increase. With advances in technology and the need for more secure and accurate identity management, biometrics will become mainstream and widely used. Additionally, the use of "federated identity management systems" will become more widespread. In a federated identity management environment, users will be able to link identity information between accounts without centrally storing personal information. The user can control when and how their accounts and attributes are linked and shared between domains and service providers, allowing for greater control over their personal data.

Advanced technical security measures, such as data-at-rest encryption, granular auditing, vulnerability assessment, and intrusion detection to protect private personally identifiable data will become more wide spread. Database security continues to be a major concern for developers, vendor and customers. Organizations demand more secure code and vendors and developers will try to accommodate that demand. In addition to more secure code, the demand for an explicit focus on unified application security architecture will force vendors and developers to seek further interoperability. This is the direct result of increase in sophistication of malware. Malware will morph and become more sophisticated than ever. The new breed of malware will be able to take advantage of operating systems and browsers' vulnerabilities to infect end user computers with malicious codes for key logging that monitor and track end users' behaviors such as web surfing habits and other behaviors. Malware sophistication will include vulnerability assessment tools for scanning and penetrating corporate network defenses to look for weaknesses. Phishing will grow in frequency and sophistication and phishing techniques will morph and become more advanced. Phishing is defined as a method where private information such as social security numbers, usernames, and passwords are collected from users under false pretenses by criminals masquerading as legitimate organizations. Malicious websites that are intended to violate end users' privacy by intentionally modifying end users' configurations such as browser settings, bookmarks, homepage, and startup files without their consent will gain popularity among the hacker community. Sophisticated malware code can infect the users' computers simply by users visiting these sites. These infections can range from installing adware and spyware on a user's computers, installing dialers, keyloggers and Trojan horses on a user's machine. Keyloggers have the ability to be installed remotely by bypassing firewalls and email scanners and in most cases may not be detected by antivirus software. The most sophisticated keyloggers will be able to capture all keystrokes, screenshots, passwords encrypt them and send these information to remote sites undetected. Malicious code such as BOTs will be a growing problem for network administrators. BOT applications are used to capture users' computers and transform them into BOT networks (botnets). These BOT networks can then be used for illegal network uses such as SPAM relay, generic traffic proxies, Distributed Denial of Service (DDoS) attacks, and hosting phishing (and other malicious code) websites.

The proliferation of Internet use will accelerate. People, companies, governments will conduct more and more of their daily business on the Internet. Not only will the Internet be used for more, but it will also be used for more complex and previously unimagined purposes. This will be partly fueled by advances in the Internet technologies that will be more complex and far reaching. However, the pace of advances in security technology will be able to keep pace with the Internet's growth and complexity. As social computing networks such Peer-to-Peer, Instant Messaging, and Chat gain more popularity and continued adoption of these technologies, organizations will be exposed to new and more disruptive threats. These social computing networks will drain more and more of the corporate bandwidth and will require additional technologies to combat. For example, it was estimated that in 2007, Instant Messaging would surpass e-mails as the most dominate form of electronic communication. Yet, Instant Messaging is not regulated in most companies and is not subject to the same level of scrutiny as the e-mail systems are. Similarly, individuals are not as vigilant when using Instant Messaging tools. Therefore, these social computing technologies are fast becoming very popular with attackers. According to a recent study, the most popular malicious use of Instant Messaging is to send the user a link to a malicious, phishing or fraudulent website which then installs and runs a malicious application on the user's computer in order to steal confidential information.

There are serious concerns that current technology and technology being developed, will allow governments extraordinary ability to monitor their citizens. There is a legitimate concern that "Big Brother" has arrived. Proper oversight and usage is essential to limit abuses. Concerns about surveillance tools were abundant prior to 9/11, since then they have lessened with the understanding that the technology will be used for national security. However the new legislation increasing law enforcement and governmental powers are not limited solely to terrorism. In our rush to protect ourselves we must be certain not to trample on individual rights in such a way that we regret it in the future. The balance between individual rights vs. national security should be carefully weighed. Those mining data obtained by business or governmental surveillance tools need to consider how the data is obtained, its accuracy and the limitations of the tools. They must be especially aware of the potential use of their analysis. Reliance on inaccurate results could have profound effects on individuals or our society as a whole.

Yet Another Security and Privacy Concern: Medical Data

Another area of concern is the growth in the use of information technology for medical purposes. Confidentiality is sacrosanct in any physician-patient relationship and rules governing this relationship going back millennia are meant to protect patient's privacy. Confidentiality, a major component of information security, is a significant mechanism by which a patient's right to privacy is maintained and respected. However, in the era of Electronic Medical Record (EMR), it is hard to achieve. Although the use of information technologies for medical purposes shows potential for substantial benefits, it is fraught with concern related to security and privacy. Since there are so many points along the EMR life cycle where security and or privacy of medical data can be compromised, wide spread use of EMR is not possible without a thorough understanding and resolution of such issues (Hunt, et. al, 1998; Johnston, et. al, 1994).

One of the most far reaching laws with privacy implication impacting electronic medical data research and practitioner communities is Health Insurance Portability and Accountability Act of 1996. It provides a standard for electronic health care transactions over the Internet. As the integrity and confidentiality of patient information is critical, this requires being able to uniquely identify and authenticate an individual. Health information is subject to HIPPA. The original legislation went into effect in 2001 and the final modifications took effect in April, 2003. A core aspect of HIPAA is to appropriately secure electronic medical records. The act applies to health information created or maintained by health care providers who engage in certain electronic transactions, health plans, and health care clearinghouses. The Office for Civil Rights (OCR) is responsible for implementing and enforcing the HIPPA privacy regulation. HIPAA has strict guidelines on how healthcare organizations can manage private health information. This includes: Authentication: A unique identification for individuals using the health care system; Access control: Manage accounts and restrict access to health information; Password management: Centrally define and enforce a global password policy; Auditing: Centralize activity logs related to the access of health information. The act sets standards to protect privacy in regards to individuals' medical information. The act provides individuals access to their medical records, giving them more control over how their protected health information is used and disclosed, and providing a clear avenue of recourse if their medical privacy is compromised (Anonymous, 2006). Improper use or disclosure of protected health information has the potential for both criminal and civil sanctions. For example, fines up to $25,000 for multiple violations of a single privacy standard in a calendar year and the penalties for intentional or willful violations of the privacy rule are much more severe with fines up to $250,000 and/ or imprisonment up to 10 years for knowing misuse of personal health data. There are more immediate risks of private lawsuits relying on the HIPAA standard of care. Security and privacy of electronic medical records constitute major regulatory compliance issues. Security must be in compliance with the "security rule" of the Health Insurance Portability and Accountability Act (HIPAA). There are five guiding principles of HIPPA's security rule: scalability, comprehensives, technological neutrality, and consideration of both external and internal security threats, and risk analysis (HIPPA, 2010). Scalability ensures that compliance with security does not depend on the size or scope of the medical entity and requires that covered entities (CE), regardless of their size, must comply with rules. Comprehensiveness requires for a CE to develop a "comprehensive" approach to all aspects of electronic medical records' security. Neutrality of the technology provides flexibility to a CE in determining the most appropriate technology and the onus is on the CE to justify the technology that is used. The CE is required to protect its data from both internal and external security threats, to regularly conduct security risk analysis and to provide appropriate documentation. In addition, the security rule requires the CE to be in full compliance; partial compliance is not acceptable. There are a number of other key concepts to assure the security of medical records. One requirement is the establishment and formal documentation of security processes, policies, and procedures. Another is the "reasonableness" requirement. Reasonableness requires the CE to certify and document that reasonable measures have been taken to protect electronic medical records. Lastly, CEs must provide regular security training, awareness to its workforce and revise its security policies and procedures as needed. These compliance security challenges stem from the fact that patient data sets are large, complex, heterogeneous, hierarchical, time series, nontraditional, and originate from a verity of sources with differing levels of quality and format. Further, data sources may have incomplete, inaccurate and missing elements, some may be erroneous due to human and equipment error and lastly, the data may lack canonical consistencies within and between sources (Ciosa, et al, 2002). Patient data are voluminous and are collected from various sources including medical images, patient interviews, laboratory data, and the physicians' observations and interpretations of patients' symptoms, and behavior (Ciosa, et al, 2002). Securing such diverse and voluminous type of data housed on multiple heterogeneous systems with diverse data stewardship is not a trivial task and requires a whole set of different and difficult considerations. For example, medical data lack the underlying data structures needed for mathematically based data encryption techniques. Unlike data collected using other processes, medical data consists of word descriptions by physician and nurses, with very few formal constraints on the vocabulary, medical images, hand written charts and others. Additionally, medical data also lack a canonical form that encapsulates all equivalent forms of the same concept and is the preferred notation used in most encryption algorithms. For example, all the following are medically equivalent: Colon adenocarcinoma, metastatic to liver; Colonic adenocarcinoma, metastatic to liver; Large bowel adenocarcinoma, metastatic to liver. (Ciosa, et al, 2002). Lastly, medical data are time sensitive and may have been collected at different times using different data collection methodologies. As a result, they may reside on heterogeneous systems with differing representation and stewardship. Massive quantities of patient data are generated as patients undergo different medical and health care processes and procedures. As a result, these large patient databases may contain large quantity of useful information about patients and their medical conditions, possible diagnoses, prognosis and treatments. A major challenge in using these large patient databases is the ability to properly secure and anonyomize the data.

Another security and privacy issue deals with data mining of medical data. Careful and systematic mining of patient databases may reveal and lead to the discovery of useful trends, relationships and patterns that could significantly enhance the understanding of disease progression and management. This process is referred to as Data mining (DM). DM is an exciting new facet of decision support systems. Data mining derived from the disciplines of artificial intelligence and statistical analysis and covers a wide array of technologies. Using data mining, it is possible to go beyond the data explicitly stored in a database to find nontrivial relationships and information that would not have been discovered by way of standard analysis methods. Medical Data Mining (MDM) is data mining applied to patient data and has been shown to provide benefits in many areas of medical diagnosis, prognosis and treatment (Lavrac, 1999). By identifying patterns within the large patient databases, medical data mining can be used to gain more insight into the diseases and generate knowledge that can potentially lead to development of efficacious treatments. Unfortunately, given the difficulties associated with mining patient databases, the potential of these systems are yet to be realized (Lavrac, 1999). Medical Data Mining is the process of discovering and interpreting previously unknown patterns in medical databases (Lavrac, 1999). It is a powerful technology that converts data into information and potentially actionable knowledge. However, obtaining and using new knowledge in a vacuum does not facilitate optimal decision making in a medical setting. In order to develop a successful final patient treatment management, the newly extracted useful medical knowledge from MDM that appears in form of relationships and patterns should be integrated with existing knowledge and expertise that of the physician to enhance patient care. The significance of data security and privacy has not been lost to the data mining research community as was revealed in Nemati and Barko (Nemati et al., 2001) of the major industry predictions that are expected to be key issues in the future (Nemati et al., 2001). Chiefly among them are concerns over the security of what is collected and the privacy violations of what is discovered (Margulis, 1977; Smith, Milberg, & Burke, 1996).

Final Thoughts

Consider this, the privacy policy of Facebook is now longer than the US Constitution with almost 50 settings and more than 170 options available to the users. Given this large number of options and setting, how likely is for an average user to understand and to make an informed decision about which settings are most appropriate to their needs. The complexities of these privacy policies make it very difficult, if not impossible, for ordinary users to comprehend the consequences of their privacy choices. Consider this; in an attempt to make the Facebook the "social center of the web", in April 2010, Facebook announced the development of "Open Graphs", as a platform for developers to exchange ideas and information. Open Graphs is an extension of the idea of "semantic networks", which according to Tim Berners-Lee (1999), is an attempt to "bring structure to the meaningful content of Web pages thus enabling computers to understand that content and how it relates to other sites and information across the internet". Using Open Graphs, Facebook can integrate websites and web apps within its existing social network environment by allowing its partner sites to create categories based on users' interests and then exchange that information with one another. For example, Open Graph would allow the following scenario to occur. A Facebook user visits Netflex, a movie rental site, and searches for a movie to rent. Netflex, an Open Graph partner of Facebook, develops a customized review for this user based on the reviews of that movie uploaded by the user's Facebook friends. Once the user makes the final selection, Netflex in turn, can notify the user's Facebook friends that their movie reviews were used by the user and thereby revealing what movie the user rented. The privacy consequence of Open Graphs is far reaching and not yet well understood, not even by the experts, let alone the average user. The most significant privacy consequence of Open Graphs is the redefinition of what "public" means. Users need to understand that public no longer means public within the Facebook only (Warren, 2010). As Christine Warren states, "users need to assume that if [they] do something that is considered public, that action can potentially end up on a customized stream for everyone in [their] social graph"(Warren, 2010). Users need to know that they should be vigilant about protecting their privacy on-line and not just Facebook. The user needs to be confident that just because she has updated her Facebook profile saying that she is feeling down, she should not expect to receive e-mail solicitation for her to purchase Prozac. Although, ultimately, the user is responsible for protecting her own privacy, she should have some measure of confidence that the protection of her privacy is a valued objective of the on line vendors. Otherwise the user may engage in privacy protecting behaviors that may be detrimental to usefulness of the services and therefore reduce the profitability. One such behavior is misrepresentation of one's identity. Consider the following example. One of my graduate students excitedly called me one day to tell me about her Facebook experience. Being concerned about her privacy, she had created a new Facebook profile for herself and purposely had given an erroneous birth date in which her aged was calculated to be 63. To her amazement, she recalled, that within hours she had received an e-mail from AARP (American Association of Retired Persons) inviting her to join that organization. Her misrepresentation of her age, nullifies any value that AARP would get from knowing her age. This is not a criticism of Facebook's or any other company's privacy policies per-se; it is a reminder of changing landscape of privacy and its impact on our daily lives. It is a call to action. No longer should we debate whether our privacy is in danger, it is time to assume that and seek ways to protect it. Companies should remember that a good privacy policy is good business and users should never assume that their privacy is protected. They need to become a more active participant in protecting their own privacy. In practice, information privacy deals with an individual's ability to control and release personal information. The individual is in control of the release process: to whom information is released, how much is released and for what purpose the information is to be used. Consumers are likely to lose confidence in the online marketplace because of these privacy concerns. Business must understand consumers' concern about these issues and aim to build consumer trust. It is important to note that knowledge about data collection can have a negative influence on a customer's trust and confidence level online.

Privacy concerns are real and have profound and undeniable implications on people's attitude and behavior (Sullivan, 2002). Privacy considerations will become more important to customers interacting electronically with businesses. As a result, privacy will become an import business driver. People (Customers) feel 'violated' when their privacy is invaded. They respond to it differently, despite the intensity of their feelings. Given this divergent and varied reaction to privacy violation, a lot of companies still do not appreciate the depth of consumer feelings and the need to revamp their information practices, as well as their infrastructure for dealing with privacy. Privacy is no longer about just staying within the letter of the latest law or regulation. As sweeping changes in attitudes of people their privacy will fuel an intense political debate and put once-routine business and corporate practices under the microscope. Two components of this revolution will concern business the most, rising consumer fears and a growing patchwork of regulations. Both are already underway. Regulatory complexity will grow as privacy concerns surface in scattered pieces of legislation. Companies need to respond quickly and comprehensively. They must recognize that privacy should be a core business issue. Privacy policies and procedures that cover all operations must be enacted. Privacy Preserving Identity Management should be viewed as a business issue, not a compliance issue.

Hamid R. Nemati
The University of North Carolina, USA

REFERENCES

Adkinson, W., Eisenach, J., & Lenard, T. (2002). Privacy Online: A Report on the Information Practices and Policies of Commercial Web Sites. Retrieved August, 2006, from http://www.pff.org/publications/privacyonlinefinalael.pdf

Adkinson, W., Eisenach, J., & Lenard, T. (2002). Privacy Online: A Report on the Information Practices and Policies of Commercial Web Sites. Retrieved August 2009, from http://www.pff.org/publications/privacyonlinefinalael.pdf

American Institute of Certified Public Accountants (AICPA) information security tops the list of ten most important IT priorities, 2007. Accessed from: http://infotech.aicpa.org/Resources.

Anonymous. (2006). Office for Civil Rights. Retrieved August 2009, from http://www.hhs.gov/ocr/index.html

Anonymous. (2006). Privacy Legislation Affecting the Internet: 108th Congress. Retrieved August 2008, from http://www.cdt.org/legislation/108th/privacy/

Barker, William and Lee, Anabelle, Information Security, Volume II: Appendices to Guide for Mapping Types of Information and Information Systems to Security Categories, National Institute of Standards and Technology, , NIST Special Publication 800- 60 Version II, 2004. Accessed from: http://csrc.nist.gov/publications/nistpubs/800-60/SP800-60V2-final.pdf

Barker, William, Guide for Mapping Types of Information and Information Systems to Security Categories, National Institute of Standards and Technology, NIST Special Publication 800- 60 Version 1.0, 2004, Accessed from: http://csrc.nist.gov/publications/nistpubs/800-60/SP800-60V1-final.pdf

Berners-Lee, Tim, The Semantic Web, 2007. Accessed from Scientific American at www.sciam.com.

Brancheau, J. C., Janz, B. D., & Wetherbe, J. C. (1996). Key issues in information systems management: 1994-95 SIM Delphi Results. MIS Quart., 20(2), 225-242.

Brown, E. (2002, April 1). Analyze This. Forbes, 169, 96-98.

Businessweek. (2001), Privacy in an Age of Terror. Businessweek.

Chew, L., Swanson, M., Stine, K., Bartol, N., Brown, A., and Robinson, W., Performance Measurement Guide for Information Security, National Institute of Standards and Technology, NIST Special Publication 800-55 Revision 1. 2008. Accessed from: http://csrc.nist.gov/publications/nistpubs/800-55-Rev1/SP800-55-rev1.pdf.

Ciosa, K.J., & Mooree, W. (2002). Uniqueness of medical data mining. Artificial Intelligence in Medicine, 26, 1–24

Classen, D. C. (1998). Clinical Decision Support Systems to Improve Clinical Practice and Quality of Care. JAMA, 280(15),1360-1361.

Clifton, C., Kantarcioglu, M., Vaidya, J., Lin, X., & Zhu, M. (2002). Tools for privacy preserving distributed data mining. ACM SIGKDD Explorations Newsletter, 4(2), 28-34.

Committee on National Security Systems (CNSS), National Security Agency, "National Information Assurance (IA) Glossary," CNSS Instruction No. 4009, May 2003, Accessed from: http://www.cnss.gov/Assets/pdf/cnssi_4009.pdf.

Culnan, M. J. (1993). How did they get my name?" An exploratory investigation of consumer attitudes toward secondary information use. MIS Quart., 17(3), 341-363.

Culnan, M. J. (1993). How did they my name? An exploratory investigation of consumer attitudes toward secondary information use. MIS Quart., 17(3), 341-363.

Dhillon, G., & Moores, T. (2001). Internet privacy: Interpreting key issues. Information Resources Management Journal, 14(4).

Dictionary.com. (2010). Privacy. Retrieved from http://dictionary.reference.com/browse/privacy

Dyson, E. (1998). Release 2.0: A Design for Living in the Digital Age. Bantam Doubleday Dell Pub.

European Commission (1999). Creating a safer information society by improving the security of information infrastructures and combating computer-related crime. Accessed from http://www.cybercrime.gov/intl/EUCommunication.0101.pdf.

Eckerson, W., & Watson, H. (2001). Harnessing Customer Information for Strategic Advantage: Technical Challenges and Business Solutions, Industry Study 2000, Executive Summary. In The Data Warehousing Institute.

Economist. (2001, February 17). The slow progress of fast wires (p. 358).

Eshmawi, A., & Sadri, F. (2009). Information Integration with Uncertainty. In Proceedings of the 2009 International Database Engineering and Applications Conference (IDEAS'09).

Estivill-Castro, V., Brankovic, L., & Dowe, D. L. (1999). Privacy in Data Mining. Retrieved August 2006, from http://www.acs.org.au/nsw/articles/1999082.htm

Evfimievski, A., Srikant, R., Agrawal, R., & Gehrke, J. (2002). Privacy preserving mining of association rules. In Proceedings of the eighth ACM SIGKDD international conference on Knowledge discovery and data mining, July 2002, Edmonton, Alberta, Canada (pp. 217-228).

Findlaw.com (2010).

Garg, A.X., Adhikari, N.K.J., McDonald, H. (2005). Effects of Computerized Clinical Decision Support Systems on Practitioner Performance and Patient Outcomes: A Systematic Review. , JAMA, 293(10), 1223-1238.

Grance, T., Stevens, M., and Myers M., Guide to Selecting Information Technology Security Products, National Institute of Standards and Technology, NIST Special Publication 800-36. 2003. Accessed from: http://csrc.nist.gov/publications/nistpubs/800-36/NIST-SP800-36.pdf.

Gross, H. (1967). The Concept of Privacy, 42 New York University Law. Review. 34, 35 (1967).

Han, J., & Kamber, M. (2001). Data Mining: Concepts and Techniques. Morgan Kaufmann Publishers.

Hardy, Q. (2004). Data of Reckoning. Forbes, 173, 151-154.

Hodge, J. G., Gostin, L. O., & Jacobson, P. (1999). Legal Issues Concerning Electronic Health Information: Privacy, Quality, and Liability. The Journal of the American Medical Association, 282(15), 1466-1471.

Hunt, D. L., Haynes, R.B., Hanna, S.E., & Smith, K. (1998). Effects of Computer-Based Clinical Decision Support Systems on Physician Performance and Patient Outcomes: A Systematic Review. JAMA, 280, 1339-1346

IDC Report (2010). The Digital Universe Decade: Are You Ready? Retrieved May 2010 from http://www.emc.com/collateral/demos/microsites/idc-digital-universe/iview.htm

Iyengar, V. S. (2002). Transforming data to satisfy privacy constraints. Paper presented at the KDD.

Johnston, M. E., Langton, K. B., Haynes, R. B., & Mathieu, A. (1994). Effects of Computer-based Clinical Decision Support Systems on Clinician Performance and Patient Outcome: A Critical Appraisal of Research. Ann Intern Med, 120(2), 135-142

Kakalik, MA and Wright, JS. (1997), "The Erosion of Privacy," Computers and Society, 22-26.

Kantarcioglu, M., & Clifton, C. (2004). Privacy-Preserving Distributed Mining of Association Rules on Horizontally Partitioned Data. IEEE Trans. Knowledge Data Eng., 16(9), 1026-1037.

Lavrac, N. (1999). Selected techniques for data mining in medicine. Artif Intell Med, 16, 3-23.

Lawson, J. (2010), "What Do People Actually Do Online?" "ColderICE" Blog, accesses from: http://3rdpoblogs.com/colderice/press/

Lindell, Y., & Pinkas, B. (2002). Privacy Preserving Data Mining. J. Cryptology, 15(3), 177-206.

Liu, J. T., Marchewka, J. L., & Yu, C. S. (2004). Beyond concern: a privacy-trust-behavioral intention model of electronic commerce. Information & Management, 42, 127-142.

Machlis, S. (1997). Web sites rush to self-regulate. Computerworld, 32, 19.

Margulis, S. T. (1977). Conceptions of privacy: current status and next steps. J. of Social Issues (33), 5-10.

Mason, R. O. (1986). Four ethical issues of the information age. MIS Quart., 10(1), 4-12.

HIPPA (2010), Accessed from http://www.hhs.gov/ocr/privacy/

McKinsey, 2007. How Businesses are using Web 2.0: A McKinsey Global Survey. Accessed from http://www.mckinseyquarterly.com/.

Miklau, G., & Suciu, D. (2004). A Formal Analysis of Information Disclosure in Data Exchange. In SIGMOD 2004 (pp. 575-586).

Milberg, S. J., S. J., B., Smith, H. J., & Kallman, E. A. (1995). Values, personal information privacy, and regulatory approaches. Comm. of the ACM, 38, 65-74.

Milberg, S. J., S. J., B., Smith, H. J., & Kallman, E. A. (1995). Values, personal information privacy, and regulatory approaches. Comm. of the ACM, 38, 65-74.

National Information Assurance Training and Education Center (NIATEC), 2006. Accessed from http://niatec.info/index.aspx?page=215&glossid=2265.

Nemati, H., Barko, R., & Christopher, D. (2001). Issues in Organizational Data Mining: A Survey of Current Practices. Journal of Data Warehousing, 6(1), 25-36.

NetIQ, (2004) Controlling your Controls: Security Solutions for Sarbanes-Oxley, Accessed at: http://download.netiq.com/Library/White_Papers/NetIQ_SarbanesWP.pdf , 2004.

Niederman, F., Brancheau, J. C., & Wetherbe, J. C. (1991). Information systems management issues for the 1990's. MIS Quart., 15, 474-500.

Nielson (2010) "Top 10 Sectors by Share of U.S. Internet Time," Accessed from: (http://blog.nielsen.com/nielsenwire/online_mobile/what-americans-do-online-social-media-and-games-dominate-activity/)

NIST, Special Publication 800-12: (2003) An Introduction to Computer Security - The NIST Handbook National Institute of Standards and Technology. Accessed from http://csrc.nist.gov/publications/nistpubs/800-12/800-12-html/index.html

OWASP, Testing for Authentication. Accessed from http://www.owasp.org/index.php/Testing_for_authentication.

Pan, S. L., & Lee, J.-N. (2003). Using E-CRM for a Unified View of the Customer. Communications of the ACM, 46(4), 95-99.

Pinkas, B. (2002). Crytographic techniques for privacy-preserving data mining. SIGKDD Exploreations, 4(2), 12-19.

Pitofsky, R. (2006). Privacy Online: Fair Information Practices in the Electronic Marketplace, a Report to Congress. Retrieved August 2006, from http://www.ftc.gov/reports/privacy2000/privacy2000.pdfFTC

Richards, G., Rayward-Smith, V.J., Sonksen, P.H., Carey, S., & Weng, C. (2001). Data mining for indicators of early mortality in a database of clinical records. Artif Intell Med, 22, 215-31.

Ripley, B.D. (1996). Pattern recognition and neural networks. Cambridge: Cambridge University Press.

Rockart, J. F., & DeLong, D. W. (1988). Executive Support Systems: The Emergence of Top Management Computer Use. Paper presented at the Dow Jones-Irwin, Homewood, IL.

Smith, H. J. (1993). Privacy policies and practices: Inside the organizational maze. Comm. of the ACM, 36, 105-122.

Smith, H. J., Milberg, S. J., & Burke, S. J. (1996). Information privacy: Measuring individuals' concerns about organizational practices. MIS Quart., 167-196.

Sullivan, B. (2002). Privacy groups debate DoubleClick settlement. Retrieved August, 2006, from http://www.cnn.com/2002/TECH/internet/05/24/doubleclick.settlement.idg/index.html.

Vaidya, J., & Clifton, C. (2004). Privacy-Preserving Data Mining: Why, How, and When. IEEE Security and Privacy, 2(6), 19-27.

Van Bemmel, J., & Musen, M. A. (1997). Handbook of Medical Informatics. New York: Springer-Verlag.

Verykios, V. S., Bertino, E., Fovino, I. N., Provenza, L. P., Saygin, Y., & Theodoridis, Y. (2004). State-of-the-art in privacy preserving data mining. SIGMOD Record, 33, 50-57.

Watson, H. J., Rainer Jr, R. K., & Koh, C. E. (1991). Executive information systems: a framework for development and a survey of current practices. MIS Quart., 13-30.

Wells, David (1996). Accessed from http://www.objs.com/survey/authent.htm.

Westin, A. (1967). Privacy and Freedom. New York: Atheneum.

Whitman, Michael and Mattord, Herbert, Principles of Information Security, Course Technology, 2004.

World Wide Web Consortium (W3C), 2004. Accessed from http://www.w3.org/TR/ws-gloss/.

Chapter 1
Re-Evaluation of On-Line Hot Topic Discovery Model

Hui-min Ye
University of Vermont, USA

Sushil K. Sharma
Ball State University, USA

Huinan Xu
Ernst & Young, USA

ABSTRACT

As a major medium for information transmission, Internet plays an important role in diffusing and spreading news on web. Some governments attach great importance and pay lot of effort trying to detect, track the development of events and forecast emergency on internet. On the basis of the researches in the field of topic detection and tracking, we proposed a model for hot topic discovery that would pick out hot topics by automatically detecting, clustering and weighting topics on the websites within a time period. We also introduced a topic index approach in following the growth of topics, which is useful to analyze and forecast the development of topics on web.

INTRODUCTION

The web has become indispensible part of modern life and has unbelievable influence in our real society. It spreads and provides sources of hundreds of millions of news and information, in which some topics that are growing in interest over time have great impact on our real life, sometimes even affect the development of events in a way. In order to pick out these influencing news and topics on the web, we built an intelligent system that can automatically and effectively discover hot topics embedded on the web within a period. Earlier we took bulletin board system (BBS) into consideration in our model in terms of discovering hot topic on internet. It's true that some messages or topics on BBS are concerned with the mainstream news or topics, however, we discover later on that most messages on BBS are too trivial and irrelevant to serious issues, the meaningful hot topics selected from BBS are almost amount to nothing compared with large number of data collection, which means it contributes little in picking out hot

DOI: 10.4018/978-1-60960-200-0.ch001

topics. Therefore in our modified topic model we ignore the contribution of messages from BBS.

The algorithm we proposed for hot topics discovery is based on the principle of Term Frequency * Proportional Document Frequency (TF*PDF). Research on TF*PDF (Term Frequency * Proportional Document Frequency) algorithm has been described in (Khoo and Ishizuka, 2001a, 2001b). The algorithm has been adapted in our article in a way that assigns heavy weight to those topics that discussed in many documents from many sources concurrently. Based on the principle of stock index, we use topic index to manifest the developing process of hot topics.

The hot topic discovery model takes a collection of data as input and identifies topic areas that are growing in importance with collected information (Allan et al. 2000, Fiscus & Doddington, 2002). It includes two stages, the first stage is topic detection and clustering stage, the second stage is hot topic discovery and generation of topic index. In the following sections, we first briefly depict the first stage in which we adopt existing algorithm to realize this task of topic detection and clustering. The second stage explains the modified model we propose to detect hot topics and the topic index method to follow the growth of topics. Then we discuss and compare the results of experiments based on two models. The flow of information in the system is illustrated in Figure 1.

The objective of topic detection is to identify topically related stories without positive or negative training stories. It is basically a problem related to clustering, where the goal is to group stories discussing the same event (Wayne, 2000). Detection is similar to tracking with the exception that no any training stories are provided for a particular topic, and all the topics that are mentioned in stream have to be identified (Allan et al., 2003, Allan, et al, 1999, Yang et al. 1999, Yang et al, 2000). Topic detection can be accomplished using any clustering algorithm as long as it is on-the-fly and nonoverlapping clustering (Wayne, 2000, Martin et al., 1997). In the process of detection we make use of *tf·idf* weighting scheme and the *cosine* similarity metric. The *idf* component of the weighting is based on incremental statistics to emulate the online nature of the task.

Document Representation

A document is represented with a *tf·idf* feature weights where

$$\text{tf} = \frac{t}{t + 0.5 + 1.5\frac{dl}{dl_{avg}}} \tag{1}$$

$$\text{idf} = \frac{\log(\frac{N + 0.5}{df})}{\log(N + 1)} \tag{2}$$

Figure 1. System information flow topic detection stage

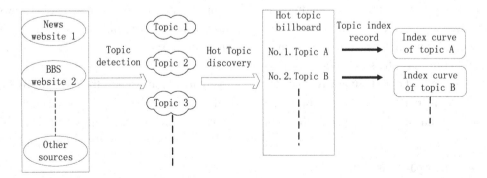

t is the number of times feature f_i occurs in the document, dl is the document's length, dl_{avg} is the average document length in the collection. N is the number of documents in the collection. Term frequency component fl represents the degree to which the term describes the contents of a document. The *idf* component is the logarithm of the inverse document frequency in the collection, it is intended to discount very common words in the collection, since they have little discrimination power. N denotes the total number of documents in the collection, df is the number of documents in which the feature appears in the collection.

Topic Similarity

With the feature weight, we use cosine coefficient to measure the similarity of a given new story to the topic representation. Cosine coefficient is a classic measure used in information retrieval. Suppose D is a document vector and T is a topic representation vector. The cosine similarity is defined as

$$Sim(D, T) = \frac{\sum_{i \in H} q_i d_i}{\sqrt{(\sum_{i \in H} q_i^2)(\sum_{i \in H} d_i^2)}} \qquad (3)$$

H is the feature collection. q_i and d_i reflect the weights assigned to feature i in the document and topic vectors, respectively.

Online Clustering Algorithm

In this modified model we still use the *single-link* incremental (single pass) clustering algorithm which has been proved to have slightly better performance in TDT's formal evaluations (Allan, et. al., 2003, Allan, et. al, 1999). It is also effective and faster than average link or complete link (Allan, et al., 2003). When a new document appears on the stream, if the story is not novel, it is put into one of the existing clusters, or if it is sufficiently dissimilar from all past stories, it becomes the seed of a new cluster. We used a threshold of θ = 0.20 based on experiments.

SECOND STAGE

Hot Topic Discovery

The number of documents relevant to a specific topic is not necessarily the only factor in defining the popularity or hot level. Major websites sources should also be seen as an important contributor for hot degree of a topic. We suppose topics being discussed by many websites are more important than those that only being discussed by only few website, even though these topics maybe contain many documents. Previously we also took the messages or topics posted on BBS into consideration for hot topic judgment, but it has been ignored in modified algorithm based on our observation that the contribution from BBS is too trivial to be worthy computed.

Research on TF*PDF (Term Frequency * Proportional Document Frequency) algorithm has been reported in several papers (Khoo and Ishizuka, 2001a, 2001b). It also has been adapted in (Khyou & Ishizuka, 2002) to extract topic on a number of newswire sources on the web. Based on the principle of TF*PDF, we propose the following algorithm to decide the hot topic among various news and sources, in which we adopt DF (document frequency) to substitute TF in TF*PDF,

Topic weight (j_t)=

$$\left(\sum_{s=1}^{s=K} | D_{js_{(t)}} | \times \exp\left(\frac{D_{js_{(t)}}}{N_{s(t)}}\right) \times W_s\right) \times WB \qquad (4)$$

$$| D_{js(t)} | = \frac{D_{js(t)}}{\sqrt{\sum_{c=1}^{c=C} D_{cs(t)}^2}} \qquad (5)$$

Topic weight (j_t) is the weight of topic j within t time period, which is used to measure the hot level of a topic. The t time period can be any part of time, say a day, a week or a month. $D_{js(t)}$ is the document number of topic j within t time period on website s, $N_{s(t)}$ is the total number of documents on website s. W_s is the weight of website s, it is 1.0 if the website is a common news website s or we attribute 2.0 to W_s if the website s is a popular website (we predefined some websites that are supposed to be very popular and well known). C is the total number of topics on a website.

There are altogether four major compositions in the algorithm. Based on the assumption that hot topic generally discussed in majority of the websites, the first part is the "summation" of the topic weight gained from each website, which significantly contributes to the weight of a topic. The larger the number of websites, the more accurate will be this algorithm in recognizing the emerging hot topics.

The second, third and forth compositions are combined to give the weight of a topic on a website. The second composition is $|D_{js(t)}|$, which is the normalized topic frequency of a topic on a website. The topic frequency needs to be normalized because when different website has different size of archive, the topic from a website with more documents will have a proportionally higher probability to appear more frequently. We suggest however, to give equal importance to the same topic from each website, thus normalization is necessary.

The third composition is

$$\exp\left(\frac{D_{js(t)}}{N_{s(t)}}\right),$$

which is the PDF (proportional document frequency) of a topic on a website. It is the exponential of the number of documents on topic j to the total number of documents on website s. We deem that topics that have many documents are more valuable than those that have few, hence the documents about a topic appear more frequently in documents archive on a website should have higher possibility to be a hot topic on this website. PDF thus should grow exponentially in respect to the number of documents about a topic, instead of linearly, so that we can give a more significant weight to the topic that being discussed in many documents compare to those that have only a few documents. Mathematically, larger the number of documents of a topic on a website, higher will be the grow rate of the PDF of the topic on the website. Here the PDF has a value ranges from (e^0) to 2.718 (e^1) exponentially.

The forth composition is the weight of a website W_s. Normal news website and popular website has different weight respectively. We decide 1.0 as the weight of news websites, and 2.0 as the weight of popular websites.

The total weight of a topic is equal to the summation of the weight of the topic in each website respectively. The algorithm proposed in this article gives significance to those topics that have many documents in majority websites.

Topic Index

We still use the same topic index algorithm to track the development of topics as before. The idea behind topic index is based on stock market index. A stock market index is a number that indicates the relative level of prices or value of securities in a market on a particular day compared with a base-day figure. It is benchmark that is used to gauge the performance of stock. Similarly, we adopt topic index to reflect a topic's developing history. Our basic idea is to use a topic index to indicate the development of a hot topic. The topic index is computed as follows,

Topic index(t_x) =

$$\frac{\text{The } x\text{th day's topic weight}}{\text{Base Day's topic weight}} \times \text{Base Day's index}$$

(6)

Topic index (t_x) represents the index of the *xth* day of a topic *t*. Both the Base day's topic weight and the *xth* day's topic weight are calculated with the same formula (4), but with different parameter values determined by base day and the *xth* day. We take the day when the topic *t* being detected in section 1 as the base day for topic *t*. The value assigned to the base day index is 100 in our experiment.

With topic index, it is easy and obvious to understand the changing range of a topic in different time compared with its base day weight. An increasing index of a topic implies the increasing popularity or importance of that topic, a sign of an emerging hot topic that should be attached attention. The information of topic index is also helpful for experts to infer the future development of some topics.

Experiment

In order to testify the modified model, our experiments have been run on the same data as had been used by previous hot topic system. Because we ignore the BBS factor in new model, so we only chose online news data and deleted messages from BBS websites in the experiment. The news websites include www.people.com.cn, www.xinhuanet.com and www.sina.com.cn, The archives collected within 7 days (dated from December 25 to December 31 in 2004) consist of 10026 news. This period includes the occurrence of the devastating tsunami that erupted in the Indian Ocean on Dec. 26.

After the clustering process on the first stage, 1806 different clusters have been clustered. On the base of those clusters, the topics have been weighted by the second stage. Table 1 shows the top 10 most heavily weighted topics calculated by the modified model where Table 2 is the result from the previous model.

Compared with the two tables we can see that all the top 10 hot topics listed in Table 2 are all included in Table 1, the only difference is the orders of some topics. The news and reports related to the tsunami disaster still occupy the top orders. The post-war situation in Iraq listed in Table 1 is No.7 while it was No.4 in Table 2. The reason for that order change is because we ignore the related messages from BBS which contributed a little to the weight of this topic. The order of the topic of relationship between China and America changed from No.8 to No.9. The reason for that change is also because of ignoring the contribution of related BBS messages.

In order to find out the fluctuation differences of topic in both two models on daily bases, we use topic index to show the changes of those 10 topics.

Table 1. Top 10 topics

No.	Topic	Topic weight
1	Reports about tsunami and earthquake happened in south Asia	2.4688
2	Tsunami disaster situation related Thailand	1.3890
3	Ukraine's general election	1.0082
4	Donation for the relief of tsunami disaster from around world	0.8524
5	Aftermath of tsunami disaster in Sri Lanka	0.8009
6	Tsunami disaster in Indonesia	0.8007
7	Post-war situation in Iraq	0.7560
8	General election in Palestine	0.6672
9	Relationship between America and China	0.6255
10	NPC Standing Committee's discussion on the drafts of several important laws	0.4504

Table 2. Top 10 topics

No.	Topic	Topic weight
1	Reports about tsunami and earthquake happened in south Asia	2.5588
2	Tsunami disaster situation related to Thailand	1.4099
3	Ukraine's general election	1.1199
4	Post-war situation in Iraq	0. 9533
5	Donation for the relief of tsunami disaster from around world	0.9308
6	Aftermath of tsunami disaster in Sri Lanka	0.8227
7	Tsunami disaster in Indonesia	0.8109
8	Relationship between America and China	0.7504
9	General election in Palestine	0.5423
10	NPC Standing Committee's discussion on the drafts of several important laws	0.4605

TOPIC INDEX

Because different topic may appear on different date, their base days have been set as the date when the topic first appeared. Topic base day's value was calculated with formula (4) where t=1. Table 3 is the topic index of those top 10 topics in Table 1. Table 3 indicates the fluctuation of every topic in the top list from date Dec 25 to Dec 31. In order to compare the fluctuation of topic generated from two models, we made topic index curve for topic No.1 in Table 1. Figure 2 and Figure 3 are the index curves for the No.1 topic based on two models respectively.

From Figure 2 and Figure 3 we can see that the curves in two figures are very similar, they have peaks and troughs on the same dates. The peak value of the two curves for topic tsunami is on 27th, after dropping a little on 28th, both curves ascended again to a second peak value. On 31st they dropped sharply. The two figures indicate the same development process and tendency of the same topic. From the comparison, we can come to the conclusion that the modified model has the same the tracking effect as previous one.

Table 3. Topic index from Dec 25 to Dec 31

Topic No.	Base day's value (date)	Topic index						
		25	26	27	28	29	30	31
1	1.8509(26)	—	100	106.24	86.7	102.8	98.3	86.22
2	0.6002(26)	—	100	258.6	143.2	88.96	142.8	68.37
3	0.4620(25)	100	57.88	329.2	190.3	233.8	45.37	90.20
4	0.1249(26)	—	100	200.68	309.65	579.78	618.3	476
5	0.3429(26)	—	100	133	380	102	130	58.2
6	0.3382(26)	—	100	122	258.2	58.3	88.06	102.3
7	0.5512(25)	100	109.3	198.3	99.8	156.7	275.3	76.83
8	1.0272(25)	100	86.2	73.4	105.6	62.9	90.3	37.6
9	1.0610(25)	100	35.65	101.3	52.79	48.56	48.65	32.89
10	0.5177(25)	100	90.63	83.4	69.40	66.38	99.6	56.72

Figure 2. The curve for topic No.1 Based on Table 1

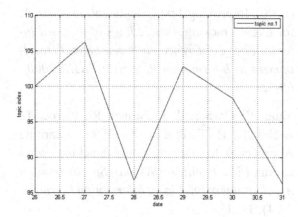

CONCLUSION

The system designed and modified in this article is effective in discovering the hot topics on websites periodically. We have shown that by ignoring the factor of BBS contribution, the modified algorithm still performs well in picking out hot topics that appear frequently in many documents from multiple website sources. In comparison, the modified model runs faster and costs less computing resources. Also, we applied topic index approach to observe the difference between the two models. The experiments show that topic indexes do not change much and also indicate the same development and trend for the same topic. The hot topic

Figure 3. The curve for topic No.1 Based on Table 2

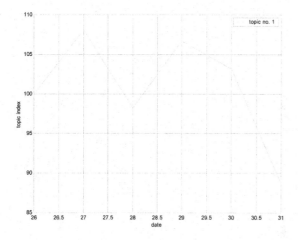

model proposed in this article is also useful to discover the trend of some sensitive topics and understand the public interest tendency timely.

REFERENCES

Allan, J.,.Papka, R., &.Lavrenko, V. (1999). On-line New Event Detection and Tracking. Graduate School of the University of Massachusetts.

Allan, J., Lavrenko, V., & Connell, M. E. (2003). A month to topic detection and tracking in Hindi. [TALIP]. *ACM Transactions on Asian Language Information Processing*, 2(2), 85–100. doi:10.1145/974740.974742

Allan, J., Lavrenko, V., & Jin, H. (2000). First Story Detection in TDT is Hard, *Proceedings of 9th Conference on Information Knowledge Management* CIKM, 374-381.

Beeferman, D., Berger, A., & Lafferty, J. (1999). Statistical models for text segmentation. *Machine Learning*, *34*, 1–34. doi:10.1023/A:1007506220214

Fiscus, J. G., & Doddington, G. R. (2002). Topic detection and tracking evaluation overview. In *James Allan* (pp. 17–31). Boston: Kluwer Academic Publishers.

Khoo, K. B., & Ishizuka, M. (2001a). *Emerging Topic Tracking System, Proceedings of Web Intelligent (WI 2001), LXAI 2198* (pp. 125–130). Machashi, Japan: Springer.

Khoo, K. B., & Ishizuka, M. (2001b). Information Area Tracking and Changes Summarizing *Proceedings of WebNet 2001*, International Conference on WWW and Internet, Orlando, Florida,680-685

Khyou, K., & Ishizuka, B. M. (2002). Topic Extraction from News Archive Using TF*PDF Algorithm. The third International Conference on Web Information Systems Engineering(WISE'00),Singapore, 73.

Martin, A., Doddington, G., Kamm, T., Ordowski, M., & Przybocki, M. (1997). The DET Curve in Assessment of Detection Task Performance. *Proceedings of Eurospeech, 1997*, 1895–1898.

Wayne, C. (2000). Multilingual Topic Detection and Tracking: Successful Research Enabled by Corpora and Evaluatio, Language Resources and Evaluation Conference (LREC), 1487-1494.

Yang, Y., Ault, T., Pierce, T., & Lattimer, C. W. (2000). Improving Text Categorization Methods for Event Tracking, *Proceedings of the 23rd International Conference on Research and Development in Information Retrieval (SIGIR-2000)*, 65-72.

Yang, Y., Carbonell, J., Brown, R., Pierce, T., Archibald, B. T., & Liu, X. (1999). Learning Approaches for Detecting and Tracking News Events. *IEEE Intelligent Systems: Special Issue on Applications of Intelligent Information Retrieval, 14*(4), 32–43.

This work was previously published in International Journal of Information Security and Privacy (IJISP), edited by Hamid Nemati, pp 1-10, copyright 2009 by IGI Publishing (imprint of IGI Global)

Chapter 2
Understanding User Behavior towards Passwords through Acceptance and Use Modelling

Lee Novakovic
Murdoch University, Australia

Tanya McGill
Murdoch University, Australia

Michael Dixon
Murdoch University, Australia

ABSTRACT

The security of computer systems that store our data is a major issue facing the world. This research project investigated the roles of ease of use, facilitating conditions, intention to use passwords securely, experience and age on usage of passwords, using a model based on the Unified Theory of Acceptance and Use of Technology. Data was collected via an online survey of computer users, and analyzed using PLS. The results show there is a significant relationship between ease of use of passwords, intention to use them securely and the secure usage of passwords. Despite expectations, facilitating conditions only had a weak impact on intention to use passwords securely and did not influence actual secure usage. Computing experience was found to have an effect on intention to use passwords securely, but age did not. The results of this research lend themselves to assisting in policy design and better understanding user behavior.

INTRODUCTION

Computer security is a major issue facing the world we inhabit. Computer systems in a multitude of institutions and organizations hold our personal information. Furthermore, we rely on the safe working of computer systems to not only protect that data, but allow us to take advantage of the benefits technology has to offer. Various kinds of security technology protect these systems. However, the development of security technology has not kept pace with suggested usability guidelines (Nielson, 1990). It has been shown that despite all of the advances in computer security technol-

DOI: 10.4018/978-1-60960-200-0.ch002

ogy, lack of suitable user compliance has led to a marked decrease in the overall levels of security (Adams & Sasse, 1999). Users find security measures difficult to use properly (Adams & Sasse, 1999). It is therefore in the interests of all levels involved with operating and using computer systems that the security measures in place have the appropriate factors affecting acceptance and use studied. The broad aim of the research described in this article was to investigate the effect of the ease of use of passwords on users' intentions to behave securely, and on their actual secure usage of passwords. The help and assistance available to users and its effect on secure usage was also of interest. To address these aims, a model derived from the Unified Theory of Acceptance and Use of Technology (UTAUT) (Venkatesh, Morris, Davis, & Davis, 2003) was developed and tested.

BACKGROUND

Computer security has traditionally focused on securing technology. This encompasses securing it from physical theft, from intrusion (both internal and external threats), compromised integrity and the system's level of availability. This is covered by the basic "Confidentiality, Integrity and Availability" (CIA) security model (Stanton, Stam, Mastrangelo, & Jolton, 2005). This model works well when the sole focus is on securing technology with minimal consideration for the users.

The users of a system are often neglected from consideration when planning the security schema of a network of systems (Adams & Sasse, 1999; Braz & Robert, 2006; Singh, Cabraal, & Hermansson, 2006; Zurko & Simon, 1996). In many instances, the failings of the security plan are seen as a failing of the users (Adams & Sasse, 1999; Zurko & Simon, 1996), rather than the failing of the technology. Since systems are provided for users to use, this shift of responsibility is crucial and the reason for many computer security failings.

A commonly held belief is that there is an inherent trade off between the usability and the security of any given system. However, "if people are unable to use secure computers, they will use computers that are not secure. At the end of the day, computers that are theoretically secure but not usable do little to improve the security of their users…the converse is also true: systems that are usable but not secure are, in the end, not very usable either" (Cranor & Garfinkel, 2005, p. x).

A commonly used security model is the AAA model. This refers to three parts of computer security: Authentication, Authorization and Accounting (Langsford, Naemura, & Speth, 1983). Authentication can be summarized with the phrase "who you are". Authentication aims to validate who a user claims to be. Once authenticated, a user's credentials may allow them to perform certain actions in certain areas of the system. An example of authorization is the difference between the level of access a regular user has on a system and the level of access an administrator has. Accounting can be summarized with "what you did". Once a user has been authenticated and authorized to do certain tasks, the accounting part records what that person did. Commonly, this is in the form of log files. Whilst all three components (among others) are important to effective computer and network security, authorization and accounting are beyond the scope of this research project. Most problems relating to the usability of security devices and techniques from the user perspective are concerned with the authentication phase (Adams & Sasse, 1999; Braz & Robert, 2006; Patrick, Long, & Flinn, 2003).

There are a number of authentication methods available to users. There are three ways for users to prove their identity to a computer system. These consist of "knowing" something, "having" something or "being" something. Respectively these can be broken down to passwords, security tokens and biometric details.

Despite the fact that they are invariably less secure than ideal, the most prevalent and widespread forms of authentication are the password (or passphrase) and personal identification number (PIN). A password can contain the alphanumeric values and special characters available on a computer system. A PIN is however limited to the ten available digits (0 – 9) (Braz & Robert, 2006). Both schemes offer easy deployment, but are easily forgotten. There are a number of commonly used rules relating to proper password creation and management. These rules are defined as part of the service. Some of these rules include using a minimum of eight characters comprised of alphanumeric characters and special symbols. A password should be easy to remember and able to be typed quickly (Garfinkel, Spafford, & Schwartz, 2003). Further to this, there are a number of rules relating to what should not be in a password. This list includes names (such as spouses and children), favorite sporting teams, favorite fictional character names and unique information about the user (Garfinkel et al., 2003). These are but a few of the recommended constraints on password design.

It is obvious that these requirements are numerous and can demand serious mental effort to create a password that fits all the criteria. For this and other related reasons users find security measures difficult to use properly (Adams & Sasse, 1999) and this can make compliance an issue. Security policies commonly have clauses which demand users change their passwords after a set period of time (Garfinkel et al., 2003; Mainwald, 2003). It has been found that there is a counterproductive effect to these security policies. Demanding passwords be changed frequently and be of strong composition can place too much cognitive load on users. As a result, users choose easy-to-remember passwords, and the system suffers a lower level of security (Adams & Sasse, 1999; Besnard & Arief, 2004; Braz & Robert, 2006). There is also a correlation between the complexity of the password regime and the insecure actions undertaken by users, with 50% of users writing down their passwords (Adams & Sasse, 1999; Besnard & Arief, 2004; Halderman, Waters, & Felten, 2005).

The survey carried out by Adams and Sasse (1999) found that the stricter the restrictions and guidelines on password content, the less memorable the resultant password. It is estimated that a large percentage of helpdesk and support requests are related to password difficulties, often a forgotten password (Brostoff & Sasse, 2000). This inability of the user to effectively deal with the password requirements laid down for them has also been used as a measure of a system's level of usability in relation to security (Brostoff & Sasse, 2000).

Adams and Sasse (1999) also found that users lack security knowledge, and that their lack of knowledge and understanding contributes to their "insecure" behavior. In part this can be traced back to an assumption that the more that is known about a security mechanism, the easier it is to attack. However, their results suggest that lack of knowledge creates more problems than it solves.

As previously mentioned, there are a number of areas in which users fail to act in the most secure way possible. It is important to make the distinction between deliberately malicious users, who may aim to misuse systems or intentionally destroy data and information and users who cause detrimental outcomes to computer security through naïve mistakes, such as poor password hygiene. The latter group of users are the focus of this research. In the survey carried out by Stanton et al. (2005), it was found that 62.5% of participants did not use any punctuation marks in their password, 48.5% of participants had not changed their password in the previous month and that 27.9% wrote down their passwords. This demonstrates the widespread occurrence of naïve mistakes made by users.

The overall security of a system which relies on passwords is not solely dependent on the complexity of user passwords. There exists a multitude of threats to a network's security once a password has been set, regardless of the user's behavior towards it. A "man-in-the-middle" attack could be used to intercept transmitted passwords in network traffic. Password based network security can also be threatened by an exposed password store, such as the "shadow file" on UNIX systems. Data loss of this sort could be through the introduction of malicious code, such as viruses or Trojan horses or theft of hardware and software (Mainwald, 2003).

There are other significant user factors that influence the overall level of security on a computer network and associated systems. These issues are out of the scope, yet complementary to the area of research involving ease of use of passwords. The first such issue is the matter of user error. As information security and the mechanisms which serve this function become increasingly more common, the possibility for user error having an impact becomes more apparent (Zurko, 2005). This could be viewed as a matter of awareness of current security concerns and the effects mitigated through education and training (Mainwald, 2003).

One must not disregard the other "class" of user which can have a great impact on computer security: the system administrator. As this class of user is responsible for the setup and maintenance of a computer network, data backup, maintaining a patching regimen, proper configuration and enforcement of computing policy through technical methods, their action or inaction can have fantastic ramifications on a network's security (Mainwald, 2003).

A system's security is also at risk through users whose confidence and trust is exploited by attackers. This is a process known as "social engineering". Social engineering is a psychological attack on the user, undertaken by tricking them to divulge some information (Orgill, Romney, Bailey, & Orgill, 2004). The effectiveness of social engineering is not due to users being overburdened by the security technologies they are forced to use, it is through a lack of compliance to the security policy. This threat is so serious that some organizations hire individuals to audit their policy by infiltrating their organization (Ceraolo, 1996; Orgill, Romney, Bailey, & Orgill, 2004). Orgill et al.'s (2004) study consisted of a one

week experiment, which consisted of infiltrating an organization and convincing employees to participate in a "survey". Of those interviewed, 81.3% willingly gave their username and 59.4% gave their passwords. The study also discovered that of the surveyed employees many were not skeptical or suspicious of the researcher's (posing as an insider of the organization) claims of authority and requests for information.

There also exists a significant social trust component in the area of password sharing and social engineering. The study performed by Weirich and Sasse (2001) showed that divulging one's password to colleagues is a sign of trust between the individuals. Not divulging a password has the unexpected outcome of appearing suspicious of fellow workmates. Similarly, the study performed by Singh, Cabraal and Hermansson. (2006) found that the sharing of bank access codes in married and de facto couples was seen as an expression of trust.

MODELING SECURITY BEHAVIOR

There are a number of models designed for computer security. However, these focus primarily on the technical aspects of computer security, such as access control within a system. Two such models are the Bell and LaPadula Model (1973) and the High-Water Mark model by Weissmann (1969).

As previously stated, the user is the key component to any system. There have been numerous models proposed, such as the Technology Acceptance Model (TAM) (Davis, 1989), to model the acceptance and use of a new technology. However, there has been little emphasis on user behavior studies in the security arena (Adams & Sasse, 1999; Braz & Robert, 2006; Singh et al., 2006; Zurko & Simon, 1996). This however is an important area and more needs to be known about the acceptance and usability of security measures, and models such as TAM can provide a valuable framework for such research.

Technology acceptance relies upon a degree of volition and freedom. However, often in the field of technology, the ability for an individual's free will to play a significant part is limited. Often, system use is mandated, and the user complies, purely due to a requirement for them to do so (Brown, Massey, Montoya-Weiss, & Burkman, 2002). Security is similar in its modus operandi as policies dictate what a user is allowed to do, and how they are required to do it. However, a differentiation needs to be made in relation to security. As stated, security is often a mandatory requirement, but its effective operation relies upon user action. The problem arises that secure user behavior is often hampered by the very system that requires secure behavior. The following section describes the major research that has attempted to model aspects of security behavior.

A study carried out by Aytes and Connolly (2004) proposed a rational choice model to study unsafe computing practices of undergraduate students. They found that users provided with information regarding their insecure actions did little to change their behavior. Cazier, Wilson and Medlin (2007) also investigated the security behaviors of students. They extended TAM (Davis, 1989) to include measures of privacy risk harm and privacy risk likelihood and found that privacy risk factors negatively influenced students' intentions to use technology. TAM was also used by Lu, Hsu and Hsu (2005) to examine the perceived risk of online applications. They surveyed 1,259 users who had used a free trial version of an online antivirus application and found that perceived risk indirectly influenced intentions to use online antivirus tools under security threats.

Lee and Lee (2002) proposed the Theory of Planned Behavior (TPB) (Ajzen, 1991) as a framework to investigate computer abuse. Ng and Rahim (2005) subsequently used a model derived from the TPB to investigate home users' intentions to practice security. The areas of security focused on were users' habits for keeping anti-virus software up-to-date, backing up their critical data and the use of a personal firewall. They found that perceived usefulness of security actions and peer influence were important factors in attitudes to security and decision to practice security.

Going beyond user behavior to the behavior of other stakeholders, several studies have proposed and tested behavioral models of security. Woon and Kankanhalli (2007) investigated the intention of programmers to develop applications that are written with security in mind. This study compared models based on the TPB and the Theory of Reasoned Action (TRA) (Fishbein & Ajzen, 1975). They found that a developer's attitude was the biggest factor in their decision to develop applications in a secure manner. Interestingly, given the heavy importance of security, organizations did little to assist their developers, beyond allowing them to go to seminars. Woon and Kananhalli (2007) also found that the help and assistance available to developers had no significant impact on intention to practice secure development of applications.

Knapp, Marshall, Rainer and Ford have undertaken several studies that model the role of top management in security effectiveness (Knapp, Marshall, Rainer, & Ford, 2006; Knapp, Marshall, Rainer, & Ford, 2007). Knapp et al. (2006) proposed and tested a model of the influence of top management support on an organization's security culture and level of security policy enforcement. They found that top management support is a significant predictor of an organization's security culture and level of policy enforcement. Their subsequent study explored the variables through which top management can positively influence security effectiveness. User training, security culture, policy relevance, and policy enforcement were all found to influence security effectiveness (Knapp et al., 2007).

RESEARCH QUESTIONS

The primary objective of the research described in this article is to explore how ease of use of passwords and facilitating conditions, such as the help and assistance available to users, influence user behavior in regards to their passwords. Three research questions were posed. To answer these research questions, a model derived from the Unified Theory of Acceptance and Use of Technology (UTAUT) (Venkatesh et al., 2003) was developed (see Figure 1). The UTAUT attempts to forge a unified view of technology acceptance, and was developed through a review and consolidation of models that had previously been proposed to explain information systems usage behavior. The UTAUT is based on eight prior technology acceptance and use models: TRA (Fishbein & Ajzen, 1975), TAM (Davis, 1989), motivational model (Vallerand, 1997), TPB (Ajzen, 1991), a combined theory of planned behavior/technology acceptance model (Taylor & Todd, 1995), model of PC utilization (Thompson, Higgins, & Howell, 1994), innovation diffusion theory (Rogers, 1962), and social cognitive theory (Bandura, 1986). The UTAUT captures a wider range of influences than any previous model and was found to account for 70% of the variance in usage in a longitudinal study (Venkatesh et. al., 2003).

The performance expectancy, social influence and voluntariness constructs of UTAUT have not been included in the research model. This research is looking specifically at the concepts of ease of use and facilitating conditions and their effect on intention and usage. Therefore performance expectancy, social influence and voluntariness are outside the scope of the project. Gender, a part of the original UTAUT model, is also not considered a factor of secure computer usage due to it becoming significantly less important as a factor in technology acceptance (Morris, Venkatesh, & Ackerman, 2005) and it was thus not included.

Consistent with the UTAUT and previous research relating to the acceptance of technology, the relationships described below were initially hypothesized in order to answer the research questions.

The first research question of interest was:

What effect does the ease of use of passwords have on users' intentions to use passwords securely and on actual secure usage?

Ease of use (also known as effort expectancy) is the extent to which a user believes that using a system will be free of effort (Davis, 1989). It is defined in this study as the ease of use of passwords. Consistent with the UTAUT and other models of technology and use, the ease of use of passwords should play a role in a user's intention to behave securely. In the current research, ease of use is thought to affect users' intentions to use

Figure 1. Research model

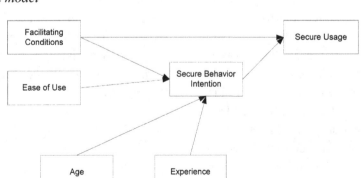

their passwords in a secure fashion, such that the easier passwords are to use, the more likely users are to intend to act in a secure manner. The following hypothesis was therefore proposed.

H1: *Ease of use will have a positive effect on secure behavior intention.*

It was expected that users' intentions to act securely would have an impact on actual secure usage. Intention influencing actual behavior is a long held relationship and was a key concept in Fishbein and Ajzen's (1975) TRA and Davis's (1989) TAM. In this research, usage is defined as actually using passwords in a secure manner. The following hypothesis was therefore proposed.

H2: *Secure behavior intention will have a positive effect on secure usage.*

The second research question addressed in the study was:

Do facilitating conditions have an impact on secure usage of passwords?

Facilitating conditions is the help and assistance available to users when encountering problems with their passwords, and the usage there of. The help and assistance available to users is considered an essential part of usable security (Besnard & Arief, 2004). Consistent with the UTAUT, it was expected that the facilitating conditions available to users would have a direct effect on their secure usage of passwords. However, as facilitating conditions may also play a role in predicting intention under certain conditions (Venkatesh et al., 2003), any indirect effect via intentions was also of interest. The following hypotheses were therefore proposed.

H3: *Facilitating conditions will have a direct positive effect on secure usage.*

H4: *Facilitating conditions will have a positive effect on secure behavior intention.*

The third research question addressed in the study was:

What effect do external factors such as age and experience have on intention to use passwords securely and actual secure usage?

Anecdotally, it is thought that the older an individual the more they will encounter difficulty in using technology. This may be due to lack of confidence and/or lack of skill (Harrison & Rainer, 1992; Janvrin & Morrison, 2000). It was expected that a user's age may have an effect on their intention to use passwords in a secure fashion, as per the results by Morris and Venkatesh (2000). Therefore, the following hypothesis was proposed.

H5 *Age will have a negative effect on secure behavior intention.*

Users' prior general computing experience is expected to have an effect on their intention to behave securely. Taylor and Todd (1995) found significant differences in intention to use technology between experienced and inexperienced users, and Thompson, Higgins and Howell (1994) found that experience had a significant positive influence on use. This distinction is expected to apply in the computer security context. Experienced users are believed to understand the importance of security measures and have a greater intention to behave securely. The following hypothesis was therefore proposed.

H6: *Computing experience will have a positive effect on secure behavior intention.*

METHODS

To answer the research questions posed, data was collected via an online survey. As the primary focus of the survey was how people use their passwords, the potential user base found online was expected to have experience with this topic.

Participants

The target population for this research was all computer users, both in a workplace or home environment. A wide range of age and computing background was desired to get a more complete representation of attitudes towards password security. A link to the survey was posted on a number of websites, each having a wide variety of users. Additional participants were recruited via flyers on university notice boards and word of mouth. A total of 111 responses were obtained.

Data Collection

The software used to create the survey was LimeSurvey (http://www.limesurvey.org). This software allows for the creation of surveys and management of survey data. The gathered data is supplied via a Comma Separated Values (CSV) file. The survey was hosted on a privately run server, accessible by the general internet. Participants were invited to participate in the study by clicking on a link to complete a questionnaire on the web. The questionnaire contained 32 questions and took approximately 10 minutes to complete. Completion of the questionnaire was voluntary and all responses anonymous.

Measurement

Items to measure the constructs of interest were developed for the security domain using instruments from previous research on the UTAUT and other related technology acceptance models as a starting point, with new items being developed as

needed. The measurement of each of the constructs is discussed below. The questionnaire completion process was pilot tested by 11 people and slight changes made to clarify questions. The Appendix contains a list of the items included in the final measurement model.

Ease of Use

Ease of use was measured using 8 items. These items are based on items from Pikkarainen, Pikkarainen, Karjaluoto and Pahnila (2004), Brown, Massey, Montoya-Weiss and Burkman, (2002) and Morris and Venkatesh (2000) and were measured on a 5 point Likert scale ranging from "strongly disagree" to "strongly agree".

Facilitating Conditions

Facilitating conditions refers to the help and assistance that is available to users as they use their passwords. Facilitating conditions was measured using 6 items which are based on items from Aytes and Connolly (2004). Simple statements and a scenario involving a forgotten password were provided and the participants asked to rate their degree of agreement or disagreement using a 5 point Likert scale ranging from "strongly disagree" to "strongly agree". The scenario posed was: "You have forgotten the password to a computer system, rendering you unable to login and use it, delaying your work".

Secure Behavior Intention

Secure behavior intention relates to a participant's intention to use their passwords in a secure fashion. The items used to measure secure behavior intention are based on items from Aytes and Connolly (2004), Ng and Rahim (2005), and Brown et al. (2002). Secure behavior intention was measured using 7 items relating to a scenario based around proper password hygiene. This scenario was: "Good password hygiene recommends a password of 12 characters, alphanumeric (letters and numbers), mixed case and other characters (such as ?, $, ^, #), changed every 30 days and not divulged to any party. A password such as "5gY?r4fTy`/q" satisfies these conditions." This scenario applied to all the secure behavior intention survey items. Simple statements were provided and the participant asked to rate their degree of agreement or disagreement using a 5 point Likert scale ranging from "strongly disagree" to "strongly agree".

Secure Usage

Secure usage refers to a participant's actual usage of their passwords. The same scenario used to measure secure behavior intention was used for this construct. The items used were adapted from Aytes and Connolly (2004). Secure usage was measured using 8 items on a Likert scale. Six items had the scale ranging from "strongly disagree" to "strongly agree", and the final 2 questions used a scale ranging from "very infrequently" to "very frequently".

Age

Age was measured as the participant's age in years.

Experience

Experience was measured as the participant's general computing experience. It was not limited to their experience with computer security issues. A 5 point scale was used ranging from 1 "Basic (basic word processing, email, web skills)" to 5 "Advanced (Use of programming languages, use of multiple network types, confident user of new systems)".

DATA ANALYSIS

Structured Equation Modeling (SEM) is a multivariate statistical technique that attempts to explain the relationship between many variables, by evaluating the interrelationships between latent constructs. SEM has the ability to model the interactions of latent constructs. The data analysis in this study was performed using Partial Least Squares (PLS), an alternative estimation approach to traditional SEM. Compared to SEM, PLS is not as sensitive to smaller sample sizes (Hair, Black, Babin, Anderson, & Tatham, 2006).

A two-step approach commonly used in SEM techniques was applied. The approach involves first testing the fit and construct validity of the proposed measurement model and then only once a satisfactory measurement model is obtained, the structural model is estimated. The measurement model is thus "fixed" when the structural model is estimated (Hair et al., 2006). SmartPLS version 2.0 was used to assess the measurement model and the structural model.

Outer loadings of the measurement items were assessed against the suggested cut-off value of 0.4 as suggested by Hulland (1999). Several items which did not meet the desired 0.4 cut-off were discarded. To ensure the reliability of the measurements, the collected data was tested using three common indicators of reliability. These were Cronbach's Alpha, composite reliability and average variance extracted (AVE). The suggested cut-off value for reliability, when using both Cronbach's Alpha and the composite reliability technique is 0.7, and for AVE it is 0.5 (Hair et al., 2006). Table 1 summarizes the results of the reliability tests and demonstrates that acceptable reliability was obtained for each construct.

Two criteria were used to assess structural model quality: the statistical significance of estimated model coefficients and the ability of the model to explain the variance in the dependent variables. If the model is a valid representation of the influences on secure usage behavior, all proposed relationships in the model should be significant. The bootstrapping technique implemented in SmartPLS 2.0 was used to evaluate the significance of these hypothesized relationships.

Table 1. Reliability of measurement

	Cronbach's Alpha	Composite Reliability	AVE
Ease of Use	0.85	0.89	0.56
Facilitating Conditions	0.70	0.82	0.61
Secure Behavior Intention	0.81	0.86	0.50
Secure Usage	0.88	0.91	0.62
Age	N/A*	N/A*	N/A*
Experience	N/A*	N/A*	N/A*

* indicates a single item measurement

The R^2 of the structural equations for the dependent variables provide an estimate of variance explained (Hair et al., 2006), and therefore an indication of the success of the model in explaining these variables.

RESULTS AND DISCUSSION

Background Statistics

A total of 111 people (34.2% females and 65.8% males) participated in the study. The youngest participant was 17 years old, and the oldest was 88 years old (with an average age of 35.3 years). The wide age range is indicative of the growing level of participation in computing. The level of computing experience was rated between 1 (basic user) and 5 (advanced user). The average experience, using this scale was 3.49 (min=1, max.=5), indicating a relatively high degree of computer competency.

Figure 2 shows the standardized coefficients for each hypothesized path in the model and the R^2 for each dependent variable. Four of the six hypotheses were supported.

As hypothesized there was a significant positive relationship between ease of use of passwords and secure behavior intention. Thus, support was found for hypothesis H1. This is consistent with a great deal of literature relating to technology acceptance, that as something is easier to use, the intention to use it rises (Davis, 1989; Venkatesh et al., 2003). Therefore, in the context of this study,

Figure 2. Structural model results (* $p < 0.05$, ** $p < 0.01$, *** $p < 0.001$)

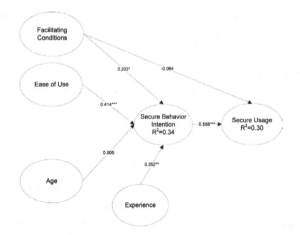

as passwords become easier to use, the intention to use them securely becomes higher. This complements previous literature about password use, which has shown that many users found passwords too difficult to use, leading to poorer usage (Adams & Sasse, 1999; Tari, Ozok, & Holden, 2006).

Secure behavior intention was also found to have a positive influence on secure usage. Thus, hypothesis H2 was supported. That is, in the context of passwords, as the intention to use them securely increases, passwords are used more appropriately. This is consistent with previous technology acceptance research which has found that intention leads to actual usage (Davis, 1989; Venkatesh et al., 2003). Or, to look at the situation holistically, as passwords become easier to use, the intention to use them properly rises, which in turn has a positive influence on actual secure usage.

The second research question addressed in the study related to the role of facilitating conditions. Contrary to expectations, facilitating conditions did not directly influence secure usage of passwords, therefore hypothesis H3 was not supported. However, facilitating conditions was found to have a weak significant effect on secure behavior intention. Although hypothesis H4 was supported, post hoc analysis of total effects showed that even though facilitating conditions influenced secure behavior intention, there was no indirect effect on secure usage. Provision of support for secure usage of passwords increased users' intentions to use passwords securely, but didn't increase their actual secure usage. This result is inconsistent with the UTAUT (Venkatesh et al., 2003) which postulates that the influence of facilitating conditions is primarily a direct one and inconsistent with Besnard and Arief's (2004) claim that the help and assistance available to users is an essential part of usable security, but consistent with Woon and Kankanhalli's (2007) study of developers' intentions to develop applications with security in mind which found that facilitating conditions had no significant effect. Also, in a study under-

taken by Ng and Rahim (2005) it was found that facilitating conditions had no effect on a user's perception of the task they were performing as being under their control.

The third research question addressed in the study related to the possible effects of external factors such as age and experience on intention to use passwords securely and actual secure usage. The results indicate that age had no significant effect on secure behavior intention. Thus, hypothesis H5 was rejected. It appears that personal computing and associated actions (such as passwords) have become commonplace, and differences due to age may be declining (Munro, Huff, Marcolin, & Compeau, 1997; Parish & Necessary, 1996).

It was hypothesized that computing experience would influence password usage. A significant positive relationship was found between an individual's prior computing experience and their intention to act in a secure way. Consequently, hypothesis H6 was accepted. This result is consistent with prior research (Taylor & Todd, 1995). Post hoc analysis also showed that experience had an indirect influence on secure usage via secure behavior intention ($t = 2.51$, $p < 0.05$). Thus, as users become more experienced, they gain knowledge about the systems they work with and the security implications of usage. With this knowledge, they become more aware of concerns about the possible security implications of their behavior and their intention to behave securely increases, which in turn leads to more secure behavior.

Model's Ability to Explain Variability in Dependent Variables

Although two of the hypothesized paths were not found to be significant, the model showed reasonable explanatory power. The variance in secure behavior intention explained by the model was 34% ($R^2 = 0.34$) and the variance explained in secure behavior was 30% ($R^2 = 0.30$). This compares well with Ng and Rahim's (2005) results and demonstrates the research model's ability to predict secure behavior. Whilst Ng and Rahim did not study the usage of passwords, they tested three common security tasks and the intention of home users to perform each. The variance explained by their model for intention to carry out each of the security tasks was: anti-virus software updating (23%), data backup (18%), and firewall usage (39%).

The model makes a valuable contribution to the field of usable security. Whilst the existing literature has established that users find their passwords hard to use, this model demonstrates that the intention to use passwords in a secure way is predicated upon ease of use. In a more practical sense, it should give food for thought to system administrators and IT managers to review their guidelines regarding passwords.

CONCLUSION

This research project aimed to determine the roles of ease of use, facilitating conditions, intention to use passwords securely, experience and age on users' usage of passwords. Data was collected via an online survey, and analyzed using PLS.

Figure 3 presents the research model with non-significant paths removed. The final model demonstrates the fundamental interest of this study, that difficult passwords have an impact on their usage. It also shows that an individual's intention to behave securely is a good indicator of their actual behavior. The model also shows that a user's prior computing experience influences their intention to act securely and though this, their actual secure usage. That is, the more experienced a person is, the more likely they are to behave securely. It is interesting to note that while available assistance had a weak impact on intention to use passwords securely, it did not influence actual secure usage.

The secure usage of computer systems is a key concern for many parties. System administrators' efforts are in vain if the technology reduces the ability of users to act securely. This concern is not just a technical administration and management issue. The dealings of individuals, business, government and society rely on secure transfer of information, and it is vital that the ability to do so is made as effective as possible. The results of this research highlight the importance of ensuring that passwords are easy to use. As one participant stated "Secure passwords are by definition transient and difficult to remember. This is a fundamental flaw in the password mechanism for everyday use". This highlights the main theme of this research and illustrates the false dichotomy often found in application development: it can be secure, or it can be usable.

Figure 3. Relationships supported by this study

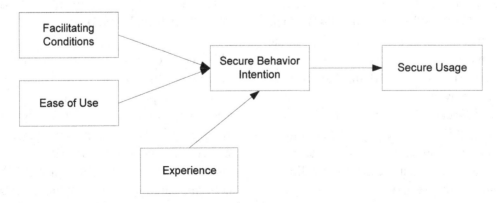

REFERENCES

Adams, A., & Sasse, M. A. (1999). Users are not the enemy. *Communications of the ACM, 42*(12), 40–46. doi:10.1145/322796.322806

Ajzen, I. (1991). The theory of planned behavior. *Organizational Behavior and Human Decision Processes, 50*(2), 179–211. doi:10.1016/0749-5978(91)90020-T

Aytes, K., & Connolly, T. (2004). Computer security and risky computing practices: A rational choice perspective. *Journal of Organizational and End User Computing, 16*(3), 22–40.

Bandura, A. (1986). *Social foundations of thought and action: A social cognitive theory.* Englewood Cliffs, NJ: Prentice-Hall.

Bell, D. E., & LaPadula, L. J. (1973). *Secure Computer Systems: Mathematical Foundations.* Bedford, Massachusetts: MITRE Corporation.

Besnard, D., & Arief, B. (2004). Computer security impaired by legitimate users. *Computers & Security, 23*(3), 253–264. doi:10.1016/j.cose.2003.09.002

Braz, C., & Robert, J. (2006). Security and usability: The case of the user authentication methods. In *Proceedings of the 18th International Conference of the Association Francophone d'Interaction Homme-Machine* (pp. 199-203). New York, USA: ACM Press.

Brostoff, S., & Sasse, M. A. (2000). Are passfaces more usable than passwords? A field trial investigation. In *Proceedings of HCI 2000* (pp. 405-424). Sunderland, UK.

Brown, S. A., Massey, A. P., Montoya-Weiss, M. M., & Burkman, J. R. (2002). Do I really have to? User acceptance of mandated technology. *European Journal of Information Systems, 11*(4), 283–295. doi:10.1057/palgrave.ejis.3000438

Cazier, J. A., Wilson, E. V., & Medlin, B. D. (2007). The role of privacy risk in IT acceptance: An empirical study. *International Journal of Information Security and Privacy, 1*(2), 61–73.

Ceraolo, J., P. (1996). Penetration testing through social engineering. *Information Systems Security, 4*(4), 37–49. doi:10.1080/10658989609342519

Cranor, L. F., & Garfinkel, S. (2005). *Security and usability: Designing secure systems that people can use.* Sebastopol: O'Reilly.

Davis, F. D. (1989). Perceived usefulness, perceived ease of use, and user acceptance of information technology. *Management Information Systems Quarterly, 13*(3), 319–340. doi:10.2307/249008

Fishbein, M., & Ajzen, I. (1975). *Belief, Attitude, Intention and Behavior: An Introduction to Theory and Research.* Reading, WA: Addison-Wesley.

Garfinkel, S., Spafford, G., & Schwartz, A. (2003). *Practical unix & internet security.* Sebastopol: O'Reilly.

Hair, J. F., Black, W. C., Babin, B. J., Anderson, R. E., & Tatham, R. L. (2006). *Multivariate Data Analysis* (6th Edition ed.). Upper Saddle River, NJ, USA: Pearson Education.

Halderman, J. A., Waters, B., & Felten, E. W. (2005). A convenient method for securely managing passwords. In *Proceedings of the 14th International Conference on World Wide Web* (pp. 471-479). New York NY, USA: ACM Press.

Harrison, A. W., & Rainer, K. (1992). The influence of individual differences on skill in end-user computing. *Journal of Management Information Systems, 9*(1), 93–111.

Hulland, J. (1999). Use of partial least squares (PLS) in strategic management research: A review of four recent studies. *Strategic Management Journal, 20*(2), 195–204. doi:10.1002/(SICI)1097-0266(199902)20:2<195::AID-SMJ13>3.0.CO;2-7

Janvrin, D., & Morrison, J. (2000). Using a structured design approach to reduce risks in end user spreadsheet development. *Information & Management, 37*(1), 1–12. doi:10.1016/S0378-7206(99)00029-4

Knapp, K. J., Marshall, T. E., Rainer, R. K., & Ford, F. N. (2006). Information security: management's effect on culture and policy. *Information Management & Computer Security, 14*(1), 24–36. doi:10.1108/09685220610648355

Knapp, K. J., Marshall, T. E., Rainer, R. K., & Ford, F. N. (2007). Information security effectiveness: Conceptualization and validation of a theory. *nternational Journal of Information Security and Privacy, 1*(2), 37-60.

Langsford, A., Naemura, K., & Speth, R. (1983). OSI management and job transfer services. *Proceedings of the IEEE, 71*(12), 1420–1424. doi:10.1109/PROC.1983.12790

Lee, J., & Lee, Y. (2002). A holistic model of computer abuse within organizations. *Information Management & Computer Security, 10*(2/3), 57–63. doi:10.1108/09685220210424104

Mainwald, E. (2003). *Network security: A beginner's guide*. New York: McGraw Hill/Osborne.

Morris, M. G., & Venkatesh, V. (2000). Age differences in technology adoption decisions: Implications for a changing workforce. *Personnel Psychology, 53*(2), 375–403. doi:10.1111/j.1744-6570.2000.tb00206.x

Morris, M. G., Venkatesh, V., & Ackerman, P. L. (2005). Gender and age differences in employee decisions about new technology: An extension to the theory of planned behavior. *IEEE Transactions on Engineering Management, 52*(1), 69–84. doi:10.1109/TEM.2004.839967

Munro, M. C., Huff, S. L., Marcolin, B. L., & Compeau, D. R. (1997). Understanding and measuring user competence. *Information & Management, 33*, 45–57. doi:10.1016/S0378-7206(97)00035-9

Ng, B. Y., & Rahim, M. A. (2005). A socio-behavioral study of home computer users' intention to practice security. In C. Saunders (Ed.), *Proceedings of The Ninth Pacific Asia Conference on Information Systems*. Bangkok, Thailand: Pacific Asia Conference on Information Systems.

Nielson, J. (1990). Heuristics for User Interface Design. Retrieved 5 February 2008, from http://www.useit.com/papers/heuristic/heuristic_list.html

Orgill, G. L., Romney, G. W., Bailey, M. G., & Orgill, P. M. (2004). The urgency for effective user privacy-education to counter social engineering attacks on secure computer systems. In *Proceedings of the 5th Conference on Information Technology Education* (pp. 177-181). New York NY, USA: ACM Press.

Parish, T. S., & Necessary, J. R. (1996). An examination of cognitive dissonance and computer attitudes. *Educational Technology Research and Development, 116*(4), 565–566.

Patrick, A. S., Long, A. C., & Flinn, S. (2003). HCI and security systems. In *Conference on Human Factors in Computing Systems* (pp. 1056-1057). New York NY, USA: ACM Press.

Pikkarainen, T., Pikkarainen, K., Karjaluoto, H., & Pahnila, S. (2004). Consumer acceptance of online banking: An extension of the technology acceptance model. *Internet Research, 14*(3), 224–235. doi:10.1108/10662240410542652

Rogers, E. M. (1962). *Diffusion of Innovation*. New York: Free Press.

Singh, S., Cabraal, A., & Hermansson, G. (2006). What is your husband's name? Sociological dimensions of internet banking authentication. In *Proceedings of the 20th conference of the computer-human interaction special interest group (CHISIG) of Australia on Computer-human interaction: design: activities, artefacts and environments* (pp. 237-244). New York, USA: ACM Press.

Stanton, J. M., Stam, K. R., Mastrangelo, P., & Jolton, J. (2005). Analysis of end user security behaviors. *Computers & Security, 24*(2), 124–133. doi:10.1016/j.cose.2004.07.001

Tari, F., Ozok, A. A., & Holden, S. H. (2006). A comparison of perceived and real shoulder-surfing risks between alphanumeric and graphical passwords. In *SOUPS '06: Proceedings of The Second Symposium on Usable Privacy and Security* (pp. 56-66). New York NY, USA: ACM Press.

Taylor, S., & Todd, P. (1995). Assessing IT usage: The role of prior experience. *Management Information Systems Quarterly, 19*(4), 561–570. doi:10.2307/249633

Thompson, R. L., Higgins, C. A., & Howell, J. M. (1994). Influence of experience on personal computer utilization: Testing a conceptual model. *Journal of Management Information Systems, 11*(1), 167–188.

Vallerand, R. J. (1997). Toward a Hierarchical Model of Intrinsic and Extrinsic Motivation. []. New York: Academic Press.]. *Advances in Experimental Social Psychology, 29*, 271–360. doi:10.1016/S0065-2601(08)60019-2

Venkatesh, V., Morris, M. G., Davis, G. B., & Davis, F. D. (2003). User acceptance of information technology: Toward a unified view. *Management Information Systems Quarterly, 27*(3), 425–478.

Weirich, D., & Sasse, M. A. (2001). Pretty good persuasion: A first step towards effective password security in the real world. In *NSPW '01: Proceedings of the 2001 Workshop on New Security Paradigms* (pp. 137-143). New York, USA: ACM Press.

Weissmann, C. (1969). Security controls in the ADEPT-50 timesharing system. In *AFIPS Conference Proceedings* (pp. 119-133). Santa Monica CA, USA: System Development Corporation.

Woon, I. M. Y., & Kankanhalli, A. (2007). Investigation of IS professionals' intention to practise secure development of applications. *International Journal of Human-Computer Studies, 65*(1), 29–41. doi:10.1016/j.ijhcs.2006.08.003

Zurko, M. E. (2005). User-centered security: Stepping up to the grand challenge. In *Proceedings of the 21st Annual Computer Security Applications Conference* (pp. 187-202). Washington, DC, USA: IEEE Computer Society.

Zurko, M. E., & Simon, R. T. (1996). User-centered security. In *NSPW '96: Proceedings of the 1996 Workshop on New Security Paradigms* (pp. 27-33). New York NY, USA: ACM Press.

APPENDIX

Final Items Used to Measure Constructs

Table 2. Ease of use

I find my password(s) are difficult to use?
I find my password(s) impede my ability to do my work?
If I faced multiple systems, each with their own password, I would feel this required a large amount of mental effort
If I faced multiple systems, each with their own password, I would be able to remember each password*
If I faced multiple systems, each with their own password, I would write down each password
If I faced multiple systems, each with their own password, I would see password(s) as being too complicated

Table 3. Facilitating conditions

The assistance available to me is helpful
I am able to get assistance
I am able to get prompt assistance

Table 4. Secure behavior intention

I intend to create strong password(s)
I intend to periodically update my password(s) to maintain a high level of password security
I intend to keep my password(s) secret from friends
I intend to keep my password(s) secret from family
I intend to keep my password(s) secret from co-workers (if applicable)
I intend to keep my password(s) secret from system administrators (if applicable)
I intend to avoid creating a written note of my password(s) to aid remembering

Table 5. Secure usage

I follow these guidelines
I feel these guidelines are too hard
If I followed these guidelines, I feel I would not be able to remember my password(s)
If I followed these guidelines, I would write down my password(s)
If I was mandated to follow these guidelines, I would make additional effort to remember my password(s)
After establishing a user account, do you regularly change your password(s)?
How regularly are you willing to change your password(s)?
Do you ever divulge your password(s) to a family member, friend, colleague or other individual?

Chapter 3
Privacy Loss:
An Expanded Model of Legal and Illegal Data Exchange[1]

Joanne H. Pratt
Joanne H. Pratt Associates, USA

ABSTRACT

Considerable research shows that personal information privacy has eroded over the last 30 years. Prior research, however, takes a consumer-centric view of personal information privacy, a view that leads to the conclusion that the individual is responsible for his/her own information. This research presents a comprehensive personal information privacy model of extra-organizational data sharing and use in ecommerce and social networking. It incorporates how data is actually passed and leaked to entities of which the individual has no knowledge and no control. This research presents support for the existence of legal, illegal, and legally-grey area extra-organizational parties and the need for more complete comprehension of personal information privacy. In addition, the research identifies the magnitude of privacy violations in spite of legal and self-protection policies. The model can serve as a guide for privacy research and for social discussion and legislation to manage and regulate use of data once collected.

INTRODUCTION

Personal privacy is a vague concept generally applied to keeping confidential anything an individual does not want known (Solove, 2006; Spinello, 1998). This research adopts the definition offered by Westin (1967, p. 7.), who defines privacy as the claim to determine for oneself when, how and to what extent personal information is released.

That perspective leads to the assumption that we each have rights to keep private anything about us that we wish, ceding access rights in exchange for societal participation (Culnan & Bies, 2003). As Posner (2008, p.248) points out, "a person would have to be a hermit to be able to function in our society without voluntarily disclosing a vast amount of personal information to a vast array of public and private demanders." To gain the benefits of citizenship and employment, and connectedness with "friends," for example, we

DOI: 10.4018/978-1-60960-200-0.ch003

cede rights of identity, domicile location, and family arrangements (Debatin, Horn, & Hughes, 2009). Through transactions we cede the rights to personal transaction information to aggregators who, until recently, limited their data collection and aggregation. Recently, because of new and maturing technologies, we are unknowingly giving away much more than just identity, location, and transaction information (Nissenbaum, 1998; Shilton, Burke, Estrin, Hansen, & Srivastava, 2008). Now our information can swiftly be integrated and aggregated, which was impossible before the Internet (Posner, 2008). Privacy is eroding as new technologies enable this massive collection, aggregation, and sale of everything about everyone (Spinello, 1998; Gleick, 1996; Inside Facebook Gold, 2010).

Data integration has led to functional, economic, and social benefits but also to abuses of individual privacy. Questions are being raised as to whether abuses to personal information privacy (PIP) are beginning to outweigh the benefits obtained by widespread data integration and sale (Thiesse, 2007; Stanton, Nemati, Chun, & Chen, 2007; Conger, Mason, Mason, & Pratt, 2005; Kling, 1995; Eldon, 2010). Legal data integrators are being pre-empted by illegal entities seeking accessibility to minutia on every facet of individuals' lives.

To understand the implications of data release and integration, this research presents an expanded privacy model that contributes to the literature in several ways. First, it presents a model of data exchange that includes all parties: the 1st party individual holding personal private data; the 2nd party vendor/provider(s) to whom data is initially released; 3rd party legal data integrators, which include legally grey area government and private data miners, and 4th party illegal data collectors. While these constructs have individually been the topic of some research, none of the research found ties the subject matter to PIP, thus presenting an incomplete view of the data relationships among organizations. Second, the model in this research

integrates and enlarges separate frameworks that model privacy and online transaction processing.

The article first presents an expanded PIP model, defining extra-organizational data-sharing entities along with the threats they pose to PIP. Then, proof of the existence and extent of losses to PIP from legal and legally grey area third parties and clearly illegal fourth parties is offered from the academic literature. Loss of control of PIP by the individual in varying degrees is illustrated with examples from current media, including loss that occurs from social networking. A review of privacy laws in the section, Safeguarding Privacy, describes the effectiveness of attempts to safeguard PIP by legislation, privacy-enhancing technologies, and self-protection. Finally, the importance of awareness of PIP issues for developing policy and possible actions are presented.

AN EXPANDED MODEL OF INFORMATION PRIVACY

Decision Calculus

The model begins with the decision calculus that the individual makes prior to releasing any personal information. Each box leading to the decision calculus in Figure 1 and the arrows depicting the relationships between them represent areas in which significant research has already been conducted (Culnan & Armstrong, 1999; Cheung, Chan, & Moez, 2005; Conger, et al., 2005; and Xu, Dinev, Smith, & Hart, 2008). The individual's judgment of the vendor, medium, environment, consumer, and product or service characteristics enters into his or her calculation. Personal privacy as modeled by Culnan and Armstrong (1999) shows the individual as consumer disclosing information based on the expectation of achieving benefits that exceed risks. Published before web maturity, the 1999 model does not specifically treat online transactions. The model is presented from a corporate vendor/provider point of view

Figure 1. Expanded model of personal information privacy (adapted from Cheung, et al, 2005; Conger, et al., 2005; Culnan & Armstrong, 1999)

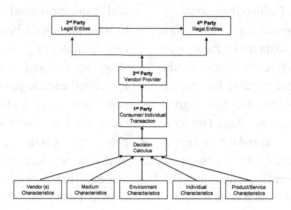

and emphasizes feedback that enables the vendor to predict subsequent behavior such as consumer retention, defection, or the attraction of new customers. The corporation gains in being able to offer products or services that will lead to sales; the consumer benefits by learning about products and services he or she might want to buy. In their model Cheung et al., (2005) present a consumer point of view and treat online transactions without incorporating privacy issues.

The Cheung model emphasizes the individual as consumer, the product, the vendor, and the environment. A third model examines how individuals' private concerns are raised in the context of online commerce, finance, health, and also addresses social networking (Xu et al., 2008). For each, a set of characteristics (Figure 1, bottom row) is used to model the individual's intention, adoption, and continuance to engage online.

Overview of Expanded Model

The expanded model assumes the individual has made the benefit/cost decision calculus based on those characteristics delineated by prior research. In contrast to earlier models, it starts at the point the trade-off has been made (1st party consumer/ individual transaction) and traces what happens to the data thereafter. It incorporates both the vendor/

provider (2nd party) and the individual points of view but focuses on the privacy implications in the exchange of information between them. The expanded model changes the focus from the individual to the data, based on the proposition that the data has an independent existence apart from the individual, once passed to the 2nd party. As it is transferred from the 2nd party to 3rd, and 4th parties, integrated, and mined, it is transformed into information that could benefit the 1st party, or as daily media coverage makes clear, subject the 1st party or others to harm (New York Times, 2007; Stanton et al., 2007; Lawyers.com, 2010; Krishnamurthy & Wills, 2009; Malin, 2005; Bonneau, Anderson, & Danezis, 2009).

Part of the 1st party individual's decision includes what data to provide to the 2nd party vendor/provider based on the expected life and use of that data, perceived relevance of the data collected, expected benefits, and expectations of corporate use of the collected data (Conger, et al., 2005; McKnight, Vivek, & Kacmar, 2004; Gross & Acquisti, 2005). A personal example provided by Bennett (2005) who tracked his own data shadow illustrates how the model can be applied: Bennett (1st party) travels by air within Canada and internationally to the U.S. He books flights with a travel agent (2nd party) who legally shares information with the Galileo reservation system and database (3rd party), the "central hubs which link all providers of travel services" (Bennett 2005, p. 116). Third party Galileo then contacts the airline (2nd party) that Bennett, the 1st party, has chosen. At this point in the data trail a Passenger Name Record (PNR) with five mandatory fields plus optional data has been created for the 1st party. The PNR then travels into the legally grey area where various data items are shared under a mixture of intertwined national and international laws from agencies concerned with international travel, customs, and homeland security. Applying the model helps clarify that at each node it is possible to analyze the privacy protection that applies, such as the practices that legalize exchanges to 3rd parties, or with more difficulty, those falling within the legally grey area. In this case history the data was kept safe from 4th party hackers.

On social networking sites exchange of personal information with family, friends, friends of friends, and communities enters into social commerce because the information has value to merchants. For example, Facebook has a "like" plug-in, presented to users as a way to tell friends they like their new Levi's. But users may be unaware that the plug-in links to the online retailer who uses their endorsements to promote its products (eMarketer, 2010, July 6). The following sections describe the model in more detail.

1st and 2nd Party Data Sharing

Figure 1 presents the expanded model of personal information privacy. Perceived relevance of data is a key construct in the decision calculus. Before making a transaction, the 1st party individual draws conclusions about the reasonableness of the 2nd party vendor/provider's request for data to be collected based on its perceived relevance. The decision calculus results in an assessment of trust and risk to either consummate or cancel the transaction and, if consummated, which data to share and the assumed sharing duration (Berlanger, Hller, & Smith, 2002; Malhotra, Kim, &

Agarwal, 2004; Thiesse, 2007; Gross & Acquisti, 2005; Fogel & Nehmad, 2008). It is a tradeoff in which the individual 1st party gives up privacy to gain perceived benefits from the 2nd party. For example, to gain the convenience of online shopping for books or for an airline ticket, the individual exchanges at a minimum her name, street and email addresses, and telephone and credit card numbers with a 2nd party vendor/provider. In exchange for providing their name, birth date, relationship status, interests, and photo to the 2nd party social networking websites (SNS) such as Facebook, MySpace, and Linked In, users gain the benefit of connection with widening circles of "friend" or professional relationships (Young & Quan-Haase, 2009; Lewis, Kaufman, & Christakis, 2008). SNS are of increasing concern as Facebook, the current leading provider, reports over 500 million active users worldwide, including both older persons–the fastest growing group–and students (Facebook.com, 2010a;. Inside Facebook. com, 2010; McCarthy, 2010). Fifty percent of all users log on every day, spending over 700 billion minutes per month. The average user has 130 "friends." More than 80 percent of social media users exchange gender, email address, name, and names of friends (eMarketer, 2010, June 29).

Mandated fields prevent the 1st party from completing the online transaction without providing all required information. However, on SNS, although the user sets boundary controls when he or she first joins, most users of Facebook, for example, leave the default settings or do not update their permission (Bilton, 2010). Engaging on Facebook, unlike the ecommerce examples, is a process of agreeing by default to a continuing series of transactions. In both cases, the problem is that once the data is released, privacy cannot be restored. Before ecommerce, face-to-face cash transactions had minimal impact on individual privacy since little record keeping was involved. In contrast, transactions based on credit, require records to complete payment. The data collected includes personal information. But data collection goes beyond requests for name, address, telephone number, and credit card, all relevant to a simple purchase. For example, as the individual 1st party browses online while conducting banking, medical or other personal business, corporate use of smart technologies can surreptitiously collect such data as click streams, personal movements, food and medicine usage, genetic markers, DNA, health, or other biological data, and criminal, genealogical, or financial history (Conger, et al., 2005; McKnight, et al., 2004; Thiesse, 2007; Culnan & Bies, 2003). The data collection may be known or unknown by the consumer. Data held by the 1st party may be collected before, during, or after an actual business transaction. Combined with other transactional and post-transactional data, this data enables, for example, the building of a consumption profile for the 1st party's family that could affect their insurance or medical coverage (Spinello, 1998). Individuals appear reluctant to read time-consuming statements of corporate privacy policies and rely heavily on organizations that vouch for the trustworthiness of the vendor (McKnight, et al., 2004). From the consumer's perspective, stewardship is inherent in the exchange of privacy for benefits. Stewardship implies vendor protection of customers' personal information (Wernick, 2006). As discussed below, stewardship can be superseded legally without the 1st party's knowledge.

In the case of SNS, although data transfer from the 2nd party is stated to be anonymous, in fact, an individual is "betrayed by [his] shadow" (Malin, 2005). By a process Malin calls "trail matching," reidentification can occur when data is aggregated with data provided by the individuals in multiple other locations (Malin, 2005). Facebook, appearing to be "free" to the user, is actually a multimillion dollar collection entity that sells information. As Facebook states, it "is no longer simply a social networking website – it has become a broad online ecosystem, supporting thousands of related businesses and on track to doing over $1 billion in revenues this year" (Inside Facebook Gold, 2010 p. 1). Inside Facebook Gold will provide "developers, brand marketers, advertisers, and investors," all 3rd parties, with weekly in-depth analysis of information collected from Facebook users, who have grown from a community of Harvard students into a global database constituting a valuable "platform and ecosystem." The data is voluntarily input and updated by the 1st party users who registered their names, email, gender, and birth date as a requirement to participate (Facebook.com, 2010, April 22a). Moreover, Facebook's terms of use forbid falsifying one's personal information implying that the data is both current and accurate and thus particularly valuable for market research (Facebook.com, 2010, April 22b).

3rd and 4th Party Data Sharing

Both private and government parties collect and use data that is not contained securely by the 2nd Party vendor/provider. The 3rd and 4th parties by definition are, respectively, legal (until their actions are proved otherwise in the courts) or illegal. Third party data integrators operate legally sanctioned businesses such as credit bureaus set up in the 1960s to provide added information about their consumer bases to vending organizations. On the one hand, benefits of widespread legal data integration can be lifesaving. An individual arrested for murder retrieved time records from his MetroCard, E-Z Pass, and surveillance cameras that proved his innocence (Weiser, 2008). On the other hand, illegal data use by 4th parties can be life-threatening. Fourth party illegal data invaders are hackers or other illegal users of vendor data including terrorists. People who steal computers and who leak names, addresses, and financial or medical information, fall into this category (Zeller, 2005, May 18). Fourth-party usage also results from non-compliant employee behaviors that result in leakages or illegal activities by others such as curious Verizon employees who hacked President-elect Obama's telephone records (AFP,

2008), and unauthorized hospital staff who viewed medical records of a slain TV anchorwoman (Dallas News, 2008). On Facebook, rogue applications "scrape and store information, then resell it on the black market…leading to phishing and other scams" (Eldon, 2010 p. 5). Fourth-party data users obtain data without permission or knowledge of the data holders, which may be 1st, 2nd, or 3rd parties (ACLU, 2003; Albrecht, 2004; Carlson, 2006).

Legally Grey Area

Problems arise when 3rd-party appropriators use data without 1st -party and/or 2nd -party permission. Examples of operating in a legally grey area might be governmental pre-emption of data, which has come under increasing scrutiny as violating constitutional rights to privacy provisions (Nissenbaum, 1998; Ahrens, 2006; Cauley 2006; Seffers, 2000; Waller, 2002). In the private sector, 3rd party legal compliance is via self-regulation but increasing activity falls into a legally gray area (Cate, 2006; Culnan, 2000). In addition, some 3rd -party partners sharing data either legitimately violate the terms of their agreements (Hoofnagle, 2005) or broadly interpret "legitimate business purposes" allowed under the Fair Credit Reporting Act (Spinello, 1998 p. 728). The rapid growth of SNS combined with increasing recognition of the economic potential of leveraging a global, up-to-date, potentially longitudinal database has raised what even Facebook calls "underlying complexities and unknowns." What happens to the data after Facebook, the 2nd party, sells it to 3rd parties? This constitutes a legally grey area as users, government officials, and researchers question the legality of data aggregation effectively without user permission (Bilton, 2010); Lawyers. com, 2010; Bonneau et al., 2009; Krishnamurthy & Wills, 2009).

PROOF OF CONSTRUCTS FROM THE LITERATURE AND CURRENT MEDIA

One issue in developing a new model of PIP is to provide proof of the existence of all constructs. Since the 1970's researchers have addressed issues of cyber security, (See, for example, Westin, 1967; Culnan & Bies, 2003; Denning, 2001; Gouldson, 2001; Granville, 2003). The connection of Denning, Gouldson, and Granville research to personal information privacy was unclear. The research of Culnan, Smith and others was the genesis of PIP understanding but the extent of transgressions enabled by the Internet was not yet mature so the understanding of the issues was necessarily limited (cf. Culnan, 1993; Culnan & Armstrong, 1999; Smith & Milberg, 1996). A flood of instances of privacy violations are so recent that they are not yet documented in published research. Many stem from the extraordinary growth of the Facebook SNS (cf. Bonneau et al. 2009; emarketer. com, 2010, June 29; Krishnamurthy et al., 2009; Levin & Abril, 2009; Posner, 2008; Lawyers.com, 2010). Thus, this section relies largely on media sources to present evidence supporting the role of parties in PIP violations beyond the 2nd party vendor/provider.

Legal 3rd Party Data Users

The 1st party individual's information is shared with any number of legal data-sharing entities, that is, the 3rd -party data users who are known external data-sharing partners such as a credit reporting company. The individual online shopper understands that sharing details of her transaction with a credit bureau gives her the advantage of building a personal credit record that will allow her to "buy now; pay later." In the context of marketing, data sharing is referred to as "secondary use of personal information from those who do not object" and governed by fair information practices (Culnan, 1993, p. 341). However, recently, data integrators have come under fire because of their seemingly unstoppable appetite for data for all companies about virtually every aspect of their consumers' lives (Hoofnagle, 2005). For example, Experian legally purchases, aggregates, and sells data with 2nd -party permission. Data brokers such as Experian generate their revenues by matching consumer information to transaction information, profiling consumers, and reselling the expanded information. As Spinello (1998, p. 733) points out "…like other forms of property, information can have a monetary value; it can also be produced, upgraded, shared, and transferred to others." Data brokers are not necessarily the problem unless their use or access to data violates their legal and contractual agreements (Cate, 2006; Hoofnagle, 2005). But, Experian, for instance, cannot ensure proper use since compliance is self-reported. Thus, vulnerabilities arise from exchanges with data-sharing partners who obtain data without permission or knowledge of their sources (Carlson, 2006; Zeller, 2005, March 10; Gross & Acquisti, 2005).

Legally Grey Area 3rdParty Data Users

Third parties include entities operating in a legally grey area whose practices cannot be classified unambiguously as legal or illegal. These organizations share two primary characteristics: Collection and/or use of PI are without 1st or 2nd party permission and may be unknowable by the 1st party owner of the personal data. The 1st party may not gain knowledge of data mining until long after trespass occurs (New York Times, 2007). For instance, the TJ Max leakage of 45 million consumer records over a four-year period became known to users only after significant publicity and reporting under California laws. Some 3rd party grey area actions may eventually be redefined by the courts as illegal (4th party)

Two types of data miners collect and/or use personal information: Governments and business

organizations. A disclosure by the director of national intelligence illustrates 3rd party trespass by the government (New York Times, 2007). After 9/11/2007 in violation of the 1978 Foreign Intelligence Surveillance Act (FISA) and The Patriot Act of 2001, the National Security Agency (NSA) intercepted "tens of millions" of communications between the U. S. and abroad (Cauley, 2006, p. 1; New York Times, 2007). At first glance an illegal 4th party example, it is not, because the President of the United States ordered the interception. Instead, this is a case of government/private sector grey area 3rd party action because telephone companies gave call data to the National Security Agency, which may be illegal (New York Times, 2007) or retroactively declared legal (Commondreams.com, 2007). Another factor that places this example in the grey area is that the actions were classified and secret, although the details eventually were being revealed (New York Times, 2007). Other legally grey area federal actions have involved, for example, the Department of Defense (Seffers, 2000), the Federal Bureau of Investigation (Ahrens, 2006), and other federal agencies including the U.S. Postal Service (Memott, 2007). In spite of its stated commitment to individual privacy (Justice News 2010), the Obama administration wants Congress to authorize the FBI to collect "electronic communication transactional records" without a judge's approval by amending the Electronic Communications Privacy Act (Nakashima, 2010). That would require companies not only to provide information, but also to keep the request secret.

The second type of legally grey area data miners is private sector, business organizations that obtain data without the consent or knowledge of the persons on whom data is collected or the companies from which the data is obtained, and integrate, sell or otherwise use the data in ways unknown to the individual data owner. Many organizations are 3rd parties, legal in their operations to collect and integrate 'free' information such as sex offender records, real estate sale records, and published phone records, to establish a profile that someone might buy (Nissenbaum, 1998). However, these organizations enter the legally grey area when they obtain data through deception using both legal and illegal means. For instance, 3rd party data collection is practiced by Aggregate Knowledge, a company that works with online vendors to develop shopping profiles through use of cookies, unobtrusively downloaded 'spyware,' keystroke trackers, and other online methods (Takahashi, 2007). While cookies, per se, are neither illegal nor unethical, the trackings of movements and clickstreams, that then are aggregated with other lifestyle, psychographic and demographic information may provide more information than a consumer wants known. During U.S. Congressional hearings, 11 practicing brokers invoked the 5th Amendment to avoid self-incrimination about their data collection practices (Matlin, 2006). Facebook has introduced even greater ambiguity into the issue of privacy protection by continually changing its terms of service. New policies favor innovation—taking advantage of new business opportunities—over maintaining the original agreement that "No personal information…will be available to any user of the Web Site who does not belong to at least one of the groups specified by you in your privacy settings." As of April 2010, Facebook stated that it would share "you and your friends' names, profile pictures, gender, connections, and any content shared using the Everyone privacy setting'—with 'pre-approved' third parties without asking for user permission first" (Eldon, 2010 p. 6). This step frees Facebook to sell all data collected to 3rd parties. One privacy issue is how the altered terms apply to users who registered before they were instituted.

4th Party Illegal Data Collection and Use

Data miners, such as the government and private sector data brokers, override personal privacy concerns by justifying their action as necessary for the public good, product enhancement, or to prevent acts of terrorism. Data invaders have no such rationale for their transgressions. Fourth party data invaders may be hackers, thieves or those taking opportunities created by inadequate security practices. Denning (2001) documents criminal and terrorist activity and data vulnerability, examining, for example, the benefits and drawback of encryption to control interactions with suppliers and partners (both 3rd parties) and customers (1st party). "Hacktivism," defined as hacking fused with activism, has become a frequent occurrence worldwide such that hackers now routinely sell data to the mafia and other organized crime syndicates for their use. The Open Security Foundation maintains the Internet database of data loss incidents formerly provided by Attrition.org. In 2009, over 221 million records were compromised (Open Security Foundation, 2009). Carelessness accounts for significant amounts of data loss. In 2007, thousands of records were found in discarded boxes, in purchased used furniture and in trash behind buildings. (Privacy Rights Clearinghouse, 2007; Attrition.org, 2007). If all lost information was reported, virtually every person in the United States has had their information compromised--at increasing privacy and dollar cost. The cost of cybercrime was more than $67 billion in 2005, according to FBI estimates (McMillan 2006 p. 1). Further, estimates of the cost of poor privacy control on the part of organizations that are hacked, leaked, or otherwise compromised is $90 to $305 per record for the 2nd party organization suffering the loss (Gaudin, 2007).

SAFEGUARDING PRIVACY

The central construct of the expanded model of information privacy is that the individual holds her own personal data until she consciously or unwittingly makes the trade-off of releasing that data in order to gain desired benefits. The willingness of individuals to engage in online e-commerce, which implies trade-offs in "trusting and risk beliefs" (Malhotra et al., 2004 p. 351; associated with collection, control, and awareness of use of personal information is the focus of marketing literature (See, for example, Tang, Hu, & Smith, 2008; Cheung et al., 2005, Malhotra et al., 2004). In online shopping or banking, for instance, the consumer controls the data being collected and by signing privacy agreements, gives permission and is aware that the information may legally be shared. However, to safeguard privacy, a central issue is individual control of personal information and legality when control of the information is taken without his permission and/or knowledge. More formal data protection was promised through the fair information practice principles, which were developed in the 1970s and 1980s and guided privacy law development throughout the world. However, the ensuing directives and guidelines, whether in the U.S. or elsewhere, are rarely invoked and often superseded, for example, by The Homeland Security Act (HSA) of 2002 and The Patriot Act of 2001 in the U.S. (Cate, 2006; Greenleaf, 2006; OECD, 2003). Thus, policies enacted in 1974 to curb illegal surveillance have shifted from issues raised during Watergate to concerns of further life threatening terrorism after 9/11/2001. The Patriot Act of 2001, a fundamental basis of privacy law, justified expanded surveillance at the cost of individual privacy.

Concern about privacy is increasing as personal information is willingly revealed on social networking sites such as Facebook and YouTube (Dwyer, Hiltz, & Passerini, 2007; Lewis et al., 2008; Stanton et al., 2007). Contrary to the assumption that the younger generation does not care about privacy, studies of college students have found that they do care about who receives personal information they post on SNS sites such as Facebook (See, for example, Fogel & Nehmad, 2008; Young & Quan-Hasse, 2009; Tufekci, 2008; Gross & Acquisti, 2005.) Users of social networking sites are given the option of managing the boundary that allows conditional access to information they differentiate as being personal or public. (Lewis et al., 2008). The greater problem is that users do not pay sufficient attention to the nuances of controlling release of PIP, either accepting the defaults preset by Facebook and/or once registered, neglecting to take another look at their settings. Users seem unaware of how easy they are making it for 3rd parties to create digital dossiers of themselves (Gross & Acquisti, 2005).

Another concern is the control of personal data as technologies such as RFID are used by, for example, retailers to control inventory (Thiesse, 2007), animal shelters to control dogs (Nielsen, 2007), and by security-conscious companies to tag employees (Citywatcher.com, 2007).

The Privacy Protection Study Commission authorized under The Privacy Act stated: "If the individual is to serve as a check on unreasonable demands for information or objectionable methods of acquiring it, he must know what to expect so that he will have a proper basis for deciding whether the trade-off is worthwhile for him" (Privacy Protection Study Commission, 1977 p.16). The Privacy Act attempts to balance the government's need for information about individuals against protection of their privacy. Protection may take the form of public policy carried out by federal and state legislation or it may occur by individual PIP management, for example, by response to "opt-out" or "opt-in" provisions offered by vendors as their own self-protection.

Legal Protection

In response to "technological changes in computers, digitized networks, and the creation of new information products," privacy law attempts to protect "against unauthorized use of the collected information and government access to private records" (BBBOnLine, Inc. and the Council of Better Business Bureaus, Inc., 2007 p. 1). Thirty-four states have notification laws (Wernick, 2006). Typically, the state laws cover combinations of an individual's name with unencrypted data items ranging from social security number to DNA profile. However, statutes exclude information available to the public in federal, state, or local records. California created a State Office of Privacy Protection in 2000 and has enacted laws that protect citizens' privacy across many facets of their lives. State regulations, for example, include limits to retrieval of information from automobile "black boxes" (California Department of Consumer Affairs 2006, p. 1), disclosure of personal information on drivers' licenses, protection of confidentiality of library circulation records, and bans on embedding social security numbers on "a card or document using a bar code, chip, magnetic strip…" (p. 3). The State also defines a "specific crime of identity theft" (p. 4). California residents have sued Facebook under state privacy laws, arguing that "Facebook doesn't do enough to protect private photos and information from misuse by third party applications" (Lawyers.com, 2010 p. 1).

Similarly, Federal privacy laws afford privacy protection of cable subscriber information, drivers' license and motor vehicle registration records, ban "persons from tampering with computers or accessing certain computerized records without authorization," and require protection of medical records (BBBOnLine, Inc. and the Council of Better Business Bureaus, Inc., 2007 p. 3). In reaction to SNS user complaints, U. S. federal regulation has been proposed that would address how owners of websites use and control data (Eldon, 2010). The European Commission also is investigating control of PIP. Privacy protection is also available under a tort of breach of confidentiality when trust is broken by a recipient of disclosed personal data (Solove, 2006).

Yet the problem remains that "there is a patchwork of various legislations at the state and federal levels but unfortunately there is no comprehensive set of laws or regulations that clearly delineates the parameters on one's privacy rights" (Spinello, 1998 p. 728). Second, the government

has the power to "trump" those laws via, for instance, The Homeland Security Act (HSA) of 2002. Once data integration occurs in the context of a short-term emergency, such as ferreting out terrorists, individual privacy cannot be restored. In fact, known transgressions of HSA by the government have led to records of innocent parties being propagated through generations of federal databases of suspected terrorists (Gellman, 2005).

1st Party Individual and 2nd Party Vendor/Provider PIP Management

Two arguments against government regulation of PIP are that individuals should manage their own privacy or that vendors should be held responsible, since it is in their own interest to avoid potential liabilities and costs (Wernick, 2006). However, with increasing use of invisible, unknown means of surveillance and tracking by unknown legal, legally grey area, and illegal parties, individuals are unable to manage their information. In one demonstration, an individual was tracked by means of over 120 readings of radio-frequency identification (RFID) and smart card chips, the global positioning system (GPS) in the cell phone, and other methods in a single day to show how tracking becomes possible (Nakashima, 2007). The increasing use of such technologies leads the 1st party individuals to distrust even beneficial retail and medical applications of RFID (Thiesse, 2007). Further, with legal relationships (and illegal ones), far removed from the original transacting vendor, even the vendors do not know where their data goes once it leaves their confines.

In the case of RFID chips, various privacy-enhancing technologies (PET) have been proposed such as physical shielding from hackers' transponders, tag deactivation, and bug-safe radio frequency protocols (Thiesse, 2007). These do not reassure the individual who "kills" the RFID tag by throwing it into the microwave and seeing sparks (Thiesse et al., 2007).

Touted as a solution that gives individuals management of their PIP and maintains their implied stewardship of data, one 2nd party corporate answer has been to offer the consumer the option to "opt out" or "opt in" to releasing PIP. Although meritorious in principle the Fair Information Practice Principles (FIPPS) developed in the 1970's and 1980's, have proven to be narrow and legalistic as applied, and further, annoy and burden individuals while giving a false illusion that 1st party privacy is protected (Cate, 2006). On the other hand, by appearing ignorant of corporate privacy policies, individuals fail to take responsibility for their own role in 1st party/2nd party transactions. The "reality recognized by almost everyone, is that the vast majority of Internet users" do not read the terms of service (Phil Malone, Director of Cyberlaw Clinic, Harvard Law School quoted in Stelter, 2008).

Opt-Out

In general, opt-out is at the discretion of the vendor with each vendor developing its own rules. Opting out of a database registry may be as simple as emailing a request (Aristotle, 2007) or as complex as proving one is at risk of bodily harm. Four examples suggest the range of privacy agreements: The Ameridex Information Systems (Ameridex, 2007, p. 1) requires the individual to "…email… the following information…formatted as shown: First-name, middle initial, last-name, city, state, year-of-birth, month-of-birth, day-of-birth…." and cautions "Note: We cannot block retrievals of listed telephone numbers. You must notify your telephone company to delist your telephone number." Intelius (2006) spells out the difficulty of removing personal information that has been captured in public databases: "If you have a compelling privacy or security issue, you may wish to contact the official custodians of those public records that contain sensitive information about you, such as your county's land records office, to determine how to remove your information from the public record (The process of having public records sealed typically requires a court order.)." To opt out of LexisNexis (2005), you must prove that you are a law enforcement officer, victim of identity theft, or under the threat of death.

On Facebook "To opt out of full disclosure of most information, it is necessary to click through more than 50 privacy buttons, which then require choosing among a total of more than 170 options" (Bilton, 2010 p. 1) The 5,830 word Privacy Policy and more than 45,000 word FAQ at best discourage users to exert the offered "control."

Opt-In

Opt-in provisions typically pertain to information that the individual supplies for inclusion in a database. Genealogy.com (2004) specifies that "content that you submit…to Virtual Cemetery, may become part of an online archive…database that may be reproduced by Genealogy.com in any format…for distribution, sale, or any other purpose." Social networking sites, such as Facebook, operate in a similar once loaded, always loaded, manner. Facebook stresses that individuals can maintain their privacy by setting boundary controls that limit information flow to three designated categories: "Everyone," Friends of Friends, or Friends only. Listed first in the permission matrix, accepting Everyone" cedes permission for Facebook to use any information the users post. The Instructions emphasize that the user is in control, but state. that "Information you've shared with everyone -as well as your name, profile, picture, gender and networks-could be seen by anyone on the Internet." Facebook.com 2010b p. 2). The stated benefit to the user of making information publicly visible to everyone is that "it is essential to helping people find and connect with you on Facebook" However, to see the mindboggling benefits of this information to Facebook, the user must find the company's marketing page, Inside Facebook Gold (2010). Supplying demographic and behavior information to marketers is one way the sites monetize their popularity (Aspan, 2008). In 2010, the information voluntarily entered by 500 million users was expected to generate more than $1 billion for Facebook, a company with an estimated worth of $25 billion (Facebook Gold, 2010; Leonard, 2010).

A seeming third approach are the data gatherers who offer neither an opt-out or opt-in provision such as DocuSearch: "You cannot opt out [or in] …Public records, by law, must be available…to anyone who requests them…our service is used by investigators, law enforcement agents… it would defeat the purpose of our service if we gave [criminals, debtors and other bad actors] the ability to opt out of being found" (DocuSearch, 2007). Therefore, the consumer has opted in, whether voluntarily or not.

PIP is increasingly important in a world of technologies that support tracking, monitoring, and the ability to collect information about every facet of private life. As the model presented in this research clarifies, the reason is that the data takes on its own life once ceded to a vendor. In this world, public safety must be balanced against the need for personal privacy. Problems arise when consumers unknowingly become targets of data collection of which they are unaware. By opting for the benefits of data sharing in a transaction, the individual takes risks that unknown data will be collected, sold or shared, and become part of the public record.

The intent of the model is to help sort out the "Social and individual risk [which] is governed by a complicated set of organizational, cultural, technological, political and legal factors" (Bennett 2005, p. 133). Added to that is the economic potential revealed with the growth of SNS, particularly Facebook innovations (Helft, 2010; Inside Facebook Gold, 2010). The expanded model of information privacy contributes to policy formation by identifying the participating parties, 1st through 4th, and their interactions. Addressing data surveillance, Bennett (2005) calls for empirical case studies to distinguish "surveillance"

from benign data integration that offers benefits to individuals in society. A final example vividly dramatizes that the core of the privacy debate is the tug of war between a need to protect the individual versus the need to protect society. Messages sent on MySpace (2nd party) from an adult posing as a teen age boy (1st party) led to a teen girl's suicide (Stelter, 2008). Although claiming she never read the terms of service requiring "truthful and accurate" registration to enter the website, the woman was convicted of "unauthorized access" in violation of the Computer Fraud and Abuse Act of 1986. Such a crime had not been anticipated when policy regulating 4th party hacker crime was legislated. Clearly, the issues of who can or should control data life, integration, and use need further discussion and resolution. The resolution may be a long time in coming as it will likely require some extent of social and cultural change. Even in societies, such as European Union members, that place a high premium on personal privacy, PIP erosion remains an issue. In the meantime, knowledge that data has its own life should be better understood to inform individual decisions.

SUMMARY

This research described in this chapter presents an expanded privacy model, incorporating extra-organizational data sharing, data leakages, and transgressions. It clarifies relationships between known and unknown parties to individual transactions and underscores the outcome that once released, data takes on a life of its own. The literature and media reports cited above offer little hope that privacy once lost can be restored or that trust can be regained.

One function of the model is that it reveals nodes and transactions where privacy loss occurs and therefore aids in developing policy and legislation that will help safeguard the individual. The model highlights the need to safeguard 1st party private information by paying attention to data collection and sharing practices by 2nd party vendors/providers. Examples of 3rd party legally grey area government data mining and 4th party illegal data collection support the existence of these parties and emphasize this growing problem. Data integration and appropriation generate risks to privacy, which have become pervasive throughout society. Data invasion has become an everyday occurrence. With these changes to PIP, the expanded privacy model shows that attention to all parties accessing information is needed to accurately comprehend the process that leads to the sharing of personal information. To protect themselves, individuals must be aware of both legal and illegal data exchange. Once the data is provided, individuals should expect that their data might be shared or sold with any number of other organizations, including organizations that have negative intentions.

REFERENCES

ACLU (2003, November 30). *RFID position statement of consumer privacy and civil liberties organizations*. New York: American Civil Liberties Union.

AFP (2008, November 21). *Verizon employees wrongly accessed Obama phone records.*

Ahrens, F. (2006, June 3). *Government, Internet firms in talks over browsing data.* Washington, DC: The Washington Post. (p. D3).

Albrecht, K. (2002). Supermarket cards: The tip of the retail surveillance iceberg. *Denver University Law Review. 79*(4, 15), 534-554.

Ameridex (2007, February 27). Privacy statement. *Ameridex Information Systems.*

Aristotle. com (2007). *Privacy policy: privacy statement for* www. Aristotle.com.

Aspan, M. (2008, February 11). *How Sticky Is Membership on Facebook? Just Try Breaking Free*. New York: The New York Times.

Attrition.org (2007, March 3). *Attrition.org, data loss archive and database (DLDOS).*

BBBOnLine, Inc. & the Council of Better Business Bureaus, Inc. (2007, March). A review of federal and state privacy laws.

Belanger, F., Hiller, J. S., & Smith, W. J. (2002). Trustworthiness in electronic commerce: the role of privacy, security, and site attributes. *The Journal of Strategic Information Systems, 11*(3/4), 245–270. doi:10.1016/S0963-8687(02)00018-5

Bennett, C. J. (2005). What happens when you book an airline ticket? The collection and processing of passenger data post-9/11. In Zureik, E., & Salter, M. B. (Eds.), *Global Surveillance and Policing* (pp. 113–138). Portland: Wilan.

Bilton, N. (2010, May 12). *Price of Facebook privacy? Start clicking*. New York: The New York Times.

Bonneau, J., Anderson, J., & Danezis, G. (2009). Prying data out of a social network. *Conference: Advances in Social Network Analysis and Mining.*

California Department of Consumer Affairs (2006, February 14). Privacy laws.

Carlson, C. (2006, February 1). Unauthorized sale of phone records on the rise. *eWeek.*

Cate, F. H. (2006). The failure of fair information practice principles. In Winn, J. K. (Ed.), *Consumer Protection in the Age of the 'Information Economy*. Ashgate.

Cauley, L. (2006, May 11). *NSA has massive database of Americans' phone calls*. Washington, DC: USA Today.

Cheung, C. M. K., Chan, G. W. W., & Moez, L. (2005). A critical review of online consumer behavior: empirical research. *Journal of Electronic Commerce in Organizations, 3*(4), 1–19.

Citywatcher.com (2007, July 22). The Answer to Immigration – "Chip them?"

Commondreams.org (2007). *ACLU condemns phone companies' role in FBI datamining, reaffirms no amnesty for telecoms.*

Conger, S., Mason, R. O., Mason, F., & Pratt, J. H. (2005 August). The connected home: poison or paradise. *Proceedings of Academy of Management Meeting.* Honolulu, HI.

Culnan, M. J. (1993). How did they get my name? An exploratory investigation of consumer attitudes toward secondary information use. *Management Information Systems Quarterly, 17*(3), 341–363. doi:10.2307/249775

Culnan, M. J. (2000). Protecting privacy online: Is self-regulation working? *Journal of Public Policy & Marketing, 19*(1), 20–26. doi:10.1509/jppm.19.1.20.16944

Culnan, M. J., & Armstrong, P. K. (1999). Information privacy concerns, procedural fairness, and impersonal trust: An empirical investigation. *Organization Science, 10*(1), 104–115. doi:10.1287/orsc.10.1.104

Culnan, M. J., & Bies, R. J. (2003). Consumer privacy: balancing economic and justice considerations. *The Journal of Social Issues, 59*(2), 323–342. doi:10.1111/1540-4560.00067

Dallas News.com (2008, November 21). *Arkansas hospital staffers fired for improperly accessing slain TV anchor's records.*

Debatin, B., Lovejoy, J., Horn, A., & Hughes, B. (2009). Facebook and online privacy: Attitudes, behaviors, and unintended consequences. *Journal of Computer-Mediated Communication, 15,* 83–108. doi:10.1111/j.1083-6101.2009.01494.x

Denning, D. (2001, Summer). Cyberwarriors: activists and terrorists turn to cyberspace. *Harvard International Review, 23*(2), 70–75.

DocuSearch.com (2007). *Privacy Statements: Opting Out.*

Dwyer, C., Hiltz, R., & Passerini, K. (2007, August 09 - 12). Trust and privacy concern within social networking sites: A comparison of Facebook and MySpace. *Proceedings of the Thirteenth Americas Conference on Information Systems,* Keystone, Colorado.

Eldon, E. (2010, May 11). Analysis: Some Facebook privacy issues are real, some are not. *Inside Facebook.* eMarketer.com (2010, June 29). *Privacy Concerns Fail to Slow Social Activity.* eMarketer.com (2010, July 6). *Online merchants love Facebook's 'Like.'*

FacebookInside.com (2010).

Facebook.com (2010, April 22a). *Privacy Policy.*

Facebook.com (2010, April 22b). *Statement of Rights and Responsibilities.*

Facebook.com (2010a). *Controlling How You Share.*

Facebook.com. (2010b). *Statistics.* Press Room.

Fogel, J., & Nahmad, E. (2008). Internet social network communities: Risk taking, trust, and privacy concerns. *Computers in Human Behavior, 25,* 153–160. doi:10.1016/j.chb.2008.08.006

Gaudin, S. (2007, April 11). Security breaches cost $90 to $305 per lost record. *Information Week.*

Gellman, B. (2005, November 6). The FBI's secret scrutiny. Washington, DC: *The Washington Post,* (p. A01).

Geneology.com. (2004, July 21). *Privacy Statement: Home pages, family trees, virtual cemetery and the world family tree.*

Gleick, J. (1996, September 29). Behind closed doors; Big Brother is us. New York: *The New York Times Sunday Magazine*, (Sec. 6), 130.

Gouldson, T. (2001, July 27). Hackers and crackers bedevil business world. *Computing Canada*, *27*(16), 13.

Granville, J. (2003, January). Review article on global governance. *Global Society*, *17*(1), 89–97. doi:10.1080/0953732032000054033

Greenleaf, G. (2006). APEC's privacy framework sets a new low standard for the Asia-Pacific. In Richardson, M., & Kenyon, A. (Eds.), *New Dimensions in Privacy Law: International and Comparative Perspectives*. Cambridge, UK: Cambridge University Press. doi:10.1017/CBO9780511494208.006

Gross, R., & Acquisti, A. (2005, November 7). Information revelation and privacy in online social networks. *Proceedings of the 2005 ACM workshop on privacy in the electronic society*. Alexandria, VA.

Helft, M. (2010, July 7). Facebook makes headway around the world New York: *The New York Time*s.

Hoofnagle, J. (2005, March 4). Privacy self regulation: A decade of disappointment. *Electronic Privacy Information Center*.

Inside Facebook Gold (2010). Analysis, data and reports on Facebook.

Intelius. (2006, February 16). Welcome to the Intelius privacy FAQ: How can I remove my information from the Intelius public records databases?

Justice News. (2010, April 8). Attorney General Eric Holder signs agreement to strengthen U. S. Spanish cooperation, pushes for terrorist financing tracking program agreement.

Kling, R. (1995). Information technologies and the shifting balance between privacy and social control. Part VI, Article A of: *Computerization and Controversy: Value Conflicts and Social Choices*. Academic Press, (pp. 614-636).

Krishnamurthy, B., & Wills, C. (2009, April 20-24). Privacy diffusion on the web: A longitudinal perspective. WWW, Madrid, Spain.

Lawyers.com. (2010). *Lawsuit targets Facebook privacy issues*. LexisNexis.

Leonard, D. (2010, July 19). Another Suit over the Spoils of Facebook. *Bloomberg Businessweek*, *25*, 42–43.

Levin, A., & Abril, P. (2009). Two notions of privacy online, 11 *Vand. J. Ent. & Tech.*, *L*, 1001–1035.

Lewis, K., Kaufman, J., & Christakis, N. (2008). The taste for privacy: An analysis of college student privacy settings in an online social network. *Journal of Computer-Mediated Communication*, *14*, 79–100. doi:10.1111/j.1083-6101.2008.01432.x

LexisNexis. (2005, March 29). "Data privacy policy" Opt-Out requests.

Malhotra, N. K., Kim, S. S., & Agarwal, J. (2004, December). Internet Users' Information Privacy Concerns (IUIPC): The Construct, the Scale, and a Causal Model. *Information Systems Research*, *15*(4), 336–355. doi:10.1287/isre.1040.0032

Malin, B. (2005). *Betrayed by my shadow: Learning data identity via trail matching*. Journal of Privacy Technology. 20050609001.

Matlin, C. (2006, June 21). 'Data Broker' reveals ID theft secrets. *ABC News*.

McCarthy, C. (2010, July 21). *Who will be Facebook's next 500 million?* The Social - CNET News.

McKnight, H., Vivek, C., & Kacmar, C. (2004). Dispositional and distrust distinctions in predicting high and low risk internet expert advice site perceptions. *E-Service Journal*, *3*(2), 35–59. doi:10.2979/ESJ.2004.3.2.35

McMillan, R. (2006, August 6).] Defcon: Cybercriminals taking cues from Mafia, says FBI. Computerworld Security.

Memott, M. (2007, January 4). Bush says feds can open mail without warrants. *USA Today.*

Nakashima, E. (2010, July 29). White House proposal would ease FBI access to records of Internet activity. Washington, DC: *Washington Post.*

New York Times. (2007, August 26). The spy chief speaks.

Nielsen, J. (2007, July 16). *City dog rules may bite.* Dallas, TX: Dallas Morning News.

Nissenbaum, H. (1998). Protecting Privacy in an Information Age: The Problem of Privacy in Public. *Law and Philosophy*, *17*, 559–596.

OECD. (2003) *Privacy online: Policy and practical guidance.*

Open Security Foundation. (2009). Data Loss Database - 2009 yearly report.

Posner, R. A. (2008, Winter). Privacy, surveillance, and law. *The University of Chicago Law Review. University of Chicago. Law School*, *75*, 245–260.

Privacy Protection Study Commission. (1977). Personal Privacy in an Information Society.

Privacy Rights Clearinghouse. (2007, February 24). A chronology of data breaches.

Seffers, G. (2000, November 2). *DOD database to fight cybercrime.* Federal Computer Week.

Shilton, K., Burke, J., Estrin, D., Hansen, M., & Srivastava, M. (2008, April 21). *Participatory privacy in urban sensing.* Presented at the International Workshop on Mobile Device and Urban Sensing (MODUS 2008), St. Louis, MO, Smith, H. J., & Milberg, S. J. (1996, June). Information privacy: measuring individuals' concerns about organizational practices. *Management Information Systems Quarterly*, *20*(2), 167–196.

Solove, D. J. (2006, January). A Taxonomy of privacy. *University of Pennsylvania Law Review*, *154*(3), 477–560. doi:10.2307/40041279

Spinello, R. A. (1998). Privacy Rights in the information economy. *Business Ethics Quarterly*, *8*(4), 723–742. doi:10.2307/3857550

Stanton, J. M., Nemati, H., Chun, S. A., & Chen, J. V. (2007, August 09 - 12) Privacy in the YouTube era: Evolving concepts in the protection of personal information. *Proceedings of the Thirteenth Americas Conference on Information Systems (AMCIS)*, Keystone, Colorado.

Stelter, B. (2008, November 27). Guilty verdict in cyberbullying case provokes many questions over online identity. New York: *The New York Times.*

Takahashi, D. (2007, January 30). Demo: Aggregate knowledge knows what you want to buy. *San Jose Mercury News.*

Tang, Z., Hu, Y., & Smith, M. (2008). Gaining trust through online privacy protection: Self-regulation, mandatory standards, or *caveat emptor. Journal of Management Information Systems*, *24*(4), 153–173. doi:10.2753/MIS0742-1222240406

Thiesse, F. (2007). RFID, privacy and the perception of risk: A strategic framework. *The Journal of Strategic Information Systems*, *16*, 214–232. doi:10.1016/j.jsis.2007.05.006

Thiesse, F., Floerkemeier, C., & Fleisch, E. (2007, August 09 - 12). Assessing the impact of privacy-enhancing technologies for RFID in the retail industry. *Proceedings of the Thirteenth Americas Conference on Information Systems,* Keystone, Colorado.

Tufekci, Z. (2008). Can you see me now? Audience and disclosure management in online social network sites. *Bulletin of Science and Technology Studies, 11*(4), 544–564.

Waller, J. M. (2002, December 24). Fears mount over 'total' spy system: Civil libertarians and privacy-rights advocates are fearful of a new federal database aimed at storing vast quantities of personal data to identify terrorist threats – Nation: homeland security. *Insight Magazine.*

Weiser, B. (2008, November 19). *Murder suspect has witness: A MetroCard.* New York: The New York Times.

Wernick, A. S. (2006, December). Data Theft and State Law. *Journal of American Health Information Management Association,* 40–44.

Westin, A. (1967). *Privacy and Freedom* (p. 487). NY: Atheneum.

Xu, H., Dinev, B., Smith, H., & Hart, P. (2008). Examining the formation of individual's privacy concerns: Toward an integrative view. *International Conference on Information Systems (ICIS), Proceedings.*

Young, A., & Quan-Haase, A. (2009, June 25-27). Information revelation and Internet privacy concerns on social network sites: A case study of Facebook, *Proceedings of the 4th International Conference on Communities and Technologies (C&T),* University Park, PA, 265-274.

Zeller, T., Jr. (2005, March 10). Another data broker reports a breach. New York: *The New York Times.*

Zeller, T., Jr. (2005, May 18). Personal data for the taking. New York: *The New York Times.*[1] This chapter is an enhanced version of the article Pratt, J. & Conger, S. Without permission: Privacy on the line. International Journal of Information Security and Privacy 3(1), 30-44.

Chapter 4

Do Privacy Statements Really Work?
The Effect of Privacy Statements and Fair Information Practices on Trust and Perceived Risk in E–Commerce

Hamid R. Nemati
The University of North Carolina, USA

Thomas Van Dyke
The University of North Carolina, USA

ABSTRACT

Companies today collect, store and process enormous amounts of information in order to identify, gain, and maintain customers. Electronic commerce and advances in database and communication technology allow business to collect and analyze more personal information with greater ease and efficiency than ever before. This has resulted in increased privacy concerns and a lack of trust among consumers. These concerns have prompted the FCC to call for the use of Fair Information Practices in electronic commerce. Many firms have added privacy statements, formal declarations of privacy and security policy, to their e-commerce web sites in an attempt to reduce privacy concerns by increasing consumer trust in the firm and reducing the perceived risk associated with e-commerce transactions. This article describes an experiment designed to determine the efficacy of that strategy.

INTRODUCTION

In today's highly competitive global marketplace e-commerce companies collect, store, and process enormous amounts of information. The marketing strategies of many successful firms increasingly depend on the use of detailed customer informa-tion to build relationships with current customers, attract new customers, and stimulate sales (Bessen, J., 1993; Culnan, M. J., & Armstrong, P. K., 1999). These strategies are abetted by the internet environment which allows business to collect and analyze more personal information with greater ease and efficiency than ever before. E-commerce firms use several methods to collect information about visitors to their sites. These methods include

DOI: 10.4018/978-1-60960-200-0.ch004

registration forms, web surveys, order forms and cookies. The information thus gathered serves as an important input into marketing, advertising, customer service and product-related decisions made by on-line retailers. However, the collection of this information creates the risk of possible misuse and generates concerns over information privacy. In a report to congress the FTC cited a survey showing that 92% of households with Internet access stated that they do not trust online companies to keep their personal information confidential (Federal Trade Commission, 2000).

These privacy concerns reflect a lack of trust that has serious negative impact on e-commerce (Hoffman, D. L., Novak, T. P., & Peralta, M., 1999). In a survey by AC Neilson, consumers rated the disclosure of personal information and security issues concerning using a credit card online as the biggest barriers to online purchasing (ACNielson). Because of these concerns, many consumers simply refuse to make purchases online. The Federal Trade Commission estimates that on-line retail sales in 2003 were reduced by up to $18 Billion due to concerns over privacy (2000).

While considerable progress has been made in the development of technological mechanisms for secure payment, they have done little to alleviate privacy concerns.

There is evidence that consumer's concerns about privacy risks associated with e-commerce are justified. In January 2000, the merger of the online advertising company DoubleClick and the database marketing firm Abacus Direct started a federal investigation when it was revealed that the company had compiled profiles of over 100,000 online users, without their consent, and intended to sell the information (Kristol, D. M., 2001). More recently, the FTC reported 214,905 instances of identity theft in 2003. This represented 42% of all complaints up from 40% in 2002 (Federal Trade Commission). Clearly, some threats to privacy and security related to internet shopping and on-line information gathering are real.

It is clear that consumers do not trust companies to keep their personal information private and they do not trust internet technology to secure their financial transactions (Hoffman, D. L., Novak, T. P., & Peralta, M., 1999). This lack of trust is costing e-retailers billions in lost sales. As an article in the Wall Street Journal put it "It seems that trust equals revenue, even on-line (Petersen, A., 2001). It is trust that must be created in order to counter the effects of privacy and security concerns. Two factors must be balanced in order for a customer to do business with an online vendor. Customer trust in the firm must be high enough and the perceived risk associated with performing the transaction over the internet must be low enough to meet the comfort threshold of the consumer before that consumer will disclose information and engage in an e-commerce transaction with a specific vendor.

The purpose of this investigation is to determine the efficacy of using privacy statements to alleviate customer's privacy concerns related to e-commerce. In this article we examine the pattern of change in perceived risk and customer trust related to the reading of privacy statements. We also investigate the effect of varying the content of privacy statements. Specifically, we examine the differential impact of various components of the fair information practices guidelines (e.g. Notice, Security, Access, and Choice) on perceived risk and customer trust.

In the following sections we first review the literature on privacy, fair information practices, trust, perceived risk, and privacy statements. We then describe our experimental methodology. Next, data analysis results are presented. Finally we will discuss the findings and their implications.

BACKGROUND

Privacy Rights

According to Justice Brandeis of the U.S. Supreme Court, the right to privacy is "the right to be left alone – the most comprehensive of rights, and the right most valued by civilized men" (1928). Westin (1967) defined the right to privacy as "the right of the individuals... to determine for themselves when, how, and to what extent information about them is communicated to others." Information privacy has been described as the claim that individually identifiable information not be generally available to other individuals or organizations, and in cases where that data is possessed by another party, the individual must be able to exercise a substantial degree of control over the data and its use (Clarke, R., 1999).

Governments use many different models to secure privacy rights. Banisar (2000) suggests several including Comprehensive Laws, Sectoral Laws, and Self-Regulation. Some government institutions such as the European Union have adopted the Comprehensive Laws model to ensure compliance with privacy standards. In the United States, a combination of Sectoral and Self-Regulation models is currently in place. Sectoral laws are used to protect privacy on an industry or population segment specific basis. An example of an industry specific standard is HIPAA, the Health Insurance Portability and Accountability Act. It is the first comprehensive Federal protection for the privacy of personal health information and has had a major impact on the health care and health insurance industries. The Children On-Line Privacy Protection Act (COPPA) applies only to Web sites or ISPs that may collect information on minors under the age of thirteen. While these and several other laws regulate specific industries or types of information, the current U.S. policy toward e-commerce and privacy is one of self-regulation. According to Swire (1997), Self-regulation differs from a purely voluntary or market solution. A pure market solution would rely on consumers patronizing those firms that implemented adequate privacy policies and avoiding those that did not protect individual privacy. Under a self-regulation model, business, not the government, creates rules and implements enforcement mechanisms to protect individual privacy.

Informed Consent and Fair Information Practices

Informed consent is an important element of fair information practices (Shapiro, B., & Baker, C. R., 2001). Consent has been defined as "any freely given specific and informed indication of his wishes by which the data subject signifies his agreement to personal data relating to him being processed" (European Union Data Protection Directive, 1995, Ch.1, Article2, para.h) (1995). Informed consent is based on the concept of freedom of contract whereby autonomous free agents know their preferences and reach a mutual agreement about each parties rights and obligations (Etzioni A., 1999).

Unfortunately it is difficult for individuals in practice to achieve informed consent in the context of electronic commerce. Individuals must make decisions without a full understanding of the technology of data collection or of how technology can be used to combine information (Burkert, H., 1997). Consumers often incorrectly believe that they are protected by existing legislation such as the 'privacy act' (Gellman, R., 2002). Many consumers are not aware that companies use their information for purposes other than that for which it was collected. This is especially true of information sharing with third parties (Shapiro, B., & Baker, C. R., 2001).

In order to help overcome these problems, many nations have developed privacy policies based on the concept of Fair Information Practices (FIPs). The current standards for FIPs were first developed by the Organization for Economic

Cooperation and Development (OECD) in 1980 in a document entitled "Guidelines on the protection of privacy and trans-border flows of personal data". Fair information practices are principles that balance the legitimate need for business to collect and use personal information with the privacy interests of consumers to be able to exercise control over the disclosure and subsequent use of their personal information (Milne, G. R., & Culnan, M. J., 2002).

In the mid-1990's, the Federal Trade Commission (FTC) added internet privacy to its agenda. The FTC held a series of workshops to promote self-regulation and the implementation of industry-imposed standards to implement FIPs. Originally, the Federal Trade Commission (FTC) believed that self-regulation would adequately protect consumer's on-line privacy. Over the years, the FTC commissioned surveys and held hearings to determine whether industries were voluntarily implementing fair information practices. The commission's first online privacy survey of commercial web sites found that while 92% of the comprehensive random collected personal information, only 14% disclosed their privacy policies (Federal Trade Commission, 2000). This performance had improved in 2000 by which time 88% of the random sample were posting a privacy disclosure statement. However only 20% of web sites in the random sample that collected personal information implemented, at least in part, all of the Fair Information Practices of notice, access, security and choice (Federal Trade Commission, 2000). After analyzing the results of the 2000 survey, the FTC was disappointed in industry efforts to protect privacy. Thereafter the FTC recommended that congress pass comprehensive on-line privacy legislation. (Federal Trade Commission, 2000; Yang, H., & Chiu, H., 2002).

In their recommendation to congress, the FTC suggested that all consumer-oriented commercial web sites that collect personally identifiable information should be required to comply with four widely-accepted fair information practices; notice, choice, access and security. The following definition of these four practices is quoted from the executive summary of the 2000 FTC report (Federal Trade Commission, 2000):

- **Notice:** Web sites would be required to provide consumers clear and conspicuous notice of their information practices, including what information they collect, how they collect it (e.g. directly or through non-obvious means such as cookies), how they use it, how they provide Choice, Access, and Security to consumers, whether they disclose the information collected to other entities, and whether other entities are collecting information through the site.

- **Choice:** Web sites would be required to offer consumers choices as to how their personal identifying information is used beyond the use for which the information was provided (e.g., to consummate a transaction). Such choice would encompass both internal secondary uses (such as marketing back to consumers) and external secondary uses (such as disclosing data to other entities).

- **Access:** Web sites would be required to offer consumers reasonable access to the information a Web site has collected about them, including a reasonable opportunity to review the information and to correct inaccuracies or delete information.

- **Security:** Web sites would be required to take reasonable steps to protect the security of the information they collect from consumers.

As of this writing, congress has not yet passed any comprehensive law requiring the use of privacy statements on all commercial web sites. However a great majority of commercial sites, especially among the most popular web sites, now contain some form of privacy statement. Although not required by law there may be other legal reasons to provide disclosure of privacy policy. For example disclosure might give the firm the ability to argue informed consent on part of the consumer if later disagreements arise concerning the use of personally identifiable information. Firms also include privacy statements and join privacy seal programs such as TRUSTe and BBBOnline as part of an industry effort to create a system of self-regulation that would preclude legislation aimed at restricting online data collection and use. Opponents of additional privacy regulation argue that most web disclosure practices (e.g. privacy statements) and current security precautions adequately protect consumers and therefore additional legislation is not needed (Shapiro, B., & Baker, C. R., 2001; Swindle, O., 2000).

Privacy Concerns Related to E-Commerce

In order to compete in a highly competitive global economy, companies rely on the large amounts of information to build relationships with current customer and to attract new customers. The marketing strategies of many successful firms increasingly depend on the use of detailed customer information (Bessen, J., 1993; Culnan, M. J., & Armstrong, P. K., 1999). Therefore it is not surprising that companies wish to maintain the right to collect, use and in some cases sell customer information.

There are two potential problems for the firm associated with the ever-increasing collection and use of detailed personal information. First is the potential of precipitating legal restrictions on information collection and use. The other potential problem stems from the fact that the very techniques of information collection and use that provide value to organizations and to their customers also raise privacy concerns among consumers (Bloom, P. N., Milne G. R., & Alder, R., 1994).

Smith et al. (1996) suggest several dimensions of concern related to information privacy. Collection is a general concern that large amounts of

personally identifiable data are being collected and stored. Unauthorized Secondary Use (internal) is the concern that information collected for one purpose could be used for another, unauthorized purpose by the same organization. Unauthorized Secondary Use (external) is the concern that information collected for one purpose could be used for another, unauthorized purpose after disclosure to an external organization. Improper Access is the concern that personal data are available to people not properly authorized to view the data. Errors names the concern that the protections against deliberate or accidental errors are not adequate. One concern that Smith et al. listed as tangential to the privacy issue, but which seems relevant in an e-commerce setting is Combining Data. This is the concern that several seemingly innocuous pieces of information in disparate databases may be combined to create personally identifying information that the user does not wish to disclose.

Even though all of these specific concerns have been identified, most consumers cannot articulate specific threats to privacy but rather speak of a vague feeling that there is too much information about them "out there". Unstructured interviews with Internet users show that many have a vague fear that unspecified people unknown to them will have access to personal information. Interviews also indicate that many web users have little understanding of the technology involved. For example they don't really know what a cookie is or how it works. There is also evidence of confusion over privacy rights. Many consumers mistakenly believe that they are protected by "the privacy act" (Gellman, R., 2002) or that privacy statements are mandated by law.

Privacy concerns are not merely psychological constructs. There is ample evidence that privacy concerns actually alter consumer behavior in a number of negative ways. According to a survey by AT Kearny, 52% of respondents reported abandoning an on-line purchase transaction due to privacy concerns (Ragnathan, C., & Grandon, E., 2002). Total avoidance of online shopping, refusal to provide information and abandoning transactions are not the only responses to privacy concerns. Polls show that 30-40% (Hoffman, D. L., Novak, T. P., & Peralta, M., 1999) of web users provide false information online. Reasons given include the desire to remain anonymous, avoidance of spam e-mail, and concern about how the website will use the information. A consequence of this on-line lying is that much of the information collected by websites is wrong. This both increases the cost and decreases the value of the data collected (Gellman, R., 2002). The Federal Trade Commission estimates that on-line retail sales were reduced by up to $18 Billion in 2002 due to concerns over privacy Federal Trade Commission (2000). The FTC also cited a survey showing that 92% of households with Internet access stated that they do not trust online companies to keep their personal information confidential Federal Trade Commission (2000). In order to alleviate privacy concerns and encourage information sharing, companies must increase trust and decrease perceived risk (Culnan, M. J., & Armstrong, P. K., 1999).

Customer Trust

Trust can be defined as the willingness to make oneself vulnerable to actions taken by the trusted party based on the feeling of confidence or assurance (Gefen, D., 2002). Trust is complex, multi-dimensional and context specific. (See McKnight and Cherveny (2002), for a typology of trust in e-commerce.) Lee and Turban (2001) proposed a model of 'consumer trust in internet shopping' that included trust in the merchant and trust in the internet shopping medium along with contextual factors such as the effectiveness of the security infrastructure. Tan and Thoen (2001) proposed a generic model of trust for electronic commerce that likewise identifies 'transaction trust' as being dependent on both trust in the other party and trust in control mechanisms. Party trust is equivalent to trust in the internet merchant and control trust includes trust in the procedures and

protocols that monitor and control the performance of the transaction. Tan and Thoen suggest that control trust can be a substitute for party trust when attempting to create a level of transaction trust necessary to encourage participation in an e-commerce transaction. It is generally agreed that some level of trust is required in order for people to engage in e-commerce transaction. The development of trust between businesses and consumers is seen as crucial to the expansion of e-commerce markets (Hoffman, D. L., Novak, T. P., & Peralta, M., 1999).

So and Sculli (2002) provide a comprehensive review of the many advantageous effects of customer trust on business related behavior including:

a. Reduction in transaction complexity – trust helps consumers reduce their set of choices and thus increases the probability of a purchase transaction (Sheth, J. N., & Pravatiyar, A., 2000).

b. Reduction in transaction costs. – New products are more readily accepted from trusted companies. Costs of selling and negotiating are reduced (Fukuyama, F., 1995; Hart, C. W., & Johnson, M. D., 1999).

c. The development of long-term relationships is based on trust. Long-term relationships with customers are important elements in long-term profits (Hart, C. W., et al., 1999; Gefen, D., 2000).

d. Trust can reduce the level of concern for the confidential information sharing that is necessary for business transactions. Customers are less reluctant to disclose their information to firms that they trust (Hart, C. W., et al., 1999).

e. Trust also reduces the need for comprehensive legislation and enforced regulation (Fukuyama, F., 1995).

f. Trust leads to a reduction of perceived risk (Larson, A., 1992).

Several factors have been shown to affect customer trust. The most common factor for increasing customer trust is satisfactory experience with a retailer. Familiarity, which is often based on past experience, has also been shown to impact customer trust (Gefen, D., 2000). Current customers can have their level of trust increased through positive experiences with the firm. However, in order to build trust with new or potential customers other factors must be utilized. Factors unrelated to experience that have been shown to be positively related to customer trust in the store include disposition to trust (McKnight, D. H., & Chervany, N., 2002), perceived size and reputation (Jarvenpaa, S., Tactinsky, N., & Vitale, M., 2000).

Trust is a critical factor in stimulating purchases over the internet (Quelch, J. A., & Klien, L. R., 1996). Although traditionally trust has been defined in interpersonal terms, when salespeople are absent from the purchase transaction, as in internet shopping, then the primary focus of the customer's trust is on the firm itself (Chow, S., & Holden, R., 1997). In an e-commerce context, trust in an internet retailer has been shown to reduce the perceived risk associated with purchasing from that retailer (Jarvenpaa, S., Tactinsky, N., & Vitale, M., 2000). Also important in the context of e-commerce is the fact that multiple studies have shown that customer trust is a significant antecedent of a customer's willingness to transact business with an on-line vendor (Gefen, D., 2000; (Jarvenpaa, S., et al., 2000).

Perceived Risk

Perceived risk is a person's belief in the likelihood that they will be harmed as a consequence of taking a particular action. The perceived risk associated with an e-commerce transaction is in itself a complex concept including the risk associated with the channel, (i.e. the internet and its related hardware, software and systems) and risks associated with the information demands of the transaction (i.e. the need to supply personal

information). The perception of risk has been shown to inhibit the willingness of consumers to disclose personal information (Olivero, N., & Lunt, P., 2002). An increase in perceived risk may also lead to an increase in the demand for control over information, thus further complicating the relationship between the on-line vendor and the consumer (Olivero, N. et al., 2002). A reduction in perceived risk has been shown to be associated with more favorable attitudes towards an internet store and an increase in consumers' willingness to transact business with an online vendor (Jarvenpaa, S., et al., 2000).

Several factors have been shown to affect perceived risk. One powerful method of decreasing perceived risk is by increasing trust in the firm (Gefen, D., 2002). Likewise, a track record of satisfactory experiences can greatly reduce perceived risk (So, M. W. C., et al., 2002). There is also evidence that the reputation of the firm can reduce perceived risk associated with e-commerce (Olivero, N., et al., 2002). Where there is no existing familiarity or previous experience firms can utilize other strategies to reduce perceived risk such as the use of privacy seals, 100% money back guarantees, or privacy statements.

Privacy Statements

One of the actions taken by on-line retailers to ameliorate the concerns of customers is the addition of privacy statements to their web sites. A privacy statement is a formal declaration of privacy policies that is accessible to the consumer. A review of the requirements for major privacy (web assurance) seals TRUSTe, WebTrust, and BBBOnline suggest that a general consensus has emerged concerning the principles of fair information practice. These have been developed based on the concepts of Notice, Choice, Access and Security as stated in the Federal Trade Commission's 2000 report to Congress entitled "Privacy Online: Fair Information Practices in the Electronic Marketplace" (Federal Trade Commission,

Figure 1. Suggested contents of a privacy statement

A Privacy Statement should contain information about:
1) What personally identifiable information is collected.
2) How information is collected (e.g. cookies).
3) How information is used.
4) If the information may be shared with third parties.
5) An option for customers to choose how their information is used, if at all, for any use beyond the use for which the information was originally provided. (Opt In/ Opt Out)
6) Access measures to allow customers to view personal information and correct errors.
7) Policies to ensure data security.
8) Enforcement mechanisms – a system for customers to submit questions or complaints and to provide complaint resolution.

2000). Guidelines for the suggested content of an effective privacy statement are listed in Figure 1.

Privacy statements should be easy to locate and easy to access. Links to the privacy statement should be provided on the site's home page and on any page that requests or collects information.

A recent national survey of online consumers reported that 83% of the subjects said that they read privacy notices at least rarely. Anecdotal comments by subjects indicated that they were more likely to read privacy statements when they were unsure of the reputation of the web site or the site requested information that the subjects felt were either sensitive or not really needed (Culnan, M. J., et al., 2002).

There is some evidence that having access to the information in privacy statements might increase consumer's trust in a firm and hence their willingness to transact business with that firm. For example, in one study 72% of Web users said they would give Web sites their demographic information if the sites would only provide a statement regarding how the information would be used (Hoffman, D. L., et al., 1999) Research has also shown that the presence of a clear privacy statement is significantly and positively associated with online sales (Ragnathan, C., et al., 2002). Lee and Turban (2001) suggest that internet merchants who want to increase consumer trust in shopping with them should focus on increasing the merchant's

integrity in the minds of the consumers. Integrity is demonstrated through honesty and strict adherence to a set of principles accepted by consumers (e.g. privacy protection principles and consumer protection principles). They recommend that marketing plans should make these principles visible to customers. One way to do this is to have these principles displayed up front on the company's internet storefront (Lee, M. K. O., et al., 2001). Their findings suggest that privacy statements should have a positive impact on consumer trust.

Similarly, Culnan and Armstrong (1999) posit that companies that establish fair information practices and disclose these practices before collecting personal information from customers can greatly reduce perceived risks and the subsequent negative consequences associated with privacy concerns. They suggest that fair information practices operationalize procedural fairness and by incorporating them into a privacy statement and living up to their requirements, the firm can create a 'privacy leverage point'. This privacy leverage point "provides an intervention opportunity for firms to build trust with their customers as they collect and use personal information, therefore making customers willing to disclose personal information by minimizing the risks of disclosure to these individuals" (Culnan, M. J., et al., 1999). Their conclusions suggest that in this way such a privacy leverage point could provide the firm with a competitive advantage.

METHODOLOGY

This study utilized an experimental, pre-test, post-test design. The subjects included 227 graduate and undergraduate students in the college of business at a university in the southeast region of the United States. Participation in the study was voluntary. Each subject was given a survey instrument with a specified URL for an e-commerce website. Over 80 different web sites were utilized representing a wide range of products, and services. Subjects were then instructed to access the site. Respondents were directed to inspect the layout of the page, the availability of information and the navigation of the site. They were instructed to determine what information they were required to provide in order to use the website. At this point they were required to complete the pre-test consisting of the Perceived Risk and Customer Trust scales. After completing the pre-test, the subjects were instructed to read the web site's privacy statement. After reading the privacy statement, each respondent completed the post-test consisting of the same Perceived Risk and Customer Trust scales.

Analysis was divided into two phases. The first phase examined the overall impact of reading privacy statements on the respondent's level of customer trust in the firm and level of perceived risk associated with doing business with the firm over the internet. Based on a review of the literature, we constructed the following hypothesis:

H1: Reading privacy statements will result in an increase in customer trust.
H2: Reading privacy statement will result in a decrease in perceived risk

Figure 2 shows the research framework with the hypothesized relationships between reading privacy statements and the dependent variables along with other relationships supported by previous research.

The second phase of the analysis investigated the differential impact of various components of fair information practices guidelines (e.g. Notice, Security, Access, and Choice) on perceived risk and customer trust. This portion of the analysis required that the web sites be evaluated for compliance with the four components of the Fair Information Practices. Table 1 shows the questions and rules used to assess the content of the privacy statements in regards to compliance with the Fair Information Practices concepts. Three independent judges conducted the assessment. In cases that were judgment was not unanimous, majority opinion prevailed. Inter-rater reliability was .915.

We used four different methods of statistical analysis. First was a simple bivariate correlation between the various measures to show relation-

Figure 2. Research model

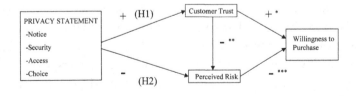

NOTE: Those relationships indicated by an * are supported by the corresponding research.
* Gefen 2000
** Morgan and Hunt, 1994, Jarvenpaa et al. 2000
*** Jarvenpaa et al. 2000

Table 1. Fair information practices assessments rules

Factor	Question(s)	Decision Rule
Notice	1. Specifies what information is collected. 2. Specifies how information is collected 3. Specifies how information is used	All three statements must be true for the web site to be considered to provide notice.
Security	1. Specifies security safeguard policy	Statement must be true.
Access	1. Specifies how the user can review or change personal information.	Statement must be true.
Choice	1. Provides opt out option for internal use 2. Provides opt out option for 3rd party use. 3. Provides opt in for 3rd party use.	If any of the three statements was true the site satisfied the requirements for choice.

ships between the variables. Next we utilized a repeated-measures T-test to examine the overall effect of the treatment (i.e. reading a privacy statement) on trust and perceived risk. The third type of analysis used was a Mixed Factorial ANOVA to examine the interaction effect between the treatment (i.e. reading the privacy statement) and the Fair Information Practices components (e.g. Notice, Security, Access and Choice). The mixed factorial design was used because we had a mixture of repeated measures and between group variables. The final method of analysis was AN-COVA. This was used for examining the between-group differences based on the varying content of the privacy statements while adjusting for the pre-treatment scores.

MEASURES

The instruments used to measure Customer Trust (CT) and Perceived Risk (PR) were adopted from Gefen (2002). The CT scale in Gefen (2002) evolved from an earlier version in Gefen (2000). The original instrument was written for a specific e-commerce company - Amazon.com. The only change made to the instrument for this study was the substitution of the generic phrase, "this company", for the original "Amazon.com" (see Appendix A). Reliability coefficients for the scales were calculated using Cronbach's alpha. The Customer Trust scale consists of 4 items with an alpha

of .935. The Perceived Risk scale also contained four items and demonstrated a reliability of .923.

RESULTS

Demographics

The study utilized 227 responses. The age of respondents ranged from 18-52 with a mean of 25.18. Respondents included 133 females (58.6%) and 94 males (41.4%). A large majority (79.3%) of the respondents reported that they have previously purchased items over the internet. Furthermore, 96.5% reported having a computer available in their home.

A correlation matrix of selected measures is shown in table 2. Notice the high correlation between pre-treatment and post-treatment scores for both the trust measure (.670) and the measure of perceived risk (.571). Given that the pre-treatment scores were measured before the reading of the privacy statements, this indicates that other factors beyond the privacy statement may account for substantial variance in the final post-treatment scores. Therefore when performing between-subjects tests on post-treatment scores we used the pre-treatment scores as a covariate in an attempt to isolate the impact of the treatment (i.e. reading the privacy statement) from differences caused by other factors that varied between subjects.

Table 2. Correlation matrix of selected measures

	Pre-trust	Post-trust	Pre-risk	Post-risk	FIP score
Pre-trust	1.00				
Post-trust	.670*	1.00			
Pre-risk	-.409*	-.320*	1.00		
Post-risk	-.382*	-.611*	.571*	1.00	
FIP score	.099	.097	-.085	-.007	1.00

* indicates significance at the.01 level

We would also like to point out the significant (p<.01) negative correlation between the measures of trust and the measures of perceived risk. This supports the contention that, in general, higher levels of customer trust are associated with lower levels of perceived risk.

Customer Trust and Perceived Risk

The results of the paired sample t-test using pre-test and post-test scores for both perceived risk and customer trust are shown in Table 3. Note that for the Perceived Risk scale, a lower score indicates more perceived risk. Similarly, a lower score on the Customer Trust scale indicates an increase in trust.

The results for Customer Trust show a statistically significant (p =.007) difference between the pre-test and post-test scores. These results demonstrate an increase in trust following the reading of the privacy statement, thus supporting H1.

The results also indicate a significant (p=.002) difference between pre-test and post-test scores for Perceived Risk. However, the direction of the change was the opposite of the a-priori hypothesized direction. The results indicate that the reading of privacy statements actually increased the perceived risk of doing business on the web site. This surprising result fails to support H2.

THE EFFECT OF FAIR INFORMATION PRACTICES CONTENT

We next pursued an exploratory investigation to determine whether the varying content of web sites relative to the components of Fair Information Practices had any impact on customer trust or perceived risk. We utilized a mixed partial factorial ANOVA design to determine the interaction effect between reading privacy statements and the presence (or absence) of each of the four components of FIP; notice, security, access, and choice. Having determined above that there exists a significant main effect of reading privacy statements, we next wanted to determine if the presence of any of the four components created a differential impact on the dependent variables. For example, would reading a privacy statement that provides choice have a significantly greater or lesser impact on trust and risk than reading a

Table 3. The effect of privacy statements on customer trust and perceived risk

	Pre-test mean (SD)	Post-test mean (SD)	N	t value	2-tail Sig.
Customer Trust	3.78 (1.42)	3.56 (1.56)	223	2.70	.007
Perceived Risk	5.05 (1.24)	4.78 (1.59)	226	3.08	.002

Table 4. Interaction effects between the treatment (reading privacy statements) and FIP components on customer trust

Effect	Between Subjects Factor	N (total = 223)	Mean Pre-Read	Mean Post-Read	F	Sig.
READ*NOTICE	Notice No Notice	140 83	3.787 3.759	3.596 3.491	.208	.649
READ*ACCESS	Access No Access	108 115	3.852 3.707	3.581 3.535	.369	.544
READ*SECURITY	Security No Security	121 102	3.899 3.632	3.659 3.436	.071	.790
READ*CHOICE	Choice No Choice	110 113	3.911 3.646	3.745 3.379	.424	.516

privacy statement that did not provide the customer with choice? Results are shown in tables 4 and 5.

The results indicate no significant differences that can be attributed to the interaction effects between reading privacy statements and the presence of any single component of the Fair Information Practices on either customer trust or perceived risk.

BETWEEN GROUP DIFFERENCES BASED ON FIP CONTENTS

Our next method of analysis was to use ANCOVA to determine if there were any between-group differences in trust and risk scores based on the presence of FIP components. This method does not use pre-treatment, post-treatment design, but rather divides the sample into groups based on content and tests for differences between the groups' post-test scores. We wanted to answer a series of questions such as "Do privacy statements that contain choice produce significantly different trust or risk scores from those that do not contain choice?"

One potential problem with using a simple t-test was that significant differences between the group's trust and risk scores might be (and in fact were) present before subjects read the privacy statements. This is due to the fact that many other factors besides the content of the privacy statements can influence the dependent variables (e.g. familiarity [Gefen, D., 2000], perceived size and reputation have been shown to affect customer trust Jarvenpaa, S., et al., 2000]) These other factors would be present after examining the

Table 5. Interaction effects between the treatment (reading privacy statements) and FIP components on perceived risk (Note: lower scores mean greater perceived risk.)

Effect	Between Subjects Factor	N (total = 226)	Mean Pre-Read	Mean Post-Read	F	Sig.
READ*NOTICE	Notice No Notice	142 84	5.041 5.069	4.829 4.685	.869	.352
READ*ACCESS	Access No Access	110 116	4.950 5.146	4.795 4.756	1.73	.189
READ*SECURITY	Security No Security	123 103	4.905 5.226	4.758 4.796	2.50	.115
READ*CHOICE	Choice No Choice	111 115	4.979 5.119	4.732 4.817	.092	.762

site but prior to reading the privacy statement. Therefore, in order to isolate the effect of the privacy statement's content, we used the pre-test scores as a covariate to adjust for the differences that existed prior to reading the statements. The high correlations between pre-treatment and post-treatment scores can be seen in Table 2. The results for customer trust are shown in table 6 and the results for perceived risk are shown in table 7. The results show no main effects of any of the four FIP components on either customer trust or perceived risk.

FIP SCORE

We have shown that while reading privacy statements has a statistically significant effect on both customer trust and perceived risk, the appearance of any individual component of Fair Information Practices does not have a significant impact either on a within subject or between subjects basis. This left us with another question related to FIP. Does the relative amount of compliance with FIP in the privacy statement affect the two dependent variables under study? In other words, we wish to determine if privacy statements that contain all four of the FIP components have a greater or lesser effect on customer trust and perceived risk than those that contain only one, two, or three or the components. We therefore calculated the FIP compliance score for each web site. The score is simply a count of the number of components ap-

pearing in the site's privacy statement. A privacy statement that contained only Notice would be scored a 1, while those that contained Notice, Access, Security and Choice would be given a FIP score of 4. A simple bi-variate correlation showed no significant correlation between FIP scores and the dependent variables (see table 2). However, as before, we recognize that the pre-treatment scores are highly correlated with the post-treatment scores (see table 2). Given that we wish to measure the effect of the treatment (i.e. reading privacy statements with various levels of FIP compliance) we attempt to reduce the bias associated with the confounding variables that are responsible for pre-treatment differences by using ANCOVA and entering the pre-treatment scores as covariates. The number of sites with each FIP score and the adjusted post-treatment means are shown in table 8 and 10. The effect of the FIP score on customer trust and perceived risk are shown in tables 9 and 11.

The results indicate no significant effect of FIP compliance score on either customer trust or perceived risk.

DISCUSSION

The analysis was divided into two phases, the hypothesis tests concerning the impact of reading privacy statements on trust and perceived risk, and an exploratory portion examining the effect of the content of the privacy statements and their

Table 6. Between subjects main effects on customer trust

Source	F	Sig.
Pre-treatment customer trust score (covariate)	169.094	.000
Notice	1.150	.285
Access	.203	.653
Security	.478	.490
Choice	.183	.669

Table 7. Between subjects main effects on perceived risk

Source	F	Sig.
Pre-treatment perceived risk score (covariate)	95.190	.000
Notice	.321	.571
Access	.052	.820
Security	.277	.599
Choice	.202	.653

Table 8. FIP scores, counts and adjusted customer trust scores

FIP SCORE	N	Adjusted Mean
0	22	3.567
1	51	3.505
2	31	3.244
3	66	3.772
4	55	3.519

Table 9. Between subjects main effects on customer trust

Source	F	Sig.
Pre-treatment Customer Trust score (covariate)	176.303	.000
FIP Score	1.176	.322

Table 10. FIP scores, counts and adjusted perceived risk scores

FIP SCORE	N	Adjusted Mean
0	22	4.810
1	52	4.561
2	31	4.871
3	67	4.845
4	54	4.827

Table 11. Between subjects main effects on perceived risk

Source	F	Sig.
Pre-treatment Perceived Risk score (covariate)	108.173	.000
FIP Score	.457	.767

compliance with the fair information practices. Overall, the impact of the FIP components was not significant. After testing for within-subjects differences, between-subjects differences, and correlations with FIP compliance scores we found no statistically significant effects based on the FIP content of the privacy statements. This may indicate that the details of privacy statement content are relatively unimportant as it pertains to effecting trust and perceived risk. Although the details of content varied greatly, the vast majority of the privacy statements shared two common elements; some type of notice about information collection and/or use, and some pledge not to abuse the information collected. These two elements may account for the effects of reading privacy statements on trust and risk.

Results of the hypothesis tests were both statistically significant and surprising. The findings related to the positive effect of reading privacy statements on customer trust were in accordance with expectations and are consistent with previous research (Culnan, M. J., & Armstrong, P. K., 1999; Lee, M. K. O., & Turban, E., 2001). Given the long list of positive effects on business-related behavior associated with increased trust (Fukuyama, F., 1995; Gefen, D., 2000;, Hart, C. W., & Johnson, M. D., 1999;, Sheth, J. N., & Pravatiyar, A., 2000; So, M. W. C., & Sculli, D., 2002, and the negative effects related to a lack of trust in the firm, it is rational to take actions that are likely to increase customer trust. As a practical matter our findings suggests that on-line vendors can use privacy statements to increase customer trust in the firm.

However, the effects of using privacy statements are not unambiguously positive. The negative effects of privacy statements on perceived risk were quite unanticipated. They were also inconsistent with Culnan and Armstrong's (1999) supposition that companies that establish and disclose fair information practices before collecting personal information from customers can greatly reduce perceived risks associated with privacy concerns. At first we were perplexed by these findings. However, an analogy might help to illustrate a plausible explanation. Imagine a patient going to see two different doctors for their opinion about the risks and pain associated with an elective surgical procedure. The first physician says "Trust me. There is nothing to worry about. It won't hurt a bit." The second physician states that the patient will experience some pain and enumerates several possible risks associated with the requested procedure. Because the second physician was straightforward about the risks involved, it is easy to understand that a patient might have a greater trust in the second physician while simultaneously increasing his or her perceived risk of the procedure.

Recall that most consumers have only vague ideas about the privacy risks involved in purchasing from an on-line vendor. Privacy statements might be educating the customer about potential risks to privacy from the misuse of information that they had not considered prior to reading the statement. For example, even if the firm promises not to sell private information to third parties, the statement sensitizes the customer to that potential risk. This could increase the customer's perceived risk in doing business on-line, while the up-front disclosure of potential risk and the firm's promise not to engage in misuse of information instills greater trust in the firm. In short it appears that privacy statements act as a warning to the consumer. Consumers are more trusting of the entity for making them aware of potential dangers. However, that awareness increases their perceived risk of transacting business with the internet vendor (see Figure 3).

FURTHER RESEARCH

Earlier studies have shown that trust is positively associated with willingness to transact business with an on-line vendor (Gefen, D., 2000; Jarvenpaa, S., Tactinsky, N., & Vitale, M., 2000). Studies have also shown that perceived risk is negatively associated with willingness to transact (Jarvenpaa, S. et al., 2000). Since our findings indicate that reading privacy statements increases both of these factors, research should be done to study the effect of reading privacy statements on willingness to transact in order to determine if the increase in trust outweighs the negative impact of increased perceived risk (see Figure 3).

The current study used real privacy statements from actual companies in order to improve the generalizability of the results. However, further research into the effect of FIP components might utilize a single company with several experimental privacy statements varying only in their FIP content. Such a design would remove several confounding variables and might display greater sensitivity to differences in content.

CONCLUSION

There is ample evidence that the lack of trust engendered by privacy concerns is constraining the growth of internet sales. Trust is an important prerequisite for many types of business activity. Moreover, an increase in trust has many advantageous effects on business related behaviors

Figure 3. Modified model based on current findings

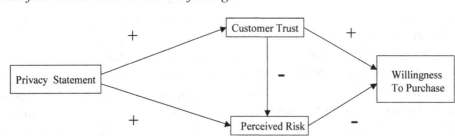

such as decreasing the concern for confidential information sharing and increasing a consumer's willingness to transact business with an online vendor. Our research has shown that when customers read privacy statements, the effect is to increase their trust in the firm. Therefore, the inclusion of privacy statements on e-commerce web sites appears to be an effective method for increasing consumer trust. Unfortunately, it appears the effect of reading privacy statements is not uniformly positive. Reading privacy statements may have the unintended consequence of increasing a customer's perceived risk associated with on-line transactions by sensitizing the customer to previously unknown privacy risks.

REFERENCES

ACNielson. ACNielsen Internet Confidence Index, http://acnielsen.com/news/corp/001/20010627b.htm

Banisar, D. (2000). *Privacy & Human Rights: An International Survey of Privacy Laws and Developments*. EPIC and Privacy International, http://www.privacyinternational.org/survey/index2000.html

Bessen, J. (1993). Riding the Marketing Information Wave. *Harvard Business Review*, *71*(5), 150–160.

Bloom, P. N., Milne, G. R., & Alder, R. (1994). Avoiding Misuses of Information Technologies: Legal and Societal Considerations. *Journal of Marketing*, *58*(1), 98–110. doi:10.2307/1252254

Burkert, H. (1997). Privacy –enhancing technologies: Typology, critique, vision. In Agre, P., & Rotenberg, M. (Eds.), *Technology and Privacy: The New Landscape* (pp. 125–142). Cambridge, MA: MIT Press.

Chow, S., & Holden, R. (1997). Toward and understanding of loyalty: The moderating role of trust. *Journal of Managerial Issues*, *9*(3), 275–298.

Clarke, R. (1999). Internet privacy concerns confirm the case for intervention. *Communications of the ACM*, *42*, 60–67. doi:10.1145/293411.293475

Culnan, M. J., & Armstrong, P. K. (1999). Information privacy concerns, procedural fairness, and impersonal trust: An empirical investigation. *Organization Science*, *10*(1), 104–115. doi:10.1287/orsc.10.1.104

Culnan, M. J., & Milne, G. R. (2001). The Culnan-Milne Survey of Consumers and Online Privacy Notices. http://intra.som.umass.edu/georgemilne/PDF_Files/culnan-milne.pdf

Etzioni, A. (1999). *The limits of Privacy*. New York: Basic Books.

European Parliament and Council of the European Union. (1995). European Union Data Protection Directive 95/45 EC. *Official Journal of the European Communities No.*, *L*(281), 31–50.

Federal Trade Commission. (2000). Privacy Online: Fair Information Practices in the Electronic Marketplace. A Report to Congress 2, Washington D.C. http://www.ftc.gov/reports/privacy2000/privacy2000.pdf

Federal Trade Commission. National and State Trends in Fraud and Identity Theft, (2004) http://www.consumer.gov/sentinel/pubs/Top-10Fraud2003.pdf

Fukuyama, F. (1995). *Trust: Social Virtues and The Creation of Prosperity*. New York: The Free Press.

Gefen, D. (2000). E-Commerce: The Role of Familiarity and Trust. *Omega*, *28*(6), 725–737. doi:10.1016/S0305-0483(00)00021-9

Gefen, D. (2002). Customer Loyalty in E-Commerce. *Journal of the Association for Information Systems*, 327–351.

Gellman, R. (2002). *Privacy, Consumers, and Costs: How the Lack of Privacy Costs Consumers and Why Business Studies of Privacy Costs are Biased and Incomplete*. http://www.epic.org/reports/dmfprivacy.html.

Hart, C. W., & Johnson, M. D. (1999). Growing the trust relationship. *Marketing Management, 8*(1), 8–19.

Hoffman, D. L., Novak, T. P., & Peralta, M. (1999). Building consumer trust online. *Communications of the ACM, 42*(4), 80–85. doi:10.1145/299157.299175

Jarvenpaa, S., Tactinsky, N., & Vitale, M. (2000). Consumer Trust in an Internet Store. *Information Technology Management, 1*, 45–71. doi:10.1023/A:1019104520776

Kristol, D. M. (2001). HTTP Cookies: Standards, Privacy, and Politics. *ACM Transactions on Internet Technology, 1*(2), 151–198. doi:10.1145/502152.502153

Larson, A. (1992). Network Dyads in Entrepreneurial settings: a study of the governance of exchange relationships. *Administrative Science Quarterly, 37*(1), 76–104. doi:10.2307/2393534

Lee, M. K. O., & Turban, E. (2001). A Trust Model for Consumer Internet Shopping. *International Journal of Electronic Commerce, 6*(1), 75–91.

McKnight, D. H., & Chervany, N. (2002). What Trust Means in E-Commerce Customer Relationships: An Interdisciplinary Conceptual Typology. *International Journal of Electronic Commerce, 6*(2), 35–59.

Milne, G. R., & Culnan, M. J. (2002). Using the Content of Online Privacy Notices to Inform Public Policy: A Longitudinal Analysis of the 1998-2001 U.S. Web Surveys. *The Information Society, 18*, 345–359. doi:10.1080/01972240290108168

Morgan, R. M., & Hunt, S. D. (n.d.). The commitment-trust theory of relationship marketing. *Journal of Marketing, 58*, 20–38. doi:10.2307/1252308

Olivero, N., & Lunt, P. (2002). Privacy versus willingness to disclose in e-commerce exchanges: The effect of risk awareness on the relative role of trust and control. *Journal of Economic Psychology, 25*, 243–262. doi:10.1016/S0167-4870(02)00172-1

Petersen, A. (2001). Private Matters: It seems that trust equals revenue, even online. *Wall Street Journal, R24*, R31.

Quelch, J. A., & Klien, L. R. (1996). The internet and international marketing. *Sloan Management Review*, 60–75.

Ragnathan, C., & Grandon, E. (2002). An Exploratory Examination of Factors Affecting Online Sales. *Journal of Computer Information Systems*, 87–93.

Shapiro, B., & Baker, C. R. (2001). Information technology and the social construction of information privacy. *Journal of Accounting and Public Policy, 20*, 295–322. doi:10.1016/S0278-4254(01)00037-0

Sheth, J. N., & Pravatiyar, A. (2000). Relationship marketing in customer markets: antecedents and consequences. In *Handbook of Relationship Marketing*. Thousand Oaks: Sage.

Smith, H. J., Milberg, S., & Burke, S. (1996). Information Privacy: Measuring Individuals Concerns About Organizational Practices. *Management Information Systems Quarterly, 20*(6), 167–196. doi:10.2307/249477

So, M. W. C., & Sculli, D. (2002). The role of trust, quality, value and risk in conducting e-business. *Industrial Management & Data Systems, 102*(9), 503–512. doi:10.1108/02635570210450181

Swindle, O. (2000). Dissenting statement of Commissioner Orson Swindle. In *Privacy Online: Fair Information Practices in the Electronic Marketplace, A Report to Congress* 2, Washington D.C.

Swire, P. P. (1997). Markets, self regulation and government enforcement in the protection of personal information. In *Privacy and self-regulation in the information age* (pp. 3–19). Washington, DC: US Department of Commerce.

Tan, Y., & Thoen, W. (2001). Toward a Generic Model of Trust for Electronic Commerce. *International Journal of Electronic Commerce, 5*(2), 61–74.

U.S Supreme court, Olmstead v. U.S., 277 U.S. 438 (1928).

Westin, A. (1967). *Privacy and Freedom*. New York: Atheneum.

Yang, H., & Chiu, H. (2002). Privacy Disclosures of Web Sites in Taiwan. [JITTA]. *Journal of Information Technology Theory and Applications, 4*(3), 15–42.

This work was previously published in International Journal of Information Security and Privacy (IJISP), edited by Hamid Nemati, pp 45-64, copyright 2009 by IGI Publishing (imprint of IGI Global)

Chapter 5
Large Key Sizes and the Security of Password-Based Cryptography

Kent D. Boklan
Queens College, USA

ABSTRACT

We expose a potential vulnerability in the common use of password-based cryptography. When employing a user-chosen password to generate cryptographic keys which themselves are larger than the digest size of the underlying hash function, a part of the resulting key is produced deterministically and this, in turn, may lead to an exploitable weakness.

INTRODUCTION

The genesis of this article came in 2006 when the author was reviewing cryptographic implementations used by certain New York City agencies to protect sensitive user-specific information - in a password-based encryption environment. It was observed that large key variants of well-established block ciphers such as Blowfish and Twofish and 3DES ('Triple DES') and the Advanced Encryption Standard (AES) Rijndael were regularly being employed. Specifically, 256 bit key Twofish was used (and not the "default" 128-bit key version). Upon inquiring why these (strong) versions were being used, the answer received was simply that,

"larger keys mean[t] greater security". This note is meant to debunk this myth in the context of password-based cryptography and to suggest that employing "exaggerated" key sizes in this kind of password-based environment may lead to a new type of security vulnerability.

PASSWORD-BASED SECURITY

Password-Based Encryption (PBE) derives an encryption key (see the Appendix for a Glossary of Technical Terms) from a user-assigned password; it is most commonly used to encrypt files which are stored locally. The Java Cryptography Extension (JCE) provides one framework for PBE. The Bouncy Castle cryptographic API (Bouncy Castle)

DOI: 10.4018/978-1-60960-200-0.ch005

is another (for both Java and C#). Coupled with a suite of available symmetric encryption schema from which to choose, one has all that is needed to protect data in such a way as that "only" the user in possession of the password can gain access.

Password-based security is invariably less secure than ideal. The primary reason for this is that there is insufficient entropy (i.e. number of bits of randomness) in a password to generate a strong cryptographic key. Keys used in symmetric encryption protocols should be randomly generated; when they are derived from a user password, there's almost always a markèd drop in security. Effective randomness in password selection is very difficult to achieve and still more difficult to demand. (We differentiate between keys for symmetric cryptography and for public key cryptography; the private keys for the latter class are mathematically dependent upon the public keys.) One of the hallmarks of cryptographic best practices is having secrets that are not biased so no information may be gained by an attacker; attacks can be mounted given even slight predisposition. Hidden Markov models are one tool used to exploit such weaknesses and build likelihood distribution models. NIST Special Publication 800-63 (NIST, 2006) suggests than an 8 character, user-chosen password, contains between 18 and 30 bits of entropy. Since an ASCII character can be regarded as a 7 bit number, a truly random 8 character password would has a (maximum) entropy of 56 bits. The average password, so, is not very random, at all. A phishing attack on MySpace reported in late 2006 (Schneier, 2006) gave further insight into password composition for 34,000 users. The good news for security: 'password' was no longer the most commonly used password (it ranked 4th). The bad news: it's 'password1' (used in about 1 in ever 450 accounts). The average password length was 8 characters and 1 in 6 used an anemic 6 or fewer characters. MySpace did not place any structural requirements on passwords and it seems that users today have been led to believe that adding a digit to a password enhances security.

This is, unfortunately, not a practical truth. Of the MySpace passwords, about 1 in 5 were lower case letters followed by the single digit '1'. In all, 8% of users had a password that was a single dictionary word followed by a '1'. This sets the stage for a clear attack: assume a password length of 8 characters with a final digit of 1. Now you have only 7 characters to figure out and you've removed about 99% of the cases. (When users are required to change their passwords, they cycle the '1' to a '2,' a predictable path of least resistance – so, very often, no security is gained.) Forcing password structure requirements (such as the necessity of containing a number) goes to lessen password entropy and this, in turn, makes data secured by PBE less secure.

A dictionary attack has some chance of success of identifying a password. An exhaustive attack is deterministic but costly. A common measure to "block" dictionary attacks and other password crackers is to salt passwords, to add some randomness – and thereby enlarge the password space. A salt is a randomly generated character string of some fixed length k that is concatenated with the user password before it is hashed and stored. By adding k bits of salt, a dictionary-type attack should take 2^k times as long to succeed. In PBE, a password cannot be directly employed as a key in any conventional cryptosystem so some processing is required to perform cryptographic operations with it. Hashing is the operation of taking an input string into a function called a hash function (a.k.a. a message digest function) which outputs a bit string of fixed length; this amounts to a digital fingerprint which, although not unique to the input, is constructed to be one-way so cannot be (non-trivially) reversed to find the input given the hash. The most well-known and widely used hash functions are the SHA family (SHA-1 is the most famous with a digest size of 160 bits) and MD5, with a digest size (i.e. output) of 128 bits.

(N.B. The past 2 years have seen very impressive attacks against both SHA-1 and MD5. For most applications, MD5 is no longer considered secure (see (Stevens, et al., 2007)). Specifically, given a file A, one may now, very quickly, modify A by appending a few thousand bytes and, in parallel, create a "malicious file" B such that the MD5 hashes of B and the modified A are the same (i.e. we have a collision). This is very bad news for MD5 adherents. SHA-1 has been attacked too, and collisions have been found. There is a very active search underway for new, stronger hash functions with larger digest sizes.)

KEYS AND BLOCK CIPHERS

Password-based key derivation is a function of the password, a salt, and an iteration count of the hashing of the salted password (these last two are not secret). (For details of PBE, see (Kaliski, 2000).) The salt cannot itself be encrypted (you'd have to have a key to encrypt the salt and you don't have such a key or else you'd encrypt the password in the first place). The salt is usually stored in the clear (that is, unencrypted) in the user table. Even though it is public information, note that the hash of the salt is not a very helpful quantity as the hash of the "sum" of two functions is not the "sum" of the hashes. Although the length of the salted key input into SHA-1, for example, is essentially unbounded, the effective search space for the derived key will be at most 160 bits. If fewer than 160 bits are needed for the key, the hash output is truncated. If more than 160 bits are needed, a second hash is calculated (with the same password and a different salt). Iterating the hash in the key generation process increases the cost of attacking by exhaustive search (on passwords) significantly with a minimal impact in the cost of deriving individual keys; a minimum of 1000 iterations is suggested (Kaliski, 2000). Finally, it is important to note that hashing does not add entropy: 20 bits of randomness into MD5 produces 128 bits of output but still only 20 bits worth of uncertainty. You can't get something from nothing.

Block ciphers, which perform, by far, the majority of encryption of data today, are composed of repetitions of complex actions, called rounds. The cryptographic key, the secret to unlocking the data encrypted by a block cipher algorithm, is subdivided by some sort of schedule into round keys.

Twofish has 16 rounds for the three different key size implementations of 128, 192 and 256 bits.

AES has 10 rounds for the 128-bit key version, 12 rounds for 192-bit key, and 14 rounds for 256-bit key.

For an attacker against PBE, it is more sensible to attack the password domain space that generated the keys rather than brute force search the whole key space; the security of information rests primarily on the entropy of the user-selected password, which is typically very low. One may roughly tally the degrees of randomness in a password (or better, passphrase) to see if it is robust enough to withstand an exhaustive attack: 6 characters can be brute-forced on a laptop and 7 is not out of reach. When you get to 8 character random passwords, it's a matter of the strength and resources of the attacker. In the PBE key generation setting, the iteration count makes this very hard in the maximum entropy case. If a user-supplied password is not deliberately made very strong, following NIST's estimates (NIST, 2006), confident PBE security in 2008 would require a password of at least 16 characters.

(It is very difficult to generate sufficient entropy to properly protect a 128-bit key not to mention a 256-bit key! To obtain 128 bits of entropy, you'd need a random 19 character password.)

On the other side of things, the strength of cryptographic algorithms is not absolute. A worst case attack is to try every possible key to see if one produces a sensible result (and that result has to be recognized – which may involve language recognition). This is called brute force and for a key length k, this involves (at most) 2^k cases. The size of k determines the feasibility of this approach and, so, a first threshold for security. DES (the former Data Encryption Standard), for example, a 16 round block cipher, is now insecure as it's 56 bit key size is simply small enough that the key can be brute forced. There is no efficient attack against DES better than brute force but (FPGA-based) DES crackers can be built for $10,000 (COPACOBANA, 2008) that exhaust the key space in less than a week. (At Queens College, we're trying to build a $1000 cracker but it's still under development.) There are classes of attacks that can break certain block ciphers with less complexity than a brute-force search: differential cryptanalysis is the most important of these. Differential cryptanalysis is the study of how differences in the input can affect the resulting differences in the output. For block ciphers, this corresponds to a series of techniques for tracing differences through the rounds of transformations in order to find non-random behavior and exploiting such properties to recover the key. Sometimes a complete break is too much to obtain but partial success comes in the form of gaining any information from a block cipher with a reduced number of rounds. Such analyses give insight into how many rounds are needed for security and how much of a security margin buffer the full version retains. Any information leakage is generally regarded as unacceptable.

As of 2006, the best successful attacks on AES were on 7 rounds for the 128 bit key version, 8 rounds for 192-bit key version, and breaking up to 9 rounds for the 256-bit key variant. (Some cryptographers, the author included, are concerned about AES since that the gap between the number of rounds in the design and the best publicly known attacks is uncomfortably small.)

WEAKNESSES IN KEY GENERATION

And this brings us back to New York City and large password-based key sizes and potential new weaknesses. Suppose a password p is going to be used to derive a large key and the user choice of hash function is MD5 or SHA-1 or any hash function of digest size smaller than the desired key size. For instance, to generate a 256-bit Twofish key with MD5, the key is formed by concatenation: key = derived (key1) || derived (key 2). Similarly, if SHA-1 is used – and this seems to be most often the case in PBE – the key is the same type of concatenation with the second part truncated after 96 of the 160 bits. As key1=p||salt1 and key2=p||salt2 and the salt values are not protected, consider P=p||salt1 and s= 0 ||salt2 XOR salt1 so

$$key = derived (P) \| derived (P XOR s).$$

Here find that all of the entropy in p, the password, may be viewed as being in the first part (half, perhaps) of the generated key so the latter bits of the key are determined, through the iterated hash, by the earlier. In the case of generating a 256-bit key from two MD5 hashes, the second 128 bits of key are (complex) functions of the first 128, independent of the entropy of the password. This means that we're really only getting 128 free bits of key even if we use a key size of 256-bits. Whether the complicated dependency can be exploited in any context aside from brute forcing is not apparent.

An interesting case arises if SHA-1 is used to generate a 3DES key in the stronger 3 key (168-bit key) variant form. (3DES is DES applied three times.) A second hash is needed to produce one byte of key. Is there bias in the first order byte of SHA-1 output? In general, over all inputs, there's probably not. But, modulo the use of the salt, we can certainly gain some insight given a user's natural predisposition towards the use of certain passwords (as in the MySpace hack) and from these, find some skewed first byte in SHA-1. This would be an interesting investigation to undertake, with the use of a concatenated salt. If there is some predisposition, of course, this points to the makings of an attack; the final byte in the 168 bit 3-key 3DES key is relevant to some rounds (based upon the key schedule) in the third application of DES in 3DES. Prejudice in one byte (of the seven) in the latter key would be a basis for an attack model.

Weak keys lead to attacks. What qualifies as a weak key is complex but, approximately, a weak key leaves traces of influence deeper into the sequence of rounds than a non-weak key. If MD5 were used to generate the 3DES key, an additional 40 bits (5 bytes) would be needed. As 3DES uses round keys of size 48 bits, almost a full one round worth of key bits can be regarded as dependent – against a brute force attack (on a 128 bit space). Is it possible to employ a (chosen-plaintext) differential cryptanalytic approach exploiting the deterministic nature of some of the key bits to regard the cipher as being reduced by a round? Can such a round key be developed as a weak key?

BETTER PRACTICES

One possible way to block the types of attacks suggested in the last section – if they are feasible attacks – and to engage in strong (best) PBE practices, is to use a hash function in the key derivation process whose digest size is larger than the desired key size. If you want 128 bits of key, use a hash function like SHA-1. If you want a large key with more than 160 bits (but no more than 256), don't use SHA-1 but try, say, SHA-256 (with a 256 bit digest size). Crucially, if you want X bits of key, have at least X bits of entropy in your passphrase or password; this is the hard part, choosing a "random" and long password. If you don't do that, as the hash function can't add entropy, your key is as strong as your password and for 256 bit keys you want at least (the equivalent of) 37 "random" characters in your password. And since that's not going to be the case, go for 128 bit variants of AES or 112 for 3DES and choose a good, unpredictable and long password and your symmetric key will be about as strong as it gets: "random."

REFERENCES

Bouncy Castle www.bouncycastle.org. Last Accessed Dec. 2008

Copacobana (2008). http://www.copacobana.org/. Last Accessed Dec. 2008

Kaliski, B. (September, 2000). PKCS #5: Password-Based Cryptography Specification, Version 2.0, RFC 2898

NIST. (April, 2006) http://csrc.nist.gov/publications/nistpubs/800-63/SP800-63V1_0_2.pdf. Last Accessed Dec. 2008

Schneier, B. (December 14, 2006). Passwords Aren't So Dumb. Wired News.

Stevens, M., Lenstra, A., & de Weger, B. (Nov. 30, 2007). Vulnerability of software integrity and code signing applications to chosen-prefix collisions for MD5. http://www.win.tue.nl/hashclash/SoftIntCodeSign/ Last Accessed Dec. 2008

APPENDIX: A GLOSSARY OF TECHNICAL TERMS

AES: (Also known, with a very slight alteration, as Rijndael) A block cipher. The current (US) Advanced Encryption Standard (as of 2001). AES comes in three variant forms: with a key length of 128, 192 or 256 bits. AES is probably responsible for more encryption performed today than any other algorithm.

Block Cipher: A term meant to signify a class of algorithms which encrypt (fixed size) blocks of text at a time. The size of the block (the block size) varies. A block cipher with block size one bit is called a stream cipher. Usually, the block size (in bits) is 64 or 128 (or larger). Block ciphers are usually designed to be composed of rounds, iterations of some complex mixing function. The more rounds, the more "random" the output (ideally), up to a point.

Brute Force: In cryptography, the process of trying every possibility. In breaking a code, this may mean trying every possible key. Brute force is deterministic but usually very (computationally) expensive and not practical.

Chosen-Plaintext: A class of cryptanalytic attacks where the attacker can ask that certain plaintexts of her choosing be encrypted. She may then analyze the pairs of plaintext and corresponding cipher texts.

DES: A block cipher. The (former) US Government Data Encryption Standard (a title now called the AES). DES has a key size of 56 bits and the smallness of $2^{\{56\}}$, the size of the key space, leads to encryption by DES no longer being considered secure.

Deterministic: An algorithm type that will come to a conclusion, though perhaps not for a very long time. This may be compared to probabilistic, which is usually much faster but not guaranteed to get you an absolute answer. As an example, a dictionary attack on a password is not guaranteed to succeed. Trying every password (every string, whether "random" looking or not) is a deterministic attack and will work, but it's very costly (and may not end in your lifetime).

Dictionary Attack: A general term for attempting to break a password (or equivalent) by assuming that a word from the dictionary – or something "word-like" – was used and running through all of these possibilities.

Entropy: The amount (often measured in bits) of randomness. In a fair coin flip, there's one bit of entropy. In a single ASCII character (chosen from 128 possible outcomes, each equally likely), there are seven bits of entropy as $2^7=128$. Unfortunately, humans do not choose random passwords so in an average six character ASCII password, there is, realistically, far less than the maximum entropy of 42 bits.

Hash Function: A fundamental tool, a hash is an algorithm that takes any input and outputs a fixed length string (called the message digest). A (good) hash function should be one-way meaning that given the digest, it is (computationally) infeasible to find an input that hashes to that output. Also, it should be infeasible to find two different inputs that hash to the same value (this is called a collision). Examples of hash functions include the SHA family (notable SHA-1) and MD5.

Hidden Markov Model: A statistical model in which observed information is used to determine system parameters. Each state has a probability distribution associated with it over the possible outcomes. The sequence of outputs leads to learning the sequence of states, or, more accurately, their likelihoods.

Key: In cryptography, the key is the secret. The size of the key, in bits, gives a sense of the security of the algorithm –but the security is also heavily reliant upon the algorithm used. In block ciphers, the key is divided up into sub keys, called round keys, each of which is used in each successive round of the algorithm.

Key Schedule: The process whereby a block cipher key is "divided up" into round keys.

MD5: See Hash Function

Password Cracker: A computer program designed to determine a password (given, usually, a simple hash of the password). Brute force is usually used for passwords of short length and modified dictionary attacks are employed against longer passwords.

Probabilistic: See Deterministic

Public Key Cryptography: (Also known as Asymmetric Cryptography): See Symmetric Cryptography

Round: See Block Cipher

Salt: In cryptography, a salt is a "random" string of some length that is appended to a password in order to add entropy to the password (making it more "random" and, thus, harder to attack – and immune to dictionary attacks).

SHA (Secure Hash Algorithm): See Hash Function

Symmetric Encryption: In symmetric cryptography, the same key that is used to encrypt (along with some algorithm, the detailed workings of which are public) is the same or easily derived from the key that is used to decrypt. Block ciphers are symmetric schema. Asymmetric cryptography, also called Public Key Cryptography, differs in that the key used to decrypt cannot be (efficiently) obtained given the key used to encrypt.

3DES: A block cipher. 3DES is the DES algorithm applied three times (using two or three different keys, depending on the variation). 3DES, unlike DES, is considered secure.

Twofish: A block cipher. There are there versions of Twofish with key sizes of 128, 192 and 256 bits. Twofish has a block size of 128 bits and has 16 rounds.

Weak Key: A term related to certain keys for certain block ciphers that should not be used as they lead to round keys with certain exploitable properties. An example of a weak key is using a key of all 0 bits in DES. There are no known weak keys for AES.

This work was previously published in International Journal of Information Security and Privacy (IJISP), edited by Hamid Nemati, pp 65-72, copyright 2009 by IGI Publishing (imprint of IGI Global)

Chapter 6
Information Systems Security Assurance Management at Municipal Software Solutions, Inc.

Virginia Franke Kleist
West Virginia University, USA

Bonnie Morris
West Virginia University, USA

James W. Denton
West Virginia University, USA

ABSTRACT

Based on an actual company, this case focuses on Business Continuity Planning issues for a small but growing software company, Municipal Software Solutions, Inc. (MSS). The firm experienced a catastrophic fire which completely eliminated all aspects of the information systems infrastructure, including the software product code repository, the client access infrastructure, the hardware operations center, and the software design facility. Fortunately, no one was harmed, and the firm survived despite the fact that it did not have a formal disaster recovery plan in place. MSS was very lucky. The case can be used in conjunction with coverage of risk assessment concepts in the context of the availability component of systems reliability and trust of services management. Accordingly, it is appropriate for use in courses covering information systems security, accounting information systems, or IT audit.

INTRODUCTION

Effective disaster recovery planning, execution, and testing are essential to manage the risk of business interruption that arises from a myriad of sources such as fire, natural or manmade disasters, sabotage, or technical or human operational failures. The Municipal Software Services, Inc (MSS) case describes a company that was faced with a catastrophic fire. The MSS case provides a realistic and easy-to-understand context for discussing risk management and systems reliability--

DOI: 10.4018/978-1-60960-200-0.ch006

two very important topics within the Management Information Systems curriculum.

The MSS case is based on the experiences of a real company. It includes photographs of what fire damage can do to information systems equipment which enhances the realism for the students. The fire at MSS completely eliminated all aspects of the information systems infrastructure, including the software product code repository, the client access infrastructure, the hardware operations center, and the software design facility. Fortunately, no one was harmed, and the firm survived despite the fact that it did not have a formal disaster recovery plan in place. MSS was very lucky. It is often cited that 40 percent of businesses that face a disaster do not reopen, and 25 percent fail within two years.[1]

Information systems and IT auditing textbooks provide students with general information about physical security threats and vulnerabilities and disaster recovery planning. The MSS case provides students with an opportunity to *apply* that knowledge in a realistic setting.

The MSS case has been used successfully in both undergraduate MIS and accounting courses and graduate level courses in MBA and Master of Professional Accountancy (MPA) programs using two main approaches: reading followed by class discussion, and as a basis for a writing assignment followed by class discussion.

The remainder of the article is organized as follows: Section II provides the case narrative and Section III is the Teaching Note.

MUNICIPAL SOFTWARE SYSTEMS, INC.[2]

Case Introduction

Municipal Software Solutions, Inc., or MSS, is a small, privately held software firm located in Cleveland, OH that supplies tailor made financial and personnel management software for large and small municipal governments in the US and Canada. MSS, Inc. is the acknowledged leader in the municipal software market. Through hard work, price competition, and a superior product, competitors have been reduced from a field of many down to a field with only two strong contenders for dominance. MSS is currently in the lead in terms of market share in the US within this niche industry. MSS revenues range from $2 million to $4 million annually, and the company employs a staff of 21. The firm has evolved over a twenty five year time period from its original inception as a systems consulting business, to a hardware solutions provider, to a LAN networking firm in the early '90s, but has settled into the specialized municipal market software engineering role for well over a decade. This case discusses the firm's business strategy, their operations and organizational structure.

MSS Background

The firm is owned, financed and managed by the 57 year old President, assisted by a senior management staff as shown in Figure 1.

The company's evolution to market leadership is a testament to the excellence of the management team, and in particular to the long range visionary skills of the President and CEO, Paul Teitelbaum. Paul was originally an employee of PricewaterhouseCoopers, with an Industrial Engineering degree from MIT. Early career moves in many large corporations gave him the ability to know and understand complex systems issues from an implementation and operational perspective, both successful and unsuccessful in nature. Paul is a strong personality, tall and thin, and quick to smile. He is also quick to assign credit to others for the firm's success. He is congenial and seems to genuinely enjoy his company, his employees and his business.

Paul spent years growing his business; yet there were several unprofitable years off and on before the company reached its current level of predictably positive revenue streams. In a discus-

Figure 1. MSS organization chart

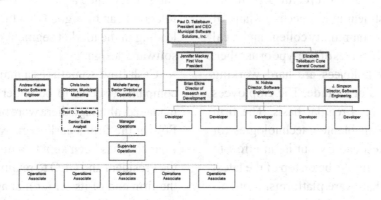

sion with the founder, Paul volunteers that some management decisions were made by the "seat of the pants," but the last decade has been one of unprecedented growth and stability. Also, the last decade was one where the senior management team formally selected the vertical market niche and narrow focus of the company into municipal markets. During a strategic planning retreat eight years ago, the senior members of the firm decided to focus on becoming the very best vendor of municipal software management programming available. That strategy has finally paid off for the firm. This tactic was a conscious and targeted approach that would allow the firm to avoid some of the cyclicality of business ups and downs in the manufacturing based Cleveland and Great Lakes regional area that had previously been their commercial client base. Municipal clients, although not glamorous or deep pocketed, usually have stable budgets from year to year, unlike traditional production businesses. Still, although the firm is no longer associated with the more virulent market turbulence of the prior decade, the firm is currently focused in one narrow applications programming niche, with a single targeted product line. Indeed, their software sales eggs are all in one basket.

The President and CEO is approaching retirement sometime in the next five to seven years. The Senior VP has been groomed to step into the senior job, but clearly there are succession issues as in any privately held company. The good news is that the firm may obtain a patent in the next two years from the US Patent Office for a product that would mean that the firm had access to a large asset, perhaps in the $15 million range in value. On the other hand, Municipal Software might not obtain the patent. Some offshore software project work is done in China to save on production costs and reduce cycle times, and copyright and patent protection legal expenses typically run about 10 percent of annual firm expense.

Paul is supported by a loyal management team, many of whom have been at the company for 15 or more years. Two of the senior team members on the technical side are also slated for retirement in the next five to seven years. Most of the staff wear many hats. For example, a person who is in sales may have skills in web design, while an operations manager may also be heavily involved in design or new implementations. Strategic planning is not comprehensive or done on a routine schedule, but it does occur when the senior staff has an off site meeting from time to time to discuss the big picture and future directions. Some of the newer staff are less experienced, but related to Mr. Teitelbaum.

The firm's culture is one that rewards and encourages each team member taking responsibility for their own areas. There is an unusual level of task delegation and assigned individual responsibility at the firm. This directed task ownership is surprising, given that the small company is run by a President with such a forceful personality and personal investment in its success. Many of the employees have community college and local university technical degrees of one type or another, and most of the employees are hard working with a 'can do' kind of attitude. The employees update their skills on a regular basis. The firm routinely makes available new technologies for the employees to test and try out in an effort to allow employees to always be on top of the latest new software and hardware platforms. Many of the employees pride themselves on being technologically astute, and enjoy this aspect of working at the firm. Both hardware and software tools are kept up to date. Employees may seek funding to learn a new technology, and employees are encouraged to learn and understand changes in the high tech environment.

The atmosphere of the firm seems to be a place of quiet professionalism mixed with pride in accomplishment and technical competence. The offices are bright with windows overlooking leafy trees, but has nothing overtly flashy or expensive in terms of furnishings. There is a full kitchen and space for lunch, and on site parking is free. Most employees live in the general area. A bus line is nearby that connects easily to the city, and there are shops handy for ease of accomplishing after work tasks such as picking up the dry cleaning. The firm has two main rooms with a four foot dividing wall between the rooms, and one side is dedicated for operations, while the other side is used for development work. Interactions between operations and development are facilitated by the low, four foot wall dividing the two spaces. Michele is capable in her role of Senior Director of Operations, and part of her responsibilities includes office management duties. The employees seem to be pleasant and get along well with each other as they do their work. The programmers interact with the technical customer representatives, so new product code writing reflects the issues that the customers may have raised with the reps. Over the years, the product has improved

and strengthened as this iterative process has unfolded. It can be argued that the MSS software is leading in the market segment due to its superior software design.

Cash flow, sometimes a major issue for small companies, seems to be under control and well managed, although there were problems with cash flow in the firm's earlier, growth years. Outside financing has been kept to a minimum, allowing the President and CEO to retain full ownership of the firm and of its senior management structure. Teitelbaum is sole owner, and debt is currently kept very low. There is a small business line of credit to cover bumps in customer payments, although Municipal Software makes an effort to not access that financial tool.

Software Development at MSS, Inc.

The software development processes seem to occur in a library like atmosphere, and, to a large degree, client crises and emergencies are few and far between. It is no surprise that this firm has established itself as the leader, given the level of professionalism in the corporate offices.

The software product runs on the municipal servers, thus reducing the network push requirements from the MSS, Inc. server room. At present, the firm has 95 clients, with a current "hot" list of five major, significant deals in process. In 2004, the company had 80 clients. Marketing occurs with an emphasis on word of mouth and a heavy presence at trade shows within the specialized market for their product. The company is known for offering and delivering a high quality product at a fair price, but they are not usually the low cost vendor. The company is also known for professionalism in the areas of support and for product development. Early in the client life cycle, the client will require a three day to one week long site visit, intense home office support, and some degree of customization work to fit the product to the municipal location needs. Income before expenses runs between approximately $150,000 to $200,000 per month, with some minor issues related to the smoothness of payments and cash flow. The billing cycle follows the classic model, with one third of billings from new license fees, one third from the annual license fee, and one third for time and billing for software customization and special project work for clients.

MSS products originally ran in the DOS environment with Paradox, evolved to an Access platform running in Windows, and now are built using a Microsoft approach with SQL, VB and ASP.net, giving users a friendly web based front end for simplicity of data access. The CEO believes that it is easier to sell a Microsoft based product, given the nature of their client base and their typically non-technical boards of directors. This strategy is a marketing decision because any non-Microsoft platform requires too much explaining to the potential buyers, according to Paul. Nearly 85 percent of clients host their own MSS products on their own municipal servers, but smaller municipalities operate on MSS servers behind a Citrix server in a classic DMZ arrangement, after running through a firewall for the remote host solution on the firm's public web server. Brian

Elkins and Andy Katula believe that their back end heavy applications run far too slowly in the remote hosted environment, but offer the hosted solution as a courtesy to smaller (less than 10 users) locations. Still, Paul Teitelbaum offers that he feels that their hosted clients are an investment in the future. Servicing the smaller clients is a way of leveraging already expended intellectual capital for very little cash outlay, although these clients do not contribute to revenues in any significant way for the firm, as shown in Figure 2.

Disaster Strikes at MSS

On the morning of July 11, 2004, a Sunday, Teitelbaum was out of town. Brian Elkins received an early morning call that a fire originating in another business had swept through the MSS rental offices, destroying the server room completely. He did not call Andrew Katula, who had responsibility for backups, but rather jumped in his car and drove to Andy's home to see if he had done the backups of all data, applications and servers. Andy was at home, out in the yard cutting the grass. Brian ran up to Andy and said, "Tell me you

Figure 2. MSS firewall schematic

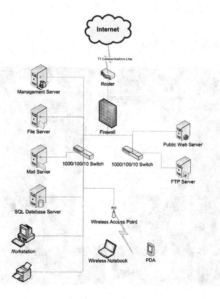

have backups?" Teitelbaum's first question after hearing the news was also to ask about the status of the backup tapes. He knew that the future of his small firm rested in the answer to that question. Fortunately, every night for years and years, Mr. Katula had done a *full* backup of all systems at the end of the day. He used a variety of backup tools, including a 40 Gigabit Exabite drive, 40 Gigabit Seagate tape drives, and two older type tape drives. Each backup device was assigned to different files, and these tapes were taken home each evening by Mr. Katula for safekeeping off the premises. When Brian and Andy went to the MSS offices, they saw complete devastation at the software company's offices as shown in Figure 3.

Teitelbaum returned from out of town by late afternoon that Sunday, and the employees met in the parking lot on Monday morning at the burned out office building to determine the best course of action. Teitelbaum's instructions to his employees were that they were to take charge of their assigned responsibilities, and to complete their aspect of the reconstruction tasks without asking for permission from anyone. For example, Brian went to Sam's Club and bought new servers and 8 personal computers. Michele met with Verizon and forwarded the central office line to a designated employee's cell phone who then routed the calls appropriately. In fact, it was almost a year before most clients were even aware that the company had had a fire. Teitelbaum met with a business associate with seasonally available extra office space, and a short term rental agreement was written out and signed on a paper restaurant placemat. Teitelbaum and the business owner with the office space had made an informal agreement years earlier that they would agree to work together if problems arose in either of their firms. On Tuesday morning, employees met at Teitelbaum's house for a logistics meeting. Remarkably, by Thursday morning, employees were at their desks in a new, temporary office space with fully functioning phones, servers, computers and management structure, having answered client questions from their cell phones over the prior few days. Although MSS was insured, Paul Teitelbaum estimated that uncompensated losses from the fire were about $30,000. He stated in an interview that he was fortunate that the company had enough resources to make the payments that were necessary to keep the firm functioning before the insurance checks were received. MSS spent about $68,000 in unexpected expenditures within the two week timeframe after the fire, including expenditures on laptops for employees, a new server, and office equipment. Teitelbaum also

Figure 3. Photographs of fire damage at MSS

Figure 4. New server room at MSS showing cooling between servers

Figure 5. Water damage of unknown origin on the ceiling in the new MSS server room

believed that his suppliers went over and above normal response times because the company had experienced a fire, and he was impressed with this.

The new server room is constructed with space between the servers in the racks for air cooling, and two temperature sensors are installed in the server room to monitor for excessive threshold temperatures, as shown in Figure 4.

If a temperature threshold is exceeded, special fans are switched on and an alarm is triggered, although no fire suppression equipment is located in the switchroom itself. The servers are single purpose only, and the phone switch choice was driven by the phones that had to be purchased to work at the temporary office location, an Avaya system.

Continuing Challenges

Today, the firm continues to lead in the municipal software markets in the United States, and is well poised to continue to land new and larger clients in many areas of the country. International products are under consideration in the same market niche, and the US Patent Office has been attentive and receptive about the patent pending information for a MSS product design for seven years. Teitelbaum is increasingly absent on international travels with his wife, and no firm succession plans

have been established. The company must decide on the next technological platform to use going forward, including their use of web hosting and web services. At the new location, Andy still backs up each evening, and he still takes the tapes home for safekeeping. Perhaps that continues to be a good strategy for MSS, Inc., as the server room ceiling has several sets of marks indicating probable, earlier water damage over the rack mounts for the dedicated mail server, application server and web server, as well as the firewall equipment.

Requirements

Evaluate the effectiveness of disaster recovery planning at MSS, Inc. Provide a qualitative assessment of the potential business impact of any weaknesses noted and make a convincing argument to support any recommendations you make. Also, identify and discuss any other business issues that may affect MSS's future viability, referring to Figure 5.

ENDNOTES

[1] US Chamber of Commerce, Business Civic Leadership Center, "The Corporate Citizen," August, 2003, see: http://

www.uschamber.com/bclc/resources/ newsletter/2003/0308fulltext.htm.

[2] Note: The name of the company, the names of the employees and the nature of the software sales have been disguised to protect the anonymity of this privately held firm.

Otherwise, all other details are accurate and true. The authors wish to express their appreciation for the "MSS, Inc." employees, who gave up time for several interviews about the case.

This work was previously published in International Journal of Information Security and Privacy (IJISP), edited by Hamid Nemati, pp 1-9, copyright 2009 by IGI Publishing (imprint of IGI Global)

Chapter 7
Chronicle of a Journey:
An E-Mail Bounce Back System

Alex Kosachev
The University of North Carolina at Greensboro, USA

Hamid R. Nemati
The University of North Carolina at Greensboro, USA

ABSTRACT

Every email that originates from outside of an organization must go through a series of firewalls and gateways before reaching the intended recipient inside the organization. During this journey, each email may get scanned for possible viruses or other malicious programming codes. In some cases, the e-mail may also receive a score based on the possibility of spam content. On any stage of this processing email can be quarantined, or moved to a spam folder for the future possible analysis or simply deleted. Understandably, such complex structure helps secure the company's internal infrastructure, however, e-mails have become an important tool in marketing for many e-commerce organizations and if marketing e-mails do not get to their intended receiver, the sending company will be disadvantaged. Therefore, from the point of view of the sender of an e-mail, it is important to understand the faith of the e-mail that was sent and whether it was received as intended. In this case study, we describe an e-mail bounce back system that was developed by a major e-commerce company in order to understand whether its e-mail based marketing was successful in delivering the intended message to its customers. In addition to the describing the development of the system, security and privacy issues are also discussed.

INTRODUCTION

E-mail was originally created as a tool for simple asynchronous communications. However, recent advances in communication technologies have made it possible for the e-mail to become ubiq-

uitous in our daily lives (Ducheneaut & Bellotti, 2001; Goodman, 2008). According to December 2008 Pew Research survey, 74% of Americans use the Internet and 91% of them use it to send and receive e-mails (Pew Research) and it is estimated that 72% of them use the Internet on daily basis and 54% of them use it to send and receive e-mail. The Radicati Group estimates that there are 1.2

DOI: 10.4018/978-1-60960-200-0.ch007

billion email users in 2007, expected to rise to 1.6 billion by 2011. At the same time, the use of e-mail as a communication tool has evolved to the point that it has become the dominant communication channel for more than just sending and receiving simple messages. It is now dominant method for the exchange of ideas and increasingly, as a critical part of conducting business (Whittaker & Sidner, 1997; Active.com, 2008).

In the current tough economic times, retailers are pressured to increase sales by all means necessary, including the use of e-mails. For business, the use of E-mail has been enormously successful; both as a communication medium and as a sales lead generator. Major retailers see e-mail as an important avenue to stay in touch with their customers and to generate new customers (Active.com, 2008). Sending the right e-mail to the right target and potential customer is a very cost effective and inexpensive method of generating sales (Active.com, 2008). Although it is difficult to have an accurate estimate of the number of e-mails sent out on daily basis, a conservative estimate would put the number to be in excess 180 billion messages are sent out per day. This means that more than 2 million emails are sent every second (Tscgabitscher, 2008). Radicati Group estimated that the number of emails sent per day (in 2008) was around 210 billion and it estimated that about 70% to 72% of them might be spam and viruses. The genuine emails are sent by around 1.3 billion email users.

According to a study of 109 of the largest e-retailers by the Email Experience Council (EEC) (Internet retailer.com, 2009), retailers sent out 45% more e-mail during the six weeks from Nov. 10 to Dec. 21 than they did during the preceding 12 weeks preceding the holiday season. The report also shows that the number of e-mails sent by retailers has grown by 45% over the past year and on average a retailer sends out 2.8 e-mails per week. According to the same EEC report, the percentage of e-retailers sending more than three e-mails per week has doubled from 14% to 28%,

and the percentage of retailers sending more than five e-mails weekly more than doubled from 4% to 10%. However such an increase in emails from merchants to potential customers has can have a significant downside (Edmunds and Morris, 2000). Customers may see this increase in e-mail frequency and traffic as an unwelcome intrusion and may view the e-mails negatively which can cause customers to opt out of e-mail lists or report e-mail as spam (Corker & Utz, 2002; Fallows 2003; Hough & Signorella, 2003).

But what happens when someone sends an e-mail out and it never reaches its destination? What happens to such e-mails? Do e-mails sometimes bounce back to the sender with an error message indicating that the e-mail was not delivered correctly to its intended recipient or do they just vanish into the Ether? Answers to these questions have a profound and important implication for organizations using e-mails not just as a communication tool but as a marketing and sales tool. Undeliverable emails, email "bouncebacks" are becoming more and more of a challenge for email marketers these days. According to a recent Association for Interactive Marketing (AIM) survey, 77% of respondents had bounce rates up to 10%, and 23% had rates greater than 10%. Every email that originates from outside of an organization must go through a series of firewalls and gateways before reaching the intended recipient inside the organization. During this journey, each email may get scanned for possible viruses or other malicious programming codes. In some cases, the e-mail may also receive a score based on the possibility of spam content. On any stage of this processing email can be quarantined, or moved to a spam folder for the future possible analysis or simply deleted. Understandably, such complex structure helps secure the company's internal infrastructure, however, e-mails have become an important tool in marketing for many e-commerce organizations and if marketing e-mails do not get to their intended receiver, the sending company will be disadvantaged. Therefore, from the point of view of the sender of an e-mail, it is important to understand the faith of the e-mail that was sent and whether it was received as intended. In this case study, we describe an e-mail bounce back system that was developed by a major e-commerce company in order to understand whether its e-mail based marketing was successful in delivering the intended message to its customers. In addition to the describing the development of the system, security and privacy issues are also discussed.

EMAIL COMMUNICATION CONCEPTS: BENEFITS, RISKS AND OBSTACLES

Email Introduction

Sending effective email campaigns on a regular basis will help increase the company's registration numbers, drive traffic to the corporate website and decrease sales cost as well as build customers' loyalty. There are a number of advantages for developing and maintaining a relationship with customers.

This is how email communication can help business succeed:

1. *Email is free*
    With no production, materials or postage expenses, the company can easily and avoidably communicate more information, more often.
2. *Email is fast*
    Time-sensitive information, including updates, announcement of events, news and promotional materials can be received by customers within minutes, not days or weeks.
3. *Email generates fast response*
    By providing links within email messages, the company marketing department gives potential customers the opportunity to effectively and in a timely

matter communicate back. The results of these efforts can be seen instantly through sales increases or growth in requests for information.

4. *Email is targeted*
    The marketing department can easily segment customer lists into groups so promotions will go to the individuals who are most likely to respond to that particular message.
5. *Email is proactive*
    Instead of passively waiting for a customer to visit the corporate website, email enables the company to aggressively communicate with and educate already existing subscribers and previous buyers.
6. *Email allows the company to foster long lasting relationships*
    Build a regular, ongoing dialogue with those customers who appreciate the routine communication. Those who do not can easily opt-out.
7. *Email will grow the company business*
    Maintaining and growing an email database will allow the company to fully utilize new communication services, including free email broadcasts, personalized quoting, selective online discounts, and expanded online promotional campaigns (active, 2008l; Mullen, 2006).

E-mail is a vital part of any business trying to expand its sales to the Internet. However, online communication has its own downside. Email systems, as any other online communication tool, are continually being threatened by viruses, spam, spoofing, phishing and others threats. All of these problems shake the confidence in email as a viable tool for communications and conducting business.

Email security, privacy, and confidentiality issues are extremely complicated subjects. Yet, it is imperative these issues and solutions for them are clearly understandable to all the readers of this case study.

Email is not a perfectly secure communication medium; and, it might be even more of a surprise to learn just how inherently insecure email can be. For example, messages that are supposed to be deleted can still exist in backup folders on remote servers years after being sent. Hackers can read and modify messages in transit, steal the email sender's usernames and passwords to login to different online services, and steal a customer's identity and/or other critical information.

As the amount of crucial business conducted via email increases, so does the amount of spam, viruses, hacking, fraud, and other malicious activity. Unless precautions are taken, email can leave anyone who uses it, as well as any business that incorporates it, open to escalating security and privacy risks. In other words, in the present world almost everybody is vulnerable. So, what are these risks?

Email Security

Spam

Until recently, spam has been an annoyance an extra load on email systems and networks, a waste of productive time and money, but these times are gone. Spam blockers are now a necessity rather than an optional utility. Rise in hijacked and spoofed email addresses symbolize an imminent threat to any company using online communication media. Due to everyday tightened rules regarding unsolicited emails, spammers try to find new ways around them. One of these ways is to send massive email broadcasts by hiding or misleading incoming IP and email addresses. If this type of spammer were able to get hold of the company's sending email and IP addresses, the business impact would be devastating. The company's Internet connection may be terminated or put on hold by Internet Service Provider (ISP), emails would be blocked without even reaching

their destination, and IP addresses would be put on a black list of known spammer addresses - all without any warnings and notifications. The whole company's online business would effectively be shutdown (Keepemailsafe, 2008; Smith, 2008).

Viruses

A computer virus is a computer program that can copy itself and infect any computer without permission or knowledge of the user. Some viruses are harmless and just replicate themselves and perhaps make their presence known by presenting text, video, or audio messages. They typically just take up computer memory used by legitimate programs and slow PC performance. However, the majority of them are much, much worse. Their intentions can be to take over a computer, send private information to attackers, destroy a hard drive, bring a computer to a standstill, or disrupt productivity in general. They are major threats to data privacy, security, and confidentiality.

Sound scary? How about spam emails that incorporate viruses as a means of transportation? An example of this type of technology is the SoBig virus whose sole purpose was to create a broad spamming infrastructure by planting code on unwilling participants' PCs, creating a mass threat to email security. This is just the tip of the iceberg. Spam will increasingly be used to spread and activate very dangerous viruses for multiple malicious purposes. (Livinginternet, 2008; Wikipedia, 2008)

Phishing

Phishing uses email messages that purport to come from legitimate businesses that one might have dealings with (banks such as Citibank or Bank of America); online portals (such as eBay and PayPal); Internet service providers (such as AOL, MSN, Yahoo and EarthLink); online retailers (such as Amazon.com or Circuit City); and insurance or credit agencies. The messages look quite authentic, featuring corporate logos and formats similar to the ones used for legitimate messages. Typically, they ask for verification of certain information, such as account numbers and passwords, allegedly for auditing purposes. Therefore, because these emails look so official, up to 20% of unsuspecting recipients respond to them. This results in financial losses, identity theft and other fraudulent activity against victims of such fraud (keepemailsafe, 2008; livinginternet, 2008; Kanga, 2008; Kay, 2008).

Email Privacy

In the digital age, securing personal information and ensuring privacy pose issues of paramount concern. At first glance, the customer might find it intriguing and pleasant that email, such as mass newsletters, sale quotes or offers, from the company that the customer agreed to receive correspondence from, greets the person by his or her first name. It is also very nice when company sends customers emails when goods of their liking are added, or it recommends goods and services based on their demographic profile, previous visits, etc. Excellent services, are they not? Sure they are; however, the intelligent computer professional will also see in these situations the privacy drawbacks of immense proportions. Who else is being provided with this information? Is there a way to ensure the security of this information? What happens with the information if the company gets into financial difficulties and has to liquidate its assets or sell some of them? Where does all of that "private information" go?

Many studies over the last few years have suggested that a majority of consumers are concerned about when, what and how their personal information is being collected and transmitted, how this information is being used and whether it is being protected. They want to know whether the information is being sold or shared with others, and if so, with whom and for what purposes. They also want to have control over their privacy in today's

digital age where advances in telecommunication, storage, and software technologies have made monitoring a person's activities effortless.

Even in cases where a company would protect a customer's information inside its databases, there is still an issue of data transmission (from customer and to customer). In the usual way that people send and receive emails, all message content (sometimes even including usernames and passwords to email accounts) is transmitted between personal computers and email servers mostly in "easily" accessible plain text. This means that anyone who has the right technology can intercept this flow of information, read emails and obtain usernames and passwords or other confidential information. Also, it is not unheard of that email interception can happen on the email server of the organization an individual works for, at the Internet Service Provider (ISP) level or at any of the many routers along the path email takes to get from source to destination. (However, unless the person who sends the email is the subject of a legal investigation or targeted by a specific attack, it is unlikely that anyone will ever actually intercept and read someone's emails. Because of the sheer volume, there are far too many, hundreds of thousands of emails passing through each email server and Internet router, for anyone to realistically read more than a small fraction of them, even if they wanted to. Unfortunately, the possibility is still there). Even more, since some people use email as a primary mean of doing business and convey all or most of the private information over the Internet, an attacker can easily gain access to a person's critical communications. Also, if a company sends some specific customer related information over the publicly available communication channels, the chances that such information can be intercepted somewhere on its journey from origination to the destination is very big. Even worse, if an attacker would gain access to such types of information and would be able to decode a user name and password to the email account, the same attacker can send email mes-

Figure 1.

Email Confidentiality Notice and Disclaimer

This email message (including attachments) contains information which may be confidential and/or legally privileged. Unless you are the intended recipient, you may not use, copy or disclose to anyone the message or any information contained in the message or from any attachments that were sent with this email, and if you have received this email message in error, please advice the sender by email, and delete the message. Unauthorized disclosure and/or use of information contained in this email may result in civil and criminal liability.

Everything in this email and attachments relating to the official business of "Company name", is proprietary to the company.

Caution should be observed in placing any reliance upon any information contained in this email, which is not intended to be a representation or inducement to make any decision in relation to "Company name". Any decision taken based on the information provided in this email, should only be made after consultation with appropriate legal, regulatory, tax, technical, business, investment, financial, and accounting advisers.

The email address of the sender may not be used, copied, sold, disclosed or incorporated into any database or mailing list for spamming and/or other marketing purposes without the prior consent of "Company name".

Neither the sender of the email, nor "Company name", shall be liable to any party for any direct, indirect or consequential damages, including, without limitation, loss of profit, interruption of business or loss of information, data or software or otherwise.

sages appearing to come from the victim. Also, by intercepting personal information, attackers can possibly steal a person's identity and create untold damage (emailprivacy, 2008).

Email Confidentiality

Probably, everyone who uses email has at least once received an email with Confidentiality Notices and Disclaimers. Please see Figure 1.

In general, the content of any email message sent or received is intended to be confidential; meaning that the content of any email message is intended to be shared only by its sender and recipients, and by any other people to whom the sender or recipients may disclose the contents of the message. The irony of this situation, is, in fact, that these messages occurred (i.e. were sent by whom, to whom, and how). For example, email messages can be saved indefinitely on receiving computer(s), copies made and forwarded to others electronically or on paper; messages sent to nonexistent or incorrect addresses may be delivered to system administrators or postmaster at an external site. These facts alone underline that confidentiality of email message content cannot be guaranteed. Confidentiality of the email cannot

be protected by simple statement about the illegality of reading email that was not sent to you (Shafer, 2004; out-law, 2008).

Sender Authentication

In light of the above information, it would not be an overestimate to say that email is not a media communication channel that should be used in transferring sensitive information. However, it does not mean that all of the above threats should be forgotten if email content does not contain private information. Email is part of our daily life, and addressing these threats is in everyone's interest. There are multiple ways to make email a little bit safer, more secure, definitely more reliable, and authenticable. We are talking about spam blockers, antivirus protection software, email encryption, and many others. However, because the primary reason for this case study is to provide detailed information describing just one part of email processing -sender obligations and duties, the authors felt that describing all of these processes in this case study would be inappropriate. So, the authors decided to describe in detail just the sender's part of the email process - sender authentication protocols. There are three major types of sender authentication protocols - Sender Policy Framework (SPF), Sender ID and DomainKeys. In the present stage of the Internet development almost every legitimate company that incorporates bulk email sending on a daily basis, has one, two or all of these services incorporated in their network infrastructure.

Sender Policy Framework (SPF)

Today, nearly all abusive email messages carry fake sender addresses. The victims whose addresses are being abused often suffer the consequences, because their reputation gets diminished and they have to disclaim liability for the abuse, or they waste their time sorting out misdirected bounce messages. Even worse, people (potential customers) who receive such types of emails try to stop any business relations with the company that allowed something like that to happen (even unknowingly) on its behalf.

Normal SMTP (Simple Mail Transfer Protocol - the underlying technology that allows email to work) without SPF allows any computer to send email claiming to be from anyone. SMTP was developed at a time where only a few clients and servers existed. SMTP has very few security features. Originally, any SMTP server would accept mail from anyone, for anyone – this is known as an open relay. This was not a problem in the early days of the Internet. Today it is a viable threat. Today, open relay is no longer an issue for the majority of companies because the network system administrators have done their work and closed them. If there are any open relays they will be relatively quickly listed on multiple blocklists.

The biggest problem today is email that gets correctly addressed to a valid email address, but come from fictitious sources (spammers). One of the solutions for this problem is SPF (Sender Policy Framework). As people may know, email messages have at least two kinds of sender addresses.

The envelope sender address (sometimes also called the return-path) is used during the transport of the message from mail server to mail server, e.g. to return the message to the sender in the case of a delivery failure. It is usually not displayed to the user by mail programs.

The header sender address of an email message is contained in the "From" or "Sender" header and is what is displayed to the user by mail programs. Generally, mail servers do not care about the header sender address when delivering a message.

SPF is an open standard specifying a technical method to prevent sender address forgery. More precisely, SPF protects the envelope sender address. The lack of security in normal SMTP makes it easy for spammers to send email from forged email addresses. It also makes it a difficult task for email administrators to trace back to where the spam actually originated from. SPF allows a domain to specify its own mail sending policy and designate which machines are authorized to send email for that domain. A domain owner publishes this information in an SPF record in the domain's DNS zone, and when someone else's mail server receives a message claiming to come from that domain, and the receiving server can check whether the message complies with the domain's stated policy. If the message comes from an unknown server, it can be considered a fake. (For example, the owner of the email domain uncg. edu can designate which systems are authorized to send email with addresses of @uncg.edu. This information is defined using special settings in DNS (Domain Name Service) records. Anyone that implements SPF would then ignore any email that claims to come from that domain but fails to come from locations that domain has authorized). With such a type of system in place, a business can finally protect its reputation and good name online (Knight, 2008; RFC 4408, 2008; RFC 2821, 2008). Please see Figure 2.

Figure 2. Mail flows (The picture is courtesy of: http://old.openspf.org/mailflows.pdf)

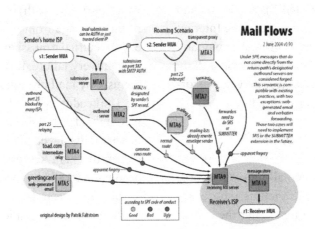

Sender ID

Sender ID seeks to verify that every email message originates from the Internet domain from which it claims to have been sent. This is accomplished by checking the address of the server sending the mail against a registered list of servers that the domain owner has authorized to send email. This verification is automatically performed by the Internet service provider (ISP) or recipient's mail server before the email message is delivered to the user. The result of the Sender ID check can be used as additional input into the filtering tasks already performed by the mail server. Once the sender has been authenticated, the mail server may consider past behaviors, traffic patterns, and sender reputation, as well as apply conventional content filters, when determining whether to deliver mail to the recipient.

It might be confusing - what is the difference between Sender ID and SPF? At first glance they work identically. However, SPF and Sender ID are not the same. Both validate email sender addresses, and both use similar methods to do so. Both publish policy records in DNS. Both use the same syntax for their policy records. They differ in what they validate and what "layer" of the email system they are concerned with.

SPF (defined in RFC 4408) validates the HELO domain and the MAIL FROM address given as part of the SMTP protocol (RFC 2821 – the "envelope" layer). The MAIL FROM address is usually displayed as "Return-Path" in the header of the email. As it was mentioned above, domain owners publish records via DNS that describe their policy for which machines are authorized to use their domains in the HELO and MAIL FROM addresses, which are part of the SMTP protocol.

Sender ID (defined in RFC 4406) on the other hand, is a Microsoft protocol which validates one of the message's address header fields defined by RFC 2822. The one it validates is selected according to an algorithm called PRA (RFC 4407 - Purported Responsible Address). The algorithm aims to select the header field with the email address "responsible" for sending the message.

Authentication is becoming a vital part of sending email for mailers who want to be seen as responsive and responsible. According to statistical analysis released at the Email Authentication Summit in April 2006, 45% of all email sent is now being authenticated. While Fortune 500 companies and email service providers have largely embraced it, many small - to medium-sized companies have yet to do so (Evers, 2005).

DomainKeys

DomainKeys is a technology proposal developed by Yahoo that uses a form of public key cryptography to authenticate the sender's domain. This authentication can give email providers a mechanism for verifying both the domain of each email sender and the integrity of the messages sent (that they were not altered during transit). It would also enable the receiving end of an email to easily filter out notes in which the sender's stated address could not be authenticated as the actual address.

The mechanism behind this solution is relatively simple: every email message that was originated from the domain that uses DomainKeys would have the originating domain private key securely embedded in its header. When the message arrives at its destination, the key can be compared to the stated domain's public key in the domain name system (DNS) listings to verify that it actually comes from where it says it comes from. Messages that originate from known sources of spam or from domains other than the one they claim to be from could be rejected by the recipient's server. Despite very prominent software features, this package has its downfalls:

- The package needs to be widely accepted to be successful;
- Even if DomainKeys package was broadly implemented it might lead to an unacceptable slowing of transmission due to the extra handling of each message;
- Spammers may try to carry out replay attacks, in which the attacker intercepts messages, steals legitimate digital signatures, and then forges messages using them.

However, it is too early to tell if DomainKeys would be successful or not. At the present moment just a few large scale providers are using it. However, authentication would be the first, but not the last step on the way to making email more safe and secure. The next step would be email reputation (Yahoo, 2008; Searchsecuirty, 2008).

Sender Reputation

Where authentication methods like SPF, Sender ID, and DomainKeys verify that a sender is who he says he is, reputation services take that sender's identity and check it against a database of their sending practices, checking for things like bounce rates, unsubscribe practices and user complaints. Unfortunately, reputation services have major obstacles in their way. One of them is that reputation calls for more subjective analysis of data taken from several sources, weighted according to a subjective decision of the provider. However, without having transparent data as the basis for reputation scores, without an established way of sharing information between sender and receiver ISPs about kinds of practices that might impact score, and without established consistent methods to manage reputation in the system, reputation services will not be implemented in the near future. This is why the Email Senders & Providers Coalition (ESPC) is working hard to create and distribute a set of best practice rules that should be followed by a reputation service provider.

Without a clear understanding of the factors that may help or harm their reputation, and a way to manage their reputation, senders will have no incentive to participate in the program.

As ISPs begin to enforce authentication and reputation, more legitimate mail will pass through to the destination with a positive reputation. That will create a true win-win situation for businesses and users, because it improves trust and confidence in email (Newcomb, 2006).

EMAIL BOUNCE BACK

Email Bounce Back Introduction

Establishing sender identity will almost always give companies a green light to deliver their message to their customers. However, it is also important to know how many emails that were sent actually ended up in the customer mailboxes. Even with multiple layers of email verification, ISPs can still block senders without a clearly defined reason or even by mistake. According to Jupiter Research, email deliverability is third on the list of the top five challenges the email marketing industry faces. However, email delivery is a manageable problem on which marketers focus right now.

Tracking data and taking corrective actions during email campaigns is vital to increasing deliverability, especially in the case of subscriptions and bounce management. Respecting subscription removals from a particular list is almost more important than any other part of the company normal communication with the customers. It is extremely important to have a process for that. Retention in terms of bounce management is also important. If a company gets an ISP's bounce back from a valid recipient based on the email address, there has to be an escalation process to pursue that.

Also, ISPs heard loud and clear from their customers that action needs to be taken to stem the tide of ever increasing spam and unsolicited emails. As a result, an ISP, after one or two accusations from customers declaring unwanted email, might suspend delivery until a more detailed investigation can take place.

If such a thing happens, an email bounce back management system is a solution to identify these situations in a timely manner and take proactive steps.

In addition, the companies would not want to send email messages to non-functioning email addresses (Sending to the wrong address is not just wasting time but wasting money as well. In contrast to a regular email user who may have unlimited Internet access and incurs no price penalty on the amount of information sent and received from his computer, all businesses that incorporate bulk email sending must pay a substantial amount of money for bandwidth and data traffic). If a company does not process bounce back messages correctly, it might result in the company's email directory having a large portion of dead addresses. This could mean lost customers and, as a consequence, lost revenue. Even worse, ISPs look at bounce information when determining whether they're being targeted by a spammer. Spammers' email lists are of very poor quality. If an ISP detects a large percentage of invalid email coming from one IP, the mail-stream may be identified as spam and blocked.

Monitoring bounce back emails can help show a potential delivery problem and help correct any irregularities if they happen. What do bounce back email consists of, and what types of bounce back emails exist?

Email Bounce Back Definitions

In computer terminology, a bounce back email is one that never arrives in the recipient's inbox and is sent back, or bounced back, to the sender with an error message that indicates to the sender that the email never transmitted successfully. To clearly understand what these error messages mean, we believe it is necessary to give a brief overview of the whole email process.

When a user attempts to send an email, he is telling his email system to look for the recipient domain's mail server. Once the sender's email system makes contact with the recipient's mail server, the sender's email server waits for the response from the receiver email server that looks at the message to determine if it will let the message pass through. If the recipient's server has predetermined that it is not accepting emails from the sender's address (for example, if it has blocked the address for anti-spamming purposes), the receiver's email server will reject the message, and it will subsequently bounce back to the sender's email server. The message will also bounce back to the sender's email server if the email server on the recipient's end is busy and cannot handle the request at that time. When an email is returned to the sender without being accepted by the recipient's email server during initial communication, this is called a hard bounce back (or internal bounce back) (extreme-messaging, 2008).

Once the email has been accepted by the recipient's mail server there are still ways for the message to be rejected. The receiver's email server has to determine if the recipient actually exists within its system and if that recipient is allowed to accept emails. If the recipient's address does not exist on the receiver's email server, then the message will be rejected because there is no one to deliver the message to. If the sender misspells the recipient's email address, then the system will recognize this as a nonexistent address and bounce the message back. If the recipient exists but does not have enough disk space to accept the message, then the message will bounce back to the sender. Some email systems have a predetermined maximum message size that they will accept and will automatically bounce email back if it exceeds that size; some email systems predetermine a maximum amount of disk space the user is allowed to occupy on the server. When an email is returned to the sender after it has already been accepted by the recipient's mail server, this can be called a soft bounce or a hard bounce back. The email bounce back type solely depends on the reason for the bounce back.

A soft bounce back would be a message that could not be delivered for a number of reasons, but the sender could not be sure that the address is invalid. In many cases, the reason for this type of email bounce back message is that a recipient's mailbox has exceeded its quota and the mail server is not placing new mail in the mailbox, network errors, DNS errors, timeouts and some

others. Eventually, mail delivered to these email addresses might succeed.

Example:

- "User mailbox exceeds allowed size"
- "The user(s) account is temporarily over quota."
- "No route found to domain "Company Name" from server "ISP Name."
- "Host unknown (Name server: "Internal Name Server": host not found)."

An email would be considered a hard bounce back if it had a fatal addressing error. No messages will ever be delivered to the email address because it is absolutely incorrect.

Example:

- "The recipient name is not recognized."
- "User not listed in public Name & Address Book"

However, there are a few other major categories of bounce back emails that exist, and it is important to be familiar with them as well.

Mail Block

A message would be considered a mail block if it was rejected by the recipient (or recipient's mail server) for security reasons. Blacklisting is one important type of mail block. If a company does not follow the "rules" for sending mail to a particular domain (for example, they BCC a lot of recipients), they may get blacklisted, and all of their messages will be rejected.

Example:

- "Remote host said: 550 Relaying is prohibited"
- "The IP address xxx.xxx.xxx.xxx is blacklisted"
- "5.7.1 You are not authorized to send to this email address: sample@abcd.com"

- "5.7.1 Spammers are NOT welcomed here"
- "Recipient address rejected: Relay access denied"

Message Restrictions

An email message faces a message restriction if the delivery failed because of a problem with the message, not with the address. There are three common reasons for email to be placed in this category: the recipient does not accept mail with attachments, the message is too long, and the message is improperly constructed (often the case when the sender has written a proprietary message-generation engine).

Example:

- "The content length of the message is too long for the recipient to take delivery"
- "Your mail to xxx could not be delivered because xxx is not accepting mail with attachments or embedded images"
- "Remote host said: 501 5.5.2 there is a stray of potential SPAM characters in the message"
- "Cannot send 8-bit data to 7-bit destination"

Out of Office Reply: Bounce Back Email

An out of office reply is a message that is automatically sent by the user's mail server indicating that the user is not currently checking his/her messages but will eventually return and do so in the future.
Example:

- "Jane Doe is currently out of the office and will return on "Day.""
- "I will return to the office on "day and month.""

Delivery Status Notification

A mail server sends a delivery status notification if it is unable to deliver the email to a recipient after some time. This is an information message stating that it has attempted to deliver the message, but it has been unsuccessful so far and some amount of time has passed since the mail was sent. The server will continue to attempt to deliver the message to the recipient. If the recipient's domain uses a relay server to receive the messages, the relay server often sends this message when the recipient's actual mail server is down.

Example:

- "Delivery to the following recipients has been delayed."
- "Warning: could not send message for past 4 hours"
- "<someone@somewhere.com>... Deferred: user over quota as of now"(Marketer, 2009)

Email Bounce Backs Management

All of the above seems to be logical and straightforward; however, in the real world things are much more complex. There are too many scenarios under which the above definitions can lead to misidentification and unprocessed bounces. Many standard bounce back code and definitions were created in the early '80s. Since then, the Internet and email have undergone enormous changes. Messages now are refused for reasons that simply did not exist back then. Even more, some ISP's or large corporations started creating their own bounce definitions and explanations. As a result, identification and categorization of the bounce back email message is far from an exact science. Worse, many domains and ISPs do not adhere to existing standards at all. In some cases, they deliberately mislead or are vague about the reason for refusing a message. Some will even return "user unknown" when they believe a message to be spam. They do this to discourage spammers from continuing to use the address. Incorrect bounce messages can be returned due to mis-configuration or system errors. If a recipient database fails all delivery attempts, it may return "user unknown" even when it's a temporary circumstance.

So, in order to incorporate as many possible emails bounce back scenarios and create effective and efficient processing system, a representation of this approach is discussed here. This is a description of the implementation that was untaken by the CrystalWare, Inc. to create Email Bounce Backs management system. (See more details about CrystalWare business for details of the company. Although the name of the company has been changed for this case, other important and relevant company related details are accurate.).

Email Bounce Back Proactive Steps

Sending bulk Emails: Email servers

First of all, the company had to create a system that mails all messages from the actual verifiable user accounts (not like nobody@ or sender@ company-a.com). It was very important for the company to send each email type from its own email address. (The reason for this decision will be explained later in this paper, in the technical details of the Email Bounce Back project). On top of it, all email servers were setup to have a reverse DNS service (lack of this service would almost positively block all emails communication from the sender). Another important aspect of bulk email system is setting accurate threshold limits on all emails servers. Some ISPs can permanently block an IP address if they detect more than allowed number of emails sends from an IP address during specified period of time. The purpose of the threshold limit concept is to not let the sending queue exceed the maximum number of waiting emails to one ISP. (Different ISPs have different approaches to calculate excessive sending. These calculations are usually secret and not published.

So, to be on the safe side, threshold limit were decided to keep on very minimum).

Sending Bulk Emails: Email Templates

The company has to change all of the existing email templates so that any mass emails can be readable by different type of recipients. Plain text emails were obvious choice because they were legible in all email clients. However, they are not as attractive as HTML ones. Unfortunately no two email clients are going to render emails in exactly the same way. So, the technical decision was made to let customers to decide what email context to receive. (The web developer team had a task to check against the most common email clients and webmail interfaces to get a "feel" for how the final product was going to look). At this point a business decision was made not to include any client-side scripting (JavaScript etc) programs or email incorporated forms. The reason for this decision is simple: email messages that have such components would be most certainly blocked by a majority of ISPs. By ensuring that HTML concept is valid, the company made a step in a right direction of assuring that outgoing emails will not be blocked by spam filters.

Sending Bulk Emails: Mailing List Management

Finally the company faced a problem of keeping email list conforming to permission based standards. The difference between senders of legitimate bulk email and spammers could not be clearer: the legitimate bulk email sender has verifiable permission from the recipients before sending, the spammer does not. So, the following infrastructure was implemented to avoid most of the possible issues:

• **The email addresses of new subscribers must be confirmed and/or verified before mailings starts**

There are two standard methods for online registration: single and double opt-in.

With single opt-in, a subscriber enters his or her email address and is then automatically registered.

Double opt-in is the preferred method for email newsletter subscriptions because it requires confirmation. No one is added to the list until he or she has replied to an email message confirming sign-up. This prevents someone from signing up an email address without the owner's knowledge.

After detail investigation, single opt-in method was chosen. The single opt-in function is simpler and requires far less system resources. However, to make it more reliable and ensure that subscribers enter their email addresses correctly, all online registration forms as well as all company's home written application that deal with email addresses were modified to include a script that checks for syntax errors upon submission. Additionally, all online registration forms were modified to require subscribers reenter their addresses in a second box.

• **Email / mailing address update**

Due to the increased number of new subscribers, the company decided to add an email address update link to any email send in bulk and a profile update form to the company web site, enabling subscribers to update/edit/disable their address and email preferences.

• **Welcome message**

Once someone subscribes, the system was programmed to send a welcome message immediately. This message includes a description of email types subscriber will receive from the company (for example: quotes of available products, newsletters, special promotions, oncoming events and some others), how frequently he or she will receive communication form the company, and how to unsubscribe from the company's mailing list.

• **Company provides a simple method for subscribers to terminate their subscriptions**

All company emails were designed to include a direct links to unsubscribe from a particular type of communication or a direct link to unsubscribe from the mailing list all together. On top of the web site unsubscribe process, each email was modified to include a separate email address implemented specifically for the unsubscribe purposes, with detailed instruction how to request the company to stop sending any individual or all types of email communication to the requester. Such requests were to be processed immediately. So, a special script was implemented to process unsubscribe request on an hourly basis

• **Contact information**

Not all customers feel comfortable enough to communicate via email or place orders online. So, it was imperative for the company to modify all standard email templates to include the company's toll-free phone number, fax, mailing and physical addresses, as well as contact emails address and company website.

Privacy Policy

To assure customers about the safety of their personal information, the company created a standard privacy policy. The link to this privacy policy was placed on every outgoing email as well as on every page on the company website that might contain questions to provide such information. This policy describes how the company handles the collected information and how people can contact the company in case they have any concerns or questions. The main purpose of this policy is to assure subscribers that the company will not share, sell, or rent individual personal information with anyone without customer advance permission or unless ordered by a court of law.

Information submitted to the company is only available to employees managing this information for purposes of contacting customers or sending customers emails based on request for information and to contracted service providers for purposes of providing services relating to our communications with the customer. Company-A also takes responsibility to protect customers' information in effective and secure matter.

Reply to Inquiries

Due to the high volume of email sent, the decision was made to allocate up to five members of the Internet Services department just to receive inquiry messages or a spam complaint, and respond to them as soon as possible. CrystalWare's customer service strategy always relied on a two-part approach: listening to customers and addressing inconsistencies in the overall consumer experience. On its website the company promised that each received message would be given individual attention and be processed within 48 hours. To fulfill this promise, a new email processing system, E-Gain, was purchased. This platform allows agents in the group process all of the inquiries and spam complains efficiently and effectively by using the following key capabilities included in email response management solution: rules-based routing, quality assurance features, management reporting, and an easy-to-use knowledge base. So, despite drastically increased email volume, the company was able to reduce its response times to all email requests to less than 24-48 hours and sustain a high quality of service without adding staff, in the face of growing email volumes.(extreme-messaging, 2008; Marketer, 2008; mail-abuse.com, 2008).

THE CRYSTALWARE, INC. INTRODUCTION

CrystalWare, Inc. is one of the world's largest retailers of discontinued and active china, crystal, silver and collectibles. The company specializes in replacing these items. The company locates hard-to-find pieces in over 175,000 patterns, some of which have not been produced for more than 100 years. The company's 12,000 square feet showroom includes a museum featuring over 2,000 rare pieces and tours of the entire building are given every half-hour.

CrystalWare, Inc. was founded in the beginning of the eighties with just one part-time assistant. The tremendous response garnered from small ads placed in national magazines such as *Southern Living* and *Better Homes and Gardens* dramatically expanded his list of potential dinnerware customers. The company sales in 1981 reached $150,000 and by 1984 were close to $4 million. In 2006, sales exceeded $77 million. Today, Company-A is serving more than 4.6 million customers nationwide, with 9.2 million pieces of available inventory. The company currently employs more than 550 people in a 225,000 square feet facility located in North Carolina.

In June 1998, CrystalWare launched a new website and published all available inventories in the top 5,000 selling patterns (approximately 200,000 SKUs). This website alone increased the company's total revenue by 20-25% over the five years following its launch. Using the company website customers could identify, register their patterns online and view available inventory but were unable to place orders (customers had to call a toll-free number and speak with the sales associate to place an order). At that time, the company had over one million visitors to the website each month. CrystalWare, has tightened their customer bond by sending email newsletters to 1.3 million customers monthly, many of whom also received a customized email catalog. The catalog features products they have expressed interest in, or similar products they are likely to be interested in. Customers who received an email newsletter/catalog containing china, silver, and collectibles on average spent 20% more per order than customers who received just mail versions of the catalog. The company's Director of Sales and Marketing stated that an email recipient's average order was $141 versus $118 for customers who received product updates via mail. The boost that CrystalWare received from expanding to the Internet came for a very moderate additional cost. It would cost millions of dollars to send the newsletter in hard copy, but with the email newsletter, there would be no increase in variable costs.

CrystalWare, Inc. has a number of competitors ranging from local antique dealers and smaller online operations up to and including the likes of eBay, Fortunoff and Ross-Simons. CrystalWare, Inc., has a competitive advantage over their competition by having one of the largest levels of inventory. Michael Lamphier, Vice president of Marketing, said that CrystalWare, Inc. "aggressively buys" products to make sure that they stock items that their competitors sometimes do not have or could not have. The main goal is to keep specialized patterns in stock so customers will be able to replace the missing or broken pieces of their collection. Their select inventory is not "just inventory" it is part of people's lives, family-history and fond memories. CrystalWare, Inc. also competes through its exclusive knowledge of almost all china patterns. The company prides itself on knowing that when a customer brings his or her pattern in for identification, there is a large likelihood that CrystalWare professionals will know what the name of the pattern is and how to best serve that customer (Wagner, 2001).

At the beginning of 2003, the company decided to make its entire inventory of more than 3.5 million SKUs publicly available through its website as well as through opening a vendor store on www.amazon.com. Making all pieces of inventory available through the website was just the first part of the business plan. The second part was to make this inventory available in real time and give customers the ability to place orders over the Internet. The initial result of this initiative was CrystalWare's ability to expand its sales and reduce operation costs with absolutely

minimal capital investments. However, the most important part of this decision was CrystalWare's success in attracting new customers. The online business was emerging as one of the most cost-effective marketing tools and its biggest source of new customers for the company. Through tracking codes attached to every visitor's file, the company segments customers as they are added to its database according to how they arrive at the website. Such techniques gave the company unique information that helped them to reorganize its online marketing strategy. From that moment on the company was able to start managing its online advertising campaigns with a precision that they never had before. It became possible to evaluate the ROI for every ad placed by the company on the Internet. At the present moment the company has more than 3 million online ads.

All of these things together saved the company thousands of dollars in marketing and operational cost. In addition approximately 280,000 new customers were obtained in the last 6 month alone. One interesting detail about these new customers is that most of them chose email as the preferred way of communication. This preference allows the company to inform the customer of any updates in the inventory status of their registered patterns, as well as inventory changes. Such updates were possible more often than it would be with a regular offline communication model. With virtually zero associated costs. (Wagener, 2001; Internetretailer. com, 2008).

At the present moment, the company's customer database contains information on more than 6 million customers, most of whom are repeat customers. More than 2 million of these 6 million customers have at least one email address on file. Based on the above information, it is safe to assume that even if CrystalWare, does not perform most of its business online, it greatly benefited from its Internet expansion (Internetretailer.com, 2008; Johnson, 2008).

So, what are the results of this recent initiative? It would not be an overestimation to say that the final results are staggering. As of now, roughly 48% of all CrystalWare's business, is coming from the Internet. Sales grew more than 10% in the past year alone. Finally, each of the first three months of the fiscal year 2007 had record breaking sales for the company. All of these numbers are even more impressive if taken into account the overall state of the business in the tableware industry. Where declining sales are the norm, and bankruptcy, along with merges have also become very common (Johnson, 2008).

As mentioned above, CrystalWare embraced computer technology in 1984 and soon became fully automated. The company's in-house built software application, ORION, does all of the daily transaction functions, including processing customer orders, managing company-supplier relationships, updating the human resources system, and the shipping and mailing processes. This proprietary system integrates many aspects of the manufacturing information platform including, but not limiting to, inventory and supply chain management.

Having a vast amount of inventory, a variety of merchandise, and offering numerous services exemplified the need for new information technology. The decision to design and implement an information system was a strategic one based on the forecast growth of customer base and inventory level and required heavy capital investments. These investments were necessary to create a software package specific enough to handle the company's offline business processes. However, in the last 5 years, the company's business model has changed dramatically. Without sacrificing its offline sales business, from a simple phone order/catalog seller merchant, the company has evolved into a completely automated Internet based seller. The reason for these changes was highly influenced by a few important factors such as: increased customer expectations, constantly emerging new technologies, and, finally, growth of offline sales cost. So, how did the company manage to efficiently coordinate offline and online

segments of its business? There are three major aspects of this transformation:

THE CRYSTALWARE, INC. BUSINESS APPROACH

Online Guided Sales System

Currently, the tableware's retail sector is facing significant changes in customer expectations, thanks to the influence of the Internet and other real time technologies. New technological innovations, like "Guided Selling" from IBM or "Personal Recommendations" from Amazon.com, are just a couple of examples of such applications that leverage these new expectations by combining technology side by side with customer-centric design.

In the last year, the company decided to go with the "Guided Selling" technology, provided by one of the affiliates of IBM. The new online initiative was designed to lead customers through the purchasing process for a simple or a complex product. The application advises about available tailoring product and it give customers a few cross-sell recommendations based on inventory availability, pricing and assortment. As a final result of this implementation, the company was able to better understand the customers motivation to buy, or not to buy, specific product, collect additional information about customers' requests of the online product availability, enhance the customers buying experience, and, above all, increase total online sales by about 3.5% (associated exclusively to this innovation) (IBM, 2008).

Know Who the Customers Are

In the last 3 years alone, CrystalWare's database of customer email addresses grew from 1.2 million in September 2003 to 5.1 million last January. The problem was that the information medium, with all of the positive sides, including the personal way to communicate with customers, ability to provide a substation amount of information about the company and its products, postage saving, delivery reliability and others, had yielded just a little information about who the customers were back to the company. It was obvious to the company's top management, that the knowledge about company's customer was less than adequate. Due to the company's approach to business and its customer relation strategy, it was vital to improve this situation.

At the same time, the company was still remembering its previous effort at researching its customer base. An extensive customer's survey generated just over 2,400 responses and cost more than $26,000. It is no surprise that management did not want to spend such a large amount of money for so little a response. However, in the last couple of years, data gathering techniques changed, and another attempt was made in the summer of 2004. This time, CrystalWare gave a customer list of approximately 100,000 recent buyers to Acxiom Corp. Its goal was to collect aggregate information of the customers' income, lifestyle characteristics, preferred magazine subscriptions, and others (Just to make this clear: the company didn't try to collect any personal information of any customers, but rather to create a collective picture of the average buyer). The survey produced interesting results that influenced CrystalWare to think about approaching its customers in new ways. For example, the survey showed that Company-A's average customer was 40 years old; female; had at least one college degree; homeowner with home value in the top 10 percents of the local markets; has some interest in foreign travel, stocks and bonds, and wines; was using the Internet and not a stranger to email types of communications (using it at least 5 to 10 times per week). The company used this data to target new online markets for advertising as well as providing a little bit more personalized information to its existing customers via personal quotes or newsletters. Within a few months of the survey, the number of new customers increased by 8% and the number of returning

customers grew by 5%. The analysis cost was $2,400 (Internetretailer.com, 2008)

Online Advertisement Strategy

As mentioned in the previous section, one of the company methods for online advertising is customer profiling. However, with emerging web technologies such strategy would have major limitations. The Internet has already proven that it can change how businesses operate. Book sales, ticket reservations, B2B marketplaces and banking are just a few examples where traditional business models virtually lost their market share and are being replaced by online substitutes. Thus, it is safe to assume that CrystalWare's customer base might change as well if the company continued moving forward with its online strategy. The company needed a new online marketing strategy. That strategy was intended to be broad-reaching and have a combination of techno-centric and customer-centric approaches. In other words, the company needed a new system to manage its online advertisement campaigns. Based on defined business goals, the targets for the new system were selected as follow: drive revenue up, increase new customer online registrations and be effective in managing the company's paid searches. Portal advertising, shopping engine commercials, and co-marketing agreements were also incorporated into the company's plan. In order to build such a system, at the beginning of 2005 the company signed a contract with Efficient Frontier, Inc., the leading provider of paid search engine marketing (SEM) solutions (wagner, 2001; efrontier. com, 2008). The proposed solution was simple and effective: apply Efficient Frontier portfolio approach to online campaigns to CrystalWare's business metrics and desired budget. The following business metrics were used in this project:

- Cost Per Acquisition (CPA) based on the total lifetime value of the customer;

- ROI levels based on sales yielded by each keyword.

Comparing the Efficient Frontier portfolio approach to the regular approach to online advertisement, this technique had a few major advantages. First of all, Efficient Frontier was able to analyze a combination of factors, like CPA vs. ROI, or usefulness of the advertisement of one particular item (or set of items) by using multiple keywords compared to the usefulness of advertising one particular keyword (Efrontier.com, 2008).

Regular approach to online paid search advertisement:

- Sets the maximum bid for a keyword
- Bids to maintain a specific position
- Manages by individual keyword

Efficient Frontier Portfolio approach

- Treats campaigns like an investment
- Optimizes to total budget and business goals
- Bids keywords based on ability to deliver the maximum performance
- Manages an infinite number of keywords

This new marketing approach gave CrystalWare, very exciting reporting capabilities of the search engine performance, trend data, and keyword level reporting. Based on this data, CrystalWare was able to analyze its online marketing efforts with overall sales data to spot correlations in performance. The project was considered successful. The company managed to increase its online sales by approximately 22% in the last year, reaching its intended target of 48% of the company's total sales. This increase was even more important because it drove sales cost down. The average online order costs from 15 to 30 cents (this amount includes all advertisement expenses as well as order processing expenditures) compare to $2 or $3 for offline orders. Because

of the success of its online marketing strategy, CrystalWare has nearly doubled its marketing expenditures to $1.5 million for the fiscal year 2007. The company also intends to bring the ratio of online to offline sales to 60:40 (Wagner, 2001)

CrystalWare is unique company, and not all of the company's business practices can be used somewhere else. In the next 10 years the marketplace will change dramatically due to constantly evolving technologies as well as market globalization and the spread of the Internet. In order for the company to sustain its current success, they have to follow some common rules:

1. Know who the customers are, so the company can address their needs better.
2. Any business oriented companies must take into consideration recent growth in Electronic commerce market. Such expansion might emphasize changes in company's customer base and differentiation of customer requirements as well as appearance of new online competitors (because the price of entering online market is lot lower than entering Brick and Mortal market).
3. The company that wants to benefit from this new market structure must allow sharing its computerized data between customers, suppliers, and other outside entities.

As a general rule, organizational size and wealth strongly determine the use of new technology and other innovations. Larger organizations typically have spare resources in the form of both expertise and money to allow them to experiment with innovations. However, as a technology becomes more widely used and standardized, its price declines and the expertise needed to deploy it become more readily available in the market. This creates numerous opportunities for smaller companies to get into the market and actively participate in the world of electronic commerce. First movers in technology often have a competitive advantage in a given market but that advantage erodes as time goes on. In order to stay successful and maintain a position as a leader in their market, CrystalWare will have to continue to be innovative in their use of technology especially as it relates to their business processes and their customers. CrystalWare is a great example of a company that was able to achieve success by adopting technology early, and they continue to be successful for that same reason. With a revamped online marketing system and strategy, the company will increase the effectiveness of its online marketing efforts and be able to better advertise relevant information to qualified potential customers. As the Internet continues to replace traditional marketing mediums such as radio and television there will be opportunities for companies that are prepared to take advantage of new technologies. Not everything was so bright just a few years ago (IBM, 2008).

Compliance with CAN-SPAM Act

On January 1, 2004, commercial email became a federally regulated activity according to CAN-SPAM (Controlling the Assault of Non-Solicited Pornography and Marketing) Act. This legislation establishes requirements for those who send commercial email, spells out penalties for spammers and companies whose products are advertised in spam, if they violate the law, and gives consumers the right to ask email senders to stop spamming them.

Even if a majority of the rules in this act does not apply directly to the company business model and business practice, compliance with the CAN-SPAM Act became a top priority for the CrystalWare.

A brief overview of the main aspects of the CAN-SPAM Act that have direct impact on CrystalWare is summarized here.

- Do not use fraudulent transmission data, such as open relays and false headers (sections 4(a), 5(a)(1), and 6).

1. IP address listed in email header should have a valid "Reverse DNS Lookup" associated with the company domain name.
2. Every associate that sends and receives business communication via email must have a properly configured email client and their outgoing email messages list their full name and email address in the "from" line.
3. Do not intentionally send commercial email from a foreign or domestic computer that the company does not have authorization to use nor use a foreign or domestic computer to "relay or retransmit" commercial email "with the intent to deceive or mislead recipients or an ISP" as to their origin (strict prohibition of open relays).
4. Do not set up email accounts or register domain names with materially false identities for the purpose of sending commercial emails from any of the above accounts or domain names.
5. Do not falsely claim ownership of any IP addresses, and then intentionally send commercial emails from these addresses.
- Do not use misleading sender or subject lines (section 5(a)(1) and 5(a)(2)). In other words, the CAN-SPAM Act prohibits use of subject lines that likely to mislead recipients about a material fact regarding the contents or subject matter of the message.
- The company postal address must be added to all business related emails (section 5(a)(3) and 5(a)(5)(A)(iii)).

The CAN-SPAM Act requires the inclusion of a valid physical postal address of the sender in every unsolicited commercial message, but does not indicate whether a PO Box will be sufficient. The same law applies to all business related emails send by employees. This means that each email account that sends business correspondence must have a sender's signature and the company postal address.

- Every broadcast email type (such as newsletter, advertisements, event announcements and so on) must contain a "clear and conspicuous" unsubscribe mechanism in every email (section 5(a)(5)(A)(ii)). A separate process should also be implemented to handle all unsubscribe requests within the 10-day window, including requests received via postal mail (or any other contact information that company posted in the email, such as phone and fax) (section 5(a)(4)). The law also allows customers to request an option to receive just some desirable email correspondence from the company they subscribed to while denying all others; along with a "global unsubscribe" option to stop all future email correspondence (section 5(a)(3)(B)).
- The Act also require from any company not to share the address (physical or email) of a person who unsubscribed with any other entity seeking to send that party email (section 5(a)(4)).

According to the CrystalWare's privacy statement, the company does not share any customer information with any affiliates or third party groups nor does the company sell it to anyone. The privacy statement can be found on the official CrystalWare's website. Every company's mass email has a link to this page as well.

- Do not harvest email addresses or use automated means to randomly generate email addresses (section 5(b)(1)).

This is a common spammers' technique and almost never used by any legitimate business organizations. This rule has no implication on the company business strategy. At the present moment CrystalWare is fully in compliance will all federal laws regulating commercial emails as well as made all necessary changes to successfully deliver all electronic correspondence to the customers. However; despite all of the above efforts, bounce back emails are unavoidable. So, in order to process these types of emails, the company started a bounce back project (Spamlaws, 2008; Squillante, 2004; Jennings, 2004).

EMAIL BOUNCE BACK PROJECT: AN OVERVIEW

Project Goals for CrystalWare, Inc.

- Provide a self-contained monitor to handle possible or actual blacklisting and/or temporary blocking.
- Redesign the company email receiving system to improve bounce back management and reporting

Project Overview

Every email that comes from outside of the company network goes through a series of firewalls and gateways before reaching the intended recipient inside. While moving through all of these devices, each email gets scanned for possible viruses or other malicious programming codes as well as scored on the Spam content. On any stage of this processing email can be quarantined, moved to a Spam folder for the future possible analysis or simply deleted. Such complex structure helps secure the company's internal infrastructure.

For the Email Bounce Back project the company decided to set up a strictly segregated email system where every type of emails set to the customers will have its own unique sending email address (these email addresses are different from the "Reply-to" email addresses). Such approach helps eliminate any confusion about an email type that might generate a bounce back. The approach also improves deliverability of the emails, and speeds up processing of the bounce back emails. Above all, if an email generates a bounce back reply, the company's gateway can seamlessly identify it and forward this email to an appropriate mailbox for processing. Such structure also prevents mass blockage or greylisting of all company's outgoing emails. If ISP decides that one email address sends too much correspondence to its servers or content of this correspondence is inappropriate (according to ISP rules), this email address will be blocked; however, this leaves all other company's sending email addresses untouched and gives supporting personnel some time to negotiate with this ISP about blockage removal. In addition, if the company knows what email context generates a blockage, it would be easy to analyze this text and try to restructure it or to re-write it in order to remove all possible causes for the blockage. This is why it is so important to have separate sending email addresses and centralized bounce back handling system.

CrystalWare's bounce back processing system was constructed using an open source programming package called Procmail. Procmail is a Unix utility, written in C, that runs non-interactively as a filter and delivery agent for incoming email. Procmail works as a mail delivery agent (MDA) or mail filter (a program that process incoming emails on a computer and widely used on the different Unix systems). Common operations carried out with Procmail include filtering and sorting of emails into different folders according to keywords in "From", "To", "Subject", text of the mail, or sending auto-replies, or more sophisticated operations. Like many open source projects, Procmail has many authors, but the primary Procmail writers are Stephen R. van den Berg and Philip A. Guenther.

Basically, Procmail package consists of four major components:

- **Procmail language pack:** This is the core of the Procmail package. Procmail takes RFC822-formatted [38] messages on stan-

dard input and processes them according to both system-wide and user-specific recipe files.

- **Lockfile:** A file locking utility that has built-in back-off mechanisms for scripts and rules that require more complex file-locking accommodations.

- **Formail:** A utility to modify and reroute incoming emails. The two main uses for formail are in scripts and in Procmail recipes. Formail can be used to split mailing list digests, to construct a reply header for any arbitrary email messages, and some others functions.

- **Mailstat:** An utility that generates a report based on the contents of Procmail logfile. The report may not be totally accurate, since Procmail (by default) does not log each multiple action taken on a single message; only the final action is logged.

- **Man pages:** Help, examples, and instructions for every part of the Procmail package. Procmail, lockfile, and formail each have man pages. The format of the Procmail recipe file is in man page as well. [36, 37]

The company implementation of the email bounce back system consists of four major elements:

1. Actual software package installed on the Linux server

2. Procmail rcfile (recipe file) that receives and processes emails. Procmail is invoked automatically, from within the mailer, as soon as mail arrives. When invoked, it first sets some environment variables to default values, reads the message from STDIN (beginning) until an EOF (end of the file), separates the body from the header, and then, if no command line arguments are present, it starts to look for a file name called.procmailrc. This file is always located in the home directory of the receiver email account. There are

two kinds of recipes: delivering and non-delivering recipes. If a delivering recipe is found to match, Procmail considers the mail delivered and will cease processing the rcfile after having successfully executed the action line of the recipe. If a non-delivering recipe is found to match, processing of the rcfile will continue after the action line of this recipe has been executed.

In the Company-A case:

- *Delivering recipes* are those that cause the header and/or the body of the email to be forwarded to an email address.
- *Non-delivering* recipes are those that cause the output of a program or filter to be captured back by Procmail or those that start a nesting block.

3. Procmail library package. This library contains multiple functional/procedural files that can be called from inside home_directory/.procmailrc. Such structure makes email processing much more efficient because the recipe file would call subprocedures to perform necessary operations *only* when mail arrives and *specific* function needs to be invoked. Such an approach makes home_directory/.procmailrc file easy to read and understand as well as saves a lot of system resources by not loading all libraries into memory at the beginning.

4. Additional scripts, to select and/or update data from the Oracle database. These files would be called from home_directory/.procmailrc file as well.

EMAIL BOUNCE BACK PROJECT: IMPLEMENTATION

Bounce Back Email Receiving

As mentioned above, the CrystalWare set up multiple sending email addresses to handle different types of email communication. For this paper I will give just a general overview of the whole process without providing specific details related to each individual account.

At the very beginning of the Procmail processing file (.procmailrc) a few global variables were defined:

- The Default mailbox where emails get received
- Root directory for the Procmail libraries
- Name of the log file (procmaillog). The file should always be located in the default mailbox folder; however, the name and amount of information recorder can be changed;
- Location of the Procmail libraries
- Location and name of the functions used in email bounce back processing:
- Function1.rc
- Function2.rc

Default values of the variables used to update the company database

BB_CORRESPONDENCE_TYPE=n(where n represents a numeric values that was assigned to different email types). Because each email type has its own sending email address, it is quite simple to identify these numbers by looking on the "To:" field of the bounce back email message.

- CUSTOMER_NUMBER= Customer number
- EMAIL_ADDRESS= Email address the company we sent email to
- BB_TYPE= Type of bounce back (hard or soft)
- BB_REASON= Reason for bounce back (mail delivery problem, content block and etc)

A level of log recording was also set by specifying YES or NO for the VERBOSE variable. VERBOSE is a variable that regulates how much information would be printed in the log file. If VERBOSE is set to NO, the amount of information in the log file would be very limited or non-existent. If VERBOSE is set to YES, the log file would contain an extensive amount of information. The VERBOSE variable can be changed multiple times anywhere in the.procmailrc file or in any of the supporting functions. When email is received for processing, it goes through the following steps inside Procmail:

1. Check for possible SPAM identifications; Check for the most common non-English email page codes (if one is found, it means that email contains non-English text); Check who was an intended recipient of the email (Sometimes, spammers use so-called "undisclosed-recipient" email addresses to send a mass broadcasts); Check for possible email loop. If any of the above criteria proves to be true, email will be deleted without processing.

2. Identification of the original receiver's email address (email address of the customer). There are multiple ways how customer's email addresses can be shown inside bounce back email. (See Figure 3). The problem with this task is the absence of the common place or structure that can identify a string as an email address. So, to overcome this obstacle, the whole new function inside Procmail processing script was developed.

3. If email address was found, the script will check this email address against the company database. If no such email address was found, the processing script (.procmailrc) will delete processed email and exit. If an email address was found, the processing script will send a request to the company database asking for the customer number.

4. Check for sender's email address ("From:").

5. If bounce back email was originated from one of the email addresses associated with the ISP's reply system (commonly called MAILER-DAEMON email addresses). procmailrc calls Function1.rc in order to identify the email bounce back reason (mailbox full/email address is bad/senders email address got blocked and etc), and email bounce back type (Soft / Hard). When both of these variables are identified, the system will assign numeric values that will represent each condition. If such identification would produce no result, default values would be substituted for the bounce back reason code and the bounce back type codes, and email

Figure 3.

Example 1
Your message did not reach some or all of the intended recipients.
Subject: Some subject
Sent: Date and time
The following recipient(s) could not be reached:

john.doe@somewhere.com on Date and Time
There was a SMTP communication problem with the recipient's email server. Please contact your system administrator.
  < mail server #5.5.0 SMTP; 571 Email from XXX.XXX.XXX.XXX is currently blocked by Provider Online's anti-spam system. The email sender or Email Service Provider may visit website and request removal of the block.>

Example 2
Your mail to the following recipients could not be delivered because they are not accepting mail from email address:
John.doe

---

would be returned back to.procmailrc file to finish processing.

6. If email came from one of the company's email servers, the Procmail processing script will set bounce back type as internal bounce back (regardless of the bounce back type identified by Function1.rc).

   a. Finally, if a customer number and an email address were found, and an email was recognized as a reply from the ISP's automatic responses system, the. procmailrc script will analyze a reason for the bounce back. There are a few possible reasons:

   b. If the bounce back reason is a blockage – the Procmail processing script will insert a new record into the bounce back processing table in the company database, identifying this bounce back as a blockage. It will also forward this email to a predefined mailbox for the future analysis and exit.

   c. If the bounce back reason is a Spam Challenge (automatic response from the ISP's subsystem that asks sender of the email to verify its identity), the Procmail processing script will forward this email for manual processing and exit.

7. If the bounce back reason is anything else except Spam Challenge and Blockage, the Procmail processing script will insert a new record into the bounce back processing table with the unprocessed status, deletes this email and exits

8. If, for any reason, one of the values: either customer number, email address, correspondence type, bounce back reason, or bounce back type cannot be explicitly determined and the email came from the ISP's automatic response system, the email will be forwarded for manual processing to predefined mailbox.

9. In some circumstances specially designated company's bounce back email addresses might receive emails that were send not by

the ISP's automatic reply systems but by the automatic response system located on top of the customer mailbox (customer automatic response system). In order to process these types of emails,.procmailrc file calls another library named Function2.rc.

10. The Function2.rc has almost the same structure as the Function1.rc function with just one exception: function1.rc was designed to processes emails that came from the ISP's automatic response system while function2. rc was designed to handle customer automatic replies.

11. In the same way as function1.rc, function2. rc tries to identify a reason behind bounce back email

    a. If the reason for the customer email is identified as a Vacation / Out of Office notice, such type of emails would be deleted without any processing;

    b. If the reason for the customer email is identified as an Email Change, this email would be forwarded for the manual processing to predefined mailbox;

    c. If the reason is a Blockage – the Procmail processing script will forward the email to predefined mailbox for the future analysis (without inserting a record into the bounce back processing table) and exit (there is no reason to record an individual mailbox block);

    d. If the reason for the customer email is identified as a Spam Challenge, the Procmail processing script will forward this email to another predefined mailbox for manual processing and exit;

    e. Finally, if bounce back email came from the customer and processing procedure was not able to identify a reason for this email, this email will be forwarded for the manual processing. Finally, if a bounce back email was not identified as any known type of bounce back emails and was not forwarder for the manual processing during the script execution, it will be dropped (See Figure 4).

As mentioned above, one of the goals for the bounce back project was an identification of the possible blockage situation. This goal was achieved by implementing an automatic script that analyzes all activities in the bounce back processing table for specific period of time (the time period since the last run). The purpose of this script is a search for the common patterns between email addresses identified as a blockage and their email correspondence types. If such pattern is identified, the script sends an alarm message to supporting personnel, briefly explaining a crisis situation.

Bounce Back Email Processing (BB_COUNT_STRIKES): Overview

One of the primary goals for the email bounce back project was verification that customer's email address is really bad before switching this customer back to mail communication. The following is an explanation of the procedure that

Figure 4. Bounce back receiving

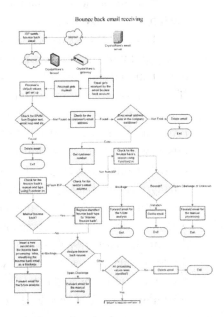

archives this goal. Based on information from the email bounce back processing best practices and incorporating its own knowledge about email bounce back handling, the company came up with the set of rules that outline the new process. The company named this process as "Bounce Back Count Strikes Rule". The rules are as follow:

1. Customer would have just one strike if no previous records of past bounce backs exist;
2. Customer would also have one strike if the most recent bounce back happened more than 2 weeks ago;
3. Customer would have two strikes if today's bounce back happened in the period that is less than two weeks from the last recorded bounce back email and customers had not had any other bounce back emails in the last two weeks prior to the last recorded bounce back incident;
4. Customer would have three strikes and switched to mail if today's bounce back happened in the period that is less than two weeks from the last recorded bounce back email and customers have at least one other bounce back emails in the last two weeks prior to the last recorded bounce back incident;
5. Customer may have immediate third strike and would be switched back to mail if the bounce back type is internal and the bounce back reason is a hard bounce back

Bounce Back Email Processing (BB_COUNT_STRIKES): Technical Implementation

1. Identify a minimum bounce back type ID and a minimum bounce back reason ID among all unprocessed records for the selected email address and customer.
   If more than one unprocessed bounce back email exists with different bounce back reasons (one that can be classified as

a soft and one that can be classified as a hard bounce backs (The hard bounce back will always have a higher reason ID than a soft bounce back)) the company would like to select a bounce back reason that would not give a customer an immediate third strike. In other words, ISP tried to deliver the company email and acknowledged that designated email address exists but may have some temporary problems (Example: mailbox is full). In this case, the company would not classify this email account as permanently undeliverable.

2. Identify possible time periods for the first, second, and third bounce backs (see Figure 5)

3. Interpret bounce back type ID as Internal or External / Hard or Soft:

    *   **INTERNAL HARD Bounce back -** emails that were rejected for delivery before even leaving the company's email servers with the reason that makes any future attempts to resend this email pointless (Example: email address does not exist). In this situation we can have the following scenarios.

        1. Customer has more than one email address on file

Delete the bounce back email address from the database;

Make secondary email address primary;

Update the bounce back processing table and replace the "Unprocessed" status to "Processed" on all records where the bounce back email address and the customer number match the entry under consideration;

2. Customer has just one email address on file

Delete the bounce back email address from the database

Switch customer communication media to mail

Update the bounce back processing table and replace "Unprocessed" status to "Processed" on all records where the bounce back email address and the customer number match the entry under consideration

3. Customer has more than one email address on file and the email address that generated bounce back email is not a primary email address on the customer profile.

Delete the bounce back email address from the database;

Update the bounce back processing table and replace the "Unprocessed" status to "Processed" on all records where the bounce back email address and the customer number match the entry under consideration

*   **INTERNAL SOFT Bounce back -** emails that were rejected for delivery before even leaving the company's email servers; however, with the reason that makes future attempts to resend logically sound (Example: mailbox is full). Such type of emails should be

Figure 5.

Bounce back three strikes rules.
Example: last bounce back happened on September 8, 2007

STRIKE1_MIN_DT	STRIKE1_MAX_DT	STRIKE2_DT	STRIKE3_DT
8/19/2007	9/3/2007	9/13/2007	9/28/2007

treated as regular external bounce back emails (see below);

- **EXTERNAL Bounce back** - emails that did not originate from the company's email servers. All external bounce back emails are treated equally without making any distinguish between soft and hard bounce backs. In this situation we can have the following scenarios.

    1. Customer has no previous bounce back record from the selected email address

- **Solution:** Update bounce back processing table and replace the "Unprocessed" status to "Processed" on all records where the bounce back email address and he customer number match the entry under consideration

    2. Customer has *only* one previous bounce back records from the selected email address where today date fell in the two week period since the last recorded bounce back incident (in other words, the second bounce back email felt into a consecutive range).

- **Solution:** Update the bounce back processing table and replace the "Unprocessed" status to "Processed" on all records where the bounce back email address and the customer number match the entry under consideration.

    3. Customer has *more* than one previous bounce back record from the selected email address where today's bounce back date felt in the two week period since the last recorded bounce back incident and the customer has at least one other recorded bounce back incident that felt in the two week period prior to the last recorded bounce back (in other words, the second and third bounce back

emails felt into a consecutive period range)

- **Solution:** Implement third strike. In this situation we can have the following scenarios:

    1. Customer has more than one email address on file:

Delete the bounce back email address from the database;

Make the secondary email address primary;

Update the bounce back processing table and replace the "Unprocessed" status to "Processed" on all records where the bounce back email address and the customer number match the entry under consideration;

    2. Customer has just one email address on file:

Delete the bounce back email address from the database;

Switch customer's communication media to mail;

Update the bounce back processing table and replace the "Unprocessed" status to "Processed" on all records where the bounce back email address and the customer number match the entry under consideration.

    3. Customer has more than one email address on file and the email address that generated bounce back wasn't primary email address on the customer profile.

Delete the bounce back email address from the database;

Update the bounce back processing table and replace the "Unprocessed" status to "Processed" on all records where the bounce back email address and the customer number match the entry under consideration (See Figure 6).

If any of the update/insert statements fail, the BB_COUNT_STRIKES procedure will raise an error flag and all of the uncommitted changes will be rollback. All records from the log table that generated an error will be updated to the status "Failure".

Figure 6. Bounce back processing

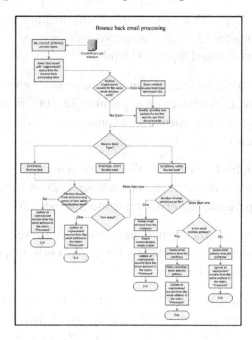

CONCLUSION

As a result of the bounce back project's implementation a couple of month ago, the company has been experiencing some remarkable transformations. The preliminary results show that the email deliverability rate increased by at least 1.5 times. Also, by surveying a list of 10 top ISPs, the company discovered that the majority of all emails originating from the company's email servers end up in the customers inboxes now rather than being blocked by the spam filters or gateways. There were a few incidents of ISP blockage but each of these was promptly discovered and fixed. The email bounce back system keeps mailing list current and accurate, and, that is very important. It also keeps user intervention to a minimum. Above all, the email bounce back project has directly increased the value of the company's business as a whole by enabling consistent and accurate ways to reach out to the customer and promote new and existing products and services.

REFERENCES

Active.com. *The Importance of E-mail in a Successful Online Campaign.* Retrieved on September 21, 2008 from http://www.active.com/images/activegiving/emailcampaign.pdf

Corker, J., & Utz, C. (2002). SCAMS and Legal Approaches to SPAM," The Cyberspace Law and Policy Series. *Continuing Legal Education Conference on International Dimensions of Internet and e-Commerce Regulation* (pp 1-14).

Ducheneaut, N., & Bellotti, V. (2001). E-mail as habitat: An exploration of embedded personal information management. *Interaction, 8*(5), 30–38. doi:10.1145/382899.383305

Edmunds, A., & Morris, A. (2000). The problem of information overload in business organizations: A review of the literature. *International Journal of Information Management, 20*(1), 17. doi:10.1016/S0268-4012(99)00051-1

Efrontier.com. *Efficient Frontier at Work. CrystalWare.* Retrieved on September 21, 2008 from: http://www.efrontier.com/efficient_frontier/

Emailprivacy.info. *Email Privacy.* Retrieved on September 30, 2008 from: http://www.emailprivacy.info/email_privacy

Evers, J. *Sender ID's fading message.* August 9, 2005 Retrieved on October 1, 2008 from: http://www.news.com/Sender-IDs-fading-message/2100-7355_3-5824234.html

Extreme-messaging.com. *Response Master Returned Message Categories.* Retrieved on October 7, 2008 from: http://www.extreme-messaging.com/extreme/docs/rmcategories.html

Fallows, D. (2003). *Spam: How It is hurting email and degrading life on the Internet* (pp. 1–43). Pew Internet and American Life Project.

Goodman, K. (2008, March). The 30-day e-mail detox. *O, The Oprah Magazine* (pp. 203-206).

Grimes, G., Hough, M., & Signorella, M. (2003, November). User Attitudes towards spam in three age groups. ACM Conference on Universal Usability (pp. 1-4), Vancouver, Canada.

Group on Unsolicited Commercial Email. (1998). Report (pp. 1-32). http://searchsecurity.techtarget. com/sDefinition/0,sid14_gci944600,00.html

IDC. (2007, April 9). *IDC reveals the future of email as it navigates through a resurgence of spam and real-time market substitutes.* Retrieved in 2009 from http://www.idc.com/getdoc. jsp?containerId=prUS20639307.

IMB. *Strengthen your customer.* Retrieved on September 21, 2008 from: http://www-03.ibm. com/innovation/us/strengthen/crm.shtml

Intentretailer.com. *E-mail communication doesn't have to be one way street.* Retrieved on September 21, 2008 from: http://www.internetretailer.com/ dailyNews.asp?id=25013

Internetretailer.com. www.CrystalWare.com *boosts its online offering to more than 1 million products.* Retrieved on September 21, 2008 from: http://www.internetretailer.com/internet/ marketing-conference/

Jennings, J. (2004, January 29). *Complying With CAN-SPAM: A 10-Point Checklist for Marketers.*, Retrieved on October 10, 2008 from: http://www. clickz.com/showPage.html?page=3305101

Johnson, E. *The Top 12 Priorities for Competitive Intelligence.* Retrieved on September 21, 2008 from: http://www.aurorawdc.com/arj_cics_pri-orities.htm

Kangas, E. *Mitigating Threats to Your Email Security and Privacy.* Retrieved on September 30, 2008 from http://luxsci.com/extranet/articles/ security-threats.html

Kay, R. *QuickStudy: Phishing.* Retrieved on September 30, 2008 from: http://www. computerworld.com/securitytopics/security/ story/0,10801,89096,00.html

Keepemailsafe.com. *Email Security and Privacy Threats.* Retrieved on September 30, 2007 from: http://www.keepemailsafe.com/security_privacy. html#1

Knight, C. *Sender Policy Framework (SPF) – Explained.* Retrieved on October 1, 2008 from: http://emailuniverse.com/ezine-tips/?id=1202

Livinginternet.com. *Email security.* Retrieved on September 30, 2008 from: http://www.livingin-ternet.com/e/es.htm

Mackay, W. E. (1988). More than just a communication system: Diversity in the use of electronic mail. *CSCW '88: Proceedings of the 1988 ACM Conference on Computer-Supported Cooperative Work* (pp. 344-353). United States.

Marketer & Agency Guide to Email Deliverability Interactive Advertising Bureau

McGough, N. *Procmail Quick Start: An introduction to email filtering with a focus on procmail.* Retrieved on October 10, 2008 from: http://www. ii.com/internet/robots/procmail/qs/

Mial-abuse.com. *Basic Mailing List Management Principles for Preventing Abuse.* Retrieved on October 10, 2008 from: http://www.mail-abuse. com/an_listmgntgdlines.html

Mullen, J. (2006, May 15). How Powerful Is E-Mail? *The ClickZ Network.*

Newcomb, K. (2006, April 17). After E-mail Authentication. *The ClickZ Network.* Retrieved on October 3, 2008 from: http://www.clickz. com/3599541

Outlaw.com. *Email notices and email footers.* Retrieved on September 30, 2008 from: http:// www.out-law.com/page-5536

RFC 2821 Simple Mail Transfer Protocol. Retrieved on October 1, 2008 from: http://www.ietf.org/rfc/rfc2821.txt

RFC 2822 Internet Message Format. Retrieved on October 1, 2008 from: http://www.ietf.org/rfc/rfc2822.txt

RFC 4406 Sender ID: Authenticating E-Mail. Retrieved on October 1, 2008 from: http://www.ietf.org/rfc/rfc4406.txt

RFC 4407 Purported Responsible Address in E-Mail Messages. Retrieved on October 1, 2008 from: http://www.ietf.org/rfc/rfc4407.txt

RFC 4408. Sender Policy Framework (SPF) for Authorizing Use of Domains in E-Mail

RFC 822 Standard for the format of ARPA Internet text messages. Retrieved October 10, 2008 from: http://www.ietf.org/rfc/rfc0822.txt

Searchsecurity.techtarget.com. *DomainKeys Definition.* Retrieved on October 23, 20087 from: http://www.searchsecurity.techtarget.com

Shafer, J. (2004, June 1). E-mail Confidential. *Who's afraid of Time Inc.'s legal disclaimer?* Retrieved on September 30, 2008 from: http://slate.com/id/2101561/

Smith, J. *How You Can Avoid The New Dangers Of Spam.* Retrieved on September 30, 2008 from: http://www.ezinearticles.com/?How-You-Can-Avoid-The-New-Dangers-Of-Spam&id=40253

SpamLaws.com. CAN-SPAM Act. Public Law 108–187—DEC. 16, 2003. Retrieved on October 10, 2008 from: http://www.spamlaws.com/f/pdf/pl108-187.pdf

Squillante, N. J. *Is Your Company CAN-SPAM Compliant?* Retrieved on October 10, 2008 from: http://www.marketingprofs.com/4/squillante3.asp?part=2

Tschabitscher, H. *How Many Emails Are Sent Every Day?* Retrieved on September 2008 from: http://email.about.com/od/emailtrivia/f/emails_per_day.htm

Wagner, M. (2001, November) *How CrystalWare looked in-house to serve a volatile inventory of china to web customers.* Retrieved on September 21, 2008 from: http://www.internetretailer.com/internet/marketing-conference/

Whittaker, S., & Sidner, C. (1997). E-mail overload: exploring personal information management of e-mail. In Kiesler, S. (Ed.), *Culture of the Internet* (pp. 277–295). Mahwah, NJ: Erlbaum.

Wikipedia. *Computer virus* Retrieved on September 30, 2008 from: http://en.wikipedia.org/wiki/Computer_virus

Wikipedia.org. *Email Privacy.* Retrieved on September 30, 2008 from: http://en.wikipedia.org/wiki/E-mail_privacy

Wikipedia.org. *Procmail.* Retrieved on October 10, 2008 from: http://en.wikipedia.org/wiki/Procmail

Williams, C., & Ferris, D. The Cost of Spam False Positives. Ferris Research Report #385, 2003.

Yahoo. com. *DomainKeys: Proving and Protecting Email Sender Identity.* Retrieved on October 23, 2008 from: http://antispam.yahoo.com/domainkeys.

This work was previously published in International Journal of Information Security and Privacy (IJISP), edited by Hamid Nemati, pp 10-41, copyright 2009 by IGI Publishing (imprint of IGI Global)

Chapter 8
Protected Health Information (PHI) in a Small Business

James Suleiman
University of Southern Maine, USA

Terry Huston
Health Care Information Technology Consultant, Canada

ABSTRACT

Compliance with regulatory guidelines and mandates surrounding information security and the protection of privacy has been under close scrutiny for some time throughout the world. Smaller organizations have remained "out of the spotlight" and generally do not hire staff with the expertise to fully address issues of compliance. This case study examines a project partnership between an information-technology (IT) consultant who specializes in small business and a diminutive medical practice that sought support with compliance issues surrounding a research study it was conducting. Other small medical practices were contributing to the research; consequently, information sharing while concurrently adhering to the regulations of the Health Insurance Portability and Accountability Act (HIPAA) of 1996 was a significant aspect of the project. It was also critical that numerous other security and privacy legislative requirements were met. The issue of data security is often neglected in IT instruction. This case study provides a foundation for examining aspects of information security from the perspective of the small-business IT consultant.

ORGANIZATION BACKGROUND

Stephanie Soule had developed a great passion toward her home state and found her undergraduate internship with several small regional businesses highly rewarding. She surprised her teachers, family, and friends when she turned down job offers from two leading U.S. technology-consulting firms. Stephanie had graduated at the top of her class with an undergraduate degree in information systems. Rather than accept a position with a large corporation, she opted to remain within her hometown of Rumford and open her own technology-consulting firm serving small businesses throughout the greater Portland, Maine region. She named her new company the Rumford

DOI: 10.4018/978-1-60960-200-0.ch008

Consulting Group (RCG) and established the firm as a subchapter S corporation, registering herself as the sole owner and employee. Arranging a loan from her parents, Stephanie began operating from an apartment above a garage belonging to her parents, which also functioned as her home. The initial goal she set for the RCG was to become profitable within 1 year and move into offices located within downtown Portland. Within days after graduation, Stephanie had her first client. The endometriosis-excision research group, led by the president of a New England center for endometriosis located in Scarborough, Maine, was referred to RCG by one of her former information-systems professors.

Endometriosis is a painful and chronic disease affecting 5.5 million women throughout the United States and Canada, as well as millions more worldwide. When the tissue lining the uterus (i.e., the endometrium) is found outside the uterus, symptoms of pain and infertility result. One method for treating endometriosis is excision, which removes such tissue beyond the visible lesion. The research group referred to the RCG was examining the efficacy of excision surgery on recurring symptoms of endometriosis. In addition to their data-collection efforts in Maine, the researchers were also collecting related data from medical practices within Atlanta, Georgia; San Antonio, Texas; and Brisbane, Australia with the possibility of contributing follow-up studies from other sites.

The endometriosis-excision research group is essentially an ad hoc virtual team of researchers that are also small-business owners. A variety of regulations affect their governance. Their studies are not conducted for profit; the goal is to advance understanding surrounding the surgical technique and effects of endometriosis excision. The research team had collected data related to preoperative symptoms, surgical techniques, postoperative results, and demographical data from nearly 1,000 patients at the time of their collaboration with RCG. They sought to share and aggregate the data for analysis while remaining compliant to HIPAA and other applicable regulations. HIPAA is a framework dictating the manner in which health care entities electronically maintain, transmit, and protect data to ensure confidentiality for patients. Failure to comply with the Act can result in fines and criminal penalty. Intentionally disclosing health-related information that concurrently identifies the respective patients can result in a fine of up to $250,000 with the possibility of imprisonment for up to 10 years. In this particular case, compliance with the HIPAA was also to be confirmed by the institutional review board for the hospital affiliated with the New England center for endometriosis.

Stephanie Soule felt well prepared for the task at hand. Her undergraduate degree in information systems had included course work in database management, programming, and systems analysis and design. Her introductory course in the management of information systems had detailed issues of compliance and risk management that specifically addressed the regulatory mandates of the Sarbanes-Oxley Act of 2002, the Graham-Leach-Bliley Act of 1999, and HIPAA. However, it would be impossible for such a course to cover all of the legislative requirements that must be addressed in an international research project. Stephanie was prepared for the necessity to "dig" for additional project-specific compliance issues.

SETTING THE STAGE

Stephanie learned in an initial phone conversation with the president of the center for endometriosis that all of the investigators participating in the research group own small practices affiliated with local or regional hospitals. Typically, a small medical practice ensures compliance with the HIPAA of 1996 by purchasing medical-office software certified as compliant by the vendor. Such software suites generally provide modules centered on practice management including billing and electronic medical records. Although these software packages are touted as HIPAA compliant, small businesses must still be cognizant of many nontechnical but management-oriented security and privacy issues. Various state; federal; and in this case, international laws and guidelines must be followed that such software will not address.

The data the researchers in this project wished to collect indeed fell beyond the scope of their current software systems. Consequently, the president of the center (i.e., the lead researcher of the group) developed a single database to support the data-collection efforts and distributed the program to each group member. Each researcher had been entering data into their local copies of the database, which was created with 127 fields to store patient demographical data and medical histories. Over 300 records had been entered by the lead researcher and each study site had entered a comparable number of records. The issue at hand was to determine how each researcher could transmit the data to the lead investigator for analysis. The ultimate process would subsequently need to be documented for the institutional review board. The lead researcher explained to Stephanie that small medical practices tend to operate without dedicated IT staff. It was therefore necessary that the solution involve minimal effort void of complexity. Stephanie met with the lead investigator to examine the database in place and to determine the project requirements.

CASE DESCRIPTION

Prior to her meeting with the lead researcher, Stephanie prepared via a thorough review HIPAA. She quickly determined that relevant rules dealt with electronically protected health information and the overarching HIPAA privacy rule. Patient health information encompasses any data relating to the physical or mental health of an individual, the provision of health care, or payments for health care that would in any way identify the respective

individual (see appendix). During the scheduled meeting, Stephanie obtained an empty copy of the database for analysis. It had been created in an Access 2000 format and all researchers had either Access 2000, 2002, or 2007 installed on their computer systems. Stephanie explained to the lead investigator that the key risk she would seek to eliminate was the exposure to any data that could be linked to specific patients. She reviewed the text of the HIPAA regulation with him and the researcher informed that such identifying information would not be needed to conduct the research.

Following the meeting, Stephanie conducted an additional review and discovered another option for transmitting protected health information (PHI) within § 164.312(e). This text stated that PHI could be transmitted electronically if the solution were to "implement technical security measures to guard against unauthorized access to electronic[ally] protected health information that is being transmitted over an electronic communications network." Stephanie interpreted this to imply that she could encrypt the PHI; however, no encryption standard was defined. In light of section § 164.514 (see appendix), she was able to identify fields within the database that appeared to contain PHI (see Table 1). Stephanie reviewed these fields and the relevant regulations with the lead researcher via a follow-up phone conversation and he made the following comments:

"Well, we don't need to know the exact date of surgery and discharge, but we do need the year of surgery and the length of stay [i.e., the difference between the discharge date and surgery date in days]. I also would prefer to have the patient's age, but would be willing to forego that for patients over 89 years of age. All the other fields that you have shown me are not necessary for the research. Please be aware that whatever recommendation you make to me should contain some assessment of how much the solution will cost. You will also need to provide a written explanation of your

Table 1. Protected health information in case database

ePHI classification	Field name	Description
Date element	dob	Date of birth
Date element	surgdate	Date of 1st surgery by investigator
Date element	dischdate	Date the patient went home after 1st surgery
Date element	age1stsurg	Patient's age at 1st surgery
Date element	surgdate2	Date of 2nd surgery, if required
Date element	surgdate3	Date of 3rd surgery
Date element	surgdate4	Date of 4th surgery
Account number	ID	Patient identifier
Name	first name	Patient first name
Name	last name	Patient last name
Social security number	SSnumber	Social security number
Address	address	Patient address
Address	city	Patient city
Address	state/province	Patient state
Address	zip postal code	Patient postal code
Address	Country	Patient country
Telephone number	Phone	Patient phone
Name	Currfirstn	Patient's 1st name if changed since initial entry
Name	Currlastna	Patient's last name if changed since initial entry
Address	Curraddres	Patient's address if changed since initial entry
Address	Currcity	City if changed since initial entry
Address	Currstatep	State or province if changed since initial entry
Address	Currzip	Zip code if changed since initial entry
Address	Currcountr	Country if changed since initial entry
Telephone number	Currphone	Telephone if changed since initial entry

Note. ePHI = electronically protected health information.

solution in detail so I can prepare a document for my review board to ensure compliance."

International Regulations

As Stephanie reviewed the relevant features HIPAA further, she discovered that privacy legislation within the United States consists of a veritable "patchwork" of laws both at state and federal levels. Her introductory course in information-systems management had also exposed her to the Sarbanes-Oxley Act of 2002 and the Graham-Leach-Bliley Act of 1999. This legislation was in response to current financial-industry debacles. The Acts partially covered health care privacy issues while placing clear pressure on the chief executive officers of large companies as holding ultimate responsibility for all organizational activities including the proper handling of sensitive information. However, Stephanie also found that, unlike other jurisdictions such as Canada, Australia, and the European Union, no overarching federal legislation existed within the United States covering the protection of such information. The enactment of additional privacy measures was left to the individual states. In these other parts of the world, federal legislation has a wider scope for compliance purposes unless individual states have also enacted legislation, in which case state law takes precedence if its content holds greater power.

Stephanie realized that, because of the multiple locations involved in the RCG project for the endometriosis-excision research group, existing law throughout Maine, Georgia, Texas, and even Australia would need to be investigated to ensure compliance beyond the HIPAA of 1996. Stephanie began her search with an investigation for any relevant compliance requirements within Australia before checking into various U.S. state laws. This was a strategic decision based upon her finding that countries such as Australia and Canada were quite advanced in their federal guidance toward protecting sensitive information. In her review of Australia federal law, she also discovered that two Australian states each mandated their own privacy legislation. Fortunately, the participating clinic in Brisbane was located just outside the states of Victoria and New South Wales. Consequently, unless clinics within these latter two states joined the research effort in the near future, concentrating solely on the Australian federal legislation was feasible.

Stephanie discovered that the Australian Federal Privacy Act contained 10 "national privacy principles" applicable to segments of the private sector and all health care providers. Several seemed to be particularly relevant to her project. The most obvious was the fourth principle, which relates to data security and mandates that an organization take reasonable steps to protect personal information it holds from loss and misuse via unauthorized access, modification, or disclosure.

The second principle addresses use and disclosure and *seems* to allow for the use of patient data for research purposes whether or not patient consent has been obtained. The 10th principle focuses on sensitive information and also *seems* to allow for use of patient data for research purposes.

Stephanie perceived the ninth principle of the Australian Federal Privacy Act to be directly applicable to her project, which addresses transborder data flow. The focus of this principle in Australia, as in Canada and the European Union, is to *prevent* the transmission of citizen data to other countries void of similar privacy legislation to provide a reasonable amount of protection from misuse of the information. The United States does *not* have similar legislation; however, the European Union recognizes *safe harbor,* which is primarily a voluntary agreement to protect information related to U.S. entities. The ninth Australian principle *seems* to allow for other exceptions that would apply in this particular case, especially with respect to part 95A of the Act, which addresses medical research and the public interest. Stephanie concluded that her review of compliance issues regarding the use of patient data for research purposes was sufficient to determine that Australian guidelines were unlikely to be any more stringent or specific than HIPAA at that point in time. Consequently, she proceeded to explore legislation and guidelines within the various U.S. states.

State Regulations

Stephanie focused her review of U.S. state legislation on the three states with clinics that would be contributing to the research of her client. With no legal background, Stephanie found the wide scope and variety of legislative information difficult to condense. She therefore turned her attention to the Internet and the Web site of the Health Privacy Project and others that appeared promising in terms of information related to the various state laws.

Maine: Stephanie found that the state of Maine was very specific in documenting that the health care information of any individual is strictly confidential and may not be disclosed without direct authorization from the respective individual. Such authorization would typically be in written form with, among other elements, the specific purpose of the disclosures identified. Maine legislation does document that disclosure without such authorization *is* permitted for research purposes; however, only when officially approved by an institutional review board. Health care practitioners and facilities are required to develop policies and procedures to protect the confidentiality of health care information to ensure that such data is not negligently or unlawfully disclosed. Penalties from $1000 to $5000 can be assessed, payable to the state and the victim; however, frequent abuses can potentially draw fines as high as $10,000 for health care practitioners and $50,000 for health care facilities. This was becoming not only complex for Stephanie, but was now presenting cause for concern because she did not know whether her client had obtained express or even implied consent for the patient information collected to date. However, she was aware that all work would be reviewed by an institutional review board for compliance with HIPAA.

Georgia: The legislative review Stephanie conducted for the state of Georgia also indicated disclosure restrictions applicable to her project. Generally, health-maintenance organizations may not disclose any information pertaining to the diagnosis, treatment, or health of any enrollee or applicant, obtained from the respective individual or any other care provider, without the express consent of the patient or applicant. Again, she was unsure as to whether such consent had been obtained by her client(s), or even if health-maintenance organizations were involved in the research project.

Georgia hospitals, physicians, and health care facilities who receive confidential or privileged medical information pursuant to a limited consent for disclosure may use the information solely for the purpose(s) for which they originally received

the data. Furthermore, any hospital, health care facility, medical or skilled nursing home, or other organization rendering patient care may provide information, reports, and other data related to the condition of an individual and the treatment received. However, such provision is restricted to solely research groups approved by the medical staff of the institution, governmental health agencies, medical associations and societies, or any in-hospital medical-staff committee. Such data may be used in any research study for the purpose of reducing morbidity or mortality rates. Recipients of the information may also use or publish it for the purpose of advancing medical research or medical education or to achieve the most effective use of health care manpower and facilities. However, the identity of the individuals whose information has been received must be held strictly confidential and may not be revealed under any circumstances.

Texas: Texas legislation indicated specific disclosure restrictions Stephanie found potentially problematic for the RCG project. Generally, health-maintenance organizations are barred from disclosing any information pertaining to the diagnoses, treatment, or health of enrollees or applicants obtained from those respective individuals or other providers without the express consent of the same enrollees or applicants. Typically, hospitals may not disclose health care information on a patient without the written authorization of that patient. A written disclosure authorization is valid only if it is dated and signed by the patient, identifies the information to be disclosed, and identifies the specific individual to whom the information is to be disclosed. The authorization is valid for 180 days unless it specifies otherwise or is revoked by the authorizing individual. Disclosures without patient authorizations are permitted only if the information released is also published in a directory, unless the patient had instructed the hospital not to include the information and it was erroneously published in the directory. Properly published data may be released to a health care provider attending the patient, a qualified organ or tissue procurement organization, and to others specified within the legislation.

Communication between a physician and patient, as well as all records of identity, diagnosis, evaluation, and treatment, are strictly confidential and may not be disclosed without the consent of the patient, except as allowed by statute. As with any data disclosed by hospitals, a written consent must be signed by the patient and must specify (a) the information or medical records authorized to be released, (b) the purpose for the disclosure, and (c) the person to whom the information is to be released. Disclosure without patient consent is permissible in a number of documented circumstances such as to individuals involved in the payment or collection of fees for medical services rendered by the attending physician. Stephanie found that a patient whose medical records have been disclosed in violation of the state statutes may bring a civil suit for injunctive relief and damages. Senate Bill 11, frequently referred to as a "super HIPAA," ultimately became the Texas Medical Privacy Act. This legislation specifically addresses the need for expressed patient consent for use of medical information; however, the requirement appears to be somewhat lax in allowing such information to be used for research purposes if approved by an institutional review board.

As Stephanie surveyed the extraordinary amount of data at her disposal, she was overwhelmed by a sense of "information overload," yet she remained uncertain as to whether her perception of each jurisdiction that could impinge on her project was complete. Her charge was to arrive at a relatively simple and inexpensive solution to move the research project forward without placing undue strain on the limited IT resources within the various participating health clinics and hospitals. If she adhered to the guidelines of the HIPAA of 1996 as closely as possible, Stephanie felt the project would be reasonably protected from any unintentional breaches. Investing fur-

ther time, and hence cost for her client, may ultimately result in *perfect* coverage; however, the needs of her client included a *rapid* solution. Consequently, uncertainty remained, but she also realized the strategic importance of recognizing when decision making must take precedence over gathering further data. Without such cognizance, decisions could be forced, producing outcomes far worse than "less than perfect." Balancing the use of IT with privacy and security concerns can be stagnating if the willingness or experience to make proactive judgment calls between information collection and decision making is absent.

CURRENT CHALLENGES

Following her legislative investigation, Stephanie felt she had a clear view of the challenge. She could focus on security aspects of the information management with the option of encrypting the data, which would involve coordinating encryption and decryption for all research participants. Alternatively, she could remove all data items that could be possibly construed as PHI, thereby insulating the research project from any unknown conflicts with privacy and security legislation. A combination of both this process and encryption could also be implemented. Stephanie remained aware of the necessity for any solution process to be exceptionally easy to maintain due to the complete lack of IT-related experience in the backgrounds of the researchers and staff.

Stephanie was fairly familiar with encryption so perceived essentially two options with this method. She could use an e-mail-based key encryption such as that provided by the PGP corporation, or she could search for a hosting company that offers secure file transfer. With the method of eliminating identifying data, Stephanie perceived the following three feasible options:

1. Provide written instructions for exporting data free of PHI.
2. Create a Microsoft Access report free of identifying data and instruct each researcher on importing and subsequently exporting the report.
3. Write an application that automatically exports data to a self-contained file.

Stephanie had additional research to conduct, but felt confident she could provide a recommendation to the lead researcher by the end of the week. She realized she was enjoying her first consulting engagement and found it invigorating. It was now time to focus on the more technical aspects of the project. Stephanie launched her Web browser and began her research on encryption software.

Alternative Encryption Solutions

While there are a wide variety of encryption and other security solutions available, Stephanie concentrated her search on low-cost solutions providing adequate security (i.e., that used a minimum of 128-bit encryption). Fitting solutions fell into the following three categories:

1. **Client-based e-mail:** While e-mail-based solutions vary in their mode of implementation, the concept of public key encryption

is fairly simple to understand. The intended recipient of secure e-mail makes their public key available to anyone wishing to send them a secure message. The key contains information on how to transform a message from *plaintext* to *ciphertext* (i.e., the key enables the sender to encrypt a message). The public key only contains information on how to encrypt messages, not on how to decrypt messages. Messages are translated from ciphertext to plaintext (i.e., *decrypted*) via the private key. Typically, only the recipient holds the private key enabling message decryption (see Figure 1). Key size is a factor in the security level of the encryption. A 128-bit key is common for electronic commerce and is considered secure and 256-bit solutions are commonly available. Public keys can be distributed to senders via a plaintext e-mail or a more secure method such as a key-distribution center to encrypt the transmission of a public key and verify its authenticity. The e-mail client must support the key-based encryption used, which usually requires the purchase of add-on or plug-in software. A variety of software options are available including Secure Multipurpose Internet Mail Extensions, Pretty Good Privacy, and Gnu Privacy Guard. An alternate e-mail-based solution would

Figure 1. Public key encryption

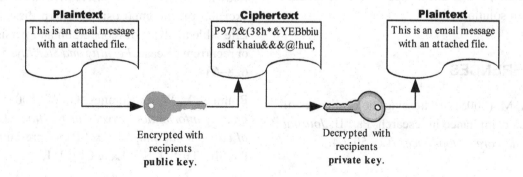

be to use a secure compression utility to create an encrypted compressed file. This is not a key-based solution. Rather than key distribution, passwords are distributed in a secure manner.

2. **Server based:** Another alternative would be to establish a server dedicated to secure file transfer and distribute clients to each sender. The encryption method used by many of these services is equal to or greater than 128-bit encryption and it is highly secure. A wide range of software solutions are available for this alternative. An example would be the WS_FTP software available from Ipswitch Corporation. Cost varies depending upon the products purchased.

3. **Hosted:** A variety of hosted, Web-based solutions exist at reasonable cost that require minimal configuration. One example is the services provided by Safety Send. This organization ensures compliance with the HIPAA of 1996 and the Graham-Leach-Bliley Act of 1999. No additional software is required. This is an economical option with services as low as $10 per month. Higher levels of encryption are also available.

4. **Secure peer-to-peer (P2P):** A fourth alternative would be to use a secure P2P client. While there are several secure P2P solutions available, many companies have policies against using P2P file sharing applications.

With her options summarized, Stephanie began preparation of her client report with her recommended solution.

REFERENCES

Arvin, M. (2005). Addressing the challenges of HIPAA compliance in research, Part II. *Journal of Healthcare Compliance, 7*(2), 59–64.

Australian federal privacy law.(n.d.). Retrieved December 28, 2005, from http://www.privacy. gov.au/act/

Berghel, H. (2005). The two sides of ROI: Return on investment vs. risk of incarceration. *Communications of the ACM, 49*(4), 15–20. doi:10.1145/1053291.1053305

Gostin, L. O., & Nass, S. (2009). Reforming the HIPAA Privacy Rule: Safeguarding Privacy and Promoting Research. *Journal of the American Medical Association, 301*(13), 1373–1375. doi:10.1001/jama.2009.424

Huston, T. (2001). Security issues for implementation of e-medical records. *Communications of the ACM, 44*(9), 89–94. doi:10.1145/383694.383712

Krohn, R. (2002). HIPAA compliance: A technology perspective. *Journal of Healthcare Information Management, 16*(2), 14–16.

Leetz, W. (2001). HIPAA: Increased efficiency in US American healthcare requires data protection and data security - an overview of the technical and organizational measures necessary. *electromedica, 69*(2), 95–100.

McCormick, V. L. (2002). HIPAA compliance options for small and mid-sized organizations. *Journal of Healthcare Compliance, 4*(6), 17–20.

Mercuri, R. T. (2004). The HIPAA-potamus in health care data security. *Communications of the ACM, 47*(7), 25–28. doi:10.1145/1005817.1005840

Redwine, D. B. (1991). Conservative laparoscopic excision of endometriosis by sharp dissection: Life table analysis of reoperation and persistent or recurrent disease. *Fertility and Sterility, 56*(4), 628–634.

Romney, V. W., & Romney, G. W. (2004). *Neglect of information privacy instruction: A case of educational malpractice?* Paper presented at the SIGITE '04, Salt Lake City, UT.

Schindler, R. G. (2001). Balancing information technology benefits with privacy and security concerns. *Journal of Healthcare Compliance, 3*(6), 44–44.

Swartz, N. (2003). What every business needs to know about HIPAA. *Information Management Journal, 37*(2), 26–34.

Wright, B. (2004). Internet break-ins: New legal liability. *Computer Law & Security Report, 20*(3), 171–175. doi:10.1016/S0267-3649(04)00032-9

APPENDIX

Health Insurance Portability and Accountability Act of 1996

§ 164.514 Privacy/Security/Enforcement Regulation Text (August 2003)

Other requirements relating to uses and disclosures of protected health information.

(a) Standard: de-identification of protected health information. Health information that does not identify an individual and with respect to which there is no reasonable basis to believe that the information can be used to identify an individual is not individually identifiable health information.

(b) Implementation specifications: requirements for de-identification of protected health information. A covered entity may determine that health information is not individually identifiable health information only if:

(1) A person with appropriate knowledge of and experience with generally accepted statistical and scientific principles and methods for rendering information not individually identifiable:

(i) Applying such principles and methods, determines that the risk is very small that the information could be used alone or in combination with other reasonably available information, by an anticipated recipient to identify an individual who is a subject of the information; and

(ii) Documents the methods and results of the analysis that justify such determination; or

(2)(i) The following identifiers of the individual or of relatives, employers, or household members of the individual, are removed:

(A) Names;

(B) All geographic subdivisions smaller than a State, including street address, city, county, precinct, zip code, and their equivalent geocodes, except for the initial three digits of a zip code if, according to the current publicly available data from the Bureau of the Census:

(1) The geographic unit formed by combining all zip codes with the same three initial digits contains more than 20,000 people; and

(2) The initial three digits of a zip code for all such geographic units containing 20,000 or fewer people is changed to 000.

(C) All elements of dates (except year) for dates directly related to an individual, including birth date, admission date, discharge date, date of death; and all ages over 89 and all elements of dates (including year) indicative of such age, except that such ages and elements may be aggregated into a single category of age 90 or older;

(D) Telephone numbers;

(E) Fax numbers;

(F) Electronic mail addresses;

(G) Social security numbers;

(H) Medical record numbers;

(I) Health plan beneficiary numbers;

(J) Account numbers;

(K) Certificate/license numbers;

(L) Vehicle identifiers and serial numbers, including license plate numbers;

(M) Device identifiers and serial numbers;

(N) Web Universal Resource Locators (URLs);

(O) Internet Protocol (IP) address numbers;

(P) Biometric identifiers, including finger and voice prints;

(Q) Full face photographic images and any comparable images; and

(R) Any other unique identifying number, characteristic, or code, except as permitted by paragraph (c) of this section;

and

(ii) The covered entity does not have actual knowledge that the information could be used alone or in combination with other information to identify an individual who is a subject of the information.

(c) Implementation specifications: re-identification. A covered entity may assign a code or other means of record identification to allow information de-identified under this section to be re-identified by the covered entity, provided that:

(1) Derivation. The code or other means of record identification is not derived from or related to information about the individual and is not otherwise capable of being translated so as to identify the individual; and

(2) Security. The covered entity does not use or disclose the code or other means of record identification for any other purpose, and does not disclose the mechanism for re-identification.

Chapter 9
Addressing Current PCI Compliance Challenges

Benjamin Ngugi
Suffolk University, USA

Glenn Dardick
Longwood University, USA

Gina Vega
Salem State University, USA

ABSTRACT

This study reviews the progress made by the introduction of the Payment Card Industry (PCI) compliance rules in the USA. Available data indicate that compliance has grown but several issues remain unresolved. These are identified within, along with an analysis of the feasibility of several solutions to the challenges that have hampered compliance with the Payment Card Industry rules. These solutions are evaluated by the extent to which they can help the merchants meet their business objectives while still safeguarding the credit card data. The first solution involves upgrading the current PCI standards as suggested by the PCI council. The second solution would require moving the burden of credit card information storage to the credit card companies and member banks, as suggested by the National Retail Federation. A third option reflects a socially responsible approach that protects the interests of all stakeholders. The study concludes by suggesting the way forward.

INTRODUCTION

Progress has been made towards compliance with rules introduced by the Payment Card Industry (PCI) in the USA. However, available data indicate that while compliance has grown, several challenges still remain unresolved. There are several options to meeting the challenges that have hampered compliance with the Payment Card Industry rules. These options can be evaluated as to the extent to which they can help merchants meet their business objectives while still safeguarding the credit card data. One option involves upgrading the current PCI standards as suggested by the PCI council. A second option would require moving the burden of credit card information storage to the credit card companies and member banks, as suggested by the National

DOI: 10.4018/978-1-60960-200-0.ch009

Retail Federation. A third option reflects a socially responsible approach that protects the interests of all stakeholders.

System breaches resulting in the theft of credit card information is still a major challenge. Not all data breaches result in such a loss; however, just a single breach can result in the loss of millions of credit card records. A recent such example was the TJX Companies, Inc. computer intrusion during which more than 45 million customer records were affected (Office of the Privacy Commissioner of Canada & Office of the Information and Privacy Commissioner of Alberta, 2007). As of August, 2007, the company had already spent about $256 million installing the necessary security systems to deter another attack and in meeting other costs associated with the intrusion, such as legal settlements and fines (TJX Companies, 2007). The figure is expected to increase, with some suggesting that the final cost may reach $1 billion (Goodin, 2007). Clearly, we are dealing with real threats that have dire financial consequences, and there is need for concerted effort from all stakeholders.

Credit card companies are struggling to fight data breaches. Statistics for four consecutive years show that the number of data breaches continue to rise (Identity Theft Resource Center, 2005, 2006, 2007, 2008). Specifically, these reports show that there were 158 cases of reported data-breaches in 2005, which rose to 315 and then to 446 cases in 2006 and 2007 respectively. As of August 2008, 449 data breaches were reported suggesting that the situation is continues to worsen.

HOW DOES THE CREDIT CARD INDUSTRY OPERATE?

There are several major players in the credit card industry chain (Shift4 Corporation, 2008). At the center of the chain is the customer who gets a credit card from the *issuer* (the financial institution that issues the credit card to the customer). The customer presents the credit card to the *merchant* in order to purchase a service or product. The merchant transmits this information to the *merchant bank* (also called the *acquirer*) for subsequent transmission to the *issuer,* who either approves or declines the request. This decision is transmitted back the same chain to the customer. The acquirer charges the merchants a fee in the form of a discount rate for acting as the middleman and then gives the issuer and the card companies a designated percentage of this fee. A significant aspect of the work of credit card companies such as VISA is to design regulations for the use and acceptance of credit cards.

Customers shopping at brick and mortar stores have to swipe their credit cards at the point of sale (POS) system when purchasing goods. This captures the full magnetic track data on the credit card (cardholder name, credit card number or primary account number (PAN), expiration date, and other optional data). This is the most precious data for data thieves because it enables them to make counterfeit cards which can be used just like the real ones. On the other hand, e-commerce customers shopping on the Internet have to enter their names, credit card numbers, expiration dates and their security codes which are transmitted over the web to the acquirer (merchant bank) via the merchant. This is the second most important set of data for the card data thieves because it enables them to make fraudulent online purchases undetected.

Merchants may want to store the credit card data for several reasons. The primary reason is to meet the requirement by the credit card companies for the merchants to store credit card information data for up to 18 months in the event that there are disputes with the customers or other retrieval requests (Hogan, 2007). Secondary reasons include the desire of online retailers to offer quick check-out and automatic bill payment options to returning customers. These options would not be possible without storing the customer credit card information during enrollment and retrieving it on demand. The reality is that the stored information accumulates over time and becomes a magnet for criminals.

Credit card companies have to protect these data, both to prevent the criminals from using them to make counterfeit cards and also to retain the integrity of the credit card system. The credit card companies initially established individual proprietary programs for the storage of this data. This meant that merchants had a different set of rules from every credit card company, resulting in confusion for the merchants who had to implement different procedures from each credit card company. The rising confusion and increasing number of data breaches prompted the five major credit card companies to form a common body to pursue their common interests in reducing card fraud (PCI Compliance Guide, 2008). The five companies (VISA, MasterCard, American Express, Discover Card and JCB International) came together and formed the PCI Council in 2004. The council created the first payment standard called Payment Card Industry Data Security Standard (PCIDSS) two years later. These regulations apply to every company that processes, stores, or transmits credit or debit card data. Failure to comply can result in fines, suspension, or revocation of the merchant's privileges to process credit/debit cards. For example, VISA collected fines of $4.6 million in 2006, up from $3.4 million in 2005 from non-compliant merchants (VISA USA, 2006).

The 12 PCI compliance rules are designed to ensure that the merchant systems storing the above data are securely protected from hackers. The next section summarizes these rules.

OVERVIEW OF THE PCI DATA SECURITY STANDARD VERSION 1.2

The PCI Data Security Standard consists of 12 requirements (PCI Security Standard Council, 2006) shown below. The requirements are clustered into six main objectives.

Build and Maintain a Secure Network

1. **Install and maintain a firewall configuration to protect cardholder data:** This requirement ensures that only trusted packets are accepted into the network.

2. **Do not use vendor-supplied defaults for system passwords and other security parameters:** This prevents hackers from exploiting the networks simply by using well known default user names, passwords, protocols, and other security parameters.

Protecting the Cardholder Data

3. **Protect stored cardholder data:** The third requirement ensures that card holder information such as the credit card number, name, and full track data are only stored when it is absolutely necessary, and even then should only be stored in an unreadable form. The requirement also prohibits the storage of the card security code (used in card-not-present transactions) to ensure that the user has physical possession of the card.

4. **Encrypt transmission of cardholder data across open, public networks:** The fourth requirement ensures that customer data is encrypted when being transmitted across different networks, the period when it is most vulnerable to exploits by hackers.

A Vulnerability Management Program

5. **Use and regularly update anti-virus software:** Requirement five ensures that the latest updates for the antivirus programs are installed to block viruses, worms, and Trojans injected into the networks by malicious hackers.

6. **Develop and maintain secure systems and applications:** Requirement six ensures that the working applications have the latest security patches and are developed using

best practices (e.g., with built-in security systems) rather than treating security as an afterthought.

Strong Access Control Measures

7. **Restrict access to cardholder data by business need-to-know:** Only users with the need-to-know are able to access customer card data information.
8. **Assign a unique ID to each person with computer access:** The eighth requirement ensures that there is accurate logging of each individual who accesses the data, to ensure accountability.
9. **Restrict physical access to cardholder data:** Requirement nine limits the number of users who gain access to card holder data. This limits the opportunity for access or copying of the data.

Monitor and Test Networks Regularly

10. **Track and monitor all access to network resources and cardholder data:** Requirement 10 ensures that an audit can be done easily, by using the logs to see who has been accessing records.
11. **Regularly test security systems and processes:** This can help detect and prosecute crimes, identify new vulnerabilities, and ensure that the network is secure at all times.

Maintain an Information Security Policy

12. **Maintain a policy that addresses information security:** Prevention is better than cure. A good security policy will help users understand what is expected of them, resulting in fewer incidents as most users are cooperative.

The above twelve requirements are well intentioned to address the needs of the payment card industry. However, their implementation has not been smooth.

PROGRESS ON PCI COMPLIANCE

VISA is the leader in pushing for PCI compliance in USA, and the path it has followed is indicative of the path that the other companies will follow. In addition to seminars and sharing data with the merchant banks, VISA used a carrot and stick program to promote PCI compliance. The company announced (VISA USA, 2006) in December, 2006 that it was going to offer $20 million as incentive to help merchants comply with PCI standards in a program called "VISA PCI Compliance Acceleration Program (PCI CAP)." This program has targeted the 1,200 largest Level 1 and 2 merchants who process more than 1 million VISA transactions per year and generate about two thirds of the total transaction volume. The merchant banks that fully complied with the PCI rules were to receive a onetime payment for each qualifying merchant and would also get a preferred interchange rate (fee paid by the merchant to the cardholders issuing bank) on their transactions.

Merchants are fined if they are involved in any data breach and also if they cannot confirm that their full track data is not being retained (VISA USA, 2006). Level 1 and 2 merchant banks have been subject to between $5,000 and $25,000 in fines per month for non-compliance since September 20, 2007 and December, 2007 respectively. Any merchant bank that could not confirm that they were not storing full track data (CVV2 or PIN data) by March 31, 2007, would be fined $10,000 per month.

The compliance program has met with some success. Table 1 shows the compliance of VISA merchants to PCI rules at the end of 2007.

At that time, 77 percent of Level 1 merchants had complied with the PCI rules, while 23 percent

Table 1. VISA PCI DSS Compliance Update as of 12/31/2007 (VISA USA, 2008)

CISP Validation Category (VISA transactions / year)	Population	Estimated % of VISA Transactions	PCI DSS Compliance Validated	Initial Validation Submitted / Re-mediating	Initial Validation In Progress	Pending Commitment
Level 1 Merchants (> 6M)	326	50%	77%	23%	0%	0%
Level 2 Merchants (1 – 6M)	709	13%	62%	30%	8%	0%
Level 3 Merchants (e-commerce only 20,000 – 1M)	2596	< 5%	54%	20%	25%	1%

had submitted their validation but were working on remediation measures. Sixty-two percent of Level 2 merchants had validated compliance; 30 percent were taking corrective measures after first submission, while the remaining eight percent had validation in progress. Fifty four percent of Level 3 merchants had completed validation, 20 percent were undergoing remediation after first submission, and 25 percent were undergoing validation. The remaining one percent had committed to comply.

The compliance of Level 4 merchants was not given. These are small merchants having (VISA USA, 2007a) fewer than one million annual VISA total transactions and fewer than 20,000 annual VISA e-commerce (online) transactions.

CHALLENGES HAMPERING PCI COMPLIANCE

A deeper examination reveals that, while compliance has grown, there are major outstanding issues that need to be addressed (Litan, 2008). Although 77 percent of the merchants have complied with PCI rules, this does not necessarily mean that their networks are totally secure. Most of the merchants have not even accounted for all the places where their cardholder data is stored, let alone encrypted

or monitored access, as there are many loopholes that allow providers with exceptions to still be PCI compliant (Carr, 2008).

Some of the storage places are not even known by the merchants. For example, some point of sale equipment is programmed to store the card data internally, unbeknownst to the merchants.

In addition, most of the available compliance statistics are from VISA which is leading the rest. This means that the state of compliance for MasterCard, Discover Card, American Express, and JCB clients is lagging behind VISA and is of major concern.

There are several challenges hampering facing PCI compliance. A number of these are discussed below.

The Cost of Compliance

PCI compliance can be costly. The rules require that technology, systems, and policies be put in place to safeguard cardholder data. This can be a significant financial undertaking. The music retailer, Guitar Center Inc., a Level 1 merchant with over 210 stores nationwide, reported that it spent more than $500,000 to purchase the technology and put in the systems and policies required to become PCI compliant. This is in line with earlier Gartner, Inc. which projected the average

PCI compliance cost for a Level 1 merchant to be about $568, 000 (Tam & Sidel, 2007).

Further, there are other added maintenance costs. For example, Level 1&2 merchants have to undergo quarterly network scanning (PCI Compliance Guide, 2008). This must be done by an approved scanning vendor (ASV). Likewise, the big merchants have to undergo an annual PCI compliance validation by a qualified security assessor (QSA).

PCI Rules are Rigid, Confusing and Keep on Changing

PCI rules are rigid and require compliance to the letter. This is forcing auditors to follow regulations to "the letter of the law" defined by the standard, but not its spirit, which might make more sense (Nolann, 2006). Previous standards such as HIPAA and SOX identified the goals to be achieved and allowed the industry and companies to work out the details of implementation themselves. Not so with PCI compliance. Further, the rules are confusing, leaving merchants with too many unanswered questions. For example, there is considerable confusion about the implications of outsourcing arrangements on the scope of PCI compliance efforts and how to segment networks adequately to reduce the scope of compliance activities (Litan, 2008). The PCI rules are also silent on whether virtualized systems are compliant, despite virtualization's ability to aid in data security.

The rules keep changing. Compliance has cost merchants enormous time and resources, and most are still struggling to reach the compliance finish line. The PCI council shifted the goals by announcing a new version 1.2 in October 2008 (PCI Council, 2008) and again by announcing the new version 2 regulations to be effective on January 1, 2011 (PCI Security Standards Council, 2010) shortly after the planned publication date of October 28, 2010. Just when the merchants thought they were done, they had to repeat the process to make sure that everything was in line with the refined standard.

Unworkable for the Smaller Merchant

The card companies and the PCI council have focused primarily on Level 1 and Level 2 merchants, and to some extent on Level 3 merchants. They have paid very little attention to Level 4 merchants. The latter are either e-commerce merchants handling fewer than 20,000 e-commerce card transactions per year or traditional brick and mortar merchants handling fewer than one million card transactions per year. Table 1 does not even provide Level 4 merchants' compliance rates. It might seem like a good strategy on the surface to avoid spending too much on the small merchants. After all, Level 1-3 merchants comprise 68 percent of all VISA transactions. A closer look reveals, however, that this strategy has been a mistake for several reasons.

First, there are more than 6 million VISA Level 4 merchant locations – about 99 percent of all VISA merchant locations. The individual transactions may be small, but total about 32 percent of VISA transactions by volume (VISA USA, 2007a). The PCI council cannot make much progress in compliance if it is not addressing the needs of 99 percent of the merchants.

Second, Level 4 merchants are the most common target of hackers. In a study that analyzed 350 cases of payment card compromises from 14 countries, it was reported that 92 percent of the card breaches targeted Level 4 merchants (Trustwave, 2008). Another study by VISA found that more than 80 percent of the identified compromises since 2005 were Level 4 merchants (VISA USA, 2007a). These merchants include the mom and pop stores scattered all over the country. Their owners often lack the technology know-how required to implement the PCI rules. They can neither afford expert security consultants to advise them on compliance nor do they have the capital to finance the heavy infrastructure required to deter data thieves. Thus,

PCI compliance remains unattainable for smaller merchants (Litan, 2008). PCI compliance security will remain weak as long as the needs of small merchants are not being addressed.

Legal Uncertainties and Conflict of Interest

There is a legal disconnect in the way PCI rules are being applied. These rules are not supposed to be laws, but rather a self regulation mechanism for those in the payment card industry (Navetta, 2008). The PCI council does not have policing or remediation powers. However, the rules are being enforced like "laws" in practice. The card companies impose fines and penalties on merchant banks for non-compliance. The merchant banks in turn impose fines and other penalties on the merchants if the latter are not PCI compliant. In this way, the card companies and the merchant banks are acting as the prosecutors, judges, and police in enforcing PCI rules.

Further, the card companies and the merchant banks have vested interests and stand to gain from the fines, making it harder to deliver fair and independent judgments. The merchant banks that are supposed to enforce the compliance of merchants for the card companies are themselves not compliant and don't really understand the problem (Nolann, 2006). The qualified security assessors (QSAs) who are supposed to validate that a merchant is compliant are a creation of the card payment industry and have products to sell which may cloud their judgment (Messmer, 2007). They also do not have any legal training and do not usually include attorneys in the validation process, increasing the possibility of key legal issues being omitted (Navetta, 2008).

Uncertainty about the issue of "Safe Harbor" as far as PCI compliance is concerned is also hindering compliance. The initial position (VISA USA, 2007b) by VISA was that a merchant was protected from VISA fines subsequent to a data breach if the member was in full compliance before the breach. However, the company seems to be shifting from this position to a new position in which the waiver of fines is subject to its own determination. This de-motivates the merchants as there is no guarantee that prior compliance will protect them from penalties.

Secure Coding

SQL injection attacks (Chong, 2002) are the cause of many computer breaches and attacks and has become commonplace because of the lack of attention on secure coding. They can be avoided with proper coding (Anley, 2002). Unfortunately, this vulnerability has historically not been well known and such attacks continue to increase over time (Swoyer, 2008). Web applications have become primary targets for such attacks as attested to by the statement, *"Hackers have realized that because networks are secure, the application is the weakest link,"*, attributed to Mandeep Khera of security firm, Cenzic (Collins, 2008).

Overlapping roles of the Database Administrator and the Data Administrator

The data administrator should deal with business decisions such as whether data is necessary and who should have access to the same. The database administrator should deal with technical IT decisions. Unfortunately, personal data is often kept and subject to a breach even though the reasons for recording and/or archiving the personal data have never been vetted. In an FTC Consent Order (FTC, 2005; In the Matter of DSW Inc., a corporation: FTC File No. 052-3096," 2005), a shoe discounter settled FTC charges of faulty data security practices when it was determined that the company retained unencrypted personal information longer than necessary (La Roche, Dardick, & Flanigan, 2006).

Newer Methods of Attack and Compromise

Many new breaches occur as a result of the discovery of new vulnerabilities. Other breaches occur as a result of existing vulnerabilities' not being addressed with current patches or best practices. The number of vulnerabilities is staggering, and there would seem to be no reasonable expectation that new vulnerabilities will not surface. These challenges need to be addressed if progress is to continue in achieving reasonable PCI compliance. The next section looks at the suggested solutions.

POSSIBLE SOLUTIONS

Two solutions have been gaining traction in the PCI compliance arena. The first solution proposed by the PCI council is to refine the PCI rules. The other solution, which has the overwhelming support of the National Retailer's Federation (Hogan, 2007), is to stop requiring the merchants to store the credit card data and shifting this burden to the credit companies. In addition to these two clearly partisan perspectives is a third proposal, one relating to stakeholder rights. All three are discussed below.

REFINEMENT OF PCI RULES TO MEET CHANGING NEEDS

The PCI council has been addressing some of the identified shortcomings in a number of ways. The first has been through a program of bulletins to merchants, providing updates and clarifications of the PCI rules. The second approach has been through the creation of a Frequently Asked Questions (FAQ) website that addresses most of the common questions. In October, 2008, the PCI council released an updated version of the PCI rules called PCI DSS Version 1.2 (PCI Council, 2008). The new standard aims to achieve several goals:

1) Incorporate existing and new best practices. 2) Provide further scoping and reporting clarification. 3) Eliminate overlapping sub-requirements and consolidate documentation. 4) Enhance the Frequently Asked Questions and glossary to facilitate understanding of the security process.

These elements may reduce confusion about the rules by eliminating overlaps and improve implementation by incorporating best practices and enhanced scoping. However, they do not go far enough in addressing the other outstanding challenges. Specifically, 1) the new version will not ease the burden on cost significantly. 2) It will not address the concerns of small merchants. 3) It will not clear the legal issues nor provide mechanism for reducing the conflict of interest. 4) Merchants still have legitimate reasons for storing credit card data to use for charging recurring bill, tips and so on, yet the above solution does not provide a secure method of doing this. In summary, the new version seems to be more of a continuation of the current situation.

SHIFTING THE DATA STORAGE BURDEN TO THE CREDIT CARD COMPANIES

The National Retail Federation (NRF) notes that the majorities of large merchants are either PCI compliant or are working towards this goal. They have invested millions of dollars into their systems to achieve compliance, yet the number of data breaches continues to rise. The NRF posits that it is unlikely that PCI rules will ever be able to keep pace with the ever evolving professional hackers or anticipate every possible variation of future attack (Hogan, 2007). This position is supported by the fact that even prior to the PCI rules companies were fighting hackers with each side trying to outdo the other.

NRF proposes that the real solution would be to stop requiring the merchants to store credit card data which acts as a magnet for criminal hackers.

Rather, the merchants would only store an authorization code provided by the acquiring bank/credit card company at the time of purchase to prove that the transaction was approved. The merchant would also store a truncated receipt in case of returns or the need for "proof of purchase." The full account and transaction data would be kept by the credit card companies and the member banks.

This proposal reduces the data storage points currently at the merchants premises to just a handful of locations determined by the credit card companies and the merchant banks. The reduced number of exposure points enhances security. The solution also addresses the small merchant problem. As stated earlier, the small merchant has neither the knowledge nor the resources required to protect stored credit card data. In the suggested solution, the data will be protected by organizations with the money and appropriate data security know-how.

This proposal gained early support from key research companies who have been struggling with PCI challenges. Gartner Research believes that the above proposal is a practical and useful step toward improving the security of sensitive data (Litan, 2007). The proposal is also technically viable as all it would require would be the development and implementation of a new payment protocol. The bulk of the processing and data storage would be passed on to the card companies and the member banks. This means that the card companies and member banks would have to upgrade their systems to be able to handle the new payment protocol as well as the increased transaction and storage capacity as they will be serving as the back end to the merchants on the credit card transactions. The merchants would also have to upgrade their point of sale systems to be able to handle the new payment protocol, likely a less expensive process than developing a secure storage system. They would also have to upgrade their internal systems in line with the new payment system and purge any credit card information stored from previous transactions. The merchants will have only to ensure that the credit card data is secure during transaction processing and transmission to the card companies and the member banks.

A STAKEHOLDER APPROACH

The two proposed solutions overlook a basic tenet of the social responsibility of business; that is the primacy of protection of the customer (in this case, the customer's personal data) from harm. The many instances of data theft and the slap-on-the-wrist industry responses to them underscore the disrespect shown to the customer by merchants, the PCI industry, and the banking system. The first principle of corporate social responsibility is trust (Richardson & McCord, 2000). Customers need to trust merchants with their sensitive credit information. The clear responsibility for protection of credit data lies with the three customer interfaces: the merchant, the credit card company, and the bank. Each of these needs to establish and maintain its own trusting relationship with its customers, or the economic system will fail to function.

The lax approach taken by all three entities to protection of the customer is shockingly casual. Most computer breaches result in losses that are incalculable to those whose identities have been stolen. They must jump through multiple financial and bureaucratic hoops to re-establish their credit and correct damaged credit scores. Banks and credit card companies assure their users that they are "only" liable for a limited amount of money, perhaps $50. "We regret any inconvenience this situation may have caused you," is a familiar component of the corporate response. This statement does little to acknowledge for the frustration they have created for the innocent credit card holders who must then attempt to reconstruct their personal identities.

Wholly distinct from legal concerns, there exist multiple economic and philosophical perspectives on consumer protection that apply to the loss of customer data. The "acceptable risk" theory suggests that our interactions, in this case our commercial interactions, are all subject to risk, and consumers evaluate as acceptable the risk of sharing their credit card data with a merchant in exchange for some other benefit – the purchase of some desired item. However, at no point in these transactions does the customer accept the risk of identity theft, because the customer believes that swiping his credit card is an acceptable risk. After all, he believes, surely the store is taking good care of my credit card information. The days of the credit card carbon paper scams are long gone.

Both parties to the exchange have the same goal; that is, they both want something from the other, and therefore each takes a limited risk about the other's good intentions (the merchant accepts the risk that the method of payment may be counterfeit, and the customer accepts the risk that his purchase may not be as anticipated once he gets it home). Both types of risk are protected from harm by implicit and explicit guarantees. When a customer pays by credit card, payment to the merchant is underwritten by the credit card company. When the shirt doesn't fit once the customer gets it home, most merchants accept the return of the item

Based on the joint concepts of trust and acceptable risk, the customer should not have to be responsible for any of the clean-up of credit loss or any financial losses. Those costs should all be borne by the entity responsible for the loss as they are all simply costs of doing business, analogous to earlier security costs like safes, padlocks, Well Fargo protection, and armed guards. Protection of the customer demands that the three interfaces stop playing "hot potato" with their basic business responsibility and either share the costs or be prepared for the inevitable government intervention.

SUGGESTING THE WAY FORWARD

The proposal to shift the burden of storing the credit card data to the card companies and the merchant's bank is a viable one. However, the reception from the card companies has been lukewarm. This may be due to the fact that the credit card companies and the merchant banks would incur additional costs in upgrading their systems to handle the resulting new protocols, increased transactions and storage requirements, yet the resulting gains would seem mostly to benefit the small (level 4) merchants.. Instead, pressure has been building for the small merchants to become compliant. The merchant banks are being asked to embark on a mission to educate the small merchant and to report to the card companies on the achievement of several set goals (VISA USA, 2007a).

We propose that the way forward is to stop searching for partisan one-size-fits-all solutions. Instead all the stakeholders, especially the PCI council, merchants, banks, credit companies and the users should work together to defeat the common data thieves. There is need for a scalable solution that can fit the needs of the smaller merchants and grow with them as they become larger. Such a solution must also meet the common goal that is critical to the whole payment card industry - protection of customer credit card information. The solution must relieve the small merchant from the burden of storing credit card information and must give big merchants the option of retaining the expensive systems that they have already implemented. The method must be acceptable to the credit card companies and require minimal changes to the current infrastructure.

In short, an acceptable solution must be a stakeholder-based solution, one that accommodates the needs of each player in the sector. The solution must also be self-sustaining and driven by the market forces. The solution must be backed by an authoritative body that already enjoys the payment industry's support and trust. No other body fits this bill better than the PCI council.

There is room for further improvements to the PCI rules especially in the area of software applications development and the web. We recommend the following improvements after analyzing the recent breaches made possible by web site vulnerabilities. The recommendations cross-reference the PCI Data Security Standard (PCI-DSS) created by the PCI Security Standard Council. While the PCI Data Security Standard was developed to protect cardholder card data, the requirements are applicable for other personal identity data as well. In fact, many breaches that exploit non-compliance with the PCI-DSS are also found to be deceptive or unfair acts or practices regarding security that could cause substantial injury to consumers under Section 5 of the Federal Trade Commission Act, 15 U.S.C. Section 45. The FTC will frequently require actions under a Consent Order consistent with the PCI-DSS recommendations.

RECOMMENDATIONS

Secure Software Development and Best Practices

Those tasked with developing applications should be trained in secure software development and best practices regarding security. In particular, attention should be given to the PCI-DSS requirement 6.

Distinguishing Between the Roles of the Database Administrator and the Data Administrator

The data administrator should deal with business decisions while the database administrator deals with technical decisions. In particular, attention should be given to the PCI-DSS requirement 3.

Encryption of Information Assets

Data stored by the organization should be protected and where possible, encrypted. In particular, attention should be given to the PCI-DSS requirement 4.

Organizational Structure

A formal organization should exist that addresses information security and policy. A formal security policy should be developed, implemented and audited on a regular basis. The security policy should encompass all uses of technology as well as software development. In particular, attention should be given to the PCI-DSS requirement 12.

IT Audits

Recurring IT audits should be implemented and conducted by an organization independent of the software development and maintenance organizations, one that is trained to audit breaches that result from new methods of attack and comprise. In particular, attention should be given to the PCI-DSS requirements - 1, 2, 5, 7, 8, 9, 10 and 11.

National Retail Federation Proposal

The NRF proposal would also address the needs of both the small and large merchants. However, judging from the lukewarm manner that the credit card companies have responded to this proposal, it can also be assumed that they don't want to take over the burden of storing credit card data. The best path would be for the PCI council to outsource the provision of the requested services as requested by NRF to authorized vendors hereafter called authorized data stewards (ADS). They could be appointed along the same lines that the PCI council appointed the current approved scanning vendors (ASVs) and qualified security assessor (QSAs). The ADS will be responsible for storing and protecting data on behalf of the merchants, especially the small merchants. The

ADS can then craft a solution that takes over the burden of storing credit card data from the small merchants while giving the big merchants the option of either storing/protecting the data themselves or having the ADS do it for them as well. The ADS can implement a solution similar to the one suggested by NRF. Working systems using such technology are already on the market. One candidate method is already being run by a company called Shift4 Corporation (Mark, 2006). The next few paragraphs describe this method.

The core of this method involves the replacement of the credit card number with a token in all transactions after the first authorization request. The token is the same size as the credit card number. The last four digits of a credit card number become the first four digits of the token. The next 12 digits are a randomly generated set of characters that is unique to each transaction. The merchant will use the token as the primary key in the storage of all transactions. The ADS will store all transactions, mapping each unique transaction to its corresponding credit card number using the unique token. The modified transaction steps are as shown follows (Figure 1):

1. The customer initiates the transaction by swiping the credit card at the merchant's POS.
2. An authorization request is generated, encrypted and sent to the payment processor via the ADS Company. The payment processor sends back an authorization/decline to the ADS.
3. The ADS replaces the credit card number with the token and sends the token together with the authorization/decline back to the merchant.
4. The merchant gives the customer a receipt if approved and stores the transactions token in the POS system for use as a reference to handle customer returns or disputes.
5. The merchant can request additional charges to be made on the card (a customer-approved tip in a restaurant or a recurring bill payment setting) by sending the old token to the ADS. The ADS will regenerate the corresponding credit card number and send it to the processor for incremental charge.
6. A new token will be generated after authorization/decline from the processor and sent back to the merchant.

Figure 1. Proposed Payment Card System adapted from Shift4 (Mark, 2006)

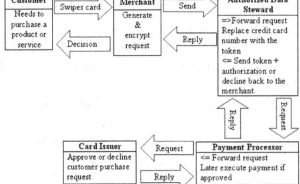

This system will only require slight adjustments to the equipment. The POS has to be reprogrammed to ask for and store the token instead of the credit card number. The token can be stored on the same field that the credit card number was stored since they are the same size. The net effect is that the small merchant will not have to store the credit card number. The request by the NRF to move the burden of storing credit card data from the merchants will have been achieved without overburdening the credit card companies.

CONCLUSION

The need for the protection of credit card data has never been greater. The introduction of the PCI DSS rules was a major step in the reduction of data breaches. However, experience has shown that more is required to address some of the developmental challenges that have hampered compliance.

The PCI council has developed recommendations which will assist organizations to improve data security. These recommendations cover practices which address the vulnerabilities of the systems adopted and implemented by organizations today. However, the PCI council now has an opportunity to take credit card data protection to the next level by giving the job of protecting credit card data to the professionals who have the knowledge and resources to do the job properly.

The recommendation regarding Secure Software Development and Best Practices states that those tasked with developing applications should be trained in secure software development and best practices regarding security. This training should not just be a stop gap effort; it needs to be an on-going effort and it requires the focus of management to assure that it is. It is important that the organization addresses information security and policy and continually audit its security and policies on an on-going basis.

The technology required is already available; all that is remaining is the political will to change the industry–not just getting the industry to adopt technical best practices and procedures, but to seek specific on-going improvement is the areas of organization and procedures - to not just apply remedial fixes to the current problem set, but to be able to anticipate and be prepared for future attempts to breach the security of the firm.

REFERENCES

Anley, C. (2002). *(more) Advanced SQL Injection*. Retrieved September 4, 2010, from http://www.ngssoftware.com/papers/more_advanced_sql_injection.pdf

Carr, J. (2008, May 1st). *Small Merchants Biggest Threat to Credit Card Fraud. S C Magazine*.

Chong, S. K. (2002). *SQL Injection Walkthrough*. Retrieved September 4, 2010, from http://www.scan-associates.net/papers/sql_injection_walkthrough.txt

Collins, H. (2008). *Cyber-Attackers Target Web Applications, Study Says*. Retrieved September 4, 2010, from http://www.govtech.com/gt/403627?topic=117671

TJX Companies, I. (2007). The TJX Companies, Inc. Announces Settlement Agreement with Visa U.S.A. Inc. and Visa Inc.; Estimated Costs Already Reflected in Previously Announced Charge. *Business Wire*.

PCI Compliance Guide. (2008). *PCI DSS: Five Guidelines for Gaining PCI Compliance*.

Council, P. C. I. (2008). *PCI Security Council to Release Version 1.2 of the PCI Security Standard in October 2008*. MA: Wakefield.

FTC. (2005). *DSW Inc. Settles FTC Charges*. Retrieved September 4, 2010, from http://www.ftc.gov/opa/2005/12/dsw.shtm

Goodin, D. (2007, October 24th). TJX Breach was Twice as Big as Admitted, Bank Says. *Channel Register*.

Hogan, D. (2007). *NRF to Credit Card Companies: Stop Forcing Retailers to Store Credit Card Data*. Wakefield, MA: National Retail Federation.

Identity Theft Resource Center. (2005). *2005 Disclosures of U.S. Data Incidents*. Retrieved September 4, 2010, from http://idtheftmostwanted. org/ITRC%20Breach%20Report%202005.pdf

Identity Theft Resource Center. (2006). *2006 Disclosures of U.S. Data Incidents*. Retrieved September 4, 2010, from http://idtheftmostwanted. org/ITRC%20Breach%20Report%202006.pdf

Identity Theft Resource Center. (2007). *2007 ITRC Breach Report*. Retrieved September 4, 2010, from http://idtheftmostwanted.org/ITRC%20 Breach%20Report%202007.pdf

Identity Theft Resource Center. (2008). *2008 ITRC Breach Report*. Retrieved September 4, 2010, from http://idtheftmostwanted.org/ITRC%20 Breach%20Report%202008.pdf

In the Matter of DSW Inc., a corporation: FTC File No. 052-3096 (United States of America Federal Trade Commission 2005).

La Roche, C., Dardick, G., & Flanigan, M. (2006). INFOSEC: What is the legal standard of care? *Journal of Business and Economic Research*, 4(7), 69–75.

Litan, A. (2007). *Proposed PCI Changes Would Improve Merchant's Data Security*. Stamford, CT: Gartner Incorporation.

Litan, A. (2008). *PCI Compliance Grows but Major Industry Problems Remain*. Stamford, CT: Gartner Incorporation.

Mark, H. (2006). *Storing Credit Card Data: A Look at the Business Needs, Regulations and Solutions Regarding the Issue*. Las Vegas, CA: Shift4 Corporation.

Messmer, E. (2007, November, 11th). PCI Compliance Mandate's Power Raises Conflict-of-interest Questions. *Network World*.

Navetta, D. (2008, April 22, 2008). The Legal Implications of the PCI Data Security Standard. *SC Magazine*.

Nolann, G. (2006, September). Seeking Compliance Nirvana. *ACM Queue; Tomorrow's Computing Today*, 71–72.

Office of the Privacy Commissioner of Canada, & Office of the Information and Privacy Commissioner of Alberta. (2007). *Report of an Investigation into the Security, Collection and Retention of Personal Information: TJX Companies Inc. / Winners Merchant International L.P.*

PCI Security Standard Council. (2006). *Payment Card Industry (PCI)*. Wakefield, MA: Data Security Standard.

PCI Security Standards Council. (2010). *PCI DSS 2.0 and PA-DSS 2.0 SUMMARY OF CHANGES - HIGHLIGHTS*. Retrieved September 4, 2010, from https://www.pcisecuritystandards.org/pdfs/ summary_of_changes_highlights.pdf

Richardson, J. E., & McCord, L. B. (2000). *Trust in the marketplace. Annual Editions: Business Ethics 2008/2009 20/e*. New York: McGraw-Hill.

Shift4 Corporation. (2008). *Credit Card 101*. Retrieved September 4, 2010, from http://www. shift4.com/players.htm

Swoyer, S. (2008). *SQL Injection Attacks on the Rise*. Retrieved September 4, 2010, from http:// redmondmag.com/articles/2008/08/13/sql-injection-attacks-on-the-rise.aspx?sc_lang=en

Tam, P.-W., & Sidel, R. (2007, Oct 2nd). Business Technology: Security-Software Industry's Miniboom; As Merchants Upgrade Systems to Meet New Rules, Tech Firms Benefit. *Wall Street Journal*.

Trustwave. (2008). *Trustwave Global Compromise Statistics: Quarterly Report March, 2008* Chicago, IL, USA.

VISA USA. (2006). *VISA USA Pledges $20 Million in Incentive to Protect Card Holder Data*. Retrieved September 4, 2010, from http://corporate.visa.com/media-center/press-releases/press667.jsphttp://corporate.visa.com/media-center/press-releases/press667.jsp

VISA USA. (2007a). *Level 4 Merchant Compliance Program*. Retrieved September 4, 2010, from http://usa.visa.com/download/merchants/level_4_merchant_compliance_program_062807.pdf

VISA USA. (2007b). *VISA Incorporation Card Holder Information Security Program*. Retrieved September 4, 2010, from http://usa.visa.com/merchants/risk_management/cisp_overview.html

VISA USA. (2008). *Visa USA Cardholder Information Security Program (CISP): PCI DSS Compliance Validation Update as of 12/31/2007*. Retrieved September 4, 2010, from http://www.usa.visa.com/download/merchants/cisp_pcidss_compliancestats.pdf

Chapter 10

Relationships between Information Security Concerns and National Cultural Dimensions:
Findings in the Global Financial Services Industry

Princely Ifinedo
Cape Breton University, Canada

ABSTRACT

This study investigates the relationships between the contextual factor of national culture and information security concerns in the global financial services industry (GFSI). Essentially, this study attempts to expand the breath of information provided in the recent 2009 Deloitte Touche Tohmatsu (DTT) survey, which reported such issues in the financial services industry. The inference from the 2009 DTT survey was that information security concerns across GFSI are being informed solely by industry-related standards or imperatives. As such, perceptions and attitudes towards such issues were thought to remain unchanged in differing contexts. Results from this study's analysis showed that the perceptions of information security concerns in GFSI compared reasonably well, but also varied by some national cultural attributes to debunk such a claim. Corporate managers in the industry may benefit from this research's findings as they formulate country-wide information security policies and strategies. As well, insights from this current effort indicate that it would be erroneous for practitioners to accept that entities in the financial services hold exactly the same view on information security issues in their industry. Future research avenues are discussed.

INTRODUCTION

It is a known fact that practitioners in the Global Financial Services Institutions (GFSI) are proactive in protecting customer data and thwarting emerging threats in their industry (Goodhue and Straub, 1991; Jung et al., 2001; Chen et al., 2008). In fact, one of the objectives of GFSI is to ensure that clients' data and information are not compromised. In other words, GFSI have an inherent need

DOI: 10.4018/978-1-60960-200-0.ch010

to be aware of the critical nature of information security (Goodhue and Straub, 1991; Kankanhalli et al., 2003). The description of GFSI as provided by the Deloitte Touche Tohmatsu (DTT) survey will be used in this work. In the DTT survey, GFSI included global financial institutions, banks, insurance companies, payment processors, and asset management companies. More precisely, a global financial services institution acts as an agent for its clients/customers (Johnson, 2000; Moshirian, 2007). It is worth noting that the term "GFSI" differs from the closely related phrase "global financial institutions", such as the World Bank and International Monetary Fund. The job of these bodies includes coordinating and regulating global financial systems at the international level (Alexander et al., 2004; Moshirian, 2007).

For businesses operating in the financial services industry, new technologies, business initiatives, and regulations often give rise to new threats and risks (Chaturvedi et al., 2000; Kankanhalli et al., 2003; DTT-Global Security Survey, 2009). A respondent in a recent DTT security survey comments, "New technologies and new business models are causing us to blindly run full speed toward the unknown. And the hot breath of threats and risk is on our necks at all times" (DTT-Global Security Survey, 2008, p. 1). The very essence of financial services business implies that various attempts must be made to secure clients' information and related resources. Kritzinger and Smith (2008, p. 224) notes that the "primary goal of information security is to protect information and ensure that the availability, confidentiality, and integrity of information are not compromised in any way." Schatz (2008, p. 94), however, asserts that "it is impossible to ever achieve a state of perfect security in which all risks are mitigated to a level that is acceptable to the business." What is advised is for corporate managers including those in the financial services industry to constantly assess their risk environments, gain an understanding of which risks need to be prioritized, and adjust their programs to address new security concerns

or threats (ISO/TR 13569, 2005; EDS, 2007; Schatz, 2008).

Threats and risks in the financial services industry may stem from both internal and external sources. Such threats can be either malicious or non-malicious in nature. Both, internal and external malicious threats can manifest in many forms, including the introduction of malwares, the theft of corporate secrets and information, and the corruption, deletion, and alteration of organizational data. This paper's focus is on internal non-malicious threats, which is understudied compared to malicious outsider threats (Theoharidoua et al., 2005; Walker, 2008; Willison and Siponen 2009). Internal non-malicious threats, encompasses human, operational, and organizational issues. Such threats can undermine the functioning and public standing of an organization if not properly managed (Goodhue and Straub, 1991; Theoharidoua et al., 2005; infoLock Technologies, 2006; Willison and Siponen 2009; Ifinedo, 2009). Examples of non-malicious internal threats include a lack of formal information security strategy, a lack of top executive support in dealing with security threats and risks, absence of commitment and funding for regulatory requirements, a lack of programs for managing privacy compliance, incompetent information security (IS) skills, and a lack of IS awareness programs, among others (Kankanhalli et al., 2003; Chang and Yeh, 2006; DTT-Global Security Survey, 2009).

The innate need to focus on information security concerns as well as gain an understanding of emerging threats in their industry have caused GFSI practitioners to start investigating and reporting such issues. The series of surveys conducted by DTT stand out in this regard (DTT - Global Security Survey, 2005; 2008; 2009). The first of the DTT surveys was published in 2003 and others have since followed. These surveys were designed to educate GFSI practitioners on IS security concerns, i.e. threats, risks, and compliance issues, compare in the global arena. A summary of the 2009 survey's findings is available online

(DTT - Global Security Survey, 2009). This present research effort paid attention to the financial services industry for two reasons. First, GFSI is one of the backbones of major economies around the world (Alexander et al., 2004; Johnson, 2000; Moshirian, 2007). Second, researchers (Goodhue and Straub, 1991; Jung et al., 2001; Kankanhalli et al., 2003; Chang and Yeh, 2006) have called for separate attention to be paid to the financial services sector as the industry's characteristics are somewhat different from other industries which also experience IS threats.

In fact, Kankanhalli et al. (2003) and Chang and Yeh (2006) found that significant differences exist across industries regarding the types and scope of information-related threats that each industry is vulnerable to (see also Jung et al., 2001). As a consequence, more useful insights will emerge by focusing attention on the realities in the GFSI industry. In the same vein, Goodhue and Straub (1991) offer several reasons why firms in the financial services sector may be more wary of breaches and threats relative to other businesses. The reasons they note include:

- Over-reliance on IS use in their operations
- Potential for large losses emanating from breaches in their operations;
- The need to maintain a good public image and assure the confidentiality and integrity of their data and IS assets.

The foregoing discussion offers insight as to why the perceptions of security concerns in the GFSI need not be lumped together with those of other industries. Of recent, scholars have started discussing IS security issues in the financial services industry (Chaturvedi et al., 2000; Ifinedo, 2008; Gupta and Sharman, 2008). Chaturvedi et al. (2000), citing the Information Security Industry Survey (1999), indicate that since 1998, upwards of 20 percent of financial institutions have suffered disruptions to their information and network systems. They add that "information security

[management], therefore, is a pivotal business and technical undertaking for any company involved [in] …. financial activities." In general, the thin volume of literature in this area partly motivates this present study.

Perhaps not intended, highlights in the 2009 DTT survey imply that the perceptions of, and attitudes toward information security concerns across GFSI are being informed solely by industry-related standards or imperatives. This thinking seems to suggest that contextual factors such as national culture, economy, and so forth may mean very little. Were this to be true, studies would not indicate that countries and even blocs of nations, for example, the European Union, establish different codes of conduct related to IS and security compliance issues, to enable them properly manage ensuing concerns in their contexts (Bia and Kalika, 2007; Chung et al., 2006; Chen et al., 2008). Further to this, contextual variables such as national culture have been reported to matter significantly in how individuals from differing cultural backgrounds accept new concepts and innovations (Shane 1993; Png et al., 2001; Straub et al., 2001; Waarts and van Everdingen, 2005; Erunbam and de Jong, 2006; Milberg et al., 1995; 2000; Chen et al., 2008)

Hofstede (2001) using different combinations of the dimensions of culture posit that organizational implicit model and views differ by country. In other words, individuals including managers in different countries have different conceptions about their organizations and issues inside them (Laurent, 1983). Prior studies have shown that country-to-country differences need to be considered when innovations and practices, including those related to IS security and privacy issues, are being discussed as well (Shane 1993; Milberg et al., 1995; 2000; Chen et al., 2008). This is because cultural norms, attitudes, and behaviors differ from one country to another (Hofstede, 2001; Dinev et al., 2009), and such differences may in some ways impact the perceptions of people on the issues being investigated.

Against this backdrop, this present research seeks to build upon the findings in the recent DTT survey as it aims to provide a layer of understanding not found in that survey. In particular, this current work is designed to examine relationships between national cultural factors and the perceptions of information security concerns by GFSI's employees in selected countries. The desire to explore this line of inquiry is informed by findings elsewhere which suggest that national cultural values are critical for organizations (and their employees) when adopting and implementing innovations and new practices, including those related to IS security concerns (Kankanhalli et al., 2004; Dinev et al., 2008; Ifinedo, 2009). Much remains to be learned about the specific nature of the relationships between cultural dimensions and information security concerns in the context of GFSI. As well, this present study seeks to complement the effort by Ifinedo (2009) who examined the relationships between national culture and perceptions of information security concerns with data obtained from the 2007 DTT survey. It can be argued that more studies are needed in this area to enhance theory development.

It is posited that country-to-country cultural differences are relevant, and should not be downplayed in the discourse of IS security concerns across GFSI. The study of the relevant literature indicates that only a handful of researchers (e.g., Milberg et al., 1995; 2000; Björck and Jiang, 2006; Schmidt et al., 2008; Dinev et al., 2008; Chen et al., 2008; Ifinedo, 2009) have written in this area. Similarly, IS security studies focusing specifically on financial services organizations have not been well represented in the extant IS literature. This present research is designed to make a contribution in both areas.

Specifically, the main objective of this research is to provide an answer to the following question: *What relationships exist between national cultural dimensions and information security concerns across GFSI?* It is hoped that this study's findings will enhance our understanding of such an issue.

This current study could also serve as a base for future investigations in the area. To the extent that new knowledge is sought and past insights reinforced, this research, to some extent, complements the emerging body of information related to the pertinence of national culture in the discourse of IS security and privacy management issues in modern organizations (Milberg et al., 1995; 2000; Björck and Jiang, 2006; Schmidt et al., 2008; Dinev et al., 2008; Ifinedo, 2009).

BACKGROUND OF THE STUDY

The advent of new technologies, the introduction of new business models, and the imposition of new government regulations have increased the threats and risks that modern organizations, including GFSI, face. As mentioned above, it is almost impossible to fashion a perfect security plan to mitigate every threat confronting an organization. What savvy corporate managers do is constantly assess their risk environments and adjust their security programs and policies accordingly (infoLock Technologies, 2006). Highly informed managers know that securing the future of their organizations is linked to how well emerging challenges are understood and subsequently contained (Ifinedo, 2009; Reinhold et al., 2009).

However, there are managers who still find it difficult to assess their risk environment and sensitize employees to information security issues (DTT - Global Security Survey, 2005; 2008; Chang and Yeh, 2006). According to the DTT - Global Security Survey (2005), about 45 percent of GFSI organizations do not adequately convey the importance of security concerns to their workers. In fact, information security awareness is one exercise among various organizational mechanisms used to contain insider or internal threat management concerns (e.g. infoLock Technologies, 2006). It can be equally argued that the inability to assess relevant security concerns and provide security awareness to employees may be inimical to the organization.

For the purpose of this study, *information security concerns* refer to threats, risks, and other vulnerabilities to IS assets in the GFSI. The scope of the definition is extended to privacy issues, which relevant literature notes are a major concern for financial services organizations (Jung et al., 2001; Kankanhalli et al., 2003; DTT - Global Security Survey, 2005; 2008). With such a broad background, it is necessary to describe the concept of risks and threats. ISACA (2006) defines risks as "events that negatively impact the accomplishment of business objectives". Regzui and Marks (2008, p. 243) cite the description of risk provided by the International Organization of Standardization (ISO) as "the potential that a given threat will exploit vulnerabilities of an asset or group of assets." A threat is an indication of an approaching or imminent danger; it could natural or man-made.

Published research on the general assessment of information security concerns in organizations is still evolving (Kritzinger and Smith, 2008; Chao et al., 2006; Sumner, 2009). Kritzinger and Smith (2008) suggest a framework for information security awareness for industry that covers both technical and non-technical issues. Chao et al. (2006) also offer an assessment of security controls for organizations. Sumner (2009) writes about the assessment of information security threats and the impacts on organizations and Hoesing (2009) discusses emerging security assessment techniques and tools in modern enterprises. The foregoing frameworks are generic and do not specifically address information security concerns in the financial services industry. This explains why they are not used in this current study. Further to this, it was decided that it will be worthwhile to scope this study's discussion to frameworks and guidelines that best fits its stated objective.

In that regard, relevant international bodies offer guidelines on how GFSI should assess or deal with emerging information security concerns in the industry. The ISO/TR 13569 (2005) has guidelines that address the development of an information security program for institutions in the financial services industry. Likewise, EDS (2007) recommends ways in which financial institutions could manage information risk and priority issues. The Control Objectives for Information and Related Technology (COBIT) guidelines from ISACA (2006) can also be tailored to the needs of GFSI. As well, a modified version of the Carnegie Mellon's Capacity Maturity Model (CMMI) can be used for assessing security programs in GFSI. Insights from the work of Schatz (2008) as well as items from the 2009 DTT survey permit us to suggest that both the CMMI and COBIT models informed the composition of items used for the DTT survey. The 13 information security concerns investigated and reported in the 2009 DTT survey are highlighted in Table 1.

The Deloitte Touche Tohmatsu (DTT) Survey and Findings

Deloitte Touche Tohmatsu (DTT) is an international firm that provides audit, tax, consulting, and financial advisory services to both public and private clients. DTT has a global network of member firms in 140 countries. The financial services sub-unit of the organization employs more than 1,500 partners and 17,000 financial services professionals in more than 40 countries. Over the past five years, this sub-unit has used its contacts, networks, and reach to research IT security concerns and issues in GFSI around the world. The first survey issued by the financial services sub-unit appeared in 2003 and four others have since followed (see DTT - Global Security Survey, 2005; DTT - Global Security Survey, 2008). Participants in the 2009 DTT study came from 31 countries and almost all regions of the world, i.e., Asia Pacific (AP) excluding Japan (JP), Europe, the Middle East & Africa (EM), Latin America and the Caribbean Region (LC), and North America (NA). The exclusion of Japan

Table 1. Summary of information security concerns in GFSI across regions

No.	Security concern	AP	JP	EM	NA	LC
#1	Respondents who feel that security has risen to executive management and/or board as a key imperative	77%	79%	70%	63%	78%
#2	Respondents who feel they have commitment and funding to address regulatory requirement	69%	65%	56%	58%	63%
#3	Respondents who indicated that they had a defined and formally documented information security strategy	62%	50%	64%	62%	68%
#4	Respondents who feel that information security and business initiatives are appropriately aligned	31%	30%	32%	28%	40%
#5	Respondents who indicated that their information security budget has increased	54%	25%	60%	65%	75%
#6	Respondents who indicated that their expenditures and information security were 'on plan' or 'ahead of requirements' based on the organization's current needs	31%	5%	50%	26%	59%
#7	Respondents who incorporated application security and privacy as part of their software development cycle	38%	40%	26%	32%	41%
#8	Respondents who feel they presently have both the required competencies to handle existing and foreseeable security requirements	23%	25%	41%	33%	33%
#9	Respondents whose employees have required at least one training and awareness session on security and privacy in the last 12 months	58%	90%	64%	82%	82%
#10	Respondents who have an executive responsible for privacy	23%	85%	58%	82%	24%
#11	Respondents who have a program for managing privacy compliance	38%	84%	43%	76%	18%
#12	Respondents who have experienced repeated internal breaches over the last 12 months	33%	17%	26%	27%	30%
#13	Respondents who have experienced repeated external breaches over the last 12 months	58%	17%	49%	51%	50%

Source: DTT-Global Security Survey (2009). The abbreviations used for the regions are provided in the paper.

from the Asia Pacific region would suggest that Japan's perceptions on theme differ significantly from the regional aggregates.

Other information in the 2009 DTT survey pertinent to this study are as follows: Their data came from 169 major GFSI, of which 29% were among the top 100 global financial institutions, 26% were among the top 100 global banks, and 14% were among the top 50 global insurance companies. The annual revenues of the respondent companies ranged from less than $1 billon to over $15 billion. The unit of analysis of the DTT survey was the organizational level of each institution. In that regard, responses from knowledgeable members such as Chief Information Security

Officers and Chief Security Officers were used. They were asked to give perceptions representative of their organizations' views or standing on the issues being investigated. Perhaps due to space limitations, the authors of the survey reported aggregate results/responses for each of the regions, which they implied provides a rough indicator of security concerns for countries in each region.

A full list of the participating counties in the DDT survey is not available online; however, DTT researchers have obliged this current study with a list of all countries in the 2009 survey. The countries and regions sampled in this study are diverse. The regions' data is shown in Table 1. It is important to relate the items in Table 1 to the issues being discussed in this study. Some of the examples of non-malicious insider threats that GFSI could encounter have been adequately reflected. For example, the absence of commitment and funding for regulatory requirements, a lack of formal information security strategy, and lack of programs for managing privacy compliance, correspond to items numbered #2, #3, and #11, respectively on Table 1.

National Cultural Values

To anthropologists, culture represents the fabric of meaning through which a society interprets the events around it (Bodley, 1994). Hofstede (2001, p. 21) defines culture as "the collective programming of the mind which distinguishes the members of one group from another." Culture relates to the habitual method of doing things over time. It is a product of assimilation, rather than of inheritance (Hofstede, 2001). Chen et al. (2008) note that competitive strategies, educational systems, training approaches, symbols, values, and managerial approaches to security issues have cultural underpinnings. Country-level adoption of innovation and new concepts does not occur in a cultural vacuum (Hofstede, 2001; Waarts and van Everdingen, 2006; Steers et al., (2008). Studies have confirmed the nexus between technological advancement, innovations, acceptance of new concepts, on the one hand, and national culture, on the other (e.g., Shane 1993; Png et al., 2001; Straub et al., 2001; Waarts and van Everdingen, 2005; Erunbam and de Jong, 2006). Similar results have been report in previous IS security studies as well (Björck and Jiang, 2006; Ifinedo, 2008)

How does cultural value compare across nations or countries? Several researchers have presented relevant, useful schemas and conceptualizations in the area (see Hall and Hall, 1990; Trompennaars, 1993; Bodley, 1994; Hofstede, 2001). However, the work of Hofstede (2001) has been widely recognized as the most dominant framework for studying technology-related issues in the context of culture and vice versa (Straub et

al., 2001; Myers and Tan, 2002; Ford et al. 2004). It is important to note that Hofstede's typology is not without criticism. Some have questioned the notion of aligning national culture with territorial boundaries (Myers and Tan, 2002) and others (e.g. Ford et al. 2003; Srite and Karahanna, 2006) express doubts as to its relevance to IS-related research. Despite its shortcomings, Hofstede's cross-cultural indices continue to be popular among IS researchers (Png et al., 2001; Waarts and van Everdingen, 2006; Erunbam and de Jong, 2006; Dinev et al., 2009) who use it to compare and contrast relevant perceptions across cultures. Studies related to IS security and privacy issues have used it as well (e.g., Milberg et al., 1995; 2000; Björck and Jiang, 2006; Chen et al., 2008; Dinev et al., 2008).

Of note is the fact that Hofstede's framework provides a lens for developing *a priori* knowledge, and comparisons of different national cultural contexts with relevant issues (Ford et al. 2003). The four main cultural dimensions in Hofstede's typology are briefly described below. Each dimension is described using descriptions obtained from a webpage dedicated to the work of Hofstede at: http://www.geert-hofstede.com/ geert_hofstede_resources.shtml (ITIM, 2010). Table 2 shows the scores of each dimension for the countries selected from the DTT 2009 security survey.

- **Power Distance Index (PDI):** "focuses on the degree of equality, or inequality, between people in the country's society. A high Power Distance ranking indicates that inequalities of power and wealth have been allowed to grow within the society" (ITIM, 2010).

- **Individualism (IDV):** "focuses on the degree the society reinforces individual or collective achievement and interpersonal relationships. A high Individualism ranking indicates that individuality and individual rights are paramount within the society. Individuals in these societies may

Table 2. The cultural dimensions' scores used in the study

Region	Country	PDI	IND	MAS	UAI
Asia Pacific, excluding Japan	India	77	48	56	40
	Indonesia	78	14	46	48
	Malaysia	104	26	50	36
Japan	Japan	54	46	95	92
Europe and Middle East	Germany	35	67	66	65
	Israel	13	54	47	81
	Switzerland	34	68	70	68
North America	Canada	39	80	52	48
	United States	40	91	62	46
Latin and Caribbean	Colombia	67	13	64	80
	Mexico	81	30	69	82
	Chile	63	23	28	86

tend to form a larger number of looser relationships. A low Individualism ranking typifies societies of a more collectivist nature with close ties between individuals" (ITIM, 2010).

- **Masculinity (MAS):** "focuses on the degree the society reinforces, or does not reinforce, the traditional masculine work role model of male achievement, control, and power. A high Masculinity ranking indicates the country experiences a high degree of gender differentiation. A low Masculinity ranking indicates the country has a low level of differentiation and discrimination between genders" (ITIM, 2010).

- **Uncertainty Avoidance Index (UAI):** "focuses on the level of tolerance for uncertainty and ambiguity within the society: i.e. unstructured situations. A high Uncertainty Avoidance ranking indicates the country has a low tolerance for uncertainty and ambiguity. A low Uncertainty Avoidance ranking indicates the country has less concern about ambiguity and uncertainty and has more tolerance for a variety of opinions" (ITIM, 2010).

The chosen countries from the 2009 DTT survey for this present study, though limited in number, is culturally diverse. Using the classification of implicit models of the organization that was used by Hofstede (2001) to categorize countries around the world into four main categories, the present study's data sample include the following four cultural subsets: village market (e.g., the US and Canada), family (e.g., India, Indonesia, and Malaysia), well-oiled machine (e.g., Germany, Israel, and Switzerland), and pyramid of people (e.g., Mexico, Colombia, and Chile). It is worth noting here that the two main national cultural dimensions used in the foregoing classification are the measures of uncertainty avoidance and power distance, which a recent IS security study found to be two most relevant dimensions to IS security concerns (Chen et al., 2008). Indirectly, the foregoing information buttresses the argument on the representative and relevance of the used data sample.

PROPOSITIONS FORMULATION

Hofstede's (2001) work indicates that countries with low uncertainty avoidance scores tend to be associated with low levels of anxiety. Perhaps as a consequence, individual's risk-taking behaviors in such countries tend to be higher than those of counterparts from high uncertainty avoidance countries. Evidence also shows that individuals from higher risk-tolerance countries are more willing to accept and use security technologies than people from countries lagging on such attributes (Chen et al., 2008; Dinev et al., 2009). Furthermore, countries exhibiting low uncertainty avoidance tendencies tend to be averse to the adoption of innovations (Hofstede, 2001). This observation extends to IS security-related innovations (Milberg et al., 1995; 2000). According to Dinev et al. (2009, p.397), "individuals in stronger uncertainty avoidance cultures often attempt to minimize risk by following established rules and norms." Against this backdrop, it might be expected that the perceptions and assessment of information security concerns will be higher for individuals in high uncertainty avoidance index (UAI) score compared to the views of counterparts from low UAI scores countries. Thus, it is proposed that:

P1: GFSI respondents in high "uncertainty avoidance" countries will exhibit higher perception levels for the information security concerns investigated.

Individuals in collectivist cultures tend to curtail individual preferences, needs and priorities in lieu of the group's interests (Hofstede, 2001). In contrast, countries with high individualism indicators accentuate individual preferences and interests. In fact, prior studies have shown that countries of the world with higher individualism– i.e. low IND scores–tend to have higher capabilities for adopting new practices and innovations (Shane, 1993; Myers and Tan, 2002; Erunbam and de Jong, 2006). Countries that emphasize individualism also tend to exhibit the belief that everyone has the right to privacy. Thus, any interference with an individual's privacy is usually

not condoned (Walczuch et al., 1995; Hofstede, 2001). The study by Walczuch et al. (1995) also showed that countries having cultural attributes underscoring individual dignity tend to uphold information privacy and security concerns at all levels. With respect to the assessment of information security concerns, it is posited that there will be marked variations in the views of GFSI employees across both sub-cultures, i.e. individualistic and collectivist. It is therefore proposed that:

P2: GFSI respondents in high "individualistic" countries will exhibit higher perception levels for the information security concerns investigated.

People in low power distant index (PDI) countries are self-oriented and they believe in taking initiatives on their own (Hofstede, 2001). To some extent, evidence suggests that people from high PDI scores countries might have an inclination towards following or taking initiatives from those with influence or authority. For example, individuals from such countries may want to try out a new idea or adopt some technological innovation if convinced of the usefulness of such concepts. In contrast, it is possible that individuals conditioned for, or inclined towards accepting initiatives from leaderships might wait for inputs on such decisions. Hofstede (2001) reported that technological adoption is higher in countries with a low-power index. Similarly, Waarts and van Everdingen (2006, p. 305) note that "centralized decision structures, authority and the use of formal rules are often the characteristics of organizations in countries with a high degree of power distance." New ideas and innovations tend to diffuse faster in countries with a low "power distance" (Shane, 1993; Png et al., 2001). Thus, in countries with high power distance scores, employees are expected to take initiatives from those in authority. This is not true for counterparts in low-power distance countries who respond with spontaneity (Hofstede, 2001). With regard to the power distant index and information security issues, Björck and Jiang (2006) found differences between two dissimilar countries when respondents in each assessed IS security implementations.

P3: GFSI respondents in high "power distance" countries will exhibit higher perception levels for the information security concerns investigated.

According to Hofstede's typology, people in masculine (MAS) cultures emphasize goal-achievement attributes more than those from more feminine societies. Thus, individuals from a more achievement oriented culture tend to accept activities or support policies that maximize their personal gains, and to some degree, their organization's aspirations as well. Consistent with Hofstede's theory, employees of GFSI based in countries with relatively high masculinity index scores would readily accept and adopt instituted policies and initiatives in their organizations that enhance stated objectives and other achievements than colleagues in countries with sub-cultures where such values are not highly regarded. Kovačić (2005, p. 147) asserts that: "it could be argued equally well that in a country with high masculinity there would also be a positive attitude toward implementing information and communication technologies [and new ideas related to IS security management] if these technologies improve performance, increase the chance of success and support competition, which are all key factors of a masculine culture." It is likely that the acceptance of new practices, including those related to IS security concerns will be lower in less-masculine cultures. Björck and Jiang (2006) found that the masculinity dimension to be a significant differentiator in the assessment of IS security implementation issues in the two differing countries that they studied. It is therefore postulated that information security concerns of employees in GFSI from countries with differing MAS scores will vary significantly. It is proposed that that:

P4: GFSI respondents in high "masculinity" countries will exhibit higher perception levels for the information security concerns investigated.

DATA SOURCES AND RESEARCH METHODOLOGY

As already mentioned, the study's data came from secondary sources. The thirteen (13) information security concerns and issues used in the survey are presented in Table 1. The cultural dimensions of each of the sampled countries were taken from Hofstede (2001); these are highlighted in Table 2. The cultural dimension indexes for each country are available online; please see (ITIM, 2010). The sample of 12 countries taken from the 2009 DTT survey, though small, is sufficient for an exploratory such as this one. Other researchers (e.g. Kovačić, 2005; Bagchi et al., 2006) have used limited samples of diverse countries to investigate comparable themes.

Although this study is exploratory in nature, its analysis of data obtained from multiple sources does not pose a major problem. The use of the multiple-sourced data for correlation analysis serves the study's objective in two main ways: a) it permits possible associations between selected variables to be examined; b) as this is a preliminary study, results from this present endeavor are intended to inform subsequent inquiries in the area. It is not presented herein as the conclusive observation on the matter. More importantly, the information security concerns in the financial services industry reported in the 2009 DTT survey compared reasonably well with those published by other practitioners for the industry (see e.g. PricewaterhouseCoopers, 2008). Thus, the reliability of the main data is assured. SPSS 15.0 was used for data analysis. Person's correlation analysis was used to assess the strength of the relationships between the study's variables.

It is worth mentioning here that an attempt was made to perform a longitudinal analysis with the data that has been accumulated over the years in the DTT surveys. This, however, was impossible because the DTT security surveys had changing information security concerns over the years (see DTT-Global Security Survey, 2005; 2008; 2009). This fact is in line with commonsense given that information security concerns have been known not to remain never static (Kritzinger and Smith; 2008; Schatz, 2008). This reality meant that this paper had to use a cross-sectional data of the 2009 DTT data.

DATA ANALYSIS AND RESULTS

With regard to relationships between the 13 information security concerns and four (4) dimensions of national culture used in the study, the analysis showed that 18 correlations yielded statistically significant results. Note that there are 52 (13 * 4) possible relationships in the correlation matrix. The correlation results are highlighted in Table 3 (the numbers in bold fonts are the ones with statistically significance results). Thus, we can say that about one third of the relationships yielded meaning results. Each of the significant

Table 3. The correlation matrix

Item	Security concern	PDI	IND	MAS	UAI
#1	Respondents [in GFSI] who feel that security has risen to executive management and/or board as a key imperative	**.685(*)**	**-.888(**)**	.025	.220
#2	Respondents [in GFSI] who feel they have commitment and funding to address regulatory requirement	**.892(**)**	**-.699(**)**	.081	-.168
#3	Respondents [in GFSI] who indicated that they had a defined and formally documented information security strategy	-.007	-.254	**-.589(*)**	.197
#4	Respondents [in GFSI] who feel that information security and business initiatives are appropriately aligned	.132	**-.661(**)**	-.226	**.612(**)**
#5	Respondents [in GFSI] who indicated that their information security budget has increased	-.035	-.231	-.391	.228
#6	Respondents [in GFSI] who indicated that their expenditures and information security were 'on plan' or 'ahead of requirements' based on the organization's current needs	-.128	-.183	-.363	.259
#7	Respondents [in GFSI] who incorporated application security and privacy as part of their software development cycle	**.794(*)**	**-.721(**)**	.031	.130
#8	Respondents [in GFSI] who feel they presently have both the required competencies to handle existing and foreseeable security requirements	**-.788(*)**	.395	-.146	.235
#9	Respondents [in GFSI] whose employees have required at least one training and awareness session on security and privacy in the last 12 months	-.064	-.227	.069	**.597(**)**
#10	Respondents [in GFSI] who have an executive responsible for privacy	**-.718(*)**	**.822(**)**	.208	-.002
#11	Respondents [in GFSI] who have a program for managing privacy compliance	-.228	**.707(**)**	.327	-.246
#12	Respondents [in GFSI] who have experienced repeated internal breaches over the last 12 months	**.601(*)**	-.403	**-.686(*)**	-.303
#13	Respondents [in GFSI] who have experienced repeated external breaches over the last 12 months	.205	-.079	**-.714(*)**	**-.643(*)**

** Correlation is significant at the 0.01 level (2-tailed).

* Correlation is significant at the 0.05 level (2-tailed).

relationships will be discussed in the next section. It is important to clarify that the aim of the study's analysis is to shed light on the possible relationships between the variables. This present study is not designed to establish causality among the variables.

DISCUSSIONS

The main objective of this study is to investigate possible relationships between the perceptions of information security concerns across GFSI and the dimensions of national culture. The study found 18 significant relationships between the variables in the study. This shows that about 35 percent (i.e., 18/52*100%) of the items in the correlation matrix offer further meaningful insights. The areas in which salient differences were noticeable are noted as follows:

1. The correlation analysis revealed that item #1 (Respondents in GFSI who feel that security has risen to executive management and/or board as a key imperative) were more prevalent in countries with relatively high power distant index scores. That is, GFSI employees in countries with high PDI scores may hold the belief that the management of information security risks and threats should not be left in the hands of junior executives. GFSI employees in countries more masculine values may hold the belief that risks, threats, and uncertainties can be attenuated by elevating the status of such issues within the organization. In contrast, the perceptions of counterparts from countries with low power distant appear to indicate a different point of view on the matter. With respect to the cultural dimension of power distance, the data is suggesting that the views of GFSI employees across the sampled countries vary considerably. This observation is consistent

with the proposition stated above on this aspect.

2. The result of the Pearson correlation also showed that the responses for item #2 (Respondents who feel that information security issues have risen to executive management and/or board as a key imperative) were higher for countries with relatively low individualistic scores (i.e. countries with collectivist cultures). Surprisingly, the need for oversight from top executives with regard to information security concerns of GFSI across sampled countries appeared to be higher in more individualist cultures. This finding is inconsistent with Hofstede's theory indicating that collectivist societies would defer to those in leaderships roles for guidance on key matters. This insight is not in tune with proposition stated above.

3. The data showed that item #2 (Respondents who feel they have commitment and funding to address regulatory requirement) were more prevalent in countries with relatively high power distant index (PDI) scores. It is expected that those in the position of influence would commit resources to ideas that they are familiar and comfortable with. In that light, given that information security issues receive the attention of more executive management in countries with relatively high PDI scores, it is not surprising that commitment and funding for regulatory requirement were higher in such countries. To some degree, this information offers preliminary support for the positive association between high PDI scores and higher levels of concern for information security commitment and funding. This finding is consistent with stated predictions.

4. The results indicated that item #2 (Respondents who feel they have commitment and funding to address regulatory requirement) were higher for countries with relatively low individualist index scores.

This information permits the suggestion that the views of financial services firms based in more individualist societies is that they have less need to look up to those in leadership roles to show commitment and provide needed resources for their information security programs more than counterparts from collectivist sub-cultures. This knowledge is not novel; others (Shane, 1993; Myers and Tan, 2002; Erunbam and de Jong, 2006) have implied that entities from individualistic have more capacity for driving such initiatives (i.e. providing necessary support and resources for technological innovations and new ideas) than counterparts in more collectivist societies. Although, the particular finding lends some support to observations elsewhere; however, it does not affirm the claim in its related proposition above. Further investigations in the area may be needed.

5. The result of the Pearson correlation showed that the number of "Respondents who indicated that they had a defined and formally documented information security strategy" (#3) was lower for countries with relatively high masculinity index scores, and vice versa. This result is somewhat unexpected given that the masculinity index provides information as to individual performances on achievement and control related issues. (It has to be noted that views from this work are preliminary in nature). Nonetheless, it is logical to expect that well defined and formally crafted information security strategies would facilitate control structures that could enhance both individual achievement and organizational objectives. A result supporting a positive relationship between this particular information security concern and the masculinity index score would have been consistent with the rationale behind the stated proposition above.

6. The data showed that the responses for item #4 (Respondents who feel that information

security and business initiatives are appropriately aligned) were more prevalent in countries with relatively low individualistic index scores (i.e. more collectivist countries). This result is at variance with findings elsewhere suggesting that the ability to adopt new ideas, practices and innovations tend to be higher in countries with low individualistic index score (Shane, 1993; Walczuch et al., 1995; Hofstede, 2001; Erunbam and de Jong, 2006). In that regard, this result contradicts the claim in the above stated proposition. Further investigation is needed to explain this uncovered observation.

7. This result revealed that numbers of "Respondents who feel that information security and business initiatives are appropriately aligned" (#4) were higher for countries with relatively high uncertainty avoidance index scores. This result is expected. As it is already known, the business climates of GFSI are often fraught with risks, threats, and uncertainty. To militate against such anomalies, GFSI practitioners that operate in more risk-averse countries of the world must appropriately align their business strategies and initiatives with their information security strategy. The fact that more respondents from high uncertainty avoidance countries feel their organizations have responded accordingly is in tune with established reasoning and insight. This finding is supportive of the stated proposition on this front.

8. The data showed that item #7 (Respondents who incorporated application security and privacy as part of their software development cycle) were higher for countries with relatively high power distant index (PDI) scores. This indicates that the perceptions of GFSI employees from countries where power inequality is a concern tend to incorporate more information security matters into their business applications development process than counterparts from low PDI scoring

countries. Again, control issues, including those designed to oversee software development processes would be more readily incorporated where power inequality exists. The result is consistent with the stated prediction.

9. The result of the Pearson correlation showed that "Respondents who incorporated application security and privacy as part of their software development cycle" (#7) were less common in individualistic countries. Once more, this result seems to be at odds with observations from elsewhere (e.g., Walczuch et al., 1995; Erunbam and de Jong, 2006) where it has been shown that the opposite hold true. That is, the result indicating that the perceptions of GFSI's respondents from more collectivist societies for this particular item are contrary to known views. More studies may be needed to illuminate knowledge of this association.

10. The data analysis seems to be indicating that item #8 (Respondents who feel they presently have both the required competencies to handle existing and foreseeable security requirements) were in greater number in countries with low power distant scores. Apparently, this result does not seem to support the suggested positive association between the study' variables. However, the result lends adequate support to observations elsewhere (Shane, 1991; Walczuch et al., 1995; Hofstede, 2001; Erunbam and de Jong, 2006) suggesting that countries in Europe and North America classified under the organizational models of the village market (e.g., the US and Canada) and the well-oiled machine (e.g., Germany, Switzerland) have relatively higher levels of instituting innovative and technological competencies, including those related to information security requirements, in this case.

11. The correlation analysis revealed that item #9 (Respondents whose employees have required at least one training and awareness session on security and privacy in the last 12 months) were in greater number in countries with high uncertainty avoidance index scores. The result could be interpreted to mean that general perception levels of information security concerns of GFSI employees from more risk tolerant countries being already higher than those of counterparts from elsewhere makes it more likely for them to appreciate the importance of training and awareness sessions in so far as such facilities help them cope with emerging threats. Thus, it makes sense for such a variation to be observed for both groupings given their differing risk tolerance, expectations, and attitudes. This result supports the above stated proposition.

12. The correlation analysis revealed that item #10 (Respondents who have an executive responsible for privacy) in their organizations were in greater number in countries with relatively low power distant index scores. This is an unexpected result. Consistent with Hofstede's conceptualization, it would seem reasonable to expect more respondents from parts of the world where authority figures are expected to lead to indicate to have an executive responsible for directing or overseeing privacy concerns in their organizations. On the contrary, the data seems to be indicating that there is more need among GFSI employees form low power distant countries, for such an executive. In some respects, the studies by Walczuch et al. (1995) and Milberg (1995; 2000) seem to echo a result similar to one the reported here.

13. The data indicated that "Respondents who have an executive responsible for privacy" (#10) in their organizations were more prevalent in countries with high individu-

alist index scores. Others (e.g. Walczuch et al., 1995; Milberg, 1995; 2000; Chen t al., 2008) have reported that privacy issues tend to be higher in individualist countries than collectivist ones. Thus, this result is consistent with prediction.

14. The results showed that item #11 (Respondents who have a program for managing privacy compliance) were more numerous in countries with relatively high individualist index scores. This information is consistent with findings in the extant IS security and related literature (Walczuch et al., 1995; Milberg, 1995; 2000), and therefore in tune with the relevant stated proposition above.

15. The data showed that item #12 (Respondents who have experienced repeated internal breaches over the last 12 months) were higher in countries with high power distant index scores. The indication of the positive association between the information security concern and this dimension of national culture is in line with the above stated proposition.

16. The result of the Pearson correlation showed that "Respondents who have experienced repeated internal breaches over the last 12 months" (#12) were prevalent countries low masculinity index scores. Such countries also appear to be the ones with higher risk-taking propensities. Thus, it is possible that the employees of GFSI in such countries might have been involved in greater business engagements (internal and external) than counterparts in less risk tolerant countries. It is reasonable to infer that those that might have been involved in more business engagements may be more susceptible to greater number of breaches. It has to be noted that in information gleaned from the DTT survey does not engender an authoritative proclamation in this matter.

17. The data analysis indicated that item #13 (Respondents who have experienced repeated external breaches over the last 12

months) tend to exist more in countries with relatively low individualistic index scores. A similar line of argument as the one presented for the preceding item may seem applicable for this particular item.

18. The correlation analysis results showed that "repeated external breaches over the last 12 months" (#13) were more prevalent in cultures with more tolerance for uncertain situations and risks. Counterparts from less risk tolerant parts of the world seemed to have reported fewer breaches. This finding, though significant, does not permit a robust discussion due to the limited information in the DTT survey for the item.

The data analysis indicates that the most statistically significant relationships were seen between selected information security concerns and the cultural dimensions of power-distance and individualism-collectivism. On the evidence of that, it is posited that perceptions of information security concerns in GFSI seem to be significantly associated with the interplay of power and the attainment of individual goal or achievement. It is somewhat surprising that uncertainty avoidance and masculinity attributes did not yield as much statistical significance as the other two dimensions of national culture. Recent studies by Björck and Jiang (2006) and Chen et al. (2008) showed that cultural dimensions of individualism and power distant are critical and deserving of attention in comparative cross-cultural studies focusing on IS security issues. To the extent that the foregoing insight is considered valid, the preliminary findings in this exploratory effort serve to support such a claim, at least in the context of the relationships between key information security concerns and cross-cultural values.

Before discussing the implications of the study, it is acknowledged that there are limitations to this research. This study is a preliminary study that has used data from secondary sources. As a consequence, it inherits perhaps all limitations from the DTT survey as well those in Hofstede's conceptualization of national culture. For example, the DTT survey researchers did not provide information about the distribution of the participants. The sample size of 12 countries, though sufficient for an initial investigation such as this one, could benefit from an increased sample size that would enhance generalizability. Further, this study was impelled to work with a cross-section of data; longitudinal studies may offer an enriched insight to this present work.

With regard to the DTT survey, the respondents in the survey were mainly from management teams; the views of lower level employees seemed not to be considered. This is limiting as both groups' views on IS-related issues often differ considerably (Ifinedo and Nahar, 2006). Thus, it is difficult to say with certainty that the findings in the DTT study can be generalized across all work groups. The lower level workers' opinion on key information security concerns in GFSI should be considered to enhance insight. The authors of the 2009 DTT survey did not provide information regarding the following: The sample size in each country, the gender mix of respondents, their ages, educational levels, and so on. The absence of such information limits the survey's results. Further to this, data analysis might have been more robust, had the data been presented on the Likert scale rather than in percentages. The diversity of GFSI used in the DTT survey might also be problematic. It is possible that opinions in the banking sector may be different from those in the area of insurance. With regard to the cultural dimension variables, there is a fundamental flaw in Hofstede's work, wherein "culture" in a nation-state is assumed to be monolithic (Myers and Tan, 2002). It is a known fact that in any single nation, there are many different cultures. In the light of the aforementioned limitations, the results discussed herein need to be interpreted with caution.

In spite of the study's limitations, this research effort adds to the growing body of knowledge on the assessment and perception of information security concerns in the financial services indus-

try and the relevance of national cultural values and norms. This preliminary investigation offers implications to both researchers and practitioners. The findings discussed above are an interesting read for practitioners who are alerted to the relevance of such contextual factors as national cultural values in their perceptions of information security issues. The paper highlighted areas where significant relationships were observed between the study's variables. In the context of this study's data, no meaningful results (i.e. variations) were seen for two items (i.e., #5 and #6) across the four cross-cultural factors. This would imply that perceptions of, and attitudes of GFSI employees toward those particular items compared perfectly.

Areas in which variations exist across the board are discussed and highlighted above. In general, given that about one third of the possible relationships showed statistical significance, it can be noted that this reality seems to be affirming the inference in the financial services industry that perception of information security compare reasonably well. Namely, GFSI (and their employees) almost adopt the same standards, practices, procedure as well as views on information security concerns in their industry. Consequently, attention needs to be paid to areas where variations were noticed (as listed above). GFSI managers may benefit from this information, and may use such as input for decision-making in the industry, especially as they implement IS security policies across countries in which they have operations. While it may be true that GFSI uphold compare view of information security issues, it is equally a reality that this is not completely true for all issues and concerns. This realization need to be understood by corporate managers in the financial services industry.

With respect to research, this effort complements the emerging studies focusing on information security assessment in modern organizations, in general (Goodhue and Straub, 1991; Kritzinger and Smith, 2008) and information security issues in financial services industry, in particular (Kankanhalli et al., 2003; Chen et al., 2008; Ifinedo, 2008).

As well, it enhances insights in prior studies that have examined the nexus between information security and privacy issues and national cultural values (Schmidt et al., 2008; Chen et al., 2008; Dinev et al., 2008; Ifinedo, 2009). As noted above, this study, in some respects, adds credence to observations about the pertinence of power distance and individualistic-collectivist indices as items of interest in the discourse of information security concerns vis-à-vis national cultural norms. Furthermore, this work lends support to Hofstede's (2001) views suggesting that prevailing perceptions and attitudes in organizations could be linked to national cultural conditioning. The observed variations in the study's variables, even for this limited sample, seem to point in that direction. As the study's data is limited, it is not possible to authoritatively ascertain whether the same differences or similarities could be noticed for other groups of countries, not considered in this study, when the relationships between information security issues and national cultural dimensions are assessed.

Future research directions may want to know whether national cultural values affect how information security concerns in GFSI are assessed or prioritized. Areas inconsistent with the stated propositions herein need further reexaminations. Studies could be designed to elaborate on some of the findings in this study; such studies could combine both quantitative and qualitative methodologies to enhance insight. Future studies could consider applying the aforementioned IS security assessment frameworks proposed Kritzinger and Smith (2008), Chao et al. (2006), and Sumner (2009) to the financial services industry to further enhance understanding in the area. The impacts of other contextual factors such as educational standards, national economic wealth, organizational managerial practices and individual attitudes towards information security compliance could also be investigated. Future study may consider using the Likert scale to facilitate research replication.

CONCLUSION

One of the critical obligations of practitioners in the financial services industry is to protect information and ensure that the availability, confidentiality, and integrity of information are not compromised in any way. New technologies, regulations, business models and other emerging threats and concerns in the industry make it almost impossible for a perfect state of security to be achieved. Nonetheless, it is advisable for corporate managers to constantly assess their risk environments, gain an understanding of what risks need to be prioritized, and adjust their programs to address new security concerns or threats. Global financial services practitioners, realizing the need to focus on information security concerns in their industry, have started to investigate and report such issues for their industry. This present study uses information provided in the 2009 DTT survey (i.e. practitioners' annual investigation of key security issues in their industry) to provide a layer of understanding, not provided in that particular survey. This present study examined the possible relationships between four cross-cultural dimensions and thirteen identified information security items. The data analysis found significant statistical relationships between some of the variables, and none for others. From the perspective of global IS security management research and practice, this research serves following objectives: a) it draws the attention management of GFSI to areas where variations may exist between countries when it comes to the perceptions of information security concerns; b) it complements the growing body of knowledge on IS security concerns vis-à-vis national culture, and c) it can be used as a baseline for future inquiry. It is not suggested that the findings presented in this preliminary investigation represent the final word in the area. More work is expected.

REFERENCES

Alexander, K., Dhumale, R., & Eatwell, J. (2004). *Global governance of financial systems. The International Regulation of Systemic Risk*. New York: Oxford University Press Inc.

Bagchi, K., Kirs, P., & Cerveny, R. (2006). Global software piracy: can economic factors alone explain the trend? *Communications of the ACM, 49*(6), 70–75. doi:10.1145/1132469.1132470

Bank of Japan. (2007). *The importance of information security for financial institutions and proposed countermeasures*. Retrieved Jan 6, 2008, from: http://www.boj.or.jp/en/type/release/zuiji/kako02/data/fsk0004b.pdf. 2007.

Bia, M., & Kalika, M. (2007). Adopting an ICT code of conduct: an empirical study of organizational factors. *Journal of Enterprise Information Management, 20*(4), 432–446. doi:10.1108/17410390710772704

Björck, J., & Jiang, K. W. B. (2006). *Information Security and National Culture: Comparison between ERP System Security Implementations in Singapore and Sweden*.Master Degree thesis submitted at the Royal Institute of Technology, Sweden.

Bodley, J. H. (1994). *Cultural Anthropology: Tribes, States, and the Global System*. Mountain View, CA: Mayfield Publishing.

Chang, A., J-T & Yeh, Q-J. (2006). On security preparations against possible IS threats across industries. *Information Management & Computer Security, 14*(4), 343–360. doi:10.1108/09685220610690817

Chao, S.-C., Chen, K., & Lin, C.-H. (2006). Capturing industry experience for an effective information security assessment. *International Journal of Information Systems and Change Management, 1*(4), 421–438. doi:10.1504/IJISCM.2006.012048

Chaturvedi, M., & Gupta, M. Mehta, S., & Valeri, L. (2000). *Fighting the wily hacker: modeling information security issues for online financial institutions using the SEAS environment, Proceedings of Inet 2000*. Retrieved Jan. 14, 2008 from: http://www.isoc.org/inet2000/cdproceedings/7a/7a_4.htm.

Chen, C. C., Medlin, B. D., & Shaw, R. S. (2008). A cross-cultural investigation of situational information security awareness programs. *Information Management & Computer Security, 16*(4), 360–376. doi:10.1108/09685220810908787

Dinev, T., Goo, J., Hu, Q., & Nam, K. (2009). User behaviour towards protective information technologies: the role of national cultural differences. *Information Systems Journal, 19*(4), 391–412. doi:10.1111/j.1365-2575.2007.00289.x

DTT-Global Security Survey. (2005). *The Global Security Survey, 2006, Deloitte Touche Tohmatsu (DTT)*. Retrieved Jan 14, 2009 from: http://www.deloitte.com/dtt/cda/doc/content/CA_FSI_2006%20Global%20Security%20Survey_2006-06-13.pdf.

DTT-Global Security Survey. (2008). *The Global Security Survey, 2007, Deloitte Touche Tohmatsu (DTT)*. Retrieved January 14, 2009 from: http://www.deloitte.com/dtt/cda/doc/content/ca_en_Global_Security_Survey.final.en.pdf.

DTT-Global Security Survey. (2009). *The Global Security Survey, 2008, Deloitte Touche Tohmatsu (DTT)*. Retrieved June 20 from: http://www.deloitte.com/dtt/cda/doc/content/dtt_en_fsi_GlobalSecuritySurvey_0901.pdf.

EDS. (2007). *Eight Financial Services Security Concerns*. Retrieved May 10, 2008 from: Http://www.eds.com/news/features/3620/. 2007.

Erunbam, A. A., & de Jong, S. B. (2006). Cross-country differences in ICT adoption: a consequence of culture? *Journal of World Business, 41*(4), 302–314. doi:10.1016/j.jwb.2006.08.005

Ford, D., Connelly, C., & Meister, D. (2003). Information systems research and Hofstede's culture's consequences: An uneasy and incomplete partnership. *IEEE Transactions on Engineering Management*, *50*(1), 8–25. doi:10.1109/TEM.2002.808265

Goodhue, D. L., & Straub, D. W. (1991). Security concerns of system users: a study of the perceptions of the adequacy of security. *Information & Management*, *20*(1), 13–22. doi:10.1016/0378-7206(91)90024-V

Gupta, M., & Sharman, R. (2008). *Social and Human Elements of Information Security*. Hershey, PA: Idea Group Inc (IGI).

Hall, E. T., & Hall, M. R. (1990). *Understanding Cultural Differences*. Yarmouth, ME: Intercultural Press.

Hofstede, G. (2001). *Culture's Consequences: Comparing Values, Behaviors, Institutions, and Organizations across Nations* (2nd ed.). Thousand Oaks, CA: Sage Publications.

Ifinedo, P. (2008). IT Security and Privacy Issues in Global Financial Services Institutions: Do Socio-economic and Cultural Factors Matter? *Sixth Annual Conference on Privacy, Security and Trust (PST2008)*, In cooperation with the IEEE Computer Society's Technical Committee on Security and Privacy, Fredericton, New Brunswick, Canada, October 1 - 3, 2008.

Ifinedo, P. (2009). Information Technology Security Management Concerns in Global Financial Services Institutions: Is National Culture a Differentiator? *Information Management & Computer Security*, *17*(5), 372–387. doi:10.1108/09685220911006678

Ifinedo, P., & Nahar, N. (2006). Do Top and Mid-level Managers View Enterprise Resource Planning (ERP) Systems Success Measures Differently? *International Journal of Management and Enterprise Development*, *3*(6), 618–635.

Information Security Industry Survey. (1999). *Information security magazine*. Retrieved Jan 14, 2008 from: http://www.infosecuritymag.com/, July 1999.

ISACA(2006). Information Systems Audit and Control Association manual, 2006 edition.

ISO/TR 13569 (2005). *Financial services - Information Security Guidelines*. http://www.iso.org/iso/iso_catalogue/catalogue_tc/catalogue_detail.htm?csnumber=3724.

ITIM. (2009). *Geert Hofstede Cultural Dimensions*. http://www.geert-hofstede.com/hofstede_dimensions.php. Retrieved June 20th.

Johnson, H. J. (2000). *Global Financial Institutions and Markets*. Malden, MA: Blackwell Publishing.

Jung, B., Han, I., & Lee, S. (2001). Security threats to Internet: A Korean multi-industry investigation. *Information & Management*, *38*(8), 487–498. doi:10.1016/S0378-7206(01)00071-4

Kankanhalli, A., Teo, H. H., Tan, B. C. Y., & Wei, K.-K. (2003). An integrative study of information systems security effectiveness. *International Journal of Information Management*, *23*(2), 139–154. doi:10.1016/S0268-4012(02)00105-6

Kritzinger, E., & Smith, E. (2008). Information security management: An information security retrieval and awareness model for industry. *Computers & Security*, *27*(5-6), 224–231. doi:10.1016/j.cose.2008.05.006

Laurent, A. (1983). The cultural diversity of Western conceptions of management. *International Studies of Management and Organization*, *13*(1-2), 75–96.

Milberg, S., Burke, S., Smith, H. J., & Kallman, E. A. (1995). Values, personal information privacy, and regulatory approaches. *Communications of the ACM*, *38*(13), 65–74. doi:10.1145/219663.219683

Milberg, S., Smith, H. J., & Burke, S. (2000). Information privacy: corporate management and national regulation. *Organization Science, 11*(1), 35–57. doi:10.1287/orsc.11.1.35.12567

Moshirian, F. (2007). Financial services and a global single currency. *Journal of Banking & Finance, 31*(1), 3–9. doi:10.1016/j.jbankfin.2006.07.001

Myers, M. D., & Tan, F. B. (2002). Beyond Models of National Culture in Information Systems Research. *Journal of Global Information Management, 10*(1), 24–32.

Pontus, E., & Erik, J. (2008). Assessment of business process information security. *International Journal of Business Process Integration and Management, 3*(2), 118–130. doi:10.1504/IJBPIM.2008.020975

PricewaterhouseCoopers. (2008). *The Global State of Information Security Survey 2008.* http://www.pwc.com/extweb/home.nsf/docid/c1cd6cc69c2676d4852574da00785949.

Rezgui, Y., & Marks, A. (2008). Information security awareness in higher education: An exploratory study. *Computers & Security, 27,* 241–253. doi:10.1016/j.cose.2008.07.008

Schatz, D. (2008). Setting priorities in your security program. In Tipton, H. F., & Krause, K. (Eds.), *Information Security Management Handbook.* Boca Raton, FL: Taylor & Francis Group.

Schmidt, M. B., Johnston, A. C., Arnett, K. P., Chen, J. Q., & Xi'an, S. L. (2008). A cross-cultural comparison of U.S. and Chinese computer security awareness. *Journal of Global Information Management, 16*(2), 91–103.

Shane, S. A. (1993). Cultural influences on national rates of innovation. *Journal of Business Venturing, 8*(1), 59–73. doi:10.1016/0883-9026(93)90011-S

Srite, M., & Karahanna, E. (2006). The role of espoused national cultural values in technology acceptance. *Management Information Systems Quarterly, 30*(3), 679–704.

Straub, D. W., Loch, K. D., & Hill, C. E. (2001). Transfer of Information Technology to Developing Countries: A Test of Cultural Influence Modeling in the Arab World. *Journal of Global Information Management, 9*(4), 6–28.

Sumner, M. (2009). Information Security Threats: A comparative analysis of impact, probability, and preparedness. *Information Systems Management, 26*(1), 2–12. doi:10.1080/10580530802384639

Trompennaars, F. (1993). *Riding the Waves of Culture.* London: The Economist Books.

Walczuch, R. M., Singh, S. K., & Palmer, T. S. (1995). An analysis of the cultural motivations for transborder data flow legislation. *Information Technology & People, 8*(2), 37–57. doi:10.1108/09593849510087994

Chapter 11
Information Security by Words Alone:
The Case for Strong Security Policies

Kirk P. Arnett
Mississippi State University, USA

Gary F. Templeton
Mississippi State University, USA

David A. Vance
Olivet Nazarene University, USA

ABSTRACT

Effective information security extends beyond using software controls that are so prominently discussed in the popular and academic literature. There must also be management influence and control. The best way to control information security is through formal policy and measuring the effectiveness of existing policies. The purpose of this research is to determine 1) what security elements are embedded in Web-based information security policy statements and 2) what security-related keywords appear more frequently. The authors use these findings to propose a density measure (the extent to which each policy uses security keywords) as an indicator of policy strength. For these purposes, they examine the security component of privacy policies of Fortune 100 Web sites. The density measure may serve as a benchmark that can be used as a basis for comparison across companies and the development of industry norms.

INTRODUCTION

Daily reports of personal information losses provide a poignant reminder of what has become one of the top security issues for the American public. For citizens, the risks loom large regardless of the precautions that are undertaken. Strategies to protect our personal information appear in all major news media. As personal information safety risks grow, so does the abundance of media advertising, postal mail, and Web-based hints available to us as to how to best protect our personal information.

We rely on businesses that have access to our personal information to protect it, and unfortunately, the protection efforts of businesses commonly fail, and we see far too many stories relating the loss of masses of personal informa-

DOI: 10.4018/978-1-60960-200-0.ch011

tion in the military, government, business, and education. Undoubtedly, business, legislative, and personal efforts are underway that promise to strengthen protection efforts. One concern lies in how effective these efforts will be.

Following widely publicized data breaches at business behemoths *AOL* and *AT&T*, *EWeek* (2006) reports on a *Ponemon Institute* study stating that two-thirds of IT professionals claim to be ineffective at the prevention of data breaches. Recently, Seltzer (2008) questioned "Can you trust *TRUSTe*?" *TRUSTe*, an organization that provides symbols of trust on the Internet and serves as a guardian of the privacy protection policy enforcement for Web sites, has come under fire as a result of allowing, what appears to be, a significant breach of individual privacy when they certified *Coupons, Inc. Coupons* violated numerous privacy standards by hiding misleading named files in the registry and by creating misleading named files in Windows™ that store information about the computers on which they reside, yet maintained full *TRUSTe* certification. The open power of the Web has allowed creation of CVV2 (Card Verification Value 2) Web sites that sell others' credit card numbers for different amounts depending on the amount of credit allowed on the card. In the legislative arena there have been several efforts aimed to encourage businesses to improve information and asset protection. Better known federal efforts include GLBA, HIPAA, and Sarbanes-Oxley, and there are also lesser known state laws as well. The *Electronic Privacy Information Center (EPIC)* presents the federal government's effort to control corporate information privacy (see http://www.epic.org/privacy/bill_track.html for real-time updates on legislative efforts underway in the U.S. Senate and House). Individuals too are making personal efforts to better patrol the collection and use of their own information, and are rightly concerned about the efforts that business is making to protect personal information.

ADDRESSING THE PROBLEM

U.S. businesses have a strong interest in data protection and the efforts that are underway to protect the personal information of its customer community. From a business standpoint, policy is used to specify the company's approach to security. Management selects and implements technology, but it is policy that guides and coordinates the selection and implementation of technologies. Security policy issues ranked sixth in an international survey of 874 certified information system security professionals (Knapp, Marshall, Rainer, and Morrow, 2006). There is no evidence that the importance of security policies should or will change in the foreseeable future.

Web-based security policies must reach beyond protecting against the threats of hackers and must extend to the causes of and solutions to insider threats. These Internal security breaches often result from worker stress brought on by organizational change or unpredictability. Events that may trigger internal breaches include "reengineering, downsizing, upsizing, mergers or acquisitions, rapid changes in markets or the economy, litigation, organized labor actions, and other traumatic phenomena" (Parker, 1996, p. 21). Although a company safeguards personal information from traditional hackers, there is evidence from the authoritative *CSI Annual Security Survey* respondents that more serious problems exist as "insider attacks edged out virus incidents as the most pressing security problem" (Richardson, 2007, p. 2).

Companies are sharing information with the public and communicating their protection efforts to the public, not only through Web site privacy policies, but also by U.S. mail, agreement forms, advertisement, etc. The flip side of this information sharing is that the public also has an interest in the policies that businesses are using for information protection. Some of these policies are widely available because they are posted on Web sites. But, as noted in a study of large U.K. organizations, although policies are common, there is considerable variety in their content (Fulford and Doherty, 2003). Because of the differences, questions that might still remain with consumers are:

- Does the business have a policy?
- What does the policy say?
- Is the policy weak or strong?
- Does the business follow its policy?

ANALYZING SECURITY POLICIES

Written policies can be analyzed by individual elements called "policy features," which are the bases for how consumers and businesses use them. Policy features are determined by examining the words contained in the policies and words are what Oliver Wendell Holmes Jr. called the "skin of a living thought." (Wordsmith, 2003) The answer to the last question above -- does the business follow its policy -- can only be determined by audit, and if the answer is *no*, then the preceding three questions are moot. But, we may examine the "skin" of policies using a content analysis approach, and this approach may be used to answer the first three questions regarding existence, content, and strength on the policy. We use a custom-developed application for this analysis which examines the wording of the Fortune 100 Web site policies by matching each word against a list of words that appear in the security suggestions part of the FTC Web site. This is a modification of a non-obtrusive data collection method applied to Fortune sites by Liu and Arnett (2002). The output from this match represents what we might *expect* in security policies based on the use of strong words or phrases used elsewhere to connote security.

Among large businesses, such as those of the *Fortune 100*, Web site privacy policies commonly contain security policy elements. The security elements provide a good starting place to examine the skin of information security in the business. Each Web site of the *Fortune 100* was visited and its policy then cut and pasted into a single data set.

This dataset was sanitized to remove extraneous material and then each of the business names was separated for begin-end recognition.

The FTC security information Web site provided a baseline keyword list that connotes security. The complete set of keywords is: access, anti-virus, backup, careless, child-predator, compromise, contingency, continuity, crime, disaster, firewall, flood, hacker, infection, misuse, password, pornography, precaution, predator, prevent, proprietary, protect, recover, risk, safeguard, safety, secure, sensitive, steal, threat, virus, worm. To illustrate the presence of these keywords in practice, a selected Fortune 100 Web site policy fragment shown below contains underlines for the words that match those selected for the FTC keyword list:

The threats *to the* security *of your information are varied – from computer* hackers *to disgruntled employees to simple* carelessness*. While* protecting *computer systems is an important aspect of information security, it is only part of the process. Here are some points to consider – and resources to help – as you design and implement your information security plan.*

Once the FTC keyword list was obtained, each of the Fortune Web site policies was searched for a match with each of the keywords or their derivatives (e.g. secure, secures, secured, security). This match yields for each Web site policy 1) which keywords are used, how many times each of the keywords is used, and 3) a density measure derived from the number of keyword occurrences in the target policy divided by total number of words. This third measure, although simple and possibly flawed because it includes counts of words such as *and, or, not, the*, etc., in the denominator, still provides a basis of comparison.

Of the 100 businesses contained in the data, 62 of their primary homepages contained usable security-related statements in their privacy policies. The remaining sites' policies were solely related to privacy and not security and thus had no relationship to the information security aspect of personal information. Rather, these 38 sites described only what information was collected, how that information could be shared, and how an individual might avoid having his or her information collected. The resulting text file consisted of 114,610 words (an average of 1849 words per policy statement). The example below illustrates the matched keywords (underlined) found in a snippet of the Washington Mutual Web-site policy.

We know that when you share your personal information online, <u>security</u> is of the highest priority. Be assured that Washington Mutual shares your concern and employs able sophisticated <u>security</u> methods. The instant you sign in to your <u>secure</u> Personal or Business Online Banking account, your user ID and <u>password</u> are encrypted using <u>Secure</u> Sockets Layer (SSL) technology. This <u>precaution</u> is intended to <u>prevent</u> anyone other than yourself and Washington Mutual from <u>accessing</u> your information.

From this policy snippet, we find that the following five keywords, with number of occurrences in parentheses. This is the method used in our analysis.

Secure (4); Password(1); Precaution(1); Prevent(1); Access(1)

Table 1 shows the policy word analysis for the entire *Fortune 100* based on the 114,610 words and the 62 Web sites that contained usable security-related statements in their privacy policies. The table illustrates the five most prevalent keywords that are used in Fortune policies, the number of times that each of the words is used in total, and the number of sites that used the keyword. Finally, the density of the keyword is presented in the rightmost column. This density is computed based on the occurrence of the word in policies where it appeared relative to the total number of words in all policies. Although the original target list included thirty-two keywords, these five keywords are the only ones that occur more than 20 times, and the arbitrary FTC keyword selection had 13 keywords that did not occur at all in the Fortune policies. Note that the data in this analysis might also be used to judge individual policy strength based on the density of all of the keywords in a particular site's policy divided by the total number of words in the site's policy so that it would be possible to state that site A, for instance, exhibits a stronger protection policy site B.

DISCUSSION

This analysis can be described as being logic-driven because it begins with the assumption that Fortune businesses will use their Web sites to promulgate information security policies to users, and that these policies will contain words similar to those that are used in FTC warnings to consumers. But, there are weaknesses with the logic-driven analysis used here. These include

Table 1. Top five most popular keywords in fortune 100 site policies

Keyword	Total Occurrences	Number of Sites	Density
Secure	314	59	0.274
Protect	114	44	0.099
Safeguard	47	31	0.041
Password	41	20	0.036
Prevent	22	14	0.019

1) the absence of context and 2) the arbitrary selection of keywords from the FTC consumer site. As the keywords are not analyzed in context, a contrary statement such as "we do not *protect* your information" would still register as a match for the keyword *protect*. The FTC statement selection, while clearly devoted to security warnings and recommendations, is not intended to represent taxonomy of security related words and certainly some important words are missing. For instance, in E-commerce environments we would expect to see *encrypted* or *SSL*, but this is not a part of the text used to form the keyword file.

Despite these limitations, these results can be used as a guide or standard of measure for policy strength, and a likeness of this density metric could be automatically generated. As noted in the study by Fulford and Doherty (2003), policy content exhibits great variety. This variety calls for analysis into the precise meaning of policy words and we believe that a word analysis metric can be a major component of such an analysis. Further, the questionable enforcement practices of *TRUSTe* strongly suggest that additional efforts are needed to examine and explain policies. The keyword density metric provides a starting base from which researchers might launch additional efforts to evaluate efforts that businesses are taking via security policy to be better stewards of consumer personal information. Yet, more needs be done. For example, the absence of specific security-related information in 38 of the Fortune 100 privacy policies begs questions -- is corporate America increasing stated security measures via policy?, and if, so to what degree is the increase taking place?

CONCLUSION

Approximately two-thirds of the Fortune 100 companies specify personal information security measures in their Web-based privacy policies. There is great variety in the wording used in these policies, and some of the words that are used seem to connote stronger degrees of security. If Web-based policies form one base of trust for consumers, then they should be crafted in such as a way as to be both understandable and meaningful. If these Web-based policies are following a fixed format, then we must insure that the words in these templates produce greater consumer confidence. More importantly, business must be committed to policy enforcement and there must be adequate external verification of policy content and actions or the words will have no meaning to readers. Additional study will be needed to determine what words and which word occurrences best convey confidence while maintaining truthfulness. As with other standards, policy wording will require cooperative efforts among government, business and consumers. If it is standards that we must create to achieve confidence, we must consider Andrew Tannenbaum's quip in Wordsmith (2003) that "The nice thing about standards is that there are so many of them to choose from." Standards alone will not solve the problem or personal information compromise that has become so prevalent, but they may very well be used to create a starting base for a policy, and the metrics used here may in this way measure the "sincerity" of the policy via count and density of policy statements words.

REFERENCES

FTC. 2008. Federal Trade Commission. Facts for Business. http://www.ftc.gov/bcp/conline/pubs/buspubs/security.shtm. Visited July 29, 2008.

Fulford, H., & Doherty, N. F. (2003). The Application of Information Security Policies in Large UK-based Organizations: An Exploratory Investigation. *Information Management & Computer Security*, *11*(3), 106–114. doi:10.1108/09685220310480381

Hines, M. (2007, December 18-25). Insuring against data loss. *EWeek the Enterprise News-weekly, 23*(50), 13.

Knapp, K. J., Marshall, T. E., Rainer, R. K. Jr, & Morrow, D. W. (2006). The Top Information Security Issues Facing Organizations: What can Government do to Help? *EDPACS: The EDP Audit. Control & Security Newsletter, 34*(4), 1–10.

Liu, C., & Arnett, K. (2002). Raising a Red Flag on Global WWW Privacy Policies. *Journal of Computer Information Systems, 43*(1), 117–127.

Parker, D. B. (1996). Information Security Controls for an Organization Undergoing Radical Changes. *Information Systems Security, 5*(3), 21–25.

Richardson, R. (2007). CSI Computer Crime and Security Survey. *Computer Security Institute.* Available from http://gocsi.com. Visited January 16, 2008.

Rothberg, D. (2006). *IT Pros Say They Can't Stop Data Breaches.* http://www. eweek.com/article2/0,1895,2010325,00. asp?kc=EWSTEEMNL083106EOAD, August 30, 2006. Visited July 29, 2008.

Seltzer, L. (2008). Can you trust TRUSTe? *PC Magazine Security Watch.* March 24, 2008, http://blogs.pcmag.com/securitywatch/2008/03/ can_you_trust_truste.php. Visited July 29, 2008.

Wordsmith (2003). http://wordsmith.org/awad/ archives/0303. Quote from Oliver Wendell Holmes, Jr. visited September 15, 2007.

This work was previously published in International Journal of Information Security and Privacy (IJISP), edited by Hamid Nemati, pp 84-89, copyright 2009 by IGI Publishing (imprint of IGI Global)

Chapter 12
The Social Network Structure of a Computer Hacker Community

Xubin Cao
Southwestern University of Finance and Economics, China

Yong Lu
Pennsylvania State University, USA

ABSTRACT

Computer hackers, both individually and as a group, have been identified as a primary threat to computer systems, users, and organizations. Although hacker groups are complex socio-technical systems, much extant research on hackers is conducted from a technical perspective and at an individual level of analysis. This research proposes a research model composed of five dimensions and their relations in order to study hacker's social organization in the whole socio-technical context. Based on this model, the researcher applies network analysis methods to disclose the structure and patterns of a significant and complex hacker group, Shadowcrew. Network analysis tools are applied for data processing and data analysis. Three network measures: degree centrality, cognitive demand, and eigenvector centrality, are utilized to determine the critical leaders. Out-degree centrality is employed to analyze the relations among the five dimensions in the research model.

INTRODUCTION

Identity theft and financial fraud conducted by hackers have evolved into serious and pervasive threats to consumers and the financial services industry (Furnell, 2002). Computer hackers, both individually and as a group, have been identified as a primary threat to computer systems and users. The CSI Computer Crime & Security Survey, the world's most widely quoted survey on computer crime, found that financial fraud, password sniffing, and malware infection cost organizations the most, with an average loss close to $289,000 for each respondent's organization (Richardson, 2009).

Academic research from a variety of disciplines has contributed to our understanding of the hacker's attack methods (Furnell, 2002), subculture (Thomas, 2002), and motivations (Taylor, 1999). Previous studies by Meyer (1989) and Holt

DOI: 10.4018/978-1-60960-200-0.ch012

(2005) found that hackers were colleagues who had relatively loose social networks that they could share information and introduce subcultural norms to new hackers. However, much extant research on hackers is conducted at the individual level of analysis. Few studies examine hackers operating in group or network contexts to reveal their social relationships and organizational patterns within hacker communities. Straub *et al.* (2008) have noted that few projects have taken from a behavioral and sociological point of view to effusively address the human aspects associated with effective decision-making for security.

Besides, considering the advancement and rapid development of computer technology and information security industry over the past decade, it is entirely possible that the nature and structure of hacker's social organization have changed. For instance, hackers have become involved in online terrorism (Williams, 2001) and organized crime (Kleen, 2001). The rapid developments of e-commerce, data warehousing, and data aggregation services have made hacking activities profitable. Hackers who once might have broken into computer systems out of curiosity or for bragging have turned to exploiting financial gains. An underground economy has developed where hackers and criminals buy and sell credit card numbers and bank account information. Hackers have shifted toward a "professionalization" of computer crimes (Richardson, 2007).

Facing the new trends in hacker groups and their activities, it is timely and important to study hacker's social network structure (Parsky, 2006). This study proposes a research model including five dimensions and their relations to study hacker's social organization. This model allows us to have a novel perspective on the social organization of hacker groups and place hackers in the whole network context to examine relations such as hacker to hacker, hacker to technology, and hacker to resource. Understanding social organizational structure of hacker groups enables us to identify vulnerabilities of the network and we have a much

better chance to thwart hacker criminal activities. This research examines a criminal hacker network, Shadowcrew, to disclose its fundamental social structure that hackers used to organize themselves to pursue hacking activities.

The remainder of this article is organized as follows. Section 2 reviews the previous research on hacker's social organization. A research model and research questions are proposed in Section 3. Section 4 is the research methodology, including data collection and data processing. Section 5 is the data analysis and results. Lastly, the researcher concludes the study in Section 6 and suggests future research directions.

SOCIAL ORGANIZATION OF HACKERS

Best and Luckenbill (1980) define social organization as the patterns of relationships among people and social organization as a network of social relations. The focus of social organization study is "a group or a pattern of social interaction, rather than the individual or the society" (Best and Luckenbill, 1994, p. 4). Therefore, the social organization of deviants refers to "the patterns of relationships among deviant actors involved in the pursuit of deviance" (p. 11). Studies of the social organization of deviants inform our understanding of the social aspects of them. Most deviants have relationships with one another and form associations. Thus, the social organization perspective allows researchers to consider how these relationships form, persist, and operate (Best and Luckenbill, 1994).

Best and Luckenbill (1994) offer a comprehensive theoretical framework for understanding the social organizational features of deviants. They classify five basic forms of deviants according to the dimension of organizational sophistication: loners, colleagues, peers, teams, and formal organizations. These organizational forms are defined in terms of four variables: mutual association,

Table 1. Characteristics of social organization of deviants

Form of Organiza-tion	Characteristic			
	Mutual association	Mutual participation	Elaborate Division of labor	Extended organization
Loners	No	No	No	No
Colleagues	Yes	No	No	No
Peers	Yes	Yes	No	No
Teams	Yes	Yes	Yes	No
Formal organizations	Yes	Yes	Yes	Yes

mutual participation, elaborate division of labor, and extended organization (Table 1).

Loners are the least sophisticated form, as they do not associate with other deviants and do not participate in deviant acts together. Colleagues differ from loners because they associate with fellow deviants. Peers not only associate with one another, but also participate in offenses together. Teams require an elaborate division of labor. Finally, the most sophisticated form, formal organizations, involves mutual association, mutual participation, an elaborate division of labor, and deviant activities extended over time and space (Best and Luckenbill, 1994).

Based on Best and Luckenbill's framework (1980), a study by Meyer (1989) found that hackers were colleagues, because they formed a subculture and shared information, but did not participate in hacking with others. Holt (2005) also applied Best and Luckenbill's framework to study the subculture and social organization of hackers. He found that hackers tended to perform hacks alone, but had loose social networks to share information and introduce subcultural norms to new hackers.

Although previous studies have provided great insight into the values and beliefs that hackers hold, they have limitations that need to be addressed. First of all, much extant research on hackers is conducted at the individual level and analyzes their relationships from an individual hacker's standpoint. They only study the elements from an individual hacker's perspective, treating elements

such as technology, knowledge, and resource as the characteristics or attributes of a hacker. These elements are not placed and analyzed in the context of the whole hacker community. Therefore, prior studies cannot answer these fundamental questions for social organization study: In what basic ways do hackers organize themselves to pursue their hacking activities? What conditions facilitate the development and transformation of hacker organizational forms? (Best and Luckenbill, 1994)

In addition, several researchers suggest that hackers have grown more sophisticated and may now in some instances constitute teams. In fact, several hacker groups appear to meet the team criteria, including the Chaos Computer Club, the Cult of the Dead Cow, and the l0pht (Furnell, 2002). There is also growing evidence that hackers are involved in organized crime (Williams, 2001), and terrorist groups (Kleen, 2001). A new pattern emerged: hacker's groups became profit-driven and exploited the holes of commercial and financial systems.

Given these limitations of previous research and new trends of hacker groups, it is vital to examine the social organization of criminal hackers with a new approach to build our understanding of the current nature of hackers' organizational relations and patterns.

RESEARCH MODEL AND RESEARCH QUESTIONS

Research Model

I propose a research model to study the social organization of hacker groups. The research model is based on the meta-matrix, an ontology defined by Carley (2002; 2003). Meta-matrix is an approach to representing the state of an organizational structure as the set of entities (agent, resources, and tasks, etc) and the relations among them. It is an extensible ontology such that new entity classes and new classes of relations can be added as needed. This model is composed of five dimensions for a hacker network: Agent, Technology, Resource, Action, and Role (Figure 1).

The following is the detailed explanation for the five dimensions and their relations.

Agent

Agent is an individual member of the hacking network or community, and is the central dimension of a hacker network. Agents need to supply themselves with whatever technology and resources are available, and conduct certain actions to accomplish their goals, with delegated responsibilities and different roles in the network.

Technology

Technology is the computing tools and skills for hacking activities, particularly computer and communications technology. Technology is the fundamental dimension of a hacker network. From the literature review, both the hacker and hacker community could not exist without technology, and technology has played a pivotal role in the formulation of hacker social networks (Taylor, 1999; Thomas, 2002). Hackers believe that technology can be turned to new and unexpected purposes, which underpins hacker's collective imagination (Jordan and Taylor, 1998).

Resource

The hacker community use Resource as channels to obtain equipment, new opportunities for engaging in hacking activities, and strategies for avoiding sanctioning.

New web communication tools, such as YouTube, MySpace and Facebook, make it much easier for hackers to communicate and collaborate. Hackers utilize these resources to recruit

Figure 1. Research model for hacker network

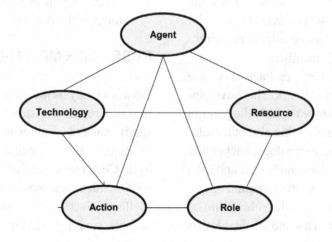

and socialize newcomers, providing training and information as well as an ideology which accounts for and justifies their activities. Besides, the wide spread of the knowledge and resources on hacking skills makes the situation worse. People can go to YouTube and easily find hacking video lessons such as "How to create real virus in 20 seconds" and "How to take a site down in under 5 min."

Action

Action means hacking activities that hackers commit. Certain types of Action include attacking computer systems, collecting system and network information, controlling computer devices, and conducting illegal selling or purchasing.

Role

Role is the position and responsibility that hackers take in their network. Some hacker networks are characterized by delegated responsibility and by routine and steady levels of productivity. In many ways, hacker networks share the same features which characterize such respectable formal bureaucracies as military organizations, churches, and business firms. They have a hierarchal division of labor, including both vertical and horizontal differentiation of positions and roles and established channels for communication. Their actions are coordinated to efficiently handle hacking activities and tasks on a routine basis. They may contain several departments with positions for administrators, coordinators, enforcers, dealers, and general members.

This research model places hackers in the context of whole hacker network. This novel approach allows us to examine not only the relation between hackers and hackers, but also other relations such as hacker and technology, hacker and resource, hacker and action, and hacker and role.

Understanding network structures and operations makes it easier to identify vulnerabilities of the hacker network. This model enables us to identify key agents who carry out the various network functions. Critical leaders in a network are ones that generally have a high level of importance and a low level of redundancy (Williams, 2001). If these agents are removed and there are no readily available communication links, then the hacker network could be severely disrupted. This model also allows us to differentiate the critical leaders and their relations to technology, resources, and activities, which makes it possible to isolate these key agents from technology and resources and thus remove the crime opportunities. This research will apply the model to a criminal hacker network to understand hacker social organizational structure.

Research Questions

Based on the proposed research model, the study intends to answer this research question: in what fundamental ways does Agent utilize Technology and Resource to coordinate their hacking Action? This central question includes the following four specific questions:

1. Are there Agents who stand out as critical leaders and what is his or her sphere of influence in the network?
2. Which Agent or which Role knows the most of the Technology?
3. Which Agent or which Role accesses the most of the Resource?
4. Which Agent or which Role conducts the most of the Action?

RESEARCH METHODOLOGY

Network analysis methodology is applied in this study to reveal the structure and patterns of a significant and complex hacker group. There are a series of toolkit for network analysis developed by the Center for Computational Analysis of Social and Organizational Systems (CASOS) of Carnegie Mellon University. Two major tools will be used for this study: AutoMap (Diesner and Carley,

2004) and ORA (Organizational Risk Analyzer) (Carley et al., 2007).

The Shadowcrew Case

The research examines the social organization of an international hacker network called Shadowcrew, which engaged in identity theft and credit card fraud. In 2004, the U.S. Secret Service concluded Operation Firewall, an 18-month investigation into members of the Shadowcrew Website, where blocks of purloined card numbers were bought and sold. This investigation led to the arrests of more than twenty individuals in the United States and several individuals in foreign countries (United States Secret Service, 2004).

The U.S. Department of Justice described the Shadowcrew Web site as "one of the largest illegal online centers" for illegitimate identification and credit information (2004). Before Shadowcrew was shut down it had members from around the globe engaged in malicious computer hacking and the dissemination of stolen credit cards, debit cards, bank account numbers and falsified identity documents. The Department of Justice alleged that Shadowcrew members bought and sold about 1.7 million stolen credit card numbers and caused losses to merchants, banks, and others in excess of $4 million. Former U.S. Attorney Scott Christie claimed that the business Shadowcrew conducted proved these gangs were "highly structured and very well organized" (McCormick & Gage, 2005).

Shadowcrew was organized into different levels of power as Administrators, Moderators, Reviewers, Vendors, and General Members. Administrators, the highest level, were the members who controlled the direction of the organization and oversaw the business functions, making sure profits were turned over (Zambo, 2007). The next level in the hierarchy consisted of Moderators, who were in charge of running the forums on Shadowcrew's Website. There were a half-dozen or more forums on the Website. A forum might discuss how to steal and forge bank cards, or how

to create identification documents, such as driver's licenses, diplomas or training certificates (Grow and Bush, 2005; Zambo, 2007).

Reviewers were the next level of the Shadowcrew network. Reviewers judged the quality of illicit merchandise and verified the identification documents and credit card information by running tests. After the goods were reviewed, they were offered for sale on the forums on Shadowcrew's Website (Zambo, 2007). Vendors were the second lowest level of Shadowcrew network. These members were responsible for the sale of stolen credit cards, as well as other services, such as money laundering (Grow and Bush, 2005). General Members, the bottom of the organization, includes thousands of individuals who typically used the Shadowcrew Website to gather and share instructions on committing credit card fraud, creating false identification documents and selling credit card and identification numbers. Registration was open to all newcomers, but more sensitive discussion areas were password-protected, and members needed a senior member to vouch for them before they were allowed to pitch sales to the group. Members were able to prove themselves and their loyalty by working their way up the ranks of the network (Grow and Bush, 2005; Zambo, 2007). Shadowcrew is a significant and complex network organization and it is an appropriate case for us to study hacker's social organization.

Data Collection

One hundred and eighty two texts were collected and formed the original data set for this Shadowcrew study. Of these texts, 157 were collected through LexisNexis Academia via an exact matching Boolean Keyword search for "Shadowcrew." The media searched with LexisNexis included major newspapers, magazines, journals, and law reviews, such as *The New York Times, The Washington Post, USA Today, Business Week, US Fed News*, and *Department of Justice Documents*. The time frame for the data set was "all available dates." The articles most relevant according to the LexisNexis sorting function were selected. Sources for the 25 other texts were open source web sites, trial transcripts, and court proceedings.

After collecting the 182 original texts, the researcher carefully reviewed each text to make sure it was relevant to the research subject. The duplicate copies were deleted and it resulted in 115 texts for data analysis, which is referred to as ShadowcrewDataSet. The following table lists the sources of the 115 texts (Table 2).

Texts are a widely used source of information to study criminal and covert groups (Carley, et al., 2003). In general, the credibility of the coding samples can be increased by using a large corpus

Table 2. List of source

Publication name	Number of text
US Fed News	12
International Herald Tribune	10
The New York Times	10
Government Publications & Documents	9
Baseline Magazine.com	8
Department of Justice Documents	8
eWeek.com	7
The Business	7
Business Week	6
Newsweek	5
USA Today	5
The Washington Post	5
Berkeley Technology Law Journal	4
CQ Federal Department and Agency Documents	4
US Newswire	4
Wall Street Journal Abstracts	3
US District Court Cases, Combined	3
CNNMoney.com	2
Kiplinger Publications	1
The New Zealand Herald	1
New England Journal on Criminal and Civil Confinement	1
Total	115

that integrates various text types from a variety of sources (Carley, 2007). This ShadowcrewDataSet is suitable to study Shadowcrew's network because this data set is from multiple different sources, such as newspapers, journals, magazines, web pages, and court proceedings. Besides, the Shadowcrew Website (http://www.shadowcrew.com) was shut down by the law enforcement agencies. Text searching is the only approach available to collect information about this hacker group from public sources.

Data Processing: From Texts to Meta-Matrix Data

AutoMap was used to extract the social organizational network from the ShadowcrewDataSet. The quality of the network (or map) extracted from the text can be enhanced by pre-processing the data prior to running analysis: Text pre-processing condenses the data to the concepts that capture the features of the texts that are relevant in a certain context or corpus. In AutoMap, pre-processing is a semi-automated process that involves four major techniques: named-entity recognition, deletion, stemming, and thesaurus creation and application (Diesner and Carley, 2005).

Named-entity recognition retrieves proper names (people, places, and organizations), numerals, and abbreviations from texts (Magnini, et al., 2002). Deletion removes non-content bearing concepts such as conjunctions and articles from text, and thus reduces the number of concepts needed to be considered when creating thesauri (Carley, 1993). Stemming detects inflections and derivations of concepts in order to convert each concept to its respective morpheme (Jurafsky & Martin, 2000). KSTEM stemmer was implemented in the pre-processing (Krovetz, 1995).

Thesaurus creation and application associates specific concepts with more abstract concepts (generalization thesaurus) or meta-matrix entities (meta-matrix thesaurus). A generalization thesaurus translates text-level concepts into higher-level concepts. The researcher created a generalization thesaurus that associates the instances of relevant named entities, aliases, and misspellings. A meta-matrix thesaurus associates text terms with meta-matrix entities, thus enabling the extraction of the structure of social and organizational networks from textual data. Based on the proposed research model for hacker network (Figure 1), the five dimensions were applied to create the meta-thesaurus list. Table 3 shows a portion of the meta-matrix network for the ShadowcrewDataSet. The first column on the left contains the individual Agent, who has links to the entities of other columns.

In the next step the researcher applied the meta-matrix thesaurus to the ShadowcrewData-Set, and ran multiple sub-matrix text analysis in AutoMap. One network for ShadowcrewDataset was extracted for network analysis.

NETWORK DATA ANALYSIS AND RESULTS

ORA (Organizational Risk Analyzer) was used to visualize the network and generate reports. Several features of the visualized network stand out (Figure 2). There are a total of twenty-three nodes (agents) and three nodes are isolates – agents who are not directly linked to other agents. They are Albert Gonzalez, Chad Hatten, and Karin Andersson, who are shown on the top-right of Figure 2. There are two agents, Alexsi Kolarov and Kaspar Kivi, who are connected with each other but separate from other agents.

The next step identified the most critical individuals in the network. Table 4 contains the top five individuals in the network with respect to measures that determine an individual's prominence or importance in the network. The meaning and a potential interpretation for each measure in Table 4 are from Carley et al. (2007, p.1340).

Degree centrality measures how many other people are connected to a particular agent researchers are interested in studying. An individual has high degree centrality if he or she is directly connected to a larger number of other agents. This individual is most likely to diffuse new information and most likely to know information. Isolation of this person will be slightly crippling the network for a short time (Wasserman and Faust, 1994; Carley, et al., 2007). In Table 4, Brandon Monchamp has the highest value of degree centrality and he is most likely to diffuse new information and most likely to know information.

Cognitive demand measures the total amount of cognitive effort expended by each agent to do his or her tasks. An Individual who is high

Table 3. Exemplary instances of meta-matrix entities

Name of individual	Meta-matrix Entity				
	Agent	Technology	Resource	Action	Role
Andrew Mantovani	Kim Taylor David Appleyard	Phishing Worm Sniffer	Server Database	Control Collect Oversee	Administrator
David Appleyard	Andrew Mantovani Anatoly Tyukanov	Trojan horse Virus	Credit card passport	Access Fraud	Administrator
Anatoly Tyukanov	David Appleyard	Spoofing Zombie	Bank account	Provide Receive	Administrator
Kim Taylor	Andrew Mantovani Wesley Lanning	Phishing Scanner	Database	Offense Generate	Moderator
Mathew Johnson	Kim Taylor Alexander Palacio	Virus	SSN	Steal Encode	Reviewer

Figure 2. Agent Network for Shadowcrew

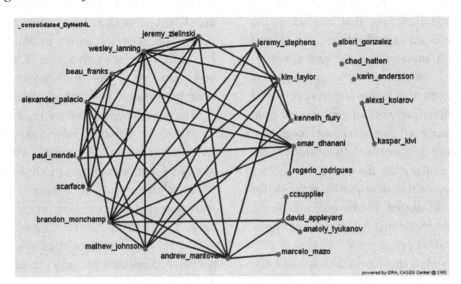

Table 4. Key actors

Measure	Rank	Value	Name of agent	Meaning	Interpretation
Degree centrality	1	0.977	Brandon Monchamp	A node has high degree centrality if it is directly connected to a larger number of other nodes.	Individual most likely to diffuse new information, most likely to know information. Isolation of this person will be slightly crippling for a short time.
	2	0.909	Andrew Mantovani		
	3	0.568	David Appleyard		
	4	0.500	Wesley Lanning		
	5	0.432	Kim Taylor		
Cognitive demand	1	0.108	Andrew Mantovani	Measures the total cognitive effort expended by each agent to do its tasks.	Individual most likely to be an emergent leader. Isolation of this person will be moderately crippling for a medium time.
	2	0.087	Kim Taylor		
	3	0.065	Wesley Lanning		
	4	0.055	Mathew Johnson		
	5	0.055	Scarface*		
Eigenvector centrality	1	0.241	Andrew Mantovani	A node has a high eigenvector centrality if the person is connected to many agents that are themselves well-connected.	Individual who is most connected to most other critical people. Isolation of this person is likely to have little effect.
	2	0.223	David Appleyard		
	3	0.143	Brandon Monchamp		
	4	0.066	Kim Taylor		
	5	0.060	Wesley Lanning		

* This is the nickname or member ID for the person.

in cognitive demand value is most likely to be an emergent leader. Isolation or Removal of the person tends to be quite disruptive to networks for a medium time (Carley, et al., 2007). In Table 4, Andrew Mantovani has the highest cognitive demand value and therefore he is most likely to be a leader for Shadowcrew network.

Eigenvector Centrality reflects one's connections to other well-connected people. An individual has a high eigenvector centrality if the person is connected to many agents that are themselves well-connected. An individual connected to many isolated people in an organization will have a much lower score. Isolation of the individual who has a high eigenvector centrality is likely to have little effect to the network (Bonacich, 1972). In Table 5, Andrew Mantovani has the highest eigenvector centrality value and he is connected to most other critical individuals.

In short, Andrew Mantovani stands out as a key actor. Andrew Mantovani is most likely to emerge as a leader (cognitive demand), and is most connected to most other critical people (eigenvector centrality). These results make sense because Andrew Mantovani was one of the co-founders and administrators of Shadowcrew network.

Table 5. Most technology (input networks: agent – technology)

Rank	Value of out-degree centrality	Agent
1	0.0196	Andrew Mantovani
2	0.0196	Albert Gonzalez
3	0.0196	Jeremy Zielinski
4	0.0196	Kenneth Flury
5	0.0196	Wesley Lanning

Because Andrew Mantovani stands out as a key agent on Table 5, a question that a researcher might ask is how this individual could be influenced, and whom he influences. To examine this, we look at the sphere of influence around Mantovani. The sphere of influence for an individual identifies the set of actors that influence and are influenced by that actor (Carley, et al., 2007). In the total twenty-three agents, there are eight agents who directly connect to Mantovani (Figure 3).

Next, the researcher applies Degree centrality to analyze the relations among the five dimensions: Agent, Technology, Resource, Action and Role. Degree centrality tells us the relative number of direct connections a particular agent might

Figure 3. Sphere of influence for Andrew Mantovani

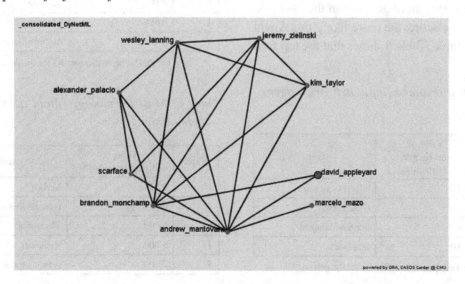

Figure 4. Formula for out-degree centrality

$$\text{row } i = \frac{1}{n} \sum_{j=1}^{n} X(i, j)$$

have in a network; the higher the score the more likely an agent might receive and potentially pass on critical knowledge, resources, or information that flows through the network (Wasserman and Faust, 1994). Consider the matrix representation X of a network with m rows and n columns. Each row i is assigned an out-degree centrality based on the sum of entries in its row (Carley, et al., 2007). The Figure 4 is the formula for out-degree centrality. This measure is also called Row degree centrality.

In the relation of Agent to Technology, the out-degree centrality shows the direct connections to Technology that Agent has in the network. The higher the score, the more likely this Agent knows or accesses Technology. Table 5 shows the top five agents who know or access most of the Technology: Andrew Mantovani, Albert Gonzalez, Jeremy Zielinski, Kenneth Flury, and Wesley Lanning.

In the connections of Agent to Resource, the out-degree centrality shows the direct connections to Resource that Agent has in the network. The higher the score, the more likely this Agent access Resource. Table 6 shows that the top four

individuals who access most of the Resource: Albert Gonzalez, Chad Hatten, Mathew Johnson and Scarface.

In the connections of Agent to Action, the out-degree centrality shows the direct ties to Action that Agent has in the network. The higher the score, the more likely this Agent conducts or implements Action. Table 7 shows the list of the top five agents. Andrew Mantovani is only the fifth on this list. From the previous analysis, even though Mantovani was the administrator and the most critical person, he was not engaged in the daily actions or activities in the network.

In the relation of Role to Technology, the out-degree centrality shows the direct connections to Technology the individuals on each Role have in the network. The higher the score, the more likely those individuals on a particular Role know or access Technology. Table 8 shows the ranking of the five roles: Vendor on the highest and Administrator on the lowest.

Table 7. Most action (input networks: agent – action)

Rank	Value of out-degree centrality	Agent
1	0.171	Paul Mendel
2	0.114	Chad Hatten
3	0.100	Scarface*
4	0.086	Kenneth Flury
5	0.086	Andrew Mantovani

* This is the nickname or member ID for the person.

Table 6. Most resource (input networks: agent - resource)

Rank	Value of out-degree centrality	Agent
1	0.071	Albert Gonzalez
2	0.036	Chad Hatten
3	0.036	Mathew Johnson
4	0.036	Scarface*

* This is the nickname or member ID for the person.

Table 8. Most technology (input networks: role – technology)

Rank	Value of out-degree centrality	Role
1	0.235	Vendor
2	0.137	General Member
3	0.000	Moderator
4	0.000	Reviewer
5	0.000	Administrator

In the relation of Role to Resource, the out-degree centrality shows the direct ties to Resource the individuals on each Role have in the network. The higher the score, the more likely those individuals on a particular Role access Resource. Table 9 shows the ranking of the five roles: General Member on the highest and Moderator on the lowest.

In the relation of Role to Action, the out-degree centrality shows the direct connections to Action the individuals on each Role have in the network. The higher the score, the more likely those individuals on a particular Role conduct or implement Action. Table 10 shows the ranking of the five roles: General Member on the highest and Administrator on the lowest.

Combining Table 8, 9 and 10 together, we can see that General Member or Vendor is on the top of the list while Administrator or Moderator is on the bottom of the list. These results imply that there are more individuals in the Role of General Member or Vendor and they know more Technology, access more Resource, and conduct more Action.

CONCLUSION AND FUTURE DIRECTIONS

This research applied network analysis methodology to disclose a hacker group, Shadowcrew's social organization from five dimensions: Agent, Technology, Resource, Role, and Action. This research revealed the fundamental ways that hackers utilize technology and resource to coordinate their action. Three network measures: cognitive demand, degree centrality, and eigenvector centrality, were used to determine the critical leaders. Out-degree centrality was employed to analyze the relations among these five dimensions.

This research is important to the information security industry and to efforts to fight against malicious hacker groups. The study not only deepens our understanding of the social organization structure on hacker groups, but also provides an approach for law enforcement agencies to analyze and monitor the activities and movements of hacker communities. A clear understanding of these structural properties in a hacker network can help law enforcement agencies target critical leaders for elimination or surveillance, and locate network vulnerabilities to destabilize the network.

The major contribution of this research is to propose a research model to study hacker's groups and this model includes five dimensions and their relations. This model places these dimensions in the whole hacker network context to allow us to have a novel perspective on the social organization of hacker's group and reveal the valuable information for decision-making, such as who is the most critical person, who knows the most of the technology, who accesses the most of the resource, and who conducts the most of the action in the hacker network. A clear understanding of

Table 9. Most resource (input networks: role – resource)

Rank	Value of out-degree centrality	Role
1	0.025	General Member
2	0.107	Vendor
3	0.036	Administrator
4	0.000	Reviewer
5	0.000	Moderator

Table 10. Most action (input networks: role – action)

Rank	Value of out-degree centrality	Role
1	1.714	General Member
2	o.429	Vendor
3	0.171	Moderator
4	0.171	Reviewer
5	0.100	Administrator

these structural properties in a hacker network can help law enforcement agencies target critical leaders for elimination or surveillance, and locate network vulnerabilities to destabilize the network.

In the future, we can extend our knowledge in two major directions to address some limitations of the current study. First, the current study only investigated a criminal hacker group, Shadowcrew. Although Shadowcrew is a significant and complex case, a further study that includes other types of hacker groups would be more comprehensive of our understanding of hacker social organization.

Second, there are five dimensions in the research model for hacker network: Agent, Technology, Resource, Action, and Role. Other dimensions could be added in the model to broaden our understanding of hacker communities. One potential dimension is Location. Although hackers are able to connect to each other through the Internet all around the world, it is still interesting to examine the physical locations that affect hacker's communication and relation.

ACKNOWLEDGMENT

This research was supported by the 211 Project for the Center of Experimental Teaching in Economics and Management at Southwestern University of Finance and Economics in China.

REFERENCES

Best, J., & Luckenbill, D. F. (1980). The Social Organization of Deviants. *Social Problems, 28*(1), 14–31. doi:10.1525/sp.1980.28.1.03a00020

Best, J., & Luckenbill, D. F. (1994). *Oragnizing Deviance* (2nd ed.). Upper Saddle River, NJ: Prentice Hall.

Carley, K. (2002). Smart Agents and Organizations of the Future. In Livingstone, L. L. S. (Ed.), *The Handbook of New Media*. Thousand Oaks, CA: Sage.

Carley, K., Dombrowski, M., & Tsvetovat, M. reminga, J., & Kamneva, N. (2003). *Destabilizing Dynamic Covert Networks*. Paper presented at the the 8th International Command and Control Research and Technology Symposium.

Carley, K. M., Diesner, J., Reminga, J., & Tsvetovat, M. (2007). Toward an interoperable dynamic network analysis toolkit. *Decision Support Systems, 43*(4), 1324–1347. doi:10.1016/j.dss.2006.04.003

Diesner, J., & Carley, K. M. (2004). *AutoMap 1.2-Extract, Analyze, Represent, and Compare Mental Models from Texts (No. CMU-ISRI-04-100)*. Carnegie Mellon University, School of Computer Science, Institute for Software Research International, Technical Reporto. Document Number.

Diesner, J., & Carley, K. M. (2005). Revealing Social structure from Texts: Metamatrix Text Analysis as a Novel Method for Network Text Analysis. In Narayanan, V. K., & Armstrong, D. J. (Eds.), *Causal Mapping for Information Systems and Technology Research: Approaches, Advances, and Illustrations* (pp. 81–108). Hershey, PA: Idea Group Publishing.

Furnell, S. (2002). *Cybercrime: Vandalizing the Information Society*. Boston: Addison-Wesley.

Grow, B., & Bush, J. (2005, May 30). Hacker Hunters: An Elite Force Takes on the Dark Side of Computing. *Business Week, 74*.

Holt, T. J. (2005). *Hacks, Cracks, and Crime: An Examination of the Subculture and Social*. St. Louis, MO: University of Missouri.

Jurafsky, D., & Marton, J. H. (2000). *Speech and Language Processing*. Upper Saddle River, NJ: Prentice Hall.

Kleen, L. J. (2001). Malicoious Hackers: A Framerwork for Analysis and Case Study [Electronic Version]. *Master's Thesis, Air Force Institutie of Technology, 2001.* Retrieved January 3, 2004, from http://www.iwar.org.uk/iwar/resources/usaf/maxwell/students/2001/afit-gor-ens-01m-09.pdf

Krovetz, R. (1995). *Word Sense Disambiguation for Large Text Databases.* Cambridge, MA: University of Massachusetts.

Legislative Hearing on H.R. 5318, the "Cyber-Security Enhancement and Consumer Data Protection Act of 2006", U.S. House of Representatives (2006).

Magnini, B., Negri, M., Prevete, R., & Tanev, H. (2002). *A WordNet-based Approach to Named Entities Recognition.* Paper presented at the SemaNet'02: Building and Using Sematic Networks.

McCormick, J., & Gage, D. (2005). *Shadowcrew: Web Mobs* [Electronic Version]. Retrieved September 26, 2008, from http://www.baselinemag.com/c/a/Security/Shadowcrew-Web-Mobs/

Parsky, L. (2006). 5318, the "Cyber-Security Enhancement and Consumer Data Protection Act of 2006". In *Committee on the Judiciary Subcommittee on Crime, Terrorism and Homeland Security, U.S. House of Representatives.* Legislative Hearing on H.R.

Richardson, R. (2007). *CSI Survey 2007: The 12th Annual Computer Crime and Security Survey.* Computer Security Institution.

Richardson, R. (2009). *CSI Survey 2008: The 14th Annual Computer Crime and Security Survey.* Computer Security Institution.

Straub, D. W., Goodman, S., & Baskerville, R. (2008). Framing of Information Security Policies and Practice. In, D. W. Straub, S. Goodman, and R. Baskerville, Eds., (ed) *Information Security Policies, Processes, and Practices.* Armonk, NY: M. E. Sharpe.

Taylor, P. A. (1999). *Hackers: Crime in the Digital Sublime.* New York: Routledge. doi:10.4324/9780203201503

Thomas, D. (2002). *Hacker Culture.* Minneapolis, MN: University of Minnesota Press.

Williams, P. (2001). *Russian Organized Crime, Russina Hacking, and U. S. Security* [Electronic Version]. Retrieved September 25, 2008, from http://www.cert.org/research/isw/isw2001/papers/Williams-06-09.pdf

Zambo, S. (2007). Digital La Cosa Nostra: The Computer Fraud and Abuse Act's Failure to Punish and Deter Organized Crime. *New England Journal on Criminal and Civil Confinement, 33*(2), 551–575.

Chapter 13
Security and Privacy Issues in Secure E–Mail Standards and Services

Lei Chen
Sam Houston State University, USA

Wen-Chen Hu
University of North Dakota, USA

Ming Yang
Jacksonville State University, USA

Lei Zhang
Frostburg State University, USA

ABSTRACT

Secure e-mail standards, such as Pretty Good Privacy (PGP) and Secure / Multipurpose Internet Mail Extension (S/MIME), apply cryptographic algorithms to provide secure and private e-mail services over the public Internet. In this article, we first review a number of cryptographic ciphers, trust and certificate systems, and key management systems and infrastructures widely used in secure e-mail standards and services. We then focus on the discussion of several essential security and privacy issues, such as cryptographic cipher selection and operation sequences, in both PGP and S/MIME. This work tries to provide readers a comprehensive impression of the security and privacy provided in the current secure e-mail services.

One of the most popular Internet services is e-mail services which provide sending and receiving electronic messages of communication networks. E-mail standards and services apply various cryptographic algorithms to achieve the security goals (Stallings, 2006; Stallings, 2007) of confi-dentiality, integrity, authentication and non-repudiation.

Data confidentiality in e-mail services is commonly made available via cryptographic encryption. Since symmetric key ciphers, such as DES, Triple-DES and AES, process data at higher rates than public key ciphers, such as RSA, they are

DOI: 10.4018/978-1-60960-200-0.ch013

preferable in protecting the secrecy of data. Hash functions, such as MD5 and SHA-1, are used to preserve data integrity. The sender hashes the data content using one or multiple hash functions and sends the message digests to the receiver who is capable to verify the message's integrity by running the same hash functions over the received message and then comparing the output digests to the received ones.

There are two types of authentication: entity authentication and data-origin authentication, both of which make use of cryptographic algorithms. Entity authentication is based on cryptographic keys, including both symmetric key-based authentication and public key-based authentication. Secure Socket Layer / Transport Layer Security (SSL/TLS) in secure web services uses this type of authentication. Data-origin based authentication is accomplished through Message Authentication Code (MAC) (Stallings, 2007) and digital signatures. Secure email services provide data-origin authentication through digital signatures.

Non-repudiation, a security feature making a communication party not able to deny the past transactions, uses public key cryptographic ciphers, such as RSA. These public key ciphers allow a party to sign a message using the private key and this signing can later be verified by applying the paired public key to the signed message. In the follow section, we review the common cryptographic ciphers and security protocols and standards in secure e-mail services.

CIPHERS AND STANDARDS

Cryptographic Ciphers and Security Protocols

Data Encryption Standard (DES) and Triple-DES

Proposals for government encryption and decryption standard were solicited in 1973 by the National Institute of Standards and Technology (NIST). In 1976, DES, based on the IBM Lucifer cipher which was developed by Feistel and his colleagues in the early nineteen seventies, was accepted as an official Federal Information Processing Standard (FIPS) for the U.S. and later other countries. DES is the predecessor of multiple cryptographic ciphers including RC5, Blowfish and CAST5.

Being an iterative symmetric key cipher, DES has relatively short key at 56 binary bits in length. In each of its 16 iterative rounds, DES takes a 64-bit data block and a 48-bit sub-key as the input and goes through a sequence of operating including Expansion, Substitution (S-Boxes) and Permutation (P-Boxes) producing 64-bit output. Only the S-Boxes are not linear in DES. Each of DES' eight different S-Boxes converts a 6-bit input to a 4-bit output. The conversion table has 4 rows and 16 columns with 64 intersections each of which holds a possible output value. With 4 binary bits, the output from each S-Box can only have 16 (2^4) possible values. Therefore, each of these 16 values appears at four different intersections, making each S-Box a one-way function. In other words, a 6-bit input, with its first and last bits as the row index and the rest bits as the column index, of an S-Box locates a single intersection in the conversion table and further determines the 4-bit output value. However, knowing an output value only helps find the four possible appearances in the conversion table leaving the input value in vague. With 8 different S-Boxes in each round and 16 rounds in total, DES is basically irreversible. Due to the limited length of key in DES, Triple-DES or 3DES was introduced extending the key length to 112-bit in EDE mode and 168-bit in EEE mode. Before the emergence of AES, DES and 3DES had been the most popular symmetric key block ciphers.

Advanced Encryption Standard (AES)

AES, also known as the Rijndael algorithm, was announced by NIST in 2001 as the new standard symmetric block cipher to replace DES and 3DES. AES was selected out of fifteen proposed candidate algorithms and has become the most popular cipher of its kind. AES offers options of 128-bit, 192-bit and 256-bit key sizes depending on the number of rounds that the algorithm goes through in the encryption process. No successful or effective attack on the algorithm has been reported so far. However, Side Channel Attacks can be used to assail the implementation of the AES cipher on system which leaks data.

Message-Digest Algorithm 5 (MD5)

MD5 is a 128-bit hash function widely used in security applications to verify the integrity of data. It was designed by Ron Rivest in 1991 to replace MD4. The output hash value is often presented in 32-bit hexadecimal format which is easy to read and compare. One of the design goals of a successful hash function is that it needs to be extremely unlikely that two different inputs will generate the same hash. In 1993, MD5 was found that two different initialization vectors produce same digest. In 2006, an algorithm was published to find collisions in one minute on an average notebook computer. It is now recommended to use more reliable hash functions such as SHA.

Secure Hash Algorithm (SHA)

SHA is a set of cryptographic hash functions designed by the National Security Agency (NSA) and published by the NIST as a U.S. Federal Information Processing Standard (FIPS). The various versions of SHA include SHA-0, SHA-1, SHA-2 and the future SHA-3. SHA-0 and SHA-1 both produce 160-bit digests and SHA-1 has been widely used in security applications and protocols since MD5 faded.

In 2005, an attack by Xiaoyun Wang and her colleagues was announced lowering the complexity of finding collisions (Wang et al, 2005) in SHA-1 to 2^{69}. In 2006, Christophe De Cannière

and his fellow researchers were able to reduce the complexity to 2^{35}. Despite of the greatly reduced complexity in theoretical attacks, no practical attack has ever been conducted making SHA-1 still the most widely used hash function. Four SHA-2 functions, each of which has a different key size, were published by NIST in 2002. However, SHA-2 has not received much attention. An open competition was announced in the Federal Register in Nov. 2007 for a new SHA-3 function which is expected to become the new government standard for hash functions in 2012.

RSA

RSA, named after its three authors, is the first algorithm suitable for both signing and encryption. It was publicly described in 1977 by Ron Rivest, Adi Shamir, and Leonard Adleman. Unlike symmetric key ciphers, RSA makes use of factoring, modular and exponential operations in mathematics to generate a pair of keys, namely public key and private key. A private key, which is only known to its owner, is used for signing data, and the paired public key can be known to everyone for verifying the signature. A public key can also be used to encrypt data destined for the party who holds the paired private key. However, due to its relatively high complexity, it is often used to protect data of small size, e.g. using a public key to encrypt and protect a symmetric key.

Diffie-Hellman (D-H) Key Exchange

D-H (Stallings, 2006) is a cryptographic protocol that enables two communication parties, without previously sharing any information, to establish, using modular and exponential operations, a shared secret key over a public communication channel such as the Internet. D-H by itself suffers from the man-in-the-middle attacks where a third party in the middle establishes two distinct D-H key exchanges with the two end communication parties. Nevertheless, the immunity to such attacks can be achieved by allowing the two end parties to authenticate themselves to each other through the use of digital signatures prior to the D-H key exchange.

Message Authentication Code (MAC)

Message Authentication Code is basically a short piece of information for authenticating a message. A MAC algorithm, a keyed hash or cipher function, takes both the shared secret key and the message to be authenticated as inputs and outputs a MAC value, or a tag. The verifiers, who also possess the shared secret key, apply the same MAC algorithm to test the data integrity and authenticity of the message received. Depending on the type of algorithm used, MAC algorithms can be further categorized into HMAC (HMAC, 2002), as in HMAC-MD5 or HMAC-SHA-1 which uses hash functions MD5 or SHA-1, and CMAC, as in AES-CMAC (Song et al., 2006) which uses symmetric key cryptographic cipher AES.

SECURITY STANDARDS

Web of Trust

The concept of Web of Trust was incorporated in the manual of Pretty Good Privacy (PGP) 2.0 by Phil Zimmermann in 1992. The concept of Web of Trust is shared by PGP, GnuPGP and other compatible systems. The core concept is to bind a public key with its owner through a decentralized trust model as opposed to a centralized trust model in Public Key Infrastructure (PKI) which relies entirely on Certificate Authorities (CA).

All OpenPGP-compliant systems have two schemes: certificate vetting and vote counting. Certificate vetting refers to the process of digitally signing the OpenPGP identity certificates (binding public keys and their owners) to endorse the association of the public key and the ID in the certificate. This process is termed a web of trust.

A user can have the right to trust or reject a certain certificate and the vote counting scheme lets users configure their trusting strategy, e.g., to decide whether in order to accept a signed certificate it will need four partially trusted endorsers or just one fully trusted endorser.

The advantage of Web of Trust is its flexibility which allows users to decide their own trusting parameters, unlike PKIs which normally require certain root certificate authorities that must be trusted. However, this also means that a user needs to be cautious and intelligent enough to manage and supervise his trusting settings. Problems of Web of Trust include losing tracking of a private keys, slow start of building trust, and being unable to find someone to endorse a new certificate, all of which are the direct consequences of the fact Web of Trust being decentralized.

The propagation of trust across the network has been an important and challenging research area over the years. Guha and colleagues (2004) developed a framework of trust propagation scheme, each of which fits in certain circumstances, and the schemes were evaluated over a large trust network of 800K trust scores among 130K users. In their research, they introduced the propagation of both trust and distrust and the algorithm starts with the atomic propagation over a basis set and then the propagation iterates until the whole network is reached. As shown in the evaluation over Epinions website, a small number of expressed trusts per individual allows the system to predict the trust between any two users in the system with high accuracy.

X.509

X.509 (Stallings, 2006) is one of the series of computer networking standards of X.500, covering electronic directory services. X.509 and the whole set of X.500 were developed by the Telecommunication Standardization Sector of the International Telecommunication Union (ITU-T). The goal of X.509 is to have formal specifications

Table 1. Trusted root certificates required by Windows XP

Issued to	Issued by	Intended purposes
1997 Microsoft Corp.	1997 Microsoft Corp.	Time Stamping
Microsoft Authenticode Root Authority	Microsoft Authenticode Root Authority	Secure E-mail, Code Signing
Microsoft Root Authority	Microsoft Root Authority	All
97 VeriSign, Inc.	97 VeriSign, Inc.	Time Stamping
VeriSign Commercial Software Publishers CA	VeriSign Commercial Software Publishers CA	Secure E-mail, Code Signing
Thawte Timestamping CA	Thawte Timestamping CA	Time Stamping
Microsoft Root Certificate Authority	Microsoft Root Certificate Authority	All

for standard formats for public key certificates, Certificate Revocation Lists (CRLs), attribute certificates, and a certification path validation algorithm in PKI. X.509 requires a strict hierarchical system of Certificate Authorities for issuing certificates. This is in contrast with Web of Trust in which everyone may sign, establish and verify the validity of other's certificates. The flexibility to support peer-to-peer or OpenPGP type Web of Trust was added in version 3 of X.509. However, in practice it is barely used in this way. Nowadays, the name X.509 broadly refers to the PKI certificate and Certificate Revocation List (CRL) (Housley, 1999) Profile of the X.509 Version 3 standard by the Internet Engineering Task Force (IETF). This latest version is often called PKIX in short.

An X.509 Version 3 digital certificate has three main parts, the certificate, the certificate signature algorithm and the certificate signature. The certificate part contains a number of attributes such as version, serial number, and algorithm ID, etc. Some of the attributes are further detailed.

A root certificate is either an unsigned public key certificate or a self-signed certificate that identifies the Root CA. If a tree is considered a proper metaphor of the hierarchy of a certificate system, then the root certificates are located at the root of the tree and hold private keys for signing other certificates. All certificates above the root certificate thus have full trust in the root certificates. Table 1 below is a list of trusted root certificates (MS-293781, 2007) required by Win-

dows XP. Different versions of operating systems may require different root certificates.

Public Key Infrastructure (PKI)

PKI is a set of hardware, software, people, policies, and procedures needed to create, manage, store, distribute and revoke digital certificates (Adams & Farrell, 1999). PKI binds public keys with their owners through Certificate Authority (CA). It is required that the user's identity must be unique for each CA.

As shown in Figure 1, instead of just requiring a Web log-in user name and password, PKI requires a valid certificate for each party of the communication. Alice sends certificate application along with her public key to the Registration Authority (RA) who verifies Alice's identity and forwards the application to the CA when the ID check is successful. For every user, the identity, the public key, their binding, validation conditions (e.g., expiration dates) and other attributes are packed in a certificate which is then signed by the CA with CA's private key. Since no one else, other than the CA, has his own private key, this certificate is unforgeable. At the other end of the communication, the online shop, who received Alice's certificate along with the electronic contract signed with Alice's private key, will verify the certificate by sending it to the Validation Authority (VA) who examines the validity of the certificate according to the information provided

Figure 1. Model of Public Key Infrastructure (PKI)

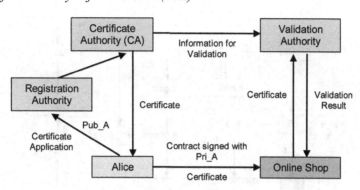

by the CA. Finally the online shop receives the validation result from the VA and decides whether to process the order.

Altough PKI seems to emerge as a promising standard for e-commerce, there have been debates and unsolved issues (Gutmann, 2006) with PKI. Carl Ellison and Bruce Schneier (2000) have pointed out in their research ten risks, of using PKI. We should note that some of these risks are not just for PKI. They are listed and briefly discusses as below:

Risk 1. A CA in PKI is often defined as "trusted". However, in cryptographic literature, it only means that a CA handles its own private keys well, and it does not mean that one can necessarily trust a certificate from that CA.

Risk 2. Most of the time, a private key is saved on a user's conventional computer and is not very well protected. Under some digital signature laws (e.g., Utah and Washington), if a signing key has been certified by an approved CA, the owner is responsible for whatever that private key does.

Risk 3. The verifying computer needs to use one or more "root" public keys to verify that the certificate was indeed signed by a CA. If an attacker can add his own public key to that list, then he can issue his own "legitimate" certificates.

Risk 4. If you received a certificate from Alice, how do you find out if the particular Alice is your friend Alice?

Risk 5. CA is not an authority on some of the information in a certificate, for example, none of the Secure Socket Layer CAs listed in the popular browsers is a DNS name authority.

Risk 6. The corporate name in the certificate is not compared to anything the user sees in the browser and there are some Web pages whose certificate is for a company that does Web hosting, not for the company whose logo appears on the displayed page.

Risk 7. CAs can have two structures: the RA+CA structure where RA is operated by the authority on the content, and the CA only structure. The RA+CA model is less secure than a system with a CA at the authority's desk and it allows some entity (the CA) to forge a certificate with that content.

Risk 8. There was a credit bureau that thought they would get into the CA business. Credit bureaus are good at business of collecting and selling facts about people, but they do not share any secret with the subjects.

Risk 9. In practice there are many unsolved questions in PKI, for example, the Certificate Revocation Lists (CRLs) are built into some certificate standards, but many implementations avoid them as they are seen as too big and too outdated to be relevant.

Figure 2. A general secure e-mail service model

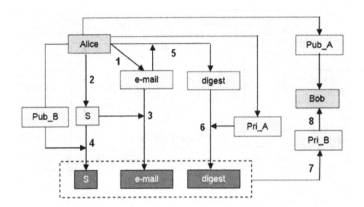

Risk 10. Implementing PKI may require massive change in the underlying system software which may introduce new security issues.

GENERAL MODEL FOR SECURE E-MAIL SERVICES

E-mails are secured (Garfinkel et al., 2005) in a quite different way from Web communication sessions. In a secure Web communication session (e.g., using Secure Socket Layer, or SSL), a sender and receiver are required to exchange multiple messages just to establish cryptographic assurances and parameters before the Web content can be transmitted; whereas in secure e-mail services, a single e-mail is the only message between the sender and receiver. Therefore, this e-mail message has to contain all information required to provide authentication, confidentiality, integrity, and non-repudiation of origin.

Authentication in e-mail services is referred to the process of identifying the sender of the e-mail and this is often done by sender signing the e-mail using his private key. Confidentiality is provided through encrypting the message content with a symmetric session key which allows much faster encryption and decryption than public key ciphers. Message digests can be generated using hash functions to verify the integrity (that the e-mail has not been altered) of the e-mail. The sender's

private key also provides non-repudiation ensuring that the sender cannot repudiate or refute the fact that he has sent the specific e-mail.

A general secure e-mail service model (Mel & Backer, 2000) is shown in Figure 2.

1. The sender (Alice) composes the e-mail.
2. Alice generates a secret session key (S) which will only be used once in encryption.
3. Alice uses S to encrypt the content of the e-mail. S needs to be protected before passed to the receiver (Bob).
4. Alice uses Bob's public key (Pub_B) to encrypt S. This is a very common way to protect a secret key over the Internet.
5. In order for Bob to verify the integrity of the e-mail, Alice generates a message digest of the e-mail plaintext and the timestamp.
6. For the purpose of providing non-repudiation, Alice signs the digest using her private key (Pri_A).
7. Alice sends the e-mail package (the encrypted e-mail, the encrypted session key, and the signed message digest) to Bob.
8. When Bob receives Alice's e-mail package, he uses his private key Pri_B to decrypt the encrypted session key S, which is then used to decrypt the e-mail message; finally Bob applies the same hash function to the e-mail message and compares the output message

Table 2. Keys used in the general secure e-mail service model

Name	Owner	Type	Function
S	Alice	Symmetric	Used to encrypt e-mail content by Alice and decrypt by Bob
Pub_A	Alice	Public	Used by Bob to "decrypt" the digest signed using Pri_A
Pri_A	Alice	Private	Used by Alice to sign the message digest
Pub_B	Bob	Public	Used by Alice to encrypt session key S
Pri_B	Bob	Private	Used by Bob to decrypt session key S

digest to the digest he received. If the two digests match, data integrity is verified.

Table 2 summarized the keys used in the above model:

In the above secure e-mail services model, data confidentiality is provided by the secret symmetric key S. Integrity can be verified by comparing the received message digest to the calculated digest on the received e-mail content. Non-repudiation is also guaranteed as Bob can prove, using Pub_A, that Alice, the only person in the world who possesses Pri_A, has signed the digest. Since Pri_A serves as the identity of Alice and Pri_B as the identity of Bob, authentication of both sides is successful. This model appears to be perfect as far as cryptography is concerned. But is it safe and sound when applied in a real environment? Is there any problem in this model that has been overlooked? We have actually made an assumption without which the above system would be insecure: both Pub_A and Pub_B must be genuine, or in other words, Pub_A and Pub_B must indeed be Alice's and Bob's public keys respectively. The way this can be handled is to use digital certificates and a trusted third party. Different programs provide various ways to retrieve digital certificates. S/MIME uses X.509 digital certificates and PGP uses OpenPGP digital certificates (called keys). More details of this will be covered in the following sections.

OPENPGP AND S/MIME

The two incompatible secure e-mail standards, OpenPGP and S/MIME (Ramsdell, 2004), both provide key security features such as confidentiality, integrity, authentication and non-repudiation. Although they both use MIME as the standard to structure messages, they are quite different in technical details.

SECURITY ISSUES IN PGP AND OPENPGP

PGP (Zimmermann, 1995) is a program that fulfills all the security goals in e-mail services. PGP was created by Philip Zimmermann in 1991 and now follows the OpenPGP standard (Callas et al., 1998). Following the general model in Figure 2, PGP applies public-key cryptography in protecting the session key and providing authentication. The initial version of PGP used Web of Trust system and in the later versions, the X.509 standard for PKI is also implemented. PGP users are allowed to both verify other users' keys and choose to trust certification statements made by other users.

Even though PGP had been quite popular in some technical communities, without a centrally managed hierarchy it suffered in trying to work with existing e-mail systems. In 1997, a commercial PGP version was introduced which included all necessary patent licenses and plug-ins in order to work with popular e-mail systems such as Microsoft Outlook and Eudora.

OpenPGP is a non-proprietary protocol for secure e-mail systems. It is based on PGP and defines standard formats for message encryption, signing, as well as certificates for exchanging public keys. The OpenPGP working group was formed in 1997 in the IETF and OpenPGP has become the biggest competitor of S/MIME (IMC-SMIME, 2006). The goal of OpenPGP is to bring companies together to promote the same standard and apply the PKI, or more accurately the OpenPGP PKI, to other non-e-mail applications.

An article by Philip Zimmermann, the author of PGP, provided another view angle on OpenPGP and PKI (Zimmermann, 2001). He indicated that the term PKI is not a synonym of CA as in X.509 systems. In OpenPGP, PKI is "an emergent property of the sum total of all the keys in the user population, all the signatures on all those keys, the individual opinions of each OpenPGP user as to who they choose as trusted introducers, all the OpenPGP client software which runs the OpenPGP trust model and performs trust calculations for each client user, and the key servers which fluidly disseminate this collective knowledge". The most important thing in OpenPGP PKI is, every user gets to choose who they trust as trusted introducers and he "should only trust honest and sophisticated introducers that understand what it means to sign a key, and will exercise due diligence in ascertaining the identity of the key holder before signing the key in question". In fact, the OpenPGP trust model is a proper superset of the centralized trust model of the X.509 systems.

The question of which to choose between Open-PGP PKI and X.509 PKI actually lies mainly on the issue of trust propagation over the Web which still was an active research topic at the time this article was written.

SECURITY ISSUES IN S/MIME

The Multipurpose Internet Mail Extensions (MIME) (Stallings, 2006) is an Internet standard created and published by the Internet Engineering Task Force (IETF). MIME supports text in character sets other than ASCII, non-text attachments, message bodies with multiple parts, header information in non-ASCII character sets. Almost all Internet e-mails are transmitted in MIME format.

The standard for e-mail security encapsulated in MIME is referred to S/MIME (Dusse et al., 1998) which utilizes public key encryption and signing of e-mails to provide confidentiality, integrity, authentication and non-repudiation. S/MIME follows the industry standard Public Key Cryptography Standards #7 (PKCS #7) for secure message format. Although both S/MIME and PGP are described in IETF standards, S/MIME seems to emerge as the industry standard for commercial and organizational use, while PGP will still remain as a choice for personal e-mail security.

The functions provided by S/MIME include:

- **Enveloped data:** encrypted data along with the corresponding keys for one or more recipients.
- **Signed data:** the message digest (hash) is signed with the private key of the signer. Both the content and the signature are encoded using base-64 encoding. Singed messages can only be viewed by recipients installed with S/MIME capability.
- **Clear-signed data:** only the digital signature is encoded using base-64. Therefore all recipients can view the message content, though those without S/MIME capability are not able to verify the signature.
- **Signed and enveloped data:** signed-only and encrypted-only data are allowed. In this way, encrypted data can be signed and signed data or clear-signed data can be encrypted.

Nowadays support for S/MIME is integrated into quite a number of e-mail clients including Microsoft Outlook and Outlook Express, Netscape Communicator, Lotus Notes, etc. But there are

Table 3. Ciphers used in S/MIME v3 and OpenPGP

Features	S/MIME v3	OpenPGP
message format	binary, based on Cryptographic Message Syntax (CMS, RFC 3852)	binary, based on previous PGP
certificate format	binary, based on X.509 v3	binary, based on previous PGP
symmetric encryption algorithm	Triple-DES	Triple-DES
signature algorithm	RSA or Diffie-Hellman	ElGamal with Digital Signature Standard (DSS)
hash algorithm	SHA-1	SHA-1
MIME encapsulation of signed data	multipart/signed or CMS	multipart/signed with ASCII armor
MIME encapsulation of encrypted data	application/pkcs7-mime	multipart/encrypted

clients, such as Yahoo, Gmail and Hotmail, and many Web-based e-mail systems that do not support S/MIME. In these systems, messages digitally signed using S/MIME will appear as conventional messages with an additional attachment named smime.p7s. E-mails that are encrypted using S/MIME are not decipherable in these systems.

CIPHER SELECTION

The cryptographic ciphers in both OpenPGP and S/MIME include Digital Signature Standard (DSS), RSA, CAST/IDEA/3DES, D-H and SHA.

For message signing in OpenPGP, SHA-1 is used to create the digest of a message. Then the digest is encrypted using either DSS or RSA with the sender's private key and attached to the message. Same as OpenPGP, S/MIME uses SHA-1 to create message digest. RFC 2119 specifies that MD5 should also be supported for backward compatibility. S/MIME also uses DSS to encrypted message digest and RSA should also be supported as described in the RFC.

For message encryption in OpenPGP, the sender generates a one-time session key which is used to encrypt the message using CAST-128 or IDEA or 3DES. The session key itself is protected using D-H or RSA with the recipient's public key and attached to the message. In S/MIME, session key is used in DES to encrypt messages.

AES and RC2-40 should also be supported. Same as OpenPGP, S/MIME also uses D-H or RSA to protect the one-time session key.

OpenPGP and S/MIME share a number of commonly used cryptographic ciphers and hash functions. S/MIME seems to require the support of more ciphers for better backward compatibility. Table 3 summarizes the ciphers used in OpenPGP and S/MIME v3.

SEQUENCE OF OPERATIONS

PGP and S/MIME basically have the same order of operations. The signing operations go as follows:

1. Sender creates a message
2. 160-bit SHA-1 message digest is generated
3. Digest is encrypted using sender's private key with RSA and attached to the message
4. Receiver decrypts and recovers the digest with sender's public key
5. Receiver generates a new digest of the message and compares it with the decrypted from step 4. If they match, the message is accepted as authentic

The operations for Confidentiality go as follows:

1. The sender generates a random 128-bit one-time session key for the current message only
2. CAST-128, IDEA or 3DES is used with the session key to encrypt the message
3. Session key is then encrypted with RSA using the receiver's public key and then attached to the message
4. The receiver uses RSA with its private key to decrypt the session key
5. Receiver decrypts the message with the recovered session key

When authentication (signing), encryption and compression are combined, the sequence of these operations should be signing, then encryption, finally compression. Signing is preferable to be the first operation for the convenience of storing a signature with a plaintext version of a message and easier verification. Encryption goes after compression because compressed messages have less redundancy than original plaintext and thus cryptanalysis becomes more difficult.

SUMMARY

In this article, we first reviewed a number of cryptographic ciphers, security protocols and standards used in secure e-mail and Web services. We then discussed a few practical systems and standards supporting the use of public keys and private keys in a real environment. For example, Web of Trust builds a flexible decentralized trust system for PGP under the standard of OpenPGP while X.509 defines a formal format of certificates used in PKI which standardizes a centralized public key and certificate system. The de facto secure e-mail standard S/MIME was introduced and compared to OpenPGP. In secure email systems, all security goals must be achieved via a single e-mail. Therefore, all necessary operations for security need to be executed in the correct order before the e-mail is sent.

REFERENCES

Adams, C., & Farrell, S. (1999). *Internet X.509 public key infrastructure: Certificate management protocols* (RFC 2510). Retrieved from http://tools.ietf.org/html/rfc2510

Callas, J., Donnerhacke, L., Finney, H., & Thayer, R. (1998). *OpenPGP message format* (RFC 2440). Retrieved from http://www.ietf.org/rfc/rfc2440.txt

Dusse, S., Hoffman, P., Ramsdell, B., Lundblade, L., & Repka, L. (1998). *S/MIME version 2 message specification* (RFC 2311). Retrieved from https://www3.ietf.org/rfc/rfc2311.txt

Ellison, C., & Schneier, B. (2000). Ten risks of PKI: What you're not being yold about public key infrastructure. *Computer Security Journal, Volume XVI.*

Garfinkel, S. L., Margrave, D., Schiller, J. I., Nordlander, E., & Miller, R. C. (2005). *How to make secure e-mail easier to use.* Paper presented at CHI 2005, Portland, OR.

Guha, R., Kumar, R., Raghavan, P., & Tomkins, A. (2004). *Propagation of trust and distrust.* Paper presented at the 13th International Conference on WWW, New York.

Gutmann, P. (2006). *Everything you never wanted to know about PKI but were forced to find out.* Retrieved from http://www.cs.auckland.ac.nz/~pgut001/pubs/pkitutorial.pdf

HMAC. (2002). The keyed-hash message authentication code (HMAC). *FIPS PUB 198*, NIST.

Housley, R., Ford, W., Polk, W., & Solo, D. (1999). *Internet X.509 public key infrastructure: Certificate and CRL profile* (RFC 2459). Retrieved from www.ietf.org/rfc/rfc2459.txt

IMC-SMIME. (2006). S/MIME and OpenPGP. *Internet Mail Consortium*

Microsoft. (2007). Trusted root certificates that are required by Windows Server 2008, by Windows Vista, by Windows Server 2003, by Windows XP, and by Windows 2000. *Microsoft Help and Support Article ID 293781.*

Ramsdell, B. (2004). *Secure/multipurpose internet mail extensions (S/MIME) version 3.1 message specification* (RFC 3851). Retrieved from https://www3.ietf.org/rfc/rfc3851.txt

Song, J. H., Lee, J., & Iwata, T. (2006). *The AES-CMAC algorithm* (RFC 4493). Retrieved from http://www.ietf.org/rfc/rfc4493.txt

Stallings, W. (2006). *Cryptography and network security* (4th ed.). Upper Saddle River, NJ: Prentice Hall. ISBN 0-13-187316-4.

Stallings, W. (2007). *Network security essentials* (3rd ed.). Upper Saddle River, NJ: Prentice Hall. ISBN 0-13-238033-1.

Wang, X. Y., Yin, Y. Q., & Yu, H. B. (2005). *Finding collisions in the full SHA-1.* Paper presented at the 25th Annual International Cryptology Conference, Santa Barbara, California, USA

Zimmermann, P. (1995). The official PGP user's guide. Cambridge, MA: MIT Press. ISBN 0-262-74017-6, 1995.

Zimmermann, P. (2001). Why OpenPGP's PKI is better than an X.509 PKI. Retrieved from http://www.openpgp.org/technical/whybetter.shtml

This work was previously published in International Journal of Information Security and Privacy (IJISP), edited by Hamid Nemati, pp 1-13, copyright 2009 by IGI Publishing (imprint of IGI Global)

Chapter 14
Advances in Security and Privacy in Wireless Sensor Networks

Dulal C. Kar
Texas A&M University-Corpus Christi, USA

Hung L. Ngo
Texas A&M University-Corpus Christi, USA

Clifton J. Mulkey
Texas A&M University-Corpus Christi, USA

Geetha Sanapala
Texas A&M University-Corpus Christi, USA

ABSTRACT

It is challenging to secure a wireless sensor network (WSN) because its inexpensive, tiny sensor nodes do not have the necessary processing capability, memory capacity, and battery life to take advantage of the existing security solutions for traditional networks. Existing security solutions for wireless sensor networks are mostly based on symmetric key cryptography with the assumption that sensor nodes are embedded with secret, temporary startup keys before deployment thus avoiding any use of computationally demanding public key algorithms altogether. However, symmetric key cryptography alone cannot satisfactorily provide all security needs for wireless sensor networks. It is still problematic to replenish an operational wireless sensor network with new sensor nodes securely. Current research on public key cryptography for WSNs shows some promising results, particularly in the use of elliptic curve cryptography and identity based encryption for WSNs. Although security is essential for WSNs, it can complicate some crucial operations of a WSN like data aggregation or in-network data processing that can be affected by a particular security protocol. Accordingly, in this chapter, the authors summarize, discuss, and evaluate recent symmetric key based results reported in literature on sensor network security protocols such as for key establishment, random key pre-distribution, data confidentiality, data integrity, and broadcast authentication as well as expose limitations and issues related to those

DOI: 10.4018/978-1-60960-200-0.ch014

solutions for WSNs. The authors also present significant advancement in public key cryptography for WSNs with promising results from elliptic curve cryptography and identity based encryption as well as their limitations for WSNs. In addition, they also discuss recently identified threats and their corresponding countermeasures in WSNs.

INTRODUCTION

Significant advancements in hardware technology have propelled the existence of Wireless Sensor Network (WSN). A WSN consists of simple, low cost yet powerful sensors. Each sensor has the ability to sense, process, and communicate data collected from the environment, in which it is deployed.

Sensors usually draw energy from a small battery, and thus energy efficiency emerges as the key issue in any WSN. The basic idea of a WSN is to deploy a large number of sensors to collectively monitor and disseminate information about a phenomenon of interest. WSNs have been designed to support a diverse range of applications. Some examples include military surveillance, habitat and weather monitoring, agricultural crop management, wildlife monitoring, target tracking, emergency rescue operations (Akyildiz, Su, Sankarasubram -aniam, & Cayirci, 2002), biosensors for health monitoring, etc. It is believed that WSNs will drastically change our lives. Not surprisingly, there is also an existing trend about integrating WSNs to the Internet (Su, & Almaharmeh, 2008).

The typical architecture of a wireless sensor node contains a sensing unit, a processing unit, a transceiver unit, a power unit, and an optional mobilizer, location finding system. The processing unit may contain a small memory unit. In addition to sensor nodes, the network may also contain a sink or base station. A sink is a node with relatively powerful communication and computation ability. It generally serves as a gateway in the network. Different kinds of communication patterns are possible between the sink and sensor

nodes (Demirkol, Ersoy, & Alagoz, 2006). However, the most common type of communication is convergecast, in which, a group of sensors communicate to a sink.

The security aspect of WSNs is very crucial and is the main focus of this paper. Security in WSNs is associated with a unique set of challenges for several reasons. Firstly, since the network is usually deployed in a hostile unattended environment, there is no physical security for the network thereby exposing it to easy attacks (Huang, Cukier, Kobayashi, Liu, & Zhang, 2003; Perrig, Szewczyk, Tygar, Wen, & Culler, 2002; Zhu, Setia, & Jajodia, 2006). Secondly, sensors are severely resource constrained. Therefore, existing security solutions are impractical and need be revised to accommodate the inherent resource constraints of WSNs. Finally, there is no trustable entity in a WSN unlike in a wired network where nodes rely on a trusted authority to securely communicate with other nodes.

Data aggregation and **passive participation** are two widely used techniques in WSN that are closely intertwined with security. Data aggregation is a method of modifying data as it flows through the network, to increase energy efficiency of the network. If encrypted data is being transmitted, the aggregating nodes must be able to access decrypted data to be able to perform aggregation. Similarly, in passive participation, a node that overhears another node transmitting the same value can choose not to transmit it. Passive participants should be able to decrypt data transmitted by neighbors, which means that the data should be encrypted with a locally shared key. However, implementing security measures on resource constrained sensor devices will further add to computation and communication overhead.

Much work has been going on in the field of security for WSNs. Cryptographic techniques such as Skipjack, RC5, Elliptic Curve Cryptography (ECC) and Identity Based Encryption (IBE) are found to be very promising for WSNs. This paper provides a comprehensive survey of these key contributions of research in applied cryptography and discusses their operations, applications, scopes, and limitations in WSNs. Some identified threats and defenses, some existing security protocols, and their limitations for security and privacy in WSNs are also presented in this paper.

The main contributions of this paper are summarized as below:

- Discuss some existing symmetric-key based protocols for WSNs.
- Examine significant developments in public-key based protocols for WSNs
- Understand specific attacks, security and privacy issues, and their solutions for WSNs.
- Identify open issues and bring up future research directions.

SYMMETRIC-KEY BASED PROTOCOLS FOR WIRELESS SENSOR NETWORKS

Since asymmetric cryptography is not energy efficient and computationally too intensive for WSNs, alternative research in symmetric-key cryptography for WSNs has led to the development of many symmetric key based security protocols for WSNs. Particularly, RC5 and Skipjack have been found very suitable for key and data encryption and decryption for WSNs. To facilitate the use of symmetric key based security protocols, sensor nodes are pre-distributed with one (or some) master secret key(s) to bootstrap the initialization of other keys.

In this section, we discuss three important symmetric-key based protocols recently developed for wireless sensor networks, namely, SPINs, LEAP, and TinySec.

Security Protocols for Sensor Networks

(SPINs)

SPINs is one of the first and well-known security protocols developed for wireless sensor networks. Perrig et al. proposed two security blocks in SPINs, which are *Secure Network Encryption Protocol* (SNEP) and *"micro" Timed Efficient Stream Loss-tolerant Authentication* (μTESLA). While SNEP provides data confidentiality, two-party data authentication, and data freshness, μTESLA is developed to provide authenticated broadcast for resource-constrained environments. However, SPINs only deals with three kinds of communication patterns:

- *Node to base station* such as sensor readings
- *Base station to node communication* such as requests from base station to a specific node
- *Base station to all nodes* such as routing beacons or queries on the entire network.

In SPINs, each sensor node shares a predistributed master secret key with the base station. All other keys are bootstrapped from the initial master secret key. The derivation procedure F is a pseudo-random function which is implemented as $F_K(x) = MAC(K,x)$. Encryption Protocol SNEP, a sub-protocol of SPINs, derives two keys from the master secret key: K_{encr} and K_{mac} where K_{encr} is used for encryption/decryption and K_{mac} is used to create message authentication code (MAC). To minimize the power requirements, the number generator key K_{rand} is also derived from master

Figure 1. Deriving keys from master secret key K

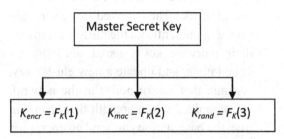

secret key K. Figure 1 shows how the master key is used to derive all these three keys.

Broadcast authentication is very important to defend wireless sensor networks from adversaries who try to take control of the network. To broadcast authenticated packets, SPINs uses μTESLA protocol. In μTESLA, the sender generates one-way key chain by using a one-way function such as MD5. The sender then chooses the last key K_n randomly and generates the other keys in reverse order from K_{n-1} to K_1 as $K_i = F(K_{i+1})$. The receiver can verify received keys by computing and comparing $F(K_{j+1})$ with K_j. A mechanism called *delayed key disclosure* is used in μTESLA to implement the authenticated broadcasting (see sub-section "Authentication and Integrity" under "Security in Wireless Sensor Networks" for more details on *Authentication*). For node-to-node comm-unications, SPINs uses the base station as a trusted agent to set up keys. Since all sensor nodes share a master secret key with the base station, they can transmit session keys securely through the base station.

Localized Encryption Authentication Protocol (LEAP)

One of the drawbacks of SPINs is that it does not consider different security requirements for different types of messages, which may reduce lifetime of sensor networks unnecessarily. For example, routing control information may not require confidentiality whereas sensor readings and aggregated reports should be encrypted be-

fore they are sent to the base station. Because of this disadvantage, different security mechanisms should be used for different types of messages in wireless sensor networks (Zhu et al., 2006). Since one single key mechanism is not enough to satisfy different security requirements, **LEAP** provides four types of keys for wireless sensor network communication:

- **Individual Key:** This is a key shared by the base station with each sensor node in the network. This key is preloaded in each sensor node before deployment and is used to secure the communication between the base station and sensor nodes.
- **Pairwise Shared Key:** This type of key is only shared by two sensor nodes. A newly added sensor node u has to follow four steps to set up a pairwise shared key with each of its neighbors.
  - **Key Pre-distribution:** Node u is loaded with an initial key K and derives a master key $K_u = f_K(u)$.
  - **Neighbor Discovery:** Node u initializes a timer with a time T_{min} and broadcasts a HELLO message to contact its neighbors where T_{min} is the minimum time necessary for an adversary to compromise a sensor node. In this phase, node u can verify the identity of its neighbors since it can easily compute its neighbors' keys. Figure 2 illustrates how node u discovers one of its neighboring node v. For example, it can compute a key for node v as

Figure 2. Neighbor discovery

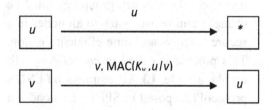

$K_v = f_K(v)$. A very important assumption in establishing this type of key is that T_{min} has to be greater than T_{est} in which T_{est} is the time to complete the key establishment process.

- **Pairwise Key Establishment:** Nodes u and v compute pairwise shared key $K_{uv} = f_{Kv}(u)$. After that, any subsequent messages exchanged between u and v are authenticated using K_{uv}.
- **Key Erasure:** When the timer T_{min} expires, node u erases the initial key K and all the master keys of its neighbors but keeps its key K_u.

Later in this paper, we discuss the requirements of establishing pairwise shared keys for two sensor nodes that are multi-hops away from each other.

- **Cluster Key:** This type of key is shared by a node and its neighbors. Unlike group keys (discussed below), a cluster key is used to broadcast messages locally. A cluster key can be easily set up by using pairwise shared keys. A node uses its pairwise keys shared with its neighbors to encrypt the cluster key. Encrypted messages, which contain the cluster key, are then sent to neighboring nodes.
- **Group Key:** This type of key is shared by all nodes in the network. A simple and most efficient way to bootstrap a group key is to pre-load it to every sensor node. Another way to establish a group key is by using cluster keys. One important issue with group keys is that when a node is compromised, the network group key must be changed and redistributed to all nodes in a secure, energy- and time-efficient fashion. This process is called *group rekeying*. To revoke a node, **LEAP** employs *μ***TESLA** protocol (proposed in SPINs) to broadcast

a revoking message to all sensor nodes in the network. The revoked node's neighbors will authenticate the message, remove their pairwise keys shared with the revoked node, and update a new cluster key. Assume that sensor nodes in the network are organized into a breadth first spanning tree, the base station can send an encrypted message that contains the new group key by using its children's cluster key. These children can then continue sending the new group key recursively down the spanning tree using their own cluster keys for encryption.

Link Layer Security Protocol: TinySec

TinySec is a security architecture, which operates on the data link layer. Unlike SPINs and LEAP, TinySec is not limited to any keying mechanism (Karlof, Sastry, & Wagner, 2004a). TinySec uses a pair of Skipjack keys to encrypt data and compute MACs of packets. Below are three different keying mechanisms that can be used with TinySec to secure sensor network applications. Each mechanism has its own advantages and disadvantages. The tradeoffs among different keying mechanisms should be considered.

- **Single network-wide key:** This type of key is shared by all authorized sensor nodes in a sensor network. It is easy to deploy by simply pre-loading shared keys into every node in the network before deployment. In a sensor network using single network-wide key mechanism, a node will reject all messages sent from unauthorized nodes. Networks using this type of keys support both passive participation and local broadcasting among authorized sensor nodes. The major drawback of network-wide keys is that if any authorized node is compromised, adversaries can eavesdrop or inject malicious codes into the networks.

- **Per-link key:** This key is shared by each pair of sensor nodes only if they need to communicate with each other. Per-link keys can be used to overcome the problem of network-wide keys because a compromised node can only inject malicious codes into its immediate neighbors and decrypt messages addressed to it. There are some drawbacks when using this keying mechanism. Not only does it limit passive participation capability, a type of in-network processing used to save energy and prolong network lifetime, but it is also not suitable for local broadcast, an important feature allowing sensor nodes to cheaply send messages to all their neighbors. Although key distribution is challenging (Karlof et al., 2004a), this problem can be solved by random key pre-distribution schemes (Chan, Perrig, & Song, 2003) or by some different pairwise key distribution mechanisms (Du, Deng, Han, Varshney, Katz, & Khalili, 2005; Liu, Ning, & Li, 2005).

- **Group key:** This key is shared by a group of neighboring nodes. When a sensor node is compromised, the extent of damage due to exposure of a group key is confined within the neighboring nodes only. The compromised node can only decrypt messages sent from sensor nodes in its group. It cannot inject malicious codes to and decrypt messages from other groups. Although this key supports passive participation and local broadcast, how to distribute and set up this type of key is still a problem.

TinySec is now fully implemented and included in TinyOS distribution (Karlof et al., 2004b). Hence, users can easily develop a secure wireless sensor network without changing application code except for some special situations. However, one should always consider the trade-off between security and network lifetime.

PUBLIC-KEY BASED PROTOCOLS IN WIRELESS SENSOR NETWORKS

Recently it has been shown that PKC (Public Key Cryptography) in wireless sensor networks is feasible to perform limited PKC operations on current sensor platforms. One notable attempted PKC system for wireless sensor networks is TinyPK proposed by Watro, Kong, Cuti, Gardiner, Lynn, and Kruss (2004). A comparative study on ECC (Elliptic Curve Cryptography) and RSA on the ATmega128 by Gura, Patel, and Wander (2004) shows that ECC outperforms RSA as a cryptosystem. Particularly, ECC has been found very amenable for wireless sensor networks due to its fast computation, small key size, and small packet overhead. For equivalent security, an ECC based scheme requires only 160-bit key in contrast to 1024-bit RSA key (NIST, 2003). Due to ECC's better computational efficiency and less power requirement compared to RSA, ECC is finding applications for security in hand-held mobile devices. Several software implementations of ECC on sensor network platforms have also been reported in literature. Some progress has been made on hardware implementation of ECC, but such solutions have not been integrated with sensor nodes yet (Batina, Mentens, Sakiyama, Preneel, & Verbauwhede, 2006; Luo, Wang, Feng, & Xu, 2008). In the following, we describe implementation of ECC based cryptosystems for wireless sensor networks.

Background on Elliptic Curve Cryptography

Elliptic curve cryptography (ECC) was proposed independently by Neal Koblitz (1987) and Victor Miller (1986) as a public key cryptosystem. Compared to RSA public key cryptography, ECC has been found advantageous in many ways including processing requirement, memory requirement, and energy requirement for its implementation (Cilardo, Coppolino, Mazzocca, & Ramno, 2006). According to NIST, for example, a 160-bit ECC key can ensure the similar level of security of a 1024-bit RSA key (NIST, 2003). The security of RSA relies on the problem of difficulty of factoring a large number, which is becoming increasingly easier to perform as researchers are working to accelerate the solution of the factorization problem, resulting to increasing vulnerability of the RSA public key cryptosystem. To cope with this, the key size for the RSA key can be used for short time but at the cost of high processing time for computation, communication, and storage. On the contrary, ECC has been found relatively less problematic and sustained a prolonged time of scrutiny and attacks as its security relies on the difficulty of the Elliptic Curve Discrete Logarithm problem.

For fast, accurate, and efficient operations for cryptography, ECC is typically defined over two finite fields: prime field F_n and binary field F_{2^m}. Specifically, ECC operations are defined over the elliptic curve:

$$y^2 = (x^3 + ax + b) \tag{1}$$

where a and b are constants such that $(4a^3 + 27b^2) \neq 0$. A point at infinity is also considered to be on the elliptic curve. Let us consider two distinct points $P = (x_p, y_p)$ and $Q = (x_q, y_q)$ on the elliptic curve defined by equation (1) on affine coordinate system. The point addition operation on the elliptic curve is defined as $R = P + Q$ where R is a point on the elliptic curve with a coordinate (x_r, y_r). If $Q = -P$ meaning $Q = (x_p, -y_p)$ then $R = P + (-P) = O$, where O is the point at infinity. If $Q = P$, then the operation $R = 2P$ is called *point doubling*. The computation of point R is summarized in Table 1 for both fields.

Elliptic Curve Discrete Logarithm Problem (**ECDLP**) is defined as $R = P + P + ... + P = k \cdot P$ where k is a scalar and P and R are two points on an elliptic curve. The corresponding operation is called point multiplication ($R = k \cdot P$) that can be achieved using a sequence of point doubling and point addition operations. Given P and R, it is computationally infeasible to find k for sufficiently large k. The scalar k is termed as the elliptic curve discrete logarithm of R to base P. The scalar k constitutes the private key component of any elliptic curve based cryptography and is kept secret. The security of ECC depends on the difficulty of computing k given P, R, and the elliptic curve parameters a and b. As can be seen from Table 1, ECC operations involve many time-consuming operations such as multiplication, squaring, and division/inversion. To expedite such operations, several hardware and software algorithms have been proposed in literature (Ciet, Joyce, Lauter, & Montgomery, 2006). In addition, to avoid division/inversion altogether, ECC operations have been proposed on projective coordinate system.

ECC Implementation for Wireless Sensor Networks

Among all ECC implementations for sensor network platforms, **TinyECC** proposed by Liu and Peng has several competitive advantages (Liu & Peng, 2008). Essentially TinyECC is a configurable software library for ECC operations for public key cryptography targeted at TinyOS for sensor platforms MICAz, TelosB, Tmote Sky, and Imote2 (Crossbow Technology, Inc., n.d.). It allows selection of specific components from its library as needed for optimization of an application on a specific sensor platform.

The following describes the optimization features of TinyECC:

- **Fast Modular Reduction:** TinyECC implements ECC over a prime field F_n and utilizes several existing optimization tech-

Table1. Operations in elliptic curve cryptography

ECC Operations over F_n	ECC Operations over F_{2^m}
A. Point Addition: 1) $R = P + Q$ $x_r = (s^2 - x_p - x_q) \bmod n$ $y_r = -y_p + s(x_p - x_r) \bmod n$ where the slope s is: $s = (y_p - y_q) / (x_p - x_q) \bmod n$. 2) If $Q = -P$ meaning $Q = (x_p, -y_p)$ then $R = P + (-P) = O$, where O is the point at infinity. B. Point Doubling 1) $R = 2P$ $x_r = s^2 - 2x_p \bmod n$ $y_r = -y_p + s(x_p - x_r) \bmod n$ where the slope s of the tangent at P is: $s = (3x_p + a) / (2y_p) \bmod n$ 2) If $y_p = 0$ then $R = 2P = O$, where O is the point at infinity.	A. Point Addition: 1) $R = P + Q$ $x_r = s^2 + s + x_p + x_q + a$ $y_r = s(x_p + x_r) + x_r + y_p$ where the slope s is: $s = (y_p + y_q) / (x_p + x_q)$. 2) If $Q = -P$ meaning $Q = (x_p, x_p + y_p)$ then $R = P + (-P) = O$, where O is the point at infinity. B. Point Doubling 1) $R = 2P$ $x_r = s^2 + s + a$ $y_r = x_p^2 + (s + 1)x_r$ where the slope s of the tangent at P is: $s = x_p + y_p / x_p$ 2) If $x_p = 0$ then $R = O$, where O is the point at infinity.

niques in its implementation for ECC operations for the sake of increased speed, reduced memory requirement, and reduced energy consumption. For modular reduction, TinyECC uses Barrett Reduction method to achieve faster speed than that can be obtained using simple division. However, Barrett Reduction implementation requires more ROM and increases RAM use in a sensor node due to its separate implementation instead of using existing division operation to carry out modular reduction.

• **Fast Modular Inversion:** As can be seen from Table 1, two essential operations, point addition and point doubling in affine coordinate system (x, y) for ECC require very expensive modular inversion operations. Using a projective coordinate system, TinyECC replaces the inversion operations with a few modular multiplications

and squares achieving faster execution of point addition and point doubling operations. However, the projective coordinate representation (x, y, z) requires a larger code size and more RAM than the affine coordinate system as it requires a point to be represented as (x, y, z) instead of (x, y) in the affine coordinate system.

• **Fast Mixed/Hybrid Operations:** To reduce execution time and program size, TinyECC uses a *mixed point addition algorithm* to add a point in projective coordinate to a second point in affine coordinate and a *repeated Doubling* algorithm for scalar multiplication (Hankerson, Menezes, & Vanstone, 2004). In addition, TinyECC utilizes a hybrid multiplication algorithm by Gura et al. (2004) and also customizes the same hybrid multiplication algorithm for squaring operations.

- **Curve Specific Optimizations:** TinyECC can also achieve curve specific optimizations particularly for the elliptic curve recommended by NIST using *pseudo-Mersenne primes* of the form $n = 2^m - c$, where c and m are positive integers such that $c \ll 2^m$.

TinyECC includes all of the above optimization modules for generating energy-efficient, storage-efficient, and time-efficient code for various sensor platforms. It may not be possible to generate code that meets all of the optimization objectives for processing time, storage requirement, and energy consumption simultaneously. Depending on the constraints of the sensor platform and the need of an application, a compromise can be achieved by selecting appropriate modules for generating code for the application. The current version of TinyECC provides support for ECDSA (Elliptic Curve Digital Signature Algorithm) for digital signatures, ECDH (Elliptic Curve Diffie-Hellman) for pairwise key establishment, and ECIES (Elliptic Curve Integrated Encryption System) for PKC-based encryption (Hankerson et al., 2004).

Elliptic Curve Diffie-Hellman Key Establishment Scheme

As mentioned earlier, the security of ECC depends on the difficulty of computing k given the curve parameters a and b and two points P and R on the curve such that $R = k \cdot P$. Accordingly the ECDH protocol can securely be used by two neighboring sensor nodes to establish a pairwise key. The following describes the protocol assuming that two sensor nodes X and Y share the curve parameters a, b and the public base point P on the curve:

1. Node X chooses a random integer x and computes a point $R_x = x \cdot P$ and sends R_x to node Y. Similarly node Y chooses a random

integer y and computers a point $R_y = y \cdot P$ and sends R_y to node X.

2. After receiving R_y, node X computes $x \cdot R_y = (xy) \cdot P$.

Similarly node Y computes $y \cdot R_x = (yx) \cdot P$.

Evidently, both nodes have computed the same point. However, an adversary will not be able to compute the point since the secret keys x and y are not known. It is to be noted that each sensor node has to perform two point-multiplications.

Regarding implementation of the protocol, it may be possible for each node to obtain the parameters a and b and the public base point P from the base station or each node can be loaded with them before deployment. Even though the protocol itself is not vulnerable, an adversarial node can exploit the protocol easily. Since a, b, P are public in either cases, an adversarial node can participate in the key establishment process as well if not checked. To prevent such an attack, it is necessary to authenticate a node from a trusted authority before accepting any key establishment request.

Identity Based Encryption

To thwart "man-in-the-middle" attacks, public key cryptosystems use a trusted certifying authority of Public Key Infrastructure (PKI) for verification and authentication of a public key and its holder. However, such practice of PKC is not feasible in a wireless sensor network environment simply due to extra overhead on sensor nodes and lack of resources prohibiting deployment of PKI. Recently, it has been shown that it is possible to have public key cryptosystems in this environment by using a technique based on random identities of the sensor nodes. The scheme is known as **Identity Based Encryption** originally introduced by Shamir a long time ago (Shamir, 1984). This is also called pairing based encryption. Due to recent development in ECC and its relation to discrete logarithm, it is now feasible to have IBE for wireless sensor networks. The mathematical theory behind pairing based cryptography can be summarized as follows (Menezes, Okamoto, & Vanstone, 1993):

Let E be an elliptic curve on a finite field F_n. A pairing e is a computable bilinear mapping for two given points P and Q on E to an integer M over $F_{n^q}^*$ that can be described as:

$$e(P, Q) \Rightarrow M \bmod n^q \qquad (2)$$

and has the following properties:

$$e(aP, bQ) = e(P, Q)^{ab} = M^{ab} \bmod n^q \qquad (3)$$

for any a and b, and

$$e(P, P) \neq 1 \qquad (4)$$

The integer q, known as the embedding degree, is the least integer such that ($n^q - 1$) is divisible by r where r is a prime order of the group of points on E over F_n (i.e., r is a prime factor that divides the number of points on E over F_n). Only a few bilinear mappings or pairings are known for small values of q that include the Weil and Tate pairings (Boneh & Franklin, 2003; Galbraith, 2005). Comparatively, the Tate paring has been found to be more efficient and amenable than the Weil pairing.

An **IBE based cryptosystem** for sensor networks can be developed based on the properties of such pairings of points on an elliptic curve. Although an IBE based public key system does not require any PKI but it requires a trusted party that is responsible to generate a public key to be used by the entire network and a secret integer corresponding to the public key. In a sensor network environment, the base station is the obvious choice for such a trusted party. The base station needs to:

1. Choose a point P on the designated elliptic curve and a secret integer s.
2. Compute a point $R = s \cdot P$ on the elliptic curve and then publish P and R both. In this case, R is the public key.

It is desirable to load each sensor node with points P and R before deployment thus avoiding any further communication from the base station to the sensor nodes for the points. In the following we describe how points P and R as well as the identity of a receiving node are used for secure communication between two sensor nodes. For the sake of simplicity, we assume that simple exclusive-or operation is used for encryption and decryption.

Encryption steps:

1. The sender computes point $Q_x = \text{Hash1}(\text{ID}_x)$ essentially by converting the identity string ID_x of a receiver X to a point Q_x on the elliptic curve by using some function Hash1.
2. The sender selects a random integer k and computes a point $U = k \cdot P$ on the elliptic curve.
3. The sender then computes an encryption key $h = \text{Hash2}(e(k \cdot R, Q_x))$ using a designated bilinear mapping function e and some hashing function Hash2.
4. For a given message m, the sender computes point $V = m \oplus h$ and then sends (U, V) to receiver X.

Decryption steps:

1. After receiving (U, V) from the sender, the receiver contacts the base station for the private key corresponding to its identity ID_x.
2. The base station first computes $Q_x = \text{Hash1}(\text{ID}_x)$ and then $d = s \cdot Q_x$ where d is the private key for receiver X.
3. Using some secure protocol, the base station sends d to the receiving node X.

4. After receiving d from the base station, the receiver reveals the plaintext m by computing $m = V \oplus \text{Hash2}(e(U, d))$.

It is to be noted that
$$e(U, d) = e(k \cdot P, s \cdot Q_x)$$
$$= e(ks \cdot P, Q_x) = e(k \cdot R, Q_x)$$
due to the properties of the bilinear mapping as mentioned earlier.
Thus, $\text{Hash2}(e(U, d))$
$= \text{Hash2}(e(k \cdot R, Q_x))$. Evidently, the
protocol eliminates the need for having a public key infrastructure for a sensor network. However, during decryption step 1, the receiving sensor node has to communicate with the base station to obtain its private key corresponding to its identity ID_x. If the receiver's identity ID_x is randomly chosen by a sender, the receiver does not have any choice but to communicate with the base station to obtain its private key each time whenever it needs to decrypt a ciphertext. The process is very expensive for a sensor node in terms of energy usage. From decryption step 3, it is evident that the security of the private key d of a receiving node X depends on a separate security protocol for key delivery from the base station to the receiving node. This step can be very expensive in terms of energy usage as well as memory usage due to extra storage required for additional code and data. In addition, the base station becomes a vulnerable point and bottleneck for the entire network. It is to be noted that the bilinear mapping function e is computationally very intensive. It is, therefore, logical to adopt IBE based public key cryptography for sensor networks only for those situations that symmetric key cryptography cannot provide a satisfactory solution in terms of security and resource usage. For example, IBE based PKC can be used to overcome the shortcomings of key establishment and key distribution using symmetric key cryptography.

Key Establishment Using IBE

The drawbacks of the IBE protocol described, in the previous section, for sensor networks can be overcome by assigning a permanent identity as well as a private key to each sensor node corresponding to its identity before deployment. As a result, a sensor node does not need to communicate with the base station to obtain its private key each time it needs to decrypt a message. Alternatively, a sensor node can choose a fixed identity and securely communicate to the base station to receive its private key once and use the key for its life time. However, a sending node must need to know the identity of the receiving node since it cannot use any arbitrary identity for the receiving node any more. One solution to the problem is to program all sensor nodes to broadcast their identity information immediately after their deployment. In the following, we summarize a protocol proposed by Oliveira, Aranha, Morais, Felipe, Lopez, and Dahab (2007) that uses a similar strategy for pairwise key establishment in a sensor network. We assume that each node in the sensor network is deployed with a unique identity string, a private key, and a common function f to derive an IBE public key from a given identity string of any node. Let us consider two nodes X and Y in a sensor network having identities ID_x and ID_y, IBE private keys S_x and S_y, and IBE public keys P_x and P_y respectively where $P_x = f(\text{ID}_x)$ and $P_y = f(\text{ID}_y)$. In order to establish a pairwise secret key between node X and node Y, the following steps are followed:

1. Node X broadcasts its identity string ID_x and a nonce N_x.
2. Each neighboring node Y upon receiving ID_x and N_x, derives the public key of X as $P_x = f(\text{ID}_x)$.
3. Each neighboring node Y generates a secret key K_{xy} to be shared between X and Y for future message transmission.

4. Each neighboring node Y encrypts the combined message K_{xy} appended with ID_y and N_x using node X's public key P_x and sends the ciphertext to node X.

5. Node X decrypts the message sent by Node Y and recovers K_{xy}.

In order to protect from replay attacks, the value of nonce N_x must indicate message freshness. The above protocol allows a sensor node to establish a pairwise secret key with each of its neighbors. Security of the pairwise key during transmission is achieved by using IBE cryptographic techniques as explained earlier. Once a pairwise secret key is established, both sensor nodes can take advantage of a suitable, fast symmetric key algorithm for future secure communications. After establishment of secret keys within a group, all private keys of all nodes can be discarded if needed. However, deletion of the private key of a node does not protect its shared secret keys from an adversary who can capture the node and reveal all shared secret keys. Another notable weakness of the protocol is that the shared secret key K_{xy} is not chosen by X but by a neighbor Y meaning that any adversarial sensor node that have access to the function f can establish a shared secret key with X since it can generate a public key for X easily. As a result, the adversary can feed wrong information to its neighboring nodes spoiling the intended purpose of the network. This is particularly a problem for data integration or in-network processing of data in which a node receives environmental data from its neighboring nodes, filters or summarizes data received, and delivers data to either the base station or some other node responsible for further data integration or in-network processing along a network path to the base station. In addition, if the adversary remains undetected it can steal information from the network. This is mainly because all neighboring nodes in the group share information among them including the unsuspected adversarial node. The problem can be solved if there is a mechanism in the protocol to check the authenticity

of a node's identity from a trusted authority such as the base station. However, this will require a separate scheme.

One way to accomplish this is to have a digitally signed identity stored in each sensor node before deployment. A node upon receiving the signed identity of its neighbor can verify the authenticity of the identity by using the public key of the signer and then engage in further communication for key exchange. There are many several public key based signature algorithms available including identity based signature schemes. However, most of them are very computationally intensive and energy consuming for a tiny sensor node. A scheme proposed by Boneh, Lynn, and Shacham for short signatures using Weil pairing seems very suitable for the purpose of node's identity verification (2001). The scheme can be described as follows for a sensor network with an ECC based solution.

A trusted party computes a point $R = s \cdot P$ on a designated elliptic curve E where s is the private key (a secret integer) and P is the base point on the elliptic curve E. It is to be noted that R, P, and the elliptic curve parameters are public.

Before Deployment, for each Node X do the following:

1. Compute point $Q_x = \mathrm{Hash}1(ID_x)$ by converting the identity string ID_x of node X on the designated elliptic curve using the hash function Hash1.

2. Compute point $V = s \cdot Q_x$ using point multiplication. Then point V is the signature for ID_x, the identity of node X.

3. Load sensor node X with ID_x, V, P, R, and the elliptic curve parameters.

Verification of Identity of Node X by Node Y: Node X sends ID_x and signature V to node Y. Node Y computes Q_x as $\mathrm{Hash}1(ID_x)$ and then checks $e(P, V) = e(R, Q_x)$.

It is to be noted that $e(P, V) = e(P, s \cdot Q_x) = e(P, Q_x)^s = e(s \cdot P, Q_x) = e(R, Q_x)$ which verifies a signed identity of node X. To verify the signature, node Y has to compute the pairing function twice, one for $e(P, V)$ and the other for $e(R, Q_x)$ which can be prohibitive in terms of computation time. However, the scheme does not require any communication with the base station since each sensor node is already provided with a fixed signed identity, public points R and P, and the curve parameters before deployment. Another notable advantage of the scheme is that it can be used to replenish an aging network with new sensor nodes as existing nodes will be able to verify authenticity of the new nodes and integrate them securely in the existing operational network. Current symmetric key based schemes lack such advantage for sensor network environment in terms of security and computational and energy cost.

IBE Implementation Examples and Issues

For the purpose of key establishment in a sensor network, recently Oliveira et al. (2007) have proposed TinyTate, an implementation of an IBE system based on elliptic curves and Tate pairing for the linear-mapping function e. It makes use of TinyECC library since it provides optimized, efficient code modules for ECC operations for popular sensor platforms. For Tate pairing computation, it uses Miller's algorithm with an embedding degree of 2 and a supersingular curve E over F_n: $y^2 = x^3 + x$ where n is 256-bit prime. It has been reported that computing a pairing by TinyTate over MICAz (8-bit, 7.3828-MHz processor, 4KB SRAM, 128KB flash memory) using TinyOS requires 30.21 seconds on average, 1,831 bytes of RAM, and 18,384 bytes of ROM (flash). Although promising, the computation time for Tate pairing presented by Oliveira et al. (2007) for wireless sensor networks is significantly high. In order to establish a pairwise secret key between two nodes, it requires computation of Tate pairing twice, one computation by the sender during

encryption and another computation by the receiver during decryption. As a result, establishing a secret key between any two pair of nodes would take over a minute (since 30.21 seconds + 31.28 seconds > 1 minute). In an application with thousands of wireless sensor nodes, it will take exorbitant amount of time for a node to establish pairwise keys with a large group of wireless sensor nodes. Hence with current sensor network technology, an IBE based PKC system has limited applications for security in wireless sensor networks.

To assess the performance of public-key cryptographic schemes, TinyPK implements RSA and Diffie-Hellman algorithms on MICA2 platform to exchange secret keys (Watro et al., 2004). While RSA makes the execution time in tens of minutes, Diffie-Hellman shows an obvious speed improvement. However, both code size and execution time are still too expensive for such energy-constrained envir-onment like wireless sensor networks. Among those above asymmetric-key based protocols, Identity-Based Encryption (IBE) and Elliptic Curve Cryptography (ECC) seem to be the most practical public key cryptographic schemes for wireless sensor networks (Law, Doumen, & Hartel, 2006; Oliveira et al., 2007).

Recent IBE Schemes

As mentioned above, the most costly operation involved with IBE is the pairing calculation. More recent implementations have shown that pairings can be calculated more efficiently using the ηT pairing, which is a reduced version of the traditional Tate pairing (Szczechowiak & Collier, 2009; Xiong, Wong, and Deng, 2010). This type of pairing operates on supersingular curves over F_{n^q} just like the original Tate pairing. This type of pairing has the bilinear property as mentioned above, as well as the commutative property, $e(A, B) = e(B, A)$ (Szczechowiak et al., 2009). This property could be used to develop other types of pairing protocols in the future. In addition to the pairing function, a fairly costly hash-to-point function is needed to implement and IBE scheme. This function provides a one way map from a random value or message to a point on the elliptic curve. One method for implementing this function efficiently is discussed below for TinyPairing.

Another drawback of using pairing based cryptography is that it allows the elliptic curve discrete logarithm problem to be transformed into a traditional discrete logarithm problem on the finite field F_{n^q} (Szczechowiak et al., 2009). This makes the IBE scheme more susceptible to a cryptanalysis attack. As a result, the size of elements in F_{n^q} need to be at least 1024 bits to make such attacks infeasible (Szczechowiak & Collier, 2009). Though these elements are large, they are not prohibitive for WSNs since there are no modular operations performed on the elements. Despite the challenges involved with implementing IBE systems, two recent implementations, TinyPairing and TinyIBE, have shown that pairing based cryptosystems are feasible for wireless sensor networks.

TinyPairing

TinyPairing is an implementation of a complete identity based cryptosystem introduced in early 2010 (Xiong, Wong, and Deng, 2010). TinyPairing comes with a complete IBE library, including support for the traditional Boneh and Franklin IBE scheme as well as two digital signature schemes.

TinyPairing uses the ηT pairing on supersingular elliptic curves. Specifically the curves used for TinyPairing reside in the ternary field $F_{3^{97}}$. Although each element in the ternary finite field require 2 bits for representation, the amount of space needed for storage is still less than that of a binary field of equivalent security level. Using a point compression technique, TinyPairing further reduces the storage requirement of elliptic curve

points by about 23% with a minimal computation overhead.

The TinyPairing hash-to-point function is required to convert a random binary number or message into an elliptic curve point on a ternary finite field. To do this, a message digest is first computed using a traditional hash algorithm like SHA. Then, every two bits of the digest is mapped to a digit of an element x in F_{3^m}. If there are not enough bits in the digest, it is rehashed and the process is repeated until there are enough digits generated for x. Finally, the elliptic curve equation is used to calculate the y value corresponding to x, thus producing a point on the elliptic curve. In addition to the pairing calculation and the hash-to-point function, TinyPairing includes optimizations for scalar point multiplication which significantly reduces calculation time.

Table 2 shows the running times of the various IBE functions in the TinyPairing library on a standard 8-bit MicaZ sensor node.

As can be seen in the table, the calculation of the ηT pairing takes 5.32 seconds. With this calculation time, the Boneh and Franklin IBE scheme requires only about 10.6 seconds for encryption and 5.4 seconds for decryption using the TinyPairing library (Xiong, Wong, and Deng, 2010). These results are much better than the previous results of TinyTate by Oliveira et. al. (2007), and further support the feasibility of IBE for sensor networks.

TinyIBE

TinyIBE is another implementation of IBE for wireless sensor networks that was presented in 2009 by Szczechowiak & Collier. The goal of TinyIBE is to provide a scheme for authenticated key distribution in WSNs. This scheme includes algorithms for IBE functions as well as a novel protocol. The TinyIBE protocol is unique in that it focuses on the the the use of Heterogeneous Sensor Networks (HSNs). An HSN is a sensor network

Table 2. Run times of TinyPairing functions (Xiong, Wong, and Deng, 2010)

	Time (sec)
Hash-to-Point (16 bytes msg)	0.89
Point compression	0.38
Point decompression	0.38
Point scalar mult (original)	7.75
Point scalar mult (optimized)	2.50
Point scalar mult (revised)	2.45
ηT pairing	5.32

that is based on a hierarchy of high power H-nodes and low power L-nodes (Szczechowiak & Collier, 2009). The nodes in this type of network form in to small groups or clusters when they are deployed. The L-nodes have the job of performing sensory functions. These nodes typically consist of Mica class or Tmote Sky motes that have a relatively slow processor and weak radio transmitter. The H-nodes act as cluster heads. These cluster heads have the job of receiving data from the L-nodes and communicating directly with the base station and other cluster heads. H-nodes may consist of Imote2 motes which have a fast processor and a powerful radio transmitter.

The TinyIBE protocol is based on the assumption that L-nodes need only encrypt and transmit data to the H-node cluster heads. The H-nodes on the other hand need to be able to decrypt messages from the L-nodes, as well as encrypt messages for communicating with the base station and other cluster heads. The overall protocol consists of four main functions: setup, extract, encrypt, and decrypt. The setup function is done by the base station before deployment and includes the establishment of curve and encryption parameters. The extract function is also done by the base station before deployment and consists assigning unique IDs and private keys to each sensor node. The encryption function is the only function that is performed by L-nodes, which involves generating a random secret key and encrypting it using the ID of its cluster head. Decryption is performed by the H-nodes and includes checking the identity

of the sending L-node and retrieving the private key using its own private key.

Like TinyPairing, TinyIBE uses the ηT pairing as its bilinear paring algorithm. The pairing for this scheme is implemented on supersingular curves over the binary field $F_{2^{271}}$. The feature of TinyIBE that makes it different from other implementations is that the encryption function does not require a pairing calculation. This offers huge advantages since the L-nodes that usually perform encryption have very limited processing power. Although decryption does require a pairing calculation, it is performed by H-nodes which have processors that can better handle the calculations. Overall, this means that only one pairing has to be calculated for each establishment of a shared key. In addition to the savings in pairing operations, the TinyIBE implementation does not require any hash-to-point function, which further reduces the overall calculation time.

Table 3 shows the time, storage, and energy usage of encryption on L-nodes and decryption on H-nodes based on an analysis performed using AVR Studio and IAR Embedded Workbench simulators.

As can be seen from the table, the performance times of TinyIBE are impressive when compared to the results from TinyTate or even TinyPairing. If these results hold when tested on the actual hardware, this shows that TinyIBE is viable and perhaps ready to be used for authenticated key distribution in working wireless sensor networks.

Table 3. Resource usage of TinyIBE encryption and decryption (Szczechowiak & Collier, 2009)

Platform	Encryption			
	Time	ROM	RAM	Energy
MicaZ (7.38MHz)	3.93s	39.6KB	2.9KB	92.67mJ
Tmote (8.19MHz)	2.62s	30.3KB	3.2KB	27.12mJ
Platform	Decryption			
	Time	ROM	RAM	Energy
Imote2 (13MHz)	462ms	32.87KB	4.12KB	12.12mJ
Imote2 (104MHz)	57.7ms	32.87KB	4.12KB	3.76mJ
Imote2 (416MHz)	14.4ms	32.87KB	4.12KB	N/A

SECURITY IN WIRELESS SENSOR NETWORKS

Since a wireless sensor network can be deployed with hundreds or thousands of sensor nodes over a large area, there is a high possibility that sensor nodes are compromised. It is impossible to prevent or protect every mote from being attacked. Having full control over compromised nodes, the attackers can read all data stored in a node's memory including information on secret keys. They can also change the behavior of captured sensor nodes to inject malicious code into the network. Although special secure memory devices can be used to prevent attackers from reading compromised nodes' memory, this solution considerably increases the cost of tiny sensor nodes (Karl & Willig, 2005). One solution to prevent such attacks is to use tamper-resistant hardware. However, this solution is not economically viable as the number of sensor nodes increases in a network (Chan & Perrig, 2003). Software, therefore, is an only possible solution at this time. Since we cannot avoid node compromise, we need mechanisms to protect healthy nodes from attacks of captured nodes. Node authentication and node revocation are two popular mechanisms to identify and exclude compromised nodes respectively. Another approach is to discard odd data. For example, we should discard the data of 100^0 F from the final result if the average result is 50^0 F. A sensor network can use one or some approaches to protect itself from node compromise and it should function effectively in all situations.

Another issue is eavesdropping. In wireless sensor network applications, nodes communicate with each other using radio signal. Hence, adversaries can easily obtain private information if they are in the range of radio signal. Encryption can solve this problem but how to exchange secret keys is still a challenging issue. Another aspect of this issue is end-to-end security. There are two main reasons that make end-to-end security very difficult to implement. First, saving all secret keys of other nodes in the network is impractical due to the large number of sensor nodes and the limited memory. Second, in-network processing (data aggregation and passive participation) requires intermediate nodes to be able to access the content of received packets. Multipath routing is a robust solution to this problem. In this mechanism, a message is divided into several parts and each part is routed to the destination over a disjoint path. The message is only reassembled at the destination. Hence, intermediate nodes cannot understand the message content if they do not have threshold parts required to reconstruct the message (like threshold scheme in Secret Splitting). Unfortunately, how to discover best disjoint paths is still a challenging issue.

Privacy of sensed data is another issue. In sensor networks, adversaries do not need to be present at a particular site to gain access to information in that area. Rather, they can gather large amount of information through remote access (Chan & Perrig, 2003). This allows adversaries to retrieve sensed data from the network in an anonymous, thus, low-risk manner. Solutions for this issue may vary. Data encryption, access control, and distributed querying can be used to solve this problem.

To address above issues in more detail, the following sections discuss several design goals for security protocols in WSNs.

Key Management

Key management is one of the most important and complex issues in every security protocol. Although public key cryptography is very promising for key management, more research is still needed to improve its performance (see section "Public-key Based Protocols in Wireless Sensor Networks"). Accordingly, most of the current security protocols use symmetric-key based instead of public-key based cryptography for key management. Key management in symmetric-key based protocols is insignificant when compared with that of public key based protocols in terms of computation complexity and power consumption (Huang et al., 2003). Unfortunately, it is more complicated and is subject to attack by adversaries.

In key distribution, how to find a good path is the most important issue. Eschenauer and Gligor (2002) proposed a random key predistribution scheme to distribute secret keys for two sensor nodes that are multi-hop away. This scheme has two main phases: initialization phase and key-setup phase. The initialization phase is conducted before a network is deployed in the environment. In this phase, a random pool of keys S is picked from the total possible key space. Each sensor node then randomly selects m keys from S and stores them in its memory. This *m-key* set is called a key ring. The number of keys in S and value of m are chosen in such a way that two random

subsets of size m in S will share at least one key with an expected probability p. After deployment, the key-setup phase is automatically performed by sensor nodes. In this phase, a sensor node discovers which neighbors share a common predistributed key with it. The simplest way to do this is to broadcast the list of key identifiers to its neighbors. When recipients receive the list, they compare the sender's list with their own list. If receivers find a common key identifier, they will send a message, which contains the shared identifier back to the sender. Another approach can be used is to establish a *private discovery*. In this approach, for each key K_i in its key ring, the node broadcasts a set $(\alpha, E_{Ki}(\alpha))$ where α is a challenge. The recipient can verify the challenge α by decrypting $E_{Ki}(\alpha)$ using the proper key. If the verification is successful, the key will be used for the respective link for later communications. A connected graph of secure links is created after the key-setup phase completes. For any communication later, a source can use this graph to reach the destination.

Instead of using a single common key, Chan et al. (2003) proposed q-composite random key predistribution scheme that needs at least q common keys. By increasing the number of shared keys in key-setup phase, the network can increase the resilience against node capture attacks. As a compromised node also stores key ring information containing secret keys for other secure links, it is important to update the communication keys for those links immediately once the compromised node is discovered. For example in Figure 3, if node N_5 which contains shared keys K_{15}, K_{45}, and K_{12} is captured, the keys of the connection N_1-N_2 need to be updated. Node N_1, in this case, cannot use the direct link N_1-N_2 and the key K_{12} to set up a new key since N_5 can use K_{12} to decrypt key-update messages and obtain the new keys. This problem can be solved by using *Multipath Key Reinforcement* scheme that splits a message into many different parts and sends them on disjoint paths to the destination (Chan et al., 2003). Es-

Figure 3. Path key establishment problem

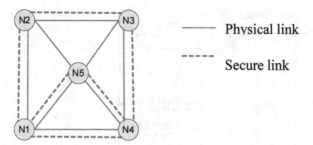

sentially, the new key K' is split into n parts where n is the number of disjoint paths from source to destination:

$K' = K \oplus v_1 \oplus v_2 \oplus ... \oplus v_n$ in which $\oplus$ is *XOR* operation.

The source sends $v_1, v_2, ... v_n$ on n disjoint paths to a destination so that adversaries cannot reveal the new key K' if they do not have all n split parts. In the above example, N_1 can send two split parts using two disjoint paths N_1-N_2 and N_1-N_4-N_3-N_2.

To produce shorter path lengths, Mehallegue, Bouridane, and Garcia (2008) proposed a novel algorithm that can quickly find common trusted nodes that are closer to both end nodes. An important assumption of this algorithm is that every sensor node has the identifier list of its first neighbors. First neighbors of N_i are defined as nodes that are one hop away from N_i and share a secret with N_i. Assuming $TIER(N_i, x)$ is the set of nodes that are x hops away from node N_i, Figure 4 shows an example for the algorithm proposed by Mehallegue et al. (2008). In the example, node N_1 wants to set up a secure link with node N_2. It initially sends a request to set up a secure link to N_2. After receiving the key identifier list from N_2, N_1 compares its own list with N_2's list (CMP_0). If there is a common key(s), N_1 and N_2 can set up a direct secure link between them. Otherwise, N_1 requests the list of N_2's first neighbors, then after receiving the list, it continues comparing its first neighbors' list and N_2's list (CMP_1). If the number of *proxies* is zero or less than *prx* which is the number of common trusted nodes required

to send the secret, N_1 will ask $TIER(N_1, 1)$ for $TIER(N_1, 2)$ and $TIER(N_2, 1)$ for $TIER(N_2, 2)$. The process becomes more and more complicated as N_1 continues finding proxies. In CMP_2, N_1 has to compare three pairs: $TIER(N_1, 1)$ with $TIER(N_2, 2)$, $TIER(N_1, 2)$ with $TIER(N_2, 1)$, and $TIER(N_1, 2)$ with $TIER(N_2, 2)$. The proxy discovery process continues until the number of proxies found is equal or greater than *prx*.

Though effective, the multipath key reinforcement scheme is complex and incurs excessive communication overhead. For a sensor node, typically communication cost is much higher than computation cost in terms of energy consumption and is the main reason of its early failure. Therefore, it is important to have a scheme that can minimize communication overhead as much as possible.

Confidentiality and Privacy

Data confidentiality is needed to protect sensitive information from being disclosed to unauthorized parties. Confidentiality plays a very important role in wireless sensor network applications such as military applications (smart uniforms, target tracking, and battlefield monitoring) or healthcare applications (to protect patient information). In wireless sensor networks, encryption is the technique used to achieve data confidentiality. Unfortunately, pure encryption may not be enough to protect data from adversaries since two same plaintexts can have the same ciphertext (Electronic

Figure 4. Process of finding trusted common sensor nodes (Adapted from Mehallegue et al., 2008)

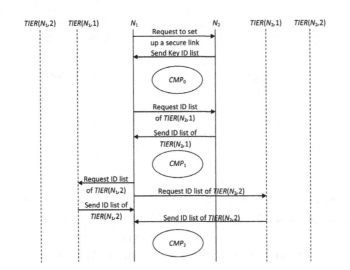

Codebook mode). To overcome this problem, the use of other operation modes such as CBC (Cipher Block Chaining) and OFM (Output Feedback Mode) is necessary.

Due to the limit in storage capacity and energy, public-key cryptography is not suitable for such energy-consuming operations like encryption and decryption. Symmetric-key cryptographic algorithms such as Skipjack or RC5, on the other hand, are proposed in many other protocols such as SPINs, LEAP, and TinySec (Karlof et al., 2004a; Law et al., 2006; Perrig et al., 2002; Zhu et al., 2006).

Another security issue that needs to be considered is end-to-end security. Because sensor nodes are energy-constrained devices, the requirement of in-network processing (data aggregation and passive participation) is the most crucial. Unfortunately, to use this mechanism, intermediate nodes need to access, aggregate, and modify information in the packets, which makes end-to-end security more difficult.

SNEP, a building block of SPINs, uses RC5, a block cipher with two counters shared by parties, to achieve confidentiality. Figure 5 illustrates the operation of RC5. To save energy for sensor nodes, the counters are not sent along with the messages.

After each block, sensor nodes increase and keep the state of the counters for themselves. SPINs can achieve *semantic security* by using the value of the counters so that even if two plaintexts are the same, the corresponding ciphertexts will be different.

Unlike SNEP, which is neither fully specified nor implemented, **TinySec** is now fully implemented and included in TinyOS distribution (Karlof et al., 2004b). TinySec is a link-layer security protocol, which means it is transparent to user. Because the encryption and decryption happen at the link layer automatically, TinySec can support in-network processing. Since RC5 requires 104 extra bytes of RAM per key, Skipjack becomes a better choice for sensor networks (Karlof et al., 2004a). In fact, the default block cipher in TinySec is Skipjack. To achieve semantic security, TinySec uses *initialization vector (IV)* with CBC mode. A TinySec-AE packet is partitioned into 7 different fields in which the combination of the first 5 fields is the *IV*. The *IV* is 8 bytes in length including destination address (2 bytes), active message handler type (1 byte), length of the data Payload (1 byte), source address (2 bytes), and 16-bit counter (2 bytes).

Figure 5. Counter mode encryption and decryption in SPINs

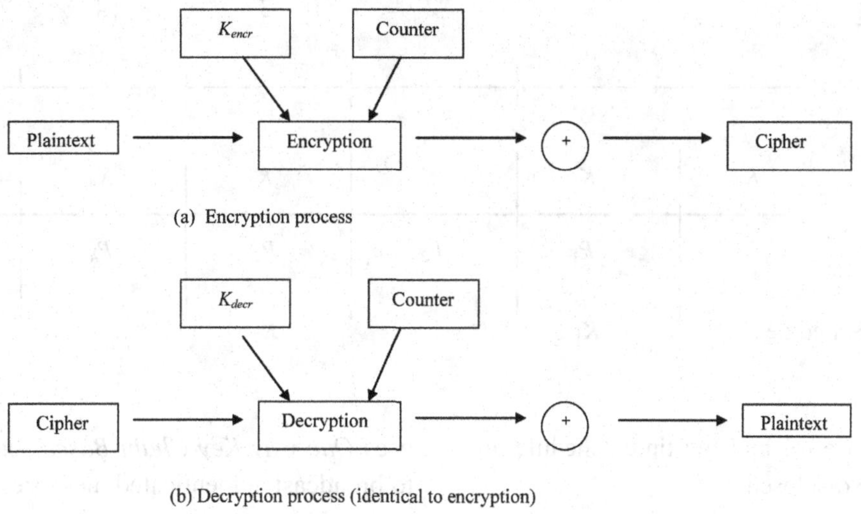

(a) Encryption process

(b) Decryption process (identical to encryption)

Authentication and Integrity

Data authentication is essential for many important functions in all sensor network applications. Controlling nodes' duty cycle and reprogramming a group of nodes or the entire network are two typical examples. Besides data confidentiality, data authentication and data integrity play crucial roles in applications that need a high level of security such as battlefield reconnaissance and surveillance applications. In applications that require data authentication and integrity, receiving nodes need to ensure that commands are sent from trusted sources (authentication) and are not modified or altered (integrity). If the communication takes place between two parties, they can simply use the message authentication code (MAC) of all communicated data to verify whether the messages originated from the trusted source (Perrig et al., 2002). Broadcast communication, on the other hand, is a much more complex situation. If one sender uses MAC and broadcasts messages to other nodes, any node, which knows the MAC key, can impersonate the sender, create fake messages, and send them to other receivers. Although asymmetric mechanisms achieve very good results in traditional networks, they are not suitable for wireless sensor networks due to high cost in terms of time and energy.

SPINs provides two sub-protocols SNEP and μ**TESLA** to deal with data authentication in two-party and broadcast communication respectively. Authentication in two-party communication is simple and based on the MAC of the message while authenticated broadcasting is more complex. μTESLA uses a mechanism called delayed disclosure of symmetric keys to broadcast authenticated Mes- sages to all sensor nodes in the network. When the base station wants to broadcast a message, it computes the MAC of the message using a key, which is not yet disclosed at that time. When a node in the network receives the message, it first saves the message in its own buffer and waits until it receives the verification key broadcasted from the base station. When the key arrives, the sensor node can authenticate the key before using that key to verify the message saved in the buffer beforehand. However, μTESLA requires that the base station and sensor nodes be loosely synchronized. Moreover, each node has to know the upper bound of the maximum

Figure 6. Source authentication using time-delayed key chain in μTESLA

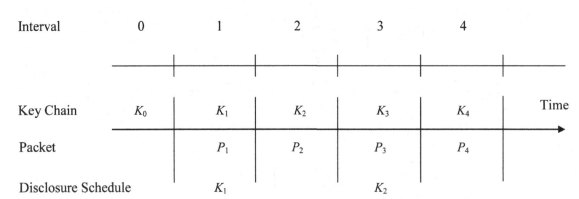

Interval	0	1	2	3	4	
Key Chain	K_0	K_1	K_2	K_3	K_4	Time
Packet		P_1	P_2	P_3	P_4	
Disclosure Schedule		K_1		K_2		

synchronization error and the time schedule at which keys are disclosed.

Figure 6 shows an example of source authentication in μTESLA. We can see that each interval has a key bound to it. The disclosure schedule here means the time at which secret keys in the key chain are disclosed. Let us consider that the sender and receiver are loosely time synchronized and the receiver knows K_0 as the commitment to the key chain. At the time interval 1 and 2, P_1, P_2, and K_1 are sent to receiver. P_1 and P_2 contain their own MACs using corresponding keys K_1 and K_2. Assume that packet containing K_1 is lost. In intervals 3 and 4, the recipient receives P_3, P_4, and K_2 successfully. By using K_2 and a one-way function F, the receiver can authenticate $K_0 = F(F(K_2))$ and compute $K_1 = F(K_2)$. Hence, the receiver can also authenticate packet P_1 using K_1 and P_2 using K_2. The time delay to broadcast authentication key (K_1 and K_2 in this example) varies from system to system. One major drawback of μTESLA is that the scheme works only when the base station (broadcaster) and sensor nodes are loosely synchronized, which may not be guaranteed in all situations in wireless sensor networks.

Like SPINS, **LEAP** also uses μTESLA for authenticated broadcasting. However, μTESLA is not an appropriate solution for local broadcasting due to the latency and storage capacity of sensor nodes (Zhu et al., 2006). Therefore, LEAP

uses *One-way Key Chain Based Authentication* to broadcast authenticated messages locally. Let us consider a communication among three nodes x, y, and z as shown in Figure 7. Node x sends a packet that contains the content M and the authentication key K. Node y will receive this packet before node z forwards its received packet to y because $|xy| < |xz| + |zy|$. Hence, if node z is an adversary, it cannot reuse the authentication key K to send another message. This approach, however, may suffer when the link between x and y is also attacked by another adversary.

Unlike SPIN which uses 8 bytes for message authentication code (MAC), TinySec uses only 4 bytes in each packet for MAC. While traditional security protocols use 8 or 16 bytes for MACs, 4-byte MACs should be enough for wireless sensor networks. On a 19.2 kb/s channel with 40

Figure 7. Local broadcast authentication in LEAP
($|xy| < |xz| + |zy|$)

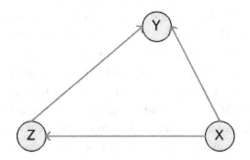

forgery attempts per second, adversaries have to spend over 20 months to try 2^{31} possibilities of a 4-byte MAC (Karlof et al., 2004). Furthermore, such attacks can be solved by a very simple heuristic. Sensor nodes should signal the base station whenever the number of MAC failures exceeds a particular threshold (Karlof et al., 2004a).

TinySec has two security options: authentication only (TinySec-Auth) and authentication-encryption (TinySec-AE). With TinySec-Auth option, the maximum size of a data packet is 37 bytes with 4 bytes for MAC. Compared to a TinyOS packet, a TinySec-Auth packet does not have 1 byte of *Group* information and 2 bytes of *Cyclic Redundancy Check (CRC)*. The 4-byte MACs in both TinySec-Auth and TinySec-AE are used for authentication and message integrity. As reported by Karlof et al. (2004a), TinySec-AE incurs 6% packet overhead and 10% energy overhead.

Non-repudiation is an important issue in traditional networks. It is used to ensure a party cannot refute or repudiate the reception or the sending of a message. In wireless sensor networks, this issue is not yet explicitly studied. The reason may be the lack of requirements for this kind of service. However, non-repudiation may become an interesting subject in the future as sensor network applications extend to all aspects of our life.

Data Freshness

The freshness of data means that the data is recent and is not replayed (Perrig et al., 2002). Data freshness is important in emergency situations and real-time applications such as forest fire detection, emergency rescue operations, and target tracking. **SPINs** defines two types of data freshness – weak freshness and strong freshness:

- Weak freshness: provides partial message ordering and carries no delay information.
- Strong freshness: provides full message ordering and carries delay information.

While weak freshness is useful for measurements (e.g. sensor readings), strong freshness can be used for time synchronization in the network. For both weak and strong freshness, protecting network from replay attacks is a big issue. Common defenses in traditional networks are to either use message timestamps or include an increasing counter to detect replayed messages. To achieve weak data freshness in SPINs, the sender simply includes a counter (CTR) in messages before sending them to the receiver. By increasing the CTR value, not only is the weak freshness achieved, but the semantic security is also accomplished. For applications that need strong freshness, the sender can create a random nonce and send it together with the request to the receiver. After receiving the request and the nonce, the receiver can include the nonce in the MAC of the response message. If the MAC of the response is verified successfully, the sender knows that the response message was created after it sent the request message, thus achieving the strong freshness. The drawback for the counter approach is that each recipient has to maintain a list (or a table) of last received counter values from other sensor nodes. This leads to the high cost of using memory resource. Since wireless sensor network applications are usually deployed with hundreds or thousands of nodes and sensor devices are very limited in memory capacity, this approach may not be a good solution.

The apparent infeasibility of public key cryptography for wireless sensor networks has motivated research to develop alternative security techniques using key distribution in sensor nodes before deployment. SPINS, LEAP, and TinySec are prime examples of such development. However, these techniques fall short of many security issues such as node compromises, revocations, and insertions of nodes, which can easily be solved using PKC.

ATTACKS AND COUNTERMEASURES

As stated earlier, wireless sensor networks are very vulnerable to attacks as they are deployed often in open, publicly accessible geographic areas where adversaries can easily access them and launch attacks. There are many identified attacks on wireless sensor networks such as replay attacks, warmhole attacks, sinkhole attacks, Sybil attacks, HELLO flood attacks, acknowledgement spoofing, and so on. Among them, the Sybil attack has been widely recognized as the most problematic one that can lead ways to many other forms of threats and attacks (Newsome, Elaine, Song, & Perrig, 2004). In the following, we describe various threats from the Sybil attack and discuss countermeasures proposed in the current literature.

The Sybil Attack

In the Sybil attack, a malicious or compromised node impersonates as multiple legitimate nodes by claiming false identities. This type of attacks could be prevented if we had a public key based trusted Certifying Authority (CA) in wireless sensor networks. The Sybil attack was originally identified by Douceur as the source of many threats for peer-to-peer networks (Douceur, 2002). In a recent paper, Newsome et al. provide taxonomy on different forms of the Sybil attack and describe

how the Sybil attack can wreak havoc on many network protocols and services in wireless sensor networks (Newsome, Elaine, Song, & Perrig, 2004). Table 4 summarizes such threats and attacks on wireless sensor networks.

Several techniques have been proposed in current literature to prevent Sybil attacks in wireless sensor networks. In the following we briefly describe some of the important techniques as reported in current literature.

Radio Resource Testing

This is a form of direct validation of a node whether it is a Sybil node or a legitimate one. In this scheme, a node assigns each of its neighbors a different channel for transmission of a message and then listens randomly to a channel. It should receive a message over the channel if the sending node is a legitimate one.

Random Key Predistribution

In the random key predistribution mechanism, each node is assigned a fixed number of random keys from a large key pool before deployment. Upon deployment, a node discovers a set of shared common keys with each of its neighbor separately. A shared common key with a neighbor can be used by a node for all secure communications with the neighbor. The identity of a node is determined by

Table 4. Forms of the Sybil attacks on protocols and services

Protocol	Description of Attack
Distributed storage	The Sybil attack can replicate or fragment data across several Sybil nodes by the same malicious node.
Routing	Multipath routing can go through a single malicious node representing several Sybil nodes.
Data aggregation	A malicious node representing enough Sybil nodes can completely alter the aggregate reading.
Voting	A malicious node representing enough Sybil nodes can affect the outcome of a voting protocol.
Fair resource allocation	The Sybil attack can allow a malicious node to deny services to legitimate nodes as the malicious node can gain unfair share of a resource.
Misbehavior detection	The Sybil attack can foil misbehavior detection by simply switching to its Sybil identities to misbehave.

the set of common keys shared with a neighbor, which can be used to authenticate a node. This basic random key pool scheme, in which keys can be issued multiple times from the same key pool, is vulnerable. This is because an attacker can capture a sufficient number of nodes and compromise a sufficient number of keys to generate a Sybil identity easily. In order to thwart such threat, Newsome et al. propose two separate key distribution schemes: 1) Single-space pairwise key distribution and 2) Multi-space pairwise key distribution. In single-space pairwise key distribution scheme, a unique key is assigned to each pair of nodes. The multi-space pairwise key distribution uses multiple key spaces, in which each sensor node is assigned k key spaces out of a set of m key spaces randomly. Any two neighboring nodes having at least one key space in common can compute their pairwise secret key. The scheme is shown to be very resilient to the Sybil attack even if hundreds of nodes are compromised in a network.

Registration

Using the base station as the central authority, each node can register its identity with the base station. Any Sybil attack can be detected by polling the network and comparing the result with the list of identities of registered nodes before deployment. To validate a node as legitimate or not, the identity of the claiming node can be checked with the list of identities of the registered nodes. The scheme is vulnerable if the list is somehow compromised.

Location Verification

Recently Mukhopadhyay and Saha describe a location verification based defense against the Sybil attack in sensor networks (Mukhopadhyay and Saha, 2006). The scheme introduces a new functional for planar triangulation defined as Inner Core for the area of deployment, which can be used to verify the claim of a sensor node in a region in the deployed area. The verification of the

location (or region) is done through a protocol run by three neighboring nodes with the claimant that involves exchanges of messages with the claimant, computation of elapsed times, and checking the times for regional validity. The scheme seems computationally intensive.

Neighboring Relations

More recently Wang et al. propose a very different mechanism to defend a wireless sensor network from Sybil attacks (Wang, Ssu, & Chang, 2010). It is based on the premise that the Sybil nodes forged by the same node will have the same set of physical neighbors that the malicious node has. By collecting the neighboring information of a suspected victim through a protocol, legitimate neighboring nodes are determined. These legitimate nodes can be utilized to identify the malicious nodes. It is reported that the detection rate of the scheme is around 95% if the network is not very sparse. It is to be mentioned that none of the above schemes have been tested in a real sensor network. For the sake of practicality, we need to study the performance of the schemes in terms of time and energy usage before applying them in a real wireless sensor network.

OPEN ISSUES AND FUTURE RESEARCH DIRECTIONS

Much of the current research on wireless sensor network security deals with key establishment, key management, and authentication schemes for WSNs. However, all these schemes become useless if a node itself in a WSN is compromised. An attacker can exploit a compromised node in several possible ways. Data on the compromised node can be interpreted, the node itself can be controlled to read vital information from the network, and so on. Although using tamper-proof hardware will help, but it is too expensive to use especially when the number of sensors deployed is large. Other existing solutions to the problem of detecting a compromised node are merely theoretical and energy inefficient. Further research in this area needs to be done, particularly on revocation of a compromised node.

One way to prevent the flow of malicious data is to use the aggregation technique to disregard any extreme values from the sensors. However, this technique will fail when several nodes are compromised and all of them report extreme values.

Many sensor applications involve transmission of highly confidential data. A standard approach for securing such data is encryption. Since public-key cryptography is resource intensive, it is desirable to use symmetric key encryption. However, this requires secure exchange of keys between the nodes, which is still an ongoing area of research.

ECC based IBE systems seem to be a very good solution for key management and distribution in WSNs. However, they may not be the most practical solutions when the network is densely deployed with large number of sensors. This is because the extended time to establish keys among all the nodes in a large WSN is exorbitantly high. How to address this problem is still an open issue. A possible solution to this could be to couple the hardware implementation of ECC with that of IBE and integrate it with the existing sensor platform. Though hardware solutions are more efficient, they are way too expensive.

In-network processing requires intermediate nodes to access decrypted values to perform further computations. This poses a serious security threat to the data. A possible solution to this problem is to split a packet into several smaller packets before transmitting it. Only the destination should be able to reassemble the packet. Intermediate nodes will, therefore, be deprived of understanding contents of the packet. However, this involves finding best disjoint paths for transmitting the packet, which is again a challenging issue.

Another open issue has to do with the secure replacement of an aged node with a new one. There has to be a way to securely accommodate this new node into the existing network without interrupting the ongoing service. A possible solution could be to deploy a new WSN in the same area and replace it with the old one once it becomes operational. Research is needed to resolve the practicality of this solution and identify any reformed solutions.

CONCLUSION

Security of wireless sensor networks is important for collection of reliable and authentic data from their deployment environment. In this paper, we provide a survey of recent, pioneering results in the development of protocols for security and privacy in wireless sensor networks. Particularly, we provide comprehensive details of most referenced symmetric key based security protocols and implementations such as SPINS, μTESLA, LEAP, and TinySec and highlight and compare their usefulness, scopes, limitations, and shortcomings. Many of these limitations can be overcome by using security protocols based on public key cryptography. However, not all public key algorithms are suitable for WSNs. Accordingly, we selectively present promising research results on public key cryptography, particularly on implementation of ECC based public key cryptosystems for WSNs. ECC based IBE cryptosystems for WSNs are found to be very promising since they do not require any public key infrastructure except the need for a trusted base station. More research is still needed, perhaps in their hardware implementation, since the existing schemes in literature are found to be still prohibitively time-consuming to be used in real wireless sensor networks. Evidently, any drastic progress in research on IBE cryptosystems for wireless sensor networks will make many current security problems easily solvable and will eliminate many existing security obstacles and concerns for wireless sensor networks.

Using current feasible symmetric key based security protocols, we provide a comprehensive summary how essential security services such as data confidentiality, node authentication, data integrity, broadcast authentication, and data freshness can be achieved in a wireless sensor network. In addition, we discuss recently identified attacks and defenses for wireless sensor networks. Finally, we also discuss open issues that require further research in protocol and algorithm development and software and hardware development for sensor network security.

REFERENCES

Akyildiz, I., Su, W., Sankarasubramaniam, Y., & Cayirci, E. (2002). A survey on sensor networks. *IEEE Communications Magazine, 40*(8), 102–114. doi:10.1109/MCOM.2002.1024422

Batina, L., Mentens, N., Sakiyama, K., Preneel, B., & Verbauwhede, I. (2006). *Low-cost elliptic curve cryptography for wireless sensor networks. Security and Privacy in Ad-Hoc and Sensor Networks* (Vol. 4357, pp. 6–17). Berlin, Germany: Springer-Verlag.

Boneh, D., & Franklin, M. (2003). Identity-based encryption from the Weil pairing. *SIAM Journal on Computing, 32*(3), 586–615. doi:10.1137/S0097539701398521

Boneh, D., Lynn, B., & Shacham, H. (2001). *Short signatures from the Weil pairing. Advances in Cryptology – ASIACRYPT 2001* (Vol. 2248, pp. 514–532). Berlin, Germany: Springer-Verlag.

Chan, H., & Perrig, A. (2003). Security and privacy in sensor networks. *Computer, 36*(10), 103–105. doi:10.1109/MC.2003.1236475

Chan, H., Perrig, A., & Song, D. (2003). Random key predistribution schemes for sensor networks. In *Proceedings of the 2003 IEEE Symposium on Security and Privacy* (pp. 197-213).

Ciet, M., Joye, M., Lauter, K., & Montgomery, P. L. (2006). Trading inversions for multiplications in elliptic curve cryptography. *Journal of Designs, Codes, and Cryptography, 39*, 189–206. doi:10.1007/s10623-005-3299-y

Cilardo, A., Coppolino, L., Mazzocca, N., & Romano, L. (2006). Elliptic curve engineering. *Proceedings of the IEEE, 94*(2), 395–406. doi:10.1109/JPROC.2005.862438

Crossbow Technology, Inc. (n.d.) *Crossbow product information*. Retrieved from http://www.xbow.com/Products/products.htm

Demirkol, I., Ersoy, C., & Alagoz, F. (2006). Mac protocols for wireless sensor networks: a survey. *Communications Magazine, IEEE, 44*(4), 115–121. doi:10.1109/MCOM.2006.1632658

Douceur, J. R. (2002). The Sybil attack, In *Proceedings of the First. International Workshop on Peer-to-Peer Systems.*

Du, W., Deng, J., Han, Y. S., Varshney, P. K., Katz, J., & Khalili, A. (2005). A pairwise key pre-distribution scheme for wireless sensor networks. [TISSEC]. *ACM Transactions on Information and System Security, 8*(2), 228–258. doi:10.1145/1065545.1065548

Eschenauer, L., & Gligor, V. D. (2002, November). *A key-management scheme for distributed sensor networks*. Paper presented at the 9th ACM Conference on Computer and Communications, Washington DC, USA.

Galbraith, S. (2005). Pairings. Blake, Seroussi, & Smart (Eds.), *Advances in elliptic curve cryptography, London Mathematical Society Lecture Notes* (chapter IX, pp. 183-213). Cambridge, UK: Cambridge University Press.

Gura, N., Patel, A., & Wander, A. (2004). Comparing elliptic curve cryptography and RSA on 8-bit CPUs. In *Proceedings of the 2004 Workshop on Cryptographic Hardware and Embedded Systems (CHES 2004)* (pp. 119-132).

Hankerson, D., Menezes, A., & Vanstone, S. (2004). *Guide to elliptic curve cryptography.* Berlin, Germany: Springer-Verlag.

Huang, Q., Cukier, J., Kobayashi, H., Liu, B., & Zhang, J. (2003, September). *Fast authenticated key establishment protocols for self-organizing sensor networks.* Paper presented at the 2nd ACM international conference on Wireless sensor networks and applications, San Diego, CA.

Karl, H., & Willig, A. (2005). *Protocols and Architecture for wireless sensor networks.* New York: John Wiley & Sons. doi:10.1002/0470095121

Karlof, C., Sastry, N., & Wagner, D. (2004a, November). Paper presented *TinySec: A link layer security architecture for wireless sensor networks* at the 2nd International Conference on Embedded Networked Sensor Systems, Baltimore, MD.

Karlof, C., Sastry, N., & Wagner, D. (2004b). *TinyOS: User manual.* Retrieved February 10, 2009, from http://www.tinyos.net/tinyos-1.x/doc/tinysec.pdf

Koblitz, N. (1987). Elliptic curve cryptosystems. *Mathematics of Computation, 48,* 203–209. doi:10.1090/S0025-5718-1987-0866109-5

Law, Y. W., Doumen, J., & Hartel, P. (2006). Survey and benchmark of block ciphers for wireless sensor networks. [TOSN]. *ACM Transactions on Sensor Networks, 2*(1), 65–93. doi:10.1145/1138127.1138130

Liu, A., & Peng, N. (2008). TinyECC: A configurable library for elliptic curve cryptography in wireless sensor networks. In *Proceedings of the 7th International Conference on Information Processing in Sensor Networks* (pp. 245-256).

Liu, D., Ning, P., & Li, R. (2005). Establishing pairwise keys in distributed sensor networks. [TISSEC]. *ACM Transactions on Information and System Security, 8*(1), 41–77. doi:10.1145/1053283.1053287

Luo, P., Wang, X., Feng, J., & Xu, Y. (2008). Low-power hardware implementation of ECC processor suitable for low-cost RFID tags. In *Proceedings of the IEEE 9th International Conference on Solid-State and Integrated-Circuit Technology (ICSICT 2008)* (pp. 1681-1684).

Malan, D., Welsh, M., & Smith, M. (2004, October). *A public-key infrastructure for key distribution in TinyOS based on elliptic curve cryptography.* Paper presented at First IEEE International Conference on Sensor and Ad Hoc Communications and Networks (IEEE SECON 2004), Santa Clara, CA.

Mehallegue, N., Bouridane, A., & Garcia, E. (2008). Efficient path key establishment for wireless sensor networks. *EURASIP Journal on Wireless Communications and Networking, 8*(3), Article No. 3.

Menezes, A., Okamoto, T., & Vanstone, S. (1993). Reducing elliptic curve logarithms to finite field. *IEEE Transactions on Information Theory, 39*(5), 1639–1646. doi:10.1109/18.259647

Miller, V. (1986). Uses of elliptic curves in cryptography. *Advances in Cryptology, CRYPTO '85 (. LNCS, 218,* 417–426.

Mukhopadhyay, D., & Saha, I. (2006). Location verification based defense against Sybil attack in sensor networks. In *Proceedings of the International Conference of Distributed Computing and Networking,* 509-521.

Newsome, J., Elaine, S., Song, D., & Perrig, A. (2004). The Sybil attack in sensor networks: analysis & defenses. In *Proceedings of the International Symposium on Information Processing in Sensor Networks,* 259-268.

NIST. (2003). *Recommendation for key management. Part1: General guidelines (Special publication 800-57)*. Washington, DC: Author.

Oliveira, L., Aranha, D., Morais, E., Felipe, D., Lopez, J., & Dahab, R. (2007). TinyTate: Computing the tate pairing in resource-constrained sensor nodes. NCA 2007. In *Proceedings of the Sixth IEEE International Symposium on Network Computing and Applications* (pp. 318-323).

Perrig, A., Szewczyk, R., Tygar, J. D., Wen, V., & Culler, D. E. (2002). SPINS: Security protocols for sensor networks. *Wireless Networks, 8*(5), 521–534. doi:10.1023/A:1016598314198

Shamir, A. (1984). Identity-based cryptosystems and signature. In *Proceedings of Cryptology* (pp. 47–53). Berlin, Germany: Springer-Verlag.

Su, W., & Almaharmeh, B. (2008). QoS integration of the internet and wireless sensor networks. W. *Trans. on Comp., 7*(4), 253–258.

Szczechowiak, P., & Collier, M. (2009). TinyIBE: Identity-Based Encryption for Heterogeneous Sensor Networks. In *5th International Conference on Intelligent Sensors, Sensor Networks and Information Processing*. 319-354.

Szczechowiak, P., Kargl, A., Scott, M., & Collier. (2009). On the Application of Pairing Based Cryptography to Wireless Sensor Networks. In *WiSec '09, Second ACM conference on Wireless Network Security*. 1-12.

Wander, A., Gura, N., Eberle, H., Gupta, V., & Shantz, S. (2005, March). *Energy analysis of public-key cryptography for wireless sensor networks*. Paper presented at the Third IEEE International Conference on Pervasive Computing and Communication (PerCom 2005), Hawaii.

Wang, W-T., Ssu, K-F., & Chang, W-C. (2010). Defending Sybil attacks based on neighboring relations in wireless sensor networks, *Security and Communication Networks*, n/a. doi: 10.1002/sec.197.

Watro, R., Kong, D., Cuti, S., Gardiner, C., Lynn, C., & Kruus, P. (2004). Tinypk: Securing sensor networks with public key technology. In *Proceedings of the Second ACM Workshop on Security of Ad-hoc and Sensor Networks (SASN'04)*, Washington, DC (pp. 59-64).

Xiong, X., Wong, D., & Deng, X. (2010). TinyPairing: A Fast and Lightweight Pairing-based Cryptographic Library for Wireless Sensor Networks. In *IEEE Wireless Communications and Networking Conference (WCNC)*. 1-6.

Zhu, S., Setia, S., & Jajodia, S. (2006). LEAP: Efficient security mechanisms for large-scale distributed sensor networks. [TOSN]. *ACM Transactions on Sensor Networks, 2*(4), 500–528. doi:10.1145/1218556.1218559

Chapter 15
Multimedia Information Security and Privacy:
Theory and Applications

Ming Yang
Montclair State University, USA

Monica Trifas
Jacksonville State University, USA

Guillermo Francia III
Jacksonville State University, USA

Lei Chen
Sam Houston State University, USA

Yongliang Hu
Taizhou University, China

ABSTRACT

Information security has traditionally been ensured with data encryption techniques. Different generic data encryption standards, such as DES, RSA, AES, have been developed. These encryption standards provide high level of security to the encrypted data. However, they are not very efficient in the encryption of multimedia contents due to the large volume of digital image/video data. In order to address this issue, different image/video encryption methodologies have been developed. These methodologies encrypt only the key parameters of image/video data instead of encrypting it as a bitstream. Joint compression-encryption is a very promising direction for image/video encryption. Nowadays, researchers start to utilize information hiding techniques to enhance the security level of data encryption methodologies. Information hiding conceals not only the content of the secret message, but also its very existence. In terms of the amount of data to be embedded, information hiding methodologies can be classified into low bitrate and high bitrate algorithms. In terms of the domain for embedding, they can be classified into spatial domain and transform domain algorithms. In this chapter, the authors have reviewed various data encryption standards, image/video encryption algorithms, and joint compression-encryption methodologies. Besides, the authors have also presented different categories of information hiding methodologies as well as data embedding strategies for digital image/video contents.

DOI: 10.4018/978-1-60960-200-0.ch015

INTRODUCTION TO ENCRYPTION

In modern information and communication systems, information security is becoming an increasingly important issue due to the threats from all different types of attacks. Traditionally, information security has been ensured with data encryption. With the development of modern information hiding theory, researchers start to resort to information hiding techniques to enhance the security level of data encryption systems. In this chapter, we will first review different encryption techniques for multimedia data, including digital image and video contents. After that, we will move to the information hiding techniques for digital multimedia contents.

General Model

Encryption is a method to protect information from undesirable attacks by converting it into a form that is non-recognizable by its attackers. Data encryption mainly is the scrambling of the content of data, such as text, image, audio, video, etc. to make the data unreadable, invisible or incomprehensible during transmission. The inverse of data encryption is data *decryption*, which recovers the original data. Figure 1 is the general model of a typical encryption/decryption system. The encryption procedure could be described as $C = E(P, K)$, where P is the plaintext (original message), E is the encryption algorithm, K is the encryption key, and C is the ciphertext (scrambled message). The ciphertext is transmitted through the communication channel, which is subject to attacks. At the receiver end, the decryption procedure could be described as $P = D(C, K')$, where C is the ciphertext, D is the decryption algorithm, K' is the decryption key (not necessarily the same as the encryption key K), and P is the recovered plaintext.

Claude Shannon pointed out that the fundamental techniques to encrypt a block of symbols are confusion and diffusion. Confusion can obscure the relationship between the plaintext and the ciphertext, and diffusion can spread the change throughout the whole ciphertext. Substitution is the simplest type of confusion, and permutation is the simplest method of diffusion. Substitution replaces a symbol with another one; permutation changes the sequence of the symbols in the block to make them unreadable. These two techniques are the foundations of encryption algorithms.

Secret-Key versus Public-Key

Kerckhoff claimed that the security of an encryption/decryption system should rely on the secrecy of the key instead of on the algorithm itself. The security level of an encryption algorithm is measured by the length of the key or the size of the key space. Based on the types of encryption/decryption key, the encryption systems can be classified into secret-key systems and public-key systems. The

Figure 1. Data encryption/decryption system

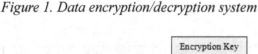

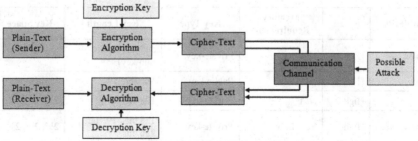

secret-key system is also called the symmetric system because the decryption key is the same as the encryption key. In a secret-key system, the encryption/decryption key has to be transmitted prior to the transmission of the ciphertext, and this requires a separate secure communication channel. The public-key system, which is also called the asymmetric system, has a decryption key that is different from the encryption key. Each person in the group knows the encryption key. This way each member can use the public key to encrypt a message, but only the person who has the decryption key can decrypt the ciphertext. With the public-key encryption system, there is no need for a secure communication channel to transmit the encryption key.

Encryption Standards

Depending on the type of plaintext, data encryption systems can be classified into text encryption, audio encryption, image encryption and video encryption. In order to have a generic cryptosystem that can encrypt different types of data, some encryption standards have been developed. Among them, DES (Data Encryption Standard), RSA (Rivest, Shamir and Adleman), AES (Advanced Encryption Standard) and IDEA (International Data Encryption Algorithm) are widely adopted. In general, these encryption standards consider all forms of multimedia data–such as text, image and video–as bit stream and encrypt them without any differentiation. A comparison of different encryption standards is illustrated in Table 1.

IMAGE ENCRYPTION

Why Not Naïve Algorithms?

As an important multimedia data type, the digital image and its encryption have attracted a lot of research interests. There are two levels of security for digital image encryption: low-level security encryption and high-level security encryption (Figure 2). In low-level security encryption, the encrypted image has degraded visual quality compared to that of the original one, but the content of the image is still visible and understandable to the viewers. In high-level security case, the content is completely scrambled and the image just looks like random noise.

If the image data is considered just as a data bitstream, there is no fundamental difference between image encryption and other types of data encryption. We can just input the image data bitstream into the standard encryption system. This type of still image encryption is called a naïve algorithm. However, considering the special properties of digital image/video data contents, more elaborate image/video encryption algorithms are desired for the following reasons:

- Considering the typical size of a digital image compared to that of a text message, the

Table 1. Comparison table

	Complexity	Speed	Memory Requirement	Key Type	Key Length	Key Space Size	Security Level
DES	Complex	High	N/A	Private-key	56 bits (48 bits Sub-key)	2^{56}	Low
RSA	Simple	High	N/A	Public-key	Variable	Variable	High
IDEA	Simple	High	N/A	Private-key	128 bits	2^{128}	High
AES	Complex	High	Very Low	Private-key	128 bits, 192 bits, 256 bits	$2^{128}, 2^{192}, 2^{256}$	High

Figure 2. Digital image encryption

| (a) Original Image | (b) Low-Level Encryption | (c) High-Level Encryption |

naïve algorithm usually cannot meet the requirements for real-time applications. Thus, we need to avoid encrypting the image bit by bit and yet ensure a secure encryption system;

- Naïve algorithms encrypt the image/video contents into a totally un-recognizable format, which may not always be necessary. Sometimes, it is enough to degrade the visual qualities of original image/video contents, and very high levels of encryption (with the standards) is not necessary;

- Digital image/video contents are usually stored and transmitted in compressed formats. It makes sense to integrate the compression and encryption procedures into one single process, which achieves both tasks. Thus, the compression process and the encryption process can enhance each other, share CPU time, and avoid processing delay.

Nowadays, many new algorithms for image/video encryption have been proposed, which exploit the properties inherent to image and video data and thus gain much higher efficiency compared to naïve algorithms. In image encryption, the following properties are always desired:

- The encryption/decryption algorithm has to be fast enough in order to meet the performance requirements of real-time applications;

- The encryption procedure should not decrease the compression ratio or increase the size of the image;

- The encryption algorithms should be robust against the general digital image processing procedures;

- The encryption/decryption procedure should not degrade the quality of the original image.

Affine Transformation Algorithms

Affine transformation basically does a one-to-one mapping between the symbols in the plaintext and the symbols in the ciphertext to protect the data content. Chuang and Lin (1999) proposed a multi-resolution approach for still image encryption. It is basically a symmetric affine cipher system, which has both multi-resolution transmission (a progressive property) and lossless reconstruction functionalities. With multi-resolution transmission, the image can be transmitted progressively with different spatial resolutions. The basic idea of this algorithm is to decompose and encrypt the original image level by level with the proposed E-transform. For each pixel, the algorithm does an affine transformation and converts the grey-level value to another one that still falls into the range of [0, 255]. In the receiver end, the image can be decrypted level by level, and the original image is recovered if the highest level is decrypted. For a 512x512 image, the size of key space is $(256!)^{87366}$. Many image encryption algorithms use similar strategies. However, affine transformation is fragile to known/chosen-plaintext attacks.

Chaotic System Based Algorithms

Scharinger (1998) proposed a fast image encryption algorithm with chaotic Kolmogorov flow, which is a class of extraordinary unstable chaotic systems. Basically, this algorithm implements a product cipher, which encrypts large blocks of plaintext by repeating intertwined applications of substitutions and permutations. Scharinger's system combined Kolmogorov flows with a pseudo-random number generator to implement a key-dependent permutation (parameterized permutation), which operates on large data blocks. This is a significant improvement compared to the product ciphers that applies fixed permutation and thus leads to higher level of security. There are three main advantages of Scharinger's algorithm: (1) the integration of a parameterized permutation into the system leads to its robustness against the differential cryptanalysis; (2) the adoption of large data blocks (maybe the whole image) makes the image structure unrecognizable, which leads to higher level of security compared to those encryption systems that operate on small data blocks; (3) this system is faster than some other comparable encryption systems because of its simplicity. However, this algorithm still tries to encrypt the whole image and thus suffers the same problem as a naïve algorithm does. Socek, Li, Magliveras, and Furht (2005) proposed a new methodology to enhance the Chaotic-Key Based Algorithm (CKBA). Their algorithm enhances the CKBA algorithm in three-fold: (1) it changes the 1-D chaotic logistic map to a piecewise linear chaotic map (PWLCM) to improve the balance property; (2) it increases the key size to 128 bits; (3) it adds two more cryptographic primitives and

extends the scheme to operate on multiple rounds so that the chosen/known plaintext attacks are no longer possible. The new cipher proved to be more secure and its performance characteristics remain very good.

Frequency Domain Algorithms

Digital images can be presented in both spatial domain and frequency domain. The term spatial domain refers to the image plane. Frequency domain processing techniques are based on modifying the Fourier transform of an image. The encryption algorithms presented in the previous sections all work in spatial domain. Since many digital image processing/compression techniques operate in the frequency domain, it would be natural to encrypt the digital image in the frequency domain for compatibility issues. Kuo (1993) proposed a novel image encryption technique by randomly changing the phase spectra of the original image. A binary phase spectra of a pseudo-noise image is added to the original phase spectra. This methodology is actually a private-key system, and the reference noise image is the encryption/decryption key. The proposed methodology is suitable for progressive transmission because of its ability to recover the original image to some extent with partial access to the encrypted image. As a result, it is a good candidate for distributed multimedia communication, which sometimes suffers from network congestion and packet loss. However, the proposed methodology has some limitations: (1) the encryption and decryption process requires FFT (Fast Fourier Transform) computation, which is very computationally demanding; (2) it is also vulnerable to known/chosen-plaintext attacks.

Comparative Results

The comparison of the image encryption algorithms discussed in previous sections is in Table 2.

Table 2. Comparative results (image encryption)

	Complexity	Speed	Key Length	Key Space Size (512*512 Image)	Security Level
Affine Transform	Simple	Low	N/A	$(256!)^{87366}$	High
Chaotic Algorithm	Simple	Low	Variable	Variable	High
Frequency Algorithm	Complex	Low	512*512	$2^{512*512}$	High

JOINT COMPRESSION-ENCRYPTION METHODOLOGIES

Since digital images are usually transmitted in a compressed format, research is focused on how to encrypt compressed digital images. It is natural to apply naïve algorithm to the compressed image to get the compressed-encrypted image. However, this will cause significant computational overhead, especially for images with low compression ratio. Thus, research efforts have been focused on integrating lossless compression and encryption algorithms to maximize the overall performance. Basically, compression and encryption can enhance each other and share the computational cost. In this section, we will first review some of the representative lossless compression techniques and then move to joint compression-encryption methodologies.

Lossless Compression Techniques

Lossless image compression can be always modeled as a two-stage procedure: decorrelation and entropy coding. The first stage removes spatial redundancy or inter-pixel redundancy by means of run-length coding, predictive techniques, transform techniques, etc. The second stage, which includes Huffman coding, arithmetic coding, LZW, etc., removes coding redundancy. The techniques employed in lossless image compression are all fundamentally rooted in entropy coding theory and Shannon's noiseless coding theorem, which guarantees that as long as the average number of bits per source symbol at the output of the encoder

exceeds the entropy (i.e. average information per symbol) of the data source by an arbitrarily small amount, the data can be decoded without error.

- **Decorrelation Techniques:** correlation between samples, which is present in nearly all kinds of signals, represents redundant information that need not be transmitted if reversible decorrelation techniques are applied. Decorrelation, also known as "whitening", can be accomplished by many techniques, such as predictive techniques, transform technique, and multi-resolution techniques.

- **Entropy Coding:** once the data has been decorrelated, more compression can be achieved by applying entropy coding as long as the Probability Mass Function (PMF) of the resulting samples is not uniform. The average bitrate can approach the entropy of the decorrelated data. Most signal compression schemes employ Huffman coding or Arithmetic coding. In addition, several compression schemes use suboptimal variable length coders that are specifically designed for speed or ease of implementation.

JOINT COMPRESSION-ENCRYPTION

Image compression can be viewed as a special type of encryption, since it converts the original image into a bitstream that is incomprehensible to human beings. The compression/decompression algorithms can be viewed as the encryption/decryption keys, because there is no way to convert the encoded bitstream back to the original image without the decompression algorithm. However, according to Kerckhoff's principle, an encryption methodology cannot rely on the secrecy of its algorithm to ensure the security of the system. Also, the compression/decompression algorithms for the existing standards are all in the public domain and supposed to be known.

Based on this observation, people start to wonder: is it possible to combine encryption key with the compression algorithms to achieve compression and encryption at the same time? The answer is "yes" and this leads to the development of joint compression-encryption algorithms. In a system that combines compression and encryption, it is better to use the parameter instead of the algorithm itself as the encryption/decryption key. In this type of systems, secret keys have been applied in the compression, and thus the compression algorithm is parameterized and becomes the joint compression-encryption algorithm. Without the private key, it is impossible to decode/decrypt the encoded bitstream and restore the original image/video contents.

Another way to implement a joint compression-encryption system is to compress the image first and then encrypt it. Different from naïve algorithm, which encrypts the whole compressed image, this type of joint compression-encryption algorithms encrypt only some of the key parameters of the encoded image. Since the key parameters of the compressed image are encrypted, the original image cannot be reconstructed even if the other parts of the compressed image are known. Thus, image data security is ensured. This type of algorithms avoids encrypting the image merely as a bitstream and thus has a reduced computational overhead compared to that of naïve algorithm.

- **Base-Switching Algorithms:** Chuang and Lin (1999) proposed a joint compression-encryption methodology for still images. The basic idea is to first decompose the original image, then use a base-switching (BS) algorithm to compress the image in a lossless manner. Finally, the base values of the compressed image will be encrypted with the affine transformation. Thus, the original image cannot be reconstructed even if the other parts of the compressed image remain unencrypted. Many available encryption algorithms could be applied to the encryption of the base value. With the proposed algorithm, theoretically there are (128!)*t possible ways to encrypt a gray-scaled image and (128!)*3t ways to encrypt a color image (t is the number of layers in the image decomposition procedure). The proposed algorithm provides very high level of security and considerable compression ratio. This methodology can be combined with other encryption methods such as the SCAN language to further improve its security level. The drawback of the algorithm is that it is vulnerable to known/chosen-plaintext attacks.

- **Entropy Coding Algorithms:** Wu and Moo (1999) proposed a joint image/video compression-encryption scheme via a high-order conditional entropy coding of wavelet coefficients. They demonstrated that wavelet image compression and conditional arithmetic coding of wavelet coefficients could be used as a framework for image encryption. Firstly, the image is transformed with the wavelet transformation. Then the wavelet coefficients are quantized and encoded with ECECOW (Embedded Conditional Entropy Coding Of Wavelet coefficients). After that, different kinds of encryption algorithms can be applied to encrypt a very small portion of the bit stream output by ECECOW. As we know, the compressed bit stream will show a certain level of randomness. This can enhance the ability to ensure a certain level of security. Encrypting only a small

Figure 3. SCAN language based joint encryption-compression

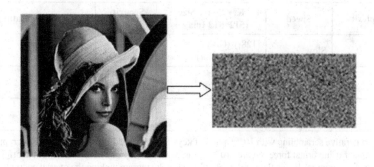

portion of the bit stream ensures the high-speed performance.

- **SCAN Language Based Algorithms:** Bourbakis and Dollas (2003) proposed a joint compression-encryption-hiding system based on the SCAN language. The name "SCAN" reflects the different ways of scanning the data of a 2D array, such as an image. The SCAN language is a formal language based on a two-dimensional spatial-accessing methodology that can represent and generate a great variety of {nxn}! scanning paths from a small set of primitive ones. The SCAN method compresses a given image by specifying a scanning path of the image in an encoded form. The core is the algorithm that determines a near-optimal or a good scanning path which minimizes the total number of bits needed to represent the encoded scanning path and the encoded bit sequence along the scanning path. After the image is compressed, the bits of the compressed image are rearranged to obtain the encrypted image (Figure 3). The rearrangement is done using a set of scanning paths that are kept secret. This set of scanning paths is actually the encryption key. The decryption/decompression procedure is the reverse of the encryption-compression procedure. An additional feature of the SCAN methodol-

ogy is the confusion function. The major functionality of the confusion function is to make the image histogram flat and look like random noise, and thus the attacks through histogram analysis will be completely disabled. The proposed methodology achieves a higher compression ratio than that achieved by a JPEG encoder (quality=100). The security level is very high and it is computationally infeasible to break the system using an exhaustive search with currently available computing power.

Comparison

A comparison of the joint compression-encryption algorithms is presented in Table 3.

VIDEO ENCRYPTION

In digital video transmission, encryption methodologies that can protect digital video from attacks during transmission become very important. Due to the huge size of digital video contents, they are usually transmitted in compressed formats such as MPEG-x, H.26x, Motion-JPEG, and Motion-JPEG2000. Thus, the encryption algorithms for digital video are usually working in the compressed

Table 3. Comparative results (image compression-encryption)

	Complexity	Speed	Key Space Size (512*512 Image)	Security Level	Compression Ratio	Compression Type
Base Switching	High	Slow	$(128!)^t$ (Gray) $(128!)^{3t}$ (Color)	High	Medium	Lossless
Entropy Coding	Low	Fast	N/A	Low	High	Lossy
SCAN * Algorithm	High	Medium	(512*512)!	High	High	Lossless

* SCAN offers not only an iterative scrambling with 10^{76000} pairs of keys for a 512x512 digital form of the encrypted information, here an image, where a supercomputer using brutal force requires 10^{75000} years with a slim probability to decrypt the original digital information, but also a confusion function that converts always flat the digital information histogram making the overall encryption process impossible. SCAN has also been efficiently used in video compression-encryption.

domain. Again, the most straightforward method to encrypt digital video data is naïve algorithm. However, the performance issues will arise. DES and RSA are obviously not fast enough to meet the real-time requirements of digital video applications such as video-on-demand and video retrieval.

Selective Encryption Algorithms

According to the Group-Of-Pictures (GOP) structure (Figure 4), the reconstruction of the B-frames and the P-frames are dependent on the availability of the preceding I-frame since they need the I-frame as reference frame. With the I-frame being encrypted, the attackers cannot reconstruct the I-frame so they will not be able to reconstruct the B-frame and the P-frame even if these frames are transmitted without being encrypted. Based on this consideration, it is natural to encrypt only the

I-frames to protect the video content. Encryption of only the I-frames will lead to much less computational overhead compared to a naïve algorithm. However, Agi and Gong (1996) have shown that the basic idea behind this method is not correct. A large portion of the encrypted video is still visible, mainly because of unencrypted I-blocks in the P and B frames and partially because of inter-frame correlation. Moreover, this methodology still adds significant computational overhead to the encoding and decoding processes.

Some approaches have been proposed to enhance the low security level caused by the I-blocks in the P- and B-frames: (1) force the MPEG encoder not to generate I-blocks inside P- and B-frames; (2) encrypt all the I-blocks inside P- and B-frames. To improve the security level of the selective algorithm, Spanos and Maples (1995) have proposed to not only encrypt the I-frames

Figure 4. The GOP (Group of Pictures) with I-, B-, and P- frames

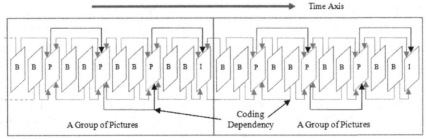

in the video stream, but also to encrypt the header information of the MPEG video and make the video stream unrecognizable to the decoder. This modification slightly increases the security level of the system. Agi and Gong (1996) found that increasing the number of I-frames and encrypting the I-frames in the selective algorithm will increase the security level, but at the price of a lower compression ratio. Encrypting the I-blocks inside the B- and the P-frames will not decrease the compression ratio but has the potential to increase security level.

When the selective algorithm is applied to MPEG video encryption, we need to take into account many factors such as computational overhead, security requirements, the sensitivity of the video data, and real-time requirements. Based on these considerations, we can choose the most suitable algorithm for the targeting application scenarios, which is actually a tradeoff between computational complexity and level of security.

Tang's Algorithm

Tang (1996) proposed a methodology in an attempt to incorporate the compression and the encryption of MPEG video streams. In the proposed system, he combines cryptographic techniques such as random permutation and probabilistic encryption with the compression/decompression algorithms. The proposed algorithm does not add much computational overhead to the encoding/decoding of the digital video but can achieve a considerable level of security for the data being processed. As we know, in the MPEG video compression algorithm, zig-zag scanning is applied to map the DCT coefficients in the 8x8 block to a 1-D vector (with 64 elements). In the encryption system proposed by Tang, a random permutation list is used. This list is actually the encryption key to implement the mapping and, thus, scramble the order of the DCT coefficients. Since mapping with the permutation list is not more computationally demanding than mapping with the zig-zag scanning, the proposed

system does not add computational overhead. This makes it a good candidate for real-time digital video applications. However, the algorithm has some drawbacks:

1. Scanning the 8x8 DCT block with a random permutation list (rather than zig-zag scanning) will decrease the performance of the subsequent run-length coding and Huffman coding and reduce the compression ratio;

2. The proposed methodology will be vulnerable to known-plaintext attack, which makes use of partial knowledge of the well-known MPEG codec structure and the distribution property of the DCT coefficients.

To fix this problem, Tang has proposed additional options. However, they increase the computational complexity and key length without significantly increasing the system's security level. Further, the methodology is not suitable in protecting highly sensitive digital video data.

Video Encryption Algorithm (VEA)

The VEA algorithm, proposed by Shi and Bhargava (1998a) is based on the modification of DCT coefficients. It uses a randomly-generated bit-stream, which is actually the encryption/ decryption key, to change the sign of the AC coefficients of the DCT transformation. Since the only operation in the encryption procedure is XOR, very limited computational overhead is added. Even the software implementation of the system is fast enough for many real-time video applications. This algorithm has some drawbacks. For example, after the encryption procedure, some AC coefficients have changed their sign while others have not. However, the video sequence is still comprehensible or understandable to some extent. Because of the well-known MPEG-x structure and the distribution property of the DCT coefficients, attackers may be able to break the system with a partial key. The algorithm is also vulnerable to known-plaintext attack. Thus, the encryption algorithm is not suitable for protecting highly sensitive video data. However, it is still suitable for protecting the commercial digital video data, since the expense that will be incurred in breaking the encryption system will be much higher than that in legitimately acquiring the video.

To increase the security level of the algorithm, Shi and Bhargava (1998b) proposed a new version of the VEA system. In the proposed system, they change the sign bits of the DC coefficients and the motion vector instead of the AC coefficients. With this modification, they obtain a higher security level while reducing the computational overhead. Since the attackers may make use of the AC coefficients to derive the DC coefficients, they suggested encrypting AC coefficients as well if a higher level of security is desired.

Qiao-Nahrstedt Algorithm

Qiao and Nahrstedt (1997) have proposed a video encryption algorithm based on the statistical analysis of the MPEG video stream. Considering the MPEG stream as a sequence of bytes, they observed that a video stream has a more uniform distribution of byte values. They analyzed the distribution of the byte value, the pair of two adjacent bytes, and the pair of two bytes with a fixed distance in between. Based on the experimental results, they concluded that there is no repeated byte pattern within any 1/16 chunk of an I-frame.

The proposed algorithm first divides a chunk of the MPEG video stream into two byte lists: an odd list and an even list. Then it performs the XOR operation to encrypt the odd list, and uses another encryption function to encrypt the even list to get the ciphertext. Since this chunk of data is a non-repeated pattern, it is considered to be perfectly secure. Some key selection approaches, which are procedures to generate random bit sequences as the keys, have been adopted to increase the security. This methodology is 47% faster than DES. Experimental results show that

the encryption/decryption time for each frame is slightly less than the frame rate time of 0.33ms. As a result, this methodology is suitable for real-time applications. Also, the security level is high enough for some sensitive video-on-demand applications. This algorithm has some drawbacks: (1) it still needs to go through all the I-frames, which is kind of computationally expensive; (2) the basic idea of this algorithm is similar to that of a selective algorithm and thus may lead to the same security issues.

Hierarchical Algorithms

Hierarchical algorithms offer different levels of security by encrypting different portions of the video data, at the price of different levels of computational cost. Li, Chen, Tan, and Campbell (1996) proposed a MPEG video stream encryption algorithm, which has three layers. The first layer encrypts only the I-frames of the MPEG video stream with the standard encryption algorithm, PGP (Pretty Good Privacy). The second layer provides higher security level by encrypting the I-frames and P-frames. The third level offers the highest security level by encrypting all of the frames.

Meyer and Gadegast (1995) have proposed a new MPEG-like video encryption algorithm called SECMPEG. This methodology incorporates selective algorithms and additional header information to enhance its level of security. It has a high-speed software implementation. SECMPEG can be combined with both DES and RSA encryption standards. SECMPEG has four levels of implementations. The algorithm for the higher level is always the superset to the algorithm immediately under it. With the increase of the layer number, the security level is increased and so is the computational overhead. In the first level, the algorithm encrypts only the header information. In the second level, the algorithm encrypts parts of the I-blocks in addition to the implementation in the first level. In the third level, I-frames and all of the I-blocks (within P-frames and B-frames) are encrypted. In the fourth level, the algorithm is the same as the naïve algorithm.

SECMPEG provides a hierarchical encryption system for digital MPEG video. We can choose different combinations of security levels and computational overhead to meet the requirements of various application scenarios. However, SECMPEG is not compatible with the standard MPEG because the header information of the video stream is changed. Thus, a special encoder/decoder would be required for the playback of unencrypted SECMPEG streams.

Comparison

The video encryption algorithms are always a tradeoff between the computational complexity and the security level. Highly secure algorithms always have to pay the price of high computational overhead; on the other hand, the fast algorithms always provide relatively low level of security. To develop efficient MPEG video encryption algorithms, we need to investigate the MPEG codec structure, search for key parameters, and try to encrypt as few as possible bits while obtaining a certain level of security according to the different applications' requirements. Comparative result among these methods is in Table 4.

INTRODUCTION TO IMAGE/VIDEO INFORMATION HIDING

With the advancements in computing power, an encryption system may be broken more easily than before. For this reason, researchers have started to use information hiding techniques to enhance encryption and increase the level of security. Information hiding conceals not only the content and location of the protected data, but also its very existence. Information hiding techniques can be used to protect the copyright of the content, track the user of the media data, and convey additional information. The following example illustrates an application of information hiding in secure communication:

• Apparently neutral's protest is thoroughly discounted and ignored. Isman hard hit. Blockade issue affects pretext for embargo on by-products, ejecting suets and vegetable oils.

This paragraph is a message sent by a spy during World War II. The content of the message is nothing secret and attracted very little or even no suspicion. However, if we extract the second letter from each word of the original message, we will be able to obtain the secret message "**Pershing sails from NY June 1**."

The generic model of an information embedding-extracting system is illustrated in Figure 5 (Yang & Bourbakis, 2005). Given a cover object

Table 4. Comparative results (video)

	Complexity	Speed	Computation Overhead	Security Level	Compression Ratio
Selective Algorithm	Low	Fast	High	Low	Unchanged
Tang	Low	Fast	Low	Low	Reduced
VEA	Low	Fast	Low	Low	Unchanged
Qiao-Nahrstedt	High	Fast	High	High	Unchanged
SECMPEG	Low-High	High	Four levels	Four levels	N/A

Figure 5. A typical information hiding and retrieval system

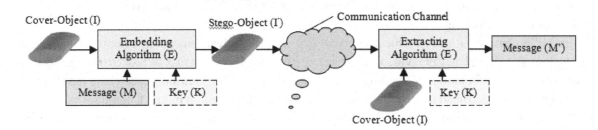

I, a message M, the embedding algorithm E, and an optional key K, the embedding process can be defined as a mapping of the form: $I \times K \times M \times E \rightarrow I'$, where I' is the stego-object. The information extraction procedure is: $I' \times K \times E' \rightarrow M'$, where I' is the stego-object, K is the key, E' is the extracting algorithm, and M' is the extracted message, which could be different from the original message M.

Digital image is one of the most popular digital multimedia data types. Thus, information hiding techniques using digital images as the host signal have attracted significant research interests. According to modern information hiding theory, the embedding capability of the host image/video frames provides an additional communication channel with a certain capacity, which could be used to transmit secure data. Compared to digital video, digital images provide less channel capacity for information embedding.

With information hiding techniques, it is possible to hide secret messages within digital image/video content without degrading its visual quality. There are lots of properties inherent to digital images and human visual system that can be utilized for information hiding. Human eyes have different levels of sensitivity to contrast in relation to spatial frequency and masking effect of edges. Moreover, human eyes are more sensitive to low-frequency components than to high-frequency components. Similarly, human eyes perceive brightness components better than chromatic information. In Figure 6, we have successfully embedded a secret image within four larger images, and as can be

seen, visually there is no difference between the original and stego images.

Different types of attacks aim to remove or disable the embedded information. In order to develop robust and efficient information hiding algorithms, it is beneficial to identify different kinds of attacks. Basically, attacks can be classified into the following categories:

- **Removal attack:** it generally tries to reduce the effective channel capacity of the information hiding scheme;
- **Geometrical attack:** it tries to degrade or cut part of the host signal and indirectly remove the embedded information;
- **Cryptographic attack:** appropriately named because of its similarity to the encryption systems attack, which tries to remove the embedded information by cryptanalysis;
- **Protocol attack:** a high-level attack which analyzes the embedding methodology on the system level and exploits the weak points of the methodology.

For information hiding systems, the definition of robustness and efficiency are always application-dependent. For example, the general information hiding schemes require robustness to all possible modifications. However, in a fragile watermarking system, the embedded information is supposed to be sensitive to any kind of modification, no matter how slight it is. In the

Figure 6. Image information hiding with SCAN based methodologies

system design procedure, it is important to take into account the applications of the system and the possible attacks for the time being.

LOW BITRATE INFORMATION HIDING

In information hiding techniques, bitrate refers to the amount of data embedded in the host signal. In terms of the amount of data to be embedded, information hiding systems can be classified as high bitrate and low bitrate algorithms. In low bitrate information hiding, relatively small amount of data is embedded in the host image to indicate some important ownership information. In high bitrate information hiding, relatively large amount of information is embedded in the host signal for covert communication, side information delivery, etc.

The most representative low bitrate information hiding application is digital watermarking, which embeds a few bits for ownership verification. Watermarking is defined (Cox, Miller, & Bloom 2002) as being the practice of imperceptibly altering a piece of data to embed information. A watermarking system should have two modules: one module that embeds the information in the host data and another module that detects and extracts the watermark. Depending on the type, quantity, and properties of the embedded infor-

mation, watermarking can serve a multitude of applications, such as:

- **Owner identification and proof of ownership**: the embedded data can carry information about the legal owner or distributor or any rights holder of a digital item and be used to warn the user that the item is copyrighted, track illegal copies, and prove the ownership of the item;
- **Broadcast monitoring**: the embedded information is utilized for various functions related to digital media (audio, video) broadcasting in order to verify whether the actual broadcasting of commercials took place as scheduled;
- **Transaction tracking**: each copy of a digital item that is distributed as part of a transaction has a different watermark. The purpose of this watermark is not only to carry information about the legal owner/ distributor of the digital item but also to mark the specific transaction copy;
- **Usage control**: the watermarking plays an active protection role by controlling the terms of use of the digital content. The embedded information can be used to prohibit unauthorized recording of a digital item or playback of unauthorized copies;
- **Authentication and tamper-proofing**: the role of the watermark is to verify the

authenticity and integrity of a digital item for the benefit of either the owner/distributor or the user;

- **Enhancement of legacy systems**: data embedded through watermarking can be used to enhance the information or functionalities provided by legacy systems while ensuring backwards compatibility.

Spatial Domain Algorithms for Low Bitrate Hiding

In terms of the embedding domain, information hiding systems can be classified as spatial domain and frequency domain algorithms. Spatial domain information hiding algorithms embed information within digital image/video contents by directly modifying the grey values of the data samples. The most straightforward spatial-domain image information hiding algorithm embeds information by modifying the least-significant-bit (LSB) of pixels. However, this algorithm is sensitive to lossy compression and the watermark can be easily removed. Duplication is a possible approach to enhance the security level of the LSB algorithm.

Koch and Zhao (1995) proposed a copyright labeling methodology called Randomly Sequenced Pulse Position Modulated Code (RSPPMC). The proposed method splits the problem into two components. The first component produces the actual copyright code and a random sequence of locations for embedding the code in the image. The second component actually embeds the code at the specified locations. It was demonstrated that a copyright label code could be embedded in several images, using pulses with sufficient noise margins to survive common processing such as lossy compression, color space conversion, and low-pass filtering.

The patchwork method was proposed by Bender, Gruhl, Morimoto, and Lu (1996), which basically embeds the message in a host image by increasing the grey level of certain pixels and decreasing the grey level of other pixels by the same amount. The pixels are chosen in pairs and thus the overall average brightness of the host image is not modified. Several modifications have been made to the original algorithm in order to improve the performance and robustness. This methodology is suitable for low bit-rate applications such as digital watermarking. Texture block coding was proposed by Bender, Gruhl, Morimoto, and Lu (1996). In this algorithm, the message is embedded within the continuous random texture pattern of a digital image. A region from a random texture pattern found in a picture is copied to an area that has similar texture. The embedded message could be extracted easily by autocorrelation, shifting, and thresholding. This methodology is robust against filtering, compression, and rotation. Possible improvements to this methodology include automatic detection and automatic texture region selection.

Bas, Chassery, and Davoine (1998) proposed a self-similarity based image watermarking scheme. Their approach is based on a fractal compression method. In the proposed methodology, the first step is to build a fractal code for the image. Therefore, each image corresponds to a fractal code, which is called "collage map". The fractal code can also be expressed in the DCT domain and is used in image compression. Image watermark is then embedded by altering the collage map. It is statistically rare to find a block equal to another one in an ordinary image. This algorithm basically adds artificial and invisible local similarities to the image in order to control the collage map.

Allen and Davidson (1998) proposed an information hiding technique, which used an image transform called Minimax Eigenvalue Decomposition (MED) to decompose an image into layered images. MED transform does not have to deal with the computational and roundoff penalties encountered in typical linear transforms. The MED transform combines message data and a subset of the layer images to create an image that is close to the original one. This technique differs from existing methodologies in that the embedded message is not the only piece of information needed for authentication. Thus, even if the message is corrupted, authentication could still be achieved.

Another technique for watermark embedding is to exploit the correlation properties of additive pseudo-random noise patterns as applied to an image (Langelaar, Setyawan & Lagendijk, 2000). To retrieve the watermark, the same pseudo-random noise generator algorithm is seeded with the same key, and the correlation between the noise pattern and possibly watermarked image is computed. If the correlation exceeds a certain threshold T, the watermark is detected. This method can be easily extended to a multiple-bit watermark by dividing the image into blocks and performing the above procedure independently on each block.

Amin, Salleh, Ibrahim, and Katmin, (2003) proposed the Secure Information Hiding System (SIHS) algorithm that is based on Least Significant Bit (LSB) technique in hiding messages in an image. The proposed method embeds the message into random positions as in (Lee & Chen, 2000). However, a different algorithm is used to determine the embedding positions.

Transform Domain Algorithms for Low Bitrate Hiding

Transform-domain algorithms embed information in the frequency domain of the host image/video. Transform domain algorithms are increasingly common because they can enhance the robustness against transform based compression, filtering, and noise. Actually, it is observed that the use of a particular transform is usually robust against compression algorithms based on the same transform. One of most popular transformations for image processing is Discrete-Cosine-Transform (DCT). The DCT allows an image to be transformed into different frequency bands.

Koch and Zhao (1995) proposed an approach to watermarking images based on the JPEG image compression algorithms. Their approach divides the image into individual 8x8 blocks. In each 8x8 block, only eight coefficients in particular positions of DCT coefficients can be marked. These comprise the low frequency components of the image block, but exclude the mean value coefficient at coordinate (0, 0) as well as the low frequencies at coordinates (0, 1) and (1, 0). Three of these coefficients are selected using a pseudo-random number generator to convey embedded information.

Cox, Kilian, Leighton, and Shamoon (1996) applied the spread spectrum theory in communication and proposed a digital watermarking system for image, audio, and video. They proposed to embed information in the perceptually significant region in order to be robust against certain procedures such as lossy compression, signal processing, and other kinds of attacks. In a digital watermarking system, the host media could be viewed as a broadband channel and as such the embedded watermark could be viewed as a signal to be transmitted through the channel. The watermark could be spread over many frequency components so that it becomes imperceptible in any certain frequency component. Thus, the visual distortion would not be noticeable. However, the presence of original cover data is needed to extract the embedded information. This problem could be fixed by a more elaborate design of an embedding/extracting algorithm.

With the standardization process of JPEG 2000 and the shift from DCT to wavelet-based image compression methods, watermarking schemes that work in the wavelet transform domain have become more interesting. The wavelet transform has a number of advantages that can be exploited for both image compression and watermarking applications.

Xia, Boncelet, and Arce (1997) proposed a multi-resolution watermarking method for digital images. Before that, most of the frequency-domain watermarking schemes were based on discrete cosine transform (DCT), where pseudo-random sequences were added to the DCT coefficients at the middle frequencies as signatures. Since wavelet image/video coding has been included in the image/video compression standard such as JPEG2000 and Motion-JPEG2000, this method works in wavelet transform domain. They added pseudo-random codes to the coefficients at the high and middle frequency bands of the discrete wavelet transform of an image. This watermarking method has multi-resolution characteristics and is hierarchical. Adding watermarking to the large coefficients in high and middle frequency bands (which correspond to the edge and texture of the image) is difficult for the human eyes to perceive. It has been shown that the proposed methodology is very robust to wavelet transform based image compression and common image distortions such as additive noise and half-toning.

Based on the multi-resolution technique introduced by Xia, Boncelet, and Arce (1997), Kim and Moon (1999) utilized Discrete Wavelet Transform (DWT) coefficients of all sub-bands (including the approximation image) to equally embed a random Gaussian distributed watermark sequence in the whole image. Perceptually significant coefficients have been selected by level-adaptive thresholding to achieve a high level of robustness.

Pereir, Voloshynovskiy, and Pun (2000) described a method based on a one-level decomposition of non-overlapping 16x16 image blocks using Haar wavelet filters. The proposed watermarking algorithm uses linear programming to optimize watermark robustness. For each bit to be embedded, a 2x2 block of neighboring coefficient is selected from a LL sub-band of size 8x8. Cheng and Huang (2001) presented an additive approach to achieve transform domain information hiding for images and video. The watermark embedding method is designed to satisfy the perceptual constraints and to improve its detectability. They proposed information hiding schemes in three transform domains: Digital Cosine Transform (DCT) domain, Digital Wavelet Transform (DWT) domain, and Pyramid Transform Domain. The embedding of the watermark into the host signal

is usually either multiplicative or additive. Their proposed system provides both good transparency and precise control of detection error.

HIGH BITRATE INFORMATION HIDING

High bitrate information hiding, unlike digital watermarking, tries to hide relatively large amounts of secure information within the host image/video contents. High bitrate information hiding techniques could be elaborately designed to cause unnoticeable visual degradation to the host signal in spite of its large data capacity. The main applications of high bitrate information hiding are secure communication, captioning, speech-in-video, video-in-video, etc. In high bitrate information hiding, four performance metrics are of interest:

1. Transparency: the embedding of protected data should not interfere with the visual fidelity of host video (Zhang, Cheung & Chen, 2005);
2. Channel capacity: how many bits can be effectively embedded within the host video (Cvejic & Seppanen, 2004; Kundur, 2000; Lin & Chang, 2001; Briffa & Das, 2002; Moulin & Mihcak, 2002);
3. The impact of embedded information on the performance of image/video compression (Chang, Chen, & Lin, 2004);
4. Robustness against lossy compression: how much hidden information can survive the lossy video codec (Gunsel, Uludag, & Tekalp, 2002; Fei, Kundur, & Kwong, 2001; Ni, Shi, Ansari, Su, Sun, & Lin, 2004).

Like low bitrate algorithms, high bitrate information hiding algorithms can be classified into spatial-domain and transform-domain algorithms.

Spatial Domain Algorithms for High Bitrate Hiding

The most commonly used spatial domain algorithm for high bitrate information hiding is the LSB algorithm. Again, it is very sensitive to lossy compression and can be removed easily. Wu and Tsai (1998) proposed a methodology where data is embedded in each pixel of a cover image by changing its grey value without exceeding a certain threshold. A multiple-based number system is proposed to convert the information in the message into values to be embedded in certain pixels of the cover image. Pseudo-random mechanisms may be used to enhance the level of security. It has been found from the experiments that the signal-to-noise ratio of the stego-images is larger than those observed in compressed images. This proves that the visual distortion caused by the data embedded is less than that caused by image compression. The proposed method can be easily applied to embed data in a color image. Maniccam and Bourbakis (2004) proposed a spatial-domain algorithm based on the texture analysis of each 3x3 neighborhood within the image. The proposed algorithm obtains higher robustness against JPEG because the modifications of non-LSB bits are more robust to lossy compression.

Chang, Chen, and Lin (2004) proposed a steganography scheme based on the search-order coding (SOC) compression method of vector quantization (VQ) indices. Their goal is to embed secret data into the compression codes of the host image such that the interceptors will not notice the existence of the secret data. In the proposed scheme, the embedding process induces no extra coding distortion and adjusts the bit rate according to the size of secret data. The receiver can efficiently receive both the compressed image and the embedded data almost at the same time. According to the experimental results, the proposed scheme yields a good and acceptable compression ratio of the image.

A novel LSB embedding algorithm for hiding encrypted messages in non-adjacent and random pixel locations in edges of images was proposed in (Singh, Singh, & Singh, 2007). It first encrypts the secret message and detects edges in the cover image. Message bits are then embedded in the least significant bits and random locations of the edge pixels. The proposed algorithm does not require the original cover-image for the extraction of the secret message. It has been shown that the blind LSB detection technique, like the gradient energy method, could not estimate the length of the secret message bits accurately for the proposed algorithm. A new improved version of Least Significant Bit (LSB) method was presented in (Kekre, Athawale, & Halarnkar, 2008). This approach is simple in implementation but still achieves a high level of embedding capacity and imperceptibility. The proposed method can also be applied to 24-bit color images and achieve embedding capacity much higher than the Pixel Value Differencing (PVD) method.

Wang and Cheng (2005) presented an efficient digital steganographic technique for three-dimensional (3D) triangle meshes. It is based on a substitutive blind procedure in the spatial domain. The basic idea is to consider every vertex of a triangle as a message vertex. They proposed an efficient data structure and advanced jump strategy to fast assign order to the message vertex. The authors provided a Multi-Level Embed Procedure (MLEP), including sliding, extending, and rotating levels, to embed information based on shifting the message vertex by its geometrical property. Experimental results showed that the proposed technique is efficient and secure, has high capacity and low distortion, and is robust against affine transformations (which include translation, rotation, scaling, or their combined operations). The technique provides an automatic, reversible method and has proven to be feasible in steganography.

Ibrahim and Zabian (2009) proposed a security mechanism that hides a message text into a digital image by converting the text to colored image. After which, the colored image is transmitted over the network to the destination. The decryption process at the destination is done in a similar but converse process.

Ren, Xia, and Ma (2009) proposed an algorithm using the prediction error to accomplish an effective information hiding. In order to restrain the error diffusion which possibly appears during the anti-predictive coding in the information hiding process, an improved predictive coding algorithm is implemented. The performances of both the basic and improved algorithms were empirically gathered. The thread correctness was established with those experiments. Clearly, the validity of the improved algorithm was achieved by an ultra large information capacity of 0.953 bits/Byte and a PSNR of 49.184dB.

Zhou, Quan, and Kang (2008) presented an information hiding algorithm based on a Radial Basis Function (RBF) neural network and LSB. The nonlinear mapping relation between input vector and original information was set up by the RBF neural network. The data used by the RBF network were embedded in the cover image as secret information. The algorithm cannot be deciphered theoretically considering the almost infinite possibilities of building the input vector. The simulation experiments confirmed the algorithm to be feasible and effective.

A fragile large capacity spatial domain information hiding algorithm, based on human visual gray sensitivity and a new calculation formula of image peak signal-to-noise ratio, was put forward by Che and Wang (2010). They proposed an adaptive embedding method which shows minimum visual gray sensitivity when massive amount of information is hidden into the original image. Experiments showed that this algorithm has excellent masking properties and that a random bit tampering will result in the incorrect recovery of the watermarking image. This indicates that the algorithm is suitable for applications that require strict information reliability.

Most of the previous works on steganography are aimed at hiding images in grayscale host images and excluded the use of color images because of their inherent complexities. Being limited by this constraint has two drawbacks. One is that only grayscale images are used to hide grayscale images. This is impractical because many valuable images are available in color. The other is the limited hiding capacity that is available in grayscale host images. This apparent difficulty is evidenced by the scarcity of published papers on steganographic techniques for color images (Chae, Mukherjee, and Manjunath, 1998; Liu and Qiu, 2002; Ni and Ruan, 2002). Moreover, the schemes presented in these papers utilize the transform domain to enable larger hiding capacity in color images.

The scheme proposed by Lin, Hu, and Chang (2002) hides large amount of data in the pixels of a true color image, which utilizes eight (8) bits to represent each color component of a color pixel. The secret image can be both a grayscale and a true color image. However, the quality of the extracted color secret image is not good with regard to the peak signal-to-noise ratio (PSNR) value and visual observation.

Yu, Chang, and Lin (2007) proposed a steganographic method which hides a color or a grayscale image in a true color image. The method has high hiding capacity and high image quality. Further, it enables the embedding of annotation data with the secret image in the host image. As for color images, the secret image can be a color image or a palette-based 256-color image, which has a color table similar to the widely used graphic interchanged format (GIF) image. In the proposed method, the local color information of an image can be preserved well through a technique of color quantization that is image dependent. The extracted secret color image is perceptibly almost identical to the original image and its PSNR value is very high. Moreover, the hiding capacity of the host image and the quality of the stego-image in the proposed method are also superior to that of the scheme described by Lin, Hu, and Chang (2002).

Visually imperceptible image hiding involves hiding one or more secret images into another non-critical image with minimal perceptible degradation. However, the hiding capacity and the distortion of cover image are trade-offs. This is because more hidden information always results in more visually perceptible degradation on the cover image. Recently, visually imperceptible data hiding schemes have been widely studied and many research reports (Chan & Cheng, 2004; Chang & Wu, 2006; Chang, Wu, & Chen, 2008; Chen, Chang, & Hwang, 1998; Chung, Shen, & Chang, 2001; Du & Hsu, 2003; Hu, 2003, 2006; Lin & Shie, 2004; Wu, Lin, & Chang, 2008) have been proposed in the literature. Among these research methods, the vector quantization (VQ) technique is most commonly applied in the procedure of data hiding. In contrast, the least-significant-bit (LSB) substitution technique is most commonly employed in data embedding.

Visually imperceptible image hiding can also be used for covert communication. In the previously described works, raw images without any compression are directly embedded into cover images. To solve the problem of inefficient utilization of hiding capacity, Chen et al. (1998) proposed a technique, called virtual image cryptosystem, where secret images are compressed, using VQ and then encrypted prior to hiding. In 2003, Hu (2003) proposed a revised version of the virtual image cryptosystem where each pixel value of the cover image was split into two parts. The significant one is used for VQ codebook training, and the insignificant one is used for data embedding by greedy substitution. Consequently, this revised version provides greater hiding capacity and lower computational cost. Nevertheless, the quality of extracted secret images is not good enough. Furthermore, the visual quality of secret images decreases badly when more secret images have to be hidden into the cover image. This is due to the fact that it is necessary to reduce the codebook size

in order to decrease the volume of each compressed secret image. Lin and Shie (2004) proposed a novel idea of transmitting a set of secret images via its corresponding VQ codebook to improve the image hiding efficiency. This scheme focuses both on the hiding capacity of the cover medium and on the quality of extracted secret images at the receiver. To achieve a high-capacity and high-quality secret image transmission scheme, the VQ technique is applied in this scheme to compact the volume of secret images. Moreover, to guarantee the visual quality of extracted secret images at the receiver, the VQ codebook utilized in the encoding procedure is adopted as cover medium. Lin and Shie's scheme provides a new and original approach to transmitting a set of secret images over a network, especially for limited-bandwidth communication channel. Although the appearance of cover medium in Lin and Shie's scheme looks like a meaningless data stream to the possible interceptors, the cover medium is a VQ codebook, not a visually recognizable image. It should be noted, however, that this may limit its practical application when the property of visually imperceptibility is required.

Shie, Lin and Jiang (2010) proposed a novel visually imperceptible image hiding scheme that improves both Hu's scheme and Lin and Shie's scheme. The VQ technique is incorporated into the previous schemes to compact the volume of secret images. Moreover, to adaptively guarantee the visual quality of extracted secret images at the receiver, the VQ codebook, which is utilized in the encoding procedure, is slightly modified and totally embedded into the cover image. The latest scheme provides a visually imperceptible image hiding approach to deliver a set of secret images to the receiver.

Kekre, et. al. (2010) proposed a data hiding method based on VQ compressed images. Codebooks of secret message and cover images have been combined using a shuffle algorithm. Experimental results indicate that this new scheme provides a 100% hiding capacity or more. This implies that a secret message can be of same size or larger than the cover image. Further, the method is claimed to deliver better image quality when compared with existing schemes that are based on VQ compressed images.

Transform Domain Algorithms for High Bitrate Hiding

Spatial domain hiding is easier to implement but it is not as robust as transform domain hiding. Transform domain hiding is more robust but the detection of hidden data is more complex. Various DCT-domain algorithms embed the information by modifying the DCT coefficients. The high bitrate frequency-domain algorithms have proven to be more robust to lossy compression compared to spatial-domain algorithms. Swanson, Zhu, and Tewfik (1997) proposed a vector projection based high bitrate information hiding algorithm, which embeds data by the projection of the DCT coefficients vector. Chae and Manjunath (1999) made use of lattice structure to code and embed information in the mid-frequency region of the DCT block. Alturki and Mersereau (2001) proposed data embedding through whitening the image and quantizing each DCT coefficient. Their algorithm significantly improved the security level and data capacity. Chang, Chen and Chung (2002) described a technique in which the medium-frequency coefficients of the DCT transformed cover image are employed to embed a secret message. The quantization table of the JPEG is also modified to further protect the embedded secret message. In the same manner, Iwata, Miyake, and Shiozaki (2004) also utilized the boundaries between zero and non-zero DCT coefficients to hide secret data.

Yang and Bourbakis (2005) proposed a novel information hiding based methodology to deliver secure information with the transmission of digital video contents. In the proposed algorithm the original host frame is first transformed into DCT domain. After that, each 4x4 DCT block is divided into sub-blocks, and then the DCT coefficients within low-frequency sub-blocks will be modified to hide the message by means of zig-zag scanning and vector quantization. Information is hidden within DCT domain in order to make the algorithm compatible to DCT-based H.264/AVC compression and obtain robustness against lossy compression. Since vector quantization is more robust to noise (including inverse DCT transform round-off noise and quantization noise) than scalar quantization, the coefficient vectors (rather than the coefficient scalars) are chosen for information hiding. Their algorithm has achieved a good balance between channel capacity and robustness against lossy compression.

Yang and Deng (2006) proposed a novel steganography method to hide a small-size gray image in a large-size gray image. Discrete Wavelet Transformation (DWT) was performed on both the cover image and the secret image. The coefficients of the wavelet decomposition of the secret image were quantized and coded into bit streams. Then, the approximation subband of secret image was embedded into the approximation subband of the cover image using an improved version of the LSB algorithm. Original image is not required for the extraction of embedded information.

A novel Discrete Wavelet Transform (DWT) domain high bitrate information hiding algorithm was proposed in (Yang, Trifas, Truitt, & Xiong, 2008). In the proposed algorithm, the coefficients within the approximation subband of the one-level wavelet decomposition have been grouped into vectors to embed information bits. Low-frequency coefficients have been chosen for information hiding due to their relatively large amplitudes and the corresponding smaller step size in JPEG2000 quantization. A mathematical model has been proposed to predict the Bit-Error-Rate (BER) of the algorithm under JPEG2000 compression.

Naoe and Takefuji (2008) proposed a new information hiding technique by using neural network trained on frequency domain. The proposed method can detect a hidden bit codes from the content by processing the selected feature sub-blocks into the trained neural network. Hidden codes can be retrieved from the neural network only if the proper extraction key is provided. The extraction keys are the coordinates of the selected feature subblocks, and the link weights are generated by supervised learning of a neural network. The supervised learning uses the coefficients of the selected feature subblocks as set of input values. The hidden bit patterns are used to train the neural network. The information hiding scheme can be combined with other algorithms to enhance the level of security.

Li (2009) proposed a novel scheme for text information hiding into a carrier image based on the Bose-Chaudhuri-Hocquenghem (BCH) code and Human Visual System (HVS) model. First, the approach uses ASCII codes to represent the text information and encodes that information using BCH code before transmitting them. The next steps are to divide the carrier image into 8×8 blocks, to transform every block into a two-dimensional DCT, to calculate the Just Noticeable Difference (*JND) threshold* value of every DCT coefficient and to choose the hiding coefficients. During the final step, the information codes are hidden into the selected coefficients in the DCT domain. The process of extracting information codes is the inverse. The experiments have proven this scheme to be secure and easy to operate.

In addition to hiding secret data in the frequency domain, another branch of research known as reversible data hiding has been recently explored for use in some sensitive applications such as military, medical and fine arts data. In the spatial domain, Tian explored redundancies in the digital content to achieve a reversible stego-image (Tian, 2003); Celik et al. used the generalized LSB of an image pixel in a cover image to design a lossless data embedding system (Celik, Sharma, Tekalp & Saber, 2005). In the compression domain, Chang et al. modified the codeword selection method of side-mach quantization vector (SMVQ) and fur-

ther proposed two reversible data hiding scheme (Chang, Tai, and Lin, 2006; Chang and Lin, 2006).

In the frequency domain, Fridrich and Goljanb (2001) presented an invertible watermarking scheme for authenticating digital images in the JPEG domain. This scheme utilizes an order-2 function, which is an inverse function, to modify the quantization table to enable lossless embedding of one bit per chosen DCT coefficient. Later, Xuan et al. (2002) proposed a high-capacity distortion-free data hiding technique based on the integer wavelet transform. Histogram modification was used in this scheme to embed secret data into the middle frequency of the wavelet domain. Their scheme is applicable to JPEG2000-compressed images because JPEG2000 is based on the wavelet transform domain.

Chang, Lin, Tseng, and Tai (2007) proposed a reversible data hiding scheme for DCT-based compressed images that increases the security of hidden secret data and enhances the hiding capacity. To maintain the quality of stego-images, the authors modified the DCT-quantized coefficients of the middle frequency components in each block because the human vision system is more sensitive to noise in the lower frequency. Moreover, they modified the quantization table to improve the quality of the stego-images without significantly decreasing the hiding capacity. Experimental results confirmed that the proposed scheme can achieve both satisfactory image quality and high hiding capacity in stego-images.

Xie, Agaian, and Noonan (2008) investigated the use of a family of transform domains in embedding hidden data. A new data hiding scheme that is based on a pair of unmatched orthogonal transforms has been developed. The hidden message signal is transmitted via the residual channel of two different parameterized slant transforms. The properties of the residual channel of parameterized slant transforms have been studied and the performance of the proposed scheme has been simulated and analyzed.

Figure. 7. Comparison between Original and Stego-Frames: "foreman_qcif.yuv"

(a) Original Frames – "foreman_qcif.yuv"

(b) Stego Frames – "stego_foreman_qcif.yuv"

In a related work, Xie, Yang, Huang, and Xie (2008) proposed a large capacity blind information hiding algorithm based on the DCT domain. Uniform spectrum processing is first used on the carrier image followed by a process using the DCT transform. At the final stage, the information is embedded into the low frequency coefficients of the DCT domain. Additionally, the information hiding is implemented by using a segment quantification method. The original image is not necessary in the extraction phase. Experimental results have shown that this scheme has a large capacity of information hiding and better imperceptibility.

INFORMATION EMBEDDING STRATEGIES FOR DIGITAL VIDEOS

A digital video is essentially a sequence of still images. Thus, it is natural to extend the digital image information hiding algorithms to corresponding approaches within digital video contents. The simplest way to implement video information hiding is to apply a still image information hiding algorithm to each frame of the video content. Figure 7 is an example of video information hiding. However, due to the inherent properties of digital video contents and the different video codec structures, information hiding within digital video has its own characteristics. In this section, the strategies of data embedding within digital video contents will be discussed.

Temporal Locations of Hidden Information

A generic video information hiding system is illustrated in Figure 8. As can be seen, a message is embedded within the host video content, resulting in a stego-video which will go through the H.264/AVC codec and the communication channel. The packet loss during the transmission on the Internet is not under consideration for the time being. Thus the only procedure that may cause hidden information loss is H.264/AVC coding.

In H.264/AVC, with the Group-Of-Pictures (GOP) structures, there are three different types of frames: I-frames, P-frames, and B-frames. Each type is compressed using a different algorithm. An I-frame is intra-coded and has the lowest compression ratio; a P-frame is inter-coded uni-directionally and has the medium compression ratio; a B-frame is inter-coded bi-directionally and has the highest compression ratio. Due to different compression algorithms, it is expected

Figure 8. Temporal location of hidden information

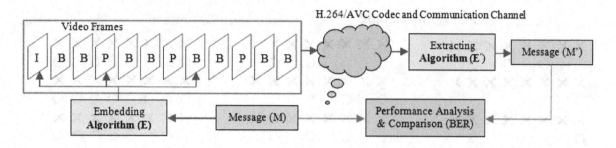

that the I-frames have the highest channel capacity for information hiding, while the B-frames have the lowest channel capacity. Accordingly, information within the I-frames has the best chance to survive, and information within the B-frames has the least chance to survive. Usually, we use the I-frames for information embedding. If higher channel capacity is desired, the P- and B- frames will also be used for information embedding.

Spatial Locations of Hidden Information in YUV Domain

In video compression, the source picture and the decoded picture are both comprised of three sample arrays: one luminance (luma) array and two chrominance (chroma) arrays. Since the human vision system is more sensitive to luminance than to chrominance, the luma array is kept as it is and the chroma arrays are down-sampled (Figure 9). With the down-sampling of chroma arrays, the data rate of the video content is largely reduced.

In order not to cause any color distortion, usually only the luma sample array is chosen as the host for information hiding. The luma array will be modified as a gray-level image to hide information. In the case that a higher channel capacity is desired, chroma samples will also be used for information hiding, at the price of slight color distortion.

Locations of Hidden Information in DCT Domain

As mentioned before, information embedded within the spatial-domain can be easily removed by a transformation based image/video codec. In order to gain robustness against lossy video codecs, it is better to embed information within the transformation domain. Two transformation domains have been investigated: Discrete Wavelet Transform (DWT) and Discrete Cosine Transform (DCT) in the research of Yang, Trifas, Truitt, and Xiong (2008). It is believed that information hiding and compression being in the same domain will make performance analysis and prediction easier. DWT based information hiding has been investigated and proven to be robust to JPEG 2000 image codec and Motion JPEG 2000 video codec.

In several studies (Yang & Bourbakis, 2005; Yang, Trifas, Truit, & Xiong, 2008), H.264/AVC was used as the video codec. Thus, the information embedding algorithm will work in the DCT domain for the following reasons: (1) H.264/AVC uses 4x4 integer transformations for decorrelation; (2) DCT is a close approximation of integer transformation. Some existing embedding algorithms proposed to embed information by modifying the whole DCT block. However, this algorithm has two drawbacks: (1) too much visual distortion due to the modification of every coefficient within the block; (2) the modification

Figure 9. YUV sampling of video contents

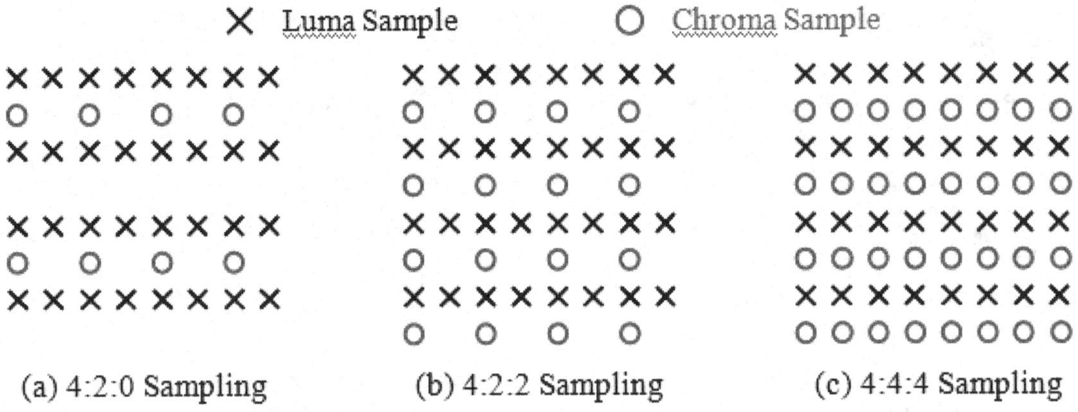

✗ Luma Sample   ○ Chroma Sample

```
✗ ✗ ✗ ✗ ✗ ✗ ✗ ✗        ✗ ✗ ✗ ✗ ✗ ✗ ✗ ✗        ✗ ✗ ✗ ✗ ✗ ✗ ✗ ✗
 ○   ○   ○   ○           ○   ○   ○   ○          ○ ○ ○ ○ ○ ○ ○ ○
✗ ✗ ✗ ✗ ✗ ✗ ✗ ✗        ✗ ✗ ✗ ✗ ✗ ✗ ✗ ✗        ✗ ✗ ✗ ✗ ✗ ✗ ✗ ✗
                          ○   ○   ○   ○          ○ ○ ○ ○ ○ ○ ○ ○

✗ ✗ ✗ ✗ ✗ ✗ ✗ ✗        ✗ ✗ ✗ ✗ ✗ ✗ ✗ ✗        ✗ ✗ ✗ ✗ ✗ ✗ ✗ ✗
 ○   ○   ○   ○           ○   ○   ○   ○          ○ ○ ○ ○ ○ ○ ○ ○
✗ ✗ ✗ ✗ ✗ ✗ ✗ ✗        ✗ ✗ ✗ ✗ ✗ ✗ ✗ ✗        ✗ ✗ ✗ ✗ ✗ ✗ ✗ ✗
                          ○   ○   ○   ○          ○ ○ ○ ○ ○ ○ ○ ○
```

  (a) 4:2:0 Sampling   (b) 4:2:2 Sampling   (c) 4:4:4 Sampling

of high-frequency coefficients will degrade the performance of run-length coding.

In order to fix the problem, current research efforts suggest to hide information within low-frequency coefficients. Preliminary experimental results also show that the proposed algorithm works best at low-frequency coefficients due to their high amplitudes. As such, the choice of the sub-block for information hiding is biased to low-frequency DCT coefficients (Figure 10). The reasons to choose low-frequency coefficients are:

1. Low-frequency coefficients have relatively larger amplitudes compared to high-frequency ones, and thus have more room for information embedding;

2. The quantization step size for low-frequency coefficients in lossy codec is relatively small, and the hidden information on low-frequency coefficients will have a better chance to survive;

3. High-frequency DCT coefficients will be easily removed by lossy compression because of their relatively low energy;

High-frequency coefficients are left unchanged and the number of non-zero coefficients in high-frequency region will not be increased. Thus, the

Figure 10. Sub-blocking Strategies of 4x4 Block; (a) Zig-Zag Scanning with no Sub-blocking, (b) 4x4 DCT Block Divided into Two Sub-blocks, (c) One Sub-block on Low-frequency Coefficients

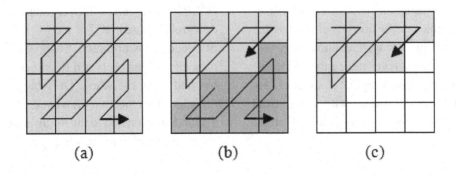

    (a)   (b)   (c)

performance of run-length coding in the video codec will not be degraded.

DIGITAL WATERMARKING TECHNIQUES AND APPLICATIONS

The preceding section is more concerned on the confidentiality of information than on its integrity. The proliferation of digital instruments and software facilitates the illegal reproduction of multimedia contents. Clearly, there is a great demand for tools and processes for integrity preservation and verification. This section will discuss the utilization of digital watermarking in the preservation of multimedia integrity.

Digital watermarking is the embedding of information into a multimedia host for the preservation and authentication of intellectual property rights. The tight integration of digital watermark information into the multimedia data provides a very secure authentication mechanism for intellectual property protection.

In Rey and Dugelay (2002), the following criteria for a generic image authentication system are proposed:

- Sensitivity to malicious manipulations.
- Tolerance to normal information loss.
- Localisation of image alterations.
- Reconstruction of altered regions.

These criteria provide the guidelines for the design of a robust image authentication system.

One of the earliest techniques in digital image watermarking is based on manipulating the least significant bit (LSB) of the image with checksum information. The algorithm, proposed by Walton (1995) and used for image tampering detection, is based on inserting check-sums into the least significant bits (LSB) of the image data. The algorithm uses a secret key to pseudo-randomly select a group of pixel, calculates the checksum of the 7 most significant bits (MSB) of the selected pixels, and embeds the checksum bits into the LSB.

The variable-watermark two-dimensional technique described by Wolfgang and Delp (1999) is based on the block-based watermarking principle. The watermarking technique consists of dividing the image into blocks of about 64 × 64 pixels and inserting a "robust" mark into each block. The integrity of an image is verified by testing the presence or absence of the mark in all blocks. If the mark is present with a high probability in each block, the image is authenticated.

Lin and Chang (2000) proposed a semi-fragile watermarking algorithm that accepts JPEG lossy compression and rejects malicious attacks. They have shown how to manipulate two invariance properties of DCT coefficients with respect to JPEG compression. The first property involves the modification of a DCT coefficient to an integral multiple of a quantization step which can be accurately reconstructed after JPEG compression. The second property is the invariant relationship between two DCT coefficients of the same coordinate position from two blocks which will not change after the quantization process. The manipulation technique can be used in embedding the signature and generating authentication bits.

Fridrich and Goljan (1999) developed a technique that essentially embeds a compressed version of the image into the LSB of its pixels. The technique divides the image into 8 x 8 block, sets the LSB of each pixel to zero, and calculates a discrete cosine transform (DCT) for each block. The quantified DCT matrix, encoded using 64 bits, corresponds to a 50% JPEG quality. To prevent deterioration of the recovery data due to tampering, the watermarked block is chosen to be sufficiently distant from the protected block. An alternative method, which enables the quality of the reconstructed image to be slightly improved, uses two LSBs for embedding the encoded quantified DCT coefficients. For most blocks, 128 bits are enough to encode almost all quantified DCT coefficients.

Schlauweg, Pröfrock, Zeibich and Müller (2006) developed a digital watermark embedding technique by geometrically shifting objects and object borders in a given host image. Without the benefit of seeing the original image for comparison, a casual observer has no way of perceiving the digital watermark that is embedded in the image. This makes this watermarking approach extremely robust to common image compression techniques. Further, they described another authentication scheme, which extends the scalar dead-zone quantization technique used in the JPEG2000 coding framework. This novel extension outperforms many existing quantization-based watermarking approaches in the wavelet-domain of JPEG2000.

Wu and Huang (2007) developed a three level decomposition wavelet-based watermarking algorithm. Their quantization based watermark is embedded in trees of coefficients. The watermark used is essentially a random binary sequence.

An application of watermarking using integer wavelet transform and companding technique augmented with genetic algorithm for intelligent coefficient selection scheme is described by Arsalan, Malik, and Khan (2010). The genetic algorithm is used to evolve a matrix of threshold information using the wavelet coefficients. The threshold matrix, which is subsequently used for image and watermark restoration, contains the optimal threshold values for a specific payload of the corresponding blocks.

Chong, Skalka, and Vaughn (2010) presented a novel approach to watermarking sensor data using probabilistic algorithms. The watermarking process that they described embeds a provenance mark, which is distributed into pieces into a dataset, and subsequently retrieved even with a corrupted dataset using a probabilistic algorithm.

A seminal work on the effects of watermarking to iris recognition performance is performed by Hammerle-Uhl, Raab, and Uhl (2010). The empirical work on the impact of applying a set of blind robust watermarking schemes on the recognition performance of two iris recognition algorithms resulted in a myriad of impacts. The significance of the result will have a tremendous influence on the way watermarking algorithms are chosen for biometric applications.

There is an implicit universal concurrence that digital watermarking must not only be robust against alterations but must also be able to withstand unauthorized removal and embedding. A paper by Schaber, et al. (2010) described a software tool that enables the semi-automatic temporal and spatial synchronization of frames and pixels of two similar videos. The process, also known as registration, is used primarily for detecting digital forensic watermarks.

Trends in H.264/AVC Video Watermarking

In the past years, the need for data hiding into digital video has attracted a great deal of interest due to copyright protection and secret communication. Early video data hiding approaches originated from still image watermarking techniques, which were extended to video by hiding the watermark into every frame independently. Traditionally, most of the data hiding techniques take place during the encoding process either in the spatial or in the transform domain (Dugelai, & Doerr, 2003). For these techniques, it is difficult to achieve real-time data hiding. Because of the large size of raw video files, video signals are usually stored and distributed in a compressed format. To embed the watermark in compressed video, it is impractical to first decode the input video stream, embed the watermark in it, and then re-encode it. Since most digital video are stored and distributed in the form of compressed bit-stream, it is more feasible and attractive to design low-complexity compressed-domain video watermarking without complete decoding of the video stream (Dai, Wang, Ye, & Zou, 2007).

H.264/AVC is the newest video coding standard with higher compression efficiency. It is expected that it will become one of the most popular video coding standard for broadcast on wireless channels and Internet media. However, to achieve better compression, new compression features such as variable block size motion estimation and compensation, directional spatial prediction in the intra-frame coding and context-adaptive entropy coding have been adopted in H.264/AVC (Bjontegaard, Luthra, Wiegand, & Sullivan 2003). These new features pose new challenges for data hiding due to less redundancy in the H.264/AVC video stream. If the conventional data hiding techniques, which were proposed for compressed bit-stream of MPEG-2/4, would be applied to the H.264/AVC video stream, some unexpected problems would occur (Dai, Wang, Ye, & Zou, 2007). Therefore, it is necessary to devise new data hiding algorithms for the H.264/AVC video bit-stream.

Recent video data hiding techniques focus on the characteristics generated by video compression standards. However, only a few data hiding algorithms have recently appeared in the literature by making full use of the properties of H.264/AVC (Mersereau & Noorkami, 2006; Li, Wang, & Zhang, 2008). In general, the existing data hiding methods for H.264/AVC can be divided into three categories in terms of the embedding carriers.

The first class of approaches only uses the quantized or un-quantized integer transform coefficients. Mersereau and Noorkami (2006) proposed a robust watermarking algorithm for H.264/AVC by modifying a subset of the 44 integer transform (HT) coefficients. The Watson visual model is adapted for the 4×4 HT block to increase the payload and robustness while limiting visual distortion. A key-dependent algorithm is used to select a subset of the coefficients that have visual watermarking capacity.

The second class of approaches utilizes motion vectors for watermark embedding. Li, Wang and Zhang (2008) proposed a video watermarking technique to hide copyright information in motion vectors. In this method, a region of the motion vector is restricted to hide watermark information. In order to obtain desirable video quality after watermark embedding, intra-mode is used to encode those macroblocks badly affected by restricting the region of the chosen motion vectors in inter-mode.

The third class of approaches makes full use of other characteristics such as context-adaptive entropy coding and intra/inter-prediction modes. Kim et al. proposed an entropy coding based watermarking algorithm to balance the capacity of watermark bits and the fidelity of the video (Hong, Won, Kim, & Kim, 2007). One bit of information is embedded in the sign bit of the trailing ones in context-adaptive variable length coding (CAVLC) of the H.264/AVC stream. Chen and Liu (2008) proposed a data hiding strategy that uses the inter- and intra-prediction modes of H.264/AVC. It uses these prediction modes to embed the watermark data. But prior to embedding, a pre-defined watermark area is determined. The block types in the inter- and intra-predictions are adequately partitioned to represent watermark bits and based on the correlations of block types.

Schlauweg, Mueller, Proefrock, and Richter (2005) proposed a video authentication scheme that utilizes some of the skipped macroblocks to embed erasable watermark. The scheme analyzes the original H.264/AVC bit-stream, computes a watermark, embeds the watermark and generates a new H.264/AVC bit-stream. A hash value is utilized to authenticate the video. Athanassios and Spyridon (2008) presented another low-complexity data hiding scheme for H.264/AVC encoded video. Embedding takes place during the encoding process and exploits the IPCM coded macroblocks in order to hide the data.

Su, Hu, and Zhang (2007) proposed an algorithm to hide one bit in each qualified intra-4×4 coded block (I4-block) by modifying the intra-4×4 prediction modes. However, the capacity of the embedded data is low. Moreover, many intra-prediction modes are changed, which leads to a significant increase in bitrate. Along the same vein, Yang, Li, He and Kang (2010) proposed an information hiding algorithm based on intra-prediction modes and matrix coding for the H.264/AVC video stream. Their algorithm utilizes the block types and modes of intra-coded blocks to embed watermark. Intra 4x4 coded blocks (I4-blocks) are divided into groups and two watermark bits are mapped to every three I4-blocks by matrix coding to map between watermark bit and intra-prediction modes. Embedding position template is utilized to select candidate I4-blocks for watermark embedding, which further enhances the security of watermark information.

MEDICAL IMAGING INFORMATION SECURITY AND PRIVACY

Patient Information Security and Privacy

The Health Insurance Portability and Accountability Act (HIPAA) requires that medical providers and insurance companies implement procedures and policies to protect patient's medical information. Also, in case of a court justification, the patient information needs to be associated with the content of the medical images. Areas to be specifically addressed include ensuring that confidential data is secured during electronic transmission, and that access is limited only to authorized personnel. Yang, Trifas, Buenos-Aires, and Elston (2009) designed a security scheme to protect patient information while making the information readily accessible when necessary. The design of the project is motivated by the following rationales:

1. Nowadays, the patient information is usually printed at the corner of the medical imaging for viewing. Thus, it is easily accessible to everybody.
2. The patient information prominently displayed may be intercepted by a third party during electronic transmission. Sometimes, this could cause a big lawsuit.
3. For scenarios such as medical imaging research, the patient information should not be accessible either.

4. For diagnosis purpose, the patient information needs to be readily accessible to the doctors.
5. In a court justification, ownership verification of the medical images is required.

System Overview

In the proposed system (Figure 11), patient information is not automatically visibly displayed in the corner of the medical image. Instead, the patient information is first encoded using ASCII character-encoding scheme and encrypted into a non-recognizable format using the RSA encryption algorithm. Next the patient information is further secured by embedding it within a section of the image that is outside the Region of Interest (ROI), which is located by using image segmentation techniques. This ensures that the embedded information will not affect the image quality and further diagnosis. This methodology effectively and securely protects patient information in scenarios such as electronic transmission and medical imaging research.

The image can be viewed in one of two forms. If the viewer does not have the authority to access the patient's personal information, for example a medical or computer researcher (or network hacker for that matter), the image is viewed with no data displayed in connection to the image. If the viewer has the authority to access the personal information, such as the patient's doctor, the information can be extracted, decrypted, decoded, and displayed upon the image with the entry of the correct encryption/decryption key. Also, in a forensic application scenario, the embedded information can be used to identify the person associated with the medical image.

Experimental Results

In the embedding procedure a simple image segmentation algorithm was first employed to identify the ROI. Figure 12 below is an X-ray of a skull

Figure 11. Flow chart of proposed methodology

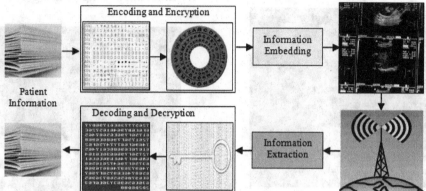

that has been analyzed by image segmentation and has only the contour lines showing. This was done using MATLAB's contour function.

Several different algorithms were experimented with to embed the data within the image. The first implementation adds an additional padding to the image to host the patient information (Figure 13). This algorithm does not alter the original image data but the viewer could clearly see where the information is located. The second method embeds the data directly in the image using the LSB technique (Figure 14). With this method the addition of the data itself could no longer be detected with the human eye. An alternative technique to embed the patient information

is a DCT based algorithm discussed by Yang and Bourbakis (2005). They proposed using a DCT on 4x4 blocks of pixels and then modifying the eight lowest frequency coefficients to embed one bit of information. With the proposed approach, patient information security and privacy can be reliably ensured during electronic transmission. It is also readily accessible when needed.

SUMMARY

Data Encryption is the backbone of information security and steganography works as the complement to data encryption. The most promising direction for the research of digital image/video encryption is to analyze the unique properties of digital image and video, make full use of the properties, and search for highly-secure algorithms that cause minimal computational overhead. Joint encryption/compression is a very promising direction. Since compression can be viewed as a special type of encryption, it can be combined with encryption to reduce the overall computational cost. The same principle applies to video encryption, too.

Information hiding techniques have attracted more and more research interests. It can be used as an enhancement to data encryption to further increase the level of security. For example, Bourbakis, Rwabutaza, Yang, and Skondras (2009) have

Figure 12. Image with Region of Interest boundary

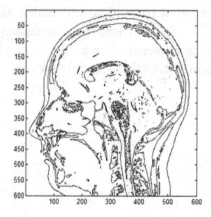

Figure 13. A Stego image with patient information

Figure 14. A Sample image with patient information embedded using LSB algorithm

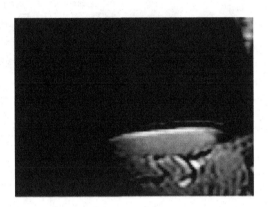

proposed a novel methodology to protect patient information during the electronic transmission of medical images. In the proposed methodology, they first adaptively identify locations to embed the patient information. After that, the locations of patient information are converted to two 2-D arrays. The 2-D arrays are compressed and encrypted using SCAN based encryption techniques. Finally, the encrypted location information is embedded with the medical images through LSB techniques. This is a very typical example of combining cryptography and steganography techniques to enhance the security of sensitive information.

The future challenges for information hiding include the following:

1. How to minimize visual distortion: the information embedding procedure should not interfere with the visual quality of the host image/video contents;
2. How to make the hiding algorithms robust to lossy compression: lossy image/video compression could possibly remove the embedded information. Existing research efforts work on how to improve the robustness of the embedded information against the lossy compression procedures;
3. How to achieve higher level of channel capacity: there is always a tradeoff between channel capacity and the robustness again

lossy compression. The more information to embed, the less level of robustness can be expected. Right now, the research challenge is: how to embed a significant amount of information while making it robust against loss compression;
4. Look for more practical applications for information hiding techniques: so far, many different information hiding techniques have been developed, and some of them are very mature in terms of the different performance metrics. Right now, the task is about how to find practical application scenarios and commercialization potentials for these research efforts.

Overall, the future trend on the development of information security techniques will be the combination of encryption, information hiding, and lossless compression. These techniques will enhance each other and increase the security level of modern information security systems.

REFERENCES

Agi, I., & Gong, L. (1996). An empirical study of secure MPEG video transmissions. *Proceedings of the Internet Society symposium on network and distributed system security*, 137-144.

Allen, C. A., & Davidson, J. L. (1998). Steganography using the Minimax Eigenvalue Decomposition. *Proceedings of the conference on mathematics of data/image coding, compression, and encryption, 3456*, 13-24.

Alturki, F., & Mersereau, R. (2001). A novel approach for increasing security and data embedding capacity in images for data hiding applications. *Proceedings of the international conference on information technology: Coding and computing*, 228–233.

Amin, M. M., Salleh, M., Ibrahim, S., & Katmin, M. R. (2003). Steganography: Random LSB Insertion Using Discrete Logarithm, *Proceedings of the Conference on Information Technology in Asia (CITA'03), Universiti Malaysia Sarawak, Sarawak, Malaysia*, 234-238.

Arsalan, M., Malik, S. A., & Khan, A. 2010. Intelligent threshold selection for reversible watermarking of medical images. In *Proceedings of the 12th Annual Conference Comp on Genetic and Evolutionary Computation* (Portland, Oregon, USA, July 07 - 11, 2010). GECCO '10. ACM, New York, NY, 1909-1914.

Athanassios, N. S., & Spyridon, K. K. (2008). Real-time data hiding by exploiting the IPCM macroblocks in H.264/AVC streams. *Journal of Real-Time Image Processing, 4*, 33–41.

Bas, P., Chassery, J., & Davoine, F. (1998). Self-similarity based image watermarking. *Proceedings of the 9th European Signal Processing Conference (EUSIPCO)*, 2277-2280.

Bender, W., Gruhl, D., Morimoto, N., & Lu, A. (1996). Techniques for data hiding. *IBM Systems Journal, 35*(3&4), 313–336. doi:10.1147/sj.353.0313

Bjontegaard, G., Luthra, A., Wiegand, T., & Sullivan, G. J. (2003). Overview of the H.264/AVC video coding standard. *IEEE Transactions on Circuits and Systems for Video Technology, 13*(7), 560–576. doi:10.1109/TCSVT.2003.815165

Bourbakis N. & Dollas, A. (2003). SCAN based multimedia-on-demand. *IEEE multimedia magazine*, 79-87.

Bourbakis, N., Rwabutaza, A., Yang, M., & Skondras, T. (2009). A synthetic stegano-crypto scheme for securing multimedia medical records", *2009 IEEE Digital signal processing and signal processing education workshop*.

Briffa, J. A., & Das, M. (2002). Channel models for high-capacity information hiding in images. *Proceedings of the SPIE, 4793*.

Celik, M. U., Sharma, G., Tekalp, A. M., & Saber, E. (2005). Lossless generalized-LSB data embedding. *IEEE Transactions on Image Processing, 14*(2), 253–266. doi:10.1109/TIP.2004.840686

Chae, J. J., & Manjunath, B. S. (1999). Data hiding in video. *Proceedings of the 6th IEEE international conference on image processing (ICIP'99), 1*, 311-315.

Chae, J. J., Mukherjee, D., & Manjunath, B. S. (1998) Color image embedding using multidimensional lattice structures, *Proceedings of IEEE International Conference on Image Processing*, Chicago, Illinois, USA, October 1998, 460–464.

Chan, C. K., & Cheng, L. M. (2004). Hiding data in images by simple LSB substitution. *Pattern Recognition, 37*(3), 469–474. doi:10.1016/j.patcog.2003.08.007

Chang, C., Chen, G., & Lin, M. (2004). Information hiding based on search-order coding for VQ indices. *Pattern Recognition Letters, 25,* 1253–1261. doi:10.1016/j.patrec.2004.04.003

Chang, C. C., Chen, T. S., & Chung, L. Z. (2002). A steganographic method based upon JPEG and quantization table modification. *Information Sciences, 141,* 123–138. doi:10.1016/S0020-0255(01)00194-3

Chang, C. C., Lin, C. C., Tseng, C. S., & Tai, W. L. (2007). Reversible hiding in DCT-based compressed images. *Information Sciences, 177,* 2768–2786. doi:10.1016/j.ins.2007.02.019

Chang, C.C., & Lin, C.Y. (2006). Reversible steganographic method using SMVQ approach based on declustering, *Information Sciences.*

Chang, C. C., Tai, W. L., & Lin, C. C. (2006). A reversible data hiding scheme based on side match vector quantization. *IEEE Transactions on Circuits and Systems for Video Technology, 16*(10), 1301–1308. doi:10.1109/TCSVT.2006.882380

Chang, C. C., & Wu, W. C. (2006). Hiding secret data adaptively in vector quantisation index tables. *IEEE Proceedings on Vision Image and Signal Processing, 153*(5), 589–597. doi:10.1049/ip-vis:20050153

Chang, C. C., Wu, W. C., & Chen, Y. H. (2008). Joint coding and embedding techniques for multimedia images. *Information Sciences, 178*(18), 3543–3556. doi:10.1016/j.ins.2008.05.003

Che, S., & Wang, H. (2010). A Fragile Information Hiding Technique Based on Human Visual Gray Sensitivity. *Journal of Advanced Materials Research, 121-122,* 1048–1051. doi:10.4028/www.scientific.net/AMR.121-122.1048

Chen, O., & Liu, C. H. (2008). Data hiding in inter- and intra-prediction modes of H.264/AVC, *Proceeding of IEEE International Symposium on Circuits and Systems,* 3205-3208.

Chen, T. S., Chang, C. C., & Hwang, M. S. (1998). A virtual image cryptosystem based upon vector quantization. *IEEE Transactions on Image Processing, 7*(10), 1485–1488. doi:10.1109/83.718488

Cheng, Q., & Huang, T. S. (2001). An additive approach to transform-domain information hiding andoptimum detection structure. *IEEE Transactions on Multimedia, 3*(3), 273–284. doi:10.1109/6046.944472

Chong, S., Skalka, C., & Vaughan, J. A. 2010. Self-identifying sensor data. In *Proceedings of the 9th ACM/IEEE international Conference on information Processing in Sensor Networks* (Stockholm, Sweden, April 12 - 16, 2010). IPSN '10. ACM, New York, NY, 82-93.

Chuang, T. J., & Lin, J.C. (1999). A new multi-resolution approach to still image encryption. *Pattern recognition and image analysis, 9* (3), 431-436.

Chung, K. L., Shen, C. H., & Chang, L. C. (2001). A novel SVD- and VQ-based image hiding scheme. *Pattern Recognition Letters, 22*(9), 1051–1058. doi:10.1016/S0167-8655(01)00044-7

Cox, I., Miller, M., & Bloom, J. (2002). *Digital watermarking.* Morgan Kaufmann Publishers.

Cox, I. J., Kilian, J., Leighton, T., & Shamoon, T. (1996). A secure, robust watermark for multimedia. *Proceedings of the first international workshop on information hiding,* 185 – 206.

Cvejic, N., & Seppanen, T. (2004). Channel capacity of high bit rate audio data hiding algorithms in diverse transform domains. *Proceedings of the international symposium on communications and information technologies (ISCIT 2004).*

Dai, Y., W., Wang Z.Q., Ye D.P., & Zou C.F. (2007). A new adaptive watermarking for real-time MPEG videos. *Applied Mathematics and Computation, 185*(2), 907–918. doi:10.1016/j.amc.2006.07.021

Du, W. C., & Hsu, W. J. (2003). Adaptive data hiding based on VQ compressed images. *IEEE Proceedings on Vision. Image and Signal Processing, 150*(4), 233–238. doi:10.1049/ip-vis:20030525

Dugelay, J. L., & Doerr, G. (2003). A guide tour of video watermarking. *Signal Processing Image Communication, 18*(4), 263–282. doi:10.1016/S0923-5965(02)00144-3

Fei, C., Kundur, D., & Kwong, R. (2001). The choice of watermark domain in the presence of compression. *Proceedings of international conference on information technology: Coding and computing,* 79-84.

Fridric, J., & Goljan, M. (1999). Protection of digital images using self embedding. *Proceedings of the Symposium on Content Security and Data Hiding in Digital Media,* New Jersey Institute of Technology, Newark, NJ, USA, May 1999.

Fridrich, J. M., & Goljanb, R. D. (2001). Invertible authentication watermark for JPEG images, Proceedings of the IEEE International Conference on Information Technology: Coding and Computing, 223–227.

Gunsel, B., Uludag, U., & Tekalp, A. M. (2002). Robust watermarking of fingerprint images. Journal of pattern recognition, 35 (12), 2739-2747.

Hämmerle-Uhl, J., Raab, K., & Uhl, A. (2010). Experimental study on the impact of robust watermarking on iris recognition accuracy. *Proceedings of the 2010 ACM Symposium on Applied Computing* (Sierre, Switzerland, March 22 - 26, 2010). SAC '10. ACM, New York, NY, 1479-1484.

Hong, Y., Won, C. S., Kim, S. M., & Kim, S. B. (2007). Data hiding on H.264/AVC compressed video. *Proceedings of International Conference on Image Analysis and Recognition, 4633,* 698–707.

Hu, Y. C. (2003). Grey-level image hiding scheme based on vector quantization. *IEEE. Electronics Letters, 39*(2), 202–203. doi:10.1049/el:20030167

Hu, Y. C. (2006). High-capacity image hiding scheme based on vector quantization. *Pattern Recognition, 39*(9), 1715–1724. doi:10.1016/j.patcog.2006.02.005

Ibrahim, A., Zabian, A., Esteteya, F. N., & Al Padawy, A. K. (2009). Algorithm for Text Hiding in Digital Image for Information Security. *International Journal of Computer Science and Network Security, 9*(6), 262–268.

Iwata, M., Miyake, K., & Shiozaki, (2004). A. Digital steganography utilizing features of JPEG images. IEICE Transactions on Fundamentals E87-A (4), 929–936.

Kekre, H. B., Athawale, A., & Halarnkar, P. N. (2008). Increased capacity of information hiding in LSB's method for text and image. *International journal of electrical, computer, and systems engineering.*

Kekre, H.B., Athawale, A., Sarode T.K. & Sagvekar K. (2010). Increased Capacity of Information Hiding using Mixed Codebooks of Vector Quantization Algorithms: LBG,

Kim, J., & Moon, Y. (1999). A robust wavelet-based digital watermark using level-adaptive thresholding. *Proceedings of the IEEE international conference on image processing (ICIP '99).*

Koch, E., & Zhao, J. (1995). Toward robust and hidden image copyright labeling. *Proceedings of IEEE workshop on nonlinear signal and image processing,* 452-455.

KPE and KMCG, *Advances in Computational Sciences and Technology, 3*(2), 245–256.

Kundur, D. (2000). Implications for high capacity data hiding in the presence of lossy compression. *Proceedings of the international conference on information technology: Coding and computing,* 16-21.

Kuo, C. J. (1993). Novel image encryption technique and its application in progressive transmission. *Journal of Electronic Imaging, 2*(4), 345–351. doi:10.1117/12.148572

Langelaar, G. C., Setyawan, I., & Lagendijk, R. L. (2000). Watermarking digital image and video data: a state-of-the-art overview. *IEEE Signal Processing Magazine, 17*(5), 20–46. doi:10.1109/79.879337

Lee, Y. K., & Chen, L. H. (2000). A Secure Robust Image Steganographic Model. *Proceedings of the Tenth National Conference on Information Security*, 275-284.

Li, C. X. (2009). A Novel Scheme for Text Information Hiding into a Carrier Image Based on BCH Code and HVS Model, Proceedings of the 2009 International Workshop on Information Security and Application (IWISA 2009), Qingdao, China.

Li, L., Wang, P., & Zhang, Z. D. (2008). A video watermarking scheme based on motion vectors and mode selection. *Proceedings of IEEE International Conference Computer Science and Software Engineering, 5*, 233–237.

Li, Y., Chen, Z., Tan, S. M., & Campbell, R. H. (1996). Security enhanced MPEG player. Proceedings of the international workshop on multimedia software development, 169-175.

Lin, C. Y., & Chang, S. F. (2000). Semi-fragile watermarking for authenticating JPEG visual content. [San Jose, CA, USA.]. *Proceedings of the SPIE International Conference on Security and Watermarking of Multimedia Contents, II*, 3971.

Lin, C. Y., & Chang, S. F. (2001). Watermarking capacity of digital images based on domain specific masking effects. Proceedings of the international conference on information technology: Coding and computing (ITCC '01).

Lin, M. H., Hu, Y. C., & Chang, C. C. (2002). Both color and gray scale secret images hiding in a color image. *International Journal of Pattern Recognition and Artificial Intelligence, 16*, 697–713. doi:10.1142/S0218001402001903

Lin, S. D., & Shie, S. C. (2004). Secret image communication scheme based on vector quantization. *IEEE Electronics Letters, 40*(14), 859–860. doi:10.1049/el:20040568

Liu, T., & Qiu, Z. D. (2002) A DWT-based color image steganography scheme, *Proceedings of* International Conference on Signal Processing, 2, 1568–1571.

Maniccam S. S., & Bourbakis, N. (2004). Lossless compression and information hiding in images. *Pattern recognition journal, 36*, 2004.

Mersereau, R. M., & Noorkami, M. (2006) Towards robust compressed-domain video watermarking for H.264/AVC. *Proceeding of the SPIE Security, Steganography, and Watermarking of Multimedia Contents*. Atlanta, USA.

Meyer, J., & Gadegast, F. (1995). Security mechanisms for multimedia-data with the example MPEG-I Video. *Proceedings (IEEE) of the international conference on multimedia computing and systems.*

Moulin, P., & Mihcak, M. K. (2002). A framework for evaluating the data-hiding capacity of image sources. *IEEE Transactions on Image Processing, 11*(9), 1029–1042. doi:10.1109/TIP.2002.802512

Naoe, K., & Takefuji, Y. (2008). Damageless information hiding using neural network on YCbCr domain. *International journal of computer science and network security, 8* (9).

Ni, R., & Ruan, Q. (2002). Embedding information into color images using wavelet, *Proceedings of* IEEE International Conference on Computers, Communications, Control and Power Engineering, 1, p. 598–601.

Ni, Z., Shi, Y., Ansari, N., Su, W., Sun, Q., & Lin, X. (2004). Robust lossless image data hiding. *International conference on multimedia & expo (ICME), 3,* 2199 – 2202.

Pereira, S., Voloshynovskiy, S., & Pun, T. (2000). Optimized wavelet domain watermark embedding strategy using linear programming. In Szu, H. (Ed.), *SPIE Aerosense 2000: Wavelet Applications VII.*

Qiao, L., & Nahrstedt, K. (1997). A new algorithm for MPEG video encryption. *Proceedings of CISST'97 international conference,* 21-29.

Ren, J., Xia, Y., & Ma, Z. (2009). Information Hiding Algorithm Based on Predictive Coding, Proceedings of the 2009 International Conference on Information Technology and Computer Science, 2, 11-14.

Ren, S., Mu, D., Zhang, T., & Hu, W. (2009). Study of Information Hiding Algorithm based on GHM and Color Transfer Theory. *Optoelectronics Letters, 5*(6), 454–458. doi:10.1007/s11801-009-9135-2

Rey, C., & Dugelay, J. (2002). A survey of watermarking algorithms for image authentication. *EURASIP Journal on Applied Signal Processing,* (6): 613–621. doi:10.1155/S1110865702204047

Schaber, P., Kopf, S., Effelsberg, W., & Thorwirth, N. (2010). Semi-automatic registration of videos for improved watermark detection. *Proceedings of the First Annual ACM SIGMM Conference on Multimedia Systems* (Phoenix, Arizona, USA, February 22 - 23, 2010). MMSys '10. ACM, New York, NY, 23-34.

Scharinger, J. (1998). Fast encryption of image data using chaotic Kolmogorov flows. *Journal of Electronic Imaging, 7*(2), 318–325. doi:10.1117/1.482647

Schlauweg, M., Mueller, E., Proefrock, D., & Richter, H. (2005). H.264/AVC video authentication using skipped macroblocks for an erasable watermark. *Proceedings of SPIE International Conference on Visual Communication and Image Processing, 5960,* 1480–1489.

Schlauweg, M., Pröfrock, D., Zeibich, B., & Müller, E. (2006). *Dual watermarking for the protection of rightful ownership and secure image authentication.* Proceedings of MCPS'06 conference, 59-66.

Shi, C., & Bhargava, B. (1998a). A fast MPEG video encryption algorithm. *ACM Multimedia, 98,* 81–88.

Shi, C., & Bhargava, B. B. (1998b). An efficient MPEG video encryption algorithm. *Proceedings of the symposium on reliable distributed systems,* 381-386.

Shie, S. C., Lin, S. D., & Jiang, J. H. (2010). Visually imperceptible image hiding scheme based on vector quantization. *Information Processing & Management, 46,* 495–501. doi:10.1016/j.ipm.2009.07.001

Singh, K. M., Singh, S. B., & Singh, S. S. (2007). Hiding encrypted message in the features of images. *International journal of computer science and network security (IJCSNS), 7* (4).

Socek, D., Li, S., Magliveras, S. S., & Furht, B. (2005). Short paper: enhanced 1-d chaotic key-based algorithm for image encryption. *First international conference on security and privacy for emerging areas in communications networks.*

Spanos, G. A., & Maples, T. B. (1995). Performance study of a selective encryption scheme for the security of networked, real-time video. *Proceedings of the 4th IEEE international conference on computer communications and networks (ICCCN '95),* 2-10.

Su, Y. T., Hu, Y., & Zhang, C. T. (2007) Information hiding based on intraprediction modes for H.264/AVC. *InProceedings of IEEE International Conference on Multimedia and Expo. 2007*, 1231–1234.

Swanson, M. D., Zhu, B., & Tewfik, A. H. (1997). Data hiding for video-in-video. *Proceedings of the 1997 international conference on image processing (ICIP '97)*, 2, 676-679.

Tang, L. (1996). Methods for encrypting and decrypting MPEG video data efficiently. *ACM Multimedia*, 96, 219–229.

Tian, J. (2003). Reversible data embedding using a difference expansion. *IEEE Transactions on Circuits and Systems for Video Technology*, 13(8), 890–896. doi:10.1109/TCSVT.2003.815962

Walton, S. (1995). Information authentication for a slippery new age. *Dr. Dobbs Journal*, 20(4), 18–26.

Wang, C. M., & Cheng, Y. M. (2005). An Efficient Information Hiding Algorithm for Polygon Models. *Computer Graphics Forum*, 24(3), 591–600. doi:10.1111/j.1467-8659.2005.00884.x

Wolfgang, R. & Delp, E. (1999). Fragile watermarking using the VW2D watermark. *Security and* Watermarking of Multimedia Contents, 3657 of SPIE Proceedings, 40–51.

Wu, D. C., & Tsai, W. H. (1998). Data hiding in images via multiple-based number conversion and lossy compression. *IEEE Transactions on Consumer Electronics*, 44(4), 1406–1412. doi:10.1109/30.735844

Wu, G. D., & Huang, P. H. (2007). Image watermarking using structure based wavelet tree quantization. *Proceedings of the 6th IEEE/ACIS International Conference on Computer and Information Science, 2007 (ICIS 2007)*, 315–319.

Wu, M. N., Lin, C. C., & Chang, C. C. (2008). An embedding technique based upon block prediction. *Journal of Systems and Software*, 81(9), 1505–1516. doi:10.1016/j.jss.2007.09.017

Wu, X., & Moo, P. W. (1999). Joint image/video compression and encryption via high-order conditional entropy coding of wavelet coefficients. *Proceedings (IEEE) of the international conference on multimedia computing and systems (ICMCS'99)*, 2, 908-912.

Xia, X. G., Boncelet, C. G., & Arce, G. R. (1997). A multi-resolution watermark for digital images. *Proceedings of IEEE international conference on image processing*, 1, 548-551.

Xie, J., Agaian, S., & Noonan, J. (2008). Secure information hiding algorithm using parametric slant-Hadamard transforms, Proceedings of the Conference on Mobile Multimedia/Image Processing, Security, and Applications.

Xie, J., Yang, C., Huang, D., & Xie, D. A. (2008). Large Capacity Blind Information Hiding Algorithm, Proceedings of the 2008 International Symposium on Electronic Commerce and Security, 934-937.

Xuan, G., Zhu, J., Chen, J., Shi, Y. Q., Ni, Z., & Su, W. (2002). Distortionless data hiding based on integer wavelet transform. *IEE Electronics Letters*, 38(25), 1646–1648. doi:10.1049/el:20021131

Yang, B., & Deng, B. (2006). Steganography in gray images using wavelet. *Proceedings of the second international symposium on communication, control and signal processing (ISCCSP)*.

Yang, G., Li, J., He, Y. & Kang, Z. (2010). An information hiding algorithm based on intra-prediction modes and matrix coding for H.264/AVC video stream, *International Journal of Electronics and Communications (AEU)*, 2010.

Yang, M., & Bourbakis, N. (2005a). A high bitrate multimedia information hiding algorithm in DCT domain. *Proceedings of the 8th world conference on integrated design and process technology (IDPT 2005)*.

Yang, M., & Bourbakis, N. (2005b). A high bitrate information hiding algorithm for digital video content under H.264/AVC compression. *Proceedings of the IEEE international midwest symposium on circuits and systems (MWSCAS 2005)*.

Yang, M., Trifas, M., Buenos-Aires, D., & Elston, J. (2009). Secure patient information in medical images. *Proceedings of the 13th world multi-conference on systemics, cybernetics and informatics*.

Yang, M., Trifas, M., Truitt, C., & Xiong, G. (2008). Wavelet domain video information embedding. *Proceedings of the 12th world multi-conference on systemics, cybernetics and informatics*.

Younes, M. A., & Jantan, A. (2003). Image encryption using block-based transformation algorithm, *IAENG International Journal of Computer Science, 35* (1).

Yu, H. Y., Chang, C. C., & Lin, I. C. (2007). A new steganographic method for color and gray-scale image hiding. *Computer Vision and Image Understanding, 107*, 183–194. doi:10.1016/j.cviu.2006.11.002

Zhang, W., Cheung, S., & Chen, M. (2005). Hiding privacy information in video surveillance system. *Proceedings of the international conference on image processing (ICIP'2005), 3*, II- 868-71.

Zhou, K., Quan, T., & Kang, Y. (2008). Study on Information Hiding Algorithm Based on RBF and LSB, Proceedings of the Fourth International Conference on Natural Computation (ICNC '08), 612-614.

Chapter 16

Cloak and Dagger:
Man-In-The-Middle and Other Insidious Attacks

Ramakrishna Thurimella
University of Denver, USA

William Mitchell
University of Denver, USA

ABSTRACT

One of the most devastating forms of attack on a computer is when the victim doesn't even know an attack occurred. After some background material, various forms of man in the middle (MITM) attacks, including ARP spoofing, fake SSL certificates, and bypassing SSL are explored. Next, rootkits and botnets, two key pieces of crimeware, are introduced and analyzed. Finally, general strategies to protect against such attacks are suggested.

INTRODUCTION

Information has always been very valuable. Computers are entrusted to maintain and process massive amounts of information. This makes them valuable targets to attackers. One of the most devastating forms of attack is when an attacker gains access to the information without the victim even being aware of it.

This paper explores some of the means by which this surreptitious access to information can occur. Background material on basics of cryptography, the Diffie-Hellman key exchange, networking, Transport Layer Security and Secure

Sockets Layer, and drive by downloads is provided in section 2. MITM attacks are defined in section 3. ARP spoofing, a form of a MITM attack, is explored in section 3.1. Futile defenses to MITM attacks are examined in section 3.2. A MITM attack on SSL using fake certificates is given in section 3.3. Even more forms of MITM attacks are explored in section 3.4. Defenses are discussed in section 3.5. Finally, a new attack known as man in the browser is detailed in section 3.6.

MITM attacks are not the only stealthy means by which information security is breached. Rootkits and botnets, which are capable of doing much more harm, can reside on victim's computer while evading detection. Rootkits are defined in section 4. An example rootkit, Mebroot, is analyzed in

DOI: 10.4018/978-1-60960-200-0.ch016

Figure 1. Process of encryption and decryption

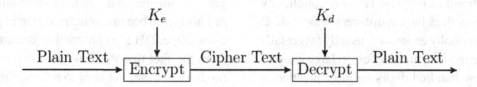

section 4.1. Defenses against rootkits are discussed in section 4.2. Botnets, which are often used in conjunction with rootkits, are defined in section 5. Attacker's motivation is examined in section 5.1. The Torpig botnet, and its recent takeover by security researchers, is investigated in 5.2.

We conclude with some general discussion on how to prevent these attacks in section 6.

Background

In this section, we begin with the basics of cryptography, pointing out the difference between symmetric and asymmetric encryption, followed by a description of the Diffie-Hellman key exchange protocol. Next, we present an abstract description of the man-in-the-middle attack. After that, we give some networking details that are necessary to understand a concrete man-in-the-middle attack on modern local-area networks. We first begin with a general discussion on cryptography.

Cryptography

When trying to communicate a message across an untrusted channel, cryptography is a natural solution. The original message, or *plain text*, is transformed into *cipher text* by encrypting the plain text with an encryption key, K_e. The cipher text will appear meaningless with no apparent relationship to the plain text. This allows the cipher text to be transferred across the untrusted channel with minimal risk of the plain text being intercepted. The cipher text can be transformed back into the plain text by decrypting it with the decryption key K_d. Collectively, the methods of

encryption and decryption are known as a *cipher*. This process, illustrated in Figure 1, can be represented symbolically as

$$P = D(K_d, E(K_e, P)).$$

If the decryption key is the same as the encryption key, or efficiently derived from it, the cipher is known as a symmetric cipher; otherwise, it is an asymmetric cipher. Popular symmetric ciphers include the Advanced Encryption Standard (National Institute of Standards and Technology, 2001) and the Triple Data Encryption Algorithm, commonly known as Triple DES (National Institute of Standards and Technology, 1999). Symmetric ciphers suffer from the key distribution problem–getting the communicating parties to agree upon a common key.

In public key cryptography, which use asymmetric ciphers, each communicating entity maintains one private key and one public key, K_{priv} and K_{pub} respectively. Extending the previous notation, public key cryptography is

$$P = D (K_{priv}, E(K_{pub}, P)).$$

As the names imply, the public key is made available freely to anyone who wishes to use it, but the private key is kept secret. If Alice wishes to communicate with Bob, she encrypts the message with Bob's public key, which is freely available, and sends the encrypted message to Bob. Anyone eavesdropping on this communication cannot decrypt the message unless they have Bob's private key. Anyone who wants to communicate with Bob can easily get access to his public key, so public key cryptography does not suffer from the key distribution problem. However, public key cryptography does have a different drawback. It is computationally expensive; usually this entails performing modular arithmetic over large integers that are few hundred digits long. In practice, a hybrid method is used: public key cryptography is used initially to exchange a random symmetric key, and this random key is used for the remainder of the session. Popular asymmetric ciphers include RSA (Rivest, Shamir, & Adleman, 1978) and El Gamal (1985).

Cryptography does more than just keep messages confidential. It can be used to authenticate the sender of a message, and verify it has not been altered (National Institute of Standards and Technology, 2009). In particular, public key cryptography can be used for this task. The public and private keys can be applied in the reverse order as

$$P = D\ (K_{pub},\ E(K_{priv},\ P)).$$

If Bob sends Alice $E(K_{priv},\ P)$, then Alice can be assured that the message P came from Bob as only Bob has access to K_{priv}. In this case, P is said to be *digitally signed* by Bob (see Ferguson & Schneier, 2003; Menezes, van Oorschot, & Vanstone, 1997; Stinson, 2005, for more background on cryptography and its applications).

2.2 Diffie-Hellman Key Exchange Protocol

The Diffie-Hellman (DH) protocol allows two parties that have no prior knowledge of each other to jointly establish a shared secret key over an insecure communication channel (Diffie & Hellman, 1976). Diffie-Hellman is also known as Diffie-Hellman-Merkle (Hellman, 2002). In short, DH is based on the fact that

$$(g^a)^b \equiv (g^b)^a \pmod{p},$$

where all computations are performed over a group of integers modulo p for some large prime p. This is true because multiplication in groups is associative. DH's cryptographic strength comes from the fact that it is easy to compute powers modulo a prime, but hard to reverse the process when large integers are involved. This intractable problem is known as the *discrete log problem*.

Alice and Bob can agree on a shared secret by performing the following steps (all arithmetic is modulo p):

1 Alice and Bob agree on a large prime p, and a generator g.
2 Alice picks a random number a,0 $<a<p$, and sends g^a to Bob. Alice keeps a private.
3 Bob picks a random number b,0 $<b<p$, and sends g^b to Alice. Bob keeps b private.
4 Alice computes $(g^b)^a$.
5 Bob computes $(g^a)^b$.

Both Alice and Bob are now in possession of g^{ab}, which is their shared secret key. Only a, b and $g^{ab} = g^{ba}$ mod p are kept private. All other values–p, g, g^a, and g^b–are public.

Networking Basics

The Transmission Control Protocol (TCP) and the Internet Protocol (IP) together are at the heart of communication protocols used for the Internet. These protocols resulted from years of research funded by Defense Advanced Research Projects Agency (DARPA). The TCP/IP suite defines a set of rules that enable computers to communicate over a network. The rules specify data formatting, addressing, shipping, routing and delivery to the correct destination.

Computers that are in close proximity and connected into the same Local Area Network (LAN) communicate with each other using Ethernet. In this protocol, frames are sent to a destination Media Access Control (MAC) address, a 48-bit address that is unique to each Network Interface Card

(NIC) on the network. The nodes on a LAN are connected using a *hub* or a *switch*. The only difference between them is that a hub is less intelligent and cheaper than a switch. It simply broadcasts every packet it receives to every computer on the LAN. For many years, hubs were very common and posed serious security problems for system administrators. Anyone on the LAN could put their NIC into "promiscuous" mode and eavesdrop on all data transferred on the LAN. Switches, on the other hand, send Ethernet frames only where they need to go instead of broadcasting to everyone. In addition to improved security, switches also increase the rate at which data can be transferred.

To connect a LAN to the Internet, one needs a more intelligent device that can route packets to the Internet. This device is called a *router*. It is smarter than a switch, in the sense that it is programmable, and usually includes an interface by which it can be configured. Routers have the ability to communicate with other routers and determine the best way to send network traffic from one point to another on the Internet. For simplicity, let us assume that there is only one router on any given LAN. Then, since all traffic from the LAN must enter and exit through the router, it provides a useful choke point. The computers on the LAN can be protected from outside attackers by running a firewall along with an intrusion detection system at this choke point. This is illustrated in Figure 2.

A *default gateway* is the node on the LAN that is chosen by the switch when it encounters an IP address that does not belong to any node on the LAN. A router usually assumes the role of a default gateway. In home networks, the functionality of a switch, router, and wireless access point are often combined into one physical unit.

TLS/SSL

Transport Layer Security (TLS) is a security protocol from the Internet Engineering Task Force (IETF) that is based on the Secure Sockets Layer (SSL) 3.0 protocol developed by Netscape. TLS

Figure 2. LAN connected to the Internet via a router. The router is seen by the switch as another host on the LAN

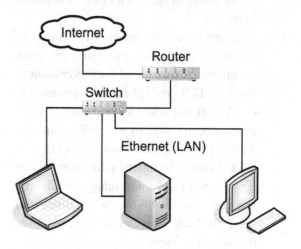

is the successor to SSL. Both protocols include cryptographic frameworks which are intended to provide secure communications on the Internet. SSL is not an industry standard as it was developed by Netscape. TLS is the widely recognized standard issued by the IETF for securing transmitted data. The current version of TLS is 1.2 and is described in RFC 5246 (Dierks & Rescorla, 2008). Version 1.1 of TLS is supported on most commercial browsers, web and email servers with support for version 1.2 forthcoming. By and large, TLS and SSL are interchangeable.

The TLS protocol runs above TCP/IP and below higher-level protocols such as HTTP or SMTP. It uses TCP/IP on behalf of the higher-level protocols, and facilitates the establishment of an encrypted connection between the client and server.

Both TLS and SSL follow a standard handshake procedure to establish communication. The handshake prior to an HTTPS session follows.

1. The client contacts a server that hosts a secured URL.
2. The server responds to the client's request and sends the server's digital certificate (X.509) to the browser.

3. The client now verifies that the certificate is valid and correct. Certificates are issued by well-known authorities (e.g., Thawte or Verisign)

4. The server could optionally choose to confirm a user's identity. Using the same techniques as those used for server authentication, TLS-enabled server software can check that the client's certificate is valid and has been issued by a certificate authority (CA) listed in the server's list of trusted CAs. This confirmation might be important if the server is a bank sending confidential financial information to a customer and wants to check the recipient's identity. (See the benefits of performing this optional step in Section 3.5.)

5. Once the certificate is validated, the client generates a random one-time session key, which will be used to encrypt all communication with the server.

6. The client now encrypts the session key with the server's public key, which was transmitted with the digital certificate. Encrypting using the server's public key ensures that others cannot eavesdrop on this sensitive exchange.

At this point, a secure session is established because the client and server both know the session key. Now, both parties can communicate via a secure channel. See Figure 3.

Drive-by downloads

A *drive-by download* is a catch-all term for software downloaded to your computer without your knowledge or intervention (Walker, 2005). Attackers often do this by exploiting the way Uniform Resource Locators (URLs) are handled by the browser. That is, a webpage link would be created that contains unusual or excessive set of characters. When a vulnerable browser attempts to parse this carefully crafted URL, the attacker can

gain access to the victim's computer by running code outside the browser environment.

Once the attacker can execute code on the victim's computer, there is little restriction as to what that code can do. For example, a rootkit could be installed. The victim could be forced to become a botnet client. Advertising software could be installed that monitors the victim's browsing behavior and bombard them with pop-ups. Keystroke loggers could be installed which could lead to the capture of logins and passwords to various things such as bank accounts, email accounts, or credit card numbers.

The best defense against drive-by downloads is to keep the operating system and web browser up to date with the latest security patches. Since these mostly exploit the web browser, it is only a matter of time before the security community learns of the specific attack used and the appropriate software is fixed.

Trust, Certificates, and Man in the Middle (MITM) Attacks

Suppose that Alice wishes to communicate with Bob using public key cryptography. Mallory, the

Figure 3. SSL/TLS protocol handshake and session key establishment (adapted from Dierks & Rescorla, 2008)

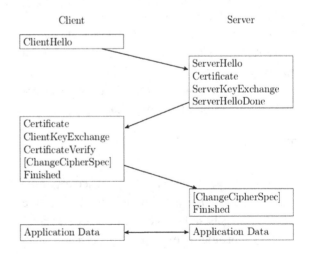

attacker, can participate actively or passively. In the latter role, she faithfully proxies the communication between Alice and Bob, while eavesdropping on their conversation–a breach of confidentiality. In the former role, Mallory can choose to edit, delete, or inject packets.

If Alice requests Bob's public key and Mallory is able to intercept it, then Mallory responds back to Alice with her public key, K_m. Alice is under the impression that she is talking to Bob and encrypts all her messages with K_m which Mallory can decrypt.

Meanwhile, Mallory, pretending to be Alice, sends K_m to Bob, telling him that it is Alice's public key and requests his public key. Bob, like Alice, encrypts all his messages with K_m which Mallory can decrypt.

Both Bob and Alice are under the impression that they are talking to each other, but all communication passes through Mallory and is completely controlled by Mallory. The attack mounted by Mallory is known as a *man in the middle attack*.

This problem arose because the public keys are sent directly by their owners. One solution is to exchange public keys through a trusted third party. This is accomplished by using *digital certificates* that contain the public key for an entity and an assurance from a trusted third party that the public key belongs to that entity. The trusted third party that issues digital certificates is called a *Certification Authority* (CA). As these certificates are digitally signed by CAs, the certificates provide protection against impersonation. Authenticity of certificates is easily verified since a CA's public key is "universally" available. For example they are embedded in browsers. When a certificate is for an individual entity (resp. CA), the certificate is a *personal* (*resp. root*) *certificate*.

Digital certificates contain at least the following information about the entity being certified:

- The public key of the certificate holder
- The common name of the certificate holder

Figure 4. Digital certificate received from PayPal web server as viewed from a browser

- The common name of the CA that is issuing the certificate
- The date certificate was issued on
- The expiration date of the certificate
- The serial number of the certificate

For obvious reasons, digital certificates do not contain the private key of the owner because it must be kept secret by the owner. See an example certificate in Figure 4.

A Public Key Infrastructure (PKI) is a system to facilitate the use of public key cryptography. Unfortunately there is some potential semantic confusion with the term (Anderson, 2008). It can mean either a key infrastructure that is public, or an infrastructure for public keys. Accordingly, there is no one standard that defines the component of a PKI. Typically, PKI refers to the former interpretations. In that case CAs and Registration Authorities (RA) normally provide the following:

- issue digital certificates
- validate digital certificates

- revoke digital certificates
- distribute public keys

The X.509 protocol suite is an International Telecommunication Union standard for a Public Key Infrastructure (Cooper, Santesson, Farrell, Boeyen, Housley, & Polk, 2008). RAs verify the information provided at the time when digital certificates are requested. If the information is verified successfully by the RA, the CA can issue a digital certificate to the requester.

MITM Attack on a Switched LAN using ARP Spoofing

How does Mallory intercept and relay communication between Alice and Bob on modern computer networks? Aren't they built on secure technology? The answer is no, unfortunately. The problem is that Ethernet, upon which virtually all modern LANs are based, was designed without any sort of authentication mechanism. An attack known as *ARP spoofing* takes advantage of this weakness and can intercept communications on a LAN running the Ethernet protocol (Wagner, 2001). This attack works against most networks that are in use at the time of this writing (see Figure 5).

Recall our discussion from Section 2.3 on how two computers communicate on a LAN using Ethernet frames. The attack works as follows. To connect to a LAN, each host must be equipped with a Network Interface Card (NIC). Each NIC is assigned a unique Media Access Control (MAC) address by the manufacturer. Communication on Ethernet takes place by sending frames to destination MAC addresses. If a MAC address is unknown, the source node broadcasts an Address Resolution Protocol (ARP) request. This request specifies an IP address and asks the host with this IP address to reply back with its physical address. In other words, ARP finds a MAC address given an IP address.

Every node on the LAN receives every ARP request, but only the host with the matching IP address replies back with its physical address; the rest simply ignore it. The response is sent back using an ARP Reply that contains the requested IP number and the corresponding MAC address. When the source node receives this information, it stores it in a table of IP and MAC address pairs. This table is known as the *ARP cache* and the mappings are considered valid for a fixed amount time, after which they expire and are removed. Every node on the LAN maintains such a cache. Note that the source node enters the IP-MAC

Figure 5. ARP request broadcast and response. Here host A is requesting a MAC (physical) address that corresponds to IP# 192.168.0.73 (host C).

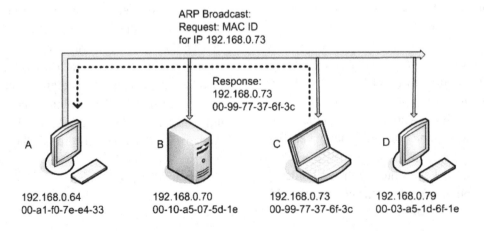

address pair contained in the ARP Reply into its cache without any validation or further checks. Put differently, there is total trust between the nodes on a LAN. To make the matters worse ARP is a *stateless protocol*, that is an ARP Reply is not matched to see if there are outstanding ARP Requests. Therefore, any malicious node can take over a LAN and route all traffic through itself by simply manipulating cache entries at various hosts. The only requirement is that the malicious node is a host on that LAN. One easy way is to accomplish this is by connecting to an insecure wireless access point. Many corporations, hospitals, and retail outlets still use easily breakable WEP encryption (Tews, Weinmann, & Pyshkin, 2007). This weakness exists within the TCP/IP stack. Hence, it is a multi-platform vulnerability.

By injecting merely two ARP reply packets into a LAN, any malicious node M can control all traffic going back and forth between any two nodes on that LAN. For example, between an unsuspecting victim node A and the default gateway G. First, M sends G a spoofed ARP Reply $\langle IP_A,$ $MAC_M \rangle$ claiming that it was assigned IP_A (which really belongs to A) but gives its own MAC address, MAC_M The gateway would blindly replace its current correct entry with the spoofed one. At the same time M would send a similar spoofed ARP Reply, $\langle IP_G, MAC_M \rangle$, to A, replacing the correct ARP cache entry for the gateway computer at A with the spoofed one. From this point on, any traffic from A bound for the default gateway would instead go to the attacking computer M. Similarly, all traffic from G destined to A is routed instead to M. Neither A nor G would be aware of the intermediary that is relaying the traffic in the middle. See Figure 6.

On a LAN with n nodes, that consists of (n − 2) nodes, 1 router, and 1 attacker, by inserting $2(n − 2)$ spoofed ARP Replies, the attacker can take full control of the traffic destined to the Internet from that LAN. This process of inserting false entries into an ARP cache is also referred to *ARP poisoning*. It is worth noting that cache

Figure 6. ARP cache values before and after poisoning by node C to insert itself between B and the Default Gateway (Router). The second column shows after ARP poisoning. The two spoofed entries are emphasized.

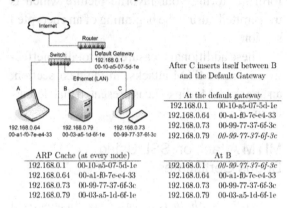

After C inserts itself between B and the Default Gateway

At the default gateway

192.168.0.1	00-10-a5-07-5d-1e
192.168.0.64	00-a1-f0-7e-e4-33
192.168.0.73	00-99-77-37-6f-3c
192.168.0.79	*00-99-77-37-6f-3c*

ARP Cache (at every node)		At B	
192.168.0.1	00-10-a5-07-5d-1e	192.168.0.1	*00-99-77-37-6f-3c*
192.168.0.64	00-a1-f0-7e-e4-33	192.168.0.64	00-a1-f0-7e-e4-33
192.168.0.73	00-99-77-37-6f-3c	192.168.0.73	00-99-77-37-6f-3c
192.168.0.79	00-03-a5-1d-6f-1e	192.168.0.79	00-03-a5-1d-6f-1e

entries are purged after a timeout period. Therefore, to keep control of the network, the attacker must periodically poison each host for the duration of the hijacked session.

In addition to compromising the confidentiality and the integrity of the data as it passes through the local network, MITM attacks can also adversely affect availability. Either by simply slowing down, or completely dropping the network communication by associating a nonexistent MAC address to the IP address of the victim's default gateway.

Futile Defenses against MITM

It has become fashionable at many financial institutions in the United States to present the online user with a set of "secret" questions, in addition to their login credentials. After a successful login, the session might proceed along the following lines:

To protect the security of your account, please answer the following questions:

Note: Your answers are NOT case sensitive.

What is the name of the school where you went to kindergarten?

Or questions such as

What is the last name of your favorite actor? What is your favorite color?

Sometimes this "extra" security comes in the form of storing your favorite picture which is transmitted during the beginning of an encrypted session.

These additional measures are totally ineffective against MITM attacks. In the next section, an attack by Marlinspike is presented that defeats them.

MITM Attack on SSL Using Bogus Certificates

A *certificate chain* is a list of certificates used to authenticate an entity. Certificate chaining is a process by which root certificate authorities delegate the certificate issuing authority to intermediate CAs for efficiency and scalability reasons. This mechanism is part of the trusted computing paradigm. When certificate chains are involved in verification, to check authenticity of a certificate for an entity, the certificate chain is used to reach the *root* CA certificate. The root CA certificate is self-signed. However, the signatures of the intermediate CAs must be verified (see Figure 7).

Chains can be longer than three. Most browsers verify certificate chains as follows:

1   Verify that the name on the certificate matches the name of the entity the client wishes to connect.
2   Check the certificate's expiration date.
3   Check the signature. If the signing certificate is in the list of root CAs in the client, stop, otherwise, move up the chain one link and repeat.

Assume an attacker is in possession of the domain attacker.com and a certificate is issued to it by CA_2. Consider the following certificate chain:

Figure 7. Certificate chain verification process by a client program (adapted from Figure 1 of IBM, 2009)

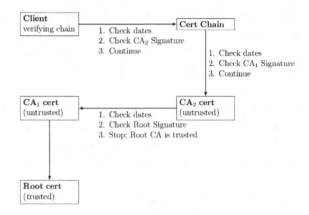

Root CA $\rightarrow$ CA_1 $\rightarrow$ CA_2 $\rightarrow$ attacker.com $\rightarrow$ victim.com

Anyone connecting to victim.com, first checks its name and expiration, and then verifies its signature by applying the public key of attacker.com. Assuming that this is successful, the process is repeated with attacker.com, CA_2, and CA_1, until Root CA is reached. In this example, all signatures and dates pass the validity test, and the Root CA would be reached successfully. Since the Root CA is always trusted, the whole chain is considered to be intact. Unfortunately there is a problem; attacker.com should not have the authority to issue certificates to other domains. This restriction is imposed in the Basic Constraints Extension of the X.509 specification (Cooper et al., 2008). It identifies whether the subject of the certificate is a CA and length of a certificate chain, including itself. The intent in the Standard is to prevent non-CAs from issuing certificates. For non-CAs, this field should be

CA:FALSE indicating that the entity to which this certificate was issued is not a CA. Unfortunately many CAs did not explicitly set this field and most browsers simply ignored it. The implication of this careless practice is that any valid certificate could create a certificate for any other domain.

In 2002, Marlinspike released a software tool, *sslsniff*, that took advantage of this weakness. This tool has the capability to dynamically generate certificates for domains that are being accessed on the fly. The new certificate becomes part of a certificate chain that is signed by any certificate provided to sslsniff.

Using sslsniff, one can perform MITM attack on an HTTPS session as follows. First, an HTTPS request from victimClient trying to connect to victimServer is intercepted using standard techniques such as ARP poisoning. The attacker then sends a bogus certificate in the name of victimServer. Unsuspecting, victimClient authenticates the certificate chain and sends a symmetric key, encrypted using the public key supplied by the attacker. The attacker decrypts the symmetric key, which is used as a session key. Simultaneously, the attacker opens an HTTPS session with victimServer and proxies the traffic between victimClient and victimServer, relaying the set "secret" questions and answers back and forth. All the data that is in transmitted between the client and the server is available to the attacker *in the clear* including sensitive information such as credit card numbers.

This weakness in the Basic Constraints field of X.509 has since been addressed by the CAs and the newer generation of popular browsers.

MITM Attack Using Other Means

Even though one may not be able to carry out MITM attacks using bogus certificates against newer web technology without raising too many red flags, there are a variety of other techniques that one can employ to launch an MITM attack and breach the confidentiality of secure web transactions. The techniques presented here are browser independent and are effective against web sites of some leading financial institutions (see Figure 8).

Since it now appears as if HTTPS has been secured, what is the best way to hijack a web session? Marlinspike (2009) provides an answer to this question by asking the following questions related to human-computer interaction (HCI):

1   How do people start an HTTPS session?
2   How are people assured that they are using a secured session?
3   How are people warned that there maybe a problem with the security of the session?

Most often, the answer to question 1 is either

1   User clicking on a button that posts to HTTPS, or
2   Through rerouting from the web server (HTTP response code 302). When the user types victimServer.com, the browser re-

Figure 8. MITM attack on secure web sessions using bogus certificates

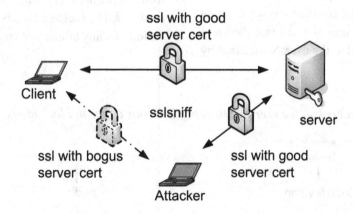

solves it to http://www.victimServer.com. For example, the exchange might look like

```
GET /index.html HTTP/1.1
Host: www.victimServer.com
```

When victimServer receives the above request, it reroutes the client as

```
HTTP/1.1 302 Found Location: https://www.
victimServer.com/index.html
```

That is, no one really types https:// before starting an online transaction. In other words, access to HTTPS is via HTTP. The strategy of the attacker becomes, attack HTTP if HTTPS is secure.

Questions 2 and 3 can be best understood by studying how browsers have evolved over the years. Seven years ago, when sslsniff was released, excessive positive feedback was given by the browser that a user was using a secure connection. There were many lock icons, the address bar or uniform resource locator (URL) bar changed color, and a number of other indicators were deployed to give a "warm-and-fuzzy" feeling to the user that the page was secure. A *favicon*, short for favorites icon, is a 16x16 pixel square icon associated with a particular website that is displayed in the URL bar. A popular favicon in the older browsers during secure sessions was a small padlock. See Figure 9.

Another example of positive feedback is as follows. When a bogus certificate is detected by the browser, a dialog similar to the one shown in Figure 10 is presented to the user. Notice that by

Figure 10. Warning dialogs routinely ignored by most online users

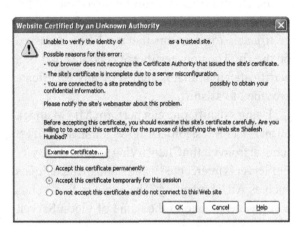

default, the certificate chain would be accepted for the session. According Marlinspike (2009), users typically click through these warning dialogs when they don't completely understand the meaning of the warning.

The trend in the newer browsers is to scale back the positive feedback while emphasizing the negative. For instance, instead of encouraging the user to simply click through the dialog as shown in Figure 10, more ominous looking dialogs like the ones shown in Figure 11 are generated when an invalid certificate is found in the certificate chain. In addition, newer browsers control the proliferation of lock icons, use plain colors for the URL bar, and employ normal favicons.

This shift in HCI with respect to online security has been referred by Marlinspike as going from giving the user *positive feedback* to *negative feedback*. His recent attack is based on the observation that any attack that triggers negative feed-

Figure 9. Positive feedback to the user by changing URL bar color and lock icons

back is bound to fail, but the absence positive
feedback during the attack is not so bad.

The attack proceeds as follows:

1. Intercept all web (HTTP) traffic and replace
   (a) <a href=https://...> by <a href=http://...>
   (b) Location: href=https://... by Location:
       href=http://...

And keep a map of all replacements.

2. If there is an HTTP request from the client for
   a resource for which there was replacement
   in the previous step, issue an HTTPS connection to the server for the same resource,
   and
3. Relay response the server using HTTP to
   the client.

The key difference between this MITM attack
and the attack described in Section 3.3 is that in
the previous attack, the attacker uses HTTPS
to connect to both the client and the server. By
comparison, in this new MITM attack, the attacker
only communicates with the server in encrypted
mode. From the point of view of the server, this
would appear like a normal secure online transaction. Compare Figures 8 and 12.

On the client side, there are no tell-tale signs
of a breach since the attack suppresses nasty dia-

Figure 12. Hijacking secure online transactions

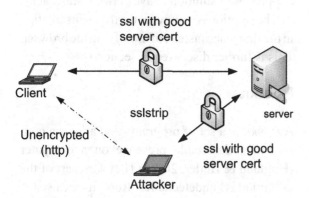

Figure 11. Negative feedback

logs from popping up. This accomplishes the goal
of not triggering any negative feedback. To complete the attack, Marlinspike adds some positive
feedback. This is done by adding a lock favicon
in the URL bar. That is, whenever a favicon request
is noticed for a URL that is in the map, a lock
favicon is returned. The only difference a security savvy user would notice is the absence of a
lock icon in the status bar and http instead of https
in the address bar.

Cached pages can pose a problem as they do
not give the attacker a chance to replace https with
http. The details on how to deal with this and other
technical problems arising from sessions, cookies,
and others can be found in Marlinspike (2009).

The results from this experiment are remarkable. The security of over a hundred email accounts, a few credit card numbers, and a few
hundred secure logins was breached in a matter of
a single *24-hour* period. Another surprising aspect
of this test was that *not a single user* attempting
to initiate a secure transaction aborted it because
the user became suspicious.

Marlinspike also showed how to extend the
homograph attack (attack that attempts to deceive remote users about what server they are
communicating with, by taking advantage of the
fact that many different characters have nearly
indistinguishable glyphs) to mount MITM against
SSL. We omit the details of this attack and the

technical problems posed by cached pages. The interested reader is referred to Marlinspike (2009).

Possible Defenses against MITM

We conclude this section by presenting some effective measures an online user can take to defend against MITM attacks. First and foremost is to educate oneself to look for signs of a breach. It is also important to understand the meaning of different warning dialogs presented by the browser.

If a web server offers its services only over HTTPS (on TCP port 443) and routinely redirects all HTTP (port 80) requests to the secure port 443, then sessions can still be hijacked. As long as HTTPS depends on HTTP, it is vulnerable because HTTP is not secure. Why not just turn off port 80? Unfortunately this would cause many Server Not Found errors for the users and it would not be good for business. One work around is to have the user type in https://... in the address bar. Alternately, the user could bookmark the secure site and issue an HTTPS request by selecting the bookmark. It is tempting to think that if browsers always try to connect over port 443 first, and only connect only to port 80 as a last resort, we can avoid the MITM attacks mentioned here. Unfortunately, the attacker can simply drop the requests to connect to port 443 and make the browsers think that the web server does not offer HTTPS. While this defense might not help in all cases, by including into browsers a select set of sites for which service over HTTPS is known to exist, one can reduce the risk of MITM attacks. The only long term solution is to secure everything, that is run only HTTPS.

Another measure that could improve security, that is not currently popular, is the verification of client certificates. By having servers verify the identity of the client, one can achieve better security. But, this requires significant changes to the existing PKI and is not immediately applicable.

Man in the Browser

Structurally similar to a MITM attack, a *man in the browser* attack is a form of a trojan that can do the following: (Gühring, 2006)

- Modify the appearance of a website before the user sees it.
- Modify the data entered by the user before it is sent to the server.
- Modify the responses of the server so that they are what the user expects.

All of the above can be done without the user having any visible effect for the user to detect.

These trojans are installed by some means, such as a drive-by download, or the user running untrustworthy programs. They then attack the browsers installed on the system by changing their configuration so the trojan is loaded when the browser starts. Browsers have this capability, known as Browser Helper Objects or Extensions depending on the browser, to allow third parties to extend and improve the browser. The trojan exploits this by creating an extension that watches the user's behavior. When a target site is visited, the trojan commences an attack. Anything entered by the user or sent by a server is vulnerable to capture. This could include login credentials, financial information, or even identity credentials sufficient for identify theft.

Philipp Gühring (2006) provides several means to prevent this type of attack. Unfortunately all of the proposed solutions have serious drawbacks. The best option is to prevent the trojan installation in the first place instead of modifying the browser. This is further discussed in section 6.

Rootkits

A *rootkit* is a set of programs that allows a consistent, undetectable presence on a computer (Hoglund & Butler, 2006). They key part of the definition is "undetectable." Rootkits are used to hide specific files, folders, processes, and network connections from the end user. They are not inherently "bad." For example, corporations could use a rootkit to monitor and enforce computer use regulations, or law enforcement could use a rootkit to collect evidence. However, as with most tools, they can also be put to nefarious purposes. For instance, an attacker could use a rootkit to hide their intrusion into a computer. This makes it much more difficult to determine if a computer has been compromised.

It is also important to understand what rootkits are not. A rootkit is not an exploit. They are often used together, and occasionally a rootkit will use an exploit to operate, but they are not an essential piece. Rootkits are not viruses. Viruses self-propagate which makes it more likely to be discovered. However, viruses do often use techniques of rootkits to slow down their detection.

Modern operating systems are object oriented. To perform a task, typically functions from several objects are invoked, creating a long call chain. To maintain their stealth, rootkits exploit this behavior. They interject themselves into the chain and change the answers as they pass by. This principle of modification, known as hooking, is at the core of most rootkits.

Binary, a readily executable program, can come in several different formats such as the Common Object File Format (COFF), the Executable and Linking Format (ELF), a.out, and the Portable Executable (PE). The format used is generally dictated by the operating system and in the case of Microsoft Windows, PE and COFF formats are used (Microsoft Corporation, 2008). All of these formats are well documented. This allows an attacker to *patch* a program so that it does what the attacker wants. This is the most common form of modification that a rootkit uses.

Source code modification is another form of modification used by rootkits. An attacker can insert malicious code directly into a program that they author. This could take the form of an overt

backdoor, or a subtle bug that the only attacker knows how to exploit.

Finally, a rootkit could use an entirely different means of modification. Operating systems are very complex leaving a multitude of places for rootkits to hide.

Despite the large varieties of potential techniques that a rootkit could use, they can still be categorized. One means of bifurcating these techniques is to classify them as either *kernel-mode* or *user-mode*. In some contexts, particularly for Microsoft Windows, these are also often known as *Ring 0* and *Ring 3*, respectively. Roughly speaking, kernel-mode code has free reign over a computer's memory and hardware, whereas user-mode code has restrictions placed upon it. It is more difficult to write kernel-mode code because the variances between computers are fully exposed. Modern rootkits will often be composed of pieces that run in kernel-mode and in user-mode.

Mebroot

During the boot process of a computer, the first physical sector of the hard drive, known as the Master Boot Record (MBR), is read and executed. It is responsible for starting the operating system. In the days when DOS was the prevalent operating system, MBR viruses were common (F-Secure Corporation, 2008).

At the Black Hat USA 2005 security conference, researchers Derek Soeder and Ryan Permeh of eEye Digital Security presented a tool called BootRoot (eEye Digital Security, 2005). This tool is a proof-of-concept of the exploit they found in the Windows NT family of operating systems whereby a user-mode program could alter the MBR.

When attempting to detect a rootkit, one very helpful thing is the order of execution. If a detection program runs prior to the rootkit, it is much easier to detect the rootkit because the detection program can detect that something has changed. In the converse, any modifications that a rootkit would employ are already completed prior to the detection program starting. Since the MBR is the first thing executed when a computer boots, a rootkit installed into the MBR gives a clear advantage.

Mebroot is a rootkit that installs itself into the MBR. It has been extensively analyzed by GMER Team (2008) and Kleissner (2008). It infects a machine with the following operations:

- Write a new kernel-mode driver to the last sectors of the hard drive.
- Copy sector 0 (MBR) of the hard drive to sector 62, and then overwrite sector 0 with a new MBR loader.
- Write new kernel loader to sector 61 of the hard drive.

The system is then forced to restart, which loads the rootkit.

Much of the MBR loader code is copied from BootRoot (GMER Team, 2008). It loads a kernel driver which patches two functions of disk.sys. In particular, it prevents the kernel from overwriting the MBR, and when the MBR is read, the contents of sector 62, the original MBR, are returned. Finally the kernel-mode driver is loaded. This kernel-mode driver includes a networking layer and can bypass local software firewalls. It contacts a server to ensure that it is running the latest version of the rootkit.

What makes Mebroot particularly stealthy is how it is stored on the hard drive. Typically, a rootkit would patch file reading functions to disguise the existence of its files. This patching is potentially a means for the rootkit to be detected. Mebroot writes itself directly to the sectors of the hard drive, bypassing the normal filesystem of the hard drive. This makes the files invisible without having to patch anything.

Defenses against Rootkits

There are two main ways to defend against rootkits: prevention and detection. As facile as it seems, preventing a rootkit from installing itself in the first place is the best way to prevent rootkits from infecting a machine. Often rootkits are only a part of an attack on a computer. They often come along with botnet clients, and other malicious software. General prevention strategies are discussed further in section 6.

Rootkit detection is very similar to virus detection. There are two main approaches: look for known rootkits, or look for suspicious behavior.

To look for a known rootkit, first one needs to know what a specific rootkit "looks like." This is referred to as its *signature*. The signature could be detected in multiple ways. A file containing the whole rootkit, or a portion thereof, can be scanned before it is protected by the rootkit. The memory of the computer can be similarly searched for fragments of a rootkit. The downside to the approach of looking for known signatures is it requires the rootkit to be known.

Detecting suspicious behavior is more difficult to do. There is the potential for both false negatives and false positives. Many forms of binary patching can be detected by looking for code that is out of place. Detection software can also patch itself into the functions that a rootkit would use to hide itself. The downside to this approach is it requires the rootkit to use a known method of attack, and the detection software checks for all known methods of attack. If the detection software misses a single method, a rootkit could pass by unnoticed.

Recall that one of the behaviors that a rootkit exploits is the idiosyncratic methods by which programs work. Rootkits interject themselves into these methods to disguise their presence. This is also a weakness. Detection software can use two different approaches to answer the same question. If the answers differ, then there is likely a rootkit of some form involved. Rootkits defend against this by patching multiple functions that could be used to detect their presence. This creates a cat and mouse style struggle between rootkits and detection software.

These techniques and more are discussed further by Hoglund and Butler (2006).

Botnets

A *botnet* is a group of individual computers, bots, under the control of a *bot herder*, also known as a *bot master*. As a practical matter, all of the bots, also known as *zombies*, are under complete control of the bot herder. A computer becomes a part of a botnet by installing a botnet client. They can be installed by techniques such as drive-by-downloads, a remote exploit on the user's system, or tricking the user into installing them.

After a botnet client is installed, the infected computer will contact a *command and control* (c&c) server. This c&c server is how the herder controls the bots. They can issue commands to tell the bots to do things such as:

- Send spam
- Be part of a denial of service attack
- Scan a network for more computers to infect
- Send all the keystrokes from the local computers including things like passwords, bank accounts, and credit card numbers
- Install additional malware on the computer

A bot can even be set up to work as a c&c server for a portion of the botnet. This makes it even harder for the bot herder to be found.

According to research by Symantec's MessageLabs, 83.2% of all spam sent in June 2009 was directly sent by botnets. Some smaller botnets direct their bots to use webmail providers to send spam, which is not accounted for in the 83.2%, making it an underestimation (MessageLabs, 2009).

Attacker's Motivation

As with much computer crime, a primary motivator is profit. There are many ways a bot herder can directly monetize their botnet. A spammer could rent out the botnet. Online businesses can be extorted under threat of a denial of service attack. The captured keystrokes on the individual bots can contain things like credit card numbers, or bank account information which can be sold on the black market. Software can be installed on the bots netting the herder a commission. The possibilities are limited only by the imagination of the herder.

However, there are also non-profit related reasons why an attacker would want a botnet. Suppose that a herder wishes to break into a system. A botnet can help them in a couple ways. One obvious goal the herder will have is to minimize any evidence that ties them to the break in. If the attack is routed through the bots, the herder can force all forensic trails to end at the bots. Further, the attack can be spread across multiple bots which makes it harder for the victim to detect that they are under attack. It is a hard enough problem to detect the precursors of an attack from a single source since often the indicators individually are benign. When the precursors come from multiple sources, the problem is even harder.

Another non-profit motive is to defeat various forms of rate-limiting. Rate-limiting is used to slow down an attacker breaking into a system. For example, when logging onto a computer, the system may force a small delay between password entry attempts. There can also be a lock out whereby after several incorrect passwords, the system prevents access for some duration of time, or even permanently. With these artificial limits, the victim system can prevent the attacker from simply using a program to try many potential passwords at a very fast rate.

Often rate-limiting is implemented on a per computer basis. That is, each bot has their own separate allotted rate. Collectively, a botnet would have a very high rate which allows the herder to perform the attacks the rate-limiting is designed to stop.

Torpig

The Torpig botnet, also known as Sinowal, was taken over for a period of ten days by researchers from the University of California, Santa Barbara (Stone-Gross et al., 2009). The botnet client operated by generating an expected location for the c&c server. The researchers exploited this by analyzing the algorithm and predicting where it will be next and placing their own c&c server there. Due to ethical considerations, the researchers made their c&c server totally passive. It never instructed the bots to do anything, and simply recorded all the data is was sent by the bots. Torpig utilizes the Mebroot rootkit to hide its existence on the infected computers.

Over the course of ten days, they recorded over 70GB of data. Their best estimate is that 180 thousand distinct infections contacted their c&c server. The botnet client was configured to send lots of data to the c&c, summarized in Figure 13

Torpig uses a man in the browser attack, described in section 3.6, on many financial institutions. It also scours the saved password cache of browsers, and records what passwords are entered by a victim. Derived from this captured data, the researchers found 8,310 accounts at 410 financial institutions. Using a heuristic validation, the researchers found 1,660 distinct credit cards. For 2008, Symantec estimated that credit cards can sell on the black market for $0.10 USD to $25 USD and bank accounts $10 USD to $1,000 USD (Symantec Corporation, 2009). Using these estimates, the researchers estimated that the Torpig controllers could have brought in between $83 thousand USD to $8.3 million USD from the captured financial data alone. The potential income for the Torpig controllers is much larger from the other means of monetization discussed in the previous section.

Best Practices to Secure Information Resources

Both physical security and computer security are fundamentally about the allocation of finite resources to maximize risk mitigation. Even if there were infinite resources, impenetrable security can not exist. The problem is that an attacker needs to find only one weakness to exploit. Preventing all attacks requires one to reinforce every potential weakness. To further complicate this, a reasonable

Figure 13. Data types captured from the Torpig botnet (adapted from Stone-Gross et al., 2009)

Data Type	Quantity
Mailbox account	54,090
Email	1,258,862
Form data	11,966,532
HTTP account	411,039
FTP account	12,307
POP account	415,206
SMTP account	100,472
Windows password	1,235,122

maxim of security is that the more complicated the system, the harder it is to secure.

Since perfect security is untenable, it is best to focus on elements that can be controlled. User education and applying security patches are the best active tactics. User education is the first and best line of defense. Many of the attacks described in this paper rely upon the user overlooking small details. Understanding what a valid SSL certificate looks like, and checking validity can prevent many forms of MITM attacks. As was shown with man in the browser attacks and the potential of rootkits a vigilant user is not always enough. Keeping software up to date and security patches applied can help with other forms of attacks. Drive by downloads, man in the browser, and botnets are often installed by exploiting a bug in the victims computer. Security patches will lessen the number of known vulnerable exploits on a computer.

Additional items that can help include virus scanners, malware scanners, rootkit scanners, and firewalls. Each one of these items has its own limitations, such as only finding known malicious software or detecting known behavior. But each provides an additional layer of defense. The more layers, the harder it is for an attacker to succeed. This principle of adding many layers is known as *defense in depth*.

Suppose that an attacker does succeed in planting malicious software onto a computer. What can be done? In general, it takes an expert to reliably, fully remove malicious software. This can often require rebuilding the computer. At this point backups are invaluable. Frequently the hard drive cannot be trusted because some forms of malicious software infect every potential file on a hard drive. Backups also need to be tested. A non-working backup is as good as no backup at all.

If an attacker succeeds only in simple MITM attack, such as ARP spoofing or a fake SSL certificate, the only harm is the loss of information. This of course could be a very costly loss, but it does not necessitate the reduilding of a victimized computer.

REFRENCES

Anderson, R. (2008). *Security engineering* (2nd ed.). Indianapolis, IN: John Wiley & Sons.

Cooper, D., Santesson, S., Farrell, S., Boeyen, S., Housley, R., & Polk, W. (2008). *Internet X.509 public key infrastructure certificate and certificate revocation list (CRL) profile* (RFC 5280). Retrieved from http://www.ietf.org/rfc/rfc5280.txt

Dierks, T., & Rescorla, E. (2008). *The transport layer security (TLS) protocol version 1.2* (RFC 5246). Retrieved from http://tools.ietf.org/html/rfc5246

Diffie, W., & Hellman, M. E. (1976). New directions in cryptography. *IEEE Transactions on Information Theory, 22*(6), 644–654. doi:10.1109/TIT.1976.1055638

eEye Digital Security. (2005). *BootRoot*. Retrieved July 10, 2009, from http://research.eeye.com/html/tools/RT20060801-7.html

El Gamal, T. (1985). A public key cryptosystem and a signature scheme based on discrete logarithms. In *Proceedings of Crypto 84 on Advances in Cryptology* (pp. 10-18). New York: Springer-Verlag.

F-Secure Corporation. (2008). *MBR rootkit, a new breed of malware*. Retrieved July 10, 2009, from http://www.f-secure.com/weblog/archives/00001393.html.

Ferguson, N., & Schneier, B. (2003). *Practical cryptography*. New York: John Wiley & Sons.

GMER Team. (2008). *Stealth MBR rootkit*. Retrieved July 10, 2009, from http://www2.gmer.net/mbr/

Gühring, P. (2006). *Concepts against man-in-the-browser attacks*. Retrieved July 10, 2009, from http://www2.futureware.at/svn/sourcerer/CAcert/SecureClient.pdf

Hellman, M. E. (2002). An overview of public key cryptography. *IEEE Communications Magazine*, (May): 42–49. doi:10.1109/MCOM.2002.1006971

Hoglund, G., & Butler, J. (2006). *Rootkits: Subverting the windows kernel*. Reading, MA: Addison-Wesley.

IBM. (2009). *Certificate chain verification*. Retrieved July 10, 2009, from http://publib.boulder.ibm.com/infocenter/tpfhelp/current/index.jsp?topic=/com.ibm.ztpf-ztpfdf.doc_put.cur/gtps5/s5vctch.html

Kleissner, P. (2008). *Analysis of sinowal*. Retrieved July 10, 2009, from http://web17.webbpro.de/index.php?page=analysis-of-sinowal

Marlinspike, M. (2009, February 16-19). *New techniques for defeating SSL/TLS*. Paper presented at Black Hat DC Briefings.

Menezes, A., van Oorschot, P., & Vanstone, S. (1997). *Handbook of applied cryptography*. New York: CRC Press.

MessageLabs. (2009). *MessageLabs intelligence: Q2/June 2009*. Retrieved July 10, 2009, from http://www.messagelabs.com/mlireport/MLIReport_2009.06_June_FINAL.pdf

Microsoft Corporation. (2008). *Microsoft portable executable and common object file format specification*. Retrieved July 10, 2009, from http://www.microsoft.com/whdc/system/platform/firmware/PECOFF.mspx

National Institute of Standards and Technology. (1999). *FIPS PUB 46-3: Data encryption standard (DES)*. Retrieved July 10, 2009, from http://csrc.nist.gov/publications/fips/fips46-3/fips46-3.pdf

National Institute of Standards and Technology. (2001). *FIPS PUB 197: Advanced encryption standard (AES)*. Retrieved July 10, 2009, from http://csrc.nist.gov/publications/fips/fips197/fips-197.pdf

National Institute of Standards and Technology. (2009). *FIPS PUB 186-3: Digital signature standard (DSS)*. Retrieved July 10, 2009, from http://csrc.nist.gov/publications/fips/fips186-3/fips_186-3.pdf

Rivest, R. L., Shamir, A., & Adleman, L. (1978). A method for obtaining digital signatures and public-key cryptosystems. *Communications of the ACM, 21*(2), 120–126. doi:10.1145/359340.359342

Stinson, D. (2005). *Cryptography: Theory and practice* (3rd ed.). New York: CRC Press.

Stone-Gross, B., Cova, M., Cavallaro, L., Gilbert, B., Szydlowski, M., Kemmerer, R., et al. (2009). *Your botnet is my botnet: Analysis of a botnet takeover* (UCSB Tech. Rep.). Retrieved July 10, 2009, from http://www.cs.ucsb.edu/%7Eseclab/projects/torpig/torpig.pdf

Symantec Corporation. (2009). *Symantec global internet security threat report: Volume XIV trends for 2008*. Cupertino, CA: Author.

Tews, E., Weinmann, R.-P., & Pyshkin, A. (2007). *Breaking 104 bit wep in less than 60 seconds* (Rep. 2007/120). Cryptology ePrint Archive.

Wagner, R. (2001). *Address resolution protocol spoofing and man-in-the-middle attacks*. Retrieved July 10, 2009, from http://www.sans.org/rr/whitepapers/threats/474.php

Walker, M. H. (2005). *Drive-by downloads: Stealthy downloads and Internet Explorer's new defense against them*. Retrived July 10, 2009, from http://www.microsoft.com/windows/ie/community/columns/driveby.mspx

This work was previously published in International Journal of Information Security and Privacy (IJISP), edited by Hamid Nemati, pp 55-75, copyright 2009 by IGI Publishing (imprint of IGI Global)

Chapter 17
A Resilient Fair Electronic Contract Signing Protocol

Harkeerat Bedi
University of Memphis, USA

Li Yang
University of Tennessee at Chattanooga, USA

ABSTRACT

Fair exchange between parties can be defined as an instance of exchange such that either all parties involved in the exchange obtain what they expected or neither one does. The authors examine a protocol by Micali that provides fair contract signing, where two parties exchange their commitments over a pre-negotiated contract in a fair manner. They show that Micali's protocol is not entirely fair and demonstrate the possibilities for one party cheating the other by obtaining the other party's commitment and not offering theirs. A revised version of this protocol by Bao which provides superior fairness by handling some of the weaknesses is also discussed. However, both these protocols fail to handle the possibilities of a replay attack. Their prior work improves upon these protocols by addressing the weakness that leads to a replay attack. This journal extends their prior work on fair electronic exchange by handling a type of attack which was not handled earlier and provides a brief survey of the recent work related to the field of fair electronic exchange. They also discuss the application of cryptography to our protocol which includes implementation of hybrid cryptography and digital signature algorithms based on elliptic curves to achieve features like confidentiality, data-integrity and non-repudiation.

INTRODUCTION

Commerce has come a long way since the beginning of our civilization. The ability to exchange goods and services for items of equivalent value has been widely exercised. Based on the kind of items exchanged between two parties, it can either be classified as a barter system where goods and services are exchanged for other goods and services, or the act of selling and buying where goods and services are sold or bought between parties in exchange for money.

The notion of *fair exchange* can be expressed as the ability to exchange goods or services for

DOI: 10.4018/978-1-60960-200-0.ch017

other goods or services in a fair manner where both the parties obtain what they expected. Being a fundamental concept, this can be implemented in various scenarios that may include exchanges based on barter system or buying and selling of goods.

With the advent of computers and the Internet, new means of performing commerce have been invented. E-commerce is one such solution where good and services are bought and sold between interested parties using computers over a network. With the rapid growth of the Internet, the magnitude of commerce performed online has also increased significantly. This increase is primarily because commerce conducted online is convenient and fast when compared to the traditional methods of trade. Even though commerce of this type offers benefits like speed and convenience, without properties like fairness and security, such services become less useful as they significantly increase the risk of failure. E-commerce cannot flourish or even sustain if it is not able to provide fairness and security. Therefore the concept of fair exchange plays a vital role in shaping such forms of commerce. When carried out online using computers and the Internet, such fair exchange is known as *fair electronic exchange*.

FAIR ELECTRONIC EXCHANGE

Fair electronic exchange can be demonstrated as e-commerce that takes place between two parties who are online and where exchange of goods and services is performed such that both either parties obtain what they expected or they obtain nothing at all. After an exchange is performed or aborted prematurely, none of the parties should have an unfair advantage over the other. If cheating takes place, where one party refuses to present their part of the exchange, other means for providing fairness should be available. These may include use of additional entities like a human judge or electronic ones that can comprehend the situation

and act accordingly to provide fairness. Protocols that provide such facilities are termed as *fair exchange protocols*. Such protocols can be used for the following purposes:

a. *Certified E-Mail (CEM)*, where a user named Alice sends a message to user a named Bob and gets a receipt from him in return. Providing the quality of fairness would include Alice getting the receipt only when Bob gets the message or Bob getting the message only when Alice gets the receipt. Associated protocols include (Zhou & Gollmann, 1996; Kremer & Markowitch, 2001; Ateniese & Nita-Rotaru, 2002; Imamoto & Sakurai, 2002)

b. *Electronic Contract Signing (ECS)*, where both Alice and Bob wish to sign a contract that has already been negotiated. This would involve Alice sending her commitment (digital signature) on the contract to Bob and him sending his commitment (digital signature) on the same in return. Providing fairness would involve Alice receiving Bob's commitment only when her commitment is received by Bob and vice versa. This example demonstrates contract signing between two parties. Protocols that provide such functionality include (Ben-Or, Goldreich, Micali, & Rivest, 1990; Damgard, 1995; Bao, Deng, & Mao, 1998; Asokan, Shoup, & Waidner, 1998; Ateniese, 1999; Garay, Jakobsson, & MacKenzie, 1999; Micali, 2003; Bao, Wang, Zhou & Zhu, 2004). However, various multi-party contract signing protocols also exist and have also been proposed in (Baum-Waidner, 2001; Ferrer-Gomila, Payeras-Capella, Huguet-Rotger, 2001; Garay & MacKenzie, 1999;

c. *Online payment systems (OPS)*, where Alice is the seller and Bob is the buyer and payment is given in return of the item of value (Cox, Tygar & Sirbu, 1995). Similar e-payment schemes in electronic commerce include

(Boyd & Foo, 1998; Park, Chong, & Siegel, 2003).

d. *Non-repudiation protocols,* where the parties involved in an exchange cannot later deny their participation or their actions performed. Protocols associated with such services include (Zhou & Gollmann, 1996; Kremer & Markowitch, 2000; Kremer, Markowitch & Zhou, 2002; Gurgens, Rudolph, & Vogt, 2003)

In the ideal case, where both Alice and Bob are guaranteed to be honest and the communication channel is secure and provides resilience, fair exchange can be achieved trivially without the aid of any external fairness provider. The above described scenarios can thus be carried out as follows:

Fair Certified E-Mail

*   Alice sends her message to Bob.
*   Bob sends his receipt for the message to Alice. The receipt may be the digital signature of Bob on the message. Being a digital signature, this step ensures non-repudiation.

Fair Electric Contract Signing

It is assumed that both parties have negotiated the contract before hand.

*   Alice sends her digital signature on the contract to Bob.
*   Bob sends his digital signature on the contract to Alice.

Fair Online Payment System

*   Alice sells goods or services online by sending it to Bob.
*   Bob buys these good or services by paying Alice online via e-check or e-money.

However in practice, honesty of the parties like Alice and Bob participating in an exchange can never be guaranteed. The availability of secure communication channels is not always possible and unsecured channels are easily prone to attacks.

Following are the types of outcomes that may take place rendering the above mentioned exchanges incomplete.

a. Cheating Bob can always refuse to send his signature on the messages to Alice after receiving her signature. In such a case, there is not much that Alice can do to obtain fairness.

b. An intruder can always stop the messages from reaching the other party. In this case the receipt or the messages signed by Bob may never reach Alice. Alice may think that she has been cheated where as Bob may be unaware of this taking place. This confusion may lead Alice to request for cancellation whereas Bob may not wish for the same.

c. An intruder who is listening to messages sent by Alice or Bob can replay those messages making the other party believe that they were sent from the original sender. In case of electronic contract signing, if the intruder replays Alice's messages, there is no way for Bob to learn that the messages are not from Alice but an intruder. This is because the signature on the intruder's message will always be verifiable using Alice's corresponding public key. Honest Bob may sign the message and think that he has signed a new contract with Alice, whereas Alice may never know of this taking place.

d. Bob can sign a fake contract is exchange of Alice's signature on the correct contract, thus cheating her by providing his commitment on a contract that does not solve her purpose.

Therefore to prevent such unwanted outcomes, external fairness providers are used to comprehend the situation if cheating is suspected and provide resolution. Such fairness providers are separate entities known as the *trusted third parties*. As the name suggests these entities are trusted by everyone. Considering the above scenarios, Alice can communicate with the external fairness provider and obtain fairness if Bob refuses to sign the contract after receiving Alice's signature. Alice can provide the provider with information relating to the contract along with the messages she sent to Bob. The provider, thus after verifying this information and being sure that Alice is not cheating can then provide fairness to her by regenerating Bob's part of exchange or issuing a certificate that can be used as a substitute for Bob's signature.

Based on their role and the method of providing fairness, either by preventing or handling such unwanted outcomes, these providers are classified into the following types:

One class of protocols depends on gathering evidence during the transaction that can later be used to provide fairness. Two parties during their transaction also send additional information along with their messages which can later be used for resolution if one believes that it has been cheated. The cheated party contacts a human judge which looks at the additional information exchanged (evidence) and provides fairness. Such protocols are classified as *weak fair-exchange protocols* due to their inability to provide fairness during the transaction.

This becomes a drawback since resolution is provided only after the transaction has been completed. In case of e-commerce where the location and availability of parties taking part in a transaction are not always fixed or known, such methods of dispute resolution may always not be possible.

To handle drawbacks like these, a second class of protocols has been defined by various researchers that provide means of avoiding disputes and obtaining resolution all within the transaction. Thus fairness can now be obtained during the transaction and such protocols are called as *strong-*

fair exchange protocols (Ray & Ray, 2002). These protocols too use a trusted third party which can provide fairness in case of a dispute.

Trusted third parties that have to involve in every transaction occurring between two parties are known as *online trusted third parties*. Exchanges using such trusted third parties suffer from the disadvantage that these trusted third parties are required to involve in every transaction occurring between the interested individuals.

Trusted third parties that are not required to involve in every transaction but only required when a dispute occurs are known as *invisible trusted third parties* or *offline trusted third parties* and the protocols implementing them are known as *optimistic protocols*. Following are the advantages provided by protocols which use an invisible trusted third party:

The invisible third party intervenes only when cheating is suspected. In such a case the invisible third party solves the conflict by providing the complaining party with what it truly deserves. Either party can initiate this procedure if they feel they have been cheated.

An invisible third party generates no congestion or bottlenecks as it intervenes only when cheating occurs; which is usually very rare. Under normal execution, transactions between two parties are carried out directly, bypassing the third party altogether.

An invisible third party generates minimal expense and minimal liabilities as it is liable only for the few messages that is sends, which is only in case of a conflict. Even if a system adds a large number of clients which carry numerous transactions, the expense generated by such a system is minimal, since the third party intervenes only with cheating occurs and stays dormant remaining of the time.

Evolution of Fair Exchange Protocols

Earliest work on exchange protocols that provided fairness was based on a class of fair exchange protocols known as *gradual exchange protocols* (Tedrick, 1983, 1985). Such protocols provided fairness as a measure directly proportional to the number of rounds of messages exchanged between the two participating parties. Thus as the number of messages exchanged between parties increases, so does the probability of fairness. These protocols were complex and made use of advanced cryptographic techniques. They also required the assumption that both parties involved in the exchange are to have equivalent computing power. This assumption was removed by the introduction of an improved set of fair exchange protocols called *probabilistic protocols* (Ben-Or, Goldreich, Micali & Rivest, 1990; Markowitch & Roggeman, 1999). These protocols did not require both the parties to have equivalent computing power. However a good number of transmissions between the parties were still required to increase the probability of fairness to acceptable levels. This downside was addressed by the introduction of a new class of protocols that used trusted third parties for providing fairness. This reduced the number of transactions required to be exchanged to a smaller number. It begun with the use of *in-line trusted third parties* (Coffey & Saidha, 1996; Ben-Or, Goldreich, Micali, & Rivest, 1990; Deng, Gong, Lazar & Wang, 1996; Zhou & Gollmann, 1996), where the third party would required to involve in every transaction between the parties participating in the fair exchange protocol. Even though the number of transactions required was reduced, the involvement of third party during the protocol was very high. This made the third party as the bottleneck, since every transaction was required to be passed through the third party. Several improvements were made in this direction of implementation, beginning with the introduction of *online trusted third parties* (Zhang & Shi,

1996; Zhou & Gollmann, 1996), where the third party was required to involve only once during an entire instance of the protocol. This was major improvement since the involvement of third party was reduced substantially. Another major breakthrough was the introduction of *offline trusted third parties* (Asokan, Schunter & Waidner, 1997; Micali, 1997; Asokan, Shoup & Waidner, 1998; Asokan, Shoup, & Waidner, 2000; Ateniese 1999; Bao, Deng, & Mao, 1998; Park, Chong, & Siegel, 2003), where the third party was required to involve only when cheating was suspected or had occurred. This was again a key improvement since now the third party was required to interfere only in case of a conflict, and therefore did not become a bottleneck during the normal execution of the protocol and such protocols as stated previously were known as *optimistic protocols*.

This approach of implementing an offline trusted third party has also been used by researchers in execution of various non-repudiation protocols (Kremer & Markowitch, 2000; Zhou & Gollmann, 1997; Zhou, Deng & Bao, 1999). Non-repudiation with respect to exchange protocols can be defined as the concept of ensuring that a party having involved in an exchange or transmission cannot later deny their involvement. The advent of public key cryptography (Diffie & Hellman, 1976) and the introduction of digital signatures served as the foundation for non-reputation. A property like non-repudiation is required by fair exchange protocols to provide fairness efficiently. However, the first set of non-repudiation protocols proposed by the International Organization for Standards (1997a, 1997b, 1998) did not support fairness exclusively.

In this journal we analyze the several optimistic fair exchange protocols and demonstrate their weaknesses. We start by explaining Micali's protocol and analyzing its weaknesses. Micali's protocol is based on the use of an offline trusted third party where it is used to demonstrate an instance of exchange that implements fair contract signing.

We discuss the revisions made by Bao et al. (Bao, Wang, Zhou & Zhu, 2004) on Micali's protocol and how his protocol handles some of its weaknesses. We then explain our protocol and demonstrate how replay attacks which are not addressed by both these protocols are identified and can be prevented.

MICALI'S ELECTRONIC CONTRACT SIGNING PROTOCOL

In 2003, during the ACM Symposium on Principles of Distributed Computing (PODC) Silvio Micali presented a fair exchange protocol that could perform electronic contract signing (Micali, 2003). The protocol was also filed under US Patent No. 5666420 in 1997. In his protocol, contract signing was achieved in a fair way by using an invisible trusted third party. Fairness in this context means that either both parties are bound to the contract (i.e. obtain each others' signature on the contract) or neither one is.

However, the protocol is not as fair as claimed by the author, since either party is able to cheat the other under certain scenarios. The protocol also does not provide any means to handle or prevent replay attacks that may take place if an intruder replays messages sent earlier by one party to another.

Some of these scenarios are also illustrated in the paper by Bao et al. (2004). Following is the actual protocol for contract signing as proposed by Micali.

Protocol

Contract signing can be implemented between two parties say, Alice and Bob in three steps. Steps 4 and 5 are required only when a dispute occurs.

Pre-Requisites

It is assumed that both parties have negotiated the contract before hand. Alice begins by selecting the contract file "*C*" that she needs to sign with Bob. She also selects a random value *M* and creates a packet "*Z*".

Packet *Z* contains the following information:

1. Identity of sender: This is basically a string that represents the sender. Public key of the sender can also be used. In this case the sender is Alice "*A*".
2. Identity of the receiver: A string that represents the receiver. Public key of the receiver can also be used. In this case the receiver is Bob "*B*".
3. Random value *M*: This can also be a number. It is a value known only to Alice and will later be used for completion of the contract signing process.

This information is encrypted using the public key of the third party, which is known to everyone.

Thus *Z* can be represented as $Z = E_{TP}(A, B, M)$, where E_{TP} is performing encryption using the trusted third party's (*TP*) public key.

Due to the practical requirements for the encryption functions to be so secure, Micali also explains the implementation of the encryption function "E^R_{TP}", where *R* emphasizes the use of a unique random value for performing encryption while using the trusted third party's (*TP*) public key.

A, *B* are the identifiers for Alice and Bob respectively and *M* is the secret random value known only to Alice.

Steps

1. Once the packet *Z* is created, Alice initiates the protocol by sending her signature on the packet *Z* and the contract *C* to Bob.

```
A1:      A → B:       SIG  (C, Z)
                         A
```

2. Upon receiving Alice's message, Bob sends his signature of *(C, Z)* and *Z* to Alice.

```
B1:      B → A:       SIG  (C, Z) + SIG
                         B                B
(Z)
```

3. After receiving Bob's message, Alice verifies his signatures on both *(C, Z)* and *Z* and if they are valid, she sends *M* to Bob.

```
A2:      A → B:       M
```

Dispute Resolution Phase

4. Bob receives the random *M* and uses it to reconstruct *Z*. If the newly created *Z* matches with the one he received in *Step 1*, he halts and the contract signing protocol is complete. Else, Bob sends his signature of *(C, Z)* and *Z* to the trusted third party.

If values of *Z* do not match:

```
B2:      B → TP:      SIG  (C, Z) +
                         B
SIG  (Z)
   B
```

5. Third Party verifies the signatures it received from Bob. If they are valid, it decrypts *Z* using its private key and sends *M* to Bob and *SIG$_B$ (C, Z) + SIG$_B$ (Z)* to Alice.

```
TP1:     TP → A:      SIG  (C, Z) +
                         B
SIG  (Z)
   B
TP2:     TP → B:      M
```

Micali defines the commitments of Alice and Bob on the contract *C* as the following:

Alice's commitment to contract *C*:

SIG$_A$ (C, Z) and M

Bob's commitment to contract *C*:

SIG$_B$ (C, Z) + SIG$_B$ (Z)

To illustrate the fairness of the above mentioned contract signing protocol, Micali provided the following argument (Micali, 2003):

"Indeed, if Bob never performs Step B1, then he is not committed to C, but neither is Alice, because Bob only has received SIG$_A$(C, Z), and has no way of learning M. However, if Bob performs Step B1, then he is committed to C, but Alice too will be so committed: either because she will honestly send M to Bob, or because Bob will get M from the invisible TP. Again, if Bob tries to cheat bypassing Step B1 and accessing directly the invisible TP to learn M, then Alice will get SIG$_B$(C, Z) and SIG$_B$ (Z) from the invisible TP, because the invisible TP will not help Bob at all unless it first receives both signatures, and because once it decrypts Z to find M, it will also discover that Alice is the first signatory, and thus that she is entitled to SIG$_B$(C, Z) and SIG$_B$ (Z)."

In case of the use of the encryption function "E^R_{TP}" during the generation of *Z*, Alice would also be required to send *R* along with *M* in Step 3.

Analysis

This section discusses the vulnerabilities in Micali's contract signing protocol and how it is unfair in certain scenarios.

Insufficient requirements for dispute resolution: Third party only requires Bob's signatures *(SIG$_B$ (C, Z) and SIG$_B$ (Z))* during the dispute resolution phase and nothing from Alice's side is required. This can cause the following attack:

After receiving Alice's signature *(SIG$_A$ (C, Z))*, dishonest Bob prepares a new contract *C'*, creates the following signatures *SIG$_B$ (C', Z)* and *SIG$_B$ (Z)* and sends them both to the third party requesting for dispute resolution. Since these two signatures are valid and third party does not require any signatures from Alice, it forwards $SIG_B (C^l, Z)$ and $SIG_B (Z)$ to Alice and M to Bob.

This result in Bob having Alice's commitment on contract C and Alice only having Bob's commitment on a contract C^l which is of no use to Alice.

Attack 1

```
A1:      A → B:       SIG_A (C, Z)
B1:      B → TP:      SIG_B (C^1, Z) + SIG_B
(Z)
```

Since Z does not contain any information about the contract C and the signature of Bob on C^l and Z are valid, the third party provides Bob with the value of M contained in Z and Alice with Bob's signature over the fake contract C^l.

```
TP1:     TP → A:      SIG_B (C^1, Z) + SIG_B
(Z)
TP2:     TP → B:      M
```

Insufficient requirements for commitment of both parties: As per Micali's definition, for Alice to show Bob's commitment on the contract C, she only requires Bob's signatures on (C, Z) and Z, which are $SIG_B (C, Z)$ and $SIG_B (Z)$. Alice is not required to provide the value M that creates Z. This flaw can be exploited such that Alice can always get Bob's commitment on a contract while Bob gets nothing. Following is the attack:

Dishonest Alice creates a random value of length Z and sends her signature of (C, Z) to Bob. Bob verifies Alice's signature and since it holds true, he sends his signatures of (C, Z) and Z to her. Alice now quits the protocol as she has received Bob's commitment. Bob on the other hand cannot get resolution form third party as Z is a random value and it cannot find M such that $Z = E_{TP} (A, B, M)$.

This leads to Alice obtaining an advantage since she is not required to present a value M that can recreate the packet Z.

Attack 2

Alice creates a random value of length Z.

```
A1:      A → B:       SIG_A (C, Z)
B1:      B → A:       SIG_B (C, Z) + SIG_B
(Z)
A2:      No response
```

Bob contacts the third party for resolution:

```
B2:      B → TP:      SIG_B (C, Z) + SIG_B
(Z)
```

The third party is not able to provide M to Bob as Z is a random value and it does not contain a value M such that $Z = E_{TP} (A, B, M)$.

```
TP:      Halts, as it is unable to
provide the value of M.
```

The above mentioned attacks are also explained in the paper by Bao et al. (2004). They handle these attacks by changing the requirements of the dispute resolution phase, the commitment parameters for both parties and the contents of Z.

Third party's dilemma: Micali's protocol does not clarify what the third party is required to do when it receives the packet Z such that decrypting it $(D_{TP} (Z))$ does not lead to the desired (A, B, M) even though the signatures $SIG_A (C, Z)$, $SIG_B (C, Z)$ and $SIG_B (Z)$ are valid. This dilemma occurs during the dispute resolution phase where $D_{TP} (Z) \neq (A, B, M)$ for any M. This indirectly means that the first two values of Z are not the identities of Alice and Bob.

In this case, the third party can either choose to ignore the request, since the identities do not match, or can proceed with dispute resolution phase and provide M to the requesting party. Bao's analysis on Micali's protocol show that either step taken by the third party leaves scope for possible attacks where one party can achieve an unfair advantage over the other.

Following is a brief overview of one of the possible attacks based on the above explained dispute resolution issue:

Attack 3

This attack takes place when the third party implements the policy of choosing to ignore the dispute resolution request if $D_{TP}(Z) \neq (A, B, M)$. To stage this attack, dishonest Alice colludes with A^1 and obtains the other party's (Bob) commitment without providing hers.

Steps

1. Alice chooses a random M and creates the packet $Z^1 = E_{TP}(A^1, B, M)$. She then initiates the protocol by creating her signature on the packet Z^1 and the contract C and sends it to Bob.

A1:   A → B: $SIG_A (C, Z^1)$

2. On receiving Alice's message, Bob verifies her signature and since it is valid, sends his signature of $SIG_B (C, Z^1)$ and $SIG_B (Z^1)$ to Alice.

B1:   B → A: $SIG_B (C, Z^1)$, $SIG_B (Z^1)$

3. After receiving Bob's message. Alice halts.

A2:   A → B: Nothing

As Bob does not receive the value of M from Alice, he contacts the third party for dispute resolution. The third party verifies the signatures which are valid but observes that $D_{TP}(Z) \neq (A, B, M)$. As per the resolution policy defined above, the third party ignores this request since the identities of both parties do not match the signatures obtained. This leads to Alice (and her colluding partner A^1) obtaining a valid commitment from Bob over the contract C with A^1 and Bob obtains nothing. This is because Bob's signatures of $SIG_B (C, Z^1)$ and

$SIG_B (Z^1)$ can be viewed as valid commitments of Bob to the contract C with the colluding party A^1 since $Z^1 = E_{TP}(A^1, B, M)$. It can be assumed that a contract usually contains the identities of both parties and that this attack can be identified since A^1 is not a part of the contract. However, such assumptions are not specified by Micali. It is not possible to identify the cheater in this type of attack since this attack can also be staged by Bob where he initiates the contract signing process and cheats in the first step by colluding with A^1.

Replay attacks: Even though the above mentioned attacks are addressed, both protocols (Micali and Bao) still leave one possible attack. These protocols provide no means of identifying a replay attack that may take place during a contract signing instance.

Since both the protocols do not handle this type of attack, one of them namely, Micali's original protocol is used for the replay attack demonstration.

Attack 4

Consider the normal execution of Micali's protocol:

A1:   A → B: $SIG_A (C, Z)$
B1:   B → A: $SIG_B (C, Z) + SIG_B (Z)$
A2:   A → B: M

Let us assume an intruder has access to the transmissions between Alice and Bob and is able to record all the messages sent by Alice. An intruder can thus replay a message that was previously sent by Alice to Bob.

Consider the following execution of the protocol by an intruder:

I1:   I → B: $SIG_A (C, Z)$
B1:   B → A: $SIG_B (C, Z) + SIG_B (Z)$
I2:   I → B: M

If the intruder replays the message *A1* as a new request, then there is no way for Bob to indentify the sender. Bob will assume the request as a genuine one since its signature will still be valid and respond back with his signature of the same. To this, the intruder can then send the message *A2*. This leads to commitment on a new contract between Alice and Bob. Bob assumes that he has signed a new contract with Alice and she on the other hand knows nothing about it.

Consider a scenario where Alice periodically purchases selected items from Bob using the above protocol. The contracts then signed by them would also be the same, which is also the case in real world transactions and if it is agreed that all contracts expire immediately upon fulfillment (i.e. Bob gets the order, he signs it, and then forgets about it), it would be hard to trace the intruder or even identify the attack. It should also be noted that the intruder does not need to involve the third party to stage this attack thus making it even harder to identify.

BAO'S ELECTRONIC CONTRACT SIGNING PROTOCOL

Micali's protocol suffers from several weaknesses due to the following design issues:

1. The packet *Z* does not contain any information about the contract the parties negotiated to sign.
2. No resolution of the third party's dilemma: where there trusted third party is not sure whether to resolve the dispute resolution request of ignore if $D_{TP}(Z) \neq (A, B, M)$.
3. The protocol provides no means or mechanisms for handling replay attacks that may take place if an intruder replays messages sent earlier from Alice to Bob.

In 2004, during the *Australasian Conference on Information Security and Privacy (ACISP)*,

Bao et al. proposed a contract signing protocol that improved upon Micali's work. Attacks made possible due to the first two design issues were identified and addressed by Bao. Our prior work (Bedi, Yang, & Kizza, 2009; Bedi & Yang, 2009) did not handle the second design issue but discussed the same in (Bedi & Yang, 2009) under the section titled "Scope for Further Improvement". Our present work now addresses this second design issue.

Attacks made possible due to the lack of contract information in packet *Z* structure were identified and addressed. Bao's protocol handled the first three types of attacks namely, Attack 1, 2 and 3, which were discussed in the previous section by changing the requirements of the dispute resolution phase, the commitment parameters for both the involved parties and the structure of the packet *Z*.

Protocol

In this protocol, contract signing between two parties, say Alice and Bob can be achieved through the following prerequisites and steps.

Prerequisites

It is assumed that both parties have negotiated the contract before hand. Alice begins by selecting the contract file "*C*" that she needs to sign with Bob and creates a hash of it *H(C)*. She also selects the random values *M* and *R* and creates a packet "*Z*".

Packet Z contains the following information:

1. Identity of sender: This is basically a string that represents the sender. Public key of the sender can also be used. In this case the sender is Alice "*A*".
2. Identity of the receiver: A string that represents the receiver. Public key of the receiver can also be used. In this case the receiver is Bob "*B*".

3. Random value M: This can also be a number. It is a value known only to Alice and will later be used for completion of the contract signing process.

4. Hash of the contract C.

This information is encrypted using the public key of the third party, which is known to everyone.

Thus packet Z can be represented as $Z = E^R_{TP}$ $(A, B, H(C), M)$, where E^R_{TP} is performing encryption using the trusted third party's (TP) public key with the randomness R.

A and B are the identifiers of Alice and Bob respectively. M is the random value known only to Alice and $H(C)$ is the hash of the contract.

Steps

1. Once the packet Z is created, Alice then initiates the protocol by creating her signature on the packet Z, the contract C, the identities of her, Bob and the third party, and sending them to Bob.

```
A1:      A → B:      SIG_A (A, B, TP, C,
Z)
```

2. On receiving Alice's message, Bob verifies her signature and if valid, sends his signature of (A, B, TP, C, Z) to Alice. Otherwise he halts.

```
B1:      B → A:      SIG_B (A, B, TP, C,
Z)
```

3. After receiving Bob's message. Alice verifies his signatures on (A, B, TP, C, Z) and if valid, she sends M and R to Bob.

```
A2:      A → B:      M, R
```

Dispute Resolution Phase

4. Bob receives the values M and R and uses them to reconstruct Z. If the newly created Z matches with the one he received in Step 1, he halts and the contract signing protocol is complete. Else, Bob sends his and Alice's signature of (A, B, TP, C, Z) to the trusted third party.

If values of Z do not match:

```
B2:      B → TP:      SIG_B (A, B, TP,
C, Z) + SIG_A (A, B, TP, C, Z)
```

5. Third Party verifies the signatures it received from Bob. If they are valid, it decrypts Z using its private key and sends $(SIG_B (A, B, TP, C, Z), M, R)$ to Alice and $(SIG_A (A, B, TP, C, Z), M, R)$ to Bob.

If contents of Z are legit and signatures are valid:

```
TP1:      TP → A:      SIG_B (A, B, TP,
C, Z) + M + R
TP2:      TP → B:      SIG_A (A, B, TP,
C, Z) + M + R
```

Else:

Halts or sends an error message

Following are the new commitments as revised by Bao:

Alice's commitment to the contract C can be defined as:

```
SIG_A (A, B, TP, C, Z), M, R
where Z = E^R_TP (A, B, H(C), M)
```

Bob's commitment to the contract C can be defined as:

```
SIG_B (A, B, TP, C, Z), M, R
where Z = E^R_TP (A, B, H(C), M)
```

The design weakness of the unavailability of a mechanism to identify and prevent replay attacks was not addressed by both Micali and Bao.

OUR FAIR CONTRACT SIGNING IMPLEMENTATION

We present a complete working implementation that provides fair electronic exchange. We implement an invisible third party that can be used to provide fairness if cheating is suspected.

Our work comprises of two parts. We begin with a revised protocol that is based on Micali's contract signing protocol. We improve upon Micali's protocol by handling certain types of weaknesses which can lead to attacks including where one party can obtain another's commitment to a contract without providing theirs. We also handle the possibilities of replay attack that can take place if an intruder replays the messages sent earlier from one party to the other.

This present work extends our prior work on fair electronic exchange (Bedi, Yang, & Kizza, 2009; Bedi & Yang, 2009) by handling a type of attack which was not handled earlier and also provides a brief survey of recent work related to the field of fair electronic exchange.

Our prior work (Bedi, Yang, & Kizza, 2009; Bedi & Yang, 2009) offered the unique contribution of handling replay attacks which were not addressed by both Micali and Bao. However one possible attack which is illustrated in the previous sections, titled "Third party's dilemma", was handled by Bao and not our protocol. Third party's dilemma was demonstrated in our prior publication (Bedi & Yang, 2009) under the section "Scope for Further Improvement" and now has been addressed in this present implementation.

To provide confidentiality, handle replay attacks and confirm the identities of both the parties, cryptography along with digital signatures is used. All messages communicated between parties involved in the contract signing process are encrypted using a hybrid cryptosystem. These two parts are explained in detail as follows.

Protocol

This section discusses our contract signing protocol and describes how it achieves fairness. Following is an adaptation of the protocol where the privacy of messages is not essential. It is assumed that both parties are not concerned about the privacy of their messages (or contracts), provided that fairness is guaranteed. This approach is taken to make the illustration of our protocol simple. Privacy of messages can be achieved using cryptography, which is explained in detail in the subsequent topics.

Following is the protocol under normal execution when both Alice and Bob are honest and there is no intruder. Contract signing between two parties, say Alice and Bob, can be achieved through following the below prerequisites and steps.

Prerequisites

It is assumed that both parties have negotiated the contract before hand. Alice selects the contract file "C" that she needs to sign with Bob. She also selects a random value M and creates a packet "Z".

Packet Z contains the following information:

1. Identity of sender: This is basically a string that represents the sender. Public key of the sender can also be used. In our case the sender is Alice "A".
2. Identity of the receiver: A string that represents the receiver. Public key of the receiver can also be used. In our case the receiver is Bob "B".
3. Random value M: This can also be a number. It is a value known only to Alice and will later be used for completion of the contract signing process.
4. Hash of the contract C, that is $H(C)$

This information is encrypted using the public key of the third party, which is known to everyone.

Thus Z can be represented as $Z = E^R_{TP} (A, B, H(C), M)$, where E^R_{TP} is performing encryption using the trusted third party's (TP) public key using the randomness R.

A and B are the identifiers of Alice and Bob respectively. $H(C)$ is the hash of the contract file C. M is the random value known only to Alice.

Steps

1. Alice sends a nonce NA_1 to Bob. Nonce is a random number used only once for the prevention of replay attacks.

A1:   A → B: NA_1

2. On receiving Alice's nonce, Bob signs it using his private key and sends it back to her along with his nonce. This step ensures Alice that it was indeed Bob who signed the message as Bob's private key is a secret known only to Bob.

B1:   B → A: $SIG_B (NA_1) + NB_1$

3. After receiving the above package Alice can verify the digital signature of Bob on NA_1 using his public key. If it matches, Alice is sure that it is indeed Bob and there is no replay attack. Alice now signs Bob's nonce using her private key so that he can be sure of the same. Alice also signs Z along with $H(C)$ and sends all of it to Bob.

This step makes Alice partially committed to the contract as she has signed the hash of contract using her private key.

A2:   A → B: $SIG_A (NB_1) + SIG_A (H(C), Z) + Z + C$

4. On receiving Alice's signatures, Bob can now verify them using her public key. If they match, Bob is sure that it is indeed Alice and there is no replay attack. It is now Bob's turn to send his commitment to Alice. Bob does this by signing the Alice's signature he received and sending it back to Alice.

B2:   B → A: $SIG_B (SIG_A (H(C), Z))$

5. After receiving the message, Alice can verify Bob's signature and if it holds true, she sends him the values M and R signed by her.

A3:   A → B: $SIG_A (M, R) + M + R$

Bob receives this package and learns the values M and R which is then used to reconstruct Z along with public values A and B. If the newly created Z matches with the one he received in Step 3, the transaction is complete and both the parties have successfully signed the contract together.

Following is the protocol under abnormal execution where Alice does not provide Bob with the correct secret values of M and R in the final step.

Dispute Resolution Phase

Upon receiving Alice's signature of Z and $H(C)$, Bob sends his signature of the same to Alice. Alice is then required to send the values of M and R to Bob to provide her complete commitment on the contract. For the purpose of discussion let us assume that Alice cheats Bob by not providing him with the correct secret values of M and R after she receives his signature on the contract.

Thus Bob is left with a partial commitment from Alice, where as Alice has Bob's complete commitment. Bob can thus execute the following steps to obtain resolution.

1. Bob sends the packet Z that he initially received from Alice, the contract C that was to be signed, Alice's signature of Z and $H(C)$ and his own signature on Alice's signature to the third party.

```
B1:     B → TP:     Z + C + SIG_A
(H(C), Z) + SIG_B (SIG_A (H(C), Z))
```

2. Third party, upon receiving Bob's request performs the following steps:
   a. Computes the value of $H(C)$ from C.
   b. Decrypts the packet Z since it knows its own private key and extracts the secret M.
   c. Verifies the contents of Z to contain the identities A for Alice and B for Bob and $H(C)$ for the hash of the contract.
   d. Verifies the signatures of Alice and Bob. Third party can do this since it knows the public keys of both Alice and Bob. If the signatures are valid, and the contents of the packet Z are verifiable with their identities and the hash of the contract, third party provides Bob with M it recovered from Z, the value R and Alice with the signature of Bob over $SIG_A (H(C), Z)$.

If contents of Z are legit and the signatures are valid:

```
TP1:     TP → B:     M + R
TP2:     TP → A:     SIG_B (SIG_A
(H(C), Z))
```
   Else:

No action or report error message.

If the secrecy of the contract is necessary, the cheating party can send the hash of the contract instead of the original contract to the third party during the dispute resolution phase. The third party then can skip the step where it is required to compute the hash of the contract, and can proceed directly with the remaining steps. This completes the resolution phase as the third party provides Bob with the correct values of M and R which gives him complete commitment from Alice on the contract.

Protocol Description

To sign a contract in theory would mean exchange of signatures from both the parties on the same contract. That is if Alice and Bob were to sign a contract with each other, Alice would need to have Bob's signature (commitment) on the contract in the form of $SIG_B(C)$ and Bob would need to have Alice's signature $SIG_A(C)$.

For this to be fair it would require that each party gets the other party's signature only when their signature is received by the other party. Implementation of this exchange may be straightforward under conventional transactions where both the parties are physically available or geographically locatable. However under e-commerce where the transactions take place over the Internet, it becomes reasonably complicated. This is because these transactions transcend geographical boundaries and it is not always possible to contact the other party for resolution or queries once the transaction is complete.

A party can always refuse to provide their signature once they receive the same from the other party. And since locating someone over the Internet or to know when the other party will be available online again is not always possible, fairness cannot be guaranteed.

Therefore to provide fairness, additional information (e.g. packet Z) is exchanged along with the contract (or messages) during these fair exchange transactions. This additional information is then examined and used for resolution if a party does not respond appropriately.

Thus the commitments for both parties are modified as follows:

For Bob to have Alice's commitment on the contract, he would need:

$$\text{SIG}_A \ (\text{H}(\text{C}), \ \text{Z}), \ \text{M and R};$$
$$\text{where Z} = \text{E}^R_{TP} \ (\text{A}, \ \text{B}, \ \text{H}(\text{C}), \ \text{M})$$

For Alice to have Bob's commitment on the contract, she would need:

$$\text{SIG}_B \ (\text{SIG}_A \ (\text{H}(\text{C}), \ \text{Z})), \ \text{M and R};$$
$$\text{where Z} = \text{E}^R_{TP} \ (\text{A}, \ \text{B}, \ \text{H}(\text{C}), \ \text{M})$$

To prove the commitments, parties will be required to present not only the signatures but also the contents M, R, A, B and H(C) that altogether satisfy $Z = E^R_{TP} (A, B, H(C), M)$. Failing to do so shall render the commitments as well as the signed contract as invalid.

The additional information used in our protocol is $Z = E^R_{TP} (A, B, H(C), M)$ and values R and M.

The packet Z is created using the following information,

1. Identities of both the parties: Those are A for Alice and B for Bob. We use text strings for this purpose. The public keys of parties or any other type of identifiable information can also be used.

2. Hash of the Contract: A Message digest created by using a cryptographic hash function. It is usually of fixed length and is unique to the data hashed. A change in hash generated would represent a change in the data hashed.

3. Random number M: Alice creates this random number that is used as a part of the contract signing process and for contract verification by Bob. Initially, Alice signs the packet Z which includes this random number M along with contract C and sends it to Bob. After receiving her signature, Bob still does not have her complete commitment over the contract as he does not know the value of M that was used to create the packet Z. Bob cannot find this value on his own since the

packet Z is encrypted using the third party's public key and the third party's corresponding private key is a secret known only to it. Bob also cannot get it from Alice unless he provides his commitment of the same to Alice. Thus the only option available to Bob is to send his commitment to Alice. Alice then verifies his signature and if valid, sends him the values M and R. Upon receiving M and R from Alice, Bob can reconstruct Z using A, B and H(C). Bob does so by encrypting these values using the third party's public key along with the random R. If the newly created Z matches with the one he received earlier, he has Alice's complete commitment on the contract.

4. The value R: It is this randomness that is used by the public-key cryptosystem during encryption to produce the same cipher text for a given data using the same public key. This is usually not the case since most public-key cryptosystems produce different cipher texts under the above scenario. In our protocol, during the final step, comparison of cipher texts is performed for contract verification purposes. Thus the production of same cipher text over the same data and same public key becomes a requirement and can only be achieved if the randomness used for encryption is stored and reused.

Our Contribution

Our contribution in the revised protocol encompasses the following design changes:

Inclusion of hash of contract in Z: Information about the hash of the contract is added in the packet Z. A Hash is basically a fixed length value returned by a cryptographic hash function that takes the contract file data as the input. These hash values are usually unique for a given message (contract) and changes if the message is altered. If one party modifies the contract during the contract signing protocol, the hash generated on the modified contract will not match with the one generated on the original contract. If the hashes on this contract do not match between the parties, it can be concluded that they have different contracts and cheating can be identified. It can be concluded so as it is extremely unlikely to find the same hash on two different contracts. We specifically assume that SIG_A () and SIG_B () are secure signing algorithms that exhibit the following four properties:

1. It is easy to compute hash for any given data.
2. It is extremely difficult to recreate the data from its hash.
3. It is extremely unlikely to find the same hash for two different data.
4. It is extremely difficult to modify a given data without changing its hash.

Exchange of random nonce prior to exchange of commitments: Random nonces are exchanged between both parties prior to exchange of the contract commitments. This step ensures that both parties are certain about the other's identity. It also helps to identify a replay attack that may occur if an intruder tries to replay messages previously sent by Alice.

This can be achieved through the following three steps. Let the two parties be Alice and Bob,

1. Alice sends a random nonce to Bob.
2. Bob signs the nonce it received from Alice using his private key and sends his random nonce to her.
3. Alice verifies the signed value using Bob's public key. If valid, she signs his nonce using her private key and sends it to Bob. Bob can verify the same using her public key.

Inclusion of hash of contract in signature: Hash of the contract instead of the actual contract is used during the digital signature generation process. This step ensures privacy of the contract between both the parties. On the contrary, if the

contract is part of the digital signature, during dispute resolution the cheated party would also have to provide the contract along with the other information to the third party. This is necessary since all information that is part of the signature is required in order to verify it which also includes the contract. If the secrecy of the contract is essential to the cheated party, executing this step would make them lose the same. Protocols by Micali and Bao both use the actual contract instead of its hash during the digital signature generation process.

Handling of Attacks

This section discusses how the attacks discovered in Micali's protocol are being handled by our protocol,

Insufficient Requirements for Dispute Resolution by the Third Party: In Micali's protocol, the third party only requires Bob's signatures $(SIG_B(C, Z)$ and $SIG_B(Z))$ during the dispute resolution phase. Nothing from Alice's side is required. This can lead to the following attack:

After receiving Alice's signature $(SIG_A(C, Z))$ dishonest Bob can prepare a new contract C^1, create the following signatures $SIG_B(C^1, Z)$ and $SIG_B(Z)$ and send them to the third party requesting for resolution. Since these two signatures are valid and third party does not require any signatures from Alice or even the contract, it forwards $SIG_B(C^1, Z)$ and $SIG_B(Z)$ to Alice and M to Bob. This result in Bob having Alice's commitment on contract C and Alice only having Bob's commitment on another contract C^1.

This attack is handled by our protocol since now the third party requires signatures of both parties participating in the contract signing process. Also, since hash of the contract file is now included in the packet Z, if Bob signs a fake contract, the hashes will change and the signature will not be verifiable.

Insufficient requirements for commitment of both parties: As per Micali's definition, for

Bob to be committed to the contract C, Alice only requires Bob's signatures on the contract C and packet Z that are $SIG_B(C, Z)$ and $SIG_B (Z)$. Alice is not required to provide the value M that creates Z. This flaw can be exploited such that Alice can always get Bob's commitment on a contract while Bob gets nothing. Following is the attack:

Dishonest Alice creates a random value of length Z and sends her signature of (C, Z) to Bob. Bob verifies Alice's signature and since it holds true, he sends his signatures of (C, Z) and Z to her. Alice now quits the protocol as she has received Bob's commitment. Bob on the other hand cannot get resolution form third party as Z is a random value and it cannot find M such that $Z = E^R_{TP} (A, B, M)$. This leads to Alice obtaining an advantage since she is not required to present a value M that can recreate the packet Z.

This attack is handled by our protocol by changing the requirements of contract commitment such that Alice is also required to provide a value of M and R such that $Z=E^R_{TP} (A, B, M)$.

Third party's dilemma: During the dispute resolution phase in Micali's protocol, it is not stated how the third party should react to a scenario where decrypting Z does not yield to the valid A, B and M values, that is, $D_{TP} (Z) \neq (A, B, M)$ for any M, even though the signatures $SIG_A (C, Z)$, $SIG_B (C, Z)$ and $SIG_B (Z)$ are valid. This indirectly means that the first two values of Z are not the identities of Alice and Bob. Bao's analysis on Micali's protocol show that either step taken by the third party leaves scope for possible attacks where one party can achieve an unfair advantage over the other.

Such attacks are handled by our protocol by changing the requirements for commitment of both the parties over the contract and by changing the contents of the packet Z to also include the hash of the negotiated contract $H(C)$. Bob is now is required to sign over Alice's signature which he received and not just the $H(C)$ and Z. Therefore, by signing over Alice's signature and not just the $H(C)$ and packet Z, Bob confirms his intention to

commit over the contract with only Alice and not anyone else. Therefore now Alice cannot collude with A^I and obtain Bob's commitment over the contract as Bob signs over Alice's signature and the packet Z contains A^I as one of the parties and not Alice. This mismatch illustrates cheating and is not allowed by our protocol.

Replay Attacks: Even though the above mentioned attacks are addressed, both protocols (Micali and Bao) still leave one possible attack. These protocols provide no means of identifying a replay attack that may take place during a contract signing instance.

Let us assume an intruder has access to the transmissions between Alice and Bob and is able to record all the messages sent by Alice. An intruder can thus always replay a message that was previously sent by Alice. Bob will assume the request as genuine as its signature will still be valid and respond back with his signature of the same. This leads to signature of a new contract between Alice and Bob. Bob assumes that he has signed a new contract with Alice and she on the other hand knows nothing about it.

This attack is handled by our protocol since both parties are required to exchange random nonce between each other before they exchange their commitments. Therefore if an intruder replays a contract signing request sent previously by Alice, Bob would respond with a nonce which has to be signed using Alice's private key. Since Alice's private key is a secret known only to Alice, the intruder will not be able to provide the signature and the contract signing process would halt, preventing the replay attack.

To recognize a replay attack Bob can also recompute Z by using previously obtained values of M from Alice. If a match occurs Bob can conclude that it is a replay attack. However, only limited values of M (or contracts) can be accessible to a party in practice due to limits on database sizes. Our use of nonce removes this limitation and does not require storage of previous values of M

or even the contract since the attack can be easily identified if nonce verification fails.

Role of Cryptography

In our protocol, cryptography is being used for two main purposes which include creation and verification of digital signatures and implementation of hybrid cryptography. Following is a brief discussion on both these purposes and their implementation in our system.

Digital Signatures

Digital signatures are derived from asymmetric cryptography where messages signed by a party using its private key can later by verified by anybody using the party's corresponding public key. This provides the property of non-repudiation where the signer cannot refuse to have signed the message since the private key used to sign the message is a secret known only to the signer. Digital signatures can be considered equivalent to traditional handwritten signatures in many aspects and when implemented properly are extremely effective. In a contract signing instance, the initiating party can sign messages using any of the various digital signature algorithms. This way during the transaction it can always be proved that the messages signed and sent by the initiating party indeed belong to it.

We implement a digital signature algorithm based elliptic curves known as Elliptic Curve Digital Signature Algorithm or ECDSA (ANSI X9.63, 1999) and our implementation produces a digital signature of 448 bits (Piotrowski, Langendoerfer & Peter, 2006) on the provided data.

Hybrid Cryptography

Our system uses hybrid cryptography for secure communication since it offers better efficiency and properties like data integrity and non-repudiation when compared individually to techniques like asymmetric and symmetric cryptography. Following is a brief discussion on both these forms of cryptography (asymmetric and symmetric) for a clear understanding of our implementation and its benefits.

Symmetric Cryptography: This process of cryptography uses the same key for encryption and decryption. The secrecy of the information is dependent on how well this secret key can be kept private. Compared to its counterpart *asymmetric cryptography* which is explained later, symmetric cryptography is fast and efficient. For this reason it is used widely for encryption and decryption of large files. Even though this process is highly efficient, it suffers from the following disadvantages:

- Key Sharing: Since an initial exchange of the secret key is required between the parties before they can begin encrypting and decryption data, safe transmission or sharing of this key becomes a problem.
- Key Management: A key is required to be shared between every two parties who are willing to exchange information securely. Therefore in a large network of users who want to exchange information with other users, a unique key is required for every user pair. This storage and management of keys become difficult for each user who wants to participate is such transactions.
- Integrity: Since the receiver cannot verify that the message has not been altered before receipt, the integrity of data can be compromised.
- Repudiation: Since the same secret key has to be shared between users, the sender can always repudiate the messages because there are no mechanisms for the receiver to make sure that the message has been sent by the claimed sender.

Asymmetric Cryptography

This process of cryptography also known as *public key cryptography* uses different keys for encrypting and decrypting information. These keys together form a key-pair and are known as public and private keys. Public keys are shared with everyone in the world. Private keys on the other are kept secret and known only to the individual to whom it belongs. For a party to send information securely to another, they need to encrypt the information using the recipient's public key. The recipient can then decrypt this data and recover the message by using their corresponding private key. Since this private key is a secret known only to the recipient, the information can be communicated securely without the requirement of initial key exchange thus handling the key sharing problem. Key management also becomes convenient since there are no unique keys that are required for each user pair willing to communicate. The user can simply use the recipient's public key and start secure communication. Non-repudiation and data integrity can be achieved by making the sender also encrypt or sign the message using their private key which can then be verified by anybody using the signer's corresponding public key.

Even though asymmetric cryptography offers features like non-repudiation and data integrity, its execution is still far slower than symmetric cryptography making it less favorable for encrypting and decrypting large files.

Hybrid Cryptography

Hybrid cryptography handles the above mentioned disadvantages in symmetric and asymmetric cryptography. It does so by using both these cryptosystems together which provides the convenience of asymmetric cryptography along with the efficiency of symmetric cryptography.

Hybrid cryptography consists of the following two stages:

1. **Data encapsulation:** The process in which data to be communicated securely is encrypted using symmetric cryptography schemes which are highly efficient.
2. **Key encapsulation:** The symmetric secret key used to encrypt the data is then encrypted using asymmetric cryptography schemes.

To encrypt a message to Bob, Alice performs the following steps:

1. Creates a random symmetric key and encrypts the message using the data encapsulation scheme.
2. Encrypts the symmetric key using Bob's public key under the key encapsulation scheme.
3. Sends both the encrypted message and the encrypted symmetric key to Bob.

To recover the message sent by Alice, Bob performs the following steps:

1. Use his private key to decrypt the encrypted symmetric key.
2. Use the recovered symmetric key to decrypt and recover the original message.

Since the major part of the transmission that includes the actual message is encrypted using symmetric cryptosystem, the efficiency of the system is improved. By encrypting only the symmetric key using asymmetric cryptography properties like key management, data integrity and non-repudiation can be addressed.

We use Elliptic Curve Integrated Encryption Scheme, also known as ECIES for performing asymmetric cryptography operations. We use Advanced Encryption Standard (AES) for symmetric cryptography. It is the current cryptography standard for symmetric cryptosystems and was announced by the National Institute of Standards and Technology (NIST) under the Federal Information Processing Standards (FIPS, 2001) 197 on November 26, 2001. It is also one of the most popular algorithms used for symmetric cryptography at present.

Elliptic Curve Cryptography Overview

Both Elliptic Curve Integrated Encryption Scheme (ECIES) and Elliptic Curve Digital Signature Algorithm (ECDSA) are part of cryptography that is based on elliptic curves. Also known as Elliptic Curve Cryptography or ECC, it is an approach to public key cryptography that is primarily based on elliptic curves which are defined over a finite field. A field is basically a mathematical group that offers operations for addition, subtraction, multiplication, and division that always construct results within the field. A finite field can be defined as a field that contains only finitely many elements. It is this property of being finite that makes it possible to perform cryptography with these elliptic curves that exists over the fields. The use of elliptic curves for cryptography was proposed independently by Neal Koblitz (1987) at the University of Washington and Victor Miller (1986) at IBM in 1985. Being grown into a mature public key cryptosystem, it is endorsed by the United States government (NIST, 1999).

The security of any cryptographic system is based on a hard mathematical problem that is computationally infeasible to solve. For example, RSA gets its security from the difficulty of factoring large numbers. The public and private keys used in RSA cryptography is a function of a pair of large prime numbers, and recovering the plain text from the cipher text that was created using the public key is believed to be computationally equivalent to finding the factors of the primes used to create the pair of public and private keys. Elliptic Curve Cryptography along with many other cryptographic systems achieves their security from the difficulty of solving the discrete logarithmic problem (DLP). ECC to be specific is based upon the difficulty of solving Elliptic Curve Discrete Logarithm Problem (ECDLP) which offers a bet-

ter implementation when compared to previous generation techniques as used by RSA. ECDLP can be demonstrated with the help of the equation $Ax = B$. For very large values of x, it gets computationally infeasible to derive its value as no efficient algorithm is available for solving it. The primitive approach of solving this would be to keep adding and/or multiplying the value of A to itself until the result matches B. This approach is used on elliptic curve groups where, a point on the group is selected and multiplied by a scalar value. When the scalar value is very large, it becomes computationally infeasible to solve the problem. The primitive approach then becomes using the addition and doubling operations together until the matching value is observed. For example, $7P$ can be expressed as $2 * ((2 * P) + P)) + P$. This calculation of a point nP is referred to as Scalar Multiplication of a point. ECDLP is based upon the intractability of scalar multiplication products.

Not all curves can provide strong security and that ECDLP for some curves can be resolved efficiently. Therefore NIST offers a set of recommended curves (NIST, 1999) whose security properties are well understood and can be safely used for cryptography. Standardization of elliptic curves also makes it convenient for interoperability and use by external third party cryptographic providers to provide cryptographic solutions that comply with the security standards.

Performance Improvements Using Elliptic Curve Cryptography

Majority of security systems still use first generation public key cryptographic algorithms like RSA and Diffie-Hellman (DH) which were developed in mid-1970. For these systems the current NIST recommended public key parameter size is 1024 bits. NIST states that these systems can be used securely till 2010 after which it is recommended to shift to other systems which provide better security. One alternative can be to keep increasing the bit size to higher values so that these systems can be used for some more time. Another option can be to shift to next generation cryptographic systems like elliptic curve cryptography which provide equivalent security for smaller key sizes and are also more efficient.

Following is Table 1 that compares ECC with schemes like RSA and Diffie-Hellman in terms of key sizes required for securing symmetric keys for varying length by NSA (2009).

We can see that NIST recommends 1024 bit key sizes for securing 80 bits symmetric keys. The same security can be provided by ECC by using 160 bit key size which makes ECC a better solution. Securing a 256 bit symmetric key would require a RSA key with the bit parameters of size 15,360 which is fifteen times the current size used in Internet today. Comparing to ECC, one would only require keys of size 521 bits which is far smaller.

ECC is also more computationally efficient when compared to RSA and Diffie-Hellman. Even though ECC has more complex arithmetic than RSA and DH, the security added per bit increase in key size does make for the extra time used to handle such complexity. Following is Table 2 that compares the computation required by ECC and schemes like Diffie-Hellman for varying key sizes by NSA (2009).

We can see that as the security level based on key sizes is increased, the difference in the computation required increases at a higher rate which makes ECC much more efficient than the first generation cryptographic algorithms.

Due to the above mentioned reasons which include smaller key sizes, better computational efficiency and greater security, Elliptic Curve Cryptography is considered as a better solution when compared to first generation techniques like RSA and DH. National Security Agency has also decided to move to Elliptic curve cryptography for protecting both classified and unclassified national security information (NSA, 2009).

CONCLUSION

In this journal we examine the notion of fair exchange and its applications. We analyze one exchange protocol by Micali that provides fair contract signing based on the concept of fair exchange. The protocol claims fairness by providing resolution if a party refuses to provide their commitment. We show that Micali's protocol is not completely fair and demonstrate scenarios where one party can cheat the other without being identified. We discuss Bao's protocol which is a revised version of Micali's protocol that provides superior fairness by handling certain types of weaknesses. Both these protocols fail to handle the possibilities of a replay attack. Our prior work improves upon these protocols by addressing the weakness that leads to a replay attack. This present work extends our prior work on fair electronic exchange by handling a type of attack which was not handled earlier and also provides a brief survey of the recent work related to the field of

Table 1. NIST recommended key sizes

Symmetric Key Size (bits)	RSA and Diffie-Hellman Key Size (bits)	Elliptic Curve Key Size (bits)
80	1024	160
112	2048	224
128	3072	256
192	7680	384
256	15360	521

Table 2. Relative computation costs of Diffie-Hellman and Elliptic Curves

Security Level (bits)	Ratio of DH Cost: EC Cost
80	3:1
112	6:1
128	10:1
192	32:1
256	64:1

fair electronic exchange. In addition to our protocol, our implementation of hybrid cryptography and digital signature algorithms which provide features like confidentiality, data-integrity and non-repudiation are also discussed.

REFERENCES

ANSI X9. 63. (1999). *Elliptic Curve Key Agreement and Key Transport Protocols*. Washington, DC: American Bankers Association.

Asokan, N., Schunter, M., & Waidner, M. (1997). Optimistic protocols for fair exchange. In T. Matsumoto (Ed.), *4th ACM Conference on Computer and Communications Security*. (pp. 6, 8–17). Zurich, Switzerland: ACM Press.

Asokan, N., Shoup, V., & Waidner, M. (1998). Optimistic fair exchange of digital signatures. *Advances in Cryptology-EUROCRYP, T98*, 591–606.

Asokan, N., Shoup, V., & Waidner, M. (2000). Optimistic fair exchange of digital signatures. *IEEE Journal on Selected Areas in Communications, 18*(4), 591–606. doi:10.1109/49.839935

Ateniese, G. (1999). Efficient verifiable encryption (and fair exchange) of digital signatures. *Proceedings of the 6th ACM conference on Computer and communications security* (pp. 138-146). ACM.

Ateniese, G., & Nita-Rotaru, C. (2002). Stateless-recipient certified e-mail system based on verifiable encryption. *Topics in Cryptology-CT-RSA, 2002*, 182–199.

Bao, F., Deng, R. H., & Mao, W. (1998). Efficient and Practical Fair Exchange Protocols with Off-line TTP. *Proceedings of IEEE Symposium on Security and Privacy*, (pp. 77-85).

Bao, F., Wang, G., Zhou, J., & Zhu, H. (2004). Analysis and Improvement of Micali's Fair Contract Signing Protocol. *Information Security and Privacy, 3108*, 176–187. doi:10.1007/978-3-540-27800-9_16

Baum-Waidner, B. (2001). *Optimistic asynchronous multi-party contract signing with reduced number of rounds. ICALP'01, LNCS 2076* (pp. 898–911). Berlin: Springer.

Bedi, H., & Yang, L. (2009). Fair Electronic Exchange Based on Fingerprint Biometrics. [IJISP]. *International Journal of Information Security and Privacy, III*(3), 76–106.

Bedi, H., Yang, L., & Kizza, J. (2009). Extended Abstract: Fair Electronic Exchange using Biometrics. *Proceedings of the 5th Annual Workshop on Cyber Security and Information Intelligence Research: Cyber Security and Information Intelligence Challenges and Strategies* (pp. 1-4). Oak Ridge: ACM.

Ben-Or, M., Goldreich, O., Micali, S., & Rivest, R. (1990). A fair protocol for signing contracts. *IEEE Transactions on Information Theory, 36*(1), 40–46. doi:10.1109/18.50372

Boyd, C., & Foo, E. (1998). *Off-line fair payment protocols using convertible signatures. Advances in Cryptology—ASIACRYPT'98* (pp. 271–285). New York: Springer.

Coffey, T., & Saidha, P. (1996, Jan.). Non-repudiation with mandatory proof of receipt. ACM SIGCOMM. *Computer Communication Review, 26*(1), 6–17. doi:10.1145/232335.232338

Cox, B., Tygar, J. D., & Sirbu, M. (1995). NetBill security and transaction protocol. In *Proc. 1st USENIX Workshop on Electronic Commerce*, 77–88.

Damgard, I. B. (1995). Practical and provably secure release of a secret and exchange of signatures. *Journal of Cryptology, 8*, 201–222. doi:10.1007/BF00191356

Deng, R., Gong, L., Lazar, A., & Wang, W. (1996). Practical protocol for certified electronic mail. *Journal of Network and Systems Management, 4*(3), 279–297. doi:10.1007/BF02139147

Diffie, W., & Hellman, M. E. (1976). New directions in cryptography. *IEEE Transactions on Information Theory, 22*(6), 644–654. doi:10.1109/TIT.1976.1055638

Ferrer-Gomila, J. L., Payeras-Capella, M., & Huguet-Rotger, L. (2001). Efficient optimistic n-party contract signing protocol. *Information Security Conference, LNCS 2200,*pp. 394-407, Berlin: Springer.

FIPS. (2001, November). *Federal Information Processing Standards.* Retrieved from http://csrc.nist.gov/publications/fips/fips197/fips-197.pdf

Garay, J., Jakobsson, M., & MacKenzie, P. (1999). Abuse-free optimistic contract signing. *Advances in Cryptology—CRYPTO'99,* (pp. 449--466).

Garay, J., & MacKenzie, P. (1999). Abuse-free multi-party contract signing. *1999 International Symposium on Distributed Computing, LNCS 1693,* pp. 151-165, Berlin: Springer.

Gurgens, S., Rudolph, C., & Vogt, H. (2003). On the security of fair non-repudiation protocols. *Information Security Conference (ISC),* LNCS 2851, pp. 193-207. Springer-Verlag, 2003.

Imamoto, K., & Sakurai, K. (2002). A certified e-mail system with receiver's selective usage of delivery authority. *Progress in Cryptology-INDOCRYPT, 2002,* 326–338.

ISO/IEC 13888-1 (1997a). *Information technology - Security techniques - Non-repudiation - Part 1: General*

ISO/IEC 13888-2 (1998). Information technology - Security techniques - Non-repudiation - Part 2: Mechanisms using symmetric techniques

ISO/IEC 13888-3 (1997b). Information technology - Security techniques - Non-repudiation - Part 3: Mechanisms using asymmetric techniques

Koblitz, N. (1987). Elliptic curve cryptosystems. *Mathematics of Computation, 48,* 203–209. doi:10.1090/S0025-5718-1987-0866109-5

Kremer, S., & Markowitch, O. (2000). Optimistic non-repudiable information exchange. In J. Biemond (Ed.), *21st Symp. on Information Theory in the Benelux, Werkgemeenschap Informatie- en Communicatietheorie.* Enschede (NL), Wassenaar (NL), 2000, (pp. 139–146).

Kremer, S., & Markowitch, O. (2001). Selective receipt in certified e-mail. *Progress in Cryptology-INDOCRYPT, 2001,* 136–148.

Kremer, S., Markowitch, O., & Zhou, J. (2002). An intensive survey of fair non-repudiation protocols. *Computer Communications, 25* (17), 1606-1621. Elsevier, Nov. 2002.

Markowitch, O., & Roggeman, Y. (1999). Probabilistic non-repudiation without trusted third party. *In Second Conference on Security in Communication Networks'99,* Amalfi, Italy.

Micali, S. (1997). *Certified E-mail with invisible post offices.* Presented at the RSA '97 conference (1997).

Micali, S. (2003). Simple and Fast Optimistic Protocols for Fair Electronic Exchange. In *Proceedings of the ACM Symposium on Principles of Distributed Computing,*pp. 12-19.

Miller, V. (1986). *Uses of elliptic curves in cryptography", Lecture Notes in Computer Science 218: Advances in Cryptology - CRYPTO '85* (pp. 417–426). Berlin: Springer-Verlag.

NIST. (1999, July). *Recommended Elliptic Curves for Federal Government Use.* Retrieved from http://csrc.nist.gov/csrc/fedstandards.html

NSA. (2009). *The Case for Elliptic Curve Cryptography*. Retrieved from http://www.nsa.gov/business/programs/elliptic_curve.shtml

Park, J. M., Chong, E. K., & Siegel, H. J. (2003). Constructing fair exchange protocols for e-commerce via distributed computation of RSA signatures. *Proceedings of 22ⁿᵈ Annual ACM Symposium on Principles Distributed Computing (PODC)*, pp. 172-181. New York: ACM press.

Piotrowski, K., Langendoerfer, P., & Peter, S. (2006). How public key cryptography influences wireless sensor node lifetime. In *Proceedings of the fourth ACM workshop on Security of ad hoc and sensor networks.*

Ray, I., & Ray, I. (2002, May). Fair Exchange in E-commerce. *ACM SIGecom Exchange, 3*(2), 9–17. doi:10.1145/844340.844345

Tedrick, T. (1983). How to exchange half a bit. In Chaum, D. (Ed.), *Advances in Cryptology: Proceedings of Crypto 83* (pp. 147–151). New York, London: Plenum Press.

Tedrick, T. (1985). Fair exchange of secrets. In G. R. Blakley, D. C. Chaum (Eds.), *Advances in Cryptology: Proceedings of Crypto 84, Vol. 196 of Lecture Notes in Computer Science*. Berlin, Germany: Springer-Verlag, (pp. 434–438).

Zhang, N., & Shi, Q. (1996). Achieving non-repudiation of receipt. *The Computer Journal, 39*(10), 844–853. doi:10.1093/comjnl/39.10.844

Zhou, J., Deng, R., & Bao, F. (1999). Evolution of fair non-repudiation with TTP. *ACISP: Information Security and Privacy: Australasian Conference.* (Vol. 1587 of Lecture Notes in Computer Science)Springer-Verlag, 1999, (pp. 258–269).

Zhou, J., & Gollmann, D. (1996). A fair non-repudiation protocol. In *IEEE Symposium on Security and Privacy, Research in Security and Privacy,* IEEE Computer Society, Technical Committee on Security and Privacy, IEEE Computer Security Press, Oakland, CA, 1996, (pp. 55–61).

Zhou, J., & Gollmann, D. (1997). An efficient non-repudiation protocol. In *Proceedings of The 10th Computer Security Foundations Workshop,* IEEE Computer Society Press, 1997, (pp. 126–132).

Chapter 18
Secure and Private Service Discovery in Pervasive Computing Environments

Feng Zhu
University of Alabama in Huntsville, USA

Wei Zhu
Intergraph Co, USA

ABSTRACT

In pervasive computing environments, service discovery is an essential step for computing devices to properly discover, configure, and communicate with each other. We introduce a user-centric service discovery model, called PrudentExposure, which automates authentication processes. Traditional authentication approaches requires much users' involvement. PrudentExposure encodes hundreds of authentication messages in a novel code word form. Moreover, we discuss how a progressive and probabilistic model can protect both users' and service providers' privacy. Perhaps the most serious challenge for pervasive service discovery is the integration of computing devices with people. In a challenging case, both users and service providers want the other parties to expose sensitive information first. Our model protects both users and service providers.

INTRODUCTION

Every year, billions of computing devices are built and seamlessly integrated into our surroundings and daily lives. In the near future, we will live in pervasive computing environments. In these environments, devices range from traditional PCs, printers, or servers, to devices that people carry, wear, and to the devices that are embedded into commodities and ambient environments. Smart phones, iPods, smartcards, RFID tags, and various sensors are already ubiquitous. New types of devices are emerging rapidly. It is predicted that within a decade one may interact with thousands of computing devices in pervasive computing environments.

Unlike traditional computing environments, pervasive computing poses at least two new challenges: a great number of devices and extremely dynamic computing environments. Unattended devices and service or partial failures may cause network services inaccessible. New networks

DOI: 10.4018/978-1-60960-200-0.ch018

services may be added and old services may be removed.

Service discovery is essential to address the two challenges in pervasive computing environments (Zhu, Mutka, & Ni, 2005). It enables devices and network services to properly discover, configure, and then communicate with each other via a network protocol. The protocol is called service discovery protocol. In next section, we provide more detailed explanation of service discovery protocols and discuss some representative protocols. These protocols greatly reduce the administrative overhead that users and system administrators have to conduct manually nowadays. Device driver installation and network service configuration are all automated by the protocols. Without service discovery protocols, administrative overhead for thousands of devices in one's vicinity is infeasible even for skilled system administrators in pervasive computing environments.

Moreover, service discovery protocols use soft states and lease-based service access to manage network services in the extremely dynamic pervasive computing environments. Soft state means that a service frequently updates its availability information. Lease-based service access allows a client device to access a service for a predetermined period of time. The client needs to renew the access request to further use the service. Both mechanisms gracefully handle failures of the unattended services and networks as well as service addition and removal.

Coupled with wireless networks, service discovery simplifies communication among devices and services. Without connecting cables and manually setting up devices or services, these devices and services can be discovered and configured automatically. Nevertheless, it creates three new security and privacy challenges.

First, computing environments are different. The boundaries are different. Physical boundaries may be disappeared. For example, at present, a digital camera in a bag is not accessible to others. But, if a digital camera communicates with other devices over wireless networks and runs a service discovery protocol, a stranger sits near the bag on a bus might be able to discover the digital camera and access its photos. As Ross Anderson points out, many security solutions failed because of the environments' change (Ross, 2008).

Second, unlike relatively homogeneous computing environments in enterprises, in pervasive computing environments, multiple service providers may co-exist at a place. For instance, in Alice's office, the company provides network services. When Alice and her colleagues carry and wear devices and shares with each other, they become service providers. In addition, services provided by the city might also be accessible from her office. Ideally, secure and private service discovery should determine who has privileges to discover and access services. At the same time, service discovery should prevent unauthorized users to discover and access pervasive services even they are in the vicinity. Without proper protection, privacy may be sacrificed. For example, a malicious attacker may find the presence of a person by querying whether a handheld device is in the vicinity. Attackers may also query the devices and services that one carries or wears to find his or her preferences. If an attacker discovers a medical device that one wears, the patient's health information might be inferred.

Third, as we own more and more devices and become service providers, the relationships among users, devices, services, and service providers become more and more complex. Usability is a serious challenge. It is infeasible to require users to memorize all identities and associated passwords or certificates from various service providers. It is also overwhelming for users to memorize the relationship between services and service providers.

With the new environments and new challenges in pervasive computing environments, the key requirements for service discovery are security, privacy, and good usability. For security, only legitimate users can discover and access

Figure 1. The client-service model

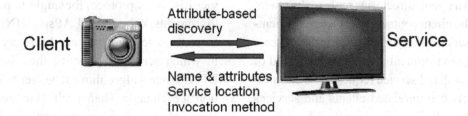

devices and services. For privacy, we need to protect service information, users' requests, users' presences information, and identities used to access devices and services. For good usability, service discovery protocols should remove the administrative overhead for owners and users to manually set up devices and services. In addition, users do not need a priori knowledge to discover and access services.

Providing security, privacy, and good usability at the same time is difficult. Usually, when security and privacy increase, usability decreases. In pervasive computing environments, however, all three requirements are necessary. We discuss two approaches to achieve the requirements.

BACKGROUND

We classify service discovery protocols into two models: client-service and client-directory-service models. Figure 1 illustrates the architecture of the client-service model. A client queries all services in the vicinity. The client specifies a list of attributes of a service that it is looking for, for example, a color display, with at least 256 colors, and resolution higher than 1024 by 768. If a service finds itself matches the request, it replies back. Then, the client starts to use the service. If there is more than one service that replies back, the client may select one service to use. With service discovery software installed, the client does not need to configure server settings. No drivers need to be pre-installed. For example, if a client is looking

for printing service, a user does not need to manually install a driver on his device to use a printer. The service discovery protocol installs the driver. Hence, people will be relieved from the burden of upgrading and installing software. In addition, service discovery provides fault tolerance. If one of the services is not available, a client will discover another service to use.

From a service's side, besides answering clients' solicitations, a service may announce its information periodically. Thus, interested clients may learn service information and select a service to use.

Client-directory-service model adds one optional layer, directories, between clients and services. Instead of asking all services directly, a client asks directories first to find related services. Figure 2 shows the architecture of the client-directory-service model.

The directories function as a surrogate for both clients and services. When directories hear a service announcement, they update and record service information. Directories can also ask

Figure 2. The client-directory-service model

around for available services. When receiving a query from a client, directories reply to the client. And then the client contacts a service. The client-directory-service model is useful in large-scale computing environments where the overhead of handling unrelated service requests and communication between unrelated clients and services are overwhelming.

Service Discovery Protocols

Research in service discovery attracts much attention in both academia and industry. In this subsection, we briefly discuss nine representative service discovery protocols. Interested readers may refer to a survey paper (Zhu, Mutka, & Ni, 2005) for detailed taxonomy and comparison of service discovery protocols.

Researchers at MIT designed Intentional Naming System (INS) (Adjie-Winoto, Schwartz, Balakrishnan, & Lilley, 1999). Unlike other approaches, services in INS are indirectly mapped to fixed service locations. INS resolves a service lookup to a service location at the delivery time. In INS/Twine (Balazinska, Balakrishnan, & Karger, 2002), service discovery is based on peer-to-peer technology, a more scalable approach to handle millions of services. Service lookups, however, may go through several directories, which may have additional search latency.

Secure Service Discovery Service (SSDS) developed at UC Berkeley puts emphasis on security and supports a huge number of services, known as wide-area support (Czerwinski, Zhao, Hodes, Joseph, & Katz, 1999). Public key and symmetric key encryptions are used for communication privacy and security. A Message Authentication Code (MAC) is used to ensure message integrity. Authentication and authorization are also addressed. For wide-area support, different hierarchical directory structures are considered. By using Bloom filters, SSDS achieves service information aggregation and filtering when building up the hierarchical directories.

IBM Research has studied and proposed a service discovery protocol for single-hop ad hoc environments, known as DEAPspace (Nidd, 2001). In contrast to other service discovery protocols in which services announce their information, DEAPspace's algorithm caches service information at each node. Then, each node broadcasts its knowledge of other services and its own services in turn. The nodes learn from each other. Service lookup is accomplished by searching one's local cache. Furthermore, energy weak devices use idle mode to save power.

Operating system vendors are shipping service discovery protocols in their operating systems. Sun Microsystems' Jini is based on Java technology (Sun Microsystems, 2003). One special feature of Jini is the mobile Java codes, which may be moved among clients, services, and directories. The advantage of Jini is its platform independency, but the disadvantage is that all the clients, services, and directories depend on the Java runtime environments directly or indirectly.

Universal Plug and Play (UPnP) is from the UPnP Forum (Miller, Nixon, Tai, & Wood, 2001). The major player is Microsoft Corporation. UPnP targets unmanaged networking environments, such as home environments. UPnP is a device-oriented service discovery protocol. All the service information and communication are in the XML format, which is platform and programming language independent, and therefore greatly increases interoperability between devices.

Apple Computer's Rendezvous is a DNS-based service discovery protocol (Cheshire, 2002). It uses the existing DNS resource record types to name and assist service discovery. Rendezvous is also known as Zero Configuration networking (Zeroconf) (Apple Computer Inc., 2003). The advantage of Rendezvous is the utilization of the ubiquity of DNS servers.

Several organizations also proposed service discovery standards. Bluetooth, from the Bluetooth Special Interest Group (SIG), enables nearby devices to communicate with each other at low cost and low power consumption (Bluetooth SIG, 2004). Part of the Bluetooth specification is the Bluetooth Service Discovery Protocol, which enables Bluetooth devices to discover each other.

The Salutation Consortium rolled out the Salutation protocol (Salutation Consortium, 1999). It is an open source protocol and is royalty-free. Its advantage is that it implements two interfaces. One interface is for applications. The other interface is designed to be independent of the transport layer, so that it is very flexible to use various underlying transport protocols and may be used in more environments. Furthermore, a mapping of Salutation over the Bluetooth Service Discovery Protocol has been specified (Miller, 1999).

Service Location Protocol (SLP) Version 2 was posted by IETF as a standard track protocol (Guttman, Perkins, Veizades, & Day, 1999). As the protocol name states, SLP only defines a way to locate a service and leaves the interaction between clients and services open. URLs are used for service locations.

Security and Privacy Support in the Service Discovery Protocols

Based on the security and privacy features, service discovery protocols may be classified into three categories. In the first category, no security and privacy features are provided by the service discovery protocol. Figure 3(a) shows this type of service discovery protocols. For example, DEAPspace and INS fall into this category.

These protocols are easy to use because there is no administrative overhead for users to discover and access the services. Easy access, however, becomes the main security and privacy problem, since anyone can discover and access anyone else' devices and services. Without security and privacy protection, devices and services are more likely to be the targets of security and privacy attacks.

In the second category, service discovery protocols directly use existing security and privacy solutions (shown in Figure 3(b)). For example, Jini, Salutation, and Bluetooth SDP fall into this category. These protocols usually require authentication. Therefore, users need to supply proper credentials such as user name and password pairs before and during the initial service discovery process. The protocols may also integrate authorization, and thus only users who have privileges can discover and access services. The procedure is the same as the traditional network service access. In pervasive computing environments, it is very difficult for users to memorize all the relations among the credentials, services, and services providers. Thus, it dramatically reduces the convenience of the service discovery protocols. In addition, if a user is not aware of a new service, she might not be able to discover the service, and therefore she will miss the opportunity to access it.

SSDS represents the third category, shown in Figure 3(c). SSDS applies strong authentication via public key certificates, encryption, and digital signatures. For access control, it uses capabilities.

Figure 3. Security, privacy, and usability features provided by the three categories of service discovery protocols (a), (b), and (c) and the PrudentExposure approach (d)

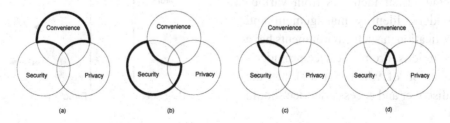

SSDS is a central server design. Suppose there are local directories that are ubiquitously available. Services register their information with local directories. On top of local directories, intermediate directories and the root directory form a hierarchical tree structure. Higher level directories aggregate service information that is available on the lower level directories. To discover and access a service, a user supplies his public key certificate for authentication and authorization. Besides security, SSDS provides convenience as well. Since wherever a user discovers services, his certificate is the only credential needed. The certificate, however, is also a disadvantage for the user. If the certificate is compromised, it affects the user for all service accesses. Privacy is also sacrificed because the server system knows when, where, and what services the user accesses.

PRUDENTEXPOSURE SERVICE DISCOVERY

PrudentExposure service discovery aims to achieve security, privacy, and good usability at the same time as shown in Figure 3(d). However, to achieve convenience, security, and privacy at the same time is challenging. As we have seen in the last section, most existing service discovery protocols either sacrifice usability to achieve security and privacy or provide good usability but sacrifice security and privacy.

Issues, Controversies, Problems

From a user's side, she may interact with hundreds or thousands of services at different places. She may have hundreds of identities from various service providers. Identity management and proper authentication in such environments have no existing solutions. From a service provider's side, determination of whether a user has the privilege to discover and access a service should be addressed.

We walk through the following scenario first. Throughout this paper, we base our discussion on this scenario.

1. At home, Bob has various wired and wireless devices, which are shared with his family members.
2. At work, Bob mainly uses his computer to perform job tasks. He shares some of his computing devices such as personal file server and printers with his colleagues. He also brings his personal devices to his office such as cell phone, MP3 player, Bluetooth headphone, etc. He might share some pieces of music on his MP3 player with his colleagues but not the cell phone. He might also access music on his colleagues' MP3 players.
3. On the way that Bob commutes between work and home, he does not want anyone riding the same bus or train to access his digital devices.

A New Service Discovery Architecture

Figure 4 illustrates a new architecture that consists of four components. Besides the components in the client-directory-service model, the PrudentExposure model has a user agent, which aggregates

Figure 4. Prudent expore model architecture

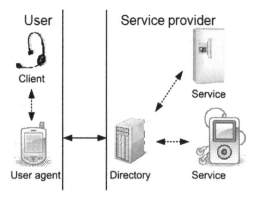

and manages all identities that a user has. A user agent may run on a PDA, a mobile phone, or other device that a user always carries or wears. The user agent acts on behalf of a user and an algorithm will select the proper identities for the authentication. A client and a user agent may establish a secure channel through side channels as discussed in (Stajano & Anderson, 1999).

Each service provider has directories. Unlike other service discovery protocols, services only register with directories that belong to the same service provider. For example, Bob may use his cell phone as a directory to manage all his wearable and handheld devices. He may use his home PC as another directory to manger the devices at home. A service and a directory establish a long term control relationship and communicate through an encrypted channel. All service accesses are via the directory and the directory instructs the services which users can access the services.

The client and the user agent may be considered as the user's side. The services and the directory may be considered as the service provider's side. Secure and proper interactions depend on the user agent and the directory. The user agent broadcasts a message to ask for available administrative domains in the vicinity. Then, all directories in the vicinity check whether the user is a valid user. If the directories find the user has privileges, they respond the user agent. Next, the directories and the user agent authenticate each other.

The novelty of PrudentExposure is that the messages exchanged between user agent and service directory are "code words" (Zhu, Mutka, & Ni, 2006). These code words are in the Bloom filter format. Hundreds of code words can easily fit in one network packet. Without loss of generality, let us assume that Bob access three domains—"Bob", "Office", and "David". David is his colleague next door. When Bob discovers a service in his office, his user agent broadcasts three code words in one network packet for the "Home", "Office", and "David" domains. The "Home" directory is not nearby, so it does not response. The "Office" directory and "David" directory hear the code words. Since the two directories understand their respective code words, they response to Bob's user agent. Another colleague, Alice, may be also in the vicinity. If Bob and Alice do not share a code word, Alice's directory does not understand any code word. And thus, it does not reply.

Generate and Verify Code Words

Figure 5 shows the code word generation. The Bloom filter is an array of bits as shown at the bottom of the figure. A code word is a combination of several bits that are set in a Bloom filter. For example, the two bits in the Bloom filter in Figure 5 consist of a code word. (All bits are initially set to zero.) We assume that a user and a service provider share a secret before a user can discover services. The shared secret and a time

Figure 5. Code word generation

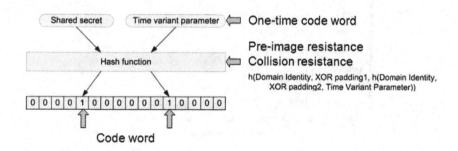

One-time code word

Pre-image resistance
Collision resistance

h(Domain Identity, XOR padding1, h(Domain Identity, XOR padding2, Time Variant Parameter))

Code word

Figure 6. Multiple code words in one message

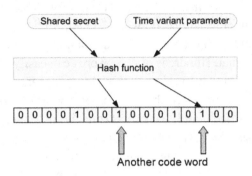

variant parameter are the two inputs to a hash function, specifically, the hash function proposed in (Bellare, Canettiy, & Krawczykz, 1996). It has the pre-image resistance and collision resistance properties. The hash result is separated into chunks. The chunk length is based on the Bloom filter size. For example, if the Bloom filter is 1024 bits, the chunk length is 10 bits. The chunk is used as an index to set bits in the Bloom filter. If a code word consists of three bits, three chunks of a hash result will be used to set the bits. Readers may find more detailed information about Bloom filter in (Bloom, 1970).

Multiple code words can be set in one Bloom filter. The user agent uses the same procedure to generate code words. The same time variant parameter and another shared secret are the two inputs as shown in Figure 6. Another code word sets two bits in the Bloom filter. If a network packet is 1,500 bytes and an average code word is 5 bits, at least 800 code words can be set in a Bloom filter.

Directories use the same procedure to generate hash results. Instead of setting the bits, directories use the same number of chunks of the hash results to verify whether all the bits of a code word are set in the Bloom filter that it receives. If all bits are set, a directory considers that there is a code word match. However, different chunks of the hash result may set the same bit in the Bloom filter. Similarly, a bit may be set by another code word. This implies that the test of domain match may result in false positive cases. The probability of reporting false positive matches when the user is not a user of this domain is:

$$P(match/nonmember) = \left(\frac{m}{n}\right)^k,$$

where n is the size of the Bloom filter, m is the number of bits set in the Bloom filter, and k is the number of bits for a domain.

The false positive cases are under user's control. Longer code words or larger Bloom filter size reduces the number of false positive cases. Figure 7 illustrates the change of the false positive rate as the length of the Bloom filter and the number of bits in a Bloom filter change. (Suppose that there are 500 bits set in a Bloom filter (m=500).)

Figure 7. False positive rate changes as k and n change

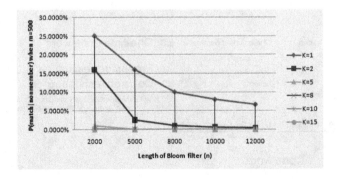

As the code word length increases, the false positive rate reduces very quickly. Similarly, as the Bloom filter size increases, the false positive rate decreases quickly.

By using one way hash functions, it is computationally difficult to find the shared secrets from the Bloom filters. More detailed analysis of mathematical properties, the secure service discovery protocol, threat analysis, and formal verification are in the authors' another work (Zhu, Mutka, & Ni, 2006).

The PrudentExposure approach is efficient. The secure service discovery protocol was implemented on PDAs with 200MHz CPU, 64MB RAM, and 2Mb wireless connections. Experiment results show that generating 100 code words takes less than 16ms, while it takes a directory about 5ms to verify a code word.

In summary, PrudentExposure achieves security via code words, authentication, and encrypted communication. Only users who share secrets with service providers can discover services. Privacy including users' and service providers' identities and their presence information is protected because those who do not know the shared secrets do not understand the communication. PrudentExposure automates the authentication process, and thus users do not need a priori knowledge to discover services and memorize hundreds of identities.

PROGRESSIVE AND PROBABILISTIC EXPOSURE

Let us revisit the example of Bob's cases and think of the following question. If Bob needs to access an electronic book on company's file server, why does David need to know what Bob is looking for? Even if Bob has a credential from David, David doesn't have the service that Bob is looking for at this time. The communication between Bob and David is wasted, until Bob's user agent learns that he cannot get the service from David. Privacy information such as his presence and his service request is unnecessarily exposed to David. If the "need to know" principle is applied, the problem will be solved. If David does not have the electronic book that Bob is looking for, Bob does not query David's directory for services.

Issues, Controversies, Problems

It is difficult in pervasive computing environments to apply the "need to know" principle. The environments are very dynamic. For example, David does not share electronic books with Bob. Tomorrow, he may share his books with Bob. It is infeasible for Bob to memorize all service and service provider relationships and to be aware of up-to-date service information.

For service providers, the ideal solution is that a user reveals her request first. If a service provider does not provide the service, she simply doesn't respond. Similarly, for users, the ideal solution is that service providers announce the services provided first. And then, the users can determine which service provider to contact. But who should reveal information first? This is a "chicken-and-egg" problem because both parties want the other party to expose their information first. How should they communicate and establish trust?

Progressively Expose Service Information and Identities

Let's further analyze the PrudentExposure model. A user queries all service providers that she shares a secret with. If the "need to know" principle is applied, a subset of the service providers need to be identified that the user shares secrets with and also provide the requested service as shown in the left side of Figure 8. Similarly, a service provider is interested in identifying a subset of users that she shares secrets with, who request an existing service, and who have privilege to access the service, as shown in the right side of Figure 8.

A novel idea is to expose users' and service providers' identity information, users' service

Figure 8. Find appropriate service providers and users during service discovery

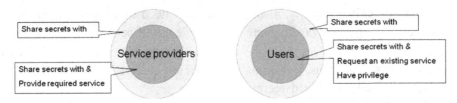

requests, and service providers' service information progressively and in multiple rounds (Zhu, Zhu, Mutka, & Ni, 2007). In each round, few bits of information are exchanged. Both a user and a service provider check whether there is any mismatch, as shown in Figure 9. The user checks whether a service provider knows the shared secret and provide the requested service, while the service provider checks whether the user knows the shared secret, has privilege, and requests an existing service. If there is any mismatch, the user and the service provider will quit the service discovery process. Since they exchanged only partial information, neither the user nor the service provider is certain about the sensitive information that she received from the other party.

During the service discovery process, a user and a service provider exchange encrypted information. Like the PrudentExposure approach, they speak code words to verify whether the other

party is the party that they want to contact. In addition, they encrypt service information and service requests before they send to the other party by using one-time secret. If the other party knows the shared secret, she can properly decrypt the information.

To generate code words and one-time secrets, a similar method that discussed in Figure 5 may be used. For code word generation, a shared secret and a time variant parameter are the two inputs to a hash function. Instead of setting the bits in a Bloom filter, the bits are directly used. In each round, several bits of the hash result is used and exchanged. Figure 10 shows an example, in which a user and a service provider share a secret and exchange a code word. The user sends the first four bits and the service provider verifies. After the service provider finds that the four bits match her code word, she sends the next two bits. Then, the user verifies. Since the user and the service provider share a secret, they keep finding the bits of the code word match. After multiple rounds, both the service provider and the user believe that the other party is extremely likely to understand the code word. Therefore, they establish the connection to provide and use the service. If a user and a service provider do not share a secret, they will find mismatch of some bits, and thus they quit the service discovery process.

Figure 10 shows a simplified version. In the actual service discovery, code words, encrypted service information, and encrypted service requests are exchanged at the same time. The detailed encoding scheme and the strategies to exchange

Figure 9. Progressively expose sensitive information between a service provider and a user

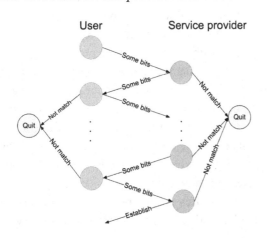

Figure 10. An example that a service provider and a user exchange code words

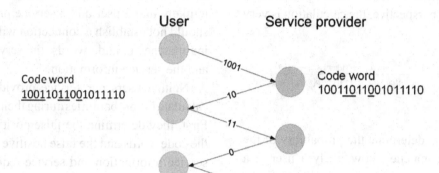

the bits can be found in (Zhu, Zhu, Mutka, & Ni, 2007).

The Probabilistic Exposures and Strategies

The progressive exposure, shown in Figure 9, may be converted into a Markov chain. Figure 11 illustrates the process. The system starts with a user sending some bits of a code word and some bits of a service request to a service provider. Then, service provider checks. If there is no mismatch, the service provider sends a few bits of the code word

and service information for the user to verify. The process repeats. If they should establish a service access session, they will always reach that state. If they should not establish a session, there is a possibility that in each step the bits exchanged are match. These matches are the false positive cases.

The probability of the false positive matches can be calculated. Without loss of generality, the following discussion is focused on code words. The equations to calculate the probability of false positive matches for the encrypted service information or service requests can be easily deduct from the equations below. Equation 1 shows the

Figure 11. The progressive exposure in the form of a Markov chain

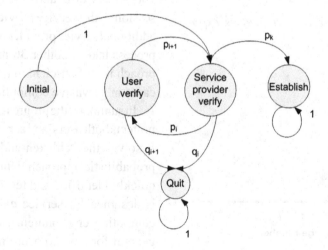

calculation from a service provider's perspective. From a user's perspective, the calculation is very similar.

$$p(not\ user\ |\ match) = \frac{p(match\ |\ not\ user) \times (1 - p(user))}{p(match\ |\ not\ user)(1 - p(user)) + p(user)}$$

(1)

Two factors determine the probability of the false positive matches: how likely a user is a valid user, *p(user)*, and the probability to find a code word match when a user is not a valid user, *p(match|not user)*. The probability, *p(user)*, is environment dependent, whereas the probability *p(match|not user)* depends on the design of the code word. Specifically, it depends on the number of bits that have been exchanged and the number of code words that a user has as shown in Equation 2. Plug in *p(user)* and *p(match|not user)*, the equation to calculate the probability of false positive matches is acquired.

$$p(match\ |\ not\ user) = 1 - (1 - \frac{1}{2^{number\ of\ bits}})^{number\ of\ codewords}$$

(2)

By further using the properties of the Markov chain, it can be shown that the false positive cases decrease exponentially. Figure 12 shows an example that after few rounds, the number of

Figure 12. False positive case decreases exponentially

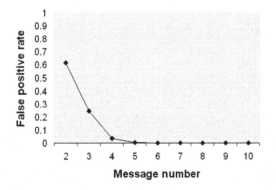

false positive cases approaches zero. Thus, it is unlikely that a user and a service provider who should not establish a connection will keep finding matches in code words, the service request, and the service information.

Neither users nor service providers need to calculate the probabilities during their interaction. First, they determine the false positive rates for the code words and the false positive rates for the service information and service requests. Then, they simply conduct table lookups. The tables are pre-calculated with the information about the number of rounds and number of bits that they need to exchange in each round. In general, a user and a service provider exchange one or two bits of a code word, service information, and a service request in a message. Although a user may interact with many service providers in some environments and they exchange few bits of information in a round, the service discovery process always converges as proved in (Zhu, Zhu, Mutka, & Ni, 2007).

Exchange partial information in multiple rounds minimizes unnecessary privacy exposure. But, the approach does introduce communication overhead between users and service providers. One round of messages becomes multiple rounds. Experiments on a set of similar PDAs (200MHz CPU, 64MB RAM, and 2 Mb wireless connections) have shown that the overhead to generate 100 code words and establish a service access session with a service provider takes 100ms. Each additional service provider involved in a discovery process takes another 30 ms. Therefore, the approach is still efficient in most service discovery cases in pervasive computing environments.

In summary, the progressive exposure approach protects both users' and service providers' privacy. It solves the "chicken-and-egg" problem via a probabilistic approach. Unnecessary exposure is quickly identified and terminated. The approach is designed for service discovery for pervasive computing environments, but it can be used in general for any exposure negotiation when two parties expect the other party to exposure information first.

FUTURE RESEARCH DIRECTIONS

The two approaches that we discussed in this paper achieve security, privacy, and good usability at the same time in general. Often in different environments or situations, there may be different emphasis on different aspects. One design might give more weight on security, whereas the other may consider usability as the highest priority. As we see in the past that emphasis on only one aspect usually sacrifices other aspects. Thus, new designs need to be properly balanced on all three aspects.

Service discovery in different environments may use different strategies for authentication and information exposure. Ideally, we want to expose appropriate amount of information to the appropriate party at the appropriate time. Nevertheless, there is no one solution fits all situations. In different situations, one might use completely different strategies for information exposure, for example, discovery of a service for medical emergency and discovery of a toy store location in a shopping mall. There is still lack of approaches to automatically select or help users to select the best strategies.

Users have many identities in pervasive computing environments. For the service providers that they have interacted before, users may have identities that associated with the service providers. Both the PrudentExposure and the progressive exposure approaches address such situations. In many situations, users and service providers are unfamiliar with each other. Users may not have identities to authenticate with the service providers. Service discovery in such environments is still an open problem. For example, one may travel to a country for the first time. It is very likely that service providers and environments are unfamiliar to the user. Although public key infrastructure might be a solution (Zhu, Mutka, & Ni, 2003),

it seems less likely that the name and public key binding provided by the public key infrastructure will solve all problems.

Trust is another critical challenge for service discovery in pervasive computing environments. The more information that a user exchanges with a service provider, the more trust they establish. Nevertheless, trust and privacy may be a conflict, since the more information exchanged the less privacy the user and the service provider may maintain. It might become very difficult for unfamiliar users and service providers to solve the conflict.

CONCLUSION

In pervasive computing environments, service discovery protocols need to provide security, privacy, and good usability at the same time. Unlike traditional computer environments, it is difficult for users to manually handle hundreds of identities and memorize complex relationships among users, services, and service providers. PrudentExposure automates the authentication process by generating and exchanging code words. Via three messages, users and service providers efficiently determine the legitimacy of each other. The approach is scalable to support hundreds of code words in one network packet.

The progressive service discovery approach extended PrudentExposure model. It applies the "need to know" principle in service discovery among users and service providers who have incomplete information about each other. Based on probabilistic and partial exposure, it protects the privacy of both users' and service providers'.

ACKNOWLEDGMENT

This paper is selected from the book, Yang and Nemati (Ed.), (in press), *Applied Cryptography for Cyber Security and Defense: Information*

Encryption and Cyphering, IGI Global. We are grateful to Guest Editor Dr. Li Yang and anonymous reviewers for their valuable comments that greatly helped us improve this paper.

REFERENCES

Adjie-Winoto, W., Schwartz, E., Balakrishnan, H., & Lilley, J. (1999). *The design and implementation of an intentional naming system*. Paper presented at the 17th ACM Symposium on Operating Systems Principles (SOSP '99), Kiawah Island, SC.

Apple Computer Inc. (2003). *Rendezvous*. Retrieved from http://developer.apple.com/macosx/rendezvous/

Balazinska, M., Balakrishnan, H., & Karger, D. D. (2002). INS/Twine: A scalable peer-to-peer architecture for intentional resource discovery. In *Proceedings of Pervasive 2002 - International Conference on Pervasive Computing*, Zurich, Switzerland (pp. 195-210). Springer-Verlag.

Bellare, M., Canettiy, R., & Krawczykz, H. (1996). Keying hash functions for message authentication. In *Advances in Cryptology–CRYPTO '96* (LNCS 1109, pp. 1-15).

Bloom, B. (1970). Space/time trade-offs in hash coding with allowable errors. *Communications of the ACM, 13*(7), 422–426. doi:10.1145/362686.362692

Bluetooth, S. I. G. (2004). Specification of the bluetooth system. Retrieved from http://www.bluetooth.org/

Cheshire, S. (2002). *Discovering named instances of abstract services using DNS, Apple Computer*. Retrieved from http://files.dns-sd.org/draft-cheshire-dnsext-dns-sd.txt

Czerwinski, S., Zhao, B. Y., Hodes, T., Joseph, A., & Katz, R. (1999). *An architecture for a secure service discovery service*. Paper presented at the Fifth Annual International Conference on Mobile Computing and Networks (MobiCom '99), Seattle, WA.

Guttman, E., Perkins, C., Veizades, J., & Day, M. (1999). Service location protocol, version 2. Retrieved from http://www.ietf.org/rfc/rfc2608.txt

Miller, B. (1999). Mapping salutation architecture APIs to bluetooth service discovery layer, bluetooth SIG. Retrieved from http://www.salutation.org/whitepaper/BtoothMapping.PDF

Miller, B. A., Nixon, T., Tai, C., & Wood, M. D. (2001). Home networking with universal plug and play. *IEEE Communications Magazine*, (December): 104–109. doi:10.1109/35.968819

Nidd, M. (2001). Service discovery in DEAPspace. *IEEE Personal Communications, August*, 39-45.

Ross, A. (2008). *Security engineering: A guide to building dependable distributed systems* (2nd ed.). New York: Wiley.

Salutation Consortium. (1999). Salutation architecture specification. Retrieved from ftp://ftp.salutation.org/salute/sa20e1a21.ps

Stajano, F., & Anderson, R. (1999). *The resurrecting duckling: Security issues for ad-hoc wireless networks*. Paper presented at the 7th International Workshop on Security protocols, Cambridge, UK.

Sun Microsystems. (2003). *Jini technology core platform specification*. Retrieved from http://wwws.sun.com/software/jini/specs/

Zhu, F., Mutka, M., & Ni, L. (2003). *Splendor: A secure, private, and location-aware service discovery protocol supporting mobile services*. Paper presented at the 1st IEEE Annual Conference on Pervasive Computing and Communications, Fort Worth, TX.

Zhu, F., Mutka, M., & Ni, L. (2005). Service discovery in pervasive computing environments. *IEEE Pervasive Computing / IEEE Computer Society [and] IEEE Communications Society, 4*(4), 81–90. doi:10.1109/MPRV.2005.87

Zhu, F., Mutka, M., & Ni, L. (2006). A private, secure and user-centric information exposure model for service discovery protocols. *IEEE Transactions on Mobile Computing, 5*(4), 418–429. doi:10.1109/TMC.2006.1599409

Zhu, F., Zhu, W., Mutka, M., & Ni, L. (2007). Private and secure service discovery via progressive and probabilistic exposure. *IEEE Transactions on Parallel and Distributed Systems, 18*(11), 1565–1577. doi:10.1109/TPDS.2007.1075

Chapter 19
Preserving Privacy in Mining Quantitative Associations Rules

Madhu V. Ahluwalia
University of Maryland Baltimore County, USA

Aryya Gangopadhyay
University of Maryland Baltimore County, USA

Zhiyuan Chen
University of Maryland Baltimore County, USA

ABSTRACT

Association rule mining is an important data mining method that has been studied extensively by the academic community and has been applied in practice. In the context of association rule mining, the state-of-the-art in privacy preserving data mining provides solutions for categorical and Boolean association rules but not for quantitative association rules. This article fills this gap by describing a method based on discrete wavelet transform (DWT) to protect input data privacy while preserving data mining patterns for association rules. A comparison with an existing kd-tree based transform shows that the DWT-based method fares better in terms of efficiency, preserving patterns, and privacy.

INTRODUCTION

Association rule mining is an important knowledge discovery technique that is used in many real-life applications. As a motivating example, we use the retail business where data collected at a central site is routinely accessed by vendors to better plan and execute their logistics processes. The most commonly used data-mining task in the retail industry is association rule mining. In the simplest cases where transactions consist of market basket data, association rules reflect buying habits of customers. By counting the different items that customers place in their shopping baskets, association rules indicate items that are frequently purchased together by customers.

In addition to the categorical association rules (over items), association rules can be also defined over quantitative values. For example, a retailer's data may hold information on quantities, discounts, and prices. A hypothetical sample of this data is shown in Table 1. Let Q be quantity, P be price, and D be discount. Figure 1 shows some quantitative association rules. A retailer may

DOI: 10.4018/978-1-60960-200-0.ch019

benefit from sharing such data with a wholesaler because such association rules may be utilized to improved supply-chain efficiency resulting in decreased pricing from the wholesaler. However, retailers may not want to reveal the exact price/unit of an item due to concerns over market competition. Thus this article focuses on preserving both the quantitative association rules and the privacy of data.

Problems with existing approaches: Privacy preserving association rule mining has been studied for categorical data by (Evfimevski et al., July 2002; Lin et al., 2007; Rizvi et al., 2002). In all these cases a randomization technique is applied to distort the original data and enforce privacy. Evfimevski et al. (2002) and Rizvi et al. (2002) (Evfimevski et al., 2002; Rizvi et al., 2002) conduct randomization on a per-transaction basis, i.e.

each original transaction is perturbed by inserting items into it or deleting items from it. Lin et al. (Lin et al., 2007) add whole new transactions to the set of original transactions. However, it is unclear how these techniques may be applied to quantitative data. For example, we cannot insert or delete items for quantitative data. Further, as pointed out in Zhang (2004), these techniques may reveal several actual items to an adversary, if a transaction consists of 10 or more items.

For transactions consisting of numerical items, Chen et al. (2005) proposed a solution that converts quantitative attributes to Boolean attributes. However, mining Boolean association rules creates a disclosure risk because input values of correlated items are restricted to 0 and 1. Also, large data sets such as point-of-sale data are not suitable for generating Boolean association rules.

One may try to use a random perturbation method (Agrawal & Srikant, 2000; Agrawal & Aggarwal, 2001) to add a random noise to the quantitative values. However, such techniques may not preserve the correlations between different attributes (e.g., between price, quantity, and discount). Thus it is unclear whether such techniques may work for quantitative association rules. Another alternative is to use micro-aggregation-based techniques. For instance, a condensation approach was proposed in (Aggarwal et al., 2004). It splits the original data into multiple groups of predefined size k. Synthetic data are generated to preserve the mean, covariance, and correlations of each group. However, there are two problems withfor this approach. First, the initial seeds used

Table 1. Sample data to illustrate quantitative association rules

Row_No.	Quantity	Price	Discount
1	25.00	125.99	0.16
2	19.00	76.95	0.12
3	8.00	49.99	0.00
4	27.00	119.49	0.17
5	15.00	51.99	0.15
6	6.00	32.45	0.05
7	47.00	150.05	0.21
8	18.00	64.25	0.13
9	35.00	105.87	0.30
10	5.00	15.25	0.10

Figure 1. Quantitative association rules derived from Table 1

> The following association rules can be derived from the sample data in Table 1.
> 1. If Q > 20 and P > 100 then D in (20%, 30%] (confidence 50%, support 20%). Rows 7 and 9 support this rule.
> 2. If Q in (10, 20] and P in (50, 100] then D in (10%, 20%] (confidence 100%, support 30%). This rule is obtained from rows 2,5, and 8.
> 3. If Q in [0,10] and P in [0, 50] then D in [0-10%] (confidence 100%, support 30%). Rows 3,6 and 10 generate this rule.

to generate these groups are randomly selected. Second, there is no backtracking mechanism to reorganize groups, in case the initial seeds are poorly selected. Therefore, there is no guarantee that this method will maximize within-groups data homogeneity. In this article, we suggest a method that maximizes within-groups data homogeneity and hence better preserves association rules.

Another micro-aggregation technique is proposed by (Li et al., 2006). It builds a kd-tree to mask a confidential attribute. This method recursively selects a non-sensitive attribute (attribute without sensitive information) with the largest variance. It splits the data into two groups using the median of the selected attribute. The splitting process continues on the partitioned sets until the leaf nodes contain the values for the sensitive attribute. Values of each attribute at a leaf are then replaced by the average of attribute values at that leaf. Figure 2 shows an example of application of this approach to the data in Table 1. Price and quantity are selected as splitting attributes based on the maximum variance criteria. The size and the value of a bubble represent the amount of discount, which may be considered a sensitive attribute (attribute with sensitive information).

However, the next example will illustrate the problem of the kd-tree approach. Table 2(a) shows the rules derived from the kd-tree perturbed sample data of Table 1. Using the kd-tree approach, the first two rules are lost due to changes in the discount values. Rule one—if Q > 20 and P > 100 then D in (20%, 30%] (confidence 50%, support 20%)—is supported by row 7, 9 in original data. The kd-tree transformation does not have a single row that satisfies this rule. Similarly, rule two - if Q in (10, 20] and P in (50, 100] then D in (10%, 20%] (confidence 100%, support 30%) is supported by row 2, 5, 8 in the original data. The kd-tree puts rows 3, 5, 8 in the same leaf. The average discount for these three rows is now 0.09, which no longer satisfies rule two (the rule says the discount is in 0.1 to 0.2). Rule 3 _ if Q in [0,10] and P in [0, 50] then D in [0-10%] (confidence 100%, support 30%) supported by rows 3,6 and 10 is the only one retained by the kd-tree approach.

The main problem of the kd-tree approach is that it works in a top-down and greedy fashion. Thus it works well only if attribute values are correlated. However, it may not work well if the attribute values are not strongly correlated. For example, in Table 1, discount is not strongly correlated with price and quantity. kd-tree approach tries to group products with similar price or quantity together, but these products may not have similar discount values. For instance, as shown in Figure 2, the product with discount 0.12 and

Figure 2. Plot of sample data in Table 1

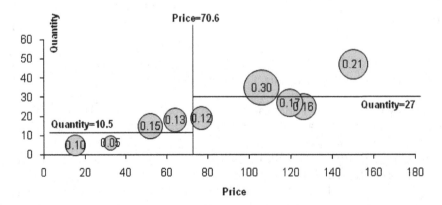

Table 2. Transformations of sample data in Table 1

(b) DWT transformed data			
Row_No.	Quantity	Price	Discount
3	11.50	50.99	0.03
6	5.50	23.85	0.03
10	5.50	23.85	0.11
2	18.50	70.60	0.11
8	18.50	70.60	0.14
5	11.50	50.99	0.14
1	26.00	138.02	0.17
4	26.00	112.68	0.17
7	41.00	138.02	0.26
9	41.00	112.68	0.26
(a) Kd-tree transformed data			
Row_No.	Quantity	Price	Discount
1	33.00	131.84	0.18
2	27.00	91.41	0.21
3	13.67	55.41	0.09
4	33.00	131.84	0.18
5	13.67	55.41	0.09
6	5.50	23.85	0.08
7	33.00	131.84	0.18
8	13.67	55.41	0.09
9	27.00	91.41	0.21
10	5.50	23.85	0.08

0.13 are put into two different groups because they have very different price values.

Our approach: In this article, we propose a bottom-up approach that uses discrete wavelet transforms (DWT) (Mallat, 1989) to hide sensitive values and preserve quantitative association rules. This first step of this approach is to sort each attribute individually and then performs a discrete wavelet transform on that attribute. This method then retains the approximation coefficients and replicates them to each row (the detail coefficients are pruned). Due to the sorting step, similar values are grouped together for each attribute. Note that this is different from kd-tree approach where similar values are grouped together only for the splitting attribute. Consequently, the underlying data patterns are preserved to a great degree of accuracy. Privacy of raw data is also preserved due to the pruning of detail coefficients (the exact data cannot be reconstructed just from the approximation coefficients. For example, Table 2 (b) shows the data perturbed by our approach. All rules in Figure 1 are retained by our approach. Rule one is kept with the same support and confidence. Rule two is kept with the same support (by rows 2, 5, and 8) but slightly lower confidence (the new confidence is 75%). The support of rule 3 drops to 10% and the confidence drops to 50%, but the rule is still kept.

Contributions: The contributions are summarized below:

- This article proposes a solution to preserve quantitative association rules while preserving privacy of numerical data. To the best of our knowledge, this is the first attempt at this problem. We believe that this problem has significant relevance in many applications areas such as supply chain management.

- The article presents empirical evidence obtained through experimental evaluation to compare the suggested method with the existing kd-tree method. The results demonstrate the superiority of our proposed method.

The rest of the article is organized as follows. Section 2 gives an overview of the closely related work. Section 3 introduces wavelet transforms. Section 4 proposes the methodology. Section 5 reports empirical results and section 6 concludes the article.

Related Work

A rich body of work on privacy preserving mining exists. Depending on the type of data privacy problems being addressed, these studies can be divided into two categories: ones that try to hide the data values when the data is sent to a third party for analyses (Agrawal et al., 2001; Agrawal et al., 2000) and others that try to hide the identity of entities when publishing data (Bayardo & Agrawal, 2005; Samarati 2001). This article falls in the first category.

To date, existing literature on the first category, focus on random perturbation approaches that add or multiply random noise to the data such that individual data values are distorted while the underlying distribution can be reconstructed with fair degree of accuracy (Agrawal & Srikant, 2000; Rizvi & Haritsa, 2002; Evfimevski et al., 2002).

There has also been work on using secure multiparty computation techniques for a wide range of data mining algorithms to address the privacy is-

sue in distributed environment (Vaidya & Clifton, 2002; Kantarcioglu & Clifton, 2004). They share intermediate mining results to calculate mining functions securely over multiple sources. We refer to (Vaidya et al., (2006) for a detailed discussion on research in PPDM. There has been work for on secure association rule mining in distributed environment. These methods build global mining models securely by following secure multi-party computation protocols (Kantarcioglu & Clifton, 2004; Vaidya & Clifton, 2002). However, this article focuses on the case when the data is sent to a third party for analysis and we assume that the data owner either does not have the capability or is not willing to do the mining himself. This assumption is often true in supply chain management environment where there are a large number of small retailers.

Security issues in the general framework of association rule mining have been pursued with much interest in recent years (Atallah et al., 1999; Evfimevski et al., 2002; Kantarcioglu & Clifton, 2004; Lin & Liu, 2007; Menon, 2007; Oliveira & Zaiane, 2002; Rizvi & Haritsa, 2002; Vaidya & Clifton, 2002; Verykios et al., 2004). The bulk of the past work on such issues deals with preventing disclosure of sensitive rules by a potential adversary (Atallah et al., 1999; Menon, 2007; Oliveira & Zaiane, 2002; Verykios et al., 2004). This work complements ours since it addresses concerns about output privacy, whereas our focus is on the privacy of the input data while disclosing the output. Since our proposed approach is more closely related to data hiding, we will limit our discussion on prior work to input data hiding.

Evfimevski et al. (2002), Lin and Liu (2007), and Rizvi and Haritsa (2002) propose solutions for mining association rules from transactions where the data is randomized to preserve privacy of individual transactions. However these solutions only work for transactions consisting of categorical items and are not applicable to quantitative data.

Random perturbation has also been used to preserve the privacy of input data in classification rule mining (Agrawal & Aggarwal, 2001; Agrawal & Srikant, 2000). Here the data is predominantly numerical. But, as in the case of categorical data, both privacy and mining results are adversely affected by randomly perturbing quantitative data. Kargupta et al. (2003) show that the privacy in perturbation approaches can be breached by the application of Independent Component Analysis (ICA) which is used extensively to split source signals from output signals. From (Wilson, 2003), it is also clear that both additive and multiplicative perturbation alter the relationships between confidential and non-confidential attributes. Therefore, generating association rules from quantitative data, which is randomly perturbed, is not advisable.

A method that does preserve correlations between attributes is suggested in (Liu, et al. 2006). It multiplies the original data with a lower dimension random matrix, but is also problem-prone, because dimensionality reduction changes the data's original form or domain. Further, this method is suggested for a distributed environment, whereas the focus in the current study is on centralized data.

Discrete Wavelet Transforms

Discrete wavelet transform is used to analyze data by decomposing it into different frequency components and then studying each component with a resolution matched to its scale. Wavelet algorithms process data at different scales or resolutions. Fine resolutions capture local features of data and coarse resolutions capture its global features. Thus information variation in the data at different levels of decomposition is obtained (Graps, 1995).

This article uses commonly used Haar wavelets due to its simplicity. For an input represented by a list of 2^n numbers, the Haar wavelet transform simply pairs up input values, storing the difference and passing the sum. The difference is called the detail coefficients and the sum is called the approximation coefficients[1]. This process can be

repeated recursively over the approximation coefficients in the previous level. In this article, we only apply one level of Haar wavelet transform.

We use DWT in our algorithm to preserve patterns and privacy of the original data. Our motivation of using DWT is based on several properties of DWT.

1.   DWT allows a multi-resolution representation of discrete data (Mallat, 1989). Important patterns in the high resolution data are usually preserved in the low resolution data (i.e., the approximation coefficients).
2.   We can prune detail coefficients to provide privacy protection. Without the detail coefficients, the exact values of original data cannot be reconstructed from transformed data because there would be infinitely many solutions towards solving for the original data from the approximation coefficients.
3.   DWT can be done very efficiently (in $O(n)$ time for n input data points).

Methodology

This section presents our approach. Our approach is based on discrete wavelet transformation. The main challenge of using DWT in this context is the order dependency of wavelet transforms. In other words, completely different sets of coefficients are generated if the dataset is ordered differently. We have devised a method that optimally groups similar data values together such that association rules can be preserved. The key idea is to sort the data on each attribute such that similar values on that attribute are brought together.

The pseudocode of our algorithm is shown in Figure 3. Let D be a data set with n rows and m columns. We also assume that all of these columns are continuous-valued. Thus, d_{ij} represents the value for column j and row i of D. Let C_j be the values of the j-th column. For each column C_j, step 1 sorts the values in C_j in ascending order.

Step 2 applies DWT over sorted C_j. We use one level of Haar Wavelet transform in this article. Essentially the approximation coefficients are the average of every two values and the detail coefficients are the differences between the two values divided by two.

Only the approximation coefficients are stored in an array C^T_j. There are n/2 such coefficients. Step 3 to 7 copy these values to the j-th column of the output (i.e., matrix P). Since there are n rows but only n/2 coefficients, each coefficient is copied to two consecutive rows. For example, the first approximation coefficient (which is computed from the first two rows in original data) is copied to both row 1 and row 2 in the output. In case there are odd number of rows, the last row just stores the last approximation coefficient (no duplication is needed). These steps are repeated over each column and finally P is returned.

Figure 4 illustrates the algorithm shown in Figure 3. Figure 4(a) shows all rows in Table 1 sorted by the first attribute Quantity. Figure 4(b) shows the data after applying DWT (we use Haar wavelet) and duplication of approximation coefficients on Quantity. Figures 4(c) and (d) show the results after processing the attribute Price. It

is obvious from Figures 4(a) and (c) that after sorting, similar values of Quantity and Price are brought together.

The privatization algorithm can be implemented in two ways. The first method is called not-in-place DWT (Nip DWT). It materializes the intermediate result matrix. It sorts the original matrix by the ith column and stores the result in an intermediate matrix. In a matrix with m attributes and n rows, the cost of sort is $O(n \log n)$. The cost of storing the intermediate matrix is $O(mn)$ for each round. Since there are m rounds (one per column), the total cost is $O((mn + n \log n) * m) = O(m^2 n + mn \log n)$. Hence, the cost of the Nip DWT grows quadratically with the number of attributes. As a result, for a large number of attributes, the execution time of the Nip DWT is very high.

The second method is called in-place DWT (Ip DWT). It does not store the intermediate results. Instead, it modifies the original matrix directly. An array is used to store the rows IDs in the sort order after the matrix is sorted on the ith column. As an example, consider rows sorted by Quantity attribute in Figure 4(a). The IDs of the first two rows in the sort order is 10 and 6. Thus the

Figure 3. Algorithm for data privatization

INPUT: a dataset D with n rows and m columns, such that d_{ij} represents the ith row and j^{th} column of D; a null set P.

OUTPUT: a privatized database P with n rows and m columns, such that p_{ij} represents the ith row and j^{th} column of P.

```
BEGIN
        For each column Cj ∈ D do
        {
 1. Sort D by column Cj
 2. Store only the approximation coefficients in CTj   // The number of values (rows)
        in CTj is n/2
        i = 1
 3. while 2i <= n
 4.     P2i-1,j = CTij   -- CTij is the ith value in CTj
 5.     P2i,j = CTij
 6.     i = i+1
 7. end
 8. if n is odd
 9.     Pn,j = CT(n+1)/2,j
 10. end
        }
    Return P
End
```

Figure 4. Example of executing the privatization algorithm

RowNo.	Quantity	Price	Discount
10	5.00	15.25	0.10
6	6.00	32.45	0.05
3	8.00	49.99	0.00
5	15.00	51.99	0.15
8	18.00	64.25	0.13
2	19.00	76.95	0.12
1	25.00	125.99	0.16
4	27.00	119.49	0.17
9	35.00	105.87	0.30
7	47.00	150.05	0.21

(a) After sort on Quantity

RowNo.	Quantity	Price	Discount
10	5.50	15.25	0.10
6	5.50	32.45	0.05
3	11.50	49.99	0.00
5	11.50	51.99	0.15
8	18.50	64.25	0.13
2	18.50	76.95	0.12
1	26.00	125.99	0.16
4	26.00	119.49	0.17
9	41.00	105.87	0.30
7	41.00	150.05	0.21

(b) After DWT and duplication on Quantity

RowNo.	Quantity	Price	Discount
10	5.50	15.25	0.10
6	5.50	32.45	0.05
3	11.50	49.99	0.00
5	11.50	51.99	0.15
8	18.50	64.25	0.13
2	18.50	76.95	0.12
9	41.00	105.87	0.30
4	26.00	119.49	0.17
1	26.00	125.99	0.16
7	41.00	150.05	0.21

(c) After sort on Price

RowNo.	Quantity	Price	Discount
10	5.50	23.85	0.10
6	5.50	23.85	0.05
3	11.50	50.99	0.00
5	11.50	50.99	0.15
8	18.50	70.60	0.13
2	18.50	70.60	0.12
9	41.00	112.68	0.30
4	26.00	112.68	0.17
1	26.00	138.02	0.16
7	41.00	138.02	0.21

(de) After DWT and duplication on Price

method directly modifies the Quantity attribute of rows 10 and 6 by taking the average. Thus the value of the Quantity attribute in both rows becomes 5. Since in each round the method only needs to update the ith column, the cost of updating values is $O(n)$. For m attributes, the total cost of Ip DWT reduces to $O(mn + mn \log n)$. The space overhead to store the row IDs is $O(n)$.

The privacy of the proposed method comes from the pruning of detail coefficients (without detail coefficients, the exact data values cannot be reconstructed). The method also generates a dataset where there are at least two rows that have identical values for any column. This produces the effect of 2-anonymity for each individual column. If necessary, we can apply more levels of DWT and produce column-level k-anonymity with the following conditions: $k = 2^i$, and $n \geq k \geq 2$. As we increase the level of decomposition, we expect a gradual degradation in the preservation of the patterns in the original dataset, but a higher privacy of the original data values. The next section will show through experiments that empirically this method preserves association rules and achieves a high degree of privacy.

Experimental Evaluation

This section presents the experimental evaluation of the proposed method. The major findings are summarized as follows:

- The proposed DWT-based method preserves the patterns of the original data to a large extent (i.e. up to 80% in most cases). A comparison with the kd-tree method proves the superiority of the DWT-based method for pattern preservation.
- The proposed method achieves a high degree of data privacy. A comparison with privacy achieved by the kd-tree and random projection methods shows that the DWT-based privacy fares better.
- Finally, the DWT-based algorithm is quite efficient and scalable. A comparison with the execution time of the kd-tree for the same number of records and attributes

shows that the kd-tree method is less efficient.

Section 5.1 describes the setup. Section 5.2 presents the results for pattern preservation. Section 5.3 reports the degree of privacy offered and the results of comparisons with two existing approaches. Section 5.4 reports the execution time of the proposed algorithm.

Setup

The experiments were conducted on a Pentium 4 machine with 3.4 GHz CPU and 4.0 GB of RAM that ran Windows XP Professional. The privatization algorithm was implemented using Matlab R2007a. For association rule mining, we used the client application, Oracle Data Miner 10.2 with Oracle application server 10g running on back-end.

Datasets: We used both real and synthetic data. The real datasets used were Cardiology, CPU, Iris, Liver and Pima Indians. While Cardiology and CPU are subsets of private datasets from the medical domain, the remaining datasets are publicly available from the UCI machine-learning repository[2]. All datasets with the exception of Cardiology contain numeric attributes. Cardiology has 6 numeric and 7 categorical attributes. We used only the numeric attributes in our experiments[3]. Since all real datasets had less than 1K records, we considered them small datasets. The two synthetic datasets were generated based on the Wine dataset from UCI machine-learning repository. Each data set contained 3 classes, the same as the Wine data. Each class was generated from a multi-dimensional Gaussian distribution with the same standard deviation and mean as a class in Wine. Table 3 reports the characteristics of these datasets. The sizes of the two synthetic data sets are much larger than the sizes of the real data sets.

Privacy-preserving algorithms: Three privacy-preserving algorithms were used: the DWT

Table 3. Data characteristics

Database name	No. of instances	No. of attributes
Cardiology	303	13
CPU	209	7
Iris	150	4
Liver	345	6
Pima Indians	768	8
Synthetic-80K	80,000	13
Synthetic-100K	100,000	13

(using Haar wavelet) method, the kd-tree method (Li & Sarkar, 2006), and the random projection method (Liu et al. (2006). Both the DWT and kd-tree based algorithms can be used for quantitative association rule mining. Thus we compare them in terms of both privacy and pattern preservation. The random projection method cannot be used for association rule mining because it does not keep the domain of data, but we compare our approach to it on privacy preservation.

Data mining parameters: Two important parameters for association rule mining are minimal support and minimal confidence. We varied both parameters in the experiments.

Rule quality metrics: We measure the quality of association rules discovered from the transformed data by comparing them to the rules discovered from the original data and determining the accuracy of the rules in both cases. The extent to which original patterns are preserved in the transformed datasets is measured by recall and precision. Recall is defined as $\sum \dfrac{(D_R \cap D'_R)}{D_R}$

and precision is defined as $\sum \dfrac{(D_R \cap D'_R)}{D'_R}$, where

D_R signifies rules generated from the original dataset and D'_R stands for rules generated from the transformed dataset. This article does not claim to determine the importance/criticality or sensitivity of the preserved rules. Such a task would call for services of a domain expert and would prove a very useful research agenda, if undertaken. Determining the importance of preserved rules constitutes one of our future research directions.

Preserving Patterns

To study pattern preservation, we computed the recall and precision measures with varying parameters for the association rules. Section 4.2.1 examines the cases of fixed minimum support and confidence. Section 4.2.2 and section 4.2.3 fix one of these two parameters and vary the other.

1.1.1 Rules at Fixed Minimum Support and Confidence Thresholds

In part 1, we examined recall and precision for all datasets with minimum rule support (sup_{min}) at 10% and minimum rule confidence ($conf_{min}$) at 50%. We also examined the results with a minimum rule support at 30% and a minimum confidence at 70%.

Tables 4 and 5 show results for small (real) and large (synthetic) datasets at $sup_{min=}$ 10% and $conf_{min=}$ 50%. Tables 6 and 7 show results for small and large datasets at $sup_{min=}$ 30% and $conf_{min=}$ 70%.

For small datasets, the average values for recall and precision of the DWT-based method remained consistently high at approximately 90% or above. In contrast, the average recall and precision measured for small kd-tree transformed datasets were in the range 69%-85%.

For large datasets, the average values for recall and precision dropped with the increase in support and confidence thresholds in the case of both the DWT and the kd-tree based methods. However, the DWT based recall and precision measures remained higher than those for the kd-tree approach. We find that in the case of synthetic-80K, recall of the DWT and the kd-tree transformed data is the same at $sup_{min=}$ 10% and $conf_{min=}$ 50%. Also, for the same data set (i.e. synthetic-80K) at $sup_{min=}$ 30% and $conf_{min=}$ 70%, our method generates more

Table 4. Comparison of association rules for small datasets at $sup_{min=}$ 10% $conf_{min=}$ 50%

Application Domain	No. of Rules Generated			Lost Rules (%)		Extraneous Rules (%)		Overlap (%)		Recall (%)		Precision (%)	
	Raw	DWT	Kd-tree	DWT	Kd-tree	DWT	Kd-tree	DWT	Kd-tree	DWT	Kd-tree	DWT	Kd-tree
Cardiology	184	178	213	8.69	16.30	5.43	32.06	91.30	83.69	91.30	83.69	94.38	72.30
CPU	147	147	156	8.16	13.60	4.76	15.64	57.82	52.38	87.63	79.38	92.39	77.00
Iris	64	64	59	6.25	17.18	6.25	6.25	90.00	79.68	93.50	82.26	93.50	92.72
Liver	115	140	138	1.73	1.73	24.34	23.47	96.52	96.52	98.23	98.23	79.86	80.44
Pima Indians	388	402	478	11.34	26.54	12.88	47.93	88.65	73.45	88.65	73.45	87.31	60.51
Average	**179.60**	**186.20**	**208.80**	**7.23**	**15.07**	**10.73**	**25.07**	**84.86**	**77.14**	**91.86**	**83.40**	**89.49**	**76.59**

Table 5. Comparison of association rules for large datasets at $sup_{min} = 10\%$ $conf_{min} = 50\%$

Application Domain	No. of Rules Generated			Lost Rules (%)		Extraneous Rules (%)		Overlap (%)		Recall (%)		Precision (%)	
	Raw	DWT	Kd-tree	DWT	Kd-tree	DWT	Kd-tree	DWT	Kd-tree	DWT	Kd-tree	DWT	Kd-tree
Synthetic-80K	2,987	2,821	3,078	13.40	13.79	7.86	16.83	86.57	86.20	86.60	86.20	91.70	83.66
Synthetic-100K	2,767	2,745	2,893	12.50	14.38	11.50	18.93	87.67	85.61	87.52	85.61	88.40	81.89
Average	**2,877.00**	**2,783.00**	**2,985.50**	**12.95**	**14.09**	**9.68**	**17.88**	**87.12**	**85.91**	**87.06**	**85.91**	**90.05**	**82.78**

Table 6. Comparison of association rules for small datasets at $sup_{min} = 30\%$ $conf_{min} = 70\%$

Application Domain	No. of Rules Generated			Lost Rules (%)		Extraneous Rules (%)		Overlap (%)		Recall (%)		Precision (%)	
	Raw	DWT	Kd-tree	DWT	Kd-tree	DWT	Kd-tree	DWT	Kd-tree	DWT	Kd-tree	DWT	Kd-tree
Cardiology	94	88	48	7.45	52.12	1.06	3.19	92.55	47.87	92.55	47.87	98.86	93.75
CPU	147	147	147	8.16	13.60	4.76	10.20	57.82	52.38	87.63	79.38	92.39	83.70
Iris	26	22	28	15.38	15.38	0.00	15.38	84.61	84.61	84.61	84.61	100.00	84.61
Liver	90	90	90	0.00	16.66	0.00	16.66	100.00	83.33	100.00	83.33	100.00	83.33
Pima Indians	233	235	156	1.71	48.06	2.57	14.59	98.28	51.93	98.28	51.93	97.45	78.06
Average	**118.00**	**116.40**	**93.80**	**6.54**	**29.16**	**1.68**	**12.00**	**86.65**	**64.02**	**92.61**	**69.42**	**97.74**	**84.69**

Table 7. Comparison of association rules for large datasets at $sup_{min} = 30\%$ $conf_{min} = 70\%$

Application Domain	No. of Rules Generated			Lost Rules (%)		Extraneous Rules (%)		Overlap (%)		Recall (%)		Precision (%)	
	Raw	DWT	Kd-tree	DWT	Kd-tree	DWT	Kd-tree	DWT	Kd-tree	DWT	Kd-tree	DWT	Kd-tree
Synthetic-80K	437	495	313	24.48	47.36	37.75	18.99	75.51	52.63	75.51	52.63	66.66	73.48
Synthetic-100K	432	475	417	26.38	43.05	36.34	39.58	73.61	56.94	73.61	56.94	66.94	58.99
Average	434.50	485.00	365.00	25.43	45.21	37.05	29.29	74.56	54.79	74.56	54.79	66.80	66.24

rules than the original data while kd-tree generates fewer rules than the original data. Thus our method has a lower precision than kd-tree, but a much higher recall. In practice, it is more important not to lose important rules than generating extra rules because there are other techniques such as interestingness measures that can be used to filter out unimportant rules.

1.1.2 Rules at Varying Minimum Support and Fixed Minimum Confidence Threshold

In this section, we varied the minimum support from 10% to 50%, while holding the minimum confidence fixed at 50%. The results for Cardiology and CPU are shown in Figures 5(a) and 5(b), respectively. The results for other data sets are similar and thus omitted.

In most cases recall and precision are both higher for DWT transformed data than for kd-tree transformed data. There is one exception where our method achieves a much higher recall but a lower precision than kd-tree. This happens in Figure 5(a) at $sup_{min} = 40\%$ and $conf_{min} = 50\%$. However, as stated earlier it is more important to preserve original rules than gaining extra rules because there are ways to filter out extraneous rules.

In the case of cardiology, recall and precision values for DWT fluctuate as support increases. However, both values remain above 70%. In contrast, the recall of kd-tree approach drops dramatically and is only 15% at support level of 50%. This indicates that a large portion of rules are missing using the kd-tree approach. Its precision gets improved. However, as mentioned above, it is often more important not to lose rules.

In the case of CPU, the recall and precision of both methods do not change much as minimal support increases, because most rules have very high support. Our method still generates better recall and precision than the kd-tree method.

Figure 5. Recall and precision for varying support

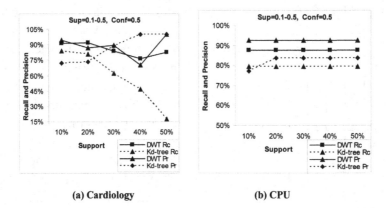

(a) Cardiology   (b) CPU

1.1.3 Rules at Varying Minimum Confidence and Fixed Minimum Support Threshold

In this section we fix the minimal support at 50% and vary the minimal confidence from 60% to 90%. Figure 6 (a) and (b) show the results for Cardiology and CPU data, respectively. The results for other data sets are similar and thus omitted.

Again, the recall for Cardiology and CPU tends to be higher for our method than for the kd-tree transformed data. For Cardiology, DWT and kd-tree have the same precision. However, DWT achieves a much higher recall than kd-tree. For CPU data, DWT also has a better recall and precision than kd-tree.

In general, we find that our method is consistently better than kd-tree in terms of rule preservation. As mentioned above, this is due to the property that our method optimally groups similar values together. Our method preserves the original rules to a very large extent. The recall of our method is over 70% in all cases and is over 80% or above in most cases. The precision is also over 80% most of the time.

Preserving Privacy

We use a metric called conditional privacy to measure the privacy. This measure was calculated using the formula $2^{h(D_i|D'_i)}$, where D_i is the i-th attribute values in the original data, D'_i is

Figure 6. Recall and precision at varying levels of confidence

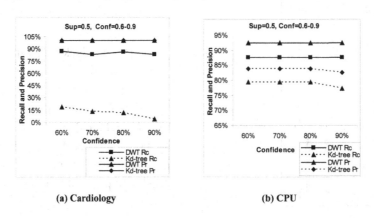

(a) Cardiology   (b) CPU

the i-th attribute values in the transformed data and $h(D_i \mid D'_i)$ is the conditional entropy of the original data D_i, given the transformed data D'_i. The conditional privacy was computed as the average over all attributes of a dataset. The conditional privacy measures the information that can be gained from perturbed data given the distribution of the original data. It ranges from 0 to 1. The larger the conditional privacy, the less information can be learned from the perturbed data.

Since there is very little work on PPDM for quantitative association rules, the privacy obtained for the DWT transformed data was compared to the conditional privacy of data perturbed using the kd-tree and random projection. The same set of real and synthetic data was used for both methods.

Figure 7 shows the conditional privacy of various methods. The results show that the privacy offered by the wavelet based method is higher than that offered by kd-tree and random projection for all datasets. According to Agrawal & Aggarwal (2001), a conditional privacy of β means that the privacy is the same as a random variable with a uniform distribution in $[0, \beta]$. Since the data has been normalized to the range of $[0,1]$, the degree of privacy reported for the wavelet-based method in Figure 7 is pretty high.

Overhead of the Proposed Method

Finally, experiments were conducted to study the efficiency and scalability of the proposed method. Several synthetic datasets were generated as in (Corney, n.d.; Mukherjee, 2006)[4]. The program to generate synthetic data contained ten clusters, each generated using a multi-dimensional Normal distribution. These datasets were used to examine the relationship between the overhead of the DWT-based privatization algorithm and the data size.

The size of the data depends on two factors: the number of records and the number of attributes. Figures 8(a) and (c) report the time in seconds to run the proposed algorithm when the number of records increased from 20,000–100,000 and the number of attributes was held constant at 100. Figures 8(b) and (d) report the time in seconds to run the proposed algorithm when the number of attributes increased from 20–100 and the number of records was held constant at 100,000. Two variants of our method (in-place and not-in-place DWT) are shown in these figures. The time of the kd-tree approach is also shown.

Since all methods spend the same amount of time to load data and save the results, Figures 8(a) and (b) show the execution time without the load and save time, and Figures 8(c) and (d) report the execution time with the load and save time.

Figure 7. Conditional privacy for wavelets and random projection

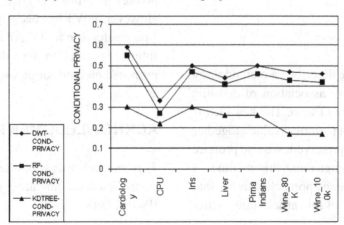

Figure 8. Execution time of DWT

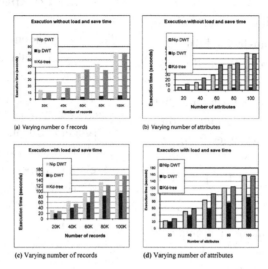

(a) Varying number o f records (b) Varying number of attributes

(c) Varying number of records (d) Varying number of attributes

Figures 8(a) and (b) show that the in-place DWT method is far more efficient than the not-in-place DWT method because the former does not store the intermediate matrix. In-place DWT is also far more efficient than kd-tree approach, largely due to the simplicity of our method. It also shows that in-place DWT scales linearly with the number of records and the number of attributes. In contrast, not-in-place DWT grows quadratically with the number of attributes.

Figures 8(c) and (d) show that when load and save time is considered, the results are similar except that the time difference between different methods are smaller because all methods spend the same amount of load and save time.

CONCLUSION

In this article we have described a methodology for mining quantitative association rules while preserving the privacy of data. The key idea is to use DWT and group similar values together such that rules can be preserved. We also propose an efficient way to implement this method. A comparison with existing approaches shows that the method proposed in this article fares better in terms of both preserving patterns and privacy. There are several possible future extensions of this work. For example, this method can be extended to a distributed setting where several parties can collaborate on generating quantitative association rules without having to share their individual data. In such distributed settings several additional issues arise including malicious attacks, gaming, and leaching, which can be studied using game theoretic models. In many real-life applications such as supply chains, other data analysis methods such as statistical regression models are frequently used. It would be interesting to study how our proposed method can be applied to such models. Lastly, there has been very little work on ensuring privacy in online analytical processing (OLAP). However, DWT has been applied as a compression mechanism for OLAP applications. Another future direction is to study the applicability of our proposed method for privacy preserving OLAP.

ACKNOWLEDGMENT

This research was supported in part by the National Science Foundation under Grant Number IIS-0713345.

REFERENCES

Aggarwal, C. C., & Yu, P. S. (2004). A Condensation Approach to Privacy Preserving Data Mining. In *Proceedings of the 9th International Conference on Extending Database Technology* (pp. 183-199).

Agrawal, D., & Aggarwal, C. (2001). On the design and quantification of privacy preserving data mining algorithms. In *Proceedings of the 20th ACM SIGMOD SIGACT-SIGART Symposium on Principles of Database Systems* (pp. 247-255).

Agrawal, R., & Srikant, R. (2000). Privacy preserving data mining. In *Proceedings of the 2000 ACM SIGMOD Conference on Management of Data* (pp. 439-450).

Atallah, M. J., Elmagarmid, A. K., Ibrahim, M., & Verykios, V. S. (1999). Disclosure Limitation of Sesitive Rules. In *Proceedings of the IEEE Knowledge and Data Engineering Workshop* (pp. 45-52).

Bayardo, R. J., & Agrawal, R. (2005). Data Privacy through Optimal k-Anonymization. In *Proceedings of the ICDE* (pp. 217-228).

Chen, Z.-Y., & Liu, G.-H. (2005). *Quantitative Association Rules Mining Methods with Privacy-preserving.* Paper presented at the Sixth International Conference on. Parallel and Distributed Computing, Applications and Technologies, PD-CAT. Corney, D. (n.d.). *Clustering with Matlab.* Retrieved from http://www.cs.ucl.ac.uk/staff/D. Corney/ClusteringMatlab.htm

Evfimevski, A., Gehrke, J., & Srikant, R. (2003). *Limiting privacy breaches in privacy preserving data mining.* Paper presented at the 22nd ACM SIGMOD-SIGACT-SIGART Symposium on Principles of Database Systems, San Diego, CA.

Evfimevski, A., Srikant, R., Agrawal, R., & Gehrke, J. (2002). Privacy preserving mining of association rules. In *Proceedings of the 8th ACM SIGKDD International Conference on Knowledge Discovery and Data Mining (KDD '02)* (pp. 217-228).

Graps, A. (1995). An introduction to wavelets. *Computational Science and Engineering, IEEE, 2*(2), 50–61. doi:10.1109/99.388960

Kantarcioglu, M., & Clifton, C. (2004). Privacy-preserving distributed mining of association rules on horizontally partitioned data. *IEEE Transactions on Knowledge and Data Engineering, 16*(9), 1026–1037. doi:10.1109/TKDE.2004.45

Kargupta, H., Datta, S., Wang, Q., & Sivakumar, K. (2003). Random data perturbation techniques and privacy preserving data mining. *Knowledge and Information Systems, 7*(4), 387–414. doi:10.1007/s10115-004-0173-6

Li, X. B., & Sarkar, S. (2006). A Tree-Based Data Perturbation Approach for Privacy-Preserving Data Mining. *IEEE Transactions on Knowledge and Data Engineering, 18*(9), 1278–1283. doi:10.1109/TKDE.2006.136

Lin, J.-L., & Liu, J. Y.-C. (2007). Privacy preserving itemset mining through fake transactions. In *Proceedings of the 2007 ACM Symposium on Applied Computing,* Seoul, Korea (pp. 375-379). New York: ACM Publishing.

Liu, K., Kargupta, H., & Ryan, J. (2006). Random projection-based multiplicative data perturbation for privacy preserving distributed data mining. *IEEE Transactions on Knowledge and Data Engineering, 18*(1), 92–106. doi:10.1109/TKDE.2006.14

Mallat, S. G. (1989). A theory for multiresolution signal decomposition:The wavelet representation. *IEEE Transactions on Pattern Analysis and Machine Intelligence, 11*(7), 674–693. doi:10.1109/34.192463

Menon, S., & Sarkar, S. (2007). Minimizing Information Loss and Preserving Privacy. *Management Science, 53*(1), 101–116. doi:10.1287/mnsc.1060.0603

Oliveira, S., & Zaiane, O. R. (2002). *Privacy Preserving Frequent Itemset Mining.* Paper presented at the IEEE International Conference on Privacy, Security and Data Mining, Maebashi City, Japan.

Rizvi, S., & Haritsa, J. R. (2002). *Maintaining Data Privacy in Association Rule Mining.* Paper presented at the VLDB.

Samarati, P. (2001). Protecting Respondents' Identities in Microdata Release. *TKDE, 13*(6), 1010–1027.

Vaidya, J., Clifton, C., & Zhu, Y. (2006). *Privacy Preserving Data Mining.* New York: Springer.

Vaidya, J. S., & Clifton, C. (2002). Privacy preserving association rule mining in vertically partitioned data. In *Proceedings of the 8th ACM SIGKDD International Conference on Knowledge Discovery and Data Mining* (pp. 639-644).

Verykios, V. S., Elmagarmid, A. K., Elisa, B., Saygin, Y., & Elena, D. (2004). Association Rule Hiding. *IEEE Transactions on Knowledge and Data Engineering, 16*(4), 434–447. doi:10.1109/TKDE.2004.1269668

Wilson, R. L., & Rosen, P. A. (2003). Protecting Data Through 'Perturbation' Techniques: The Impact on Knowledge Discovery in Databases. *Journal of Database Management, 14*(2), 14–26.

Zhang, N., Wang, S., & Zhao, W. (2004). *A New Scheme on Privacy Preserving Association Rule Mining.* Berlin Heidelberg, Germany: Springer-Verlag.

ENDNOTES

[1]   We divide the sum and difference by two in this paper.

[2]   http://www.ics.uci.edu/~mlearn/MLRepository.html

[3]   We focus on numerical input data types. However, if the data has categorical attributes in addition to the numerical attributes, then one can use existing PPDM methods for categorical data.

[4]   The class variable was removed before transformation as it is not required for association rule mining.

This work was previously published in International Journal of Information Security and Privacy (IJISP), edited by Hamid Nemati, pp 1-17, copyright 2009 by IGI Publishing (imprint of IGI Global)

Chapter 20
A New SOA Security Model to Protect Against Web Competitive Intelligence Attacks by Software Agents

Hamidreza Amouzegar
K. N. Toosi University of Technology, Iran

Mohammad Jafar Tarokh
K. N. Toosi University of Technology, Iran

Anahita Naghilouye Hidaji
Infotech Pars Company, Iran

ABSTRACT

This article presents an automata SOA based security model against competitive intelligence attacks in e-commerce. It focuses on how to prevent conceptual interception of an e-firm business model from CI agent attackers. Since competitive intelligence web environment is a new important approach for all e-commerce based firms, they try to come in new marketplaces and need to find a good customer-base in contest with other existing competitors. Many of the newest methods for CI attacks in web position are based on software agent facilities. Many researchers are currently working on how to facilitate CI creation in this environment. The aim of this paper is to help e-firm designers provide a non-predictable presentation layer against CI attacks.

INTRODUCTION

No business is an island. For success, the business will need to deal with customers, suppliers, employees, and others. In almost all cases there will also be other organizations offering similar

products to similar customers. These other organizations are competitors. And their objective is the same—to grow, make money and succeed. Effectively, the businesses are at war—fighting to gain the same resource and territory: the customer. And like in war, it is necessary to understand the enemy, how he thinks, what his strengths are, what his weaknesses are, where he is vulnerable,

DOI: 10.4018/978-1-60960-200-0.ch020

where he can be attacked, and where the risk of attack is too great(SCIP).

And like in war, the competitor will have secrets that can be the difference between profit and loss, expansion or bankruptcy for the business. Identifying these secrets is thus crucial for business survival. But all this is not new; around the year 500 BC, the great Chinese military strategist, Sun Tzu wrote a treatise on the Art of War. From a 21st-century perspective, many of Sun Tzu's approaches would be viewed as barbaric today (Gordon, 1989). Nevertheless, his views on strategy are still relevant today for both military commanders and business leaders looking at how to win against competitors.

Although elements of organizational intelligence collection have been a part of business for many years, the history of Competitive Intelligence began in the U.S. in the 1970s. In 1980 Michael Porter published the study competitive strategy: Techniques for Analyzing Industries and Competitors which is widely viewed as the foundation of modern competitive intelligence (Porter, 1998).

Business competitors are:

- Other organizations offering the same product or service now.
- Other organizations offering similar products or services now.
- Organizations that could offer the same or similar products or services in the future.
- Organizations that could remove the need for a product or service.

After the web was born, the entire competitive analysis model turned to new direction which grows by search engines and measuring the competitor web sites traffic according to customer's behavior. The big problem was how to model the web sites and customers manner which present the business intelligence of competitors (Russel & Norvig, 2002). Nowadays many researchers are working on how to facilitate CI creation in this environment and trying to use some automotive solutions with software agent approach which is used before as a method of recursive searching in e-payments.

This paper will try to introduce an automata SOA based security model against competitor agent's attacks in web environment to prevent e-firms from business model transparency.

The first section will explain CI analysis methods and their solutions in web. The second section will introduce SOA uses in web. The third section will explain the security gaps. The forth section will focus on software agent specifications. And the final part will represent the proposed model for protecting the business from attackers.

COMPETITOR ANALYSIS METHODS

Competitor Array

One common and useful technique is constructing a competitor array. The steps in web environment include:

1. Define your e-firm scope and nature of the firm.
2. Determine who your competitors are and their services URL. Divide them to two section of secure an insecure which comes from their protocol.
3. Determine who your customers are and what benefits they expect.
4. Determine what the key success factors are in your e-firm.
5. Rank the key success factors by giving each one a weighting – The sum of all the weightings must add up to one.
6. Rate each competitor on each of the key success factors – this can best be displayed on a two dimensional matrix - competitors along the top and key success factors down the side.

7. Multiply each cell in the matrix by the factor weighting.
8. Sum columns for a weighted assessment of the overall strength of each competitor relative to each other.

Competitor Profiling

Another common technique is to create detailed profiles on each of your major competitors. These profiles give an in-depth description of the competitor's background, finances, products, markets, facilities, personnel, and strategies (Nwana, 1996).

Media Scanning

We can learn a lot about the competitive environment by scanning our competitors' ads. Changes in a competitor's advertising message can reveal new product offerings, new production processes, a new branding strategy, a new positioning strategy, a new segmentation strategy, line extensions and contractions, problems with previous positions, insights from recent marketing or product research, a new strategic direction, a new source of sustainable competitive advantage, or value migrations within the industry (March, 1994). From a tactical perspective, it can also be used to help a manager implement his/her own media plan. By knowing the competitor's media buy, media selection, frequency, reach, continuity, schedules, and flights, the manager can arrange his/her own media plan so that they do not coincide (Kahneman, 2003).

There are four stages in monitoring competitors—the four "C"s:

- Collecting the information (with a first stage—deciding what to collect),
- Converting information into intelligence (with three steps: CIA—Collate and catalogue it, Integrate it with other pieces of information and Analyze and interpret it),
- Communicating the intelligence,
- Countering any adverse competitor actions like using the intelligence.

These methods of competitor analysis are the basic methods which will be used in business intelligence creation. They come from SWOT thinking method and focus on key success factors in CA, competitor's details in CP and advertising behaviors in CMS. Migrating from BI to CI begins when the firms try to find their competitor manners and put the way on competing face to face. These methods work in real physical world well and are effective if you have some informer agent in competitors' side and good pattern interceptor in entry-exit port of them.

In the web virtual world there are no choices to select and rate in competitor side. So competitor array solution will be stopped at the stage #6 and analyzing will stop too; competitor profiling will be useless because information should be gathered from a nonsense environment. Interception solution proposed in some researches will be described in the following section. It shows us how to find the competitor service cycle and how to rate each competitor key factors in web environment.

How They Solve It?

All the described methods are inherited from strategic point of view which tries to explain the competitors based on PEST analyses and needs a physical concentration for the manner detection. The main gap is in modeling the competitor behaviors in web environment which is positioned in a virtual location. Modeling the strategic actions in web requires a finite and formal detailed view, because of the complication of data gathering in this environment. We need a new model to present the manners formally which also has the possibility to be generated by agents automatically. Gathered data need to be grown to information and then be converted to intelligence.

The researchers solved this problem by representing a new modeling method which will be applicable with software agent help.

Modeling the competitor's behaviors and tricks by automata (An automaton—plural automata—is a self-operating machine. The word is sometimes used to describe a robot; more specifically, an autonomous robot, Shalyto, 1991) helps us to:

1. Find his scenario completely.
2. Increase the possibility of weighting for detailed behavior.
3. Increase the possibility of using agents automatically.
4. Discover the competitors provided services while measuring the customer's reactions.
5. Find the strength and weakness of any competitor actions.

This solution can be provided by agents or human researcher.

Figure 1 shows how you can model a competitor service and his manner in relation with customer. This model helps us to simulate consumer for competitor's web site and negotiate with its services to weigh the transitions for finding the SW (strength and weakness) of competitor.

According to Figure 2, we can compute the strength of this competitor in a provided service (use-case) for two goals. This figure describes that 0.8 of web site services need the personal information form; 0.4 of next service facilities

push the user to behave in an employee manner; 0.3 of next service facilities for employees help them to find a car and 0.2 of next service facilities direct car finders to buy the car. In other words it means approximately two (0.8 * 0.4 * 0.3 * 0.2) percents of this web-site's services aim for selling cars and one percent aims to sell films to visitors.

This also describes 0.32 (0.8 * 0.4) of services in this web site focus on employee segment of customers and 0.48 of them focus on student segment. There are many other findings from this diagram which comes from automata modeling of web site services by an agent automatically.

SOA IN WEB

One of the current approaches to software development in remote environment is service-oriented programming. Service-oriented computing represents a new generation of distributed computing platform. It contains many things, including its own design paradigm and design principles, design pattern catalogs, pattern languages, a distinct architectural model, and related concepts, technologies, and frameworks (SCIP). The vision

Figure 1. State diagrams are used to graphically represent finite state machines

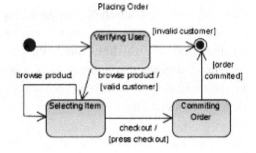

Figure 2. Automata model of one competitor's provided service

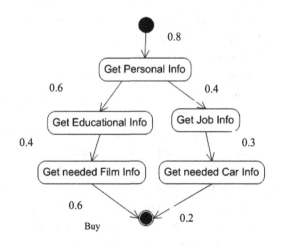

behind service-oriented computing is extremely ambitious and therefore also very attractive to any organization interested in truly improving the effectiveness of its IT enterprise. After the web was born, all the software patterns turned to new direction and have been pushed to network area with its challenges as a child. Web is a network of servers linked together by a common protocol, allowing access to millions of hypertext resources (Porter, 1998). Tracking the web shows it is going to be a fully interactive media to achieve all the needs of communication among multiple agents with or without standards. But W3C creation makes a new door in standardization of network protocols which helps fast growing of protocol generation and eases making new ideas. So service-oriented was jumped in web with some protocols, e.g. SOAP for web service. By growing use of service-oriented design, a new architecture was born which is SOA (Russel & Norvig, 2002). There is no widely-agreed upon definition of service-oriented architecture other than its literal translation that it is an architecture that relies on service-orientation as its fundamental design principle. Service-orientation describes an architecture that uses loosely coupled services to support the requirements of business processes and users. Resources on a network in an SOA environment are made available as independent services that can be accessed without knowledge of their underlying platform implementation. These concepts can be applied to business, software and other types of producer/consumer systems (March, 1994). OASIS (the Organization for the Advancement of Structured Information Standards) defines SOA as the following (Gordon, 1989):

"A paradigm for organizing and utilizing distributed capabilities that may be under the control of different ownership domains. It provides a uniform means to offer, discover, interact with and use capabilities to produce desired effects consistent with measurable preconditions and expectations."

Web 2.0 refers to a "second generation" of web sites, primarily distinguished by the ability of visitors to contribute information for collaboration and sharing. Web 2.0 applications use Web services and may include Ajax program interfaces, Web syndication, blogs, and wikis (Russel & Norvig, 2002).

There are two approaches in service presenting from server to clients:

Service Statelessness: First and the most successful approach till now in service providing is statelessness of it, which comes from four principles (SCIP); service loose coupling, service abstraction, service autonomy, service security. These principles cause SOA put its way on a locked room implemented by a procedure or function with primitive standard types in signature instead of complex data structure for parameter passing.

Service State-fullness: This approach is isolated because of the history of SOA. SOA comes to solve application negotiations together and there are no needs to long interview between two applications.

Web protocols (most popular HTTP) are stateless because of resource management for connection in both client and server side. But web servers solved application missed needs by session management. Session means a memory to save the specific client state for its life cycle.

Current leader in SOA is Web Service by means of which many applications try to communicate together. Remote Procedure Call (RPC) Web Services present a distributed function (or method) call interface that is familiar to many developers. As it is clear from the title, RPC is the director of web service concept. Thus, it is fully stateless.

The structure of web service in the anonymous networks, e.g. internet, shows that each state of FSM in interactive model can be mapped to an f(x) in Web service model, and change the complicated appearance of new form to a simple view with just an additional session management (Figures 3 and 4)

Figure 3. Web service structure

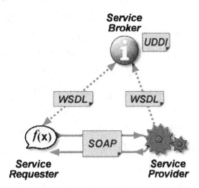

Figure 4. Mapping a business model to Web service

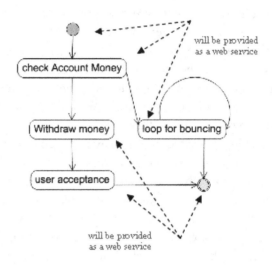

In this model, server should manage the session of each service requester in addition to its provided service responding. State of service requester in business FSM specifies where it is and where it can go (Figure 4). Also security management should be in server side which is just a business security manager.

SECYRITY GAPS

Computer security is also frequently defined in terms of several interdependent domains that roughly map to specific departments and job titles. For example "physical security" controls the comings and goings of people and materials; protection against the elements and natural disasters. Operational/procedural security covers everything from managerial policy decisions to reporting hierarchies. Personnel security hires employees, background screens, and trains, security briefs, monitoring, and handling departures. System security user access and authentication controls, assignment of privilege, maintaining file and file-system integrity, backups, monitoring processes, log-keeping, and auditing. Network security protects network and telecommunications equipment, protects network servers and transmissions, combats eavesdropping, and controls access from un-trusted networks, firewalls, and detects intrusions.

In many cases, what are called thefts may actually be the consequences of effective active CI against your company by a competitor. In some cases, a firm may even be placing competitively sensitive information in a nice, neat package, without the need for your competitors to exert any real effort to piece it together.

All of the presented models and solutions for CI in web are based on behavior modeling of competitor in business life time. According to section "competitor analysis methods", manner detection of competitor is the most important segment of intelligence, and the best model to describe their manner is state diagrams. This means that attacker agents should be state-full and they should have an embedded memory in themselves which is implemented with sessions in web servers. These attackers method are too similar to brute-forcers, but the major difference is their aim. CI attacker tries to find all the possible ways, as a human tries, from start point to end point and saves all the happen things events. So the CI agents need to find the continuity of tries in one side and in another side the continuity of tries and responses together. If anything cuts the continuity of these lines, agent's mission will not be accessible and practical.

The main security hole in these ways is predictable steps in the e-firm web site which will be found by competitors very simply. When a business flow has been found then simulation of it will be possible; this means the firm will not have a competitive advantage or comparative benefit in it.

SOFTWARE AGENT METHODOLOGY

In computer science, a software agent (see Figure 5) is a piece of software that acts for a user or other program in a relationship of agency. Such "action on behalf of" implies the authority to decide when (and if) action is appropriate. The idea is that agents are not strictly invoked for a task, but activate themselves. Related and derived concepts include intelligent agents (in particular exhibiting some aspect of Artificial Intelligence, such as learning and reasoning), autonomous agents (capable of modifying the way in which they achieve their objectives), distributed agents (being executed on physically distinct machines), multi-agent systems (distributed agents that do not have the capabilities to achieve an objective alone and thus must communicate), and mobile agents (agents that can relocate their execution onto different processors).

Various authors have proposed different definitions of agents; these commonly include concepts such as:

Figure 5. Nwana's category of software agent

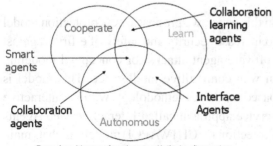

Based on Nwanna's primary attribute dimension

- **Persistence** (code is not executed on demand but runs continuously and decides for itself when it should perform some activity).
- **Autonomy** (agents have capabilities of task selection, prioritization, goal-directed behavior, decision making without human intervention).
- **Social ability** (agents are able to engage other components through some sort of communication and coordination; they may collaborate on a task).
- **Reactivity** (agents perceive the context in which they operate and react to it appropriately).

The agent concept is most useful as a tool to analyze systems, not as a prescription. The concepts mentioned above often relate well to the way we naturally think about complex tasks and thus agents can be useful to model such tasks.

A software agent should simulate a human behavior in web interaction; it goes to competitor's web site and tries to find all the possible next states from this page or form. It traverses the possible ways till the end and weights the transitions according to web facilities.

To find the competitor's web sites, agent would use these steps:

1. Link Intelligence
2. Search Term Intelligence
3. Search Engine Intelligence
4. PPC Campaign Intelligence
5. Referrer Intelligence
6. Popularity Index Report
7. Ranking Report
8. Meta Keywords

Agent will use the smart propagator methodology to influence in selected competitor's web site; and parallel completion of automata models will be handled by agent in a single or multi-agent manner. In this model the agent will check all the local reference links and buttons to find the paths and to complete the models incrementally.

PROTECTION MODEL

By comparing the software agent's methods and security holes described in section 4 & 5, some rules will be found. First, learning and reasoning need memory. Second, the knowledge comes from some correlated information. Third, the intelligence will be born from continuous knowledge. Forth, the statelessness of information is knowledge killer.

So any type of non-predictable business representation will create a secure e-commerce in web environment. SOA helps designers in this way. In the SOA point of view, e-firms can implement their business line with stateless components which will cut the auto agents finds. One of the simplest and famous ways against brute forces is rational reorganization such as alphabetical pictures used to considering the humanity of users but we cannot use this way for all the steps and all the forms, it will create an annoying web site. Another way is using email authentication to communicate with customers in some steps of business. This solution has the same problems as the previous one if it is repetitive. The third usual way is human protection by non automatic confirmation of requests at another time, step by step. This way is so expensive and customer killer for long term.

An interactive approach in SOA for providing the services is a new point of view in web environment, if interactions can be none-continues then the competitor actors cannot predict the web behaviors.

According to section "How They Solve It?" every behavior has one start state and one final state. So agents should recognize the web business manner's start state (the first page or first response of first request for business start) and final state (by continuing the steps and getting the end

response). But the main problem of the agents is finding the relative pages from start to end. There are three ways to find the relative steps (pages) in web; first, following the URLs; second, following the server side's session by client side's cookie; third, receiving the final signal from server in a standard protocol.

In this protection model, the e-firm should provide each step of its business model just by a service and should not represent any model of business flow with page flows. In other word, e-firms put their way on business driven service providing. It means business providing without web page providing. Most of Agent's approach to flow discovery is based on web http specifications which is primarily stateless, but will be state-full by session management of web server applications.

Thus, in our protection model, e-firms turn to applet based application providing or service management in server side. Absolutely this way is not fully secure but agent's modeling of business behavior takes a lot of time for discovery. Thus time consumption will help us to abort any anonymous tries. Also server side applications can randomly change the ways.

If some e-firms must provide their business in http mode and web pages and they do not like to use applet approach, they can use random authorization and authentication in multiple ways to force the agents lose time. But note that it is not a good way since it is just a breaking way for short time.

CONCLUSION

In this paper, we propose a new protection model to increase security and safety of e-firms against software agent attacks for conceptual modeling in web competitive intelligence. This model is based on SOA methodology with an interactive service approach called Interactive Web Agents Protection for CI (IWAPCI) model which its main elements are: SOA, interactive state-full service, and software agent. The aim of IWAPCI is to enable fully flexible, scalable, and secure business presentation while CI agent attackers try to be aware about e-firm's manner. We achieve this goal with an architecture that is based on three complementary principles:

- All the businesses of competitor's behavior could be modeled by a finite state machine.
- Services could be provided state-full and interactive.
- Software agents could automatically track the provided services on web if it is state-full.
- Statelessness of provided business services will confuse the automatic agents.

In the paper we also propose a model to provide a stateless manner by service dispatching for transitions of FSM model.

REFERENCES

Baeza-Yates, R., Castillo, C., Marin, M., & Rodriguez, A. (2005). Crawling a Country: Better Strategies than Breadth-First for Web Page Ordering. In *Proceedings of the Industrial and Practical Experience Track of the 14th Conference on the World Wide Web,* Chiba, Japan (pp. 864-872). New York: ACM Publishing.

Booch, G., Rambaugh, J., & Jacobson, I. (2005). *The Unified Modeling Language User Guide* (2nd ed.). Reading, MA: Addison Wesley Professional.

Castillo, C. (2004). *Effective Web Crawling*. Unpublished PhD thesis, University of Chile.

Daneshpajouh, S., Nasiri, M. M., & Ghodsi, M. (2008). *A Fast Community Based Algorithm for Generating Crawler Seeds Set*. Paper presented at the 4th International Conference on Web Information Systems and Technologies (WEBIST).

Edwards, J., McCurley, K. S., & Tomlin, J. A. (2001). An adaptive model for optimizing performance of an incremental web crawler. In *Proceedings of the Tenth Conference on the World Wide Web* (pp. 106-113). Elsevier Science.

Fowler, M. (2004). *UML Distilled* (3rd ed.). Reading, MA: Addison Wesley.

Franklin, S., & Graesser, A. (1996). *Is It an Agent, or Just a Program? A Taxonomy for Autonomous Agents*. Paper presented at the Third International Workshop on Agent Theories, Architectures, and Languages, Springer-Verlag.

Gadomski, A. M., & Zytkow, J. M. (1995). Abstract Intelligent Agents: Paradigms, Foundations and Conceptualization Problems. In *Abstract Intelligent Agent* (Vol. 2). Rome: ENEA. ISSN/1120-558X.

Gordon, I. (1989). *Beat the Competition How to Use Competitive Intelligence to Develop Winning Business Strategies*. Oxford, UK: Basil Blackwell Publishers.

Ipeirotis, P., Ntoulas, A., Cho, J., & Gravano, L. (2005). Modeling and managing content changes in text databases. In *Proceedings of the 21st IEEE International Conference on Data Engineering* (pp. 606).

Jim, S. L. (2006). *From UML Diagrams to Behavioural Source Code*. Unpublished master's thesis, Centrum voor Wiskunde en Informatica.

Kahneman, D. (2003). Maps of bounded rationality: psychology for behavioral economics. *The American Economic Review*, 1449–1475. doi:10.1257/000282803322655392

Kasabov, N. (1998). Introduction: Hybrid intelligent adaptive systems. *International Journal of Intelligent Systems*, 6, 453–454. doi:10.1002/(SICI)1098-111X(199806)13:6<453::AID-INT1>3.0.CO;2-K

March, J. G. (1994). *A Primer on Decision Making: How Decisions Happen*. New York: Free Press.

Nelson, M. L., Van de Sompel, H., Liu, X., Harrison, T. L., & McFarland, N. (2005). *mod_oai: An Apache module for metadata harvesting*. Paper presented at the 9th European Conference on Research and Advanced Technology for Digital Libraries.

Nwana, H. S. (1996). Software Agents: An Overview. *The Knowledge Engineering Review, 11*(3), 1–40. doi:10.1017/S026988890000789X

Porter, M. E. (1998). *Competitive Strategy: Techniques for Analyzing Industries and Competitors*. New York: Free Press

Powell, R. (2001, February). DM Review: A 10 Year Journey. *DM Review*. Retrieved from http://www.dmreview.com

Russell, S. J., & Norvig, P. (2002). *Artificial Intelligence: A Modern Approach* (2nd ed.). Upper Saddle River, NJ: Prentice Hall

Shalyto, A. (1991). Programmatic Implementation of control automata //Marine industry *Automation and Remote Control, 13*, 41-42.

Shoeman, M. A., & Cloete, E. (2003). Architectural Components for the Efficient Design of Mobile Agent System. In *Proceedings of SAICSIT* (pp. 48-58).

Tukkel, N., & Shalyto, A. (2001). State-Based Programming. *PC World, 8*, 116–121.

White, J. E. (1994). *Telescript Technology: The Foundation for the Electronic Marketplace*. Mountain View, CA: General Magic Inc.

Wong, J., Helmer, G., Naganathan, V., Polavarapu, S., Honovar, L., & Miller, L. (2001). SMART Mobile Agent Facility. *Journal of Systems and Software, 56*, 9–22. doi:10.1016/S0164-1212(00)00082-0

This work was previously published in International Journal of Information Security and Privacy (IJISP), edited by Hamid Nemati, pp 18-28, copyright 2009 by IGI Publishing (imprint of IGI Global)

Chapter 21
PAKE on the Web

Xunhua Wang
James Madison University, USA

Hua Lin
University of Virginia, USA

ABSTRACT

Unlike existing password authentication mechanisms on the web that use passwords for client-side authentication only, password-authenticated key exchange (PAKE) protocols provide mutual authentication. In this article, we present an architecture to integrate existing PAKE protocols to the web. Our integration design consists of the client-side part and the server-side part. First, we implement the PAKE client-side functionality with a web browser plug-in, which provides a secure implementation base. The plug-in has a log-in window that can be customized by a user when the plug-in is installed. By checking the user-specific information in a log-in window, an ordinary user can easily detect a fake log-in window created by mobile code. The server-side integration comprises a web interface and a PAKE server. After a successful PAKE mutual authentication, the PAKE plug-in receives a one-time ticket and passes it to the web browser. The web browser authenticates itself by presenting this ticket over HTTPS to the web server. The plug-in then fades away and subsequent web browsing remains the same as usual, requiring no extra user education. Our integration design supports centralized log-ins for web applications from different web sites, making it appropriate for digital identity management. A prototype is developed to validate our design. Since PAKE protocols use passwords for mutual authentication, we believe that the deployment of this design will significantly mitigate the risk of phishing attacks.

INTRODUCTION

Phishing attacks have become more widespread these days. A study by the Anti-Phising Working Group found that the password stealing malicious code URLs increased from 9529 in June of 2008 to 31173 (more than tripled) in December of 2008 (Anti-phishing Working Group, 2009). Another study showed that phishing cost the U.S. $3.2 billion in 2007 (Hodgin, 2007). Among the vic-

DOI: 10.4018/978-1-60960-200-0.ch021

tims of phishing attacks, financial institutions are hit hardest. Because of the rising online identity theft caused by phishing attacks and regulators' concerns, financial institutions are looking for better on-line security tools against phishing attacks (Richmond, 2005).

In a typical phishing attack, a user first receives an email informing him to update his online account (such as an online banking account or an online utility bill account) using an embedded URL. The email also warns that failing to conform would result in account lock-out or deletion. Struck by panic, the user may immediately click on the given link, which would lead the user's web browser to a web site that bears the right logo and a familiar appearance. The user then hastens to type in his account name and password. But actually that web site is run by an attacker, who now has the information to perform fraudulent transactions in that user's name. Phishing attacks harvest secret information for client-side authentication by impersonating a web server.

Most of today's web applications use three methods to authenticate a client, namely, *basic authentication*, *digest authentication*, and *form-based authentication*. (There is a fourth client authentication method on the web, the *certificate-based client authentication*. In this method, a client is assigned a private key, which is used in the Secure Socket Layer (SSL) protocol for client authentication. This method is not common for home users as it requires a user to manage a *random* private key and ordinary users lack the expertise to handle a private key correctly.) All these three methods are password-based authentications, in which a client remembers a password and the server stores a related *password verification data* (PVD). In basic authentication, a client's password is encoded with the (public) Base64 (Josefsson, 2003) method and sent to the server for verification. In digest authentication, the client's password is *not* sent to the server; rather, the server sends a random challenge to the client, who then responds with a value calculated

from its password and the challenge value. The server compares the received response value with a value calculated from the challenge and the corresponding PVD. In form-based authentication, a client's password is encapsulated in a HTML form and then transmitted in HTTP to the server.

Should the web server be impersonated, in basic authentication and form-based authentication, the phony web server will receive the client's password. If digest authentication is used, the phony web server will not get the password directly but having a (challenge, response) pair will allow it to mount off-line dictionary attacks: a value calculated from a guessed password and the challenge is compared against the received response; this process is repeated until a match is found, indicating that the current guessed password is the correct one.

To provide server-side authentication, the common practice is to run all these three password authentications on the top of HTTPS, which is HTTP over Secure Socket Layer (SSL). In HTTPS, each server has a domain name and a public/private key pair. Its public key is certified by some certification authorities (CA), whose public keys have already been shipped with popular web browsers such as Microsoft Internet Explorer (IE) and Mozilla. The resulting digital certificate contains the web server's public key, its domain name, and a digital signature by the CA covering both the server's public key and the domain name. After receiving a digital certificate from a server, the client uses the corresponding CA's public key to verify it. In this way, the client is ensured that the public key in the digital certificate indeed belongs to that domain name. The client then uses this public key to establish a shared session key (thus a secure connection) with the server and the server is authenticated by demonstrating the possession of the corresponding private key. Over this secure connection is the client's password credential sent for client authentication.

THE PROBLEM

However, this loose coupling of two one-way authentications, namely, *server-side* certificate-based authentication and *client-side* password authentication, lends itself to phishing attacks. A phishing server can bypass the server-side authentication by not using HTTPS. Such a server usually looks very real by assuming an appearance similar to the genuine web site and having a URL that can be easily confused with the genuine URL. For example, one would think that http://www.chase.com.1i1l0.com/start.htm?cmd=LogIn is linked to the Chase bank but it actually is not. Under these social engineering attacks, an innocent user might be fooled into trusting the phishing web site and give away his password.

Asking an end user to look for HTTPS in a URL before typing his password does not help much either. More sophisticated phishing attacks do use HTTPS. When the phishing URL is a HTTPS (say https://www.chase.com.1i1l0.com/start.htm?cmd=LogIn), a security padlock appears in the right bottom corner of the web browser window, giving the user further false sense of security. Such a phishing server either uses a self-signed digital certificate or purchases a legitimate digital certificate with certain properties. In the first case, the user will see a pop-up window warning about the self-signed digital certificate but most users usually choose to accept it (Dhamija, Tygar, & Hearst, 2006). (Some legitimate web sites do use self-signed digital certificates and thus such warnings are common, making the user to think that another one does not hurt. Also, an ordinary user usually lacks the knowledge to understand what a digital certificate is and tends to accept it (Dhamija, Tygar, & Hearst, 2006).) The second case is more subtle as the server's digital certificate is certified by a trusted third party. Popular web browsers like MS IE and Mozilla are shipped with more than 100 root CAs' public keys and a browser trusts a digital certificate issued by any of these CAs (Gutmann, 2003, 2004). A phishing web site can purchase a digital certificate with a domain name similar to the target web site. For example, it can buy a digital certificate with domain name www.ao1.com, which looks like www.aol.com. This type of attack has happened in the real world (Dunn, 2005). Worse, these days it is common practice to purchase a digital certificate with wildcards in the domain name such as *.1i1l0.com. Such a digital certificate can be abused on a host with domain name like www-chase-com.1i1l0.com for phishing without causing any pop-up alarms, as www-chase-com.1i1l0.com does match *.1i1l0.com.

In this article we explore countering phishing attacks by integrating *password-authenticated key exchange* (PAKE) protocols into the web. Like the aforementioned password authentication mechanisms, a PAKE client remembers a password and the PAKE server stores a related PVD. Unlike those password authentications, PAKE protocols use passwords for *mutual*, not one-way, authentication. PAKE protocols allow a client and a server to bootstrap, in a secure manner, from a weak password to a cryptographically strong session key. A client without the correct password or a server without the appropriate PVD will not agree on a common session key value; hence mutual authentication. In this bootstrapping process, *no* secure transport mechanisms (such as SSL) are assumed and good PAKE protocols are secure against both the simple password eavesdropping attack and (more complex) off-line dictionary attacks. PAKE protocols achieve authenticated key exchange by integrating passwords with (unauthenticated) key exchange techniques such as Diffie-Hellman. Since PAKE protocols do not assume a secure channel, they do *not* rely on PKI. The PAKE authenticated session key of a successful log-in can be used to provide both data confidentiality and data integrity for subsequent communication and prevent session hijacking.

Although implemented in several other applications, PAKE protocols have not been integrated into the web (Fu, Sit, Smith, & Feamster, 2001).

Our PAKE integration consists of the client-side integration and the server-side integration. First, we implement the client-side functionality of a PAKE protocol in a web browser plug-in. To provide strong security, PAKE protocols require secure client-side implementation and browser plug-ins meet this requirement. Other choices such as *Java Applet* and *JavaScript* are not appropriate as they are downloaded from a server and, in the absence of strong server-side authentication, their integrity and origin cannot be guaranteed. We assume that our plug-in program is distributed in a reliably way, for example shipped with web browsers or distributed through CD distribution by individual financial institution. The plug-in has a user-customizable log-in window, which can be customized in both text and graphics when it is installed. This user-specific information is stored in the local file system and is not accessible to any mobile code (like *JavaScript* mentioned above). By checking this information in a log-in window, a user can easily detect a fake log-in window created by mobile code. Our server-side integration comprises two logical components, namely two web pages and a PAKE server. These two web pages—the *log-in page* and the *activation page*—are the web interface of our server-side integration. The PAKE server component implements PAKE's server-side functionality.

The browser plug-in program is launched when the browser receives a HTTP response with a specific MIME type. It then prompts the PAKE log-in window for user's password. After receiving a password from the user, the plug-in program runs PAKE against the PAKE server and *securely* receives a *onetime ticket*. Note that the PAKE mutual authentication happens between the plug-in and the PAKE server, *not* between the web browser and the web server. The PAKE plug-in then passes the one-time ticket to the web browser and the web browser authenticates itself by presenting this ticket over HTTPS to the web server. (As its name indicates, each one-time ticket can be used only once.) Thereafter the plug-in

program fades away and subsequent web browsing remains the same. Our integration of PAKE and HTTPS has the minimal impact on existing user browsing behaviors and requires little user education.

In our design, the PAKE server can be a stand-alone program, thus a potentially distributed component. This allows our architecture to support centralized log-in for web applications from *different* web sites. Thus, our design supports digital identity management, just like Liberty (Liberty Alliance Project, 2005) and Windows Live (Microsoft Corporation, 2006), when the PAKE server is run by a separate *identity provider*. In our design, when issuing tickets, the PAKE server does *not* need direct communication with the web-page component, making it very flexible in deployment. To validate our design we build a prototype implementation. We believe that our approach can effectively counter phishing attacks.

The remainder of this article is organized as follows. In next section we give the related work. We then present our integration design, including the client-side integration and the server-side integration. In the subsequent implementation section, we share the details of a prototype implementation. Concluding remarks are given at the end of this article.

RELATED WORK

Digital Identity Management

There have been efforts to establish digital identities, including Liberty (Liberty Alliance Project, 2005) and Windows Live (Microsoft Corporation, 2006), to support single sign-on. These frameworks focus on high-level architectures by defining entities like *identity provider* and *service provider* and data flow among them. They usually adopt standard security technologies like SSL/TLS. To our best knowledge PAKE protocols have not been seriously researched in this context yet

(Fu et al., 2001). As shown in later sections, our PAKE integration design supports the concept of identity provider and thus is consistent with these frameworks.

Techniques against Phishing Attacks

Phishing attacks have been described in various places (Anti-phishing Working Group, 2009; Cao, Han, & Le, 2008; Dhamija et al., 2006; James, 2005; The Honeynet Project & Research Alliance, 2005). Dhamija et al. (2006) studied phishing attacks from the cognitive perspective and noticed that *lack of knowledge*, *visual deception*, and *lack of attention* contribute to their success. Several countermeasures have been suggested (Tally, Thomas, & Van Vleck, 2004). Some of them are essentially at the infrastructure level, such as setting up a gateway to filter out SPAM emails and other malicious content. Others are end-user-oriented, including *user education* to train ordinary users to be more suspicious and *procedures* to force users to constantly update their anti-virus software. Infrastructure-level countermeasures are more advantageous as they are invisible to ordinary users and require little user education (Odlyzko, 2003).

Chou, Ledesma, Teraguchi, Boneh, and Mitchell (2004) developed a web browser plug-in program called SpoofGuard to monitor browsing behaviors and to report and prevent possible phishing attacks. Ross, Jackson, Miyake, Boneh, and Mitchell (2005) noticed that it is common that a user employs the same password for different web sites. They propose to use a web browser extension, instead of a browser plug-in, to generate, from the same reusable password, domain-specific passwords for different web sites. In this way the compromise of one does not affect others.

RSA Security (2004) proposed the *two-factor authentication* for countering phishing attacks. In this scheme, in addition to a reusable password, a user is also equipped with a hardware token, which generates and displays a new one-time password

every minute. When the user remotely logs into the server, he types in both his reusable password and a one-time password. This two-factor authentication mitigates the risk of phishing attacks in that, even successfully stealing a user's reusable password and a one-time password, the phishing web site must use the stolen one-time password in its short validity period (one minute in the above case). However, as pointed out in (Schneier, 2005), this scheme still allows fraudulent transactions as a phishing web site could simply mount a man-in-the-middle attack. Another downside of this approach is that it requires one hardware token for each web site and thus a user may end up with many hardware tokens, which brings inconvenience.

In contrast to all existing countermeasures, the approach of this article mitigates the risk of phishing attacks by strengthening the server-side authentication. Our approach requires little user education and it does not require a user to carry any additional gadgets, making it pretty economically feasible. Like all existing countermeasures, we assume that the client machine is secure in that there are no malware such as a keylogger running on it. Otherwise, no security exists.

THE INTEGRATION DESIGN

As noted in the introduction section, it is the weak server-side authentication that makes web-based phishing attacks possible. PAKE protocols use passwords for mutual authentication, including both the server-side authentication and the client-side authentication, and the combination of these two one-way authentications in a PAKE is inherent and inseparable. Therefore, integrating PAKE into the web can mitigate the risk of phishing attacks.

The Major Challenge

Integrating a PAKE protocol into the web must overcome several barriers. First, building a browser from scratch with PAKE implementation seems infeasible. Second, existing browsers use HTTPS (i.e., SSL) for authenticated key exchange. (Both SSL and PAKE are authenticated key exchange protocols and each of them has its own way to perform entity authentications—*one-way* in SSL and *mutual* in PAKE—and establish session keys after successful authentications. SSL also defines a mode in which mutual authentication is required but this is seldom used in HTTPS by web servers.) They also depend on SSL for application data confidentiality, integrity and anti-replay services. These web browsers do *not* allow a third-party PAKE implementation to replace their native SSL implementations. This forces us to work out a way to compose PAKE with HTTPS. One natural idea is to run a PAKE authenticated key exchange first and then use the PAKE authenticated session key in SSL for application data confidentiality and integrity. However, the native SSL implementations of web browsers do *not* allow their session key to be set to a given value such as a PAKE session key. On the other hand, a simple composition of PAKE and HTTPS by running a PAKE over a possibly broken HTTPS (as is the case of self-signed certificate) at the beginning of a web session is still vulnerable to the man-in-the-middle attack. An innocent user might be fooled into connecting, in HTTPS, to the phishing web site, which then connects in HTTPS to the real web server in that user's name. The phishing web site then passes the PAKE authentication traffic between the cli-

ent and the real server without any modification, allowing the PAKE authentication to succeed. After that the phishing server can perform any fraudulent transactions in the user's name.

Another issue further complicates the web integration of PAKE. As shown in (Felton, Balfanz, Dean, & Wallach, 1996; Ye & Smith, 2002), a phishing web site could use *mobile code* like *JavaScript}* in its web pages to manipulate a user's browser window; if the user mistakes a fake log-in window created by mobile code as a genuine one and types in his password there, there will be no security.

The Data Flow

Figure 1 depicts the architecture of our integration design, with the client-side integration on the left and the server-side integration on the right. On the client side, we use a *browser plug-in* to extend a web browser to integrate PAKE. Unlike mobile code on the web, a browser plug-in provides a secure implementation base for a PAKE client. The server-side integration comprises a web interface containing two web pages and a PAKE server. The PAKE server is also configured with a list of names of the domains that are allowed to use the PAKE server for authentication.

At the very beginning, a user's browser requests a web page that requires user authentication and is redirected to the *log-in page*. In message 2, the log-in page sends back a HTTP response with a

Figure 1. PAKE Web integration data flow

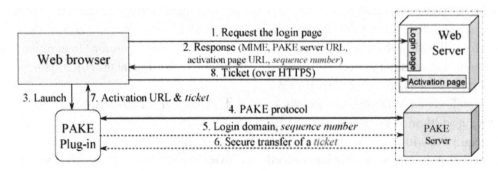

specific MIME type and two URLs—the PAKE server URL and the activation page URL—and a *sequence number*. Upon the MIME type the user's web browser will launch the plug-in program and pass it these two URLs and the sequence number. The sequence number is a 64-bit value starting from 1 and it monotonically increments by one for each request. Its design rationale will be shortly discussed in the section for server-side integration.

Then a log-in window by the browser plug-in program pops up, asking for user name and password. This log-in window should display the customization information that the user specifies when the plug-in program is installed. (If not, the user should refuse to type in his password and the log-in aborts.) After receiving user name and password, the plug-in program talks to the PAKE server in a PAKE protocol, indicated as message 4 in Figure 1, for mutual authentication. If the mutual authentication fails, the plug-in program simply exits. Otherwise, an authenticated session key (thus a secure channel) is established and in message 5, the browser plug-in program sends the log-in domain name, derived from the activation page URL, and the sequence number over the secure PAKE channel (indicated with a dash line in Figure 1) to the PAKE server. If the domain name is *not* an authorized one, the PAKE server will notify the plug-in program to abort this attempt. In message 6, the server will send back a *one-time ticket* over the secure PAKE channel. We shall describe the details of generation and verification of this *one-time ticket*} in the section for server-side integration. In message 7, the plug-in program attaches the ticket to the activation page URL and passes it to the browser, asking it to load the *activation page* URL into the current browser window. This authenticates the web browser to the web server. (An example activation page URL with an attached ticket is https://192.168.100.100/PAKEActivation.jsp?ticket=AFCD7682.) To prevent the one-time ticket from being eavesdropped in message 8, the activation page URL should be based on HTTPS and this is where HTTPS is kicked in. The activation page on the server checks both the *validity* and *freshness* of a received ticket, as described in the section for server-side integration, and stores this user's information in the session object so that the user later can browse restricted web pages. Afterwards, the user browses the web site as usual.

How are phishing attacks prevented by this integration? *First*, a phishing web site could get *no* useful information about the user's reusable password by impersonating the PAKE server. The PAKE protocol used in our design is secure against both simple (passive) eavesdropping and (active) off-line dictionary attacks. Therefore, as long as the end user types in his password to this genuine PAKE log-in window *only*, a fake PAKE server gets no information about the reusable password. On the other hand, an end user can easily detect a fake log-in window by visually checking the customization information. (More details about the customization can be found in the next section.) *Second*, a phishing web site could *not* get any useful information by impersonating the web server hosting the log-in/activation pages either. Since the domain name of the activation page URL is checked by the authenticated PAKE server, a phony web site cannot trick a user into sending a one-time ticket to it. Because the activation page URL is based on HTTPS, an attacker cannot simply eavesdrop on a one-time ticket either. Thus, even the user clicks on a phishing URL in a spam e-mail, no harm will be done.

Design of PAKE Log-in Window

Existing basic and digest authentications use browser-specific log-in windows that are common to all web sites. Figure 2 and Figure 3 are the log-in windows for basic authentication in MSIE and Mozilla respectively. (The log-in windows for digest authentication are very similar.) Both log-in windows do display web-site specific information, including the web server domain name and the

Figure 2. IE 6.0 window for HTTP basic authentication

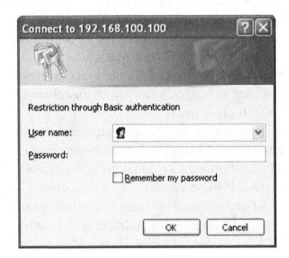

authentication realm name, but both names can be easily manipulated. The web server domain name can be modified to an IP address if the phishing URL uses an IP address, not a domain name. The authentication realm name can be set to any value by the web server.

In form-based authentication, a web site can customize its log-in window (e.g., by displaying its company logo) but this type of customization is public and can be easily copied by a phishing web site.

In our design, to prevent a user from typing his password into a fake log-in window, we add a user customization step in our client-side design. When a user installs the PAKE plug-in program, he is given a chance to customize his PAKE

log-in window. User customization information includes both a textual message (for example, "This is John Doe's Secure Log-in Window") and a graphical picture (for example, Joe Doe's favorite icon). Figure 4 shows how John Doe's PAKE log-in window looks like. The upper-left message is John Doe's customized textual warning message and the upper-right picture is John's Doe's customized icon.

SERVER-SIDE INTEGRATION

Architectural Consideration

As shown in Figure 1, the server-side integration consists of two *logical* parts, those two web pages and the PAKE server implementing PAKE server-side functionality. The *log-in page* and the *activation page* are for message 1 and message 8 of Figure 1 respectively. The PAKE server can be implemented in several forms: it can be implemented as web pages running in the same web container as the log-in page and the activation page; or it can also be implemented as a *stand-alone* application server listening on a dedicated network port.

The major benefits of having a stand-alone PAKE server are performance enhancement and cross-site log-in. We can run the stand-alone program on a fast computer. This will significantly improve the server-side computational performance as PAKE protocols are built on

Figure 3. Mozilla 3.0.10 window for HTTP basic authentication

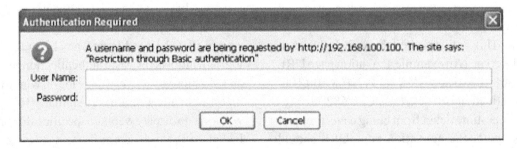

Figure 4. PAKE log-in widow

computation-intensive public key techniques. We can also direct the authentication of multiple web applications, possibly from *different* web sites, to the same stand-alone PAKE server. This is desirable as it reduces the number of passwords a user has to memorize. It also allows centralized auditing on the stand-alone PAKE server for on-line password guessing attacks.

Sequence Numbers, Tickets, and Their Security

The ticket of message 6 of Figure 1 has three elements: *the sequence number, the user name,* and *an authentication tag.* (Unlike a Kerberos ticket, a ticket here is not based on time and thus a globally synchronized clock is not required.) The inclusion of a sequence number in a ticket is to prevent a ticket from being replayed. Depending on the implementation format of the PAKE server, the generation and verification of a ticket vary.

Case 1: Embedded authentication. *When the PAKE server is implemented as a web page running in the same web container as the log-in/activation pages, the ticket generation and verification are simple. Such a PAKE server can share a common buffer with the log-in and activation pages. In*

this case, the sequence number is left empty by the log-in page. After successfully authenticating a user, the PAKE server simply generates a 128-bit random number as the authentication tag; it then stores the (user account name, the random number) pair to the common buffer. After receiving the ticket in message 8, the activation page can verify its authenticity by looking up the common buffer. This random number is removed from the common buffer after it is verified. In this way, a replayed ticket can be simply detected as there is no corresponding random number in the buffer.

Case 2: Separate identity provider. *If the PAKE server is implemented as a distributed component by a separate identity provider, care should be taken in the ticket generation and verification. In this case, a sequence number is a 64-bit monotonically increasing number starting from 1. We do not use time stamps for anti-replaying as it is hard to maintain a globally synchronized clock in a distributed environment.*

We use the symmetric key-based *message authentication code* (MAC) for the generation and verification of the *authentication tag* of a ticket, assuming that the PAKE server and the activation page share a common symmetric key, k. (A MAC is a value calculated from a symmetric key and a given message. MAC allows a message receiver who also has the same symmetric key to check the integrity of the received message. Example MAC techniques are HMAC and C-MAC.) The details of establishing k will be shortly described in the next section. This makes our design extremely efficient as MAC schemes are very fast. After successfully authenticating a user in Step 4 and verifying the log-in domain name in Step 5 of Figure 1, the PAKE server applies k to the given sequence number and the domain\user name to generate a MAC value, which is used as the authentication tag. (k is called the MAC key.)

To detect a replayed ticket, the activation page maintains a *sliding receiver sequence-number window* of a certain size (say 128). After receiving a ticket in Step 8 of Figure 1, the activation page first uses k to check the validity of the MAC value. If the MAC value is successfully verified, indicating that the ticket is authentic, the activation page checks whether the sequence number of the ticket is in the sliding window and whether it has not been used before. The sliding window has two edges, *the left edge* and *the right edge*, which is larger. If the sequence number is smaller than the left edge of this window, the ticket will be rejected. If the sequence number is between these two edges, the activation page will check whether the corresponding slot in the window has been occupied. If not, the ticket is accepted and the slot is marked as occupied. If the slot is already occupied, the ticket will be rejected as it is replayed.

If the sequence number falls outside the right edge of the sliding window, the ticket is accepted and the right edge of the window is moved to that position. To keep the sliding receiver window at a fixed size, the left edge of window also moves correspondingly. (The concept of sliding receiver window has been used in IP Security, where two parties, the sender and the receiver, are involved. Note that we have three distributed parties here,

the log-in/activation page, the web browser, and the PAKE server.)

It should be noted that the above sliding window mechanism automatically checks the freshness of a ticket. If a ticket is too old, very likely its sequence number will be smaller than the left edge of the sliding window and thus will be rejected.

The Establishment of the MAC Key

When the PAKE server is implemented as a distributed application server (that is, case 2), in the last section, we assumed that the PAKE server shares a symmetric key with the activation page. Here we describe how this symmetric key is established.

To avoid direct communication between the PAKE server and the activation page, we can piggyback the key establishment messages in the data flow of Figure 1. Below we describe one example scenario based on the authenticated Diffie-Hellman protocol to show how the piggyback works. The piggybacking of messages for other key establishment protocols is very similar.

Let's assume that the PAKE server generates a public/private key pair for digital signature and the *log-in page* has the PAKE server's public key. (This can be accomplished through either manual configuration or a small-scale public key infrastructure (PKI).) Let N be a large prime and g be a generator of finite field F_N. When the web container of the log-in page boots up, there is no shared symmetric key between the *activation page* and the PAKE server.

When the log-in page receives a log-in request, it generates a random number a, $1 \leq a \leq N$, calculates $A = g^a \mod N$, and sends A, along with the sequence number, in message 1 of Figure 1. Value A is passed to the browser plug-in program and is piggybacked in message 5 of Figure 1 to the PAKE server. The PAKE server generates a random value b, $1 \leq b \leq N$, and calculates $B = g^b \mod N$, $X = A^b \mod N$, and $k = h(X)$, where h is a cryptographic hash function like SHA-1. k is used as the MAC key discussed in the last section to generate authentication tags. The PAKE server then digitally signs the concatenation of A and B and piggybacks B and the digital signature value in message 6 of Figure 1 to the browser plug-in, which piggybacks them in message 8 to the activation page. The activation page runs in the same web container as the log-in page and thus can access value a. The activation page then checks the digital signature on $(A \| B)$; if the digital signature is verified successfully, it calculates $X = B^a$ mod N, $k = h(X)$, and uses k as the MAC key to verify the received authentication tag.

To make the *distributed* system more resilient against network delays, value A is piggybacked to the first 10 log-in requests; similarly, value B and the digital signature value are piggybacked in the first 10 responses from the PAKE server. In this way, there is no requirement on the order of the log-in requests reaching the PAKE server or on the order of the responses reaching the activation page.

PROTOTYPE IMPLEMENTATION

Plug-in Development

To validate our design, we developed a prototype. We chose the MS Windows as our client-side platform as most phishing attacks target at Windows users. The web browser that we picked was

Mozilla, an open source web browser, and we based our plug-in development on the *Gecko SDK* (Mozilla Developer Center, 2006). A browser plug-in developed this way also works with Microsoft Internet Explorer (MS IE) (Mozilla Developer Center, 2001). Figure 4 gives an example of our customizable PAKE log-in window.

We used the *CInternetSession* class of the Microsoft Foundation Classes (MFC), which supports web cookies to maintain HTTP states, for the HTTP communication between the plug-in and the PAKE server. The GMP (GNU Multiple Precision) Arithmetic Library (Granlund, 2004) was employed for big integer operations.

The PAKE protocol used in our prototype implementation was the Secure Remote Password protocol version 6 (SRP6) (IEEE P1363.2, 2005), whose data flow is given in the appendix section. The SRP6 system parameters were chosen from the IKE MODP 1024 (well-known group 2) (Orman, 1998) where N has 1024 bits and is provably prime.

The web browser plug-in exists as a *DLL* file, *nppake.dll*, and should be deployed to the *plugins* subdirectory of the Mozilla browser.

Server-Side Prototype Implementation

Our server-side ran Apache's Tomcat web server 5.5.9 (Apache Tomcat, 2003) and we used Java Server Page (JSP) as our development language. The server-side implementation comprises three JSP pages—*PAKELogin.jsp*, *PAKEActivation. jsp*, and *SRP6Login.jsp*—and one JavaBean class, *SRP6.java*. *PAKELogin.jsp* is the log-in page. It handles the request in message 1 of Figure 1 and returns message 2, which is a HTTP message with the *application/x-pake-auth* MIME type in its header and the full URLs of the *PAKEActivation. jsp* page and the *SRP6Login.jsp* page in its body. *PAKEActivation.jsp* is the activation page and it handles message 8 of Figure 1 and it checks the validity of a ticket.

SRP6Login.jsp is the front JSP page of the SRP6 server and it runs in the same web container as the log-in page and the activation page. (In other words, we implemented case 1 of the SEQUENCE NUMBERS section.) *SRP6Login. jsp* calls a JavaBean class *SRP6*, which implements the SRP6 server-side functionality. More specifically, the SRP6 class provides two methods. The first method receives I and A (see Table 1 of the Appendix section) and returns s and B. The second method receives M_1 and returns M_2 and, if the mutual authentication succeeds, an encrypted message containing a ticket. After issuing a ticket, the *SRP6* class registers this ticket to a web application-wide object, which is also accessible to the activation page.

CONCLUSION

Existing password authentication methods on the web use passwords for client-side authentication only and they need a *separate* mechanism for server-side authentication. Through exploiting a weakness in such a loose coupling, phishing attacks succeed in collecting users' passwords and conducting fraudulent transactions and have become rampant on the Internet. In this article, we explored countering phishing attacks by integrating on the web the password-authenticated key exchanged (PAKE) protocols, which use passwords for mutual authentication.

By employing one-time tickets, our design integrates PAKE with HTTPS very well and does *not* require changes to user browsing behaviors and needs *little* user education. Through a customized PAKE log-in window, an ordinary user can easily detect and stop spoofing attacks by mobile code. Our server-side integration allows a stand-alone PAKE server and thus supports centralized log-in and digital identity management.

REFERENCES

Anti-phising Working Group. (2009, March). *Phishing activity trends report for the 2nd half of 2008*. Retrieved from http://www.antiphishing. org/reports/apwg_report_H2_2008.pdf

Apache Tomcat. (2003). *The Apache Jakarta Tomcat 5 servlet/JSP container*. Retrieved from http://tomcat.apache.org/tomcat-5.0-doc/

Cao, Y., Han, W., & Le, Y. (2008). Anti-phishing based on automated individual white-list. In *Proceedings of the 4th ACM Workshop on Digital Identity Management (DIM'08)*, Alexandria, VA (pp. 51-60).

Chou, N., Ledesma, R., Teraguchi, Y., Boneh, D., & Mitchell, J. C. (2004). *Client-side defense against web-based identity theft*. Paper presented at the 11th Annual Network and Distributed System Security Symposium (NDSS '04).

Dhamija, R., Tygar, J. D., & Hearst, M. (2006). *Why phishing works*. Paper presented at the Conference on Human Factors in Computing Systems (CHI2006).

Dunn, J. E. (2005, December 30). Phishers now targeting SSL. *TechWorld*. Retrieved from http://www.techworld.com/news/index. cfm?RSS&NewsID=5069

Felton, E., Balfanz, D., Dean, D., & Wallach, D. (1996). *Web spoofing: An Internet con game* (Tech. Rep. No. TR 54096). Princeton, NJ: Princeton University.

Fu, K., Sit, E., Smith, K., & Feamster, N. (2001). *Dos and don'ts of client authentication on the web*. Paper presented at the 10th USENIX Security Symposium.

Granlund, T. (2004). *GNU MP edition 4.1.4. (The GNU Multiple Precision Arithmetic Library)*. Retrieved from http://swox.com/gmp/

Gutmann, P. (2003). *Plug-and-play PKI: A PKI your mother can use*. Paper presented at the 12nd USENIX Security Symposium.

Gutmann, P. (2004). *How to build a PKI that works*. Paper presented at the 3rd Annual PKI R&D Workshop, Gaithersburg, MD.

Hodgin, R. C. (2007, December 18). Phishing cost the U.S. $3.2 billion in 2007. *Tom's Hardware*. Retrieved from http://www.tomshardware.com/news/phishing-cost-u-s-3-2-billion-2007,4576.html

IEEE. P1363.2. (2005). *Draft standard specifications for password-based public key cryptographic techniques*. Retrieved from http://grouper.ieee.org/groups/1363/passwdPK/index.html

James, L. (2005). *Phishing exposed. uncover secrets from the dark side* (1st ed.). Burlington, MA: Syngress.

Josefsson, S. (2003, July). *The base16, base32, and base64 data encodings*. Freemont, CA: Internet IETF Request for Comments 3548.

Liberty Alliance Project. (2005, May). *Liberty ID-FF architecture overview* (Version 1.2-errata-v1.0). Retrieved from http://www.projectliberty.org/resource_center/specifications/liberty_alliance_id_ff_1_2_specifications

Microsoft Corporation. (2006). *Windows live ID service*. Retrieved from http://msdn.microsoft.com/library/default.asp?url=/library/en-us/dn-live/html/winliveidserv.asp

Mozilla Developer Center. (2001). *ActiveX control for hosting Netscape plug-ins in IE*. Retrieved from http://www.mozilla.org/projects/plugins/plugin-host-control.html

Mozilla Developer Center. (2006). *Gecko plugin API reference*. Retrieved from http://developer.mozilla.org/en/docs/Gecko_Plugin_API_Reference

Odlyzko, A. (2003). Economics, psychology, and sociology of security. In R. N. Wright (Ed.), *Proceedings of the 7th International Conference on Financial Cryptography (FC 2003)* (LNCS 2742, pp. 182-189).

Orman, H. (1998). *The OAKLEY key determination protocol* (RFC 2412). Freemont, CA: IETF.

Richmond, R. (2005, December 1). Banks seek better online security tools. *Wall Street Journal*.

Ross, B., Jackson, C., Miyake, N., Boneh, D., & Mitchell, J. (2005). *Stronger password authentication using browser extensions*. Paper presented at the 14th USENIX Security Symposium.

Schneier, B. (2005, March 15). The failure of two-factor authentication. *Crypto-Gram Newsletter*. Retrieved from http://www.schneier.com/crypto-gram-0503.html

Security, R. S. A. (2004). *Protecting against phishing by implementing strong two-factor authentication*. Retrieved from http://www.antiphishing.org/sponsors_technical_papers/PHISH_WP_0904.pdf

Tally, G., Thomas, R., Van, V., & Ieck, T. (2004). *Anti-phishing: Best practices for institutions and consumers*. Retrieved from http://www.antiphishing.org/sponsors_technical_papers/Anti-Phishing_Best_Practices_for_Institutions_Consumer0904.pdf

The Honeynet Project & Research Alliance. (2005). *Know your enemy: Phishing – behind the scenes of phishing attacks*. Retrieved from http://www.honeynet.org/papers/phishing/

Ye, Z., & Smith, S. (2002). Trusted paths for browsers. In *Proceedings of the 11th USENIX Security Symposium* (pp. 263-279).

APPENDIX

We used SRP6 in our prototype implementation. For completeness reason, we summarize here its data flow. It should be noted that SRP has many versions and this one is from (IEEE P1363.2, 2005).

Let N be a large prime and g is a generator for finite field F_N. For a user I whose password is p, his corresponding PVD is $v = g^x \bmod N$, where $x = h(s, I, p)$, h is a cryptographic hash function like SHA-1 and s is a value called *salt*. $\delta = h(N \parallel g)$ where $\parallel$ denotes string concatenation.

Given two integers a and b, $[a, b]$ denotes the set of integers between a and b, inclusive. $r \in_R [a, b]$ denotes that r is a number randomly picked from $[a, b]$. Table 1 describes the data flow of the SRP6 protocol.

Table 1. The SRP6 protocol

	CLIENT		SERVER
1	$a \in_R [1, N-2]$, $A = g^a \bmod N$	$I, A \rightarrow$	If $A \bmod N = 0$, quit
2	$x = h(s, I, p)$ If $B \bmod N = 0$, quit; $u = h(A \parallel B)$	$\leftarrow s, B$	$b \in_R [1, N-2]$, $B = \delta \times v + g^b \bmod N$ $u = h(A \parallel B)$
3	$S_c = (B - \delta \times g^x)^{a+ux} \bmod N$ $K_c = h(S_c)$		$S_s = (Av^u)^b \bmod N$ $K_s = h(S_s)$
4	$M_1 = h(0x03, A, B, S_c, v)$	$M_1 \rightarrow$	$M_1' = h(0x03, A, B, S_s, v)$ If $M_1' \neq M_1$, quit
5	$M_2' = h(0x4, A, B, S_c, v)$ If $M_2' \neq M_2$, quit	$\leftarrow M_2$	$M_2 = h(0x4, A, B, S_s, v)$

This work was previously published in International Journal of Information Security and Privacy (IJISP), edited by Hamid Nemati, pp 29-42, copyright 2009 by IGI Publishing (imprint of IGI Global)

Chapter 22
Three Models to Measure Information Security Compliance

Wasim A. Al-Hamdani
Kentucky State University, USA

ABSTRACT

This work introduces three models to measure information security compliance. These are the cardinality model, the second's model, which is based on vector space, and the last model is based on the priority principle. Each of these models will be presented with definitions, basic operations, and examples. All three models are based on a new theory to understand information security called the Information Security Sets Theory (ISST). The ISST is based on four basic sets: external sets, local strategy sets, local standard sets, and local implementation sets. It should be noted that two sets are used to create local standard sets—local expansion and local creation. The major differences between the Zermelo Fraenkel set theory and the ISST are the elimination of using empty element ϕ and empty set. This assumption is based on "there is not empty security" measure and the ϕ is substituted to be λ and is defined as "minimum security (or system default security)". The main objective of this article is to achieve new modeling system for information security compliance. The compliance measurement is defined in the first model as the cardinality between local strategy sets and the actual local implementation. The second model is looking at the security compliance as the angle θ between two sets, local implementation and local standard. The third model is based on the priority philosophy for local security standard.

1. INTRODUCTION

Compliance is one of the major issues in information security management is "to be sure been evaluated correctly". Compliance (regulation) is

DOI: 10.4018/978-1-60960-200-0.ch022

defined as, "the act of adhering to, and demonstrating adherence to, a standard or regulation" (Wikipedia.org, 2008) or "Conformity in fulfilling official requirement" (MerriamWebster.com, 2009). Many industries measure the compliance with best practices as compliance with ISO 17799 or NIST special publication 800. A normal procedure to measure compliance is to create a checklist and label two elements finding and compliance, such as in BS 7799.2:2002 Audit Checklist (Thiagarajan, 2003) or ISO 177999 checklist (Thomas, 2003). The checklist evaluator would give either a value of 1 (for YES) to element compliance and 0 (for NO) for noncompliance and the final result measured mathematically would be: "

Superior: >95 "yes" answers
Fair: 82–95 "yes" answers
Marginal: 68–81 "yes" answers
Poor: 54–67 "yes" answers
At Risk: <54 "yes" answers"

Such a model can be mathematically summarized as the sum for all elements $\sum_{i=1}^{n} x_i$ and x_i is an element in the security list.

Another issuer is to look at compliance through regulation. As Adler (2006) pointed out, "Self-regulation through the implementation of good security practices was thought to be the way to protect electronic personal information. In the latter part of the 20th century, "a sectoral approach to information security regulation started to gain favor with the passage of laws protecting health and financial information" (Adler, 2006). Most regulation compliance is with:

- Health Insurance Portability and Accountability Act (HIPAA) compliance,
- Family Educational Rights and Privacy Act (FERPA)
- Gramm-Leach-Bliley Act (GLBA)
- Payment Card Industry Data Security Standard (PCIDSS)
- Federal Information Security Management Act of 2002 (FISMA)
- OMB M-06-16 addresses the protection of agency information that is either "accessed remotely or physically transported outside

of the agency's secured, physical perimeter" (Adler, 2006).

Some have permitted information security compliance to be handled by more than one department. For example, in education campuses (Adler, 2006), the university hospital or the health center may be tasked with Health Insurance Portability and Accountability Act (HIPAA) compliance, the financial aid office or departments using credit cards may focus on compliance with the Gramm-Leach-Bliley Act (GLBA) or the Payment Card Industry Data Security Standard (PCIDSS), while the registrar may be held responsible for the privacy of student educational records under the Family Educational Rights and Privacy Act (FERPA).

On the technical level, many organizations reference their technical (configuration) standards compliance based on NIST special publications 800 series and NIST checklist (NIST, 2008). As in Special Publication 800-70, "A *security configuration checklist* (sometimes called a lockdown or hardening guide or benchmark) is in its simplest form a series of documented instructions for configuring a product to a pre-defined operational environment. It could also include templates or automated scripts and other procedures. Checklists can be developed for specific IT products and environments not only by IT vendors, but also by consortia, industry, Federal agencies and other governmental organizations, and others in the public and private sectors. The use of well-written, standardized checklists can reduce the vulnerability exposure of IT products and be particularly helpful to small organizations and individuals for securing their systems" (Souppaya, Wack, & Kent, 2005, p. 1).

To summarize these issues, there are two types of compliance measures:

- Using baseline or best practices in the industry or best standards (as using ISO

17799 or NIST Special application 800 series)

- Using legal requirements such as using HIPAA or GLBA.

Both of these techniques use a checklist or a matrix method with measure of Yes and No, and a normal auditing procedure is using the checklist as a measure of auditing compliance.

In this work, we will cover the introduction of the Information Security Sets Theory (ISST) and the three information security compliance models. The ISST set is the base of all this work. It is a classical set theory with major differences from the Zermelo Fraenkel set (Aczel, 2008). In particular, the ISST eliminates any existing of empty element ϕ and any empty set $\{\phi\}$; this assumption is based on "there is not empty security environment to be measured", the ϕ is substituted to be λ and is defined as minimum security or system default security.

The ISST model has four basic different sets. These are:

- *External sets*: sets of all national and international best practices and standard benchmarks
- *Local strategy sets*: sets of external sets that have been adopted by an organization to guide their security standards
- *Local standard sets*: sets generated using local expansion sets and /or local creation sets
- *Local implementation sets*: sets of actual security elements implemented in an organization

The first compliance model presented in this work uses a measure defined as the cardinality between *local strategy* sets and the actual *local implementation*. The second model is looking at the security compliance from vector spec's point of view and the compliance is the angle θ between two sets – *local standard* and *local implementation*. The third model is as the second using the same principles presented in the first model of the ISST with an additional element to measure the compliance; this is the priority principle. There are several ways that priorities can be assigned, which can be designated as either internal priorities or external priorities. With this model, the compliance measure is the sum of the product between the priority value and the *local standard* value.

An observation to evaluate these three models shows that the third model is the most realistic, as what is important for your organization is not important for my organization. This depends on many factors, such as organizational culture, the level required from confidentiality, integrity, availability (CIA), authenticity, non-reputation, accountability, legality, and other elements. For example, the precedence security object for a credit card company is not the same as for a small local bank, and the precedence security object for an international bank is not the same as a small local bank.

A comparison between the three models shows that the last model is most reasonable to be implemented since priority is right of precedence. This conclusion rejects the standard security compliance measure as two values of exist (=1) and not exist (=0). As suggested, the first two models and many compliance matrix measurements exist for security compliance. As a result, the priority model has mathematical definitions for fuzzy compliance measures, compliance evidence measures, compliance plausibility, possibility compliance measures, and necessity compliance measures. These definitions are based on the concept of fuzzy measure modeling.

In this work phrase, *observation* is defined as "remark or comment based on examination of different facts."

2. BASICS PRINCIPLES

Set theory principles some basic set theory definitions are:

Definition: A set is a collection of distinct objects

Definition: An object x is an element or member of a set S, written $x \in S$, if x satisfies the rule defining membership is S.

We can write $x \notin S$ if x is not an element of S.

Definition: The empty set or null set, denoted ϕ, is the set containing no elements.

Definition: The cardinality of a set S, written |S|, is the number of elements in the set.

Definition: Two sets S and T are equal, written S = T, if S and T contain exactly the same elements

Definition: A set S is a subset of another set T, written $T \subset S$ if every element of S is also an element of T.

Definition: A set S is a proper subset of T if $T \subset S$ and $T \neq S$ That is, if every element of S is also in T, but some element of T is not in S.

Other basic classical set theory can be found in Appendix 1

Information Security Set Theory (ISST) some basic definitions are

Definition: A security object is an element used to protect an organization

Example: The following are security objects: network access control, system access matrices, e-mail policy, disaster recovery plan, system recovery plan, firewall configuration management, physical security, firewall, router policy, access policy, and organization procedures.

Definition: S is the Information Security Set Theory (ISST) defined as a collection of security objects.

Observation: The ISST set does not have an empty set or an empty element, The information security set has λ as a minimal security object. The λ is defined as the system default and it has a system default set as $\{\lambda\}$. Simply, λ is a default object and $\{\lambda\}$ is a default set.

Example: An organization X does not have any security program, λ = operating system security, network access control enforced by the network operating system, system default encryption, wireless default encryption.

Example: A small business has one computer loaded with Windows XP and Office 2007; λ_1 is the XP operating default security and λ_2 is the Office 2007 default security; $\lambda_1 \cup \lambda_2 = \{default\ Windows\ XP\ and\ Office\ 2007\ patches\ updating\} = \{\lambda\}$

By this assumption, the ISST operations and axioms are the same as in the classical set theory (Zermelo-Fraenkel axioms) except for the use of λ. Assume S is an ISST, then

$$\lambda_S \cup S = S$$

$$\lambda_S \cap S = \lambda_S$$

If S and T are ISST (for different organizations), then each ISST has its λ and is defined as λ_S and λ_T, $\lambda_S \neq \lambda_T$

If $S = T$ then (possibly and not necessarily true) $\lambda_S = \lambda_T$ and $\lambda_T \cup S = S \cup \lambda_T$

If S, T and P are ISST (for a single organization), then an organization $\lambda = \{\lambda_S \cup \lambda_T \cup \lambda_P\}$

Generally if S, T are ISST, then:

$$S \cup T \neq \lambda \ iff. \ S \neq \lambda \ \text{or} \ T \neq \lambda$$

$$S \cap T \neq \lambda \ iff. \ S \neq \lambda \ \text{or} \ T \neq \lambda$$

$$S \cap T = \lambda \ iff. \ S = \lambda \ \text{or} \ T = \lambda$$

$$S = T \neq \lambda \ iff. \ (S \cup T) \subset (S \cap T)$$

U is defined as the universal set

$$\overline{U} = \lambda \ \text{ and } \ \overline{\lambda} = U$$

$$S \cup \overline{S} = U \ \text{and} \ S \cap \overline{S} = \lambda$$

$$S \subset \overline{S} \ \ iff. \ S = \lambda_S$$

All other properties from the classical set theory are applied on set ISST, such as: definition of subset, equality, intersection, reflexive, transitive symmetric, commutative, set deference (for detail definitions, see Goldrei, 1996; Jech, 2006).

3. INFORMATION SECURTY SET THEORY MODEL (ISST)

In ISST, there are four different sets. These are: *External Strategy sets* $Extr_x$, *Local Strategy sets* $Lstr_x$, *Local Standard sets* $Lsta_x$ (can be generated using *Local Standard sets* $Lsta_x$ with correlation to *Local Expansion sets* $L\exp_x$ and /or *Local Creation sets* $Lcre_x$) and the last set is the *Local Implementation sets* $Limp_x$,

Definition:*External Strategy sets* $Extr_x$ is a set including all national and international standards and best practices and standard benchmarks (existing outside an organization and has not been adopted officially to be used by the organization).

The $Extr_x$ could one or more (standard) adopted from the following list:

(a) International standardization organizations:
- *International Organization for Standardization (ISO)* (Example: ISO/IEC 17799:2005)
- *International Electrotechnical Commission (IEC)*
- *International Telecommunication Union (ITU)*

(b) National standardization organizations:
- *National Institute of Standards and Technology (NIST)*
- *American National Standards Institute (ANSI)*

(c) *British Standards Institute (BSI)*

(d) Industrial standardization organizations:
- *Institute of Electrical and Electronics Engineers (IEEE)*
- *Public-Key Cryptography Standards (PKCSs)*
- *Internet Engineering Task Force (IETF)*
- *Standards for Efficient Cryptography Group (SECG)*
- *Third Generation Partnership Project (3GPP)*
- *European Telecommunications Standard Institute (ETSI)*

(e) Legal standards
- *Health Insurance Portability and Accountability Act (HIPAA)*
- *Family Educational Rights and Privacy Act (FERPA)*
- *Gramm-Leach-Bliley Act (GLBA)*
- *Payment Card Industry Data Security Standard (PCIDSS)*
- *Federal Information Security Management Act of 2002 (FISMA)*
- *OMB M-06-16*
- *Visa Cardholder Information Security Program (CISP)*
- *American Express Data Security Standard*
- *Sarbanes-Oxley Act (SOX)*
- *California Senate Bill No. 1386*

Definition

The set $Extr_x$ is the *universal set* of all security objects (exists exterior to an organization).

Example

$Extr_x = \{$ISO17799-2005, COBIT, ISO 27001 and ISO 27002 $\}$
OR

$Extr_x = \{$COBIT, ISO 27001 and ISO 27002 $\}$
OR

$Extr_x = \{$COBIT $\}$

$Extr_x = \{$ $Gramm - Leach - BlileyAct$ $\left(GLBA\right)$ $\}$

An organization can adopt any standards to be local strategy sets

$Extr_1 = \{Federal\ Information$ Processing Standards $\left(\text{FIPS 2006}\right)\}$
OR

$Extr_2 = \{$ISO17799-2005$\}$ OR

$Extr_1 \cup Extr_2 =$
$\{$ISO17799-2005, FederalInformation Processing Standards $\left(\text{FIPS 2006}\right)\}$

$Extr_1 \cap Extr_2 = \lambda$

$\lambda = \{$Access control, P*ersonal security,..}*

Definition

Local Strategy sets $Lstg_x$ are sets of external strategies sets that have been adopted by an organization to guide their security standards and implementation with $Lstg_x \subset Extr_x$. The local strategy sets $Lstg_x$ can be defined as a collection of sets or subset of power sets[1] on external sets $\rho(Extr_1)$

Example: in set theory is $S = \left\{x, y, z\right\}$ then
$$\rho(S) = \{\{\}, \{x\}, \{y\}, \{z\}, \{x,y\}, \{x,z\}, \{y,z\}, \{x,y,z\}\}$$

While in ISST if $S = \left\{x, y, z\right\}$ then
$$\rho(S) = \{\lambda, \{x\}, \{y\}, \{z\}, \{x,y\}, \{x,z\}, \{y,z\}, \{x,y,z\}\}$$

Example:
$Lsta_{ISO17799} = \{$set of all ISO 17799 elements$\}$
$= \{$Security Policy, Organizing Information Security$\}$

Definition: the function that maps external strategies sets $Extr_x$ and local strategies sets $Lstg_x$ is $f : \rho(Extr_x) \rightarrow Lstg_x$

And

$$f = \begin{cases} 0 \ iff. \ \nexists^{Lstg} \text{Adaptation} \\ 1 \ iff. \ \exists^{Lstg} \text{Adaptation} \end{cases}$$

$\exists^{Lstg}$ Means these exist as local strategy sets adopted from the external sets

$\nexists^{Lstg}$ Means these exist as no local strategy sets adopted from the external sets

Example: An organization decides to use ISO 19977 as their local strategy. $f : Extr_{ISO19977} \rightarrow Lstg_x, f_{ISO17799} = 1$, in this case $\exists$ set of all ISO17799 class as Local standard sets, and then $Lsta_{ISO17799} = \{$set of all ISO 17799 elements$\}$ $=\{$Security Policy, Organizing Information Security, Asset Management, Human Resources Security, Physical and Environment Security, Communications and Operations Management, Access Control, Information Systems Acquisition, Development and

Maintenance, Information Security Incident Management, Business Continuity Management, Compliance}

Example

An organization defined their local strategies sets as

$$Lstg_x = \{\text{ISO17799}\} \text{ or } Lstg_x = \left\{\text{ISO17799}\right\} \cup \{NIST - SP\ 800 - 66\ \text{Rev1}\}$$

SP 800-66 Rev1 (Scholl et al., 2008) is a "DRAFT An Introductory Resource Guide for Implementing the Health Insurance Portability and Accountability Act (HIPAA) Security Rule"

Another set is call local standard sets, which represents the baseline for implementing secure functionality in an organization. This set is a collection of:

- All adopted security principles and functionality from local strategy $Lstg$
- All added and adopted security functionality from other organization called *local expansion* $L\exp$
- All local creation security principles (based on an organization cultures) called *local creation* $Lcre$

    Example: An organization's local strategy is $Lstg_x = \{\text{ISO17799}\}$, x add an adopted security policy from an organization y and added local disaster recovery plan implementation previously. However, this organization x has local standard sets.

    $$Lsta_x = \text{ISO17799} \cup$$
    security policy from y ∪ x Disaster recovery plan

Definition

Local standard sets $(Lsta_x)$ is a collection of sets of all adopted detail security objects and is generated from three types:

Type 1: Local strategies $Lstg_x$

Type 2: Local Expansion $L\exp_x$ is an object (element) existing outside an organization (element in standard or benchmark) adopted to the organization.

Example: an organization x adopts ISO17799 as their local strategy $Lstg_x = \{ISO17799\}$ and adopt an organization y awareness program to cooperate their local satrapy; till this stage x should have $Lstg_x = \{ISO17799\} \cup Lstg_{y:Awareness\ \text{Program}}$

Example: an organization x adopts sets of existing policies implemented in an organization y with their agreement; such that $L\exp_{x:policies} = L\exp_{y:policies}$

Type 3: Local creations set $Lcre_x$ is created using local resources based on organization culture.

These three sets $Lstg_x$, $Lexp_x$ & $Lcre_x$ are the essential sets to create the local standard $(Lsta_x)$ for an organization. The difference between local expansion $Lexp_x$ and local creation $Lcre_x$ are local expansion $Lexp_x$ uses an external resource (for one object or more), while the local creation $Lcre_x$ uses internal resources.

The relation between the three sets, $Lstg_x$, $Lexp_x$ & $Lcre_x$

$$Lsta_x = Lstg_x \cup Lexp_x \cup Lcre_x$$

Figure 1 shows the hierarchy relationships between different sets.

Figure 1. The hierarchy relationships between different sets

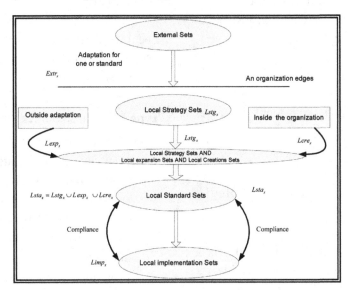

Building a complete local strategy set could be done using top down approach, as in the following example.

Example

$Lstg_{level1} = \{ISO17799\}$

$Lstg_{level2} = \{$Security Policy, *Asset Management, Human Resources Security, Physical and Environment Security, Communications and Operations Management, Access Control, Information Systems Acquisition, Development and Maintenance, Information Security Incident Management, Business Continuity Management, Compliance}*

$Lstg_{level21} = \{$Security Policy$\} =$ {hardware policy, softwarepolicy, email policy, the computer use,

Access to Information and Systems, ConfiguringNetworks ...}

$L \exp_{22} = \{AssetManagement\}$

$L \exp_{23} \{AccessControl\}$

$L \exp_{23} = Lcre_{education} = \{$student access control (graduate and undergraduate), staff, faculty, administration, IT department}

$L \exp_{23} = \{HumanResources\ Security\}$

Definition

Local implementation sets $Limp_{x}$, is the actual implemented security objects in an organization.

Example

Assume
$Lsta_{Access\ control} = \{$graduate studentaccess control, undergraduate access control, staff, faculty, administration,IT department}

$$Limp_{Access\ contol} = \{\text{student privilege, faculty privilege, ITdepartment}\}$$

$$Lsta_{Security\ Policy} = \{Hardware\ policy, Software\ policy,$$
$$software\ installation,\ software\ configuration,$$

Fax machine policy, Email policy, Emailattachments policy}

$$Limp_{Security\ Policy} = \{\text{Email Policy}\}$$

Definition: **Class** is a collection of sets

Definition: **External class** is collection of external sets and represented as: $Cls(Extr_x)$

$$Cls(Extr_x) = \{Extr_{x_1} \cup Extr_{x_2} \cup ...Extr_{x_n}\} \text{ And}$$

could be written as $Cl(Extr_x) = \bigcup_n^{i=1} Extr_{xi}, n \in \mathbb{Z}$

Example

$Extr_{x1} = \{$National Institute of Standards and technology $(NIST)$, America National Standard Institute $(ANSI)$, British Standard $(BSI)\}$

$Extr_{x2} = \{$InternationalOrganization for Standardization (ISO), International ElectrotechnicalCommission (IES), International Telecommunication Union $(ITU)\}$

An organization could select to work only with these two classes, and then their external classes are

$$Cls(Extr_x) = \{Extr_{x_1} \cup Extr_{x_2}\}$$

And generally

$$Cls(Extr_x) = \bigcup_n^{i=1} Extr_{xi}$$

Definition: An organization's top-level security is the class of all local standards.

$$Cls(Lsta_x) = \bigcup_n^{i=1} Lsta_{xi}$$

Definition: A minimum security set $MinSec_x$ is a subset from Local Class Standard $Cls(Lsta_x)$ suchthat $MinSec_x \subset Cls(Lsta_x)$

Definition: Base Line security set $Basline_x$ is a subset from the set of Local Standard $Lsta_x$ such that
$$MinSec_x \subset Basline_x \subseteq Cls(Lsta_x)$$

Observation

Two organizations with different cultures have different baseline security.

FororganizationA: $\exists\ Basline_A \subseteq Cls(Lsta_A)$ and for B: $\exists\ Basline_B \subseteq Cls(Lsta_B)$

$$Lsta_A = f(Lstg_A, L\exp_A, Lcre_A)$$

$$Lsta_A = Lstg_A + L\exp_A + Lcre_A$$

And similarly, for organization B, since the two organizations have different cultures, this means different security control understanding, then (Even with $Lstg_A = Lstg_B$)

$$Lsta_A \neq Lsta_B \text{ Because}$$
$$L\exp_A \neq L\exp_B \text{ and } Lcre_A \neq Lcre_B$$

Observation

Two organizations with different cultures have different local standards.

$Lsta_x$ For organization A: $\exists\ Lsta_A$ and for B:
$$Lsta_B$$

$$Lsta_A = f(Lstg_A, L\exp_A, Lcre_A)$$

$$Lsta_A = Lstg_A + L\exp_A + Lcre_A$$

And for organization B, since the two organizations have different cultures, this means different security control understanding, then

$Lsta_A \neq Lsta_B$ Because
$L\exp_A \neq L\exp_B$ and $Lcre_A \neq Lcre_B$

Observation

Two organizations with similar cultures do not necessarily have to have the same local standard $Lsta_x$

Because
$L\exp_A \neq L\exp_B\ and\ Lcre_A \neq Lcre_B$ (Even with $Lstg_A = Lstg_B$)

Observation

Two organizations with similar cultures have the same local standard Iff.

$Lstg_A = Lstg_B, L\exp_A = L\exp_B\ and\ Lcre_A = Lcre_B$
And then $Lsta_A = Lsta_B$

Observation

Two organizations with similar or different cultures have the same local strategies $Lstg_x$ (This because the local strategies are the highest abstract security assumption.)

4. THREE MODELS FOR LOCAL COMPLIANCE $Lcomp_x$ MEASURES

Compliance is the act or process of complying to an organization's local standard. The three models are:

4.1 Binary Relationship to Measure $Lcomp_x$ (Cardinality Model)

There is a logic relation between $Limp_x$, $Lsta_x$ and $Lcomp_x$ such as $Lcomp_x = Limp_x \wedge Lsta_x$

$Lsta_x$	$Limp_x$	$Lcomp_x$	
1	1	1	
1	0	0	Logic AND
0	1	0	
–	–	–	

The bottom lines for an organization's security are the set of local standards $Lsta_x$ and their Local implementation sets $Limp_x$. Local compliance standards are defined as the ratio of the cardinality $Limp_x$ to cardinality $Lsta_x$

$$Lcomp_x = \frac{\left|Limp_x\right|}{\left|Lsta_x\right|}$$

Strategy compliance is the ratio between local compliance and local strategy.

$$Stgcomp_x = \frac{\left|Lcomp_x\right|}{\left|Lstg_x\right|}$$

These relationships are shown in Figure 1.

Assume the $Lstg_{Policy} = \{x_1\}$, $Lsta_{Policy} = \{x_1, x_2, \ldots x_{20}\}$ and $Limp_{Policy} = \{x_3, x_6\}$

$$Lcomp_x = \frac{\left|Limp_x\right|}{\left|Lsta_x\right|} = \frac{2}{20} = 0.1$$

Since $\left|Lstg_{Policy}\right| = 1$ then the local compliance with external strategy (Strategy compliance $Stgcomp_x$) $Stgcomp_x = \frac{\left|Lcomp_x\right|}{\left|Lstg_x\right|} = \frac{0.1}{1} = 0.1$

This reads as the organization in this case has only a value of 0.1 compliance with the defined external adopter set (adopted external set) $Extr_x$

Assume that the local strategy covers two elements concerning the policy. In this case, we would have $\left|Lstg_{Policy}\right| = 2$ then

$$Stgcomp_x = \frac{\left|Lcomp_x\right|}{\left|Lstg_x\right|} = \frac{0.1}{2} = 0.05$$

0.05 is the compliance value

Assume

$Limp_{Policy} = \{x_1, x_2, x_3, x_4, x_5, x_6, x_{11}, x_{18}, x_{19}, x_{20}\},\ Lsta_x = \{x_1, \ldots x_{20}\}$

$$Lcomp_x = \frac{\left|Limp_x\right|}{\left|Lsta_x\right|} = \frac{10}{20} = 0.5$$

$$Stgcomp_x = \frac{\left|Lcomp_x\right|}{\left|Lstg_x\right|} = \frac{0.5}{1} = 0.5$$

Definition: Well-founded set $Welf_x$ of all compliance elements, set of all of one's in $Limp_x$

It is the sets of all elements $Limp_x$ which satisfy $Lsta_x$.

$$f = \begin{cases} 0 \ iff. \ \not\exists^{Limp} & \text{generate vulnerability } Vulb_x \\ 1 \ iff. \ \exists^{Limp} & \text{generate } Welf_x \end{cases}$$

Definition: vulnerability sets $Vulb_x$ all elements that are not in compliance sets

Definition: vulnerability sets $Vulb_x$ is the gap between $Lsta_x$ and $Limp_x$

$Vulb_x = Lsta_x / Limp_x \quad = \{x : x \in Lsta_x \text{ and } x \notin Limp_x\}$

$(Vulb_x)^c = Welf_x; \quad (Welf_x)^c = Vulb_x$

$Lsta_x = Welf_x \cup Vulb_x$

Definition: vulnerability sets $Vulb_x$ is none implemented security and it is outside well-founded sets

Definition: sets of all $Welf_x$ is the actual security in an organization

$$Total\ security = \bigcup_1^n Welf_x, n \in \mathbb{Z}$$

These relationships are shown in Figure 2 From the last example:

$Limp_{Policy} = \{x_1, x_2, x_3, x_4, x_5, x_6, x_{11}, x_{18}, x_{19}, x_{20}\}$
$Welf_x = \{x_1, x_2, x_3, x_4, x_5, x_6, x_{11}, x_{18}, x_{19}, x_{20}\}$
$Vulb_x = \{x_7, x_8, x_9, x_{10}, x_{12}, x_{13}, x_{14}, x_{15}, x_{16}, x_{17}\}$

$$Vulb_x = 1 - 0.5 = 0.5 = \frac{10}{20} = 0.5$$

Assume the $Lstg_{Policy} = \{x_1\}$, $Lsta_{Policy} = \{x_1, x_2, \ldots x_{10}\}$ and $Limp_{Policy} = \{x_3, x_6, x_7, x_8\}$

Figure 2. Venn diagrams or set diagrams for different sets

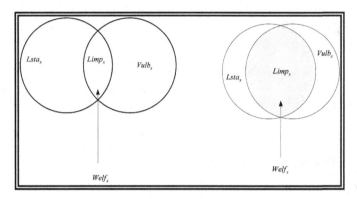

$$Lcomp_x = \frac{\left| Limp_x \right|}{\left| Lsta_x \right|} = \frac{4}{10} = 0.4 = Wef_x$$

$$Vulb_x = 1 - 0.4 = 0.6$$

Definition: Complete security is when $Lsta_x \approx Limp_x$ and $Lsta_x = Limp_x + \lambda$, λ at its minimum

From above, generally we have two binary one-dimension matrixes for local standard $Lsta_x = (x_1, x_2, ..x_n)$ and one dimension matrix for local implementation $Limp_y = (y_1, y_2, ...y_n)$

The local compliance $Lcomp_x$ is the ration between the two matrices of 1s. The vulnerabilities $Vulb_x$ or the security gape is the numbers 0s.

4.2 Vector Model

In this approach, we look at $Lsta_x = (x_1, x_2, ..x_n)$ and $Limp_y = (y_1, y_2, ...y_n)$ as each one of them is vector and has a value and a magnitude as in Figure 3.

θ is the angle between local implementation $Limp_x$ and local standard $Lsta_x$

Local compliances $Lcomp_x$ between local standard and local implementation $(Lsta_x, Limp_y)$

$$Lcomp_x(\overrightarrow{Lsta_x}, \overrightarrow{Limp_y}) = \frac{\overrightarrow{Lsta_x} \bullet \overrightarrow{Limp_y}}{\left| \overrightarrow{Lsta_x} \right| \times \left| \overrightarrow{Limp_y} \right|}$$

Figure 3. The angle between local standard and local implementation

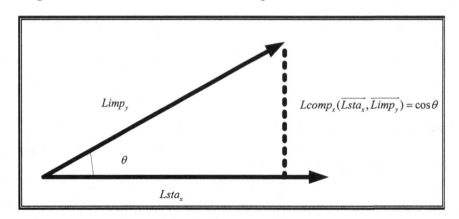

$\overrightarrow{Lsta_x} \bullet \overrightarrow{Limp_y}$ is the dot product between local implementation $Limp_x$ and local standard $Lsta_x$

$\left|\overrightarrow{Lsta_x}\right|$ and $\left|\overrightarrow{Limp_y}\right|$ are the norms of local implementation $Limp_x$ and local standard $Lsta_x$

Because

$\overrightarrow{Lsta_x} \bullet \overrightarrow{Limp_y} = \left|\overrightarrow{Lsta_x}\right| \times \left|\overrightarrow{Limp_y}\right| \times \cos\theta$ where θ is the angle between local implementation $Limp_x$ and local standard $Lsta_x$

$$Lcomp_x(\overrightarrow{Lsta_x}, \overrightarrow{Limp_y}) = \frac{\left|\overrightarrow{Lsta_x}\right| \times \left|\overrightarrow{Limp_y}\right| \times \cos\theta}{\left|\overrightarrow{Lsta_x}\right| \times \left|\overrightarrow{Limp_y}\right|} = \cos\theta$$

$$Lcomp_x(\overrightarrow{Lsta_x}, \overrightarrow{Limp_y}) = \frac{\sum_{i=1}^{n} x_i y_i}{\sqrt{\sum_{i=1}^{n} x_i^2} \sqrt{\sum_{i=1}^{n} y_i^2}}$$

$$Lcomp_x(\overrightarrow{Lsta_x}, \overrightarrow{Limp_y}) = \frac{x_1 \times y_1 + x_2 \times y_2 + \ldots + x_n \times y_n}{\sqrt{x_1^2 + x_2^2 + ..x_n^2} \times \sqrt{y_1^2 + y_2^2 + ..y_n^2}}$$

Since all values are either zeros or ones ($1^2 = 1$), the last equation could be expressed as

$$Lcomp_x(\overrightarrow{Lsta_x}, \overrightarrow{Limp_y}) = \frac{m}{\sqrt{n} \times \sqrt{m}}$$

Where n is the number of elements in $Lsta_x$ sets (cardinality) and m is the number of elements in local implementation set $Limp_y$ (cardinality). Then the last equation can be presented as

$$Lcomp_x(\overrightarrow{Lsta_x}, \overrightarrow{Limp_y}) = \frac{\left|\overrightarrow{Limp_y}\right|}{\sqrt{\left|\overrightarrow{Lsta_x}\right|} \times \sqrt{\left|\overrightarrow{Limp_y}\right|}}$$

Example

The two sets $Lsta_x$ and $Limp_y$ (see Table 1) has the following values:

And the curve between these two compliance values is local compliance 1 is $Lcomp_x = \frac{\left|Limp_x\right|}{\left|Lsta_x\right|}$ and Local compliance 2 is $Lcomp_x(\overrightarrow{Lsta_x}, \overrightarrow{Limp_y})$

In Figure 4 the $x-$axis is the local standard set $Lsta_x$ and the $y-$axis is the local implementation set $Limp_x$ and shows that the first model, the cardinality model, is a straight line, while the vector model converges from a straight line and is about 0.10675 moved out the local standard. This indicates that the mean value of

Table 1.

$Lsta_x$	$Limp_y$	$Lcomp_1 = \frac{\left|Limp_x\right|}{\left|Lsta_y\right|}$	$Lcomp_2(\overrightarrow{Lsta_x}, \overrightarrow{Limp_y})$
100	25	0.25	0.5
100	50	0.5	0.707
100	75	0.75	0.86
100	100	1	1

Figure 4. Shows the two compliance measures

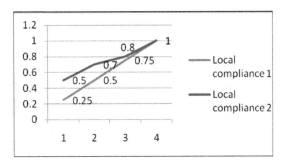

moving away from the local standard in the vector model (in this simple example) is about 0.11. This proves that the first model compliance is more to be close to the local standard (which is the ideal measure).This concludes that the cardinality model, which based on binary values, more closely represents the compliance measures.

4.3 Priority Model

Our calculation is based on the $Limp_x$ set, and this set is measured by one of two values, 0 and 1.

This assumption is absolutely correct – if all security elements are at the same level of weighty importance, this means there are high import or most critical functionality for an organization and for any elements – for example: "All elements of ISO 17799 are at the same level of impotents".

Example

$Lstg_{ISO17799}$ = {Security Policy, Organizing Information Security, Asset Management, Human Resources Security, Physical and Environment Security, Communications and Operations Management, Access Control, Information Systems Acquisition, Development and Maintenance, Information Security Incident Management, Business Continuity Management, Compliance}, and (see Table 2):

Table 2. Important level

Element	Important
Security Policy	1
Organizing Information Security	1
Asset Management	1
Human Resources Security	1
Physical and Environment Security	1
Communications and Operations Management	1
Access Control, Information Systems Acquisition	1
Development and Maintenance	1
Information Security Incident Management	1
Business Continuity Management	1
Compliance	1

And for more details for security policy is shown in Table 3:

Observation: In real secure space, the precedence, priority, or main concern element have major issues, and there are some elements more important than others.

Example: Developing firewall configuration rules are more important than developing e-mail policy; implementing a continuity plan and being reviewed on regular basis is more important than other elements. The main argument in this contest is that "what is a high security concern

Table 3A. Security policy

Element	
Securing Hardware, Peripherals, and Other Equipment	
Element	**Important**
Purchasing and Installing Hardware	1
Cabling, UPS, Printers, and Modems	1
Consumables	1
Working Off Premises or Using Outsourced	1
Processing	1
Using Secure Storage	1
Documenting Hardware	1

Table 3B. Security policy

Element	
Controlling Access to Information and Systems	
Element	**Important**
Managing Access Control Standards	1
Managing User Access	1
Securing Unattended Workstations	1
Managing Network Access Controls	1
Controlling Access to Operating System Software	1
Managing Passwords	1
Securing Against Unauthorized Physical Access	1
Restricting Access	1
Monitoring System Access and Use	1
Giving Access to Files and Documents	1
Managing Higher Risk System Access	1
Controlling Remote User Access	1

Table 4. values

Element	Im pv$_x$
Security Policy	0.5
Organizing Information Security	0.7
Asset Management	1
Human Resources Security	0.8
Physical and Environment Security	0.6
Communications and Operations Management	1
Access Control, Information Systems Acquisition	0.6
Development and Maintenance	0.5
Information Security Incident Management	0.9
Business Continuity Management	0.6
Compliance	1

for organization A is not a high security concern for organization B". For example, a credit card company's security concern is not the same as an education campus's security concern. The above observation suggests the following:

Each object in the local standard set $Lsta_x$ has important (priority) value $\mathrm{Im}\, pv_x$, such that $0.1 \leq \mathrm{Im}\, pv_x \leq 1$

Each **sub** object in the local standard set $Lsta_x$ has important (priority) value $\mathrm{Im}\, pv_{sub}$ such that $0.1 \leq \mathrm{Im}\, pv_{sub} \leq 1$

The total of each sub object in the local standard set $Lsta_x$ has important (priority) value $\mathrm{Im}\, pv_T = \mathrm{Im}\, pv_x \times \mathrm{Im}\, pv_{sub}$

The total element in the local standard set $Lsta_x$ has important (priority) value $\sum_{i=1}^{n} \mathrm{Im}\, pv_T$

Table 4 shown $\mathrm{Im}\, pv_x$ values for the above example:

Table 5 (A and B) show more details for security policy:

In reality, information security cannot be measured in precise digits. This is because information security is a range of value.

This observation suggests:

Each object in local standard set $Lsta_x$ has important (priority) value $Low_L \leq \mathrm{Impv}_x \leq Upe_L$, where Low_L is the lower level value and Upe_L is the upper level value such that $0.1 \leq Low_L$ and $Upe_L \leq 1$

Each **sub** object in the local standard set $Lsta_x$ has important (priority) value $Low_L \leq \mathrm{Impv}_{sub} \leq Upe$ such that $0.1 \leq Low_L$ and $Upe_L \leq 1$

The total of each sub object in the local standard set $Lsta_x$ has important value $\mathrm{Impv}_T = \mathrm{Impv}_x \times \mathrm{Impv}_{sub}$

Table 6, 7A and B Looking at the previous example:

And for more details for security policy:

Now Low_L set

Table 5A. The value of $\sum_{i=1}^{n} \text{Impv}_T$

Element	$Impv_x$		
Securing Hardware, Peripherals, and Other Equipment	0.5		
Element	$Impv_{sub}$	$Impv_T$	$Impv_T$
Purchasing and Installing Hardware	0.2	0.2x0.5	0.1
Cabling, UPS, Printers, and Modems	0.1	0.1x0.5	0.5
Consumables	0.3	0.3x0.5	0.15
Working Off Premises or Using Outsourced	0.5	0.5x0.5	0.25
Processing	0.6	0.6x0.5	0.36
Using Secure Storage	0.9	0.9x0.5	0.45
Documenting Hardware	1	1x0.5	0.5
$\sum_{i=1}^{n} \text{Impv}_T = 1.8$			

Table 5B. the value of $\sum_{i=1}^{n} \text{Impv}_T$

Controlling Access to Information and Systems	$Impv_x$		
Element	$Impv_{sub}$	$Impv_T$	$Impv_T$
Managing Access Control Standards	0.1	0.1x0.7	0.7
Managing User Access	0.2	0.2x0.7	0.14
Securing Unattended Workstations	0.3	0.3x0.7	0.21
Managing Network Access Controls	0.5	0.5x0.7	0.35
Controlling Access to Operating System Soft.	0.3	0.3x0.7	0.21
Managing Passwords	0.6	0.6x0.7	0.42
Securing Against Unauthorized Physical Access	0.8	0.8x0.7	0.56
Restricting Access	0.7		
Monitoring System Access and Use	0.3	0.7x0.7	0.49
Giving Access to Files and Documents	0.9	0.3x0.7	0.21
Managing Higher Risk System Access	1	0.9x0.7	0.63
Controlling Remote User Access	1	1x0.7	0.7
$\sum_{i=1}^{n} \text{Impv}_T = 9.73$		1x0.7	0.7

Table 6. Level of Impv_x

Element	Impv_x
Security Policy	0.5-0.8
Organizing Information Security	0.7-1
Asset Management	1-1
Human Resources Security	0.8-1
Physical and Environment Security	0.6-0.9
Communications and Operations Management	1-1
Access Control, Information Systems Acquisition	0.6-0.7
Development and Maintenance	0.5-0.6
Information Security Incident Management	0.9-0.9
Business Continuity Management	0.6-0.7
Compliance	1-1

5. DISCUSSION

The priority model shows the capability to be more accurate to represent compliance measures. This indicates the capability to implement this model as a fuzzy set control system. The fuzzy control is a compliance decision making indicating at any given time the level of the compliance.

These results show that the approach of compliance measure is non-classical measure; the classical measures hold the additive property. Additivity can be very effective and convenient in some applications, but can also be somewhat "inadequate in many reasoning environments of the real world as in approximate reasoning" (Garmendia, 2007, p. 2), artificial intelligence, fuzzy logic, game theory, decision making, economy, data mining, etc., that require the definition of non-additive measures and a large amount of open problems. For example, the efficiency of a set of workers is being measured; the efficiency of the same people doing teamwork is not the addition of the efficiency of each individual working on their own.

"The concept of fuzzy measure requires monotonicity related to the inclusion of sets. The concept of fuzzy measure can also be generalized by new concepts of measure that pretend to measure a characteristic not really related with the inclusion

Table 7A. Lower important

Element		$Impv_x$	
Securing Hardware, Peripherals, and Other Equipment		0.5	
Element	Impv_{sub}		Impv_T
Purchasing and Installing Hardware	0.2		0.2×0.5
Cabling, UPS, Printers, and Modems	0.1		0.1×0.5
Consumables	0.3		0.3×0.5
Working Off Premises or Using Outsourced	0.5		0.5×0.5
Processing	0.6		0.6×0.5
Using Secure Storage	0.9		0.9×0.5
Documenting Hardware	1		1×0.5
$\sum_{i=1}^{n} \text{Impv}_T = 1.8$			

Table 7B. High important

Element	$Impv_x$	
Securing Hardware, Peripherals, and Other Equipment	0.5	
Element — $Impv_{sub}$		$Impv_T$
Purchasing and Installing Hardware — 0.2		0.2x0.5
Cabling, UPS, Printers, and Modems — 0.1		0.1x0.5
Consumables — 0.3		0.3x0.5
Working Off Premises or Using Outsourced — 0.5		0.5x0.5
Processing — 0.6		0.6x0.5
Using Secure Storage — 0.9		0.9x0.5
Documenting Hardware — 1		1x0.5

$$\sum_{i=1}^{n} \text{Impv}_T = 1.8$$

of sets" (Garmendia, 2007, p. 3). On the other hand, those new measures can show that 'x has a higher degree of a particular quality (and in our case high level of security) than y' (p. X), when x and y are ordered by a preorder (not necessarily the set inclusion preorder). The term fuzzy integral uses the concept of fuzzy measure, other important fuzzy integrals, as *Choquet* integral. (The Choquet integral is a generalization of the Lebesgue integral with respect to a non-classical measure, non-additive measure often called fuzzy measure.)

The major important for practical of this work is: "the compliance measures are related to the priority of control for an organization"; this means that the compliance for an organization is completely different values for other organization even within the same culture.

Preliminaries

A *measurable space* is a couple $(X, \wp)$ where X is a set and $\wp$ **algebra** or set of subsets of X (power set) such that

1. $X \in \wp$
2. Let $A \subset X$. If $A \in \wp$ Then $A' \in \wp$
3. If $A_n \in \wp$ Then $\bigcup_{n=1}^{\infty} A_n \in \wp$

Definition of Normal Compliance Measure

Let $(X, \wp)$ be a measurable space. A measure $M : \wp \to [0,1]$ is a normal compliance measure if there exists a minimal set A_n and maximum set A_m in $\wp$ э

1. $M(A_0) = \lambda$
2. $M(A_m) = 1$

For example, minimum security compliance is default system security λ and maximum security satisfies all required from the local standard.

DEFINITION OF COMPLIANCE FUZZY MEASURE

Let $\wp$ be an δ - algebra on a universe X. A **compliance fuzzy measure** is $C : C \rightarrow [0,1]$ Verifying:

1. $C(\phi)=\lambda$, $C(X)=1$
2. If $A,B \in \wp$ *and* $A \subseteq B$ Then $C(A) \leq C(B)$

Theory of Compliance Evidence

The theory of compliance evidence is based on two dual, non-additive measures: belief measures and plausibility measures. Given a measurable space, a belief of compliance measure is a function $Cb : \wp \rightarrow [0,1]$ verifying the following properties:

1. $Cb(\phi) = \lambda$
2. $Cb(X) = 1$
3. $Cb(A \cup B) \geq Cb(A) + Cb(B)$

Property 3 is called **superadditivity**. When X is infinite, the superior continuity of the function Cb is required.

For every $A \in \wp$ the $Cb(A)$ is read as a compliance belief degree for some element to be in the set A.

From the definition of compliance belief measure, it can be proved that $Cb(A) + Cb(B) \leq 1$

Given a compliance belief measure, its dual compliance plausibility measure can be defined as

$Cp(A) = 1 - Cred(A')$ (*Cred* is credibility measures; credibility measures and plausibility measures are Sugeno measures. The possibility measures introduced by *Zadeh* (1978) gives Sugeno measures.)

Given compliance measurable space $(X, \wp)$, a measure of **compliance plausibility** Cp is a function $Cp : \wp \rightarrow [0,1]$ ∋

1. $Cp(\phi)=\lambda$
2. $Cp(X)=1$
3. $Cp(A \cup B) \leq Cp(A)+Cp(B)$

Property 3 is called **subadditivity**.

The measures of **compliance credibility** and **compliance plausibility** are defined as $M : \wp \rightarrow [0,1]$ ∋ $M(\phi)=\lambda$ and $\sum_{A \in \wp} M(A) = 1$

Where M represents a proportion of the show's evidence that an element of X is in a subset A.

We can define further **possibility compliance measure** and **necessity compliance measure** as the theory of possibility is a branch of theory of evidence where the compliance plausibility measures verify that $Cp(A \cup B) = \max\left\{Cp\left(A\right), Cp\left(B\right)\right\}$ Such plausibility measures are called **possibility compliance measures**. In the theory of possibility, the belief compliance measures satisfy that $Cb(A \cap B) = \min\left\{Cb\left(A\right), Cb\left(B\right)\right\}$ and are called **necessity compliance measures**.

6. CONCLUSION

Three models to measure information security compliance were presented in this work. These were cardinality measures, the vector model, and priority based. The last model shows it is the most accurate model to measure compliance since it takes the environment requirement rather than just adding satisfaction compliance. The last part of this work is simple presentation for defining fuzzy compliance measure, compliance evidence measures, compliance plausibility, possibility compliance measure and necessity compliance measure. These definitions are based on the concept of fuzzy measure modeling. This definition proved that there is a high possibility to create a more advanced mathematical model to measure compliance and eventually building complete control software to measure compliance validation whenever it's accrued.

REFERENCES

Aczel, P. (2008). *Variants of Classical Set Theory and their Applications*. Retrieved from http://www.cs.man.ac.uk/~petera/

Adler, M. P. (2006). A Unified Approach to Information Security Compliance. *EDUCAUSE Review*, *41*(5), 46–61.

FIPS. (2006). *Minimum Security Requirements for Federal Information and Information Systems*. Retrieved from http://csrc.nist.gov/

Garmendia, L. (2007). *The Evolution of the Concept of Fuzzy Measure*. Retrieved from http://www.fdi.ucm.es/profesor/lgarmend/SC/Congresos/

Goldrei, D. C. (1996). *Classic Set Theory: For Guided Independent Study*. London: Chapman & Hall.

MerriamWebster.com. (2009). *Compliance definition*. Retrieved from http://www.merriam-webster.com/

Murofushi, T. (1989). An interpretation of fuzzy measures and the Choquet integral as an integral with respect to a fuzzy measure. *Fuzzy Sets and Systems*, 201–227. doi:10.1016/0165-0114(89)90194-2

Murofushi, T. (1991). Fuzzy t-conorm integral with respect to fuzzy measures: Generalization of Sugeno integral and Choquet integral. *Fuzzy Sets and Systems*, *42*, 57–71. doi:10.1016/0165-0114(91)90089-9

Murofushi, T., Sugeno, M., & Machida, M. (1994). Non-monotonic fuzzy measures and the Choquet integral. *Fuzzy Sets and Systems*, *64*, 73–86. doi:10.1016/0165-0114(94)90008-6

Murofushi, T. A. (1991). A theory of fuzzy measures: Representations the Choquet integral and null sets. *Journal of Mathematical Analysis and Applications*, *159*, 532–549. doi:10.1016/0022-247X(91)90213-J

NIST. (2008). *NIST Security Configuration Checklists*. Retrieved from http://csrc.nist.gov/checklists/

Scholl, M., Scholl, K., Hash, J., Bowen, P., Johnson, A., & Smith, C. D. (2008). *An Introductory Resource Guide for Implementing the Health Insurance Portability and Accountability Act (HIPAA) Security Rule*. Retrieved from http://csrc.nist.gov/publications/nistpubs/800-66-Rev1

Souppaya, M., Wack, J. P., & Kent, K. (2005). *Security Configuration Checklists Program for IT Products – Guidance for Checklists Users and Developers* (NIST Special Publication No. 800-70). Gaithersburg, MD: NIST.

Stoll, R. R. (1979). *Set Theory and Logic*. Mineola, NY: Dover Publications.

Thiagarajan, V. (2003). *Information Security Management BS 7799.2:2002 Audit Check List*. Retrieved from http://www.sans.org/score/checklists/ISO_17799_checklist.pdf

Thomas, P. R. (2003). *Preparing for ISO 17799*. Retrieved from http://www.uaslp.mx/PDF/2042_183.pdf

Wikipedia.org. (2008). *Compliance*. Retrieved from http://en.wikipedia.org/

Zadeh, L. (1978). Fuzzy sets as a basis for a theory of possibility. *Fuzzy Sets and Systems*, 28.

ENDNOTE

[1]   power set is complete list of subsets of set S

APPENDIX 1

Basic set theory definitions and properties:

Properties If R, S, and T are any sets, the following properties hold:

$S = S$ (Reflexive)
If $S = T$, then $T = S$ (Symmetric).
If $R = S$ and $S = T$ then $R = T$ (Transitive).

$\lambda \in S$

$S \subset S$ (Reflexive)

If $R \subset S$ and $S \subset R$ then $R \subset T$ (Transitive).
$S \subset T$ and $T \subset S$ if and only if $S = T$
If $S \subset T$, then $|S| \leq |T|$ and if $S \subsetneq T$ then $|S| < |T|$.
Definition: The intersection of two sets S and T, written $S \cap T$ is the set of elements common to both
    S and. $S \cap T = \{x \in S \text{ and } x \in T\}$
Definition: The union of two sets S and T, written $S \cup T$, is the set of elements that are in either S or
    T or both and $S \cup T = \{x \in S \text{ or } x \in T\}$

Properties

$S \cup T = T \cup S$ (Commutative)

$S \cap T = T \cap S$ (Commutative)
$S \subset S \cup T$
$\phi \cup S = S$
$\phi \cap S = \phi$
$S \cup S = S \cap S = S$
$S \subset T$ iff. $S \cup T = T$
If $R \subset T$ and $S \subset T$ then $R \cup S \subset T$
If $R \subset S$ and $R \subset T$ then $R \subset (S \cap T)$
If $S \subset T$ then $R \cup S \subset R \cup T$ and $R \cap S \subset R \cap T$
$S \cup T \neq \phi$ iff. $S \neq \phi$ or $T \neq \phi$
$S \cap T \neq \phi$ iff. $S \neq \phi$ or $T \neq \phi$
$S \cap T = \phi$ iff. $S = \phi$ or $T = \phi$
$S = T \neq \phi$ iff. $(S \cup T) \subset (S \cap T)$

$$\left|S + T\right| = \left|S\right| + \left|T\right| - \left|S \cap T\right|$$

Definition: The difference between S and T, written $S \setminus T$, is the set of elements in S but not also in T $S \setminus T = \{x : x \in S \text{ and } x \notin T\}$

Properties

$$S \setminus T = S \setminus (S \cap T)$$
$$\left|S \setminus T\right| = \left|S\right| - \left|S \cap T\right|$$

The first property states that the elements of T that are not in S play no role in the construction of $S \setminus T$. The second property states that the number of elements removed from S to produce $S \setminus T$ is the same as the number of elements that S and T have in common

Definition: The symmetric difference between S and T is $(S \cup T) \setminus (S \cap T)$ i.e., the set of elements in S or T, but not both.

The cardinality of a symmetric difference satisfies: $\left|(S \cup T) \setminus (S \cap T)\right| = \left|S\right| + \left|T\right| - 2\left|S \cap T\right|$

Definition: Relative to a universe U, the complement of S, written $\overline{S}$, is the set of all elements of the universe not contained in S, i.e. $\overline{S} = \{x : x \in U \text{ and } x \notin S\}$

Cardinality property of complements

$$\left|\overline{S}\right| = \left|U\right| - \left|S\right|$$

Properties of complements and differences:

APPENDIX 2

Symbols

| OR

∋ or: Such that
∈ Member of
∉ Not member of
iff. If and only if
↔ If and only if
∀ For every
→ Implies; if … then
∪ Union
∩ Intersection

$\subset$ Subset

$\subseteq$ Subset or equal

$| \ |$ Cardinality

$Extg_x$ External strategy sets

$Lstg_x$ Local strategy sets

$Lsta_x$ Local standard sets

$L\exp_x$ Local expansion sets

$Lcre_x$ Local creation sets

$Limp_x$ Local implementation

$\mathbb{Z}$: set of integer numbers

$\exists^{Lstg}$ Means these exist local adopted from the external sets

$\nexists^{Lstg}$ Means these exist no local strategy adopted from the external sets

$\text{Im } pv_x$ Object important (priority) value,

$\text{Im } pv_{sub}$ Sub object important (priority) value

Low_L Lower level value

Upe_L Upper level value

$\wp$ Power set of X

M Measurable space

A_n Minimal compliance set

A_m Maximum compliance set

C Compliance fuzzy measure

Cb Compliance measure

Cp Possibility compliance measure

This work was previously published in International Journal of Information Security and Privacy (IJISP), edited by Hamid Nemati, pp 43-67, copyright 2009 by IGI Publishing (imprint of IGI Global)

Chapter 23

Do You Know Where Your Data Is?
A Study of the Effect of Enforcement Strategies on Privacy Policies

Ian Reay
University of Alberta, Canada

Patricia Beatty
University of Alberta, Canada

Scott Dick
University of Alberta, Canada

James Miller
University of Alberta, Canada

ABSTRACT

Numerous countries around the world have enacted privacy-protection legislation, in an effort to protect their citizens and instill confidence in the valuable business-to-consumer E-commerce industry. These laws will be most effective if and when they establish a standard of practice that consumers can use as a guideline for the future behavior of e-commerce vendors. However, while privacy-protection laws share many similarities, the enforcement mechanisms supporting them vary hugely. Furthermore, it is unclear which (if any) of these mechanisms are effective in promoting a standard of practice that fits with the social norms of those countries. We present a large-scale empirical study of the role of legal enforcement in standardizing privacy protection on the Internet. Our study is based on an automated analysis of documents posted on the 100,000 most popular websites (as ranked by Alexa.com). We find that legal frameworks have had little success in creating standard practices for privacy-sensitive actions.

DOI: 10.4018/978-1-60960-200-1.ch023

INTRODUCTION

Business-to-consumer (B2C) electronic commerce is a vital part of the world economy. B2C sales in the USA were $138.6 billion in 2005 (Graumann & Neinert, 2006), $51 billion combined in Japan, South Korea, India and China in 2005 (Grau, 2007), and $87.8 billion combined in the UK, Germany, and France (the three largest B2C economies in Europe) in 2006 (Grau, 2006) (all figures USD). This vital industry is utterly dependent on the willingness of consumers to entrust sensitive personal and financial data to faceless online vendors. Conversely, distrust of websites and web services is a major deterrent to Internet use and e-commerce (Patil & Kobsa, 2009). A recent study by Consumer Web Watch reported that 86% of Internet users have changed their online behavior, while 29% have reduced their online purchases because of concerns about identity theft (Princeton Survey Research Associates International, 2005). A Pew Internet report (Fallows, 2004) found that although 75% of people thought that the Internet was a good place to conduct important transactions, only 55% had in fact done so—and then only to purchase low-value items such as concert or sports tickets. When the trust consumers have placed in a website is betrayed, the consequences can range from the merely annoying (telemarketing, differential pricing) to the financially crippling (identity theft).

We have previously argued (Reay, Dick, & Miller, 2009a) that the relationship between a consumer and a website contains a great deal of information asymmetry: the consumer has essentially no foreknowledge of how their private information might be utilized, while the website operator knows exactly what they intend to do with it (including holding the data for future uses). There is also a major inequality in power; the consumer *must* surrender their personal information to complete a transaction, but they cannot compel the website to use or refrain from using that information in any manner. In response to this inequality, the Organization for Economic Co-operation and Development long ago proposed a set of privacy-protection principles for the benefit of consumers (OECD, 1980). Today, websites will generally publish "privacy policies" on their websites, informing consumers of how their data will be used and their rights in relation to that data; the OECD privacy principles are the basis for the terms of these policies. In theory, at least, the OECD principles ought to form the basis of any standard of practice in online privacy protection.

A policy, however, is only a piece of paper; without external enforcement, it is meaningless. This "enforcement" takes many forms, and is dictated in part by the social norms of different countries. Thus, for instance, the United States has only enacted a hodgepodge of state and industry-specific privacy legislation, in keeping with the generally anti-government sentiment of U.S. society (Sun, 1994). Enforcement of those laws is not centralized in any one regulatory body; the Federal Communications Commission has the statutory authority to enforce a privacy policy once it is posted, but violations of other privacy legislation would fall under the purview of other agencies, or the states Attorneys-General. In the most general sense, "enforcement" in the United States is generally allowed to take the form of private litigation. European Union nations, on the other hand, have been far more willing to enact comprehensive privacy-protection laws, and the EU Data Protection Directive (European Commission, 1995) is the benchmark to which other privacy-protection legislation (e.g., Office of the Privacy Commissioner of Canada, 2000) and Japan (Government of Japan, 2003) is compared. These nations usually implement ombudsmen, registration offices, or licensing bureaus to enforce these laws; these are consolidated governmental enforcement mechanisms. Still other nations (notably Russia and China) have not enacted any privacy-protection legislation, and consumers have essentially no recourse when websites abuse their trust. There is currently no evidence on which (if any) of these mechanisms are effective in promoting a standard of practice amongst websites in a nation.

Our goal in this article is to examine the effect of these different enforcement regimes, seeking to understand how they succeed (or fail) in creating accepted standards of practice. In effect, we are asking whether the social norms embodied in the laws and enforcement mechanisms affect the declared practices of websites in those jurisdictions. Norms are a key element of every society, part of the cultural milieu that influences each decision a person makes. Prior research (Hsu & Kuo, 2003; Shaw, 2003) has shown that social norms will influence the behavior of employees in an organization, and so it is reasonable to inquire whether this effect is observed in the area of privacy protection. We have studied the 100,000 most popular sites of the Internet (as ranked by Alexa.com), and harvested P3P documents from these sites. P3P documents are a machine-readable encoding of a privacy policy, and as such should provide evidence on whether a standard of practice with respect to privacy protection has evolved. As norms are particular to a given culture, we expect that the evolution of such standards would be very uneven. Our study covers 15 nations that represent the range of enforcement mechanisms, from the hands-off approach of Russia to France's mandatory licensing bureau for data collectors.

The remainder of this paper is organized as follows. In Section 2, we review key background and related work on current privacy protections on the Web. In Section 3, we develop our hypotheses concerning the effects of different enforcement regimes on the content of P3P policies. In Section 4, we discuss our study methodology, and we present and discuss our results in Section 5. We offer a summary and discussion of future work in Section 6.

CURRENT STATE OF ONLINE PRIVACY

Online Consumer Behaviors

Online consumers must constantly face the risk of betrayal; they must surrender their personal information to an entity (or entities) that they have no personal interaction with, in order to complete any transaction. Consumers are therefore confronted with the need to determine if the privacy risks of a transaction outweigh the benefits of the transaction, where the future actions of the vendor are uncertain. There is a growing body of work showing that online consumers deal with this uncertainty by making assumptions about the future behavior of the vendor – and that these assumptions are deeply flawed (Consumer Reports Web Watch, 2002; Earp, Anton, Aiman-Smith, & Stufflebeam, 2005; Turow, Feldman, & Meltzer, 2005). For example, Turow et al. (2005) found that:

- 59% of respondents believed incorrectly that "When a website has a privacy policy, it means that the site will not share my information with other websites or companies"
- 55% of respondents believed incorrectly that "When I give personal information to a bank, privacy laws say that the bank has no right to share that information, even with companies owned by the bank"
- 47% of respondents believed incorrectly that "When I give money to a charity, by law that charity cannot sell my name to another charity unless I give it permission"

We can interpret the findings in Turow et al. (2005) as a lack of common ground between the online stores and the consumer, defined as the information or tools assumed to exist when they transact (Clark, 1996). Online stores commonly post privacy policies, which often explicitly state that they will undertake some or all of the actions studied in Turow et al. (2005); consumers, however, do not incorporate these facts into their assumptions. Common ground concerning privacy in online transactions could include shared expectations of legal protections or business practices. When this common ground does not exist, it can be created through the standardization of business practices via standards development (Anton et al., 2004), creating laws (Bracey, 2006; Ellickson, 2001) or applying social pressure (Horne, 2001). For instance, Larose and Rifon (2007) suggest modifying privacy policies to include a "safety warning" prominently displayed at the start of the privacy policy. Miyazaki (2008) found that disclosure of cookie use *did* reduce consumer's negative perception of cookies, also indicating that better implementations of privacy policies could better align consumer expectations with vendor behavior. The current lack of common ground on privacy-sensitive actions damages consumer trust in online stores, which in turn impacts their willingness to transact with online stores (Greenspan, Goldberg, Weimer, & Basso, 2000; Kaplan & Nieschwietz, 2003). As an example, (Chau, Hu, Lee, & Au, 2007) found that e-commerce customers frequently drop out of transactions; the "shopping cart abandon rate" varies from 20% to as high as 90% on some sites, while 78% of consumers report having abandoned some shopping activities; this is likely due to insufficient trust in the given vendor.

Recent calls for standardization of privacy policies (Anton et al., 2004) and alignment of website privacy sensitive actions (Earp et al., 2005) attempt to address this issue. We interpret these calls as an effort to create standards of practice, which consumers can then use as the basis of their expectations. The Internet, however, provides an environment where geographic, cultural, and legal restraints are marginalized, thus removing incentives to align and standardize practice. Findings by Shaw (2003) and Hsu and Kuo (2003) indicate that a wide range of cultural, legal, and organizational influences affect the privacy sensitive decisions made by employees of organizations, while consumers' privacy preferences are also culturally dependent (Capurro, 2005; Kumaraguru & Cranor, 2005). Together, these lines of evidence indicate that the social norms governing the behaviors of websites (and thus, whatever standards of practice might evolve) may vary widely between cultures.

Social Approaches to Privacy Protection

Social privacy protections attempt to create common ground between vendor and consumer via communication. Specifically the vendor will provide assurances about their personal information handling practices, which are in some sense binding upon them. Consumers can then form accurate behavioral expectations about the practices of a specific website. Currently, these methods include the use of human readable privacy policies (Anton et al., 2004; Jensen & Potts, 2004; Lichtenstein, Swatman, & Babu, 2003) and third party assurance services (WebTrust, 2006; Better Business Bureau, 2006; Truste.org, 2006). While these mechanisms provide means to develop common ground between the consumer and website operator, recent empirical evidence (discussed below) indicates that these mechanisms are insufficient for the *average* user to develop accurate behavioral expectations.

Human readable privacy policies (HRPP) are intended to inform website patrons of the privacy sensitive actions undertaken by a website. In many jurisdictions, the vendor controlling the website is legally bound to follow the practices disclosed in this document. However, recent studies (Anton et al., 2007; Jensen & Potts, 2004) have found HRPPs to be beyond the reading comprehension of average Internet users. HRPPs are constructed using legal terminology, as one would expect of an enforceable legal document. The terminology that is used is thus opaque to most users. Additionally, HRPPs also lack a standardized format, are rarely read (Acquisti & Grossklags, 2005; Jensen,

Potts, & Jensen, 2005), time consuming to analyze (Earp et al., 2005), and are potentially deceptive (Lichtenstein et al., 2003). Furthermore, even when privacy policies are posted, they may not fully comply with privacy protection legislation (O'Connor, 2007). These findings suggest that HRPP's currently do not generate adequate common ground between vendors and consumers, and do not solve the problem of privacy protection.

Third party assurance (TPA) services are another attempt to solve many of the aforementioned usability problems with HRPP's. These services create an auditable standard to which member organizations adhere. Often TPA services provide a trademarked certification to organizations, which can be posted on their websites proving they satisfy the provider's requirements. Truste (Truste.org, 2006), BBBOnline (Better Business Bureau, 2006), CPA Web Trust (WebTrust, 2006), and Verisign (Verisign, 2008) represent the most popular TPA authorities. While TPA services provide consumers with an assurance that the vendor follows the requirements of the TPA authority, they require individuals to be aware of the certification's existence, implications, and limitations. Since only a minority of individuals can identify the Truste (42% of individuals), BBBOnline (28.7%), or CPA Web Trust (7.7%) certifications (Moores, 2005), it would appear unlikely that Internet users can discern the differences between certifications let alone interpret their meaning. Furthermore, effective use of privacy seals again requires users to read the website's privacy policy, which only a small number of users do (Jensen et al., 2005; Larose & Rifon, 2007).

Technological Approaches to Privacy Protection

In contrast to the predominantly social mechanisms above, a number of privacy-enhancing technologies (PETs) such as P3P (L. Cranor, Langheinrich, Marchiori, Presler-Marshall, & Reagle, 2002), anonymization tools (Bruckner &

Voss, 2005; Dingledine, Mathewson, & Syverson, 2007; Gritzalis, 2004), cookie managers (Bruckner & Voss, 2005; Goecks & Mynatt, 2005), and encryption (Garfinkel, 1995; Gritzalis, 2004) (P3P is often referred to as a PET; we discuss this further below). Ad-hoc strategies (such as providing fake or unused email addresses to a website) are also employed by some users (Cases, Fournier, Dubois, & Tanner Jr., in press). However, usability issues plague their widespread adoption since these mechanisms currently demand a high degree of technical sophistication from their user. PETs require the user to develop a *desired* behavioral model, and then assist the user in *enforcing* that model in their online transactions. The common ground created in this latter case is essentially adversarial rather than cooperative, but it can result in fairly accurate behavioral expectations. PETs are rarely part of a standard system configuration, require knowledge of the threat model behind the technology, and frequently demand significant effort to configure. For example the MozPETs browser plug-in (Bruckner & Voss, 2005) for the Firefox web browser requires individuals to:

1) Know that cookies exist,
2) Determine the vulnerabilities associated with different classes of cookies
3) Create detection rules (possibly using regular expressions, see Watt, 2005)

Given that the average Internet user cannot explain the basic functionality of cookies (Jensen et al., 2005), these requirements are unrealistic for the general population. Similarly, the "Discreet Box" privacy middleware of (Lioudakis et al., 2007) also requires users to set up their privacy-protection preferences; this architecture deals with mobile browsing and location-based services, making the burden on the user even greater. Likewise, the PeopleFinder application (Sadeh et al., 2008) also requires users to determine privacy preferences, albeit using a more intuitive interface. Social networks also complicate privacy protection;

as pointed out in (Preibusch, Hoser, Gurses, & Berendt, 2007), every user's profile implicitly contains information about other users; thus, each privacy declaration may well pertain to more than one user. Current legislation implicitly assumes that there is only one data subject involved in any single privacy decision; requiring users to sort through the legal implications of deciding to share information on a social network is obviously infeasible.

Some recent research has attempted to create vendor-side PETs. A vendor-side PET will not be adversarial in nature, but instead will be more cooperative. (Kalloniatis, Kavakli, & Gritzalis, 2008) propose a requirements-engineering technique that adds privacy protection as a system attribute (much like security). The field of privacy-enhanced personalization is an effort to develop vendor-side tools that provide stronger privacy protections while maintaining the advantages of personalization technology (e.g. collaborative filtering) (Kobsa, 2007). (Anton, Bertino, Li, & Yu, 2007) call for a comprehensive privacy-protection framework, including user agents and preference-specification tools for the user, and an enterprise privacy architecture that runs from high-level privacy policies all the way to database-layer access controls based on them.

P3P (Cranor et al., 2002) is an attempt to provide a machine readable form of a website's HRPP. In the P3P protocol, HRPPs are mapped to a machine readable format by converting the semantic contents of a privacy policy into an XML document using an XML schema provided in the P3P specification. Once a HRPP is translated into a P3P document and posted on a website, these documents are retrieved and analyzed by software (within the user's browser) in the hope of providing the user with a salient summary of the policy (see Appendix A for a brief overview of the P3P protocol). P3P agents are also able to warn users when a privacy policy does not conform to the user's preferences. For this reason, P3P can be viewed as both a social and a technological mechanism;

it provides information for, and supports a user in, enforcing behavioral expectations. While the P3P protocol appears to be an improvement over HRPPs, it has not been widely adopted by websites. Researchers have found general P3P adoption to be approximately 9% and 10% in May and June of 2003 respectively (Byers, Cranor, & Kormann, 2003; Cranor, Byers, & Kormann, 2003). Recent follow up studies (Egelman & Cranor, 2006; Reay, Beatty, Dick, & Miller, 2007) describe little if any change in current adoption rates (with the exception of U.S. government websites, likely due to the 2002 E-Governance Act (America, 2002). This adoption rate, while sufficient for a survey analyzing website actions such as ours, limits P3P's impact as a privacy enhancing technology. A separate analysis solely of compact policies in Security Space (2006) found that the adoption rate was approximately 3%; however, an analysis examining only compact policies is highly problematic. Firstly, compact policies are only a string in the HTTP response header, containing a small subset of the information in the full P3P policy. Second, there is evidence (Reay, Dick, & Miller, 2009b) that compact policies are often deployed without a corresponding full policy. This is a clear violation of the P3P standard, and is believed to be an attempt to circumvent the P3P agent in Internet Explorer 6.0/7.0. This agent by default blocks third-party cookies lacking a compact P3P policy. Hence, a compact P3P policy appears to be an insufficient basis for analyzing an organization's privacy intent, and our survey only examines full policies. Preibusch et al. (2007) proposed an extension to P3P (a new INTERACTION tag) to accommodate the problem of implicit information about other users in social network profiles.

Privacy-Protection Legislation

Since the methods above appear incapable of creating sufficient common ground between website operators and average users for accurate behavioral expectations to develop, a number of nations have enacted privacy-protection legislation (Henry, 2001; Perkins & Markel, 2004). While these laws have the potential to standardize website practices, it is only reasonable to expect this standardization to exist within a legal jurisdiction. Since international consensus on the most suitable legal framework does not yet exist (Henry, 2001), we cannot currently expect privacy protection to be standardized Internet- (or world-) wide. In addition, further complications arise when legal frameworks that are similar in spirit differ in written content and enforcement measures (European Commission, 2003; Henry, 2001). As a result of these framework inconsistencies, a range of protections exist. These differences tend to imply that only some jurisdictions would possess legal protections sufficiently stringent as to foster the development of standardized practice.

This legal environment is further complicated by the findings of Turow et al (Turow et al., 2005) which indicate that even where laws exist, individuals are unaware of the protections afforded. This suggests that even where legal protections are provided, individual users are unlikely to be able to utilize them. These conjectures imply that standardized practice is likely to exist only where an effective third party enforces the legal framework. To date, third party enforcement is implemented through the creation of ombudsmen (Privacy Commissioner of Canada, 2006), registration offices (New Zealand Privacy Commissioner, 2006), or licensing bureaus (Française, 2006).

In a previous study (Reay et al., 2009b) we have compared posted privacy policies against the laws of their jurisdiction (judged by the physical location of the server). Specifically, we looked at whether websites complied with five legal mandates that could be unambiguously extracted from the E.U. Data Protection Directive (European Commission, 1995), and two additional ones from the U.S. Safe Harbor program (Export.gov, 2007), a self-certification process that allows U.S. companies to meet the requirements for exporting data from the E.U. to the U.S. We found that compliance was highly variable for the seven rules over the websites we studied, and that very few websites at all would pass all five E.U. rules, to say nothing of the two additional U.S. rules. The analysis in that paper concerns only a matching between the "letter of the law" and the specific assertions in a privacy policy. Examining the effect of *enforcement* is an important next step, as this prior work considered neither the policies declared on the website nor the law enforcement mechanisms in that jurisdiction.

HYPOTHESES OF THE STUDY

As we have previously mentioned, Hsu (Hsu & Kuo, 2003) and Shaw (Shaw, 2003) have found that employees who must make privacy-sensitive decisions on their employer's behalf are influenced *in part* by the perceived magnitude of any negative consequences of that decision. However, their employer will have put in place policies governing, and business models requiring, the collection and use of private information, and employees must respond to those needs. As there is generally no one "business model" even within a single industry, it would thus appear unreasonable to expect companies to independently adopt similar practices without external influences such as legislation or strong public opinion. However, as previously indicated, Internet users in general do not appear to have an adequate grasp of Internet privacy issues to mobilize a "grassroots" social campaign for the creation of standard practices. Thus, legislative action appears to be the only realistic means of influencing organizational choices. This influence is however contingent upon legislation being sufficiently stringent, as well as the existence of a legal framework providing effective third party enforcement. Furthermore, this implies that this influence can only reasonably be expected to cover a single legal jurisdiction (i.e. a nation).

While legislation has the *potential* to establish standards of practice, it is unrealistic to expect complete uniformity in the stated actions of websites since transaction context varies. For example, it is reasonable for an E-Commerce company to request your address, retain it until shipping is completed, and share the address with a shipping company. Similar actions undertaken by a search engine are likely to be considered unwarranted. As a consequence, similar practices should only be expected for certain sub-categories of P3P content that are often described in legislation (Office of the Privacy Commissioner of Canada, 2000; Henry, 2001; Government of Japan, 2003; European Commission, 1995; Varian, Wallenberg, & Woroch, 2005), such as accessibility of collected information, dispute resolution methods employed, remedies offered when problems occur, and *transaction independent* purposes for data collection such as administering the website, profiling individuals, telemarketing, etc. We therefore propose the following conceptual model for our study (see Figure 1). The factor *General Laws / 3rd Party Enforcement* captures whether or not national privacy laws have been enacted in a country, and whether there is a 3rd party enforcing them (this is a dichotomous variable). *Right of Access* refers to whether or not data subjects in that country have the right to access all data held about them by a data controller. *Dispute Resolution Methods* represents the means avail-

able to data subjects in that country to resolve a dispute with the data controller. *Remedies Offered* captures what compensation will be offered to a data subject in that country if the data concerning them is inaccurate. *Non-Transactional Purposes for Collection* captures the different reasons why a data controller might collect data about a subject. It excludes the purpose of "completing the current transaction," as this can be assumed true in every transaction. The relationships we posit (H1 through H4) represent "agreement," in the sense that websites hosted in nations with a "positive" value for *General Laws / 3rd Party Enforcement* should exhibit consistency on the given factor, while those with a "negative" value should exhibit no such consistency. Specifically, we propose the following hypotheses:

Hypothesis 1a: *For each nation utilizing general privacy laws with third party enforcement, a significant association with respect to whether individuals can access information collected about them should exist.*

Hypothesis 1b: *For each nation not utilizing general privacy laws with third party enforcement, a significant association should not exist*

Figure 1. Conceptual model of the study

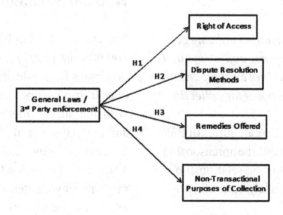

as to whether individuals can access information collected about them.

Hypothesis 2a: *For each nation utilizing general privacy laws with third party enforcement, a significant association regarding dispute resolution methods offered should exist.*

Hypothesis 2b: *For each nation not utilizing general privacy laws with third party enforcement, a significant association should not exist regarding dispute resolution methods offered.*

Hypothesis 3a: *For each nation utilizing general privacy laws with third party enforcement, significant association as to the remedies offered should exist.*

Hypothesis 3b: *For each nation not utilizing general privacy laws with third party enforcement, a significant association should not exist as to the remedies offered.*

Hypothesis 4a: *For each nation utilizing general privacy laws with third party enforcement, a significant association regarding transaction independent purposes for collection should exist.*

Hypothesis 4b: *For each not nation utilizing general privacy laws with third party enforcement, a significant association should not exist regarding transaction independent purposes for collection.*

As discussed, there are also categories of P3P tags for which we assume it would be unreasonable to expect agreement (and thus, no relationship is included in our conceptual model). To confirm this

assumption we propose the following hypotheses concerning the *absence* of agreement:

Hypothesis 5a: *For each nation, a significant association should not exist regarding categories of data collected.*

Hypothesis 5b: *For each nation, a significant association should not exist regarding how long information is retained.*

Hypothesis 5c: *For each nation, a significant association should not exist regarding who is permitted access to information.*

METHODOLOGY

The hypotheses in Section 3 are analyzed via a survey which consists of an automated analysis of P3P documents posted on the most popular 100,000 Internet websites as ranked by Alexa. com (2007). P3P policies were chosen as the unit of analysis due to the extreme time commitments required to analyze human readable privacy policies. An analysis of 100,000 human readable privacy policies using a method analogous to Earp et al. (2005) would take approximately 800 person years to complete, and is clearly not cost-effective.

Website Selection

The choice of using P3P policies from the Alexa 100,000 list (2007) instead of a random sample originates from a desire to analyze business practices from a user perspective and is in accordance with the survey methodology of previous P3P surveys (Byers et al., 2003; Cranor et al., 2003; Egelman & Cranor, 2006; Ernst and Young, 2003). The websites contained in this list comprise the vast majority of websites a user is likely to encounter and consequently have the greatest affect upon an average individual's privacy. Websites not appearing on this list have less than a 0.00125% chance of being visited by the average Internet user (Alexa, 2007). Further, the use of the Alexa 100,000 list allows for an analysis that draws upon websites from 119 countries. Hence, we view this list as a highly representative sample of the "usable" Internet. In fact, it could be argued that the list effectively represents the entire "usable" Internet.

P3P Policy Harvesting

The P3P validator (Koike & Taiki, 2002) is the official W3C P3P document verification tool. It is openly provided and provides a convenient method for retrieving, parsing, and validating P3P documents. It locates policies using the official methods defined in the P3P specification (L. Cranor et al., 2002): HTTP headers, HTML link tags, and the well-known location (/w3c/p3p.xml). Once the documents are retrieved and parsed, Perl scripts export the results to a MySQL database where information is stored as binary values (whether the tag exists or not; categorical XML tag attributes are dichotomized). A reverse DNS look-up was performed for each website using the Linux 'host' program. Once the IP address was retrieved, a database purchased from IP2Location (IP2Location.com, 2006) was used to locate the corresponding country of origin. IP2Location states their accuracy is above 95%. In this article, we assume that the legal jurisdiction having authority over a website corresponds to the physical location of the server. While this is a debatable point under international law, no better approach currently exists.

Although the Alexa 100,000 list covers 119 countries, the websites on this list are obviously not evenly distributed amongst them. Furthermore, adoption of the P3P protocol itself is uneven, with the most popular sites being as much as five times as likely to publish a P3P policy as the least popular sites (Reay et al., 2007). In addition, there are a large number of errors in P3P documents; Egelman

and Cranor (2006) found that as many as 75% of P3P documents contained some syntax errors, although the majority of these errors were not fatal to fault-tolerant P3P user agents. Reay et al. (2007) also observed high error rates in P3P documents, as did Cranor, Egelman, Sheng, McDonald, and Chowdhury (2008). For these reasons, we have limited our study to P3P full policies that are free of syntax errors (as determined by the W3C Validator), as the erroneous XML P3P documents cannot be reliably parsed. We have furthermore limited our collection to the home page of a site only. However, as pointed out in (Cranor et al., 2008; Egelman & Cranor, 2006), numerous P3P policies (which are often identical) may be deployed in various sub-sections of a single domain. As such we are using the home-page policy as a proxy for the organization's privacy "intent", as no mechanism exists to retrieve an organization's true intent; and as the most likely point of initial interaction between a user and an organization (from a privacy perspective) which can be viewed as another proxy for the point where the user is most likely to "assess" (acceptable, unacceptable) the organization's privacy intent. This approach also implies that we are only collecting a single statement (policy details including no policy) per Web site, which allows for the aggregation of individual results to the jurisdictional level; i.e. every surveyed Web site is represented exactly once when jurisdictional statements are inferred.

Data Analysis

With respect to hypotheses 1a-5c, our goal is to determine the degree of association within websites from an individual jurisdiction. Due to the potentially large number of variables, standard bivariate approaches such as Pearson or Spearman Rank correlations are not applicable. For these reasons, Cronbach's Alpha (Cronbach, 1951; Garson, 2006; Nunnally, 1978) and Intraclass Correlation (Andersen, 1990; Howell, 2002; Portney & Watkins, 1993; Sheskin, 2004; Shrout

& Fleiss, 1979) methods are utilized. Cronbach's Alpha provides a method for rating the internal consistency of a series of responses (website P3P policies) on various subjects of interest (P3P tags). However, Cronbach's Alpha is not a measure of unidimensionality. A dataset can have a high Cronbach's Alpha and still be multidimensional when clusters of highly intercorrelated items exist and weak correlation exists between these clusters (Garson, 2006). As a result, Cronbach's Alpha will be utilized as an exploratory test indicating whether a population exhibits general internal consistency. Thus, while a weak result indicates no consistency or agreement, a strong result cannot be interpreted as agreement between websites regarding privacy issues. The lower bound of 0.7, stated by Nunnally and Bernstien (1994) and Garson (2006), will be used as an indication of general internal consistency.

Intraclass correlation will be utilized to determine the degree of absolute website agreement on the subjects of interest (P3P tags). Intraclass correlation (ICC) should not be confused with standard correlation techniques; ICC allows for analysis concerning both the degree of association as well as the repeatability of the association when the observed variables are dichotomous in nature. The analysis of this paper utilizes the method generally referred to as Model 3 (Portney & Watkins, 1993; Shrout & Fleiss, 1979) using individual measurements; Model 3 is appropriate when all subjects of interest are surveyed (Portney & Watkins, 1993). This approach is reasonable since this study surveys all popular P3P adopting websites. Generalizations to all popular websites (whether they adopt P3P or not) would require the usage of Model 2 and must be made at the reader's discretion. However, as a cross check, the ICC results for Model 2 were calculated and no significant differences exist between the results from Models 2 and 3.

Interpretations of ICC results differ from those generated through standard correlation methods, the ICC value cannot be viewed as an r^2 value since it takes into account consistency *as well as* repeatability of results. We will follow the recommendations of Portney and Watkins (1993), who state that an ICC above 0.75 is an indicator of good agreement. In practice, ICC values range from 0.00 to 1.00. However, in certain circumstances, the ICC values can range from $\pm\infty$ (Portney & Watkins, 1993). This situation occurs when the data set is homogeneous, meaning a lack of significant variance between subjects of interest (P3P tags); this situation can be discovered by the application of a one-way ANOVA test (Howell, 2002). When a dataset is found to be homogenous, the test is considered inconclusive; we report the F-test results from the one-way ANOVA for completeness.

A limitation of using the ICC method is the lack of clear consensus regarding the calculation of Type I and Type II errors. For example, little guidance exists regarding the choice of a null hypothesis for an ICC test. The choice of $H_0 = 0$, for instance, provides information of little practical importance. Walter, Eliasziw, and Donner (1998) recommended setting H_0 to the minimally acceptable level of reliability. However, little guidance is given for choosing this point without making the tests overly conservative. The calculation of a minimum detectable effect (MDE) (Bloom, 1995) is a potential solution. MDE's describe the smallest effect that can be detected at a given statistical power and significance level, thus guarding against these errors. However, no formulation exists for the calculation of a MDE when using ICC. As a result of these limitations, confidence intervals will be calculated as an indicator of the degree of uncertainty in the results (Bonett, 2002). Further, this limits our ability to provide insight into the hypotheses 1b,2b,3b,4b,5a,5b and 5c; and hence, we will only make very conservative statements about our findings with regard to these hypotheses.

RESULTS AND ANALYSIS

In order to test hypotheses 1a-5c we examine the 15 nations that had the highest P3P adoption rate, constituting 95% of all the observed valid P3P full policies from the Alexa 100,000 list. This gives us a sample of 2,078 policies to examine. The analysis of hypotheses 1a-5c also requires the identification of whether general privacy laws and third party enforcement mechanisms exist in the various nations under study. General privacy laws with third party enforcement mechanisms have been implemented in the Netherlands (Dutch Data Protection Authority, 2006), Belgium (Commission for the Protection of Privacy, 2006), Spain (Spanish Data Protection Authority, 2006), Sweden (Swedish Data Inspection Board, 2006), United Kingdom (Information Commissioner's Office of the United Kingdom, 2006), Denmark (Danish Data Protection Agency, 2006), France (Française, 2006), Germany (Federal Commissioner for Data Protection and Freedom of Information, 2006), Australia (Australian Government Office of the Privacy Commissioner, 2006; Attorney-General's Department, 1988), Canada (Privacy Commissioner of Canada, 2006; Office of the Privacy Commissioner of Canada, 2000), and New Zealand (New Zealand Privacy Commissioner, 2006; New Zealand Parliamentary Counsel Office, 1993). Japan has enacted general privacy laws (Government of Japan, 2003), but does not implement a third party protection agency. The United States and Korea both implement sector specific legislation (Federal Trade Commission, 2006; Privacy International, 2004b). Russia only provides constitutional privacy protections (Privacy International, 2004a).

The results of Table 1 indicate that (with the exception of Russia), total agreement in P3P document content was not observed. It is very surprising that Russian websites, which are governed by very weak privacy protections (Privacy International, 2004a; Rajan, 2002) showed significant agreement. This agreement could be a result of an unidentified relationship either through ownership or industry sector. Another plausible independent explanation could be that due to the lack of legal protections, Russian websites all report that they undertake any action they wish. This unique agreement in Russian websites will be analyzed further in the following sections.

Evidence for Hypotheses 1a and 1b

Through analysis of Table 2, no support for hypothesis 1a is found for any nation. This is particularly surprising since the European Union's Data Protection Directive (European Commission, 1995) contains provisions concerning access privileges. For example, Article 41 requires that individuals be provided with access to information collected about themselves in order to ensure its accuracy (European Commission, 1995). This lack of consistent practice may be partly due to a lack of adherence. For instance, 18 websites from the Netherlands (31%), 19 from the United Kingdom (13%), 7 from Denmark (33%), 9 from France (26%), and 11 from Germany (15%), stated that they provided no access to selected information, which potentially violates Article 41. This potential lack of adherence to the legal framework is also observed in 15 Canadian websites (17%) who offered no access to selected information; an apparent contradiction of Principle 9 of the Personal Information Protection and Electronic Documents Act (Office of the Privacy Commissioner of Canada, 2000). A similar potential lack of adherence has recently been identified by Bowie and Jamal (2006) in UK websites. Their analysis found that many UK websites did not disclose the usage of cookies on a website; a potential violation of the Data Protection Directive. Our findings, if substantiated, provide further support for Bowie and Jamal's recommendation that formal government regulation should be resisted until it is understood why companies appear to ignore the currently enacted legislation in both the European Union and Canada.

Table 1. Intraclass correlation between all privacy related P3P tags (53 total tags)

Country	Number Of P3P policies	Cronbach's Alpha	Intraclass Correlation	95% confidence interval		F-Test		
				lower	Upper	Value	df	Significance
Nations With General Privacy Laws and Third Party Protection								
Australia	23	0.932	0.345	0.261	0.455	14.8	52	< 0.001
Belgium	11	0.877	0.387	0.290	0.508	8.1	52	< 0.001
Canada	86	0.976	0.301	0.230	0.400	41.9	52	< 0.001
Denmark	21	0.885	0.235	0.166	0.333	8.7	52	< 0.001
France	34	0.964	0.428	0.340	0.539	27.9	52	< 0.001
Germany	72	0.975	0.338	0.262	0.441	40.4	52	< 0.001
Netherlands	58	0.971	0.346	0.268	0.451	34.8	52	< 0.001
New Zealand	9	0.916	0.526	0.419	0.642	11.9	52	< 0.001
Spain	12	0.945	0.578	0.479	0.685	18.1	52	< 0.001
Sweden	12	0.896	0.360	0.260	0.482	9.6	52	< 0.001
United Kingdom	145	0.987	0.327	0.254	0.428	77.5	52	< 0.001
Nations Lacking General Privacy Laws or Third Party Protection								
Japan	30	0.940	0.308	0.231	0.413	16.7	52	< 0.001
Korea	14	0.726	0.130	0.077	0.210	3.7	52	< 0.001
Russian Federation	24	0.994	0.863	0.813	0.907	174.9	52	< 0.001
USA	1527	0.996	0.296	0.228	0.392	237.4	52	< 0.001

Table 2. Intraclass correlation between all access related P3P tags (6 total tags)

Country	Number Of websites	Cronbach's Alpha	Intraclass Correlation	95% confidence interval		F-Test		
				lower	upper	Value	df	Significance
Nations With General Privacy Laws and Third Party Protection								
Australia	23	.763	.144	.029	.562	4.2	5	.002
Belgium	11	.565	.124	-.021	.589	2.3	5	.059
Canada	86	.878	.091	.029	.402	8.2	5	< 0.001
Denmark	21	.869	.275	.095	.722	7.6	5	< 0.001
France	34	.832	.149	.042	.553	6.0	5	< 0.001
Germany	72	.960	.288	.126	.716	25.2	5	< 0.001
Netherlands	58	.899	.155	.054	.548	9.9	5	< 0.001
New Zealand	9	.911	.578	.278	.902	11.3	5	< 0.001
Spain	12	.915	.518	.242	.877	11.8	5	< 0.001
Sweden	12	.804	.291	.075	.752	5.1	5	0.001
United Kingdom	145	.906	.074	.025	.343	10.6	5	< 0.001
Nations Lacking General Privacy Laws or Third Party Protection								
Japan	30	.561	.048	-.006	.337	2.3	5	0.050
Korea	14	.872	.369	.135	.800	7.8	5	< 0.001
Russian Federation	24	.995	.915	.800	.985	217.0	5	< 0.001
USA	1527	.980	.103	.041	.413	49.0	5	< 0.001

While no support for Hypothesis 1a was found, Hypothesis 1b could only be rejected for the surveyed Russian websites. This apparent standardization of practice cannot be considered privacy protection, since 23 out of 24 websites provide individuals with no access to selected information. The OECD privacy principle of Individual Participation (OECD, 1980) requires that individuals have access to information about them, the right to challenge any information held, and to have that information updated if the challenge is successful. While the OECD privacy principles are not mandatory guidelines and Russia is not a signatory, they are a generally agreed upon framework for privacy protection supported by 30 nations.

Evidence for Hypotheses 2a and 2b

While the results in Table 3 support hypothesis 2a for the United Kingdom, France, Australia, and Spain, these nations constitute but a minority of nations surveyed that have implemented general privacy legislation and provide third party enforcement. The surveyed websites from these nations all tend to remedy their disputes through customer service. It is unknown why websites from other nations have not followed this practice, since customer service would appear to be the preferable means of resolving disputes when compared to independent arbitration, court decisions, or referencing applicable laws (Cranor et al., 2002). Hypothesis 2b could only be rejected for Russian websites, which also prefer to utilize customer service for resolving disputes.

Table 3. Intraclass correlation between all dispute resolution P3P tags (4 total tags)

Country	Number Of websites	Cronbach's Alpha	Intraclass Correlation	95% confidence interval		F-Test		
				lower	Upper	Value	Df	Significance
Nations With General Privacy Laws and Third Party Protection								
Australia	23	.992	.864	.654	.989	120.7	3	< 0.001
Belgium	11	.733	.226	.007	.846	3.8	3	0.021
Canada	86	.996	.741	.473	.976	223.7	3	< 0.001
Denmark	21	.923	.387	.134	.905	13.0	3	< 0.001
France	34	.991	.801	.551	.983	115.9	3	< 0.001
Germany	72	.995	.743	.475	.976	195.3	3	< 0.001
Netherlands	58	.989	.644	.357	.962	91.4	3	< 0.001
New Zealand	9	.853	.449	.108	.930	6.8	3	0.002
Spain	12	.992	.909	.741	.993	121.0	3	< 0.001
Sweden	12	.970	.727	.418	.975	33.0	3	< 0.001
United Kingdom	145	.998	.775	.521	.980	461.4	3	< 0.001
Nations Lacking General Privacy Laws or Third Party Protection								
Japan	30	.982	.649	.354	.963	54.2	3	< 0.001
Korea	14	.598	.092	-.018	.697	2.5	3	0.075
Russian Federation	24	.996	.913	.761	.993	253.0	3	< 0.001
USA	1527	.998	.592	.317	.953	649.5	3	< 0.001

Evidence for Hypotheses 3a and 3b

The results of Table 4 provide support for hypothesis 3a only for the United Kingdom, France, Australia, and Canada. Websites from all four of these nations predominately indicate that they offer to correct the problem. This would appear to be the preferable remedy from a business perspective when compared to the other choices of either monetary compensation, or following legally mandated remedies (L. Cranor et al., 2002). We are at a loss to explain this observed lack of uniformity in other surveyed nations. Hypothesis 3b was only rejected for Russian websites. It is surprising that websites from other nations did not follow the Russian model and offer to correct the error rather than refer to laws or paying compensation.

Evidence for Hypotheses 4a and 4b

The results of Table 5 indicate that there is no support for hypothesis 4a from any surveyed nation. This finding is especially surprising for France since they implement a strict licensing bureau (Française, 2006). The implications of these findings are significant for Internet users who do not read privacy policies (Jensen et al., 2005); no standard of practice whatsoever has evolved in the collection of non-transactional data. While legislative action may restrict unlawful actions of websites, lawful but undesirable actions may well be rampant. Clearly, consumer pressure for a standard of data-collection practice either does not exist, or is as yet ineffectual.

Hypothesis 4b can only be rejected for Russian websites. Further analysis of the agreement between Russian websites indicates that they use

Table 4. Intraclass correlation between all remedy related P3P tags (3 total tags)

Country	Number Of websites	Cronbach's Alpha	Intraclass Correlation	95% confidence interval		F-Test		
				Lower	upper	Value	df	Significance
Nations With General Privacy Laws and Third Party Protection								
Australia	23	.988	.768	.449	.992	80.3	2	< 0.001
Belgium	11	.753	.194	-.003	.926	4.0	2	0.034
Canada	86	.996	.771	.471	.993	263.7	2	< 0.001
Denmark	21	.926	.315	.082	.951	13.5	2	< 0.001
France	34	.995	.860	.613	.996	215.5	2	< 0.001
Germany	72	.985	.499	.203	.976	67.5	2	< 0.001
New Zealand	9	.865	.517	.089	.980	7.4	2	< 0.001
Netherlands	58	.959	.322	.100	.951	24.3	2	< 0.001
Spain	12	.944	.552	.195	.981	18.0	2	< 0.001
Sweden	12	.935	.500	.158	.977	15.4	2	< 0.001
United Kingdom	145	.997	.752	.448	.992	388.1	2	< 0.001
Nations Lacking General Privacy Laws or Third Party Protection								
Japan	30	.972	.572	.241	.982	35.7	2	< 0.001
Korea	14	.479	.057	-.036	.831	1.9	2	0.167
Russian Federation	24	.994	.870	.627	.996	161.0	2	< 0.001
USA	1527	.999	.694	.379	.989	1021.9	2	< 0.001

Table 5. Intraclass correlation between all purpose related P3P tags (12 total tags)

Country	Number Of websites	Cronbach's Alpha	Intraclass Correlation	95% confidence interval		F-Test		
				lower	Upper	Value	df	Significance
Nations With General Privacy Laws and Third Party Protection								
Australia	23	.910	.239	.119	.495	11.1	11	< 0.001
Belgium	11	.913	.493	.293	.752	11.5	11	< 0.001
Canada	86	.963	.209	.113	.440	27.2	11	< 0.001
Denmark	21	.883	.194	.089	.435	8.5	11	< 0.001
France	34	.941	.300	.165	.564	16.9	11	< 0.001
Germany	72	.973	.290	.165	.546	36.4	11	< 0.001
Netherlands	58	.964	.225	.121	.464	27.6	11	< 0.001
New Zealand	9	.951	.661	.462	.857	20.5	11	< 0.001
Spain	12	.960	.619	.421	.832	25.3	11	< 0.001
Sweden	12	.917	.352	.176	.634	12.0	11	< 0.001
United Kingdom	145	.985	.272	.155	.521	68.7	11	< 0.001
Nations Lacking General Privacy Laws or Third Party Protection								
Japan	30	.949	.301	.164	.566	19.5	11	< 0.001
Korea	14	.608	.067	.010	.232	2.5	11	0.006
Russian Federation	24	.995	.885	.788	.957	184.8	11	< 0.001
USA	1527	.996	.252	.144	.494	233.9	11	< 0.001

information for website administration, completion of requested activity, further development of the website, analysis of patrons in an anonymized fashion, and to make decisions about patrons in an anonymous fashion. While these results are not highly informative, it is unknown why Russian websites did not undertake more invasive analysis such as profiling of individuals, since few restraints appear to exist.

Evidence for hypothesis 5a

Hypothesis 5a can only be rejected for Russian websites given the results of Table 6. The observed Russian websites generally collected information relating to personal identification, characteristics of a patron's computer, site navigation and system state. The similarity in both types of information collected and purposes for its collection (outside of completing the current transaction) is unique

in our survey. One possible explanation is that the surveyed Russian websites are related either through ownership or services offered. However, we have been unable to confirm or refute this possibility.

Evidence for Hypothesis 5b

The results of Table 7 only allow for the rejection of hypothesis 5b for Russian websites. We summarize our data for Hypothesis 5b in Table 9, which outlines the retention periods used by surveyed websites. While general agreement was not expected, the number of websites who say they store information indefinitely is disturbing. In fact, the indefinite storage of information by 40 of 86 surveyed Canadian websites potentially violates the privacy principles outlined by the Model Code for the Protection of Personal Information (Canadian Standards Association, 1996) and appears

Table 6. Intraclass correlation between all category related P3P tags (17 total tags)

Country	Number Of websites	Cronbach's Alpha	Intraclass Correlation	95% confidence interval		F-Test		
				lower	Upper	Value	df	Significance
Nations With General Privacy Laws and Third Party Protection								
Australia	23	.842	.130	.062	.282	6.3	16	< 0.001
Belgium	11	.773	.219	.099	.437	4.3	16	< 0.001
Canada	86	.959	.153	.087	.301	24.4	16	< 0.001
Denmark	21	.804	.076	.031	.185	5.1	16	< 0.001
France	34	.951	.303	.184	.512	20.2	16	< 0.001
Germany	72	.949	.174	.100	.335	19.7	16	< 0.001
Netherlands	58	.957	.247	.148	.439	23.2	16	< 0.001
New Zealand	9	.305	.033	-.019	0.158	1.4	16	0.133
Spain	12	.858	.326	.181	.556	7.1	16	< 0.001
Sweden	12	.831	.149	.059	.330	5.9	16	< 0.001
United Kingdom	145	.979	.202	.120	.372	48.6	16	< 0.001
Nations Lacking General Privacy Laws or Third Party Protection								
Japan	30	.944	.233	.131	.428	17.9	16	< 0.001
Korea	14	.737	.120	.046	.282	3.7	16	< 0.001
Russian Federation	24	.996	.888	.810	.949	225.6	16	< 0.001
USA	1527	.993	.174	.104	.329	145.8	16	< 0.001

inconsistent with Principle 5 governing retention periods in the Personal Information Protection and Electronic Documents Act (Office of the Privacy Commissioner of Canada, 2000). Indefinite retention implies *permanent* vulnerability to security breaches within the data controllers, or privacy invasions by the data controllers themselves.

Evidence for Hypothesis 5c

From the results of Table 8, Hypothesis 5c was rejected for the populations of websites from Belgium, Spain, Sweden, France, New Zealand, and Russia. Websites from these nations (except Russia) all indicate that information will not be shared outside of the company. This agreement is unexpected since it would appear reasonable to hypothesize that many websites in the Alexa 100,000 list would be E-Commerce sites. Further it would also appear sensible that many of these

E-Commerce companies would use third parties to ship their products. While unforeseen, this finding indicates that information retained by these websites may be relatively secure since information sharing, and by extension usage, would be restricted. In contrast, Russian websites generally share information with unrelated third parties who do not follow similar privacy practices.

SUMMARY AND FUTURE WORK

We have studied the question of how different approaches to enforcement affect privacy protection on the Web. We retrieved all valid P3P policies from the 100,000 most popular websites, as ranked by Alexa.com, and investigated the level of consistency (on transaction-independent items) between them, taking into consideration the enforcement mechanisms of the hosting country. In general, we

Table 7. Intraclass correlation between all retention related P3P tags (5 total tags)

Country	Number Of websites	Cronbach's Alpha	Intraclass Correlation	95% confidence interval		F-Test		
				Lower	Upper	Value	df	Significance
Nations With General Privacy Laws and Third Party Protection								
Australia	23	0.932	0.405	.167	.858	14.8	4	< 0.001
Belgium	11	0.923	0.566	0.258	0.922	13.0	4	< 0.001
Canada	86	0.945	0.166	0.059	0.633	18.1	4	< 0.001
Denmark	21	0.752	0.148	0.021	0.651	4.0	4	0.005
France	34	0.909	0.255	0.088	0.755	11.0	4	< 0.001
Germany	72	0.856	0.083	0.022	0.463	6.9	4	< 0.001
Netherlands	58	0.972	0.396	0.180	0.848	36.2	4	< 0.001
New Zealand	9	0.892	.535	.207	.915	9.3	4	< 0.001
Spain	12	.884	.429	.151	.875	8.6	4	< 0.001
Sweden	12	.850	.355	.103	.842	6.7	4	< 0.001
United Kingdom	145	.974	.227	.091	.713	37.8	4	< 0.001
Nations Lacking General Privacy Laws or Third Party Protection								
Japan	30	0.844	0.181	0.047	0.681	6.4	4	< 0.001
Korea	14	0.421	0.054	-0.035	0.513	1.7	4	0.158
Russian Federation	24	.987	.789	.556	.969	76.2	4	< 0.001
USA	1527	.994	.263	.112	.748	159.3	4	< 0.001

Table 8. Intraclass correlation between all recipient related P3P tags (6 total tags)

Country	Number Of websites	Cronbach's Alpha	Intraclass Correlation	95% confidence interval		F-Test		
				lower	upper	Value	df	Significance
Nations With General Privacy Laws and Third Party Protection								
Australia	23	.968	.552	.304	.885	31.4	5	< 0.001
Belgium	11	.991	.914	.789	.985	117.6	5	< 0.001
Canada	86	.994	.632	.396	.912	164.6	5	< 0.001
Denmark	21	.970	.638	.383	.916	33.4	5	< 0.001
France	34	.994	.852	.640	.966	162.0	5	< 0.001
Germany	72	.995	.742	.524	.946	218.1	5	< 0.001
Netherlands	58	.994	.743	.523	.946	177.2	5	< 0.001
New Zealand	9	.987	.896	.747	.982	78.4	5	< 0.001
Spain	12	1.000	1.000	-	1.000	-	5	-
Sweden	12	.987	.862	.689	.975	76.1	5	< 0.001
United Kingdom	145	.995	.558	.326	.884	184.8	5	< 0.001
Nations Lacking General Privacy Laws or Third Party Protection								
Japan	30	.974	.388	.182	.798	38.2	5	< 0.001
Korea	14	.858	.266	.086	.716	7.0	5	< 0.001
Russian Federation	24	.994	.873	.719	.977	180.4	5	< 0.001
USA	1527	.998	.533	.307	.873	640.8	5	< 0.001

Given the absolute agreement between Spanish websites, a lower confidence interval and F-value are invalid

Table 9. Retention periods specified by surveyed websites

	No retention	Stated purpose	Legal requirement	Business practices	Indefinitely
Netherlands	**5**	**8**	**2**	**21**	**44**
Belgium	0	0	2	1	9
Spain	2	0	0	3	9
Sweden	1	1	0	6	8
United kingdom	13	24	11	66	77
Denmark	5	1	0	7	9
France	1	7	2	16	19
Germany	9	23	6	21	29
Australia	0	1	1	5	15
Canada	6	8	9	34	40
New Zealand	0	7	0	1	1
United States	120	198	78	583	852
Korea	0	0	1	3	3
Japan	4	1	1	13	11
Russian Federation	0	0	0	21	2

Note: websites may utilize different storage lengths for different types of data

found that there is no evidence of any "standards of practice" evolving no matter the enforcement regime used. There were a few exceptions: websites from a few nations with general privacy laws showed some commonality on mechanisms for dispute resolution (Hypothesis 2a), what remedies the website will offer (Hypothesis 3a), and which other entities will be allowed access to a person's data (Hypothesis 5c). However, the only nation that appeared in all three of these "exceptional" groups was France, with the United Kingdom, Spain and Australia appearing in two out of three. Furthermore, there was no evidence of standards of practice in allowing individuals to examine (and possibly challenge) information about themselves, nor in what transaction-independent purposes data will be used for. As expected, there is also no consistency in what categories of data are collected, or in how long that data will be retained. All of these elements are a part of the OECD privacy principles, and should not be adopted in isolation from one another.

Our findings indicate that, regardless of the current enforcement mechanisms employed, privacy-protection legislation seems to have made little headway in promoting a more consistent or predictable environment for on-line consumers. While this fact has often been taken for granted, it has never been empirically studied on a large scale. The actions of websites vary even where strict licensing bureaus are established such as in France (Française, 2006). These results would also appear to imply that without a novel approach to influencing websites, calls for standardization (Anton et al., 2004) and alignment (Earp et al., 2005) are unlikely to be realized. A limiting factor of our analysis, by necessity, is the usage of P3P documents as the primary information source. The limited adoption rate of these policies restricts the generalizability of the results and should be taken into account in the interpretation of the above results.

Future work on this topic will include an investigation of the exceptions we detected in our analysis. Why would French websites, for example, have a consistent approach to dispute resolution, but not to providing individuals access to stored information about them (which is how disputes will arise in the first place)? Is this a true reflection of the state of practice, or is it a quality control / maintenance issue with the P3P documents themselves? If it is a true reflection, and if the posted policies violate French law (as they seem to), are the penalties described in French law being applied? This research would require evidence beyond just self-reports such as P3P documents or surveys, as in (Bowie & Jamal, 2006). We also need to determine why Web sites provide P3P policies. Our results depict various discrepancies between and within nations, and a generally chaotic environment. So why do web site operators invest the resources to create a P3P policy in the first place? Plainly, research into the business drivers behind this choice would have to be conducted via survey questionnaires on any large scale.

ACKNOWLEDGMENT

The authors wish to thank Alexa.com for providing a copy of their Top 100,000 List for our research. This research was supported in part by the Natural Sciences and Engineering Research Council of Canada under grant G121210906 and by Alberta Innovation & Science under grant G230000066.

REFERENCES

Acquisti, A., & Grossklags, J. (2005). Privacy and Rationality in Individual Decision Making. *IEEE Security and Privacy*, *3*(1), 26–33. doi:10.1109/MSP.2005.22

Alexa. (2007). *Alexa Web Search - Top 500*. Retrieved February 21, 2007, from http://www.alexa.com/site/ds/top_500

Andersen, E. B. (1990). *The Statistical Analysis of Categorical Data*. New York: Springer-Verlag.

Anton, A. I., Bertino, E., Li, N., & Yu, T. (2007). A roadmap for comprehensive online privacy policy management. *Communications of the ACM*, *50*(7), 109–116. doi:10.1145/1272516.1272522

Anton, A. I., Earp, J. B., He, Q., Stufflebeam, W., Bolchini, D., & Jensen, C. (2004). Financial Privacy Policies and the Need for Standardization. *IEEE Security and Privacy*, *2*(2), 36–45. doi:10.1109/MSECP.2004.1281243

Anton, A. I., Earp, J. B., Vail, M. W., Jain, N., Gheen, C. M., & Frink, J. M. (2007). HIPPA's Effect on Web Site Privacy Policies. *IEEE Security and Privacy*, *5*(1), 45–52. doi:10.1109/MSP.2007.7

Attorney-General's Department. (1988). *Privacy Act 1988, Act 119*. Canberra, Australia: Office of Legislative Drafting and Publishing.

Australian Government Office of the Privacy Commisioner. (2006). *Office of the Privacy Commissioner*. Retrieved from http://www.privacy.gov.au/

Better Business Bureau. (2006). *BBBOnLine, Inc. - Promoting Trust and Confidence on the Internet*. Retrieved from http://www.bbbonline.org/

Bloom, H. S. (1995). Minimum Detectable Effects. *Evaluation Review*, *19*(5), 547–556. doi:10.1177/0193841X9501900504

Bonett, D. G. (2002). Sample Size Requirements for Estimating Intraclass Correlations with Desired Precision. *Statistics in Medicine*, *21*(9), 1331–1335. doi:10.1002/sim.1108

Bowie, N. E., & Jamal, K. (2006). Privacy Rights on the Internet: Self-Regulation or Government Regulation. *Business Ethics Quarterly*, *16*(3).

Bracey, D. H. (2006). *Exploring Law and Culture*. Long Grove, IL: Waveland Press

Bruckner, L., & Voss, M. (2005, October 2005). *MozPETs - A Privacy Enhanced Web Browser.* Paper presented at the Third Annual Conference on Privacy, Security and Trust, St. Andrews, New Brunswick, Canada.

Byers, S., Cranor, L., & Kormann, D. (2003). *Automated Analysis of P3P-Enabled Web Sites.* Paper presented at the 5th International Conference on Electronic Commerce, Pittsburgh, PA.

Canadian Standards Association. (1996). *Model Code for the Protection of Personal Information.* Retrieved May 13, 2006, from http://www.csa.ca/standards/privacy/default. asp?load=code&language=English

Capurro, R. (2005). Privacy. An Intercultural Perspective. *Ethics and Information Technology, 7,* 37–47. doi:10.1007/s10676-005-4407-4

Cases, A.-S., Fournier, C., Dubois, P.-L., & Tanner, J. F. Jr. (in press). Web Site spill over to email campaigns: The role of privacy, trust and shoppers' attitudes. *Journal of Business Research.*

Chau, P. Y. K., Hu, P. J.-H., Lee, B. L. P., & Au, A. K. K. (2007). Examining customers' trust in online vendors and their dropout decisions: An empirical study. *Electronic Commerce Research and Applications, 6,* 171–182. doi:10.1016/j. elerap.2006.11.008

Clark, H. H. (1996). *Using Language.* New York: Cambridge University Press.

Commission for the Protection of Privacy. (2006). *Commission for the Protection of Privacy-Home.* Retrieved from http://www.privacycommission. be/

Consumer Reports Web Watch. (2002). *A Matter of Trust: What Users Want From Web Sites.* Yonkers, NY: Author.

Cranor, L., Dobbs, B., Egelman, S., Hogben, G., Humphrey, J., Langheinrich, M., et al. (2006). *The Platform for Privacy Preferences 1.1 (P3P1.1) Specification.* Retrieved January 25, 2008, from http://www.w3.org/TR/P3P11/

Cranor, L., Egelman, S., Sheng, S., McDonald, A., & Chowdhury, A. (2008). P3P Deployment on Websites. *Electronic Commerce Research and Applications*

Cranor, L., Langheinrich, M., Marchiori, M., Presler-Marshall, M., & Reagle, J. (2002). *The Platform for Privacy Preferences 1.0 Specification.* Retrieved from http://www.w3.org/TR/P3P/

Cranor, L. F., Byers, S., & Kormann, D. (2003). *An Analysis of P3P Deployment on Commercial, Government and Children's Web Sites as of May 2003.* Washington, DC: Federal Trade Commission.

Cronbach, L. J. (1951). Coefficient Alpha and the Internal Structure of Tests. *Psychometrika, 16*(3), 297–334. doi:10.1007/BF02310555

Danish Data Protection Agency. (2006). *DATA-TILSYNET: Introduction to the Danish Data Protection Agency.* Retrieved from http://www. datatilsynet.dk/eng/index.html

Dingledine, R., Mathewson, N., & Syverson, P. (2007). Deploying Low-Latency Anonymity: Design Challenges and Social Factors. *IEEE Security and Privacy, 5*(5), 83–87. doi:10.1109/MSP.2007.108

Dutch Data Protection Authority. (2006). *Dutch DPA.* Retrieved from http://www.dutchdpa.nl/

Earp, J. B., Anton, A. I., Aiman-Smith, L., & Stufflebeam, W. H. (2005). Examining Internet Privacy Policies Within the Context of User Privacy Values. *IEEE Transactions on Engineering Management, 52*(2), 227–237. doi:10.1109/TEM.2005.844927

Egelman, S., & Cranor, L. F. (2006, August, 2006). *An Analysis of P3P-Enabled Web Sites among Top-20 Search Results.* Paper presented at the Eighth International Conference on Electronic Commerce, Fredericton, New Brunswick, Canada.

Ellickson, R. C. (2001). The Evolution of Social Norms: A Perspective from the Legal Academy. In M. Hechter & K.-D. Opp (Eds.), *Social Norms* (pp. 35-75). New York: Russell Sage Foundation.

Ernst and Young. (2003). *P3P Dashboard Report.* Retrieved from http://www.ey.com/global/download.nsf/US/P3P_Dashboard_January_2003/$file/E&YP3PDashboardJan2003.pdf

European Commission. (1995). *Directive 95/46/EC of the European Parliament and of the Council of 24 October 1995 on the protection of individuals with regard to the processing of personal data and on the free movement of such data* (Official Journal L 281). Brussels, Belgium: Author.

European Commission. (2003). *First Report on the Implementation of the Data Protection Directive (95/24/EC).* Brussels, Belgium: Author.

Export.gov. (2007). *Safe Harbor Program.* Retrieved February 20, 2007, from http://www.export.gov/safeharbor/doc_safeharbor_index.asp

Fallows, D. (2004). *The Internet and Daily Life.* Washington, DC: Pew Internet & American Life Project.

Federal Commissioner for Data Protection and Freedom of Information. (2006). *Welcome to the Website of the Federal Commissioner for Data Protection and Freedom of Information.* Retrieved from http://www.bfdi.bund.de/cln_029/nn_533554/EN/Home/homepage__node.html__nnn=true

Federal Trade Commission. (2002). *E-Government Act of 2002.* Washington, DC: Author.

Federal Trade Commission. (2006). *Privacy Initiatives.* Retrieved from http://www.ftc.gov/privacy/index.html

Française, C. R. (2006). *Comission Nationale De L'Informatique Et Des Libertes.* Retrieved May 10, 2006, from http://www.cnil.fr/index.php?id=4

Garfinkel, S. (1995). *PGP: Pretty Good Privacy.* Sebastopol, CA: O'Reilly.

Garson, D. (2006). *Scales and Standard Measures.* Retrieved from http://www2.chass.ncsu.edu/garson/PA765/standard.htm

Goecks, J., & Mynatt, E. D. (2005). Social Approaches to End-User Privacy Management. In L. F. Cranor & S. Garfinkel (Eds.), *Security and Usability Designing Secure Systems That People Can Use.* Beijing, China: O'Reilly.

Government of Japan. (2003). *Act on the Protection of Personal Information.* Tokyo: Author.

Grau, J. (2006). *Europe Retail E-Commerce: Spotlight on the UK, Germany, and France.* New York: eMarketer, Inc.

Grau, J. (2007). *Asia-Pacific B2C E-Commerce.* New York: eMarketer, Inc.

Graumann, S., & Neinert, F. (2006). *Monitoring the Information Economy: 9th Factual Report.* Munich, Germany: TNS Business Intelligence.

Greenspan, S., Goldberg, D., Weimer, D., & Basso, A. (2000, December). *Interpersonal Trust and Common Ground in Electronically Mediated Communication.* Paper presented at the 2000 ACM Conference on Computer Supported Cooperative Work, Philadelphia.

Gritzalis, S. (2004). Enhancing Web Privacy and Anonymity In the Digital Era. *Information Management & Computer Security, 12*(3), 255–288. doi:10.1108/09685220410542615

Henry, M. (2001). *International Privacy, Publicity & Personality Laws*. Markham, OT, Canada: Butterworths.

Horne, C. (2001). Sociological Perspectives on the Emergence of Norms. In M. Hechter & K.-D. Opp (Eds.), *Social Norms*. New York: Russell Sage Foundation.

Howell, D. C. (2002). *Statistical Methods for Psychology* (5th ed.). Pacific Grove, CA: Duxbury/Thomson Learning.

Hsu, M.-H., & Kuo, F.-Y. (2003). The Effect of Organization-Based Self-Esteem and Deindividualism in Protecting Personal Information Privacy. *Journal of Business Ethics*, *42*(4), 305–320. doi:10.1023/A:1022500626298

IP2Location.com. (2006). *Geolocation IP Address to Country City Region Latitude Longitude ZIP Code ISP Domain Name Database for Developers*. Retrieved from http://www.ip2location.com/

Information Commissioner's Office of the United Kingdom. (2006). *Information Commissioner's Office of the United Kingdom-Home*. Retrieved from http://www.ico.gov.uk/eventual.aspx

Jensen, C., & Potts, C. (2004, April 2004). *Privacy Policies as Decision-Making Tools: An Evaluation of Online Privacy Notices*. Paper presented at the CHI 2004, Vienna, Austria.

Jensen, C., Potts, C., & Jensen, C. (2005). Privacy Practices of Internet Users: Self-Reports Versus Observed Behavior. *International Journal of Human-Computer Studies*, *63*, 203–227. doi:10.1016/j.ijhcs.2005.04.019

Kalloniatis, C., Kavakli, E., & Gritzalis, S. (2008). Addressing privacy requirements in system design: the PriS method. *Requirements Engineering*, *13*(3), 241–255. doi:10.1007/s00766-008-0067-3

Kaplan, S. E., & Nieschwietz, R. J. (2003). A Web Assurance Model of Trust for B2C E-Commerce. *International Journal of Accounting Information Systems*, *4*(2), 95–114. doi:10.1016/S1467-0895(03)00005-8

Kobsa, A. (2007). Privacy-enhanced personalization. *Communications of the ACM*, *50*(8), 24–33. doi:10.1145/1278201.1278202

Koike, Y., & Taiki, S. (2002). *P3P Validator*. Retrieved from from http://www.w3.org/P3P/validator.html

Kumaraguru, P., & Cranor, L. (2005, May 2005). *Privacy in India: Attitudes and Awareness*. Paper presented at the 2005 Workshop on Privacy Enhancing Technologies, Dubrovnik, Croatia.

Larose, R., & Rifon, N. J. (2007). Promoting i-Safety: Effects of Privacy Warnings and Privacy Seals on Risk Assessment and Online Privacy Behavior. *The Journal of Consumer Affairs*, *41*(1), 127–149. doi:10.1111/j.1745-6606.2006.00071.x

Lichtenstein, S., Swatman, P. M. C., & Babu, K. (2003). *Adding Value to Online Privacy for Consumers: Remedying Deficiencies in Online Privacy Policies with an Holistic Approach*. Paper presented at the 36th Hawaii International Conference on System Sciences, Hawaii.

Lioudakis, G. V., Koutsoloukas, E. A., Dellas, N. L., Tselikas, N., Kapellaki, S., & Prezerakos, G. N. (2007). A middleware architecture for privacy protection. *Computer Networks*, *51*(16), 4679–4696. doi:10.1016/j.comnet.2007.06.010

Miyazaki, A. D. (2008). Online Privacy and the Disclosure of Cookie Use: Effects on Consumer Trust and Anticipated Patronage. *Journal of Public Policy & Marketing*, *27*(1), 19–33. doi:10.1509/jppm.27.1.19

Moores, T. (2005). Do Consumers Understand the Role of Privacy Seals in E-Commerce? *Communications of the ACM, 48*(3), 86–91. doi:10.1145/1047671.1047674

New Zealand Parliamentary Counsel Office. (1993). *Privacy Act 1993 No 28*. Wellington, New Zealand: Author.

New Zealand Privacy Commissioner. (2006). *Privacy Commissioner Home*. Retrieved from http://www.knowledge-basket.co.nz/privacy/top.html

Nunnally, J. C. (1978). *Psychometric Theory* (2nd ed.). New York: McGraw-Hill.

Nunnally, J. C., & Bernstien, I. H. (1994). *Psychometric Theory* (3rd ed.). New York: McGraw-Hill.

O'Connor, P. (2007). Online Consumer Privacy: An Analysis of Hotel Company Behavior. *The Cornell Hotel and Restaurant Administration Quarterly, 48*(2), 183–200. doi:10.1177/0010880407299541

OECD. (1980). *OECD Guidelines on the Protection of Privacy and Transborder Flows of Personal Data*. Retrieved May 20, 2006, from http://www.oecd.org/document/18/0,2340, en_2649_34255_1815186_1_1_1_1,00.html

Office of the Privacy Commissioner of Canada. (2000). [). Ottawa, ON, Canada: Public Works and Government Services Canada - Publishing.]. *Personal Information Protection and Electronic Documents Act, C-6*, 2000.

Patil, S., & Kobsa, A. (2009). Privacy Considerations in Awareness Systems: Designing with Privacy in Mind In P. Markopoulos, B. De Ruyter & W. Mackay (Eds.), *Awareness Systems: Advances in Theory, Methodology and Design* (pp. 187-206). London: Springer.

Perkins, E., & Markel, M. (2004). Multinational Data-Privacy Laws: An Introduction for IT Managers. *IEEE Transactions on Professional Communication, 47*(2), 85–94. doi:10.1109/TPC.2004.828207

Portney, L. G., & Watkins, M. P. (1993). *Foundations of Clinical Research, Applications to Practice*. Norwalk, CT: Appletop & Lange.

Preibusch, S., Hoser, B., Gurses, S., & Berendt, B. (2007). *Ubiquitous social networks – opportunities and challenges for privacy-aware user modelling*. Berlin, Germany: German Institute for Economic Research.

Princeton Survey Research Associates International. (2005). *Leap of Faith: Using the Internet Despite the Dangers*. Yonkers, NY: Consumer Reports Web Watch.

Privacy Commissioner of Canada. (2006). *Home Page - Privacy Commissioner of Canada*. Retrieved from http://www.privcom.gc.ca/index_e.asp

Privacy International. (2004a). *PHR 2004 - The Russian Federation*.

Privacy International. (2004b). *The Republic of Korea*. Retrieved from http://www.privacyinternational.org/article.shtml?cmd[347]=x-347-83785

Rajan, M. T. S. (2002). The Past and Future of Privacy in Russia. *Review of Central and East European Law, 4*, 625–638.

Reay, I., Beatty, P., Dick, S., & Miller, J. (2007). A Survey and Analysis of the P3P Protocol's Agents, Adoption, Maintenance and Future. *IEEE Transactions on Dependable and Secure Computing, 4*(2), 151–164. doi:10.1109/TDSC.2007.1004

Reay, I., Dick, S., & Miller, J. (2009a). An Analysis of Privacy Signals on the World Wide Web: Past, Present and Future. *Information Sciences, 179*(8), 1102–1115. doi:10.1016/j.ins.2008.12.012

Reay, I., Dick, S., & Miller, J. (2009b). A Large-Scale Empirical Study of Online Privacy Policies: Stated Actions Vs. Legal Obligations. *ACM Transactions on the Web, 3*(2), 34. doi:10.1145/1513876.1513878

Sadeh, N., Hong, J., Cranor, L., Fette, I., Kelley, P., & Prabaker, M. (2008). Understanding and Capturing People's Privacy Policies in a People Finder Application. *Journal of Personal and Ubiquitous Computing, 13*(6), 401–412. doi:10.1007/s00779-008-0214-3

Security Space. (2006). *P3P Compact Privacy Policy Report*. Burlington, ON, Canada: Author.

Shaw, T. R. (2003). The Moral Intensity of Privacy: An Empirical Study of Webmasters' Attitudes. *Journal of Business Ethics, 46*(4), 301–318. doi:10.1023/A:1025628530013

Sheskin, D. J. (2004). *Handbook of Parametric and NonParametric Statistical Procedures* (3rd ed.). Boca Raton, FL: Chapman and Hall/CRC.

Shrout, P. E., & Fleiss, J. L. (1979). Intraclass Correlations: Uses in Assessing Rater Reliability. *Psychological Bulletin, 86*, 420–428. doi:10.1037/0033-2909.86.2.420

Spanish Data Protection Authority. (2006). *Agencia Espanola De Proteccion De Datos*. Retrieved from https://www.agpd.es/index.php?idSeccion=8

Sun, L.-T. (1994). Government as an institution for human fulfillment. *Humanomics, 10*(4), 76–101. doi:10.1108/eb018758

Swedish Data Inspection Board. (2006). *Swedish Data Inspection Board - Information in English - Datainspektionen*. Retrieved from http://www.datainspektionen.se/in_english/start.shtml

Truste.org. (2006). *TRUSTe - Make Privacy Your Choice*. Retrieved from http://www.truste.org/

Turow, J., Feldman, L., & Meltzer, K. (2005). *Open To Exploitation: American Shoppers Online and Offline*. Philadelphia: University of Pennsylvania's Annenberg School for Communication.

Varian, H., Wallenberg, F., & Woroch, G. (2005). The Demographics of the Do-Not-Call List. *IEEE Security and Privacy, 3*(1), 34–39. doi:10.1109/MSP.2005.28

Verisign. (2008). *VeriSign - Security (SSL Certificates), Intelligent Communications, and Identity Protection*. Retrieved from http://www.verisign.com/

Walter, S. D., Eliasziw, M., & Donner, A. (1998). Sample size and optimal designs for reliability studies. *Statistics in Medicine, 17*(1), 101–110. doi:10.1002/(SICI)1097-0258(19980115)17:1<101::AID-SIM727>3.0.CO;2-E

Watt, A. (2005). *Beginning Regular Expressions*. Indianapolis, IN: Wiley Publishing, Inc.

WebTrust. (2006). *WebTrust / SysTrust*. Retrieved from http://www.webtrust.org/

Wenning, R., & Cranor, L. (2006). *The Platform for Privacy Preferences (P3P) Project*. Retrieved February 21, 2007, from http://www.w3.org/P3P/

APPENDIX A

The P3P 1.0 (Cranor et al., 2002) specification became an official W3C recommendation in 2001. Through the use of XML documents and a XML schema provided by the W3C, websites are able to encode their human readable privacy policies in a machine-readable manner. These documents are retrieved by a P3P user agent, interpreted and displayed to the user. P3P does not enforce privacy standards. It is through the use of written laws, situational context, and legal precedence that the legality of organizational actions is determined. The role of the user agent is to request the P3P documents (Figure 2) and display any relevant information to the user. The information that is passed in a P3P document transfer can be represented as a series of classes (Table 10). These classes are composed of tags that can be viewed as an approximation to the concepts, and information, contained in the human readable privacy policies that are posted on websites.

There are two types of P3P policies. Full P3P policies provide an approximate mapping from a HRPP to an XML document, based on the XML schema published by the W3C as a part of their P3P 1.0 specification (Cranor et al., 2002). Compact P3P policies, on the other hand, only contain information relevant to cookies set during an HTTP request/response sequence. Cookies were a significant concern for P3P architects since they allow users to be tracked across Web sites and can be used to store sensitive information. Since multiple cookies from first and third parties can be set during a HTTP transaction, multiple privacy policies may need to be requested to determine how the information collected will be used. To limit bandwidth usage and time delays, P3P compact policies are simply a string transmitted in the HTTP response header. The P3P specification contains a complete description of both full and compact policies (Cranor et al., 2002). The P3P 1.1 standard (Cranor et al., 2006) has been published as a Working Group note; however, the W3C has decided not to proceed with the candidate recommendation process as of November 2006 (Wenning & Cranor, 2006).

Figure 2. Activity diagram for the P3P protocol

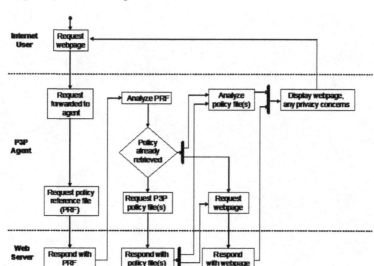

Table 10. Primary P3P XML tag classes

TAG	DESCRIPTION
CATEGORY	Categories of data that are collected by a website
PURPOSE	The reason(s) why data is being collected by the website. All tags are transaction independent with the exception of a single tag that indicates information is collected to complete the requested transaction.
RECIPIENT	Personnel the website will permit to access collected data
ACCESS	Type of access the website provides a user to collected data concerning them
RETENTION	Period of time collected information will be kept by the website
DISPUTES	Recourses available to the user if the website does not abide by its posted privacy policy
REMEDIES	Remedies the website will offer to the user if there is a breach of the website's privacy policy

This work was previously published in International Journal of Information Security and Privacy (IJISP), edited by Hamid Nemati, pp 68-95, copyright 2009 by IGI Publishing (imprint of IGI Global)

Compilation of References

ACLU (2003, November 30). *RFID position statement of consumer privacy and civil liberties organizations.* New York: American Civil Liberties Union.

ACNielson. ACNielsen Internet Confidence Index, http://acnielsen.com/news/corp/001/20010627b.htm

Acquisti, A., & Grossklags, J. (2005). Privacy and Rationality in Individual Decision Making. *IEEE Security and Privacy*, 3(1), 26–33. doi:10.1109/MSP.2005.22

Active.com. *The Importance of E-mail in a Successful Online Campaign.* Retrieved on September 21, 2008 from http://www.active.com/images/activegiving/email-campaign.pdf

Aczel, P. (2008). *Variants of Classical Set Theory and their Applications.* Retrieved from http://www.cs.man.ac.uk/~petera/

Adams, A., & Sasse, M. A. (1999). Users are not the enemy. *Communications of the ACM*, 42(12), 40–46. doi:10.1145/322796.322806

Adams, C., & Farrell, S. (1999). *Internet X.509 public key infrastructure: Certificate management protocols* (RFC 2510). Retrieved from http://tools.ietf.org/html/rfc2510

Adjie-Winoto, W., Schwartz, E., Balakrishnan, H., & Lilley, J. (1999). *The design and implementation of an intentional naming system.* Paper presented at the 17th ACM Symposium on Operating Systems Principles (SOSP '99), Kiawah Island, SC.

Adler, M. P. (2006). A Unified Approach to Information Security Compliance. *EDUCAUSE Review*, 41(5), 46–61.

AFP (2008, November 21). *Verizon employees wrongly accessed Obama phone records.*

Aggarwal, C. C., & Yu, P. S. (2004). A Condensation Approach to Privacy Preserving Data Mining. In *Proceedings of the 9th International Conference on Extending Database Technology* (pp. 183-199).

Agi, I., & Gong, L. (1996). An empirical study of secure MPEG video transmissions. *Proceedings of the Internet Society symposium on network and distributed system security*, 137-144.

Agrawal, D., & Aggarwal, C. (2001). On the design and quantification of privacy preserving data mining algorithms. In *Proceedings of the 20th ACM SIGMOD SIGACT-SIGART Symposium on Principles of Database Systems* (pp. 247-255).

Agrawal, R., & Srikant, R. (2000). Privacy preserving data mining. In *Proceedings of the 2000 ACM SIGMOD Conference on Management of Data* (pp. 439-450).

Ahrens, F. (2006, June 3). *Government, Internet firms in talks over browsing data.* Washington, DC: The Washington Post. (p. D3).

Ajzen, I. (1991). The theory of planned behavior. *Organizational Behavior and Human Decision Processes*, 50(2), 179–211. doi:10.1016/0749-5978(91)90020-T

Akyildiz, I., Su, W., Sankarasubramaniam, Y., & Cayirci, E. (2002). A survey on sensor networks. *IEEE Communications Magazine*, 40(8), 102–114. doi:10.1109/MCOM.2002.1024422

Albrecht, K. (2002). Supermarket cards: The tip of the retail surveillance iceberg. *Denver University Law Review. 79*(4, 15), 534-554.

Alexa. (2007). *Alexa Web Search - Top 500*. Retrieved February 21, 2007, from http://www.alexa.com/site/ds/top_500

Alexander, K., Dhumale, R., & Eatwell, J. (2004). *Global governance of financial systems. The International Regulation of Systemic Risk*. New York: Oxford University Press Inc.

Allan, J., Lavrenko, V., & Connell, M. E. (2003). A month to topic detection and tracking in Hindi. [TALIP]. *ACM Transactions on Asian Language Information Processing, 2*(2), 85–100. doi:10.1145/974740.974742

Allan, J., .Papka, R., &.Lavrenko, V. (1999). On-line New Event Detection and Tracking. Graduate School of the University of Massachusetts.

Allan, J., Lavrenko, V., & Jin, H. (2000). First Story Detection in TDT is Hard, *Proceedings of 9th Conference on Information Knowledge Management* CIKM, 374-381.

Allen, C. A., & Davidson, J. L. (1998). Steganography using the Minimax Eigenvalue Decomposition. *Proceedings of the conference on mathematics of data/image coding, compression, and encryption, 3456*, 13-24.

Alturki, F., & Mersereau, R. (2001). A novel approach for increasing security and data embedding capacity in images for data hiding applications. *Proceedings of the international conference on information technology: Coding and computing*, 228–233.

Ameridex (2007, February 27). Privacy statement. *Ameridex Information Systems*.

Amin, M. M., Salleh, M., Ibrahim, S., & Katmin, M. R. (2003). Steganography: Random LSB Insertion Using Discrete Logarithm, *Proceedings of the Conference on Information Technology in Asia (CITA'03), Universiti Malaysia Sarawak, Sarawak, Malaysia*, 234-238.

Andersen, E. B. (1990). *The Statistical Analysis of Categorical Data*. New York: Springer-Verlag.

Anley, C. (2002). *(more) Advanced SQL Injection*. Retrieved September 4, 2010, from http://www.ngssoftware.com/papers/more_advanced_sql_injection.pdf

ANSI X9. 63. (1999). *Elliptic Curve Key Agreement and Key Transport Protocols*. Washington, DC: American Bankers Association.

Anti-phising Working Group. (2009, March). *Phishing activity trends report for the 2nd half of 2008*. Retrieved from http://www.antiphishing.org/reports/apwg_report_H2_2008.pdf

Anton, A. I., Bertino, E., Li, N., & Yu, T. (2007). A roadmap for comprehensive online privacy policy management. *Communications of the ACM, 50*(7), 109–116. doi:10.1145/1272516.1272522

Anton, A. I., Earp, J. B., He, Q., Stufflebeam, W., Bolchini, D., & Jensen, C. (2004). Financial Privacy Policies and the Need for Standardization. *IEEE Security and Privacy, 2*(2), 36–45. doi:10.1109/MSECP.2004.1281243

Anton, A. I., Earp, J. B., Vail, M. W., Jain, N., Gheen, C. M., & Frink, J. M. (2007). HIPPA's Effect on Web Site Privacy Policies. *IEEE Security and Privacy, 5*(1), 45–52. doi:10.1109/MSP.2007.7

Apache Tomcat. (2003). *The Apache Jakarta Tomcat 5 servlet/JSP container*. Retrieved from http://tomcat.apache.org/tomcat-5.0-doc/

Apple Computer Inc. (2003). *Rendezvous*. Retrieved from http://developer.apple.com/macosx/rendezvous/

Aristotle. com (2007). *Privacy policy: privacy statement for* www. Aristotle.com.

Arsalan, M., Malik, S. A., & Khan, A. 2010. Intelligent threshold selection for reversible watermarking of medical images. In *Proceedings of the 12th Annual Conference Comp on Genetic and Evolutionary Computation* (Portland, Oregon, USA, July 07 - 11, 2010). GECCO '10. ACM, New York, NY, 1909-1914.

Arvin, M. (2005). Addressing the challenges of HIPAA compliance in research, Part II. *Journal of Healthcare Compliance, 7*(2), 59–64.

Asokan, N., Shoup, V., & Waidner, M. (2000). Optimistic fair exchange of digital signatures. *IEEE Journal on Selected Areas in Communications, 18*(4), 591–606. doi:10.1109/49.839935

Asokan, N., Schunter, M., & Waidner, M. (1997). Optimistic protocols for fair exchange. In T. Matsumoto (Ed.), *4th ACM Conference on Computer and Communications Security.* (pp. 6, 8–17). Zurich, Switzerland: ACM Press.

Aspan, M. (2008, February 11). *How Sticky Is Membership on Facebook? Just Try Breaking Free.* New York: The New York Times.

Atallah, M. J., Elmagarmid, A. K., Ibrahim, M., & Verykios, V. S. (1999). Disclosure Limitation of Sesitive Rules. In *Proceedings of the IEEE Knowledge and Data Engineering Workshop* (pp. 45-52).

Ateniese, G., & Nita-Rotaru, C. (2002). Stateless-recipient certified e-mail system based on verifiable encryption. *Topics in Cryptology-CT-RSA, 2002,* 182–199.

Ateniese, G. (1999). Efficient verifiable encryption (and fair exchange) of digital signatures. *Proceedings of the 6th ACM conference on Computer and communications security* (pp. 138-146). ACM.

Athanassios, N. S., & Spyridon, K. K. (2008). Real-time data hiding by exploiting the IPCM macroblocks in H.264/AVC streams. *Journal of Real-Time Image Processing, 4,* 33–41.

Attorney-General's Department. (1988). *Privacy Act 1988, Act 119.* Canberra, Australia: Office of Legislative Drafting and Publishing.

Attrition.org (2007, March 3). *Attrition.org, data loss archive and database (DLDOS).*

Australian federal privacy law.(n.d.). Retrieved December 28, 2005, from http://www.privacy. gov.au/act/

Australian Government Office of the Privacy Commisioner. (2006). *Office of the Privacy Commissioner.* Retrieved from http://www.privacy.gov.au/

Aytes, K., & Connolly, T. (2004). Computer security and risky computing practices: A rational choice perspective. *Journal of Organizational and End User Computing, 16*(3), 22–40.

Baeza-Yates, R., Castillo, C., Marin, M., & Rodriguez, A. (2005). Crawling a Country: Better Strategies than Breadth-First for Web Page Ordering. In *Proceedings of the Industrial and Practical Experience Track of the 14th Conference on the World Wide Web,* Chiba, Japan (pp. 864-872). New York: ACM Publishing.

Bagchi, K., Kirs, P., & Cerveny, R. (2006). Global software piracy: can economic factors alone explain the trend? *Communications of the ACM, 49*(6), 70–75. doi:10.1145/1132469.1132470

Balazinska, M., Balakrishnan, H., & Karger, D. D. (2002). INS/Twine: A scalable peer-to-peer architecture for intentional resource discovery. In *Proceedings of Pervasive 2002 - International Conference on Pervasive Computing,* Zurich, Switzerland (pp. 195-210). Springer-Verlag.

Bandura, A. (1986). *Social foundations of thought and action: A social cognitive theory.* Englewood Cliffs, NJ: Prentice-Hall.

Banisar, D. (2000). *Privacy & Human Rights: An International Survey of Privacy Laws and Developments.* EPIC and Privacy International, http://www.privacyinternational.org/survey/index2000.html

Bank of Japan. (2007). *The importance of information security for financial institutions and proposed countermeasures.* Retrieved Jan 6, 2008, from: http://www.boj.or.jp/en/type/release/zuiji/kako02/data/fsk0004b.pdf. 2007.

Bao, F., Wang, G., Zhou, J., & Zhu, H. (2004). Analysis and Improvement of Micali's Fair Contract Signing Protocol. *Information Security and Privacy, 3108,* 176–187. doi:10.1007/978-3-540-27800-9_16

Bao, F., Deng, R. H., & Mao, W. (1998). Efficient and Practical Fair Exchange Protocols with Off-line TTP. *Proceedings of IEEE Symposium on Security and Privacy,* (pp. 77-85).

Bas, P., Chassery, J., & Davoine, F. (1998). Self-similarity based image watermarking. *Proceedings of the 9ᵗʰ European Signal Processing Conference (EUSIPCO)*, 2277-2280.

Batina, L., Mentens, N., Sakiyama, K., Preneel, B., & Verbauwhede, I. (2006). *Low-cost elliptic curve cryptography for wireless sensor networks. Security and Privacy in Ad-Hoc and Sensor Networks* (*Vol. 4357*, pp. 6–17). Berlin, Germany: Springer-Verlag.

Baum-Waidner, B. (2001). *Optimistic asynchronous multi-party contract signing with reduced number of rounds. ICALP'01, LNCS 2076* (pp. 898–911). Berlin: Springer.

Bayardo, R. J., & Agrawal, R. (2005). Data Privacy through Optimal k-Anonymization. In *Proceedings of the ICDE* (pp. 217-228).

BBBOnLine, Inc. & the Council of Better Business Bureaus, Inc. (2007, March). A review of federal and state privacy laws.

Bedi, H., & Yang, L. (2009). Fair Electronic Exchange Based on Fingerprint Biometrics. [IJISP]. *International Journal of Information Security and Privacy, III*(3), 76–106.

Bedi, H., Yang, L., & Kizza, J. (2009). Extended Abstract: Fair Electronic Exchange using Biometrics. *Proceedings of the 5th Annual Workshop on Cyber Security and Information Intelligence Research: Cyber Security and Information Intelligence Challenges and Strategies* (pp. 1-4). Oak Ridge: ACM.

Beeferman, D., Berger, A., & Lafferty, J. (1999). Statistical models for text segmentation. *Machine Learning, 34*, 1–34. doi:10.1023/A:1007506220214

Belanger, F., Hiller, J. S., & Smith, W. J. (2002). Trustworthiness in electronic commerce: the role of privacy, security, and site attributes. *The Journal of Strategic Information Systems, 11*(3/4), 245–270. doi:10.1016/S0963-8687(02)00018-5

Bell, D. E., & LaPadula, L. J. (1973). *Secure Computer Systems: Mathematical Foundations*. Bedford, Massachusetts: MITRE Corporation.

Bellare, M., Canettiy, R., & Krawczykz, H. (1996). Keying hash functions for message authentication. In *Advances in Cryptology–CRYPTO '96* (LNCS 1109, pp. 1-15).

Bender, W., Gruhl, D., Morimoto, N., & Lu, A. (1996). Techniques for data hiding. *IBM Systems Journal, 35*(3&4), 313–336. doi:10.1147/sj.353.0313

Bennett, C. J. (2005). What happens when you book an airline ticket? The collection and processing of passenger data post-9/11. In Zureik, E., & Salter, M. B. (Eds.), *Global Surveillance and Policing* (pp. 113–138). Portland: Wilan.

Ben-Or, M., Goldreich, O., Micali, S., & Rivest, R. (1990). A fair protocol for signing contracts. *IEEE Transactions on Information Theory, 36*(1), 40–46. doi:10.1109/18.50372

Berghel, H. (2005). The two sides of ROI: Return on investment vs. risk of incarceration. *Communications of the ACM, 49*(4), 15–20. doi:10.1145/1053291.1053305

Besnard, D., & Arief, B. (2004). Computer security impaired by legitimate users. *Computers & Security, 23*(3), 253–264. doi:10.1016/j.cose.2003.09.002

Bessen, J. (1993). Riding the Marketing Information Wave. *Harvard Business Review, 71*(5), 150–160.

Best, J., & Luckenbill, D. F. (1980). The Social Organization of Deviants. *Social Problems, 28*(1), 14–31. doi:10.1525/sp.1980.28.1.03a00020

Best, J., & Luckenbill, D. F. (1994). *Oragnizing Deviance* (2nd ed.). Upper Saddle River, NJ: Prentice Hall.

Better Business Bureau. (2006). *BBBOnLine, Inc. - Promoting Trust and Confidence on the Internet*. Retrieved from http://www.bbbonline.org/

Bia, M., & Kalika, M. (2007). Adopting an ICT code of conduct: an empirical study of organizational factors. *Journal of Enterprise Information Management, 20*(4), 432–446. doi:10.1108/17410390710772704

Bilton, N. (2010, May 12). *Price of Facebook privacy? Start clicking*. New York: The New York Times.

Bjontegaard, G., Luthra, A., Wiegand, T., & Sullivan, G. J. (2003). Overview of the H.264/AVC video coding standard. *IEEE Transactions on Circuits and Systems for Video Technology, 13*(7), 560–576. doi:10.1109/TCSVT.2003.815165

Björck, J., & Jiang, K. W. B. (2006). *Information Security and National Culture: Comparison between ERP System Security Implementations in Singapore and Sweden.* Master Degree thesis submitted at the Royal Institute of Technology, Sweden.

Bloom, P. N., Milne, G. R., & Alder, R. (1994). Avoiding Misuses of Information Technologies: Legal and Societal Considerations. *Journal of Marketing, 58*(1), 98–110. doi:10.2307/1252254

Bloom, B. (1970). Space/time trade-offs in hash coding with allowable errors. *Communications of the ACM, 13*(7), 422–426. doi:10.1145/362686.362692

Bloom, H. S. (1995). Minimum Detectable Effects. *Evaluation Review, 19*(5), 547–556. doi:10.1177/0193841X9501900504

Bluetooth, S. I. G. (2004). Specification of the bluetooth system. Retrieved from http://www.bluetooth.org/

Bodley, J. H. (1994). *Cultural Anthropology: Tribes, States, and the Global System.* Mountain View, CA: Mayfield Publishing.

Boneh, D., & Franklin, M. (2003). Identity-based encryption from the Weil pairing. *SIAM Journal on Computing, 32*(3), 586–615. doi:10.1137/S0097539701398521

Boneh, D., Lynn, B., & Shacham, H. (2001). *Short signatures from the Weil pairing. Advances in Cryptology – ASIACRYPT 2001* (Vol. 2248, pp. 514–532). Berlin, Germany: Springer-Verlag.

Bonett, D. G. (2002). Sample Size Requirements for Estimating Intraclass Correlations with Desired Precision. *Statistics in Medicine, 21*(9), 1331–1335. doi:10.1002/sim.1108

Bonneau, J., Anderson, J., & Danezis, G. (2009). Prying data out of a social network. *Conference: Advances in Social Network Analysis and Mining.*

Booch, G., Rambaugh, J., & Jacobson, I. (2005). *The Unified Modeling Language User Guide* (2nd ed.). Reading, MA: Addison Wesley Professional.

Bouncy Castle www.bouncycastle.org. Last Accessed Dec. 2008

Bourbakis N. & Dollas, A. (2003). SCAN based multimedia-on-demand. *IEEE multimedia magazine,* 79-87.

Bourbakis, N., Rwabutaza, A., Yang, M., & Skondras, T. (2009). A synthetic stegano-crypto scheme for securing multimedia medical records", *2009 IEEE Digital signal processing and signal processing education workshop.*

Bowie, N. E., & Jamal, K. (2006). Privacy Rights on the Internet: Self-Regulation or Government Regulation. *Business Ethics Quarterly, 16*(3).

Boyd, C., & Foo, E. (1998). *Off-line fair payment protocols using convertible signatures. Advances in Cryptology—ASIACRYPT'98* (pp. 271–285). New York: Springer.

Bracey, D. H. (2006). *Exploring Law and Culture.* Long Grove, IL: Waveland Press

Braz, C., & Robert, J. (2006). Security and usability: The case of the user authentication methods. In *Proceedings of the 18th International Conference of the Association Francophone d'Interaction Homme-Machine* (pp. 199-203). New York, USA: ACM Press.

Briffa, J. A., & Das, M. (2002). Channel models for high-capacity information hiding in images. *Proceedings of the SPIE, 4793.*

Brostoff, S., & Sasse, M. A. (2000). Are passfaces more usable than passwords? A field trial investigation. In *Proceedings of HCI 2000* (pp. 405-424). Sunderland, UK.

Brown, S. A., Massey, A. P., Montoya-Weiss, M. M., & Burkman, J. R. (2002). Do I really have to? User acceptance of mandated technology. *European Journal of Information Systems, 11*(4), 283–295. doi:10.1057/palgrave.ejis.3000438

Bruckner, L., & Voss, M. (2005, October 2005). *MozPETs - A Privacy Enhanced Web Browser.* Paper presented at the Third Annual Conference on Privacy, Security and Trust, St. Andrews, New Brunswick, Canada.

Burkert, H. (1997). Privacy –enhancing technologies: Typology, critique, vision . In Agre, P., & Rotenberg, M. (Eds.), *Technology and Privacy: The New Landscape* (pp. 125–142). Cambridge, MA: MIT Press.

Byers, S., Cranor, L., & Kormann, D. (2003). *Automated Analysis of P3P-Enabled Web Sites.* Paper presented at the 5th International Conference on Electronic Commerce, Pittsburgh, PA.

California Department of Consumer Affairs (2006, February 14). Privacy laws.

Callas, J., Donnerhacke, L., Finney, H., & Thayer, R. (1998). *OpenPGP message format* (RFC 2440). Retrieved from http://www.ietf.org/rfc/rfc2440.txt

Canadian Standards Association. (1996). *Model Code for the Protection of Personal Information.* Retrieved May 13, 2006, from http://www.csa.ca/standards/privacy/default.asp?load=code&language=English

Cao, Y., Han, W., & Le, Y. (2008). Anti-phishing based on automated individual white-list. In *Proceedings of the 4th ACM Workshop on Digital Identity Management (DIM'08),* Alexandria, VA (pp. 51-60).

Capurro, R. (2005). Privacy. An Intercultural Perspective. *Ethics and Information Technology, 7,* 37–47. doi:10.1007/s10676-005-4407-4

Carley, K. M., Diesner, J., Reminga, J., & Tsvetovat, M. (2007). Toward an interoperable dynamic network analysis toolkit. *Decision Support Systems, 43*(4), 1324–1347. doi:10.1016/j.dss.2006.04.003

Carley, K. (2002). Smart Agents and Organizations of the Future . In Livingstone, L. L. S. (Ed.), *The Handbook of New Media.* Thousand Oaks, CA: Sage.

Carley, K., Dombrowski, M., & Tsvetovat, M. reminga, J., & Kamneva, N. (2003). *Destabilizing Dynamic Covert Networks.* Paper presented at the the 8th International Command and Control Research and Technology Symposium.

Carlson, C. (2006, February 1). Unauthorized sale of phone records on the rise. *eWeek.*

Carr, J. (2008, May 1st). *Small Merchants Biggest Threat to Credit Card Fraud. S C Magazine.*

Cases, A.-S., Fournier, C., Dubois, P.-L., & Tanner, J. F. Jr. (in press). Web Site spill over to email campaigns: The role of privacy, trust and shoppers' attitudes. *Journal of Business Research.*

Castillo, C. (2004). *Effective Web Crawling.* Unpublished PhD thesis, University of Chile.

Cate, F. H. (2006). The failure of fair information practice principles . In Winn, J. K. (Ed.), *Consumer Protection in the Age of the 'Information Economy.* Ashgate.

Cauley, L. (2006, May 11). *NSA has massive database of Americans' phone calls.* Washington, DC: USA Today.

Cazier, J. A., Wilson, E. V., & Medlin, B. D. (2007). The role of privacy risk in IT acceptance: An empirical study. *International Journal of Information Security and Privacy, 1*(2), 61–73.

Celik, M. U., Sharma, G., Tekalp, A. M., & Saber, E. (2005). Lossless generalized-LSB data embedding . *IEEE Transactions on Image Processing, 14*(2), 253–266. doi:10.1109/TIP.2004.840686

Ceraolo, J., P. (1996). Penetration testing through social engineering. *Information Systems Security, 4*(4), 37–49. doi:10.1080/10658989609342519

Chae, J. J., & Manjunath, B. S. (1999). Data hiding in video. *Proceedings of the 6th IEEE international conference on image processing (ICIP '99), 1,* 311-315.

Chae, J. J., Mukherjee, D., & Manjunath, B. S. (1998) Color image embedding using multidimensional lattice structures, *Proceedings of IEEE International Conference on Image Processing,* Chicago, Illinois, USA, October 1998, 460–464.

Chan, H., & Perrig, A. (2003). Security and privacy in sensor networks. *Computer*, *36*(10), 103–105. doi:10.1109/MC.2003.1236475

Chan, C. K., & Cheng, L. M. (2004). Hiding data in images by simple LSB substitution. *Pattern Recognition*, *37*(3), 469–474. doi:10.1016/j.patcog.2003.08.007

Chan, H., Perrig, A., & Song, D. (2003). Random key predistribution schemes for sensor networks. In *Proceedings of the 2003 IEEE Symposium on Security and Privacy* (pp. 197-213).

Chang, A., J-T & Yeh, Q-J. (2006). On security preparations against possible IS threats across industries. *Information Management & Computer Security*, *14*(4), 343–360. doi:10.1108/09685220610690817

Chang, C., Chen, G., & Lin, M. (2004). Information hiding based on search-order coding for VQ indices. *Pattern Recognition Letters*, *25*, 1253–1261. doi:10.1016/j.patrec.2004.04.003

Chang, C. C., Chen, T. S., & Chung, L. Z. (2002). A steganographic method based upon JPEG and quantization table modification. *Information Sciences*, *141*, 123–138. doi:10.1016/S0020-0255(01)00194-3

Chang, C. C., Lin, C. C., Tseng, C. S., & Tai, W. L. (2007). Reversible hiding in DCT-based compressed images . *Information Sciences*, *177*, 2768–2786. doi:10.1016/j.ins.2007.02.019

Chang, C. C., Tai, W. L., & Lin, C. C. (2006). A reversible data hiding scheme based on side match vector quantization. *IEEE Transactions on Circuits and Systems for Video Technology*, *16*(10), 1301–1308. doi:10.1109/TCSVT.2006.882380

Chang, C. C., & Wu, W. C. (2006). Hiding secret data adaptively in vector quantisation index tables . *IEEE Proceedings on Vision Image and Signal Processing*, *153*(5), 589–597. doi:10.1049/ip-vis:20050153

Chang, C. C., Wu, W. C., & Chen, Y. H. (2008). Joint coding and embedding techniques for multimedia images. *Information Sciences*, *178*(18), 3543–3556. doi:10.1016/j.ins.2008.05.003

Chang, C.C., & Lin, C.Y. (2006). Reversible steganographic method using SMVQ approach based on declustering, *Information Sciences*.

Chao, S.-C., Chen, K., & Lin, C.-H. (2006). Capturing industry experience for an effective information security assessment. *International Journal of Information Systems and Change Management*, *1*(4), 421–438. doi:10.1504/IJISCM.2006.012048

Chaturvedi, M., & Gupta, M. Mehta, S., & Valeri, L. (2000). *Fighting the wily hacker: modeling information security issues for online financial institutions using the SEAS environment, Proceedings of Inet 2000*. Retrieved Jan. 14, 2008 from: http://www.isoc.org/inet2000/cdproceedings/7a/7a_4.htm.

Chau, P. Y. K., Hu, P. J.-H., Lee, B. L. P., & Au, A. K. K. (2007). Examining customers' trust in online vendors and their dropout decisions: An empirical study. *Electronic Commerce Research and Applications*, *6*, 171–182. doi:10.1016/j.elerap.2006.11.008

Che, S., & Wang, H. (2010). A Fragile Information Hiding Technique Based on Human Visual Gray Sensitivity. *Journal of Advanced Materials Research*, *121-122*, 1048–1051. doi:10.4028/www.scientific.net/AMR.121-122.1048

Chen, C. C., Medlin, B. D., & Shaw, R. S. (2008). A cross-cultural investigation of situational information security awareness programs. *Information Management & Computer Security*, *16*(4), 360–376. doi:10.1108/09685220810908787

Chen, T. S., Chang, C. C., & Hwang, M. S. (1998). A virtual image cryptosystem based upon vector quantization. *IEEE Transactions on Image Processing*, *7*(10), 1485–1488. doi:10.1109/83.718488

Chen, O., & Liu, C. H. (2008). Data hiding in inter- and intra-prediction modes of H.264/AVC, *Proceeding of IEEE International Symposium on Circuits and Systems*, 3205-3208.

Chen, Z.-Y., & Liu, G.-H. (2005). *Quantitative Association Rules Mining Methods with Privacy-preserving.* Paper presented at the Sixth International Conference on. Parallel and Distributed Computing, Applications and Technologies, PDCAT. Corney, D. (n.d.). *Clustering with Matlab.* Retrieved from http://www.cs.ucl.ac.uk/staff/D. Corney/ClusteringMatlab.htm

Cheng, Q., & Huang, T. S. (2001). An additive approach to transform-domain information hiding and optimum detection structure. *IEEE Transactions on Multimedia, 3*(3), 273–284. doi:10.1109/6046.944472

Cheshire, S. (2002). *Discovering named instances of abstract services using DNS, Apple Computer.* Retrieved from http://files.dns-sd.org/draft-cheshire-dnsext-dns-sd.txt

Cheung, C. M. K., Chan, G. W. W., & Moez, L. (2005). A critical review of online consumer behavior: empirical research. *Journal of Electronic Commerce in Organizations, 3*(4), 1–19.

Chong, S. K. (2002). *SQL Injection Walkthrough.* Retrieved September 4, 2010, from http://www.scan-associates.net/papers/sql_injection_walkthrough.txt

Chong, S., Skalka, C., & Vaughan, J. A. 2010. Self-identifying sensor data. In *Proceedings of the 9th ACM/IEEE international Conference on information Processing in Sensor Networks* (Stockholm, Sweden, April 12 - 16, 2010). IPSN '10. ACM, New York, NY, 82-93.

Chou, N., Ledesma, R., Teraguchi, Y., Boneh, D., & Mitchell, J. C. (2004). *Client-side defense against web-based identity theft.* Paper presented at the 11th Annual Network and Distributed System Security Symposium (NDSS '04).

Chow, S., & Holden, R. (1997). Toward and understanding of loyalty: The moderating role of trust. *Journal of Managerial Issues, 9*(3), 275–298.

Chuang, T. J., & Lin, J.C. (1999). A new multi-resolution approach to still image encryption. *Pattern recognition and image analysis, 9* (3), 431-436.

Chung, K. L., Shen, C. H., & Chang, L. C. (2001). A novel SVD- and VQ-based image hiding scheme. *Pattern Recognition Letters, 22*(9), 1051–1058. doi:10.1016/S0167-8655(01)00044-7

Ciet, M., Joye, M., Lauter, K., & Montgomery, P. L. (2006). Trading inversions for multiplications in elliptic curve cryptography. *Journal of Designs, Codes, and Cryptography, 39,* 189–206. doi:10.1007/s10623-005-3299-y

Cilardo, A., Coppolino, L., Mazzocca, N., & Romano, L. (2006). Elliptic curve engineering. *Proceedings of the IEEE, 94*(2), 395–406. doi:10.1109/JPROC.2005.862438

Citywatcher.com (2007, July 22). The Answer to Immigration – "Chip them?"

Clark, H. H. (1996). *Using Language.* New York: Cambridge University Press.

Clarke, R. (1999). Internet privacy concerns confirm the case for intervention. *Communications of the ACM, 42,* 60–67. doi:10.1145/293411.293475

Coffey, T., & Saidha, P. (1996, Jan.). Non-repudiation with mandatory proof of receipt. ACM SIGCOMM *. Computer Communication Review, 26*(1), 6–17. doi:10.1145/232335.232338

Collins, H. (2008). *Cyber-Attackers Target Web Applications, Study Says.* Retrieved September 4, 2010, from http://www.govtech.com/gt/403627?topic=117671

Commission for the Protection of Privacy. (2006). *Commission for the Protection of Privacy-Home.* Retrieved from http://www.privacycommission.be/

Commondreams.org (2007). *ACLU condemns phone companies' role in FBI datamining, reaffirms no amnesty for telecoms.*

Conger, S., Mason, R. O., Mason, F., & Pratt, J. H. (2005 August). The connected home: poison or paradise. *Proceedings of Academy of Management Meeting.* Honolulu, HI.

Consumer Reports Web Watch. (2002). *A Matter of Trust: What Users Want From Web Sites.* Yonkers, NY: Author.

Copacobana (2008). http://www.copacobana.org/. Last Accessed Dec. 2008

Corker, J., & Utz, C. (2002). SCAMS and Legal Approaches to SPAM," The Cyberspace Law and Policy Series. *Continuing Legal Education Conference on International Dimensions of Internet and e-Commerce Regulation* (pp 1-14).

Council, P. C. I. (2008). *PCI Security Council to Release Version 1.2 of the PCI Security Standard in October 2008.* MA: Wakefield.

Cox, I., Miller, M., & Bloom, J. (2002). *Digital watermarking*. Morgan Kaufmann Publishers.

Cox, B., Tygar, J. D., & Sirbu, M. (1995). NetBill security and transaction protocol. In *Proc. 1st USENIX Workshop on Electronic Commerce*, 77–88.

Cox, I. J., Kilian, J., Leighton, T., & Shamoon, T. (1996). A secure, robust watermark for multimedia. *Proceedings of the first international workshop on information hiding*, 185 – 206.

Cranor, L. F., & Garfinkel, S. (2005). *Security and usability: Designing secure systems that people can use.* Sebastopol: O'Reilly.

Cranor, L. F., Byers, S., & Kormann, D. (2003). *An Analysis of P3P Deployment on Commercial, Government and Children's Web Sites as of May 2003.* Washington, DC: Federal Trade Commission.

Cranor, L., Dobbs, B., Egelman, S., Hogben, G., Humphrey, J., Langheinrich, M., et al. (2006). *The Platform for Privacy Preferences 1.1 (P3P1.1) Specification.* Retrieved January 25, 2008, from http://www.w3.org/TR/P3P11/

Cranor, L., Egelman, S., Sheng, S., McDonald, A., & Chowdhury, A. (2008). P3P Deployment on Websites. *Electronic Commerce Research and Applications*

Cranor, L., Langheinrich, M., Marchiori, M., Presler-Marshall, M., & Reagle, J. (2002). *The Platform for Privacy Preferences 1.0 Specification.* Retrieved from http://www.w3.org/TR/P3P/

Cronbach, L. J. (1951). Coefficient Alpha and the Internal Structure of Tests. *Psychometrika, 16*(3), 297–334. doi:10.1007/BF02310555

Crossbow Technology, Inc. (n.d.) *Crossbow product information*. Retrieved from http://www.xbow.com/Products/products.htm

Culnan, M. J. (1993). How did they get my name? An exploratory investigation of consumer attitudes toward secondary information use. *Management Information Systems Quarterly, 17*(3), 341–363. doi:10.2307/249775

Culnan, M. J. (2000). Protecting privacy online: Is self-regulation working? *Journal of Public Policy & Marketing, 19*(1), 20–26. doi:10.1509/jppm.19.1.20.16944

Culnan, M. J., & Armstrong, P. K. (1999). Information privacy concerns, procedural fairness, and impersonal trust: An empirical investigation. *Organization Science, 10*(1), 104–115. doi:10.1287/orsc.10.1.104

Culnan, M. J., & Bies, R. J. (2003). Consumer privacy: balancing economic and justice considerations. *The Journal of Social Issues, 59*(2), 323–342. doi:10.1111/1540-4560.00067

Culnan, M. J., & Armstrong, P. K. (1999). Information privacy concerns, procedural fairness, and impersonal trust: An empirical investigation. *Organization Science, 10*(1), 104–115. doi:10.1287/orsc.10.1.104

Culnan, M. J., & Milne, G. R. (2001). The Culnan-Milne Survey of Consumers and Online Privacy Notices. http://intra.som.umass.edu/georgemilne/PDF_Files/culnan-milne.pdf

Cvejic, N., & Seppanen, T. (2004). Channel capacity of high bit rate audio data hiding algorithms in diverse transform domains. *Proceedings of the international symposium on communications and information technologies (ISCIT 2004).*

Czerwinski, S., Zhao, B. Y., Hodes, T., Joseph, A., & Katz, R. (1999). *An architecture for a secure service discovery service*. Paper presented at the Fifth Annual International Conference on Mobile Computing and Networks (Mobi-Com '99), Seattle, WA.

Dai, Y., W., Wang Z.Q., Ye D.P., & Zou C.F. (2007). A new adaptive watermarking for real-time MPEG videos . *Applied Mathematics and Computation, 185*(2), 907–918. doi:10.1016/j.amc.2006.07.021

Dallas News.com (2008, November 21). *Arkansas hospital staffers fired for improperly accessing slain TV anchor's records.*

Damgard, I. B. (1995). Practical and provably secure release of a secret and exchange of signatures. *Journal of Cryptology, 8,* 201–222. doi:10.1007/BF00191356

Daneshpajouh, S., Nasiri, M. M., & Ghodsi, M. (2008). *A Fast Community Based Algorithm for Generating Crawler Seeds Set.* Paper presented at the 4th International Conference on Web Information Systems and Technologies (WEBIST).

Danish Data Protection Agency. (2006). *DATATILSYNET: Introduction to the Danish Data Protection Agency.* Retrieved from http://www.datatilsynet.dk/eng/index.html

Davis, F. D. (1989). Perceived usefulness, perceived ease of use, and user acceptance of information technology. *Management Information Systems Quarterly, 13*(3), 319–340. doi:10.2307/249008

Debatin, B., Lovejoy, J., Horn, A., & Hughes, B. (2009). Facebook and online privacy: Attitudes, behaviors, and unintended consequences. *Journal of Computer-Mediated Communication, 15,* 83–108. doi:10.1111/j.1083-6101.2009.01494.x

Demirkol, I., Ersoy, C., & Alagoz, F. (2006). Mac protocols for wireless sensor networks: a survey. *Communications Magazine, IEEE, 44*(4), 115–121. doi:10.1109/MCOM.2006.1632658

Deng, R., Gong, L., Lazar, A., & Wang, W. (1996). Practical protocol for certified electronic mail. *Journal of Network and Systems Management, 4*(3), 279–297. doi:10.1007/BF02139147

Denning, D. (2001, Summer). Cyberwarriors: activists and terrorists turn to cyberspace. *Harvard International Review, 23*(2), 70–75.

Dhamija, R., Tygar, J. D., & Hearst, M. (2006). *Why phishing works.* Paper presented at the Conference on Human Factors in Computing Systems (CHI2006).

Diesner, J., & Carley, K. M. (2004). *AutoMap 1.2- Extract, Analyze, Represent, and Compare Mental Models from Texts (No. CMU-ISRI-04-100).* Carnegie Mellon University, School of Computer Science, Institute for Software Research International, Technical Reporto. Document Number.

Diesner, J., & Carley, K. M. (2005). Revealing Social structure from Texts: Metamatrix Text Analysis as a Novel Method for Network Text Analysis . In Narayanan, V. K., & Armstrong, D. J. (Eds.), *Causal Mapping for Information Systems and Technology Research: Approaches, Advances, and Illustrations* (pp. 81–108). Hershey, PA: Idea Group Publishing.

Diffie, W., & Hellman, M. E. (1976). New directions in cryptography. *IEEE Transactions on Information Theory, 22*(6), 644–654. doi:10.1109/TIT.1976.1055638

Dinev, T., Goo, J., Hu, Q., & Nam, K. (2009). User behaviour towards protective information technologies: the role of national cultural differences. *Information Systems Journal, 19*(4), 391–412. doi:10.1111/j.1365-2575.2007.00289.x

Dingledine, R., Mathewson, N., & Syverson, P. (2007). Deploying Low-Latency Anonymity: Design Challenges and Social Factors. *IEEE Security and Privacy, 5*(5), 83–87. doi:10.1109/MSP.2007.108

DocuSearch.com (2007). *Privacy Statements: Opting Out.*

Douceur, J. R. (2002). The Sybil attack, In *Proceedings of the First. International Workshop on Peer-to-Peer Systems.*

DTT-Global Security Survey. (2005). *The Global Security Survey, 2006, Deloitte Touche Tohmatsu (DTT).* Retrieved Jan 14, 2009 from: http://www.deloitte.com/dtt/cda/doc/content/CA_FSI_2006%20Global%20Security%20Survey_2006-06-13.pdf.

DTT-Global Security Survey. (2008). *The Global Security Survey, 2007, Deloitte Touche Tohmatsu (DTT)*. Retrieved January 14, 2009 from: http://www.deloitte.com/dtt/cda/doc/content/ca_en_Global_Security_Survey.final.en.pdf.

DTT-Global Security Survey. (2009). *The Global Security Survey, 2008, Deloitte Touche Tohmatsu (DTT)*. Retrieved June 20 from: http://www.deloitte.com/dtt/cda/doc/content/dtt_en_fsi_GlobalSecuritySurvey_0901.pdf.

Du, W., Deng, J., Han, Y. S., Varshney, P. K., Katz, J., & Khalili, A. (2005). A pairwise key pre-distribution scheme for wireless sensor networks. [TISSEC]. *ACM Transactions on Information and System Security, 8*(2), 228–258. doi:10.1145/1065545.1065548

Du, W. C., & Hsu, W. J. (2003). Adaptive data hiding based on VQ compressed images. *IEEE Proceedings on Vision . Image and Signal Processing, 150*(4), 233–238. doi:10.1049/ip-vis:20030525

Ducheneaut, N., & Bellotti, V. (2001). E-mail as habitat: An exploration of embedded personal information management. *Interaction, 8*(5), 30–38. doi:10.1145/382899.383305

Dugelay, J. L., & Doerr, G. (2003). A guide tour of video watermarking. *Signal Processing Image Communication, 18*(4), 263–282. doi:10.1016/S0923-5965(02)00144-3

Dunn, J. E. (2005, December 30). Phishers now targeting SSL. *TechWorld*. Retrieved from http://www.techworld.com/news/index.cfm?RSS&NewsID=5069

Dusse, S., Hoffman, P., Ramsdell, B., Lundblade, L., & Repka, L. (1998). *S/MIME version 2 message specification* (RFC 2311). Retrieved from https://www3.ietf.org/rfc/rfc2311.txt

Dutch Data Protection Authority. (2006). *Dutch DPA*. Retrieved from http://www.dutchdpa.nl/

Dwyer, C., Hiltz, R., & Passerini, K. (2007, August 09-12). Trust and privacy concern within social networking sites: A comparison of Facebook and MySpace. *Proceedings of the Thirteenth Americas Conference on Information Systems,* Keystone, Colorado.

Earp, J. B., Anton, A. I., Aiman-Smith, L., & Stufflebeam, W. H. (2005). Examining Internet Privacy Policies Within the Context of User Privacy Values. *IEEE Transactions on Engineering Management, 52*(2), 227–237. doi:10.1109/TEM.2005.844927

Edmunds, A., & Morris, A. (2000). The problem of information overload in business organizations: A review of the literature. *International Journal of Information Management, 20*(1), 17. doi:10.1016/S0268-4012(99)00051-1

EDS. (2007). *Eight Financial Services Security Concerns*. Retrieved May 10, 2008 from: Http://www.eds.com/news/features/3620/. 2007.

Edwards, J., McCurley, K. S., & Tomlin, J. A. (2001). An adaptive model for optimizing performance of an incremental web crawler. In *Proceedings of the Tenth Conference on the World Wide Web* (pp. 106-113). Elsevier Science.

Efrontier.com. *Efficient Frontier at Work. CrystalWare.* Retrieved on September 21, 2008 from: http://www.efrontier.com/efficient_frontier/

Egelman, S., & Cranor, L. F. (2006, August, 2006). *An Analysis of P3P-Enabled Web Sites among Top-20 Search Results.* Paper presented at the Eighth International Conference on Electronic Commerce, Fredericton, New Brunswick, Canada.

Eldon, E. (2010, May 11). Analysis: Some Facebook privacy issues are real, some are not. *Inside Facebook.* eMarketer.com (2010, June 29). *Privacy Concerns Fail to Slow Social Activity.* eMarketer.com (2010, July 6). *Online merchants love Facebook's 'Like.'*

Ellickson, R. C. (2001). The Evolution of Social Norms: A Perspective from the Legal Academy. In M. Hechter & K.-D. Opp (Eds.), *Social Norms* (pp. 35-75). New York: Russell Sage Foundation.

Ellison, C., & Schneier, B. (2000). Ten risks of PKI: What you're not being yold about public key infrastructure. *Computer Security Journal, Volume XVI.*

Emailprivacy.info. *Email Privacy.* Retrieved on September 30, 2008 from: http://www.emailprivacy.info/email_privacy

Ernst and Young. (2003). *P3P Dashboard Report.* Retrieved from http://www.ey.com/global/download.nsf/US/P3P_Dashboard_January_2003/$file/E&YP3PDashboardJan2003.pdf

Erunbam, A. A., & de Jong, S. B. (2006). Cross-country differences in ICT adoption: a consequence of culture? *Journal of World Business, 41*(4), 302–314. doi:10.1016/j.jwb.2006.08.005

Eschenauer, L., & Gligor, V. D. (2002, November). *A key-management scheme for distributed sensor networks.* Paper presented at the 9th ACM Conference on Computer and Communications, Washington DC, USA.

Etzioni, A. (1999). *The limits of Privacy.* New York: Basic Books.

European Commission. (1995). *Directive 95/46/EC of the European Parliament and of the Council of 24 October 1995 on the protection of individuals with regard to the processing of personal data and on the free movement of such data* (Official Journal L 281). Brussels, Belgium: Author.

European Commission. (2003). *First Report on the Implementation of the Data Protection Directive (95/24/EC).* Brussels, Belgium: Author.

European Parliament and Council of the European Union. (1995). European Union Data Protection Directive 95/45 EC. *Official Journal of the European Communities No., L*(281), 31–50.

Evers, J. *Sender ID's fading message.* August 9, 2005 Retrieved on October 1, 2008 from: http://www.news.com/Sender-IDs-fading-message/2100-7355_3-5824234.html

Evfimevski, A., Gehrke, J., & Srikant, R. (2003). *Limiting privacy breaches in privacy preserving data mining.* Paper presented at the 22nd ACM SIGMOD-SIGACT-SIGART Symposium on Principles of Database Systems, San Diego, CA.

Evfimevski, A., Srikant, R., Agrawal, R., & Gehrke, J. (2002). Privacy preserving mining of association rules. In *Proceedings of the 8th ACM SIGKDD International Conference on Knowledge Discovery and Data Mining (KDD'02)* (pp. 217-228).

Export.gov. (2007). *Safe Harbor Program.* Retrieved February 20, 2007, from http://www.export.gov/safeharbor/doc_safeharbor_index.asp

Extreme-messaging.com. *Response Master Returned Message Categories.* Retrieved on October 7, 2008 from: http://www.extreme-messaging.com/extreme/docs/rmcategories.html

FacebookInside.com (2010).

Facebook.com (2010, April 22a). *Privacy Policy.*

Facebook.com (2010, April 22b). *Statement of Rights and Responsibilities.*

Facebook.com (2010a). *Controlling How You Share.*

Facebook.com. (2010b). *Statistics.* Press Room.

Fallows, D. (2003). *Spam: How It is hurting email and degrading life on the Internet* (pp. 1–43). Pew Internet and American Life Project.

Fallows, D. (2004). *The Internet and Daily Life.* Washington, DC: Pew Internet & American Life Project.

Federal Commissioner for Data Protection and Freedom of Information. (2006). *Welcome to the Website of the Federal Commissioner for Data Protection and Freedom of Information.* Retrieved from http://www.bfdi.bund.de/cln_029/nn_533554/EN/Home/homepage__node.html__nnn=true

Federal Trade Commission. (2000). Privacy Online: Fair Information Practices in the Electronic Marketplace. A Report to Congress 2, Washington D.C. http://www.ftc.gov/reports/privacy2000/privacy2000.pdf

Federal Trade Commission. National and State Trends in Fraud and Identity Theft, (2004) http://www.consumer.gov/sentinel/pubs/Top10Fraud2003.pdf

Federal Trade Commission. (2002). *E-Government Act of 2002*. Washington, DC: Author.

Federal Trade Commission. (2006). *Privacy Initiatives*. Retrieved from http://www.ftc.gov/privacy/index.html

Fei, C., Kundur, D., & Kwong, R. (2001). The choice of watermark domain in the presence of compression. *Proceedings of international conference on information technology: Coding and computing*, 79-84.

Felton, E., Balfanz, D., Dean, D., & Wallach, D. (1996). *Web spoofing: An Internet con game* (Tech. Rep. No. TR 54096). Princeton, NJ: Princeton University.

Ferrer-Gomila, J. L., Payeras-Capella, M., & Huguet-Rotger, L. (2001). Efficient optimistic n-party contract signing protocol. *Information Security Conference, LNCS 2200*, pp. 394-407, Berlin: Springer.

FIPS. (2001, November). *Federal Information Processing Standards*. Retrieved from http://csrc.nist.gov/publications/fips/fips197/fips-197.pdf

FIPS. (2006). *Minimum Security Requirements for Federal Information and Information Systems*. Retrieved from http://csrc.nist.gov/

Fiscus, J. G., & Doddington, G. R. (2002). Topic detection and tracking evaluation overview . In *James Allan* (pp. 17–31). Boston: Kluwer Academic Publishers.

Fishbein, M., & Ajzen, I. (1975). *Belief, Attitude, Intention and Behavior: An Introduction to Theory and Research*. Reading, WA: Addison-Wesley.

Fogel, J., & Nahmad, E. (2008). Internet social network communities: Risk taking, trust, and privacy concerns. *Computers in Human Behavior, 25*, 153–160. doi:10.1016/j.chb.2008.08.006

Ford, D., Connelly, C., & Meister, D. (2003). Information systems research and Hofstede's culture's consequences: An uneasy and incomplete partnership. *IEEE Transactions on Engineering Management, 50*(1), 8–25. doi:10.1109/TEM.2002.808265

Fowler, M. (2004). *UML Distilled* (3rd ed.). Reading, MA: Addison Wesley.

Française, C. R. (2006). *Comission Nationale De L'Informatique Et Des Libertes*. Retrieved May 10, 2006, from http://www.cnil.fr/index.php?id=4

Franklin, S., & Graesser, A. (1996). *Is It an Agent, or Just a Program? A Taxonomy for Autonomous Agents*. Paper presented at the Third International Workshop on Agent Theories, Architectures, and Languages, Springer-Verlag.

Fridric, J., & Goljan, M. (1999). Protection of digital images using self embedding. *Proceedings of the Symposium on Content Security and Data Hiding in Digital Media*, New Jersey Institute of Technology, Newark, NJ, USA, May 1999.

Fridrich, J. M., & Goljanb, R. D. (2001). Invertible authentication watermark for JPEG images, Proceedings of the IEEE International Conference on Information Technology: Coding and Computing, 223–227.

FTC. (2005). *DSW Inc. Settles FTC Charges*. Retrieved September 4, 2010, from http://www.ftc.gov/opa/2005/12/dsw.shtm

FTC. 2008. Federal Trade Commission. Facts for Business. http://www.ftc.gov/bcp/conline/pubs/buspubs/security.shtm. Visited July 29, 2008.

Fu, K., Sit, E., Smith, K., & Feamster, N. (2001). *Dos and don'ts of client authentication on the web*. Paper presented at the 10th USENIX Security Symposium.

Fukuyama, F. (1995). *Trust: Social Virtues and The Creation of Prosperity*. New York: The Free Press.

Fulford, H., & Doherty, N. F. (2003). The Application of Information Security Policies in Large UK-based Organizations: An Exploratory Investigation. *Information Management & Computer Security, 11*(3), 106–114. doi:10.1108/09685220310480381

Furnell, S. (2002). *Cybercrime: Vandalizing the Information Society*. Boston: Addison-Wesley.

Gadomski, A. M., & Zytkow, J. M. (1995). Abstract Intelligent Agents: Paradigms, Foundations and Conceptualization Problems. In *Abstract Intelligent Agent* (Vol. 2). Rome: ENEA. ISSN/1120-558X.

Galbraith, S. (2005). Pairings. Blake, Seroussi, & Smart (Eds.), *Advances in elliptic curve cryptography, London Mathematical Society Lecture Notes* (chapter IX, pp. 183-213). Cambridge, UK: Cambridge University Press.

Garay, J., & MacKenzie, P. (1999). Abuse-free multiparty contract signing. *1999 International Symposium on Distributed Computing, LNCS 1693,* pp. 151-165, Berlin: Springer.

Garay, J., Jakobsson, M., & MacKenzie, P. (1999). Abuse-free optimistic contract signing. *Advances in Cryptology—CRYPTO'99,* (pp. 449--466).

Garfinkel, S., Spafford, G., & Schwartz, A. (2003). *Practical unix & internet security.* Sebastopol: O'Reilly.

Garfinkel, S. (1995). *PGP: Pretty Good Privacy.* Sebastopol, CA: O'Reilly.

Garfinkel, S. L., Margrave, D., Schiller, J. I., Nordlander, E., & Miller, R. C. (2005). *How to make secure e-mail easier to use.* Paper presented at CHI 2005, Portland, OR.

Garmendia, L. (2007). *The Evolution of the Concept of Fuzzy Measure.* Retrieved from http://www.fdi.ucm.es/profesor/lgarmend/SC/Congresos/

Garson, D. (2006). *Scales and Standard Measures.* Retrieved from http://www2.chass.ncsu.edu/garson/PA765/standard.htm

Gaudin, S. (2007, April 11). Security breaches cost $90 to $305 per lost record. *Information Week.*

Gefen, D. (2000). E-Commerce: The Role of Familiarity and Trust. *Omega, 28*(6), 725–737. doi:10.1016/S0305-0483(00)00021-9

Gefen, D. (2002). Customer Loyalty in E-Commerce. *Journal of the Association for Information Systems,* 327–351.

Gellman, B. (2005, November 6). The FBI's secret scrutiny. Washington, DC: *The Washington Post,* (p. A01).

Gellman, R. (2002). *Privacy, Consumers, and Costs: How the Lack of Privacy Costs Consumers and Why Business Studies of Privacy Costs are Biased and Incomplete.* http://www.epic.org/reports/dmfprivacy.html.

Geneology.com. (2004, July 21). *Privacy Statement: Home pages, family trees, virtual cemetery and the world family tree.*

Gleick, J. (1996, September 29). Behind closed doors; Big Brother is us. New York: *The New York Times Sunday Magazine,* (Sec. 6), 130.

Goecks, J., & Mynatt, E. D. (2005). Social Approaches to End-User Privacy Management. In L. F. Cranor & S. Garfinkel (Eds.), *Security and Usability Designing Secure Systems That People Can Use.* Beijing, China: O'Reilly.

Goldrei, D. C. (1996). *Classic Set Theory: For Guided Independent Study.* London: Chapman & Hall.

Goodhue, D. L., & Straub, D. W. (1991). Security concerns of system users: a study of the perceptions of the adequacy of security. *Information & Management, 20*(1), 13–22. doi:10.1016/0378-7206(91)90024-V

Goodin, D. (2007, October 24th). TJX Breach was Twice as Big as Admitted, Bank Says. *Channel Register.*

Goodman, K. (2008, March). The 30-day e-mail detox. *O, The Oprah Magazine* (pp. 203- 206).

Gordon, I. (1989). *Beat the Competition How to Use Competitive Intelligence to Develop Winning Business Strategies.* Oxford, UK: Basil Blackwell Publishers.

Gostin, L. O., & Nass, S. (2009). Reforming the HIPAA Privacy Rule: Safeguarding Privacy and Promoting Research. *Journal of the American Medical Association, 301*(13), 1373–1375. doi:10.1001/jama.2009.424

Gouldson, T. (2001, July 27). Hackers and crackers bedevil business world. *Computing Canada, 27*(16), 13.

Government of Japan. (2003). *Act on the Protection of Personal Information.* Tokyo: Author.

Granlund, T. (2004). *GNU MP edition 4.1.4. (The GNU Multiple Precision Arithmetic Library)*. Retrieved from http://swox.com/gmp/

Granville, J. (2003, January). Review article on global governance. *Global Society, 17*(1), 89–97. doi:10.1080/0953732032000054033

Graps, A. (1995). An introduction to wavelets. *Computational Science and Engineering, IEEE, 2*(2), 50–61. doi:10.1109/99.388960

Grau, J. (2006). *Europe Retail E-Commerce: Spotlight on the UK, Germany, and France*. New York: eMarketer, Inc.

Grau, J. (2007). *Asia-Pacific B2C E-Commerce*. New York: eMarketer, Inc.

Graumann, S., & Neinert, F. (2006). *Monitoring the Information Economy: 9th Factual Report*. Munich, Germany: TNS Business Intelligence.

Greenleaf, G. (2006). APEC's privacy framework sets a new low standard for the Asia-Pacific . In Richardson, M., & Kenyon, A. (Eds.), *New Dimensions in Privacy Law: International and Comparative Perspectives*. Cambridge, UK: Cambridge University Press. doi:10.1017/CBO9780511494208.006

Greenspan, S., Goldberg, D., Weimer, D., & Basso, A. (2000, December). *Interpersonal Trust and Common Ground in Electronically Mediated Communication*. Paper presented at the 2000 ACM Conference on Computer Supported Cooperative Work, Philadelphia.

Grimes, G., Hough, M., & Signorella, M. (2003, November). User Attitudes towards spam in three age groups. ACM Conference on Universal Usability (pp. 1-4), Vancouver, Canada.

Gritzalis, S. (2004). Enhancing Web Privacy and Anonymity In the Digital Era. *Information Management & Computer Security, 12*(3), 255–288. doi:10.1108/09685220410542615

Gross, R., & Acquisti, A. (2005, November 7). Information revelation and privacy in online social networks. *Proceedings of the 2005 ACM workshop on privacy in the electronic society*. Alexandria, VA.

Group on Unsolicited Commercial Email. (1998). Report (pp. 1-32). http://searchsecurity.techtarget.com/sDefinition/0,sid14_gci944600,00.html

Grow, B., & Bush, J. (2005, May 30). Hacker Hunters: An Elite Force Takes on the Dark Side of Computing. *Business Week, 74.*

Guha, R., Kumar, R., Raghavan, P., & Tomkins, A. (2004). *Propagation of trust and distrust*. Paper presented at the 13th International Conference on WWW, New York.

Gunsel, B., Uludag, U., & Tekalp, A. M. (2002). Robust watermarking of fingerprint images. Journal of pattern recognition, 35 (12), 2739-2747.

Gupta, M., & Sharman, R. (2008). *Social and Human Elements of Information Security*. Hershey, PA: Idea Group Inc (IGI).

Gura, N., Patel, A., & Wander, A. (2004). Comparing elliptic curve cryptography and RSA on 8-bit CPUs. In *Proceedings of the 2004 Workshop on Cryptographic Hardware and Embedded Systems (CHES 2004)* (pp. 119-132).

Gurgens, S., Rudolph, C., & Vogt, H. (2003). On the security of fair non-repudiation protocols. *Information Security Conference (ISC)*, LNCS 2851, pp. 193-207. Springer-Verlag, 2003.

Gutmann, P. (2003). *Plug-and-play PKI: A PKI your mother can use*. Paper presented at the 12nd USENIX Security Symposium.

Gutmann, P. (2004). *How to build a PKI that works*. Paper presented at the 3rd Annual PKI R&D Workshop, Gaithersburg, MD.

Gutmann, P. (2006). *Everything you never wanted to know about PKI but were forced to find out*. Retrieved from http://www.cs.auckland.ac.nz/~pgut001/pubs/pkitutorial.pdf

Guttman, E., Perkins, C., Veizades, J., & Day, M. (1999). Service location protocol, version 2. Retrieved from http://www.ietf.org/rfc/rfc2608.txt

Hair, J. F., Black, W. C., Babin, B. J., Anderson, R. E., & Tatham, R. L. (2006). *Multivariate Data Analysis* (6th Edition ed.). Upper Saddle River, NJ, USA: Pearson Education.

Halderman, J. A., Waters, B., & Felten, E. W. (2005). A convenient method for securely managing passwords. In *Proceedings of the 14th International Conference on World Wide Web* (pp. 471-479). New York NY, USA: ACM Press.

Hall, E. T., & Hall, M. R. (1990). *Understanding Cultural Differences*. Yarmouth, ME: Intercultural Press.

Hämmerle-Uhl, J., Raab, K., & Uhl, A. (2010). Experimental study on the impact of robust watermarking on iris recognition accuracy. *Proceedings of the 2010 ACM Symposium on Applied Computing* (Sierre, Switzerland, March 22 - 26, 2010). SAC '10. ACM, New York, NY, 1479-1484.

Hankerson, D., Menezes, A., & Vanstone, S. (2004). *Guide to elliptic curve cryptography*. Berlin, Germany: Springer-Verlag.

Harrison, A. W., & Rainer, K. (1992). The influence of individual differences on skill in end-user computing. *Journal of Management Information Systems, 9*(1), 93–111.

Hart, C. W., & Johnson, M. D. (1999). Growing the trust relationship. *Marketing Management, 8*(1), 8–19.

Helft, M. (2010, July 7). Facebook makes headway around the world New York: *The New York Tim*es.

Henry, M. (2001). *International Privacy, Publicity & Personality Laws*. Markham, OT, Canada: Butterworths.

Hines, M. (2007, December 18-25). Insuring against data loss. *EWeek the Enterprise Newsweekly, 23*(50), 13.

HMAC. (2002). The keyed-hash message authentication code (HMAC). *FIPS PUB 198*, NIST.

Hodgin, R. C. (2007, December 18). Phishing cost the U.S. $3.2 billion in 2007. *Tom's Hardware*. Retrieved from http://www.tomshardware.com/news/phishing-cost-u-s-3-2-billion-2007,4576.html

Hoffman, D. L., Novak, T. P., & Peralta, M. (1999). Building consumer trust online. *Communications of the ACM, 42*(4), 80–85. doi:10.1145/299157.299175

Hofstede, G. (2001). *Culture's Consequences: Comparing Values, Behaviors, Institutions, and Organizations across Nations* (2nd ed.). Thousand Oaks, CA: Sage Publications.

Hogan, D. (2007). *NRF to Credit Card Companies: Stop Forcing Retailers to Store Credit Card Data*. Wakefield, MA: National Retail Federation.

Holt, T. J. (2005). *Hacks, Cracks, and Crime: An Examination of the Subculture and Social*. St. Louis, MO: University of Missouri.

Hong, Y., Won, C. S., Kim, S. M., & Kim, S. B. (2007). Data hiding on H.264/AVC compressed video . *Proceedings of International Conference on Image Analysis and Recognition, 4633*, 698–707.

Hoofnagle, J. (2005, March 4). Privacy self regulation: A decade of disappointment. *Electronic Privacy Information Center*.

Horne, C. (2001). Sociological Perspectives on the Emergence of Norms. In M. Hechter & K.-D. Opp (Eds.), *Social Norms*. New York: Russell Sage Foundation.

Housley, R., Ford, W., Polk, W., & Solo, D. (1999). *Internet X.509 public key infrastructure: Certificate and CRL profile* (RFC 2459). Retrieved from www.ietf.org/rfc/rfc2459.txt

Howell, D. C. (2002). *Statistical Methods for Psychology* (5th ed.). Pacific Grove, CA: Duxbury/Thomson Learning.

Hsu, M.-H., & Kuo, F.-Y. (2003). The Effect of Organization-Based Self-Esteem and Deindividualism in Protecting Personal Information Privacy. *Journal of Business Ethics, 42*(4), 305–320. doi:10.1023/A:1022500626298

Hu, Y. C. (2003). Grey-level image hiding scheme based on vector quantization. *IEEE . Electronics Letters, 39*(2), 202–203. doi:10.1049/el:20030167

Hu, Y. C. (2006). High-capacity image hiding scheme based on vector quantization. *Pattern Recognition, 39*(9), 1715–1724. doi:10.1016/j.patcog.2006.02.005

Huang, Q., Cukier, J., Kobayashi, H., Liu, B., & Zhang, J. (2003, September). *Fast authenticated key establishment protocols for self-organizing sensor networks.* Paper presented at the 2nd ACM international conference on Wireless sensor networks and applications, San Diego, CA.

Hulland, J. (1999). Use of partial least squares (PLS) in strategic management research: A review of four recent studies. *Strategic Management Journal, 20*(2), 195–204. doi:10.1002/(SICI)1097-0266(199902)20:2<195::AID-SMJ13>3.0.CO;2-7

Huston, T. (2001). Security issues for implementation of e-medical records. *Communications of the ACM, 44*(9), 89–94. doi:10.1145/383694.383712

Ibrahim, A., Zabian, A., Esteteya, F. N., & Al Padawy, A. K. (2009). Algorithm for Text Hiding in Digital Image for Information Security . *International Journal of Computer Science and Network Security, 9*(6), 262–268.

IDC. (2007, April 9). *IDC reveals the future of email as it navigates through a resurgence of spam and real-time market substitutes.* Retrieved in 2009 from http://www.idc.com/getdoc.jsp?containerId=prUS20639307.

Identity Theft Resource Center. (2005). *2005 Disclosures of U.S. Data Incidents.* Retrieved September 4, 2010, from http://idtheftmostwanted.org/ITRC%20Breach%20Report%202005.pdf

Identity Theft Resource Center. (2006). *2006 Disclosures of U.S. Data Incidents.* Retrieved September 4, 2010, from http://idtheftmostwanted.org/ITRC%20Breach%20Report%202006.pdf

Identity Theft Resource Center. (2007). *2007 ITRC Breach Report.* Retrieved September 4, 2010, from http://idtheftmostwanted.org/ITRC%20Breach%20Report%202007.pdf

Identity Theft Resource Center. (2008). *2008 ITRC Breach Report.* Retrieved September 4, 2010, from http://idtheftmostwanted.org/ITRC%20Breach%20Report%202008.pdf

IEEE. P1363.2. (2005). *Draft standard specifications for password-based public key cryptographic techniques.* Retrieved from http://grouper.ieee.org/groups/1363/passwdPK/index.html

Ifinedo, P. (2009). Information Technology Security Management Concerns in Global Financial Services Institutions: Is National Culture a Differentiator? *Information Management & Computer Security, 17*(5), 372–387. doi:10.1108/09685220911006678

Ifinedo, P., & Nahar, N. (2006). Do Top and Mid-level Managers View Enterprise Resource Planning (ERP) Systems Success Measures Differently? *International Journal of Management and Enterprise Development, 3*(6), 618–635.

Ifinedo, P. (2008). IT Security and Privacy Issues in Global Financial Services Institutions: Do Socio-economic and Cultural Factors Matter? *Sixth Annual Conference on Privacy, Security and Trust (PST2008),* In cooperation with the IEEE Computer Society's Technical Committee on Security and Privacy, Fredericton, New Brunswick, Canada, October 1 - 3, 2008.

Imamoto, K., & Sakurai, K. (2002). A certified e-mail system with receiver's selective usage of delivery authority. *Progress in Cryptology-INDOCRYPT, 2002,* 326–338.

IMB. *Strengthen your customer.* Retrieved on September 21, 2008 from: http://www-03.ibm.com/innovation/us/strengthen/crm.shtml

IMC-SMIME. (2006). S/MIME and OpenPGP. *Internet Mail Consortium*

In the Matter of DSW Inc., a corporation: FTC File No. 052-3096 (United States of America Federal Trade Commission 2005).

Information Commissioner's Office of the United Kingdom. (2006). *Information Commissioner's Office of the United Kingdom-Home*. Retrieved from http://www.ico.gov.uk/eventual.aspx

Information Security Industry Survey. (1999). *Information security magazine*. Retrieved Jan 14, 2008 from: http://www.infosecuritymag.com/, July 1999.

Inside Facebook Gold (2010). Analysis, data and reports on Facebook.

Intelius. (2006, February 16). Welcome to the Intelius privacy FAQ: How can I remove my information from the Intelius public records databases? Justice News. (2010, April 8). Attorney General Eric Holder signs agreement to strengthen U. S. Spanish cooperation, pushes for terrorist financing tracking program agreement.

Intentretailer.com. *E-mail communication doesn't have to be one way street*. Retrieved on September 21, 2008 from: http://www.internetretailer.com/dailyNews.asp?id=25013

Internetretailer.com. www.CrystalWare.com *boosts its online offering to more than 1 million products*. Retrieved on September 21, 2008 from: http://www.internetretailer.com/internet/marketing-conference/

IP2Location.com. (2006). *Geolocation IP Address to Country City Region Latitude Longitude ZIP Code ISP Domain Name Database for Developers*. Retrieved from http://www.ip2location.com/

Ipeirotis, P., Ntoulas, A., Cho, J., & Gravano, L. (2005). Modeling and managing content changes in text databases. In *Proceedings of the 21st IEEE International Conference on Data Engineering* (pp. 606).

ISACA(2006). Information Systems Audit and Control Association manual, 2006 edition.

ISO/IEC 13888-1 (1997a). *Information technology - Security techniques - Non-repudiation - Part 1: General*

ISO/IEC 13888-2 (1998). Information technology - Security techniques - Non-repudiation - Part 2: Mechanisms using symmetric techniques

ISO/IEC 13888-3 (1997b). Information technology - Security techniques - Non-repudiation - Part 3: Mechanisms using asymmetric techniques

ISO/TR 13569 (2005). *Financial services - Information Security Guidelines*. http://www.iso.org/iso/iso_catalogue/catalogue_tc/catalogue_detail.htm?csnumber=3724.

ITIM. (2009). *Geert Hofstede Cultural Dimensions*. http://www.geert-hofstede.com/hofstede_dimensions.php. Retrieved June 20th.

Iwata, M., Miyake, K., & Shiozaki, (2004). A. Digital steganography utilizing features of JPEG images. IEICE Transactions on Fundamentals E87-A (4), 929–936.

James, L. (2005). *Phishing exposed. uncover secrets from the dark side* (1st ed.). Burlington, MA: Syngress.

Janvrin, D., & Morrison, J. (2000). Using a structured design approach to reduce risks in end user spreadsheet development. *Information & Management*, *37*(1), 1–12. doi:10.1016/S0378-7206(99)00029-4

Jarvenpaa, S., Tactinsky, N., & Vitale, M. (2000). Consumer Trust in an Internet Store. *Information Technology Management*, *1*, 45–71. doi:10.1023/A:1019104520776

Jennings, J. (2004, January 29). *Complying With CAN-SPAM: A 10-Point Checklist for Marketers.*, Retrieved on October 10, 2008 from: http://www.clickz.com/showPage.html?page=3305101

Jensen, C., Potts, C., & Jensen, C. (2005). Privacy Practices of Internet Users: Self-Reports Versus Observed Behavior. *International Journal of Human-Computer Studies*, *63*, 203–227. doi:10.1016/j.ijhcs.2005.04.019

Jensen, C., & Potts, C. (2004, April 2004). *Privacy Policies as Decision-Making Tools: An Evaluation of Online Privacy Notices*. Paper presented at the CHI 2004, Vienna, Austria.

Jim, S. L. (2006). *From UML Diagrams to Behavioural Source Code*. Unpublished master's thesis, Centrum voor Wiskunde en Informatica.

Johnson, H. J. (2000). *Global Financial Institutions and Markets*. Malden, MA: Blackwell Publishing.

Johnson, E. *The Top 12 Priorities for Competitive Intelligence*. Retrieved on September 21, 2008 from: http://www.aurorawdc.com/arj_cics_priorities.htm

Josefsson, S. (2003, July). *The base16, base32, and base64 data encodings*. Freemont, CA: Internet IETF Request for Comments 3548.

Jung, B., Han, I., & Lee, S. (2001). Security threats to Internet: A Korean multi-industry investigation. *Information & Management*, 38(8), 487–498. doi:10.1016/S0378-7206(01)00071-4

Jurafsky, D., & Marton, J. H. (2000). *Speech and Language Processing*. Upper Saddle River, NJ: Prentice Hall.

Kahneman, D. (2003). Maps of bounded rationality: psychology for behavioral economics. *The American Economic Review*, 1449–1475. doi:10.1257/000282803322655392

Kaliski, B. (September, 2000). PKCS #5: Password-Based Cryptography Specification, Version 2.0, RFC 2898

Kalloniatis, C., Kavakli, E., & Gritzalis, S. (2008). Addressing privacy requirements in system design: the PriS method . *Requirements Engineering*, 13(3), 241–255. doi:10.1007/s00766-008-0067-3

Kangas, E. *Mitigating Threats to Your Email Security and Privacy*. Retrieved on September 30, 2008 from http://luxsci.com/extranet/articles/security-threats.html

Kankanhalli, A., Teo, H. H., Tan, B. C. Y., & Wei, K.-K. (2003). An integrative study of information systems security effectiveness. *International Journal of Information Management*, 23(2), 139–154. doi:10.1016/S0268-4012(02)00105-6

Kantarcioglu, M., & Clifton, C. (2004). Privacy-preserving distributed mining of association rules on horizontally partitioned data. *IEEE Transactions on Knowledge and Data Engineering*, 16(9), 1026–1037. doi:10.1109/TKDE.2004.45

Kaplan, S. E., & Nieschwietz, R. J. (2003). A Web Assurance Model of Trust for B2C E-Commerce. *International Journal of Accounting Information Systems*, 4(2), 95–114. doi:10.1016/S1467-0895(03)00005-8

Kargupta, H., Datta, S., Wang, Q., & Sivakumar, K. (2003). Random data perturbation techniques and privacy preserving data mining. *Knowledge and Information Systems*, 7(4), 387–414. doi:10.1007/s10115-004-0173-6

Karl, H., & Willig, A. (2005). *Protocols and Architecture for wireless sensor networks*. New York: John Wiley & Sons. doi:10.1002/0470095121

Karlof, C., Sastry, N., & Wagner, D. (2004a, November). Paper presented *TinySec: A link layer security architecture for wireless sensor networks* at the 2nd International Conference on Embedded Networked Sensor Systems, Baltimore, MD.

Karlof, C., Sastry, N., & Wagner, D. (2004b). *TinyOS: User manual*. Retrieved February 10, 2009, from http://www.tinyos.net/tinyos-1.x/doc/tinysec.pdf

Kasabov, N. (1998). Introduction: Hybrid intelligent adaptive systems. *International Journal of Intelligent Systems*, 6, 453–454. doi:10.1002/(SICI)1098-111X(199806)13:6<453::AID-INT1>3.0.CO;2-K

Kay, R. *QuickStudy: Phishing*. Retrieved on September 30, 2008 from: http://www.computerworld.com/securitytopics/security/story/0,10801,89096,00.html

Keepemailsafe.com. *Email Security and Privacy Threats*. Retrieved on September 30, 2007 from: http://www.keepemailsafe.com/security_privacy.html#1

Kekre, H. B., Athawale, A., & Halarnkar, P. N. (2008). Increased capacity of information hiding in LSB's method for text and image. *International journal of electrical, computer, and systems engineering*.

Kekre, H.B., Athawale, A., Sarode T.K. & Sagvekar K. (2010). Increased Capacity of Information Hiding using Mixed Codebooks of Vector Quantization Algorithms: LBG,

Khoo, K. B., & Ishizuka, M. (2001a). *Emerging Topic Tracking System, Proceedings of Web Intelligent (WI 2001), LXAI 2198* (pp. 125–130). Machashi, Japan: Springer.

Khoo, K. B., & Ishizuka, M. (2001b). Information Area Tracking and Changes Summarizing *Proceedings of WebNet 2001*, International Conference on WWW and Internet, Orlando, Florida,680-685

Khyou, K., & Ishizuka, B. M. (2002). Topic Extraction from News Archive Using TF*PDF Algorithm. The third International Conference on Web Information Systems Engineering(WISE'00),Singapore, 73.

Kim, J., & Moon, Y. (1999). A robust wavelet-based digital watermark using level-adaptive thresholding. *Proceedings of the IEEE international conference on image processing (ICIP '99)*.

Kleen, L. J. (2001). Malicoious Hackers: A Framerwork for Analysis and Case Study [Electronic Version]. *Master's Thesis, Air Force Institutie of Technology, 2001*. Retrieved January 3, 2004, from http://www.iwar.org. uk/iwar/resources/usaf/maxwell/students/2001/afit-gor-ens-01m-09.pdf

Kling, R. (1995). Information technologies and the shifting balance between privacy and social control. Part VI, Article A of: *Computerization and Controversy: Value Conflicts and Social Choices*. Academic Press, (pp. 614-636).

Knapp, K. J., Marshall, T. E., Rainer, R. K., & Ford, F. N. (2006). Information security: management's effect on culture and policy. *Information Management & Computer Security, 14*(1), 24–36. doi:10.1108/09685220610648355

Knapp, K. J., Marshall, T. E., Rainer, R. K. Jr, & Morrow, D. W. (2006). The Top Information Security Issues Facing Organizations: What can Government do to Help? *EDPACS: The EDP Audit . Control & Security Newsletter, 34*(4), 1–10.

Knapp, K. J., Marshall, T. E., Rainer, R. K., & Ford, F. N. (2007). Information security effectiveness: Conceptualization and validation of a theory. *nternational Journal of Information Security and Privacy, 1*(2), 37-60.

Knight, C. *Sender Policy Framework (SPF) – Explained*. Retrieved on October 1, 2008 from: http://emailuniverse. com/ezine-tips/?id=1202

Koblitz, N. (1987). Elliptic curve cryptosystems. *Mathematics of Computation, 48*, 203–209. doi:10.1090/S0025-5718-1987-0866109-5

Kobsa, A. (2007). Privacy-enhanced personalization. *Communications of the ACM, 50*(8), 24–33. doi:10.1145/1278201.1278202

Koch, E., & Zhao, J. (1995). Toward robust and hidden image copyright labeling. *Proceedings of IEEE workshop on nonlinear signal and image processing*, 452-455.

Koike, Y., & Taiki, S. (2002). *P3P Validator*. Retrieved from from http://www.w3.org/P3P/validator.html

KPE and KMCG, *Advances in Computational Sciences and Technology, 3*(2), 245–256.

Kremer, S., & Markowitch, O. (2001). Selective receipt in certified e-mail. *Progress in Cryptology-INDOCRYPT, 2001*, 136–148.

Kremer, S., & Markowitch, O. (2000). Optimistic non-repudiable information exchange. In J. Biemond (Ed.), *21st Symp. on Information Theory in the Benelux, Werkgemeenschap Informatie- en Communicatietheorie*. Enschede (NL), Wassenaar (NL), 2000, (pp. 139–146).

Kremer, S., Markowitch, O., & Zhou, J. (2002). An intensive survey of fair non-repudiation protocols. *Computer Communications, 25*(17), 1606-1621. Elsevier, Nov. 2002.

Krishnamurthy, B., & Wills, C. (2009, April 20-24). Privacy diffusion on the web: A longitudinal perspective. WWW, Madrid, Spain.

Kristol, D. M. (2001). HTTP Cookies: Standards, Privacy, and Politics. *ACM Transactions on Internet Technology, 1*(2), 151–198. doi:10.1145/502152.502153

Kritzinger, E., & Smith, E. (2008). Information security management: An information security retrieval and awareness model for industry. *Computers & Security, 27*(5-6), 224–231. doi:10.1016/j.cose.2008.05.006

Krohn, R. (2002). HIPAA compliance: A technology perspective. *Journal of Healthcare Information Management, 16*(2), 14–16.

Krovetz, R. (1995). *Word Sense Disambiguation for Large Text Databases*. Cambridge, MA: University of Massachusetts.

Kumaraguru, P., & Cranor, L. (2005, May 2005). *Privacy in India: Attitudes and Awareness.* Paper presented at the 2005 Workshop on Privacy Enhancing Technologies, Dubrovnik, Croatia.

Kundur, D. (2000). Implications for high capacity data hiding in the presence of lossy compression. *Proceedings of the international conference on information technology: Coding and computing,* 16-21.

Kuo, C. J. (1993). Novel image encryption technique and its application in progressive transmission. *Journal of Electronic Imaging, 2*(4), 345–351. doi:10.1117/12.148572

La Roche, C., Dardick, G., & Flanigan, M. (2006). IN-FOSEC: What is the legal standard of care? *Journal of Business and Economic Research, 4*(7), 69–75.

Langelaar, G. C., Setyawan, I., & Lagendijk, R. L. (2000). Watermarking digital image and video data: a state-of-the-art overview. *IEEE Signal Processing Magazine, 17*(5), 20–46. doi:10.1109/79.879337

Langsford, A., Naemura, K., & Speth, R. (1983). OSI management and job transfer services. *Proceedings of the IEEE, 71*(12), 1420–1424. doi:10.1109/PROC.1983.12790

Larose, R., & Rifon, N. J. (2007). Promoting i-Safety: Effects of Privacy Warnings and Privacy Seals on Risk Assessment and Online Privacy Behavior. *The Journal of Consumer Affairs, 41*(1), 127–149. doi:10.1111/j.1745-6606.2006.00071.x

Larson, A. (1992). Network Dyads in Entrepreneurial settings: a study of the governance of exchange relationships. *Administrative Science Quarterly, 37*(1), 76–104. doi:10.2307/2393534

Laurent, A. (1983). The cultural diversity of Western conceptions of management. *Internnational Studies of Management and Organization, 13*(1-2), 75–96.

Law, Y. W., Doumen, J., & Hartel, P. (2006). Survey and benchmark of block ciphers for wireless sensor networks. [TOSN]. *ACM Transactions on Sensor Networks, 2*(1), 65–93. doi:10.1145/1138127.1138130

Lawyers.com. (2010). *Lawsuit targets Facebook privacy issues.* LexisNexis.

Lee, J., & Lee, Y. (2002). A holistic model of computer abuse within organizations. *Information Management & Computer Security, 10*(2/3), 57–63. doi:10.1108/09685220210424104

Lee, M. K. O., & Turban, E. (2001). A Trust Model for Consumer Internet Shopping. *International Journal of Electronic Commerce, 6*(1), 75–91.

Lee, Y. K., & Chen, L. H. (2000). A Secure Robust Image Steganographic Model. *Proceedings of the Tenth National Conference on Information Security,* 275-284.

Leetz, W. (2001). HIPAA: Increased efficiency in US American healthcare requires data protection and data security - an overview of the technical and organizational measures necessary. *electromedica, 69*(2), 95–100.

Legislative Hearing on H.R. 5318, the "Cyber-Security Enhancement and Consumer Data Protection Act of 2006", U.S. House of Representatives (2006).

Leonard, D. (2010, July 19). Another Suit over the Spoils of Facebook. *Bloomberg Businessweek, 25,* 42–43.

Levin, A., & Abril, P. (2009). Two notions of privacy online, 11 *Vand. J. Ent. & Tech., L,* 1001–1035.

Lewis, K., Kaufman, J., & Christakis, N. (2008). The taste for privacy: An analysis of college student privacy settings in an online social network. *Journal of Computer-Mediated Communication, 14,* 79–100. doi:10.1111/j.1083-6101.2008.01432.x

LexisNexis. (2005, March 29). "Data privacy policy" Opt-Out requests.

Li, L., Wang, P., & Zhang, Z. D. (2008). A video watermarking scheme based on motion vectors and mode selection. *Proceedings of IEEE International Conference Computer Science and Software Engineering, 5,* 233–237.

Li, X. B., & Sarkar, S. (2006). A Tree-Based Data Perturbation Approach for Privacy-Preserving Data Mining. *IEEE Transactions on Knowledge and Data Engineering, 18*(9), 1278–1283. doi:10.1109/TKDE.2006.136

Li, C. X. (2009). A Novel Scheme for Text Information Hiding into a Carrier Image Based on BCH Code and HVS Model, Proceedings of the 2009 International Workshop on Information Security and Application (IWISA 2009), Qingdao, China.

Li, Y., Chen, Z., Tan, S. M., & Campbell, R. H. (1996). Security enhanced MPEG player. Proceedings of the international workshop on multimedia software development, 169-175.

Liberty Alliance Project. (2005, May). *Liberty ID-FF architecture overview* (Version 1.2-errata-v1.0). Retrieved from http://www.projectliberty.org/resource_center/specifications/liberty_alliance_id_ff_1_2_specifications

Lichtenstein, S., Swatman, P. M. C., & Babu, K. (2003). *Adding Value to Online Privacy for Consumers: Remedying Deficiencies in Online Privacy Policies with an Holistic Approach.* Paper presented at the 36th Hawaii International Conference on System Sciences, Hawaii.

Lin, C. Y., & Chang, S. F. (2000). Semi-fragile watermarking for authenticating JPEG visual content. [San Jose, CA, USA.]. *Proceedings of the SPIE International Conference on Security and Watermarking of Multimedia Contents, II,* 3971.

Lin, M. H., Hu, Y. C., & Chang, C. C. (2002). Both color and gray scale secret images hiding in a color image. *International Journal of Pattern Recognition and Artificial Intelligence, 16,* 697–713. doi:10.1142/S0218001402001903

Lin, S. D., & Shie, S. C. (2004). Secret image communication scheme based on vector quantization. *IEEE Electronics Letters, 40*(14), 859–860. doi:10.1049/el:20040568

Lin, C. Y., & Chang, S. F. (2001). Watermarking capacity of digital images based on domain specific masking effects. Proceedings of the international conference on information technology: Coding and computing (ITCC '01).

Lin, J.-L., & Liu, J. Y.-C. (2007). Privacy preserving itemset mining through fake transactions. In *Proceedings of the 2007 ACM Symposium on Applied Computing,* Seoul, Korea (pp. 375-379). New York: ACM Publishing.

Lioudakis, G. V., Koutsoloukas, E. A., Dellas, N. L., Tselikas, N., Kapellaki, S., & Prezerakos, G. N. (2007). A middleware architecture for privacy protection. *Computer Networks, 51*(16), 4679–4696. doi:10.1016/j.comnet.2007.06.010

Litan, A. (2007). *Proposed PCI Changes Would Improve Merchant's Data Security.* Stamford, CT: Gartner Incorporation.

Litan, A. (2008). *PCI Compliance Grows but Major Industry Problems Remain.* Stamford, CT: Gartner Incorporation.

Liu, C., & Arnett, K. (2002). Raising a Red Flag on Global WWW Privacy Policies. *Journal of Computer Information Systems, 43*(1), 117–127.

Liu, D., Ning, P., & Li, R. (2005). Establishing pairwise keys in distributed sensor networks. [TISSEC]. *ACM Transactions on Information and System Security, 8*(1), 41–77. doi:10.1145/1053283.1053287

Liu, K., Kargupta, H., & Ryan, J. (2006). Random projection-based multiplicative data perturbation for privacy preserving distributed data mining. *IEEE Transactions on Knowledge and Data Engineering, 18*(1), 92–106. doi:10.1109/TKDE.2006.14

Liu, A., & Peng, N. (2008). TinyECC: A configurable library for elliptic curve cryptography in wireless sensor networks. In *Proceedings of the 7th International Conference on Information Processing in Sensor Networks* (pp. 245-256).

Liu, T., & Qiu, Z. D. (2002) A DWT-based color image steganography scheme, *Proceedings of* International Conference on Signal Processing, 2, 1568–1571.

Livinginternet.com. *Email security.* Retrieved on September 30, 2008 from: http://www.livinginternet.com/e/es.htm

Luo, P., Wang, X., Feng, J., & Xu, Y. (2008). Low-power hardware implementation of ECC processor suitable for low-cost RFID tags. In *Proceedings of the IEEE 9th International Conference on Solid-State and Integrated-Circuit Technology (ICSICT 2008)* (pp. 1681-1684).

Mackay, W. E. (1988). More than just a communication system: Diversity in the use of electronic mail. *CSCW '88: Proceedings of the 1988 ACM Conference on Computer-Supported Cooperative Work* (pp. 344-353). United States.

Magnini, B., Negri, M., Prevete, R., & Tanev, H. (2002). *A WordNet-based Approach to Named Entities Recognition.* Paper presented at the SemaNet'02: Building and Using Sematic Networks.

Mainwald, E. (2003). *Network security: A beginner's guide.* New York: McGraw Hill/Osborne.

Malan, D., Welsh, M., & Smith, M. (2004, October). *A public-key infrastructure for key distribution in TinyOS based on elliptic curve cryptography.* Paper presented at First IEEE International Conference on Sensor and Ad Hoc Communications and Networks (IEEE SECON 2004), Santa Clara, CA.

Malhotra, N. K., Kim, S. S., & Agarwal, J. (2004, December). Internet Users' Information Privacy Concerns (IUIPC): The Construct, the Scale, and a Causal Model. *Information Systems Research, 15*(4), 336–355. doi:10.1287/isre.1040.0032

Malin, B. (2005). *Betrayed by my shadow: Learning data identity via trail matching.* Journal of Privacy Technology. 20050609001.

Mallat, S. G. (1989). A theory for multiresolution signal decomposition:The wavelet representation. *IEEE Transactions on Pattern Analysis and Machine Intelligence, 11*(7), 674–693. doi:10.1109/34.192463

Maniccam S. S., & Bourbakis, N. (2004). Lossless compression and information hiding in images. *Pattern recognition journal, 36,* 2004.

March, J. G. (1994). *A Primer on Decision Making: How Decisions Happen.* New York: Free Press.

Mark, H. (2006). *Storing Credit Card Data: A Look at the Business Needs, Regulations and Solutions Regarding the Issue.* Las Vegas, CA: Shift4 Corporation.

Marketer & Agency Guide to Email Deliverability Interactive Advertising Bureau

Markowitch, O., & Roggeman, Y. (1999). Probabilistic non-repudiation without trusted third party. *In Second Conference on Security in Communication Networks '99,* Amalfi, Italy.

Martin, A., Doddington, G., Kamm, T., Ordowski, M., & Przybocki, M. (1997). The DET Curve in Assessment of Detection Task Performance. *Proceedings of Eurospeech, 1997,* 1895–1898.

Matlin, C. (2006, June 21). 'Data Broker' reveals ID theft secrets. *ABC News.*

McCarthy, C. (2010, July 21). *Who will be Facebook's next 500 million?* The Social - CNET News.

McCormick, V. L. (2002). HIPAA compliance options for small and mid-sized organizations. *Journal of Healthcare Compliance, 4*(6), 17–20.

McCormick, J., & Gage, D. (2005). *Shadowcrew: Web Mobs* [Electronic Version]. Retrieved September 26, 2008, from http://www.baselinemag.com/c/a/Security/Shadowcrew-Web-Mobs/

McGough, N. *Procmail Quick Start: An introduction to email filtering with a focus on procmail.* Retrieved on October 10, 2008 from: http://www.ii.com/internet/robots/procmail/qs/

McKnight, H., Vivek, C., & Kacmar, C. (2004). Dispositional and distrust distinctions in predicting high and low risk internet expert advice site perceptions. *E-Service Journal, 3*(2), 35–59. doi:10.2979/ESJ.2004.3.2.35

McKnight, D. H., & Chervany, N. (2002). What Trust Means in E-Commerce Customer Relationships: An Interdisciplinary Conceptual Typology. *International Journal of Electronic Commerce, 6*(2), 35–59.

McMillan, R. (2006, August 6).] Defcon: Cybercriminals taking cues from Mafia, says FBI. Computerworld Security.

Mehallegue, N., Bouridane, A., & Garcia, E. (2008). Efficient path key establishment for wireless sensor networks. *EURASIP Journal on Wireless Communications and Networking, 8*(3), Article No. 3.

Memott, M. (2007, January 4). Bush says feds can open mail without warrants. *USA Today.*

Menezes, A., Okamoto, T., & Vanstone, S. (1993). Reducing elliptic curve logarithms to finite field. *IEEE Transactions on Information Theory, 39*(5), 1639–1646. doi:10.1109/18.259647

Menon, S., & Sarkar, S. (2007). Minimizing Information Loss and Preserving Privacy. *Management Science, 53*(1), 101–116. doi:10.1287/mnsc.1060.0603

Mercuri, R. T. (2004). The HIPAA-potamus in health care data security. *Communications of the ACM, 47*(7), 25–28. doi:10.1145/1005817.1005840

MerriamWebster.com. (2009). *Compliance definition.* Retrieved from http://www.merriam-webster.com/

Mersereau, R. M., & Noorkami, M. (2006) Towards robust compressed-domain video watermarking for H.264/AVC. *Proceeding of the SPIE Security, Steganography, and Watermarking of Multimedia Contents.* Atlanta, USA.

Messmer, E. (2007, November, 11th). PCI Compliance Mandate's Power Raises Conflict -of-interest Questions. *Network World.*

Meyer, J., & Gadegast, F. (1995). Security mechanisms for multimedia-data with the example MPEG-I Video. *Proceedings (IEEE) of the international conference on multimedia computing and systems.*

Mial-abuse.com. *Basic Mailing List Management Principles for Preventing Abuse.* Retrieved on October 10, 2008 from: http://www.mail-abuse.com/an_listmgntgdlines.html

Micali, S. (1997). *Certified E-mail with invisible post offices.* Presented at the RSA '97 conference (1997).

Micali, S. (2003). Simple and Fast Optimistic Protocols for Fair Electronic Exchange. In *Proceedings of the ACM Symposium on Principles of Distributed Computing,* pp. 12-19.

Microsoft Corporation. (2006). *Windows live ID service.* Retrieved from http://msdn.microsoft.com/library/default.asp?url=/library/en-us/dnlive/html/winliveidserv.asp

Microsoft. (2007). Trusted root certificates that are required by Windows Server 2008, by Windows Vista, by Windows Server 2003, by Windows XP, and by Windows 2000. *Microsoft Help and Support Article ID 293781.*

Milberg, S., Burke, S., Smith, H. J., & Kallman, E. A. (1995). Values, personal information privacy, and regulatory approaches. *Communications of the ACM, 38*(13), 65–74. doi:10.1145/219663.219683

Milberg, S., Smith, H. J., & Burke, S. (2000). Information privacy: corporate management and national regulation. *Organization Science, 11*(1), 35–57. doi:10.1287/orsc.11.1.35.12567

Miller, V. (1986). Uses of elliptic curves in cryptography. *Advances in Cryptology, CRYPTO '85 (. LNCS, 218,* 417–426.

Miller, V. (1986). *Uses of elliptic curves in cryptography", Lecture Notes in Computer Science 218: Advances in Cryptology - CRYPTO '85* (pp. 417–426). Berlin: Springer-Verlag.

Miller, B. A., Nixon, T., Tai, C., & Wood, M. D. (2001). Home networking with universal plug and pIay. *IEEE Communications Magazine,* (December): 104–109. doi:10.1109/35.968819

Miller, B. (1999). Mapping salutation architecture APIs to bluetooth service discovery layer, bluetooth SIG. Retrieved from http://www.salutation.org/whitepaper/BtoothMapping.PDF

Milne, G. R., & Culnan, M. J. (2002). Using the Content of Online Privacy Notices to Inform Public Policy: A Longitudinal Analysis of the 1998-2001 U.S. Web Surveys. *The Information Society, 18,* 345–359. doi:10.1080/01972240290108168

Miyazaki, A. D. (2008). Online Privacy and the Disclosure of Cookie Use: Effects on Consumer Trust and Anticipated Patronage. *Journal of Public Policy & Marketing, 27*(1), 19–33. doi:10.1509/jppm.27.1.19

Moores, T. (2005). Do Consumers Understand the Role of Privacy Seals in E-Commerce? *Communications of the ACM, 48*(3), 86–91. doi:10.1145/1047671.1047674

Morgan, R. M., & Hunt, S. D. (n.d.). The commitment-trust theory of relationship marketing. *Journal of Marketing, 58*, 20–38. doi:10.2307/1252308

Morris, M. G., & Venkatesh, V. (2000). Age differences in technology adoption decisions: Implications for a changing workforce. *Personnel Psychology, 53*(2), 375–403. doi:10.1111/j.1744-6570.2000.tb00206.x

Morris, M. G., Venkatesh, V., & Ackerman, P. L. (2005). Gender and age differences in employee decisions about new technology: An extension to the theory of planned behavior. *IEEE Transactions on Engineering Management, 52*(1), 69–84. doi:10.1109/TEM.2004.839967

Moshirian, F. (2007). Financial services and a global single currency. *Journal of Banking & Finance, 31*(1), 3–9. doi:10.1016/j.jbankfin.2006.07.001

Moulin, P., & Mihcak, M. K. (2002). A framework for evaluating the data-hiding capacity of image sources. *IEEE Transactions on Image Processing, 11*(9), 1029–1042. doi:10.1109/TIP.2002.802512

Mozilla Developer Center. (2001). *ActiveX control for hosting Netscape plug-ins in IE*. Retrieved from http://www.mozilla.org/projects/plugins/plugin-host-control.html

Mozilla Developer Center. (2006). *Gecko plugin API reference*. Retrieved from http://developer.mozilla.org/en/docs/Gecko_Plugin_API_Reference

Mukhopadhyay, D., & Saha, I. (2006). Location verification based defense against Sybil attack in sensor networks. In *Proceedings of the International Conference of Distributed Computing and Networking*, 509-521.

Mullen, J. (2006, May 15). How Powerful Is E-Mail? *The ClickZ Network*.

Munro, M. C., Huff, S. L., Marcolin, B. L., & Compeau, D. R. (1997). Understanding and measuring user competence. *Information & Management, 33*, 45–57. doi:10.1016/S0378-7206(97)00035-9

Murofushi, T. (1989). An interpretation of fuzzy measures and the Choquet integral as an integral with respect to a fuzzy measure. *Fuzzy Sets and Systems*, 201–227. doi:10.1016/0165-0114(89)90194-2

Murofushi, T. (1991). Fuzzy t-conorm integral with respect to fuzzy measures: Generalization of Sugeno integral and Choquet integral. *Fuzzy Sets and Systems, 42*, 57–71. doi:10.1016/0165-0114(91)90089-9

Murofushi, T., Sugeno, M., & Machida, M. (1994). Non-monotonic fuzzy measures and the Choquet integral. *Fuzzy Sets and Systems, 64*, 73–86. doi:10.1016/0165-0114(94)90008-6

Murofushi, T. A. (1991). A theory of fuzzy measures: Representations the Choquet integral and null sets. *Journal of Mathematical Analysis and Applications, 159*, 532–549. doi:10.1016/0022-247X(91)90213-J

Myers, M. D., & Tan, F. B. (2002). Beyond Models of National Culture in Information Systems Research. *Journal of Global Information Management, 10*(1), 24–32.

Nakashima, E. (2010, July 29). White House proposal would ease FBI access to records of Internet activity. Washington, DC: *Washington Post*.

Naoe, K., & Takefuji, Y. (2008). Damageless information hiding using neural network on YCbCr domain. *International journal of computer science and network security, 8* (9).

Navetta, D. (2008, April 22, 2008). The Legal Implications of the PCI Data Security Standard. *SC Magazine*.

Nelson, M. L., Van de Sompel, H., Liu, X., Harrison, T. L., & McFarland, N. (2005). *mod_oai: An Apache module for metadata harvesting*. Paper presented at the 9th European Conference on Research and Advanced Technology for Digital Libraries.

New York Times. (2007, August 26). The spy chief speaks.

New Zealand Parliamentary Counsel Office. (1993). *Privacy Act 1993 No 28*. Wellington, New Zealand: Author.

New Zealand Privacy Commissioner. (2006). *Privacy Commissioner Home*. Retrieved from http://www.knowledge-basket.co.nz/privacy/top.html

Newcomb, K. (2006, April 17). After E-mail Authentication. *The ClickZ Network*. Retrieved on October 3, 2008 from: http://www.clickz.com/3599541

Newsome, J., Elaine, S., Song, D., & Perrig, A. (2004). The Sybil attack in sensor networks: analysis & defenses. In *Proceedings of the International Symposium on Information Processing in Sensor Networks*, 259-268.

Ng, B. Y., & Rahim, M. A. (2005). A socio-behavioral study of home computer users' intention to practice security. In C. Saunders (Ed.), *Proceedings of The Ninth Pacific Asia Conference on Information Systems*. Bangkok, Thailand: Pacific Asia Conference on Information Systems.

Ni, R., & Ruan, Q. (2002). Embedding information into color images using wavelet, *Proceedings of* IEEE International Conference on Computers, Communications, Control and Power Engineering, 1, p. 598–601.

Ni, Z., Shi, Y., Ansari, N., Su, W., Sun, Q., & Lin, X. (2004). Robust lossless image data hiding. *International conference on multimedia & expo (ICME), 3*, 2199–2202.

Nidd, M. (2001). Service discovery in DEAPspace. *IEEE Personal Communications, August*, 39-45.

Nielsen, J. (2007, July 16). *City dog rules may bite*. Dallas, TX: Dallas Morning News.

Nielson, J. (1990). Heuristics for User Interface Design. Retrieved 5 February 2008, from http://www.useit.com/papers/heuristic/heuristic_list.html

Nissenbaum, H. (1998). Protecting Privacy in an Information Age: The Problem of Privacy in Public. *Law and Philosophy, 17*, 559–596.

NIST. (2003). *Recommendation for key management. Part1: General guidelines (Special publication 800-57)*. Washington, DC: Author.

NIST. (1999, July). *Recommended Elliptic Curves for Federal Government Use*. Retrieved from http://csrc.nist.gov/csrc/fedstandards.html

NIST. (2008). *NIST Security Configuration Checklists*. Retrieved from http://csrc.nist.gov/checklists/

NIST. (April, 2006) http://csrc.nist.gov/publications/nistpubs/800-63/SP800-63V1_0_2.pdf. Last Accessed Dec. 2008

Nolann, G. (2006, September). Seeking Compliance Nirvana. *ACM Queue; Tomorrow's Computing Today*, 71–72.

NSA. (2009). *The Case for Elliptic Curve Cryptography*. Retrieved from http://www.nsa.gov/business/programs/elliptic_curve.shtml

Nunnally, J. C. (1978). *Psychometric Theory* (2nd ed.). New York: McGraw-Hill.

Nunnally, J. C., & Bernstien, I. H. (1994). *Psychometric Theory* (3rd ed.). New York: McGraw-Hill.

Nwana, H. S. (1996). Software Agents: An Overview. *The Knowledge Engineering Review, 11*(3), 1–40. doi:10.1017/S026988890000789X

O'Connor, P. (2007). Online Consumer Privacy: An Analysis of Hotel Company Behavior . *The Cornell Hotel and Restaurant Administration Quarterly, 48*(2), 183–200. doi:10.1177/0010880407299541

Odlyzko, A. (2003). Economics, psychology, and sociology of security. In R. N. Wright (Ed.), *Proceedings of the 7th International Conference on Financial Cryptography (FC 2003)* (LNCS 2742, pp. 182-189).

OECD. (1980). *OECD Guidelines on the Protection of Privacy and Transborder Flows of Personal Data*. Retrieved May 20, 2006, from http://www.oecd.org/document/18/0,2340,en_2649_34255_1815186_1_1_1_1,00.html

OECD. (2003) *Privacy online: Policy and practical guidance.*

Office of the Privacy Commissioner of Canada, & Office of the Information and Privacy Commissioner of Alberta. (2007). *Report of an Investigation into the Security, Collection and Retention of Personal Information: TJX Companies Inc. /Winners Merchant International L.P.*

Office of the Privacy Commissioner of Canada. (2000). [). Ottawa, ON, Canada: Public Works and Government Services Canada - Publishing.]. *Personal Information Protection and Electronic Documents Act, C-6, 2000.*

Oliveira, L., Aranha, D., Morais, E., Felipe, D., Lopez, J., & Dahab, R. (2007). TinyTate: Computing the tate pairing in resource-constrained sensor nodes. NCA 2007. In *Proceedings of the Sixth IEEE International Symposium on Network Computing and Applications* (pp. 318-323).

Oliveira, S., & Zaiane, O. R. (2002). *Privacy Preserving Frequent Itemset Mining.* Paper presented at the IEEE International Conference on Privacy, Security and Data Mining, Maebashi City, Japan.

Olivero, N., & Lunt, P. (2002). Privacy versus willingness to disclose in e-commerce exchanges: The effect of risk awareness on the relative role of trust and control. *Journal of Economic Psychology, 25*, 243–262. doi:10.1016/S0167-4870(02)00172-1

Open Security Foundation. (2009). Data Loss Database - 2009 yearly report.

Orgill, G. L., Romney, G. W., Bailey, M. G., & Orgill, P. M. (2004). The urgency for effective user privacy-education to counter social engineering attacks on secure computer systems. In *Proceedings of the 5th Conference on Information Technology Education* (pp. 177-181). New York NY, USA: ACM Press.

Orman, H. (1998). *The OAKLEY key determination protocol* (RFC 2412). Freemont, CA: IETF.

Outlaw.com. *Email notices and email footers.* Retrieved on September 30, 2008 from: http://www.out-law.com/page-5536

Parish, T. S., & Necessary, J. R. (1996). An examination of cognitive dissonance and computer attitudes. *Educational Technology Research and Development, 116*(4), 565–566.

Park, J. M., Chong, E. K., & Siegel, H. J. (2003). Constructing fair exchange protocols for e-commerce via distributed computation of RSA signatures. *Proceedings of 22nd Annual ACM Symposium on Principles Distributed Computing (PODC)*, pp. 172-181. New York: ACM press.

Parker, D. B. (1996). Information Security Controls for an Organization Undergoing Radical Changes. *Information Systems Security, 5*(3), 21–25.

Parsky, L. (2006). 5318, the "Cyber-Security Enhancement and Consumer Data Protection Act of 2006". In *Committee on the Judiciary Subcommittee on Crime, Terrorism and Homeland Security, U.S. House of Representatives.* Legislative Hearing on H.R.

Patil, S., & Kobsa, A. (2009). Privacy Considerations in Awareness Systems: Designing with Privacy in Mind In P. Markopoulos, B. De Ruyter & W. Mackay (Eds.), *Awareness Systems: Advances in Theory, Methodology and Design* (pp. 187-206). London: Springer.

Patrick, A. S., Long, A. C., & Flinn, S. (2003). HCI and security systems. In *Conference on Human Factors in Computing Systems* (pp. 1056-1057). New York NY, USA: ACM Press.

PCI Compliance Guide. (2008). *PCI DSS: Five Guidelines for Gaining PCI Compliance.*

PCI Security Standard Council. (2006). *Payment Card Industry (PCI).* Wakefield, MA: Data Security Standard.

PCI Security Standards Council. (2010). *PCI DSS 2.0 and PA-DSS 2.0 SUMMARY OF CHANGES - HIGHLIGHTS.* Retrieved September 4, 2010, from https://www.pcisecuritystandards.org/pdfs/summary_of_changes_highlights.pdf

Pereira, S., Voloshynovskiy, S., & Pun, T. (2000). Optimized wavelet domain watermark embedding strategy using linear programming . In Szu, H. (Ed.), *SPIE Aerosense 2000: Wavelet Applications VII.*

Perkins, E., & Markel, M. (2004). Multinational Data-Privacy Laws: An Introduction for IT Managers. *IEEE Transactions on Professional Communication, 47*(2), 85–94. doi:10.1109/TPC.2004.828207

Perrig, A., Szewczyk, R., Tygar, J. D., Wen, V., & Culler, D. E. (2002). SPINS: Security protocols for sensor networks. *Wireless Networks, 8*(5), 521–534. doi:10.1023/A:1016598314198

Petersen, A. (2001). Private Matters: It seems that trust equals revenue, even online. *Wall Street Journal, R24,* R31.

Pikkarainen, T., Pikkarainen, K., Karjaluoto, H., & Pahnila, S. (2004). Consumer acceptance of online banking: An extension of the technology acceptance model. *Internet Research, 14*(3), 224–235. doi:10.1108/10662240410542652

Piotrowski, K., Langendoerfer, P., & Peter, S. (2006). How public key cryptography influences wireless sensor node lifetime. In *Proceedings of the fourth ACM workshop on Security of ad hoc and sensor networks.*

Pontus, E., & Erik, J. (2008). Assessment of business process information security. *International Journal of Business Process Integration and Management, 3*(2), 118–130. doi:10.1504/IJBPIM.2008.020975

Porter, M. E. (1998). *Competitive Strategy: Techniques for Analyzing Industries and Competitors.* New York: Free Press

Portney, L. G., & Watkins, M. P. (1993). *Foundations of Clinical Research, Applications to Practice.* Norwalk, CT: Appletop & Lange.

Posner, R. A. (2008, Winter). Privacy, surveillance, and law. *The University of Chicago Law Review. University of Chicago. Law School, 75,* 245–260.

Powell, R. (2001, February). DM Review: A 10 Year Journey. *DM Review.* Retrieved from http://www.dmreview.com

Preibusch, S., Hoser, B., Gurses, S., & Berendt, B. (2007). *Ubiquitous social networks – opportunities and challenges for privacy-aware user modelling.* Berlin, Germany: German Institute for Economic Research.

PricewaterhouseCoopers. (2008). *The Global State of Information Security Survey 2008.* http://www.pwc.com/extweb/home.nsf/docid/c1cd6cc69c2676d-4852574da00785949.

Princeton Survey Research Associates International. (2005). *Leap of Faith: Using the Internet Despite the Dangers.* Yonkers, NY: Consumer Reports Web Watch.

Privacy Commissioner of Canada. (2006). *Home Page - Privacy Commissioner of Canada.* Retrieved from http://www.privcom.gc.ca/index_e.asp

Privacy International. (2004a). *PHR 2004 - The Russian Federation.*

Privacy International. (2004b). *The Republic of Korea.* Retrieved from http://www.privacyinternational.org/article.shtml?cmd[347]=x-347-83785

Privacy Protection Study Commission. (1977). Personal Privacy in an Information Society.

Privacy Rights Clearinghouse. (2007, February 24). A chronology of data breaches.

Qiao, L., & Nahrstedt, K. (1997). A new algorithm for MPEG video encryption. *Proceedings of CISST'97 international conference, 21-29.*

Quelch, J. A., & Klien, L. R. (1996). The internet and international marketing. *Sloan Management Review,* 60–75.

Ragnathan, C., & Grandon, E. (2002). An Exploratory Examination of Factors Affecting Online Sales. *Journal of Computer Information Systems,* 87–93.

Rajan, M. T. S. (2002). The Past and Future of Privacy in Russia. *Review of Central and East European Law, 4,* 625–638.

Ramsdell, B. (2004). *Secure/multipurpose internet mail extensions (S/MIME) version 3.1 message specification* (RFC 3851). Retrieved from https://www3.ietf.org/rfc/rfc3851.txt

Ray, I., & Ray, I. (2002, May). Fair Exchange in E-commerce. *ACM SIGecom Exchange, 3*(2), 9–17. doi:10.1145/844340.844345

Reay, I., Beatty, P., Dick, S., & Miller, J. (2007). A Survey and Analysis of the P3P Protocol's Agents, Adoption, Maintenance and Future. *IEEE Transactions on Dependable and Secure Computing, 4*(2), 151–164. doi:10.1109/TDSC.2007.1004

Reay, I., Dick, S., & Miller, J. (2009a). An Analysis of Privacy Signals on the World Wide Web: Past, Present and Future. *Information Sciences, 179*(8), 1102–1115. doi:10.1016/j.ins.2008.12.012

Reay, I., Dick, S., & Miller, J. (2009b). A Large-Scale Empirical Study of Online Privacy Policies: Stated Actions Vs. Legal Obligations. *ACM Transactions on the Web, 3*(2), 34. doi:10.1145/1513876.1513878

Redwine, D. B. (1991). Conservative laparoscopic excision of endometriosis by sharp dissection: Life table analysis of reoperation and persistent or recurrent disease. *Fertility and Sterility, 56*(4), 628–634.

Ren, S., Mu, D., Zhang, T., & Hu, W. (2009). Study of Information Hiding Algorithm based on GHM and Color Transfer Theory. *Optoelectronics Letters, 5*(6), 454–458. doi:10.1007/s11801-009-9135-2

Ren, J., Xia, Y., & Ma, Z. (2009). Information Hiding Algorithm Based on Predictive Coding, Proceedings of the 2009 International Conference on Information Technology and Computer Science, 2, 11-14.

Rey, C., & Dugelay, J. (2002). A survey of watermarking algorithms for image authentication. *EURASIP Journal on Applied Signal Processing,* (6): 613–621. doi:10.1155/S1110865702204047

Rezgui, Y., & Marks, A. (2008). Information security awareness in higher education: An exploratory study. *Computers & Security, 27,* 241–253. doi:10.1016/j.cose.2008.07.008

RFC 2821 Simple Mail Transfer Protocol. Retrieved on October 1, 2008 from: http://www.ietf.org/rfc/rfc2821.txt

RFC 2822 Internet Message Format. Retrieved on October 1, 2008 from: http://www.ietf.org/rfc/rfc2822.txt

RFC 4406 Sender ID: Authenticating E-Mail. Retrieved on October 1, 2008 from: http://www.ietf.org/rfc/rfc4406.txt

RFC 4407 Purported Responsible Address in E-Mail Messages. Retrieved on October 1, 2008 from: http://www.ietf.org/rfc/rfc4407.txt

RFC 4408. Sender Policy Framework (SPF) for Authorizing Use of Domains in E-Mail

RFC 822 Standard for the format of ARPA Internet text messages. Retrieved October 10, 2008 from: http://www.ietf.org/rfc/rfc0822.txt

Richardson, J. E., & McCord, L. B. (2000). *Trust in the marketplace. Annual Editions: Business Ethics 2008/2009 20/e.* New York: McGraw-Hill.

Richardson, R. (2007). *CSI Survey 2007: The 12th Annual Computer Crime and Security Survey.* Computer Security Institution.

Richardson, R. (2009). *CSI Survey 2008: The 14th Annual Computer Crime and Security Survey.* Computer Security Institution.

Richardson, R. (2007). CSI Computer Crime and Security Survey. *Computer Security Institute.* Available from http://gocsi.com. Visited January 16, 2008.

Richmond, R. (2005, December 1). Banks seek better online security tools. *Wall Street Journal.*

Rizvi, S., & Haritsa, J. R. (2002). *Maintaining Data Privacy in Association Rule Mining.* Paper presented at the VLDB.

Rogers, E. M. (1962). *Diffusion of Innovation.* New York: Free Press.

Romney, V. W., & Romney, G. W. (2004). *Neglect of information privacy instruction: A case of educational malpractice?* Paper presented at the SIGITE '04, Salt Lake City, UT.

Ross, A. (2008). *Security engineering: A guide to building dependable distributed systems* (2nd ed.). New York: Wiley.

Ross, B., Jackson, C., Miyake, N., Boneh, D., & Mitchell, J. (2005). *Stronger password authentication using browser extensions*. Paper presented at the 14th USENIX Security Symposium.

Rothberg, D. (2006). *IT Pros Say They Can't Stop Data Breaches*. http://www.eweek.com/article2/0,1895,2010325,00.asp?kc=EWSTEEMNL083106EOAD, August 30, 2006. Visited July 29, 2008.

Russell, S. J., & Norvig, P. (2002). *Artificial Intelligence: A Modern Approach* (2nd ed.). Upper Saddle River, NJ: Prentice Hall

Sadeh, N., Hong, J., Cranor, L., Fette, I., Kelley, P., & Prabaker, M. (2008). Understanding and Capturing People's Privacy Policies in a People Finder Application. *Journal of Personal and Ubiquitous Computing, 13*(6), 401–412. doi:10.1007/s00779-008-0214-3

Salutation Consortium. (1999). Salutation architecture specification. Retrieved from ftp://ftp.salutation.org/salute/sa20e1a21.ps

Samarati, P. (2001). Protecting Respondents' Identities in Microdata Release. *TKDE, 13*(6), 1010–1027.

Schaber, P., Kopf, S., Effelsberg, W., & Thorwirth, N. (2010). Semi-automatic registration of videos for improved watermark detection. *Proceedings of the First Annual ACM SIGMM Conference on Multimedia Systems* (Phoenix, Arizona, USA, February 22-23, 2010). MMSys '10. ACM, New York, NY, 23-34.

Scharinger, J. (1998). Fast encryption of image data using chaotic Kolmogorov flows. *Journal of Electronic Imaging, 7*(2), 318–325. doi:10.1117/1.482647

Schatz, D. (2008). Setting priorities in your security program . In Tipton, H. F., & Krause, K. (Eds.), *Information Security Management Handbook*. Boca Raton, FL: Taylor & Francis Group.

Schindler, R. G. (2001). Balancing information technology benefits with privacy and security concerns. *Journal of Healthcare Compliance, 3*(6), 44–44.

Schlauweg, M., Mueller, E., Proefrock, D., & Richter, H. (2005). H.264/AVC video authentication using skipped macroblocks for an erasable watermark . *Proceedings of SPIE International Conference on Visual Communication and Image Processing, 5960*, 1480–1489.

Schlauweg, M., Pröfrock, D., Zeibich, B., & Müller, E. (2006). *Dual watermarking for the protection of rightful ownership and secure image authentication*. Proceedings of MCPS'06 conference, 59-66.

Schmidt, M. B., Johnston, A. C., Arnett, K. P., Chen, J. Q., & Xi'an, S. L. (2008). A cross-cultural comparison of U.S. and Chinese computer security awareness. *Journal of Global Information Management, 16*(2), 91–103.

Schneier, B. (2005, March 15). The failure of two-factor authentication. *Crypto-Gram Newsletter*. Retrieved from http://www.schneier.com/crypto-gram-0503.html

Schneier, B. (December 14, 2006). Passwords Aren't So Dumb. Wired News.

Scholl, M., Scholl, K., Hash, J., Bowen, P., Johnson, A., & Smith, C. D. (2008). *An Introductory Resource Guide for Implementing the Health Insurance Portability and Accountability Act (HIPAA) Security Rule*. Retrieved from http://csrc.nist.gov/publications/nistpubs/800-66-Rev1

Searchsecurity.techtarget.com. *DomainKeys Definition*. Retrieved on October 23, 20087 from: http://www.searchsecurity.techtarget.com

Security Space. (2006). *P3P Compact Privacy Policy Report*. Burlington, ON, Canada: Author.

Security, R. S. A. (2004). *Protecting against phishing by implementing strong two-factor authentication.* Retrieved from http://www.antiphishing.org/sponsors_technical_papers/PHISH_WP_0904.pdf

Seffers, G. (2000, November 2). *DOD database to fight cybercrime.* Federal Computer Week.

Seltzer, L. (2008). Can you trust TRUSTe? *PC Magazine Security Watch.* March 24, 2008, http://blogs.pcmag.com/securitywatch/2008/03/can_you_trust_truste.php. Visited July 29, 2008.

Shafer, J. (2004, June 1). E-mail Confidential. *Who's afraid of Time Inc.'s legal disclaimer?* Retrieved on September 30, 2008 from: http://slate.com/id/2101561/

Shalyto, A. (1991). Programmatic Implementation of control automata //Marine industry *Automation and Remote Control, 13,* 41-42.

Shamir, A. (1984). Identity-based cryptosystems and signature . In *Proceedings of Cryptology* (pp. 47–53). Berlin, Germany: Springer-Verlag.

Shane, S. A. (1993). Cultural influences on national rates of innovation. *Journal of Business Venturing, 8*(1), 59–73. doi:10.1016/0883-9026(93)90011-S

Shapiro, B., & Baker, C. R. (2001). Information technology and the social construction of information privacy. *Journal of Accounting and Public Policy, 20,* 295–322. doi:10.1016/S0278-4254(01)00037-0

Shaw, T. R. (2003). The Moral Intensity of Privacy: An Empirical Study of Webmasters' Attitudes. *Journal of Business Ethics, 46*(4), 301–318. doi:10.1023/A:1025628530013

Sheskin, D. J. (2004). *Handbook of Parametric and NonParametric Statistical Procedures* (3rd ed.). Boca Raton, FL: Chapman and Hall/CRC.

Sheth, J. N., & Pravatiyar, A. (2000). Relationship marketing in customer markets: antecedents and consequences . In *Handbook of Relationship Marketing.* Thousand Oaks: Sage.

Shi, C., & Bhargava, B. (1998a). A fast MPEG video encryption algorithm. *ACM Multimedia, 98,* 81–88.

Shi, C., & Bhargava, B. B. (1998b). An efficient MPEG video encryption algorithm. *Proceedings of the symposium on reliable distributed systems,* 381-386.

Shie, S. C., Lin, S. D., & Jiang, J. H. (2010). Visually imperceptible image hiding scheme based on vector quantization . *Information Processing & Management, 46,* 495–501. doi:10.1016/j.ipm.2009.07.001

Shift4 Corporation. (2008). *Credit Card 101.* Retrieved September 4, 2010, from http://www.shift4.com/players.htm

Shilton, K., Burke, J., Estrin, D., Hansen, M., & Srivastava, M. (2008, April 21). *Participatory privacy in urban sensing.* Presented at the International Workshop on Mobile Device and Urban Sensing (MODUS 2008), St. Louis, MO, Smith, H. J., & Milberg, S. J. (1996, June). Information privacy: measuring individuals' concerns about organizational practices. *Management Information Systems Quarterly, 20*(2), 167–196.

Shoeman, M. A., & Cloete, E. (2003). Architectural Components for the Efficient Design of Mobile Agent System. In *Proceedings of SAICSIT* (pp. 48-58).

Shrout, P. E., & Fleiss, J. L. (1979). Intraclass Correlations: Uses in Assessing Rater Reliability . *Psychological Bulletin, 86,* 420–428. doi:10.1037/0033-2909.86.2.420

Singh, K. M., Singh, S. B., & Singh, S. S. (2007). Hiding encrypted message in the features of images. *International journal of computer science and network security (IJCSNS), 7* (4).

Singh, S., Cabraal, A., & Hermansson, G. (2006). What is your husband's name? Sociological dimensions of internet banking authentication. In *Proceedings of the 20th conference of the computer-human interaction special interest group (CHISIG) of Australia on Computer-human interaction: design: activities, artefacts and environments* (pp. 237-244). New York, USA: ACM Press.

Smith, H. J., Milberg, S., & Burke, S. (1996). Information Privacy: Measuring Individuals Concerns About Organizational Practices. *Management Information Systems Quarterly, 20*(6), 167–196. doi:10.2307/249477

Smith, J. *How You Can Avoid The New Dangers Of Spam.* Retrieved on September 30, 2008 from: http://www. ezinearticles.com/?How-You-Can-Avoid-The-New-Dangers-Of-Spam&id=40253

So, M. W. C., & Sculli, D. (2002). The role of trust, quality, value and risk in conducting e-business. *Industrial Management & Data Systems, 102*(9), 503–512. doi:10.1108/02635570210450181

Socek, D., Li, S., Magliveras, S. S., & Furht, B. (2005). Short paper: enhanced 1-d chaotic key-based algorithm for image encryption. *First international conference on security and privacy for emerging areas in communications networks.*

Solove, D. J. (2006, January). A Taxonomy of privacy. *University of Pennsylvania Law Review, 154*(3), 477–560. doi:10.2307/40041279

Song, J. H., Lee, J., & Iwata, T. (2006). *The AES-CMAC algorithm* (RFC 4493). Retrieved from http://www.ietf. org/rfc/rfc4493.txt

Souppaya, M., Wack, J. P., & Kent, K. (2005). *Security Configuration Checklists Program for IT Products – Guidance for Checklists Users and Developers* (NIST Special Publication No. 800-70). Gaithersburg, MD: NIST.

SpamLaws.com. CAN-SPAM Act. Public Law 108–187—DEC. 16, 2003. Retrieved on October 10, 2008 from: http://www.spamlaws.com/f/pdf/pl108-187.pdf

Spanish Data Protection Authority. (2006). *Agencia Espanola De Proteccion De Datos.* Retrieved from https://www.agpd.es/index.php?idSeccion=8

Spanos, G. A., & Maples, T. B. (1995). Performance study of a selective encryption scheme for the security of networked, real-time video. *Proceedings of the 4th IEEE international conference on computer communications and networks (ICCCN '95),* 2-10.

Spinello, R. A. (1998). Privacy Rights in the information economy. *Business Ethics Quarterly, 8*(4), 723–742. doi:10.2307/3857550

Squillante, N. J. *Is Your Company CAN-SPAM Compliant?* Retrieved on October 10, 2008 from: http://www. marketingprofs.com/4/squillante3.asp?part=2

Srite, M., & Karahanna, E. (2006). The role of espoused national cultural values in technology acceptance. *Management Information Systems Quarterly, 30*(3), 679–704.

Stajano, F., & Anderson, R. (1999). *The resurrecting duckling: Security issues for ad-hoc wireless networks.* Paper presented at the 7th International Workshop on Security protocols, Cambridge, UK.

Stallings, W. (2006). *Cryptography and network security* (4th ed.). Upper Saddle River, NJ: Prentice Hall. ISBN 0-13-187316-4.

Stallings, W. (2007). *Network security essentials* (3rd ed.). Upper Saddle River, NJ: Prentice Hall. ISBN 0-13-238033-1.

Stanton, J. M., Stam, K. R., Mastrangelo, P., & Jolton, J. (2005). Analysis of end user security behaviors. *Computers & Security, 24*(2), 124–133. doi:10.1016/j.cose.2004.07.001

Stanton, J. M., Nemati, H., Chun, S. A., & Chen, J. V. (2007, August 09 - 12) Privacy in the YouTube era: Evolving concepts in the protection of personal information. *Proceedings of the Thirteenth Americas Conference on Information Systems (AMCIS),* Keystone, Colorado.

Stelter, B. (2008, November 27). Guilty verdict in cyberbullying case provokes many questions over online identity. New York: *The New York Times.*

Stevens, M., Lenstra, A., & de Weger, B. (Nov. 30, 2007). Vulnerability of software integrity and code signing applications to chosen-prefix collisions for MD5. http://www.win.tue.nl/hashclash/SoftIntCodeSign/ Last Accessed Dec. 2008

Stoll, R. R. (1979). *Set Theory and Logic.* Mineola, NY: Dover Publications.

Straub, D. W., Loch, K. D., & Hill, C. E. (2001). Transfer of Information Technology to Developing Countries: A Test of Cultural Influence Modeling in the Arab World. *Journal of Global Information Management, 9*(4), 6–28.

Straub, D. W., Goodman, S., & Baskerville, R. (2008). Framing of Information Security Policies and Practice. In, D. W. Straub, S. Goodman, and R. Baskerville, Eds., (ed) *Information Security Policies, Processes, and Practices.* Armonk, NY: M. E. Sharpe.

Su, W., & Almaharmeh, B. (2008). QoS integration of the internet and wireless sensor networks. W. *Trans. on Comp., 7*(4), 253–258.

Su, Y. T., Hu, Y., & Zhang, C. T. (2007) Information hiding based on intraprediction modes for H.264/AVC. *InProceedings of IEEE International Conference on Multimedia and Expo.* 2007, 1231–1234.

Sumner, M. (2009). Information Security Threats: A comparative analysis of impact, probability, and preparedness. *Information Systems Management, 26*(1), 2–12. doi:10.1080/10580530802384639

Sun, L.-T. (1994). Government as an institution for human fulfillment. *Humanomics, 10*(4), 76–101. doi:10.1108/eb018758

Sun Microsystems. (2003). *Jini technology core platform specification.* Retrieved from http://wwws.sun.com/software/jini/specs/

Swanson, M. D., Zhu, B., & Tewfik, A. H. (1997). Data hiding for video-in-video. *Proceedings of the 1997 international conference on image processing (ICIP '97), 2,* 676-679.

Swartz, N. (2003). What every business needs to know about HIPAA. *Information Management Journal, 37*(2), 26–34.

Swedish Data Inspection Board. (2006). *Swedish Data Inspection Board - Information in English - Datainspektionen.* Retrieved from http://www.datainspektionen.se/in_english/start.shtml

Swindle, O. (2000). Dissenting statement of Commissioner Orson Swindle. In *Privacy Online: Fair Information Practices in the Electronic Marketplace, A Report to Congress* 2, Washington D.C.

Swire, P. P. (1997). Markets, self regulation and government enforcement in the protection of personal information . In *Privacy and self-regulation in the information age* (pp. 3–19). Washington, DC: US Department of Commerce.

Swoyer, S. (2008). *SQL Injection Attacks on the Rise.* Retrieved September 4, 2010, from http://redmondmag.com/articles/2008/08/13/sql-injection-attacks-on-the-rise.aspx?sc_lang=en

Szczechowiak, P., & Collier, M. (2009). TinyIBE: Identity-Based Encryption for Heterogeneous Sensor Networks. In *5th International Conference on Intelligent Sensors, Sensor Networks and Information Processing.* 319-354.

Szczechowiak, P., Kargl, A., Scott, M., & Collier. (2009). On the Application of Pairing Based Cryptography to Wireless Sensor Networks. In *WiSec '09, Second ACM conference on Wireless Network Security.* 1-12.

Takahashi, D. (2007, January 30). Demo: Aggregate knowledge knows what you want to buy. *San Jose Mercury News.*

Tally, G., Thomas, R., Van, V., & Ieck, T. (2004). *Antiphishing: Best practices for institutions and consumers.* Retrieved from http://www.antiphishing.org/sponsors_technical_papers/Anti-Phishing_Best_Practices_for_Institutions_Consumer0904.pdf

Tam, P.-W., & Sidel, R. (2007, Oct 2nd). Business Technology: Security-Software Industry's Miniboom; As Merchants Upgrade Systems to Meet New Rules, Tech Firms Benefit. *Wall Street Journal.*

Tan, Y., & Thoen, W. (2001). Toward a Generic Model of Trust for Electronic Commerce. *International Journal of Electronic Commerce, 5*(2), 61–74.

Tang, Z., Hu, Y., & Smith, M. (2008). Gaining trust through online privacy protection: Self-regulation, mandatory standards, or *caveat emptor. Journal of Management Information Systems, 24*(4), 153–173. doi:10.2753/MIS0742-1222240406

Tang, L. (1996). Methods for encrypting and decrypting MPEG video data efficiently. *ACM Multimedia, 96,* 219–229.

Tari, F., Ozok, A. A., & Holden, S. H. (2006). A comparison of perceived and real shoulder-surfing risks between alphanumeric and graphical passwords. In *SOUPS '06: Proceedings of The Second Symposium on Usable Privacy and Security* (pp. 56-66). New York NY, USA: ACM Press.

Taylor, S., & Todd, P. (1995). Assessing IT usage: The role of prior experience. *Management Information Systems Quarterly, 19*(4), 561–570. doi:10.2307/249633

Taylor, P. A. (1999). *Hackers: Crime in the Digital Sublime*. New York: Routledge. doi:10.4324/9780203201503

Tedrick, T. (1983). How to exchange half a bit. In Chaum, D. (Ed.), *Advances in Cryptology: Proceedings of Crypto 83* (pp. 147–151). New York, London: Plenum Press.

Tedrick, T. (1985). Fair exchange of secrets. In G. R. Blakley, D. C. Chaum (Eds.), *Advances in Cryptology: Proceedings of Crypto 84, Vol. 196 of Lecture Notes in Computer Science*. Berlin, Germany: Springer-Verlag, (pp. 434–438).

The Honeynet Project & Research Alliance. (2005). *Know your enemy: Phishing – behind the scenes of phishing attacks*. Retrieved from http://www.honeynet.org/papers/phishing/

Thiagarajan, V. (2003). *Information Security Management BS 7799.2:2002 Audit Check List.* Retrieved from http://www.sans.org/score/checklists/ISO_17799_checklist.pdf

Thiesse, F. (2007). RFID, privacy and the perception of risk: A strategic framework. *The Journal of Strategic Information Systems, 16,* 214–232. doi:10.1016/j.jsis.2007.05.006

Thiesse, F., Floerkemeier, C., & Fleisch, E. (2007, August 09 - 12). Assessing the impact of privacy-enhancing technologies for RFID in the retail industry. *Proceedings of the Thirteenth Americas Conference on Information Systems,* Keystone, Colorado.

Thomas, D. (2002). *Hacker Culture*. Minneapolis, MN: University of Minnesota Press.

Thomas, P. R. (2003). *Preparing for ISO 17799.* Retrieved from http://www.uaslp.mx/PDF/2042_183.pdf

Thompson, R. L., Higgins, C. A., & Howell, J. M. (1994). Influence of experience on personal computer utilization: Testing a conceptual model. *Journal of Management Information Systems, 11*(1), 167–188.

Tian, J. (2003). Reversible data embedding using a difference expansion . *IEEE Transactions on Circuits and Systems for Video Technology, 13*(8), 890–896. doi:10.1109/TCSVT.2003.815962

TJX Companies, I. (2007). The TJX Companies, Inc. Announces Settlement Agreement with Visa U.S.A. Inc. and Visa Inc.; Estimated Costs Already Reflected in Previously Announced Charge. *Business Wire.*

Trompennaars, F. (1993). *Riding the Waves of Culture*. London: The Economist Books.

Truste.org. (2006). *TRUSTe - Make Privacy Your Choice.* Retrieved from http://www.truste.org/

Trustwave. (2008). *Trustwave Global Compromise Statistics: Quarterly Report March, 2008* Chicago, IL, USA.

Tschabitscher, H. *How Many Emails Are Sent Every Day?* Retrieved on September 2008 from: http://email.about.com/od/emailtrivia/f/emails_per_day.htm

Tufekci, Z. (2008). Can you see me now? Audience and disclosure management in online social network sites. *Bulletin of Science and Technology Studies, 11*(4), 544–564.

Tukkel, N., & Shalyto, A. (2001). State-Based Programming. *PC World, 8,* 116–121.

Turow, J., Feldman, L., & Meltzer, K. (2005). *Open To Exploitation: American Shoppers Online and Offline.* Philadelphia: University of Pennsylvania's Annenberg School for Communication.

U.S Supreme court, Olmstead v. U.S., 277 U.S. 438 (1928).

Vaidya, J. S., & Clifton, C. (2002). Privacy preserving association rule mining in vertically partitioned data. In *Proceedings of the 8th ACM SIGKDD International Conference on Knowledge Discovery and Data Mining* (pp. 639-644).

Vaidya, J., Clifton, C., & Zhu, Y. (2006). *Privacy Preserving Data Mining.* New York: Springer.

Vallerand, R. J. (1997). Toward a Hierarchical Model of Intrinsic and Extrinsic Motivation. [). New York: Academic Press.]. *Advances in Experimental Social Psychology, 29*, 271–360. doi:10.1016/S0065-2601(08)60019-2

Varian, H., Wallenberg, F., & Woroch, G. (2005). The Demographics of the Do-Not-Call List. *IEEE Security and Privacy, 3*(1), 34–39. doi:10.1109/MSP.2005.28

Venkatesh, V., Morris, M. G., Davis, G. B., & Davis, F. D. (2003). User acceptance of information technology: Toward a unified view. *Management Information Systems Quarterly, 27*(3), 425–478.

Verisign. (2008). *VeriSign - Security (SSL Certificates), Intelligent Communications, and Identity Protection.* Retrieved from http://www.verisign.com/

Verykios, V. S., Elmagarmid, A. K., Elisa, B., Saygin, Y., & Elena, D. (2004). Association Rule Hiding. *IEEE Transactions on Knowledge and Data Engineering, 16*(4), 434–447. doi:10.1109/TKDE.2004.1269668

VISA USA. (2006). *VISA USA Pledges $20 Million in Incentive to Protect Card Holder Data.* Retrieved September 4, 2010, from http://corporate.visa.com/media-center/press-releases/press667.jsphttp://corporate.visa.com/media-center/press-releases/press667.jsp

VISA USA. (2007a). *Level 4 Merchant Compliance Program.* Retrieved September 4, 2010, from http://usa.visa.com/download/merchants/level_4_merchant_compliance_program_062807.pdf

VISA USA. (2007b). *VISA Incorporation Card Holder Information Security Program.* Retrieved September 4, 2010, from http://usa.visa.com/merchants/risk_management/cisp_overview.html

VISA USA. (2008). *Visa USA Cardholder Information Security Program (CISP): PCI DSS Compliance Validation Update as of 12/31/2007.* Retrieved September 4, 2010, from http://www.usa.visa.com/download/merchants/cisp_pcidss_compliancestats.pdf

Wagner, M. (2001, November) *How CrystalWare looked in-house to serve a volatile inventory of china to web customers.* Retrieved on September 21, 2008 from: http://www.internetretailer.com/internet/marketing-conference/

Walczuch, R. M., Singh, S. K., & Palmer, T. S. (1995). An analysis of the cultural motivations for transborder data flow legislation. *Information Technology & People, 8*(2), 37–57. doi:10.1108/09593849510087994

Waller, J. M. (2002, December 24). Fears mount over 'total' spy system: Civil libertarians and privacy-rights advocates are fearful of a new federal database aimed at storing vast quantities of personal data to identify terrorist threats – Nation: homeland security. *Insight Magazine.*

Walter, S. D., Eliasziw, M., & Donner, A. (1998). Sample size and optimal designs for reliability studies. *Statistics in Medicine, 17*(1), 101–110. doi:10.1002/(SICI)1097-0258(19980115)17:1<101::AID-SIM727>3.0.CO;2-E

Walton, S. (1995). Information authentication for a slippery new age. *Dr. Dobbs Journal, 20*(4), 18–26.

Wander, A., Gura, N., Eberle, H., Gupta, V., & Shantz, S. (2005, March). *Energy analysis of public-key cryptography for wireless sensor networks.* Paper presented at the Third IEEE International Conference on Pervasive Computing and Communication (PerCom 2005), Hawaii.

Wang, C. M., & Cheng, Y. M. (2005). An Efficient Information Hiding Algorithm for Polygon Models. *Computer Graphics Forum*, 24(3), 591–600. doi:10.1111/j.1467-8659.2005.00884.x

Wang, W-T., Ssu, K-F., & Chang, W-C. (2010). Defending Sybil attacks based on neighboring relations in wireless sensor networks, *Security and Communication Networks*, n/a. doi: 10.1002/sec.197.

Wang, X. Y., Yin, Y. Q., & Yu, H. B. (2005). *Finding collisions in the full SHA-1*. Paper presented at the 25th Annual International Cryptology Conference, Santa Barbara, California, USA

Watro, R., Kong, D., Cuti, S., Gardiner, C., Lynn, C., & Kruus, P. (2004). Tinypk: Securing sensor networks with public key technology. In *Proceedings of the Second ACM Workshop on Security of Ad-hoc and Sensor Networks (SASN'04),* Washington, DC (pp. 59-64).

Watt, A. (2005). *Beginning Regular Expressions*. Indianapolis, IN: Wiley Publishing, Inc.

Wayne, C. (2000). Multilingual Topic Detection and Tracking: Successful Research Enabled by Corpora and Evaluatio, Language Resources and Evaluation Conference (LREC), 1487-1494.

WebTrust. (2006). *WebTrust / SysTrust*. Retrieved from http://www.webtrust.org/

Weirich, D., & Sasse, M. A. (2001). Pretty good persuasion: A first step towards effective password security in the real world. In *NSPW '01: Proceedings of the 2001 Workshop on New Security Paradigms* (pp. 137-143). New York, USA: ACM Press.

Weiser, B. (2008, November 19). *Murder suspect has witness: A MetroCard*. New York: The New York Times.

Weissmann, C. (1969). Security controls in the ADEPT-50 timesharing system. In *AFIPS Conference Proceedings* (pp. 119-133). Santa Monica CA, USA: System Development Corporation.

Wenning, R., & Cranor, L. (2006). *The Platform for Privacy Preferences (P3P) Project*. Retrieved February 21, 2007, from http://www.w3.org/P3P/

Wernick, A. S. (2006, December). Data Theft and State Law. *Journal of American Health Information Management Association*, 40–44.

Westin, A. (1967). *Privacy and Freedom* (p. 487). NY: Atheneum.

Westin, A. (1967). *Privacy and Freedom*. New York: Atheneum.

White, J. E. (1994). *Telescript Technology: The Foundation for the Electronic Marketplace*. Mountain View, CA: General Magic Inc.

Whittaker, S., & Sidner, C. (1997). E-mail overload: exploring personal information management of e-mail . In Kiesler, S. (Ed.), *Culture of the Internet* (pp. 277–295). Mahwah, NJ: Erlbaum.

Wikipedia. *Computer virus* Retrieved on September 30, 2008 from: http://en.wikipedia.org/wiki/Computer_virus

Wikipedia.org. (2008). *Compliance*. Retrieved from http://en.wikipedia.org/

Wikipedia.org. *Email Privacy*. Retrieved on September 30, 2008 from: http://en.wikipedia.org/wiki/E-mail_privacy

Wikipedia.org. *Procmail*. Retrieved on October 10, 2008 from: http://en.wikipedia.org/wiki/Procmail

Williams, C., & Ferris, D. The Cost of Spam False Positives. Ferris Research Report #385, 2003.

Williams, P. (2001). *Russian Organized Crime, Russina Hacking, and U. S. Security* [Electronic Version]. Retrieved September 25, 2008, from http://www.cert.org/research/isw/isw2001/papers/Williams-06-09.pdf

Wilson, R. L., & Rosen, P. A. (2003). Protecting Data Through 'Perturbation' Techniques: The Impact on Knowledge Discovery in Databases. *Journal of Database Management*, 14(2), 14–26.

Wolfgang, R. & Delp, E. (1999). Fragile watermarking using the VW2D watermark. *Security and* Watermarking of Multimedia Contents, 3657 of SPIE Proceedings, 40–51.

Wong, J., Helmer, G., Naganathan, V., Polavarapu, S., Honovar, L., & Miller, L. (2001). SMART Mobile Agent Facility. *Journal of Systems and Software, 56*, 9–22. doi:10.1016/S0164-1212(00)00082-0

Woon, I. M. Y., & Kankanhalli, A. (2007). Investigation of IS professionals' intention to practise secure development of applications. *International Journal of Human-Computer Studies, 65*(1), 29–41. doi:10.1016/j.ijhcs.2006.08.003

Wordsmith (2003). http://wordsmith.org/awad/archives/0303. Quote from Oliver Wendell Holmes, Jr. visited September 15, 2007.

Wright, B. (2004). Internet break-ins: New legal liability. *Computer Law & Security Report, 20*(3), 171–175. doi:10.1016/S0267-3649(04)00032-9

Wu, D. C., & Tsai, W. H. (1998). Data hiding in images via multiple-based number conversion and lossy compression. *IEEE Transactions on Consumer Electronics, 44*(4), 1406–1412. doi:10.1109/30.735844

Wu, M. N., Lin, C. C., & Chang, C. C. (2008). An embedding technique based upon block prediction . *Journal of Systems and Software, 81*(9), 1505–1516. doi:10.1016/j.jss.2007.09.017

Wu, G. D., & Huang, P. H. (2007). Image watermarking using structure based wavelet tree quantization. *Proceedings of the 6th IEEE/ACIS International Conference on Computer and Information Science, 2007 (ICIS 2007)*, 315–319.

Wu, X., & Moo, P. W. (1999). Joint image/video compression and encryption via high-order conditional entropy coding of wavelet coefficients. *Proceedings (IEEE) of the international conference on multimedia computing and systems (ICMCS'99), 2*, 908-912.

Xia, X. G., Boncelet, C. G., & Arce, G. R. (1997). A multi-resolution watermark for digital images. *Proceedings of IEEE international conference on image processing, 1*, 548-551.

Xie, J., Agaian, S., & Noonan, J. (2008). Secure information hiding algorithm using parametric slant-Hadamard transforms, Proceedings of the Conference on Mobile Multimedia/Image Processing, Security, and Applications.

Xie, J., Yang, C., Huang, D., & Xie, D. A. (2008). Large Capacity Blind Information Hiding Algorithm, Proceedings of the 2008 International Symposium on Electronic Commerce and Security, 934-937.

Xiong, X., Wong, D., & Deng, X. (2010). TinyPairing: A Fast and Lightweight Pairing-based Cryptographic Library for Wireless Sensor Networks. In *IEEE Wireless Communications and Networking Conference (WCNC)*. 1-6.

Xu, H., Dinev, B., Smith, H., & Hart, P. (2008). Examining the formation of individual's privacy concerns: Toward an integrative view. *International Conference on Information Systems (ICIS), Proceedings.*

Xuan, G., Zhu, J., Chen, J., Shi, Y. Q., Ni, Z., & Su, W. (2002). Distortionless data hiding based on integer wavelet transform . *IEE Electronics Letters, 38*(25), 1646–1648. doi:10.1049/el:20021131

Yahoo. com. *DomainKeys: Proving and Protecting Email Sender Identity.* Retrieved on October 23, 2008 from: http://antispam.yahoo.com/domainkeys.

Yang, Y., Carbonell, J., Brown, R., Pierce, T., Archibald, B. T., & Liu, X. (1999). Learning Approaches for Detecting and Tracking News Events . *IEEE Intelligent Systems: Special Issue on Applications of Intelligent Information Retrieval, 14*(4), 32–43.

Yang, H., & Chiu, H. (2002). Privacy Disclosures of Web Sites in Taiwan. [JITTA]. *Journal of Information Technology Theory and Applications, 4*(3), 15–42.

Yang, B., & Deng, B. (2006). Steganography in gray images using wavelet. *Proceedings of the second international symposium on communication, control and signal processing (ISCCSP).*

Yang, G., Li, J., He, Y. & Kang, Z. (2010). An information hiding algorithm based on intra-prediction modes and matrix coding for H.264/AVC video stream, *International Journal of Electronics and Communications (AEU)*, 2010.

Yang, M., & Bourbakis, N. (2005a). A high bitrate multimedia information hiding algorithm in DCT domain. *Proceedings of the 8th world conference on integrated design and process technology (IDPT 2005)*.

Yang, M., & Bourbakis, N. (2005b). A high bitrate information hiding algorithm for digital video content under H.264/AVC compression. *Proceedings of the IEEE international midwest symposium on circuits and systems (MWSCAS 2005)*.

Yang, M., Trifas, M., Buenos-Aires, D., & Elston, J. (2009). Secure patient information in medical images. *Proceedings of the 13th world multi-conference on systemics, cybernetics and informatics*.

Yang, M., Trifas, M., Truitt, C., & Xiong, G. (2008). Wavelet domain video information embedding. *Proceedings of the 12th world multi-conference on systemics, cybernetics and informatics*.

Yang, Y., Ault, T., Pierce, T., & Lattimer, C. W. (2000). Improving Text Categorization Methods for Event Tracking, *Proceedings of the 23rd International Conference on Research and Development in Information Retrieval (SIGIR-2000)*, 65-72.

Ye, Z., & Smith, S. (2002). Trusted paths for browsers. In *Proceedings of the 11th USENIX Security Symposium* (pp. 263-279).

Younes, M. A., & Jantan, A. (2003). Image encryption using block-based transformation algorithm, *IAENG International Journal of Computer Science, 35* (1).

Young, A., & Quan-Haase, A. (2009, June 25-27). Information revelation and Internet privacy concerns on social network sites: A case study of Facebook, *Proceedings of the 4th International Conference on Communities and Technologies (C&T)*, University Park, PA, 265-274.

Yu, H. Y., Chang, C. C., & Lin, I. C. (2007). A new steganographic method for color and grayscale image hiding. *Computer Vision and Image Understanding, 107*, 183–194. doi:10.1016/j.cviu.2006.11.002

Zadeh, L. (1978). Fuzzy sets as a basis for a theory of possibility. *Fuzzy Sets and Systems*, 28.

Zambo, S. (2007). Digital La Cosa Nostra: The Computer Fraud and Abuse Act's Failure to Punish and Deter Organized Crime. *New England Journal on Criminal and Civil Confinement, 33*(2), 551–575.

Zeller, T., Jr. (2005, March 10). Another data broker reports a breach. New York: *The New York Times.*

Zeller, T., Jr. (2005, May 18). Personal data for the taking. New York: *The New York Times.*[1] This chapter is an enhanced version of the article Pratt, J. & Conger, S. Without permission: Privacy on the line. International Journal of Information Security and Privacy 3(1), 30-44.

Zhang, N., & Shi, Q. (1996). Achieving non-repudiation of receipt. *The Computer Journal, 39*(10), 844–853. doi:10.1093/comjnl/39.10.844

Zhang, N., Wang, S., & Zhao, W. (2004). *A New Scheme on Privacy Preserving Association Rule Mining*. Berlin Heidelberg, Germany: Springer-Verlag.

Zhang, W., Cheung, S., & Chen, M. (2005). Hiding privacy information in video surveillance system. *Proceedings of the international conference on image processing (ICIP '2005), 3*, II- 868-71.

Zhou, J., & Gollmann, D. (1996). A fair non-repudiation protocol. In *IEEE Symposium on Security and Privacy, Research in Security and Privacy*, IEEE Computer Society, Technical Committee on Security and Privacy, IEEE Computer Security Press, Oakland, CA, 1996, (pp. 55–61).

Zhou, J., & Gollmann, D. (1997). An efficient non-repudiation protocol. In *Proceedings of The 10th Computer Security Foundations Workshop*, IEEE Computer Society Press, 1997, (pp. 126–132).

Zhou, J., Deng, R., & Bao, F. (1999). Evolution of fair non-repudiation with TTP. *ACISP: Information Security and Privacy: Australasian Conference*. (Vol. 1587 of Lecture Notes in Computer Science)Springer-Verlag, 1999, (pp. 258–269).

Zhou, K., Quan, T., & Kang, Y. (2008). Study on Information Hiding Algorithm Based on RBF and LSB, Proceedings of the Fourth International Conference on Natural Computation (ICNC '08), 612-614.

Zhu, S., Setia, S., & Jajodia, S. (2006). LEAP: Efficient security mechanisms for large-scale distributed sensor networks. [TOSN]. *ACM Transactions on Sensor Networks*, 2(4), 500–528. doi:10.1145/1218556.1218559

Zhu, F., Mutka, M., & Ni, L. (2005). Service discovery in pervasive computing environments. *IEEE Pervasive Computing / IEEE Computer Society [and] IEEE Communications Society*, 4(4), 81–90. doi:10.1109/MPRV.2005.87

Zhu, F., Mutka, M., & Ni, L. (2006). A private, secure and user-centric information exposure model for service discovery protocols. *IEEE Transactions on Mobile Computing*, 5(4), 418–429. doi:10.1109/TMC.2006.1599409

Zhu, F., Zhu, W., Mutka, M., & Ni, L. (2007). Private and secure service discovery via progressive and probabilistic exposure. *IEEE Transactions on Parallel and Distributed Systems*, 18(11), 1565–1577. doi:10.1109/TPDS.2007.1075

Zhu, F., Mutka, M., & Ni, L. (2003). *Splendor: A secure, private, and location-aware service discovery protocol supporting mobile services*. Paper presented at the 1st IEEE Annual Conference on Pervasive Computing and Communications, Fort Worth, TX.

Zimmermann, P. (1995). The official PGP user's guide. Cambridge, MA: MIT Press. ISBN 0-262-74017-6, 1995.

Zimmermann, P. (2001). Why OpenPGP's PKI is better than an X.509 PKI. Retrieved from http://www.openpgp.org/technical/whybetter.shtml

Zurko, M. E. (2005). User-centered security: Stepping up to the grand challenge. In *Proceedings of the 21st Annual Computer Security Applications Conference* (pp. 187-202). Washington, DC, USA: IEEE Computer Society.

Zurko, M. E., & Simon, R. T. (1996). User-centered security. In *NSPW '96: Proceedings of the 1996 Workshop on New Security Paradigms* (pp. 27-33). New York NY, USA: ACM Press.

About the Contributors

Hamid Nemati is Associate Professor of Information Systems at the Information Systems and Operations Management Department of The University of North Carolina at Greensboro. He holds a doctorate from the University of Georgia. Before coming to UNCG, he was on the faculty of J. Mack Robinson College of Business Administration at Georgia State University. Dr. Nemati has extensive professional experience as a consultant business analyst, and system developer and has consulted with a number of major corporations. extensive professional experience as a consultant. His research articles has appeared in a number of major scholarly and professional journals.

***

Kirk P. Arnett, D.B.A. CCP, GSEC, is professor emeritus of Information Systems for Mississippi State University's College of Business and Industry in the Department of Management and Information Systems. Prior to his 25 years of service with the College of Business and Industry, Dr. Arnett worked in the information processing area for 17 years. His research and creative achievement highlights include over 150 publications through journals, proceedings, and miscellaneous academic outlets, and several funded grants for research, service, and teaching.

Madhu Ahluwalia is a doctoral student at the University of Maryland, Baltimore County. She is primarily interested in privacy protecting techniques applicable in association rule mining and the practical significance of this area in business contexts such as the supply chain management. Her current focus is on problems associated with maintaining different kinds of summary information on evolving databases. Madhu's other research interests include data warehousing and database systems, in particular database replication, database synchronization and database performance tuning. Her research contributions lie in the fields of privacy preserving data mining and database synchronization. She has recently completed an Academic Research Center fellowship at SAP Corp.

Patricia Beatty is a network engineer in San Francisco. Her research interests include trust and standards compliance in web-based systems. Patricia has a B.Sc. and an M.Sc. in Computer Engineering, both from the University of Alberta. Contact her at plbeatty@gmail.com.

Harkeerat Bedi is a graduate student pursuing his Ph.D. in computer science at the University of Memphis. He earned his master's in computer science from the University of Tennessee at Chattanooga in August 2009. His master's work included research on Fair Electronic Exchange where he, with guidance from his mentors Dr. Li Yang and Dr. Joseph Kizza aimed to improve an existing fair exchange protocol by handling several possible attacks and creating software that facilitated the same. His current research involves the application of game theory in network security for its analysis and improvement.

Kent D. Boklan is an NSA-trained cryptographer. He received his SB from MIT and PhD from the University of Michigan (in analytic number theory) and has written about twenty research papers in cryptography and cryptanalysis [but most of them are CLASSIFIED]. Dr. Boklan is presently on the faculty of Queens College and the City University of New York Graduate Center. He also provides data security and cryptographic consulting services to a variety of clients including Nike, the NYC Police Department, the NYC Sanitation Department and the NYC Department of Buildings. In his spare time, he breaks (historical) codes.

Xubin Cao is the Director of the Center of Experimental Teaching in Economics and Management at Southwestern University of Finance and Economics in China. His research interests include information security, knowledge management, e-learning, and e-business.

Lei Chen received his B.Eng. degree in Computer Science from Nanjing University of Technology, China, in 2000, and Ph.D. degree in Computer Science from Auburn University, USA, in Aug. 2007. He has been with Sam Houston State University as an Assistant Professor in Computer Science since 2007. Dr. Chen has been actively working in research in computer networks, network security and wireless and multimedia networking. In the past twelve months, he had eight papers/chapters published in major journals and conferences, and books. He also serves as reviewer of a number of books, journals and conferences.

Zhiyuan Chen is an Assistant Professor at Information Systems department, UMBC. He has a PhD in Computer Science from Cornell University. His research interests include privacy preserving data mining, semantic search and navigation, XML, automatic database tuning, and database compression.

Glenn S. Dardick is an Associate Professor of Information Systems within the College of Business and Economics at Longwood University in Farmville, Virginia USA and. Adjunct Associate Professor of Information Systems within the secAU Security Research Center at Edith Cowan University in Perth, Western Australia. He has over 35 years experience in the IT Industry and began working with microcomputers 29 years ago while serving as an original member of the IBM PC development team. Dr. Dardick is responsible for the Digital Forensics, Security and Law program at Longwood University teaching Digital Forensics and IT courses at the undergraduate and postgraduate levels. Dr. Dardick frequently consults with attorneys in matters concerning Digital Forensics and IT. He has testified in Federal, State and Sectarian courts within the United States. Dr. Dardick is also the Editor of the Journal of Digital Forensics, Security and Law and is the founder of the Association of Digital Forensics, Security and Law (ADFSL) and the annual ADFSL Conference on Digital Forensics, Security and Law.

James W. Denton is an Associate Professor in the College of Business and Economics at West Virginia University where he has taught courses, in basic information systems, programming, operations research and operations management. Prior to receiving his Ph.D. from Kent State University, Dr.

Denton worked in Engineering and Quality Assurance in several industrial settings. He has previously published research on neural networks and information systems education in the Journal of Computer Information Systems, the European Journal of Operational Research, Accounting, Management, and Information Technologies, the Journal of Information Systems Education and others.

Scott Dick is an Associate Professor of Computer Engineering at the University of Alberta. His research interests include computational intelligence, data mining, and machine learning. Scott has a Ph.D. in Computer Science and Engineering from the University of South Florida. He is a member of the IEEE and the ACM. Contact him at dick@ece.ualberta.ca

Michael Dixon is a Senior Lecturer in Information Technology at Murdoch University in Western Australia. He holds a PhD from Murdoch University and a MBA in Telecommunications Management from Golden Gate University. He is also a certified Cisco Certified Network Professional (CCNP), Cisco Certified Design Professional (CCDP), and Cisco Certified Academy Instructor (CCAI). His major research interests include information technology education, data communications and neural networks.

Guillermo A. Francia, III received his Ph.D. in Computer Science from New Mexico Tech. In 1996, Dr. Francia received one of the five national awards for Innovators in Higher Education from Microsoft Corporation. Dr. Francia served as a Fulbright scholar to Malta in 2007. His research interests include computer security, digital forensics, visualization, data mining, and performance dashboards. He has published extensively in books, journals, and conference proceedings and has delivered the keynote speech in several conferences. Currently, Dr. Francia is serving as Professor of Computer Science and Director of the Center for Information Security and Assurance at JSU.

Aryya Gangopadhyay is a Professor of Information Systems at the University of Maryland Baltimore County (UMBC). He has a PhD in Computer Information Systems from Rutgers University. His research interests include privacy preserving data mining, data cube navigation, and core and applied research on data mining. He has co-authored and edited three books, many book chapters, and numerous papers in peer-reviewed journals.

Wasim A Al-Hamdani, holds a Ph.D. in Computer Science (1985) from the University of East Anglia, Norwich, UK. He is currently an Associate Professor of Cryptography and Information Security at Kentucky State University (KSU).He has published six textbooks and more than 53 papers dealing with Computer Science and Cryptography. For the past 19 years, he has concentrated his research in cryptography and information security.

Wen-Chen Hu received a BE, an ME, an MS, and a PhD, all in Computer Science, from the Tamkang University, Taiwan, the National Central University, Taiwan, the University of Iowa, Iowa City, and the University of Florida,Gainesville, in 1984, 1986, 1993, and 1998, respectively. Currently, he is an associate professor in the Department of Computer Science of the University of North Dakota, Grand Forks. He is the Editor-in-Chief of the International Journal of Handheld Computing Research (IJHCR), and has been over 20 editors and editorial advisory/review board members of international journals/books and more than 10 track/session chairs and program committee members of international conferences. Dr. Hu has published over 70 articles in refereed journals, conference proceedings, books, and encyclopedias, edited three books, and solely authored a book entitled "Internet-enabled handheld devices, computing, and programming: mobile commerce and personal data applications." His current research interests include handheld computing, electronic and mobile commerce systems, Web technologies, and databases.

Yongliang Hu received his B.S. in Computer Science from Sichuan University, China, in 1997, and M.S. degree in Computer Science from Hangzhou Dianzi University, China, in 2003. He has been with Taizhou University as an Associate Professor in Computer Science since 2007. He has been actively working in research in computer networks, network security and image processing. He has published over twenty papers/chapters in books, journals, and conference proceedings. He is currently leading a group in Taizhou University to conduct research on software theoretics and technology. Currently, Prof. Hu is serving as vice Director of School of Mathematic and Inforamtion Engineering at Taizhou University.

Terry Huston, Ph.D. is an optometrist with 15 years of clinical experience including over five years active duty with the U.S. Air Force in addition to civilian private practice. He holds a Ph.D. in Management Information Systems from the University of Pittsburgh and has spent 13 years in academia, teaching and doing research in various areas of Information Technology with a special interest in Security and Privacy issues. He is presently a health care information technology consultant in Canada and the U.S.

Princely Ifinedo is an Associate Professor at the Shannon School of Business, Sydney, Cape Breton University, Canada. He earned his PhD in Information Systems Science from the University of Jyväskylä, Finland. He obtained an MBA in International Management from Royal Holloway College, University of London, UK. His current research interests include Global IT management, IS security issues, IT and SMEs, and ERP success measurement. His research papers have appeared in such journals as Computers in Human Behavior, Journal of Computer Information Systems, Information Management & Computer Security, Enterprise Information Systems, International Journal of Information Security and Privacy, and Journal of Global Information Technology Management, and Information for Development. He has authored (and co-authored) about 70 peer-reviewed papers, and he is affiliated with AIS, CIPS, DSI, and ISACA.

Dulal C. Kar received the B.Sc.Engg. and the M.Sc.Engg. degrees from Bangladesh University of Engineering and Technology, Dhaka, Bangladesh and the MS and the Ph.D. degrees from North Dakota State University, Fargo, North Dakota. Currently he is working as an associate professor in the Department of Computing Sciences at Texas A&M University – Corpus Christi, Texas. Previously, he was a faculty in the Department of Computer Science at Virginia Polytechnic Institute and State University, Virginia; Mountain State University, West Virginia; and Bangladesh University of Engineering and Technology, Bangladesh. He is an associate editor of the International Journal of Distance Education Technologies published by IGI Global. His research interests include wireless sensor networks, signal and image processing algorithms, network architecture and performance measurement, network and information security, information retrieval, and educational technology.

Virginia Kleist is an Associate Professor at the College of Business and Economics at West Virginia University. Her research area includes investigating the information goods industries and cost versus benefit issues of biometrics, network security and knowledge management technologies. Recent publications include work on modeling technological based electronic trust and security in the digital economy and research on the adoption, assessment and payoff of electronic information systems projects. She holds a BA from Duke University in Economics, an MBA from Marquette University, and an MA in Economics, MS in MIS and PhD in MIS and telecommunications from the University of Pittsburgh. Dr. Kleist spent 10 years as a manager of technology systems applications, including responsibility for multimillion dollar budgets and 24/7 operations. Dr. Kleist was awarded the 2000 ICIS Best Doctoral Dissertation Award, the 2003 WVU Foundation Outstanding Teaching Award, and was recently the Chair of the WVU Faculty Senate.

Alex Kosachev is a business analyst with CrystalWare, Inc. a private company specializing in marketing and selling active and discontinued China, Crystal, Silver, and Collectible products. Prior to joining Replacements, Ltd in the year 2000, he worked as a network specialist at the Customs Information Center in Ukraine. I hold M.S. in Electrical Engineering from the National Technical University of Ukraine in Kiev and M.S. in Information Technology and Management from the University of North Carolina in Greensboro.

Hua Lin is a senior software engineer at the School of Nursing, University of Virginia. She has over a decade's experience in software engineering, web development, and information security. Hua received her M. S. degree in Software Engineering from George Mason University and is a certified database administrator.

Yong Lu is an assistant professor of Information Sciences and Technology at Pennsylvania State University. His research interests center around virtual communities, social capital, and information security. He has published papers in journals including Computers & Education, Communications of AIS, International Journal of Mobile Learning and Organisation, International Journal of Information Security and Privacy and others.

Tanya McGill is a Senior Lecturer in Information Technology at Murdoch University in Western Australia. She has a PhD from Murdoch University. Her major research interests include information technology education and end user computing. Her work has appeared in various journals including Decision Support Systems, Journal of Research on Computing in Education, European Journal of Psychology of Education, Information Resources Management Journal and Journal of Organizational and End User Computing

James Miller is a Professor of Computer Engineering at the University of Alberta. His research interests include software verification and validation embedded, Web-based, and ubiquitous environments. James has a Ph.D. in Computer Science from the University of Strathclyde. He is a member of the IEEE. Contact him at jm@ece.ualberta.ca

William Mitchell is a doctoral student in the Department of Computer Science at the University of Denver. He earned his master's degree in mathematics from the University of Illinois at Urbana Champagne and bachelor's from University of Colorado at Denver, majoring also mathematics. His research interests include information security, mathematical foundations of security, and graph theory.

Bonnie Morris is the Go-Mart Professor of Accounting Information Systems in the College of Business and Economics at West Virginia University. Dr. Morris' research interests are in the areas of forensic accounting, IT audit, and privacy policy compliance. Recent research projects have focused on continuous auditing, privacy issues, auditing electronic data interchange (EDI) systems, financial EDI, and case-based reasoning systems for auditing and financial statement analysis. She teaches courses in accounting systems, information systems auditing, and fraud data analysis. Dr .Morris holds a Ph.D. in Accounting with a Minor in Artificial Intelligence from the University of Pittsburgh, as well as an M.B.A. from the University of Pittsburgh and a B.A. in Mathematics from West Virginia University.

Clifton J. Mulkey graduated from Eastern New Mexico University in 2009 with a double major Bachelor's degree in Computer Science and Mathematics. He is currently pursuing a Master's degree in Computer Science at Texas A&M University – Corpus Christi. His current research interests include Identity Based Encryption as well as Quantum Key Distribution. He is also active in information assurance, cyber defense, and system administration

Hung Ngo received his B.S. degree in Computer Science from University of Natural Sciences, Vietnam in August 2006. He worked in industry for two years before going back to school to pursue his M.S. in Computer Science. He is now a graduate student in the Department of Computing Sciences at Texas A&M University – Corpus Christi. His current research interests include Wireless Sensor Networks, Wireless Security, and Digital Signal Processing.

Benjamin Ngugi is an Assistant Professor in the Information Systems and Operations Management at the Sawyer Business School, Suffolk University in Boston. He received his Ph.D. in Information Systems from New Jersey Institute of Technology and his Bachelors in Electrical and Electronics Engineering from University of Nairobi, Kenya. He conducts his research in the areas of biometrics, legal data security compliance, business intelligence and technology adoption. Ben brings over eleven years of professional experience initially as a system engineer and then as a Technical Director in charge of technical sales, installations and training in computer networks, security systems and satellite systems. He has published his research in journals including Decision Support Systems, International Journal of Information Security and Privacy, The Case Journal and the ACM Journal of Data quality.

Lee Novakovic is in a graduate program with a governmental consumer affairs agency. He has an Honours degree in Computer Science from Murdoch University. His research interests include information security, data communications and human factors in computing.

Filippo Passerini studied Physics at the University of Florence. His graduate work on physics was done at the Perimeter Institute for Theoretical Physics and University of Waterloo under the supervision of Professor Jaume Gomis. He is presently postdoctoral researcher at the Humboldt University Berlin. His research interests are focused on String Theory, with particular attention to the holographic duality between gauge theories and string models.

Joanne Pratt is president of her consulting firm, Joanne H. Pratt Associates. She is recognized as a futurist for her research on new work patterns enabled by technology. Her research includes the impacts of remote work on corporate work patterns, work/life, and privacy issues. She was the only US member of the European Union funded team studying telework and information-age employment. She has conducted research for the US Small Business Administration, the Bureau of Transportation Statistics, and other federal agencies, and has led research projects for private sector clients. Her research publications include E-Biz.com: Strategies for Small Business Success, Counting the New Mobile Workforce, Impact of Location on Net Income, and Homebased Business: the Hidden Economy. Her degrees are from Oberlin College and Harvard University.

Ian Reay is a software developer with Hitachi ID in Calgary, Alberta. His research interests lie in privacy preservation, computer security, and identity management systems. He has a B.Sc. and an M.Sc. in Computer Engineering from the University of Alberta. Contact him at shakennotstir69@hotmail.com.

Geetha Sanapala received her M.Sc. degree in Information Systems from Osmania University, India in July 2003. She is currently pursuing Masters degree in Computer Science from the Texas A&M University of Corpus Christi. As part of her degree program, she is working as a Research Assistant with focus on security aspects of Wireless Sensor Networks. Prior to this, she had a chance to work with United Online Ltd (India). in the department of Information Security and Anti-Spam operations.

Simone Severini studied Chemistry at the University of Siena and Philosophy at the University of Florence. He obtained a Ph.D. in Mathematics under the supervision of Richard Jozsa. He has been postdoctoral researcher in the Department of Combinatorics & Optimization at the University of Waterloo. He is currently a Newton International Fellow at University College London. His research interests are in Quantum Theory, Discrete Mathematics, and Complex Systems.

Sushil K. Sharma is a Professor of Information Systems at Ball State University, Muncie, Indiana, USA. Co-author of two textbooks and co-editor of six books, Dr. Sharma has authored over 100 refereed research papers in many peer-reviewed national and international MIS and management journals, conferences proceedings and books. His primary teaching and research interests are in e-commerce, computer-mediated communications, community informatics, information systems security, e-government, ERP systems, database management systems, web services and knowledge management. He has a wide consulting experience in information systems and e-commerce and has served as an advisor and consultant to several government and private organizations including projects funded by the World Bank.

James Suleiman, Ph.D. (www.usm.maine.edu/~suleiman) is an Associate Professor of Information Systems at University of Southern Maine's School of Business and a Senior Research Associate at the Center for Business and Economic Research. He received his B.S. in Finance from Lehigh University, his M.B.A. from University of South Florida and his Ph.D. in MIS from University of Georgia. He was a consultant for Cap Gemini Ernst & Young's division of Telecommunications Media and Networks, worked for IBM and consulted for various Fortune 500 firms. His research interests include information systems education, computer security, and computer supported cooperative work.

Gary F. Templeton is an Associate Professor of Management Information Systems at Mississippi State University. He earned his BS in Finance, MBA, MMIS and PhD in MIS from Auburn University. Among his peer-reviewed publications, he has published in the Journal of Management Information Systems, the Journal of the AIS, the European Journal of Information Systems, and Communications of the ACM. His research focuses on topics that advance organizational learning and information security.

Ramakrishna Thurimella received his PhD in Computer Science from the University of Texas at Austin. He is currently the Director of Colorado Research Institute for Security and Privacy, an NSA designated Center for Academic Excellence in Information Assurance Education, at the University of Denver. He is also an associate professor of Computer Science at the University of Denver where he regularly teaches courses on information security and forensics. His research interests include network security, intrusion detection, and mathematical foundations of information security. He has made fundamental contributions to algorithmic graph connectivity, and other areas in theoretical computer science. His current focus is on applying some of the existing theory from graph connectivity to identify weaknesses in the Internet infrastructure. He is a member of ACM and IEEE.

Monica Trifas received her BS and MS in Computer Science degrees from University of Bucharest, Bucharest, Romania in 1996. She joined Jacksonville State University (JSU) in Fall 2005, after she completed the Ph.D. in Computer Science at Louisiana State University (LSU). Her dissertation, "Medical Image Enhancement", focused on contrast enhancement for medical images. Dr. Trifas' research interests include Digital/Video Image Processing, Medical Imaging, Human Computer Interaction, Bioinformatics, Artificial Intelligence, Data Mining, and Visualization. She is the author of over 15 publications on medical image enhancement methods, visualization, data security, video coding in leading computer science journals and conference proceedings. She is the reviewer of various international journals and conferences. Currently, Dr. Trifas is serving as Director of the Center for Information Security and Assurance at JSU. Dr. Trifas' complete background information can be found in http://mcis.jsu.edu/faculty/atrifas/.

Thomas P. Van Dyke is an assistant professor of Information Systems and Operations Management at the University of North Carolina, Greensboro. He received his Ph.D. in business computer information systems at the University of North Texas. His current research interests include Privacy and Security, IT leadership and Human factors. His previous publications appear in journals such as MIS Quarterly, Decision Sciences, and Electronic Markets.

David A. Vance, Ph.D, Southern Illinois University, is Professor of Information Systems and head of the Business Information Systems program at Olivet Nazarene University. He is a former executive in the telecommunications and computer technology industries. His research interest is the influence of information policy on organizational behavior. Dr. Vance is the founding editor of the AIS-ISWorld Internet pages on computer ethics education.

Gina Vega, Ph.D. is Professor of Management and founding Director of the Center for Entrepreneurial Activity at the Bertolon School of Business at Salem State University. She conducts her research in three complementary streams revolving around organizational structure: entrepreneurship and business transitions, ethics, and the evolving world of work. Dr. Vega is widely published in academic journals, including Entrepreneurship Theory & Practice, Journal of Management Education, Journal of Business Ethics and others, and she has presented papers nationally and internationally on issues of business transitions, technology, and corporate social responsibility. She has written three books (A Passion for Planning: Financials, Operations, Marketing, Management, and Ethics [University Press of America, 2001], Managing Teleworkers and Telecommuting Strategies [Praeger Publishers, 2003]), and Moral Courage in Organizations: Doing the Right Thing at Work (with D.R. Comer) [M.E. Sharpe, forthcoming]. Dr. Vega is currently a CASE Fellow, Editor of The CASE Journal, and Associate Editor for the Journal of Management Education. She teaches Small Business Management and Corporate Social Responsibility.

Xunhua Wang is an Assistant Professor of computer science at James Madison University (JMU) in Virginia, USA, and teaches cryptography and information security courses there. He received his Ph.D. from George Mason University in 2002. Dr. Wang's research interests include applied cryptography, network security, and software engineering. He has published a dozen of refereed papers in information security and his work was sponsored by Cisco. He is a member of IEEE.

Huinan Xu now is an executive manager at Ernst&Young. His current focus is on areas of Information Systems auditing and security assurance advisory practices. Prior to E&Y, he was a senior consultant with IBM Global Business Services. Dr. Xu received his Ph.D in MIS from Brunel University, UK.

Hui-min Ye is now studying in Computer Science as Ph.D. student at University of Vermont, United States. Her current focus is data provenance, specifically about semantics of data provenance and ways to guarantee users of data understand the background of the data. Previously, Ms. Ye has worked on several state-sponsored research projects at Chinese Academy of Science, Beijing China.

Li Yang is an Associate Professor in the Department of Computer Science and Electrical Engineering at University of Tennessee at Chattanooga. Her research interests include network and information security, databases, and engineering techniques for complex software system design. She authored papers on these areas in refereed journal, conferences and symposiums. She is a member of the ACM.

Ming Yang received his B.S. and M.S. degrees in Electrical Engineering from Tianjin University, China, in 1997 and 2000, respectively, and Ph.D. degree in Computer Science and Engineering from Wright State University, Dayton, Ohio, USA in 2006. He is currently with Montclair State University as an Assistant Professor in Computer Science. His research interests include Digital Image/Video Coding, Multimedia Communication & Networking, and Information Security. He is the author/co-author of over twenty publications in leading computer science journals and conference proceedings. He also serves as reviewer of numerous international journals and conferences.

Lei Zhang is an assistant professor of computer science, Frostburg State University, University System of Maryland. She received M.S. and Ph.D. from Auburn University in 2005 and 2008. Before she pursued her graduate study in the U.S, she worked as an instructor at school of Electrical Engineering & Automation, Tianjin University, China. Her current research interests include Wireless Networks Protocols Design and Applications, Distributed Algorithm, Information Security, Data Mining and Human Computer Interaction. She is a member of IEEE/ACM. She has been a technical reviewer for numerous international journals and conferences

Feng Zhu received the B.S. degree in computer science from East China Normal University in 1994, the M.S. degree in computer science and engineering from Michigan State University in 2001, the M.S. degree in statistics from Michigan State University in 2005, and the Ph.D. degree from Michigan State University in 2006. He is an assistant professor at The University of Alabama in Huntsville. He was a program manager at Microsoft from 2006 to 2008, and a software engineer at Intel from 1997 to 1999. His current research interests include pervasive computing, security and privacy, computer networks, and statistical system analysis and design.

Wei Zhu received the Ph.D. degree in computer science and engineering from Michigan State University in 2006, the M.S. degree in statistics from Michigan State University in 2004, the M.S. degree in computer science and engineering from Michigan State University in 2001, and the B.S. degree in computer science from East China Normal University in 1994. Her research interests include human-computer interaction, pervasive computing, computer graphics, augmented reality, and multimedia systems. She is currently a software consultant at Intergraph Corporation. She was a software design engineer at Microsoft Corporation from 2006 to 2008.

Index